The BCPC International Congress
Crop Science & Technology 2003

10-12 November 2003

Congress Proceedings

Volume 2

Proceedings of an international congress
held at the SECC, Glasgow, Scotland, UK

BCPC

© 2003 The British Crop Protection Council
7 Omni Business Centre
Omega Park
Alton
Hampshire
GU34 2QD
UK

Tel: +44 (0) 1420 593 200
Fax: +44 (0) 1420 593 209
Email: gensec@bcpc.org
Web: www.bcpc.org

British Library Cataloguing in Publication Data - A catalogue record for this book
is available from the British Library.

ISBN 1 901396 63 0   Set of two volumes

100361 3740

Cover design by m360° Ltd, Nottingham
Printed in Great Britain by Page Bros, Norwich

CONTENTS

Page

BCPC Council Members XXI
BCPC XXII
The BCPC Congress 2003 Programme Committee XXIII
Author Index XXV
Abbreviations XXXI

VOLUME 1

SESSION 1A
KEYNOTE LECTURES

Session   Page

Increased crop productivity from renewable inputs –
a scientific challenge for the 21st century
I R Crute 1A-1 3

The impact of genomics on the food chain
P J Lillford 1A-2 15

Meeting consumer demand for food safety,
quality and environmental protection
C M Bruhn 1A-3 27

Balancing bio-diversity and agriculture
G R Potts 1A-4 35

SESSION 2A
NEW COMPOUNDS, NEW CONCEPTS AND NEW USES

A novel formulation of clomazone for use in rice
D T Schulteis and J Heier...2A-1 47

Efficacy of a pyrethroid and systemic neonicotinoid to
manage an insect and pathogen complex
J D Bradshaw, M E Rice and J H Hill 2A-2 53

Transgenic mycoherbicides for effective, economic weed control
J Gressel and Z Amsellem...2A-3 61

Genetically engineered Cry3Bb1 corn for controlling Diabrotica
rootworms: estimating the agronomic, economic and
environmental benefits of transgenic biotechnology
M E Rice...2A-4 69

Penoxsulam, a new broad spectrum rice herbicide for
weed control in European Union paddies
D Larelle, R Mann, S Cavanna, R Bernes et al. 2A-5 75

Metamifop: a new post-emergence grass killing herbicide
for use in rice
T J Kim, H S Chang, J W Ryu, Y K Ko et al. 2A-6 81

Flucetosulfuron: a new sulfonylurea herbicide
D S Kim, S J Koo, J N Lee, K H Hwang et al. 2A-7 87

SYP-Z071: a new broad spectrum fungicide candidate
L Zhang, Z CH Li, B Li, K Sun et al. 2A-8 93

MTF-753: a novel fungicide
K Tomiya and Y Yanase 2A-9 99

The effects of novel fungicide benthiavalicarb-isopropyl
on Oomycete fungal diseases
Y Miyake, J Sakai, I Miura, K Nagayama and M Shibata 2A-10 105

SESSION 2B
BIOTECHNOLOGY APPROACHES TO OPTIMISE CROP DEVELOPMENT AND QUALITY

Genomics and molecular breeding for crop plant improvement
G J Bryan 2B-1 115

Designer tubers for the production of novel compounds
U Sonnewald, M-R Hajirezaei, S Biemelt and M Müller 2B-2 123

Transgenic approaches to study quality traits in cereals
H D Jones, H Wu, C Sparks and P R Shewry 2B-3 133

Cereal functional genomics and the cell cycle: improving yield
V Frankard, C Reuzeau, A Sanz, Y Hatzfeld et al. 2B-4 141

SESSION 2C
NEW EU ENVIRONMENTAL POLICIES: ISSUES FOR PESTICIDES STAKEHOLDERS

EU strategy on sustainable use of pesticides
E Liégeois 2C-1 149

The impact on pesticides use of the water framework directive
A Croxford, A S Chapman and D Foster 2C-2 155

Developing a national pesticides strategy
D P E Williams 2C-3 163

The Pesticides Forum and its role in encouraging a reduction
in the impacts arising from pesticide use
E Gallagher 2C-4 171

SESSION 3A
REGISTRATION OF PLANT PROTECTION PRODUCTS IN EUROPE: EMERGING ISSUES

Revision of Directive 91/414
L Smeets 3A-1 179

Re-registration of plant protection products in Europe
D J Flynn..3A-2 187

Progress with resolving minor use crop protection
issues in Europe
A J W Rotteveel and V Powell 3A-3 195

The UK perspective on comparative risk assessment
S C Popple, T J Davis and D J Hussey 3A-4 203

SESSION 3B
CROP MANAGEMENT FOR FARMLAND BIODIVERSITY

What biodiversity should we expect from farmland?
M I Avery and D Moorcroft 3B-1 211

Weeds: their impact and value in arable ecosystems
P J Lutman, N D Boatman, V K Brown and E J P Marshall 3B-2 219

Sustainable arable farming for an improved environment:
the effects of novel winter wheat sward management
on skylarks (*Alauda arvensis*)
A J Morris, R B Bradbury and A D Evans 3B-3 227

Meeting the margins – for profit – for biodiversity
C Drummond and J Boxall 3B-4 233

A risk assessment framework for determining the effects
of pesticides on farmland biodiversity
D Boatman, A Hart, M Clook, V K Brown et al. 3B-5 239

SESSION 3C
SPRAY APPLICATION TECHNIQUES

The current and future role of application in improving
pesticide use
P C H Miller...3C-1 247

Pesticide formulation and drift potential
A Herbst 3C-2 255

Effect of drop evaporation on spray drift and buffer zone
risk assessments
C S Parkin, P J Walklate and J W Nicholls..3C-3 261

Defining the size of target for air induction nozzles
E S Powell, J H Orson, P C H Miller, P N Kudsk and S Mathiassen 3C-4 267

Evaluation of nozzles for the application of a late
fungicide spray
T H Robinson, M C Butler Ellis and J D Power 3C-5 273

The deposit characteristics of pesticide sprays applied
at low volumes
M C Butler Ellis, I M Scotford and D A Webb...3C-6 279

SESSION 4A
THE IMPACT OF EUROPEAN ENLARGEMENT

An introduction to the enlargement of the European Union:
policy objectives and instruments in the fields of
agriculture and rural development
R D E Gooch 4A-1 287

Increasing the cost-competitiveness of wheat production
in Northern Europe
J H Orson, G Lemaitre and D Hanus...4A-2 293

A UK farmer's experience of farming in Hungary
M J Jenkins 4A-3 301

The economic impact of European enlargement
A J Dickie..4A-4 307

SESSION 4B
PREDICTION, MONITORING AND PRECISION IN CROP MANAGEMENT

Early assessment of herbicide efficacy after application
with ALS inhibitors – a first exploration
I Haage Riethmuller, L Bastiaans, M J Kropff, J Harbinson et al. 4B-1 317

Automatically recording sprayer inputs to improve traceability and control
A J Watts, P C H Miller and R J Godwin 4B-2 323

WMSS: Improving the precision and prediction of weed
management strategies in winter dominant rotations
L V Collings, D Ginsburg, J H Clarke, A E Milne et al. 4B-3 329

A risk management system for controlling the
foliar pests of Brassica crops
R H Collier, A Mead, W E Parker and S A Ellis 4B-4 335

Combinatorial approaches to model development for
predicting emergence and crop-weed competition
D S Kim, P Brain, J E Marshall, J C Caseley and Y W Kwon 4B-5 341

PLATFORM SESSION 4C
ADVANCES IN RESIDUE ANALYSIS, METABOLISM AND TOXICOLOGY

Emerging technologies in the analytical laboratory
S Cram..4C-1 349

Uncertainty of sample processing of tomato and olive samples
B Maestroni, A Ambrus and S Culin 4C-2 355

Relevant metabolites in soil, water, plants and animals
C R Leake 4C-3 365

Safety of genetically modified crops for food and animal feed
G A Kleter and H A Kuiper..4C-4 371

SESSION 4D
BIOREMEDIATION OF ORGANIC AND INORGANIC CONTAMINANTS

Soil bioremediation: bioavailability, biofilms and complexity
R G Burns...4D-1 381

Soil microbial response during the phytoremediation
of PAH contaminated soil
D L Johnson and S P McGrath 4D-2 393

The use of short rotation coppice in the bioremediation
of municipal wastewater
W M Dawson and F E A Wilson...4D-3 399

Perspectives for the use of cattail (*Typha* spp) in phytoremediation
P Schröder, J Neustifter, S Peis and B Huber...............................4D-4 405

POSTER SESSION 5A
NEW COMPOUNDS, NEW CONCEPTS AND NEW USES

New fungicide benthiavalicarb-isopropyl + mancozeb for
foliar use in potatoes in Europe
T W Hofman, S M Boon, G Coster, Z van Oudheusden *et al*............................5A-1 413

Control of Fusarium oxysporum and *Meloidogyne* spp.
with *Pseudomonas oryzihabitans*
I K Vagelas, F T Gravanis and S R Gowen 5A-2 419

Potential of *Bacillus thuringiensis* subsp. *kurstaki* (3a 3b)
on young larval instars of rice stem borer *Chilo suppressalis*
J Karimi, H Abbasipour and D Talei 5A-3 425

POSTER SESSION 5B
NON-CHEMICAL CROP PROTECTION

Arbuscular mycorrhizal fungi: their role in the ability
of crops to cope with stress
Z Dunsiger, C A Watson and D Atkinson 5B-1 433

The effect of increased crop diversity on colonisation by
pest insects of brassica crops
R H Collier and S Finch 5B-2 439

The efficacy of high temperature and diatomaceous earth
combinations against adults of the red flour beetle
Tribolium castaneum (Coleoptera: *Tenebrionidae*) and the grain
weevil *Sitophilus granarius* (Coleoptera: *Curculionidae*)
D A Cook 5B-3 445

Seed consumption by ground beetles
A Honek and Z Martinkova...5B-4 451

Reduction of invertebrate contamination of salad crops
using directed airstreams
M J Lole..5B-5 457

Use of Salix genotype mixtures for the control of rust in
short rotation coppice willow
A R McCracken and W M Dawson..5B-6 463

Integrated biological control of powdery mildew and grey mould
of cucumber and tomato using Brevibacillus brevis combinations
E J Allan, I Lazaraki, D Dertzakis, S Woodward et al. 5B-7 469

Comparison of brassica tissues for control of
soil-borne and tuber diseases in vitro
K G Sutherland, E J Booth and A McCubbin-Green 5B-8 475

Strategies to control Cirsium arvense in organic farming systems
A Verschwele and A Häusle..5B-9 481

POSTER SESSION 5C
SPRAY APPLICATION TECHNIQUES

Evaluating the potential of a weed wiper for
Molinia caerulea (L.) Moench control in upland moorland
A L Milligan, P D Putwain and R H Marrs 5C-1 489

Effect of adjuvants on fruit and leaf calcium concentrations
in Golden Delicious apple following calcium nitrate applications
for the control of bitter pit
M North, J Wooldridge and J Mudzunga.......................................5C-2 495

Assessment of environmental concentrations
of pesticide from spray drift
A G Lane and M C Butler Ellis 5C–3 501

Comparison of operator exposure for five different
greenhouse spraying operations
D Nuttyens, S Windey, P Braekman, A De Moor and B Sonck........5C-4 507

Influence of adjuvants on the emission of pesticides
to the atmosphere. Review, methodology and perspectives
H de Ruiter, H G J Mol, J J de Vlieger and J C van de Zande 5C-5 513

POSTER SESSION 5D
PREDICTION, MONITORING AND PRECISION IN CROP MANAGEMENT

Modelling the soil seed bank as an aid to crop management
in Integrated Arable Farming Systems
A J Murdoch, S J Watson and J R Park.......................................5D-1 521

Prediction of residues of crop protection products on crops
K Hyder and K Z Travis 5D-2 527

POSTER SESSION 5E
CROP MANAGEMENT FOR FARMLAND BIODIVERSITY

Non-inversion tillage and farmland birds in winter
H M Cunningham, K Chaney, A Wilcox and R B Bradbury..............................5E-1 533

Managing weeds for environmental benefit in GMHT sugar beet
G T Champion and M J May 5E-2 537

POSTER SESSION 5F
ADVANCES IN RESIDUE ANALYSIS, METABOLISM AND TOXICOLOGY

Chemistry of organic matter in some New Zealand soils:
correlation with pesticide sorption
R Ahmad, A Rahman and S J Hill...5F-1 545

Analytical support of the DuPont quality program stewardship
initiatives in the Nordic region
C R Powley, G Magnusson and M Christerson 5F-2 551

Laboratory studies on flumioxazin sorption and persistence in soil
J A Ferrell, W K Vencill and T L Grey 5F-3 555

Validation of analytical methods for the determination of
agrochemical residues in air, using a simulated sampling technique
J M Wimbush...5F-4 561

POSTER SESSION 5G
REGISTRATION OF PLANT PROTECTION PRODUCTS: EMERGING ISSUES

Maximum residue levels: a critical investigation
K Hyder and K Z Travis 5G-1 569

The effects of refining consumer exposure assessments
of glyphosate residues
C A Harris and C P Gaston 5G-2 575

Cooperative facilitation of registrations of crop protection
chemicals in fruit, vegetables and other speciality crops
in the United States and Canada
J J Baron, D L Kunkel, R E Holm, C Hunter et al. 5G-3 583

The Render-4 Project – start of the 4th stage
of the EU review programme
A Verschwele and U Pingel 5G-4 589

POSTER SESSION 5H
BIOREMEDIATION OF ORGANIC AND INORGANIC CONTAMINANTS

Practical on-farm bioremediation systems to
limit point source pesticide pollution
S C Rose, W D Basford, A D Carter and P J Mason.......................................5H-1 597

Biodegradation of simazine in olive groves under
laboratory and field conditions
M J Martínez, R De Prado, R Santiago, A R Franco and F Peña......................5H-2 603

POSTER SESSION 5I
POSTGRADUATE STUDENT POSTERS

Growth reduction of cotton (*Gossypium hirsutum*, L)
caused by bermudagrass (*Cynodon dactylon*, L). A case of allelopathy
P Bouchagier and P Efthhimiadis 5I-1 611

Compatiblity of the candidate bioherbicide *Microsphaeropsis*
amaranthi with chemical herbicides and adjuvants in tank mixture
D A Smith and S G Hallett...5I-2 615

The structure-activity relationship of herbicidal 3-phenyl
substituted 1,2,3-benzotriazin-4-ones, 4(3H)-quinazolinones
and 2,4(1H, 3H)-quinazolinediones
B Li and H Z Yang 5I-3 619

Efficacy of four different formulations of plant protection
products containing the botanical antifeedant azadirachtin
against the large pine weevil (*Hylobius abietis*)
W Bryan 5I-4 623

Northern bobwhite chick-arthropod food abundance in
insect resistant GM cotton crops
D A Butler and M P Cook 5I-5 627

The survival of Chinese pesticide companies in a
global marketplace – an international marketing perspective
S Kong 5I-6 631

Influence of *Pseudomonas oryzihabitans* on growth of tomato
plants and development of root-knot nematode *Meloidogyne javanica*
S V Leontopoulos, S R Gowen, I K Vagelas and F T Gravanis.........................5I-7 635

Ultrastructural and cytochemical observations of *Musa* spp.
in relation to susceptibility to nematodes
H A Kalorizou, S R Gowen and L J Bonner...5I-8 639

Crude protein and lipid concentration in grains from oats
infected with barley yellow dwarf virus
T Persson and H Eckersten 5I-9 643

Control of brassica clubroot using modern fungicides
possessing ant-protozoal activity
D Townley and R T V Fox...5I-10 647

Mechanisms in the biological control of lentil vascular wilt
(*Fusarium oxysporum* f.sp. *lentis*) by *Trichoderma hamatum*
S A El-Hassan and S R Gowen 5I-11 651

Seed treatment with a bacterial antagonist for reducing cotton
damping-off caused by *Pythium* spp.
A V Kapsalis, S R Gowen and F T Gravanis....................................5I-12 655

Disease control and the consequences of timing
on the yield of oilseed rape
A Coules and S Rossall...5I-13 659

Integrated control of Fusarium ear blight
M Guingouain and S Rossall...5I-14 663

Suppressing weed competition: the interaction of seed quality
and seed rate in spring wheat
M D Alallgi and A J Murdoch 5I-15 667

DISCUSSION SESSION 1
FUTURE CROP PROTECTION NEEDS

Future crop protection needs
P Ryan DS-1 673

DISCUSSION SESSION 2
THE FUTURE EDUCATIONAL NEEDS FOR CROP PROTECTION DS-2 678

VOLUME 2

SESSION 6A
RESISTANCE: SCIENCE INTO PRACTICE

Insecticide resistance: from science to practice
M S Williamson, J A Anstead, G J Devine, A L Devonshire *et al.* 6A-1 681

Qol resistance development in populations
of cereal pathogens in the UK
B A Fraaije, J A Lucas, W S Clark and F J Burnett 6A-2 689

The issues facing industry in the management of resistance in Europe
R Thompson...6A-3 695

The role and impact of the regulator in resistance management
O C Macdonald, I Meakin and D M Richardson 6A-4 703

SESSION 6B
PESTICIDE RESIDUES IN FOOD

Pesticide residues – better early than never?
G N Foster, D Atkinson and F J Burnett 6B-1 711

Removing hazardous products from the food chain
K Barker 6B-2 719

The grower's perspective on strategies for the minimisation
of pesticide residues in food
C J C Wise and A Findlay 6B-3 723

The role of biotechnology in the management of pesticide residues
P Rylott...6B-4 727

SESSION 6C
NOVEL AND INDUSTRIAL CROPS: REALISING THEIR POTENTIAL

An overview of opportunities and factors affecting exploitation
of crops for industrial use
M F Askew 6C-1 735

Issues affecting development of non-food crops – an industry view
C Spencer...6C-2 741

Development of flax and hemp agronomy for industrial fibre production
J P R E Dimmock, G R Hughes, R D Western and D Wright.............................6C-3 749

Liquid biofuels – an opportunity for UK agriculture?
D B Turley...6C-4 757

POSTER SESSION 7A
RESISTANCE: SCIENCE INTO PRACTICE

Gene flow from Bt transgenic corn to non Bt corn:
can refuges speed the evolution of pest resistance?
C F Chilcutt 7A-1 765

Study of resistance to ALS inhibitors in the weed
species *Echinochloa crus-galli*
B Konstantinovic, M Meseldzija, S Popovic and Bo Konstantinovic 7A-2 771

Differential sensitivity of Jordanian *Amaranthus retroflexus*
populations to post-emergence herbicides
H Z Ghosheh and K Hurle 7A-3 777

Characterisation of neonicotinoid resistance in
Bemisia tabaci from Spain
K Gorman, J Wren, G J Devine and I Denholm...7A-4 783

Negative cross-resistance between indoxacarb and
pyrethroids in the cotton bollworm, *Helicoverpa armigera*,
in Australia: a tool for resistance management
R V Gunning and A L Devonshire 7A-5 789

Biological evaluation of spiromesifen against *Bemisia tabaci*
and an assessment of resistance risks
F Guthrie, I Denholm, G J Devine and R Nauen 7A-6 795

Fluoxastrobin: risk assessment and anti-resistance
management strategy for seed treatment application in winter wheat
I Haeuser-Hahn, K H Kuck, A Suty-Heinze, A Mehl and P Evans....................7A-7 801

The response of *Echinochloa colona* populations from Nigeria
to oxadiazon, propanil and pendimethalin
F B Jafun, S A M Perryman and S R Moss 7A-8 807

A mutation in the C domain of the acetolactate synthase (ALS)
gene of *Bidens pilosa* confers resistance to imazethapyr
M Duran, G Plaza, M D Osuna, R De Prado and A Rodríguez-Franco...............7A-9 813

A new mutation site in the acetolactate synthase (ALS)
gene in *Amaranthus quitensis* resistant to imazethapyr
M D Osuna, C Casado, R De Prado, J Wagner and K Hurle 7A-10 819

POSTER SESSION 7B
MODE OF ACTION AND METABOLISM

Duration of yellow nutsedge (*Cyperus esculentus*) competitiveness
after treatment with various herbicides
J A Ferrell, W K Vencill and H J Earl 7B-1 825

Metamifop: mechanism of herbicidal activity and selectivity
in rice and barnyardgrass
T J Kim, H S Chang, J S Kim, I T Hwang *at al.* 7B-2 833

Herbicide resistance in *Lolium multiflorum* Lam.
(Italian rye-grass): involvement of glutathione S-transferases
J P H Reade and A H Cobb 7B-3 839

Structure of dichloromethyl-ketal safeners affects the
expression of glutathione S-transferase isoforms
T Matola, I Jablonkai, D Dixon, I Cummins and R Edwards...........................7B-4 845

Mode of action of the rediscovered fumigant – ethyl formate
G Dojchinov and V S Haritos 7B-5 851

Two different vacuolar enzymes are responsible for degradation
of glutathione-S-conjugates in barley (*Hordeum vulgare* L.)
P Schröder and C E Scheer...7B-6 857

Can picoxystrobin protect winter wheat from environmental stress?
J P H Reade, L J Milner and A H Cobb...7B-7 863

POSTER SESSION 7C
NOVEL AND INDUSTRIAL CROPS: REALISING THEIR POTENTIAL

IENICA – Interactive European Network for Industrial Crops
and their Applications
C A Holmes...7C-1 871

Identification of opportunities for under-utilised crop
in Wales – a novel approach
L V Hodsman, D B Turley and M G Ceddia.....................................7C-2 877

[^{14}C] glyphosate: uptake into Echium plantagineum
following pre-emergent application
A B McEwen, E B Whittle, R G Parsons and K McCurrie 7C-3 883

POSTER SESSION 7D
ASPECTS OF HORTICULTURAL CROP PROTECTION

Control of field thrips, Thrips angusticeps,
in vining peas, Pisum sativum
R L Ward and A J Biddle 7D-1 889

Alternative methods for controlling onion thrips
L Jensen, B Simko, C Shock and L Saunders..7D-2 895

Slug control by molluscicide and herbicide applications
prior to planting iceberg lettuce
D M Glen, C W Wiltshire, D A Bohan, R Storer et al. 7D-3 901

An IPM strategy for slugs in vegetable and salad crops
G R Port, M D F Shirley, R H Collier, D A Bohan et al. 7D-4 907

Aggressiveness of cucumber isolates of Pythium aphanidermatum
on tomato and pepper in the Sultanate of Oman, and the relationship
between aggressiveness and resistance to the fungicide metalaxyl
A M Al-Saadi, M L Deadman, I Khan and J R M Thacker 7D-5 913

Forecasting and control of Alternaria blight in carrots
J E Thomas, D M Kenyon and D Martin..7D-6 919

Can crab shells protect roses from blackspot?
A M Hall, A Ali and B Pascoe 7D-7 925

Evaluation of oxadiargyl herbicide in various
Australian horticultural crops
P R Frost, I L Macleod and E M Hanlon..7D-8 929

Possible future herbicide options in green beans, Phaseolus vulgaris
J Scrimshaw...7D-9 933

POSTER SESSION 7E
ASPECTS OF PRODUCTION, PROTECTION AND REGULATION IN ARABLE CROPS

Flucetosulfuron: a new tool to control Galium aparine
and broadleaf weeds in cereal crops
D S Kim, J N Lee, K H Hwang, T Y Kim et al...7E-1 941

The effect of downy mildew (Peronospora viciae) on the yield
of spring sown field beans (Vicia fabae) and its control
A J Biddle, J Thomas, D Kenyon, N V Hardwick and M C Taylor 7E-2 947

Terbuthylazine in maize – a model example
of product stewardship and safe use
T Kuechler, B Duefer, H Resseler, M Schulte and D Cornes............................7E-3 953

Mixed maize and soya bean cropping as an
effective fodder production method
L Prijic, G Cvijanovic, M Srebric and D Glamoclija 7E-4 959

Biological action of some herbicides on teluric microflora
development from sugar beet cultivated soil
S Stefan, I Horia, M Oprea, E Bucur et al. 7E-5 963

Influence of calcium ion on the efficacy of selected herbicides
C Gauvrit...7E-6 969

The effects of fungicides on grain water and dry matter
contents during maturation of winter wheat
S Pepler, M J Gooding and R H Ellis...7E-7 975

Optimising the benefits of fluquinconazole seed treatment
in sequences of winter wheat crops
G L Bateman, J F Jenkyn and R J Gutteridge 7E-8 979

POSTER SESSION 7F
CROP PRODUCTION AND PROTECTION IN TROPICAL CROPS

Population dynamics and control of the dubas bug
Ommatissus lybicusi in the Sultanate of Oman
J R M Thacker, I H S Al-Mahmooli and M L Deadman 7F-1 987

Weed management options for resource
poor maize-dairy farmers in Central Kenya
J M Maina, B M Kivuva, M W K Mburu, A J Murdoch et al. 7F-2 993

Epidemiology and maize crop resistance to head smut disease
with reference to small-scale maize-dairy farmers in Central Kenya
J G M Njuguna, P M Njoroge and A N Jama 7F-3 999

Solving weed management problems in maize-rice
wetland production systems in semi-arid Zimbabwe
A B Mashingaidze, O C Chivinge, S Muzenda, A P Barton et al. 7F-4 1005

Scaling-up improved Imperata management practices in
the sub-humid Savannah of Nigeria
J Ellis-Jones, J Power, D Chikoye, O K Nielsen et al.......................................7F-5 1011

Farmers, farms and physiology: an integrated approach
to Striga research
S Pierce, G Ley, A M Mbwaga, R I Lamboll et al. 7F-6 1017

Promoting integrated Striga management practices
in maize in northern Nigeria
I Kureh, M A Hussaini, D Chikoye, A M Emechebe et al.................................7F-7 1023

Improving rice-based cropping systems in north-west
Bangladesh: diversification and weed management
M Mazid, M A Jabber, M Mortimer, L Wade et al. 7F-8 1029

Direct seeding as an alternative to transplanting rice
for the rice-wheat systems of the Indo-Gangetic plains:
sustainability issues related to weed management
G Singh, Y Singh, V P Singh, R K Singh et al. 7F-9 1035

Glyphosate and carfentrazone-ethyl mixtures for the control
of hard to kill weeds in zero-tillage systems in Brazil
L L Foloni, V A Gangora, E D Vellini, P J Christoffoleti et al. 7F-10 1041

Modulation of seed dormancy in Ocimum basilicum
by light, gibberellins (GA3) and abscisic acid (ABA)
D A Dawoud, E A Ahmed, H Khalid and A G T Babiker 7F-11 1047

Response of some important citrus weeds to two formulations
of glyphosate applied at three growth stages
M Singh and S Singh...7F-12 1053

Rhizotron study on soil moisture and plant population
effect on root competition of cotton and mungbean
with Trianthema portulacastrum and Echinochloa crus-galli
S Singh, A Yadav, R K Malik and M Singh 7F-13 1059

DISCUSSION SESSION 3
REGULATION OF ADJUVANTS – CURRENT STATUS AND FUTURE PROSPECTS

Market and regulatory trends affecting the use of tank mix adjuvants
R H Sohm...DS-3 1067

Trends in the chemicals regulatory arena affecting tank mix
adjuvant markets
J A Rosenblom DS-3 1069

DISCUSSION SESSION 4
DOES UK PLANT BIOTECHNOLOGY HAVE A COMMERCIAL FUTURE?.............DS-4 1072

SESSION 8A
THE ENVIRONMENTAL IMPACT OF GM CROPS: COSTS AND BENEFITS A DECADE AFTER COMMERCIALISATION

An assessment of the environmental impact of
genetically modified crops in the US
M J McKee, S Fernandez, T E Nickson and G P Head....................................8A-1 1075

The environmental impact of controlling weeds using broad
spectrum herbicides in genetically modified herbicide tolerant
crops: the farm scale evaluations explained
A Dewar...8A-2 1085

Evaluation of transgenic herbicide-resistant oilseed rape and
maize with respect to integrated pest management strategies
B Hommel and B Pallutt 8A-3 1087

Life cycle and gene dispersal of oilseed rape volunteers
(*Brassica napus* L.)
S Gruber, C Pekrun and W Claupein 8A-4 1093

SESSION 8B
CROP PRODUCTION WITH REDUCED INPUTS

A rational basis for the design of wheat canopy ideotypes
S R Parker, P M Berry, N D Paveley, F van den Bosch and D J Lovell..............8B-1 1101

Novel sensors for measuring soil nitrogen,
water availability and strength
A J Miller, D M Wells, J Braven, L Ebdon *et al.* 8B-2 1107

Adjusting the fungicide input in winter wheat
depending on variety resistance
L N Jørgensen, L Hagelskjær and G C Nielsen..8B-3 1115

SESSION 8C
NEW APPROACHES TO CROP PROTECTION BY EXPLOITING
STRESS-RELATED SIGNALLING IN PLANTS

Exploring multi-trophic plant-herbivore interactions
for new crop protection methods
H J Bouwmeester, I F Kappers, F W A Verstappen, A Aharoni *et al.* 8C-1 1123

Plant activation of barley by intercropped conspecifics
and weeds: allelobiosis
J Pettersson, V Ninkovic and R Glinwood 8C-2 1135

Plant-fungal interactions mediated by volatile signals
J A Lucas 8C-3 1145

Registration opportunities for natural product versus
synthetic plant stress signals (or plant activators) for crop protection
T E Tooby...8C-4 1149

SESSION 9A
THE ENVIRONMENTAL IMPACT OF GM CROPS: SAFETY TESTING,
RISK ASSESSMENT AND REGULATION

The use of ecological endpoints and other tools from
ecological risk assessment to create a more conceptual
framework for assessing the environmental risks of GM plants
G M Poppy 9A-1 1159

Rethinking the herbicide development and regulation
process post GM crop environment impact studies
J Pidgeon 9A-2 1167

An assessment of the level of crop to crop gene flow
in forage maize crops in the UK
R Weekes, C Henry, D Morgan, R Daniels and C Boffey..................................9A-3 1169

Containment and mitigation of transgene flow from crops
J Gressel and H I Al-Ahmad...9A-4 1175

SESSION 9B
IMPACT OF CHANGING WEATHER PATTERNS ON
CROP PROTECTION AND CROP PRODUCTION

Linking climate change predictions with crop simulation models
M A Semenov...9B-1 1181

Climate change and decreasing herbicide persistence
S W Bailey 9B-2 1189

Turning up the heat on pests and diseases:
a case study for Barley yellow dwarf virus
R Harrington..9B-3 1195

Predicting the potential distribution of alien pests in the
UK under global climate change: *Diabrotica virgifera virgifera*
R H A Baker, R J C Cannon and A MacLeod..9B-4 1201

SESSION 9C
NEW APPROACHES TO CROP PROTECTION BY EXPLOITING
STRESS-RELATED SIGNALLING IN PLANTS

Plant defense-inducing N-acylgutamines from insect guts:
structural diversity and microbe-assisted biosyntheses
L Ping, D Spiteller and W Boland 9C-1 1211

Synthetic herbivore-induced plant volatiles as field
attractants for beneficial insects
D G James 9C-2 1217

Evaluation of the plant defence booster, acibenzolar-S-methyl,
for use in Australian agriculture
I L Macleod, R Walker and I M Inglis 9C-3 1223

New chemical signals in plant protection against herbivores and weeds
M Matthes, J A Napier, J A Pickett and C M Woodcock 9C-4 1227

BCPC COUNCIL MEMBERS

President	Mr H Oliver-Bellasis
Chairman	Dr B Thomas
Vice-chairmen	Prof D Atkinson
	Mr J MacLeod
Honorary Treasurer	Mr P C Moring

Corporate Members

Agricultural Engineers Association
Association of Applied Biologists
Association of Independent Crop Consultants
Biotechnology and Biological Sciences Research Council
British Institute of Agricultural Consultants
British Society for Plant Pathology
British Society of Plant Breeders
Campden & Chorleywood Food Research Association
Crop Protection Association
Department for Environment, Food and Rural Affairs represented by
  • Pesticides Safety Directorate
Department of Agriculture and Rural Development for Northern Ireland
Environment Agency
Imperial College, London
Lantra
National Association of Agricultural Contractors
National Consumer Association
National Farmers' Union
National Institute of Agricultural Botany
Natural Environment Research Council
Scottish Executive Environment and Rural Affairs Department
Society of Chemical Industry – Pest Management Group
United Kingdom Agricultural Supply Trade Association

Individual Member

Dr D V Alford	Mr R Joice
Mr M Askew	Prof G Marshall
Dr K J Brent	Dr R Morrod
Mr J R Finney	Dr A R Thompson
Dr J Gilmour	

General Secretary

Dr J P Fisher

BCPC

BCPC is a registered charity. It was founded in 1968 when the British Weed Control Council (set up in 1953) and the British Insecticide and Fungicide Council (set up in 1962) merged to form a single body. Although essentially a British organisation, its work is international in outlook.

BCPC brings together a wide range of organisations interested in the improvement of crop protection. The members of the Board represent the interests of government departments, the agrochemical industry, farmers' organisations, the advisory services and independent consultants, distributors, the research councils, agricultural engineers, environment interests, consumer groups, training and overseas development.

Objectives

The mission of the BCPC is to promote the development, use and understanding of effective and sustainable crop protection practice.

The BCPC has four objectives:

- To examine current and developing issues in the science and practice of crop protection;

- To promote improved, environmentally-sensitive crop protection practices to produce wholesome food;

- To foster and support crop protection science and practice through conferences, symposia and publications and through the presentation of its views to government and other organisations;

- To present independent information to the general public on the place of crop protection in agriculture and horticulture and to encourage and contribute to education and training.

Further information

Further information about the BCPC, its organisation and its work can be obtained from:

7 Omni Business Centre
Omega Park
Alton
Hampshire
GU34 2QD
UK

Tel: +44 (0) 1420 593 200
Fax: +44 (0) 1420 593 209
Email: gensec@bcpc.org
Web: www.bcpc.org

THE BCPC CONGRESS 2003
PROGRAMME COMMITTEE

Congress Programme Chairman

Dr Ken Pallett   *Bayer CropScience, Cambridge, UK*

Congress Co-Chairman

Professor Phil Russell   *Consultant, Cambridge, UK*

Congress Vice Chairman

Naresh Atreya   *Consultant, Maidenhead, UK*
Chris Furk   *Plant Health and Seeds Inspectorate, York, UK*
Cathy Knott   *Consultant, Peterborough, UK*

Congress Co-Chairman

Dr Geoff Bateman   *Rothamsted Research, Harpenden, UK*
Dr Anthony Biddle   *PGRO, Peterborough, UK*
Dr Fiona Burnett   *SAC, Edinburgh, UK*
Dr Clare Butler Ellis   *Silsoe Research Institute, Bedford, UK*
Dr John Caseley   *Castan Consultants, Bristol UK*
Peter Chapman   *Pesticides Safety Directorate, York, UK*
James Clarke   *ADAS Boxworth, Cambridge, UK*
Dr Leonard G Copping   *LGC Consultants, Saffron Walden, UK*
Dr William Cormack   *ADAS Terrington, Kings Lynn, UK*
Professor Howard Davies   *Scottish Crop Research Institute, Dundee, UK*
Dr Fergus Earley   *Syngenta, Bracknell, UK*
Dr Jean Fitzgerald   *Horticulture Research International, East Malling, UK*
Caroline Harris   *Exponent International, Harrogate, UK*
Kerry Hutchinson   *Pesticides Safety Directorate, York, UK*
Dr David Johnson   *International Rice Research Institute, Metro Manila, Philippines*
Dr Roy Kennedy   *Horticulture Research International, Wellesbourne, UK*
Martin Lainsbury   *Morley Research Centre, Wymondham, UK*
Professor Paul Miller   *Silsoe Research Institute, Bedford, UK*
Dr Rod Morrod   *BCPC Biotech2020 Organising Group Chair, Maidenhead, UK*
Professor Bob Naylor   *Trelareg Consultants, Banchory*
Professor John Pickett   *Rothamsted Research, Harpenden, UK*
Dr Alan Raybould   *Syngenta, Bracknell, UK*
Dr Charlie Riches   *Natural Resources Institute, University of Greenwich, Chatham, UK*
Dr Pat Ryan   *Syngenta Crop Protection UK, Cambridge, UK*
David Turley   *Central Science Laboratory, York, UK*
Dr Keith Walters   *Central Science Laboratory, York, UK*
Duncan Webb   *Health and Safety Laboratory, Sheffield, UK*
Dr Fangjie Zhao   *Rothamsted Research, Harpenden, UK*

On behalf of BCPC

Dr David Alford — *Director, Programme Policy*
Frances McKim — *Editor-in-Chief & Press Manager*
Dr Colin Ruscoe — *Exhibitions Director*
Chris Todd — *BCPE, Managing Director*

BCPC Congress Secretariat

Rachel Price — *The Event Organisation Company*

AUTHOR INDEX

Author	Paper
A	
Abbasipour, H	5A-3
Aharoni, A	8C-1
Ahmad, R	5F-1
Ahmed, E A	7F-11
Al-Ahmad, H I	9A-4
Alallgi, M D	5I-15
Ali, A	7D-7
Allan, E J	5B-7
Al-Mahmooli, I H S	7F-1
Al-Saadi, A M	7D-5
Ambrus, A	4C-2
Amsellem, Z	2A-3
Anstead, J A	6A-1
Archambault, S	5G-3
Askew, M F	6C-1
Atkinson, D	5B-1, 6B-1
Avav, T	7F-5
Avery, M I	3B-1
B	
Babiker, A G T	7F-11
Bailey, S W	9B-2
Baker, R H A	9B-4
Barela, J F	7F-10
Barker, K	6B-2
Baron, J J	5G-3
Barton, A P	7F-4
Basford, W D	5H-1
Bastiaans, L	4B-1
Bateman, G L	7E-8
Benjamin, L R	4B-3
Bernes, R	2A-5
Berry, P M	8B-1
Biddle, A J	7D-1, 7E-2
Biemelt, S	2B-2
Boatman, N D	3B-2, 3B-5
Boddis, W	5G-3
Boffey, C	9A-3
Bohan, D A	7D-3, 7D-4
Boland, W	9C-1
Bonner, L J	5I-8
van den Boogaard, R	4B-1
Boon, S M	5A-1
Booth, E J	5B-8

Author	Paper
van den Bosch, F	8B-1
Bouchagier, P	5I-1
Bouwmeester, H J	8C-1
Boxall, J	3B-4
Bradbury, R B	3B-3, 5E-1
Bradshaw, J D	2A-2
Braekman, P	5C-4
Brain, P	4B-5
Braven, J	8B-2
Broekaert, W	2B-4
Brown, V K	3B-2, 3B-5
Bruhn, C M	1A-3
Bryan, G J	2B-1
Bryan, W	5I-4
Bucur, E	7E-5
Burnett, F J	6A-2, 6B-1
Burns, R G	4D-1
Butler, D A	5I-5
Butler Ellis, M C	3C-5, 3C-6, 5C-3
C	
Cannon, R J C	9B-4
Carter, A D	5H-1
Casado, C	7A-10
Caseley, J C	4B-5, 7E-1
Cavanna, S	2A-5
Ceddia, M G	7C-2
Champion, G T	5E-2
Chaney, K	5E-1
Chang, H S	2A-6, 7B-2
Chapman, A S	2C-2
Chikoye, D	7F-5, 7F-7
Chilcutt, C F	7A-1
Chivinge, O C	7F-4
Cho, J H	2A-7
Cho, K Y	2A-6, 7B-2
Christerson, M	5F-2
Christoffoleti, P J	7F-10
Chung, B J	2A-6, 7B-2
Clark, L J	8B-2
Clark, W S	6A-2
Clarke, J H	4B-3
Clarkson, S	7D-3
Claupein, W	8A-4
Clook, M	3B-5

Author	Paper
Cobb, A H	7B-3, 7B-7
Collier, R H	4B-4, 5B-2, 7D-4
Collings, L V	4B-3
Cook, D A	5B-3
Cook, M P	5I-5
Cornes, D	7E-3
Coster, G	5A-1
Coules, A	5I-13
Cram, S	4C-1
Croxford, A	2C-2
Crute, I R	1A-1
Culin, S	4C-2
Cummins, I	7B-4
Cunningham, H M	5E-1
Cvijanovic, G	7E-4

D

Author	Paper
Daniels, R	9A-3
Davies, D H K	4B-3
Davis, T J	3A-4
Dawoud, D A	7F-11
Dawson, W M	4D-3, 5B-6
De Moor, A	5C-4
De Prado, R	5H-2, 7A-9, 7A-10
De Wolf, J	2B-4
Deadman, M L	7D-5, 7F-1
Denholm, I	6A-1, 7A-4, 7A-6
Dertzakis, D	5B-7
Devine, G J	6A-1, 7A-4, 7A-6
Devonshire, A L	6A-1, 7A-5
Dewar, A	8A-2
Dicke, M	8C-1
Dickie, A J	4A-4
Dillen, W	2B-4
Dimmock, J P R E	6C-3
Dixon, D	7B-4
Dojchinov, G	7B-5
Droual, A-M	2B-4
Drummond, C	3B-4
Duefer, B	7E-3
Dunsiger, Z	5B-1
Duran, M	7A-9
Duriatti, A	2A-5

E

Author	Paper
Earl, H J	7B-1
Ebdon, L	8B-2
Eckersten, H	5I-9

Author	Paper
Edwards, R	7B-4
Efthhimiadis, P	5I-1
El-Hassan, S A	5I-11
Ellis, R H	7E-7
Ellis, S A	4B-4
Ellis-Jones, J	7F-4, 7F-5, 7F-7
Emechebe, A M	7F-7
Evans, A D	3B-3
Evans, P	7A-7

F

Author	Paper
Fernandez, S	8A-1
Ferrell, J A	5F-3, 7B-1
Field, L M	6A-1
Finch, S	5B-2
Findlay, A	6B-3
Flynn, D J	3A-2
Foloni, L L	7F-10
Foster, D	2C-2
Foster, G N	6B-1
Foster, S P	6A-1
Fox, R T V	5I-10
Fraaije, B A	6A-2
Franco, A R	5H-2
Frankard, V	2B-4
Franke, A C	7F-7
Frost, P R	7D-8

G

Author	Paper
Gallagher, E	2C-4
Gangora, V A	7F-10
Gaston, C P	5G-2
Gauvrit, C	7E-6
Ghinea, L	7E-5
Ghosheh, H Z	7A-3
Ginsburg, D	4B-3
Glamoclija, D	7E-4
Glen, D M	7D-3, 7D-4
Glinwood, R	8C-2
Godwin, R J	4B-2
Gooch, R D E	4A-1
Gooding, M J	7E-7
Gorman, K	7A-4
Gowen, S R	5A-2, 5I-7, 5I-8, 5I-11, 5I-12
Gowing, D J G	8B-2
Gravanis, F T	5A-2, 5I-7, 5I-12
Gressel, J	2A-3, 9A-4

Author	Paper	Author	Paper
Grey, T L	5F-3	**I**	
Gruber, S	8A-4	Ibana, S	7F-5
Guingouain, M	5I-14	Inglis, I M	9C-3
Gunning, R V	7A-5		
Guthrie, F	7A-6	**J**	
Gutteridge, R J	7E-8	Jabber, M A	7F-8
		Jablonkai, I	7B-4
H		Jafun, F B	7A-8
Haage Riethmuller, I	4B-1	Jama, A N	7F-3
Haeuser-Hahn, I	7A-7	James, D G	9C-2
Hagelskjær, L	8B-3	Jenkins, M J	4A-3
Hajirezaei, M-R	2B-2	Jenkyn, J F	7E-8
Hall, A M	7D-7	Jensen, L	7D-2
Hallett, S G	5I-2	Joe, G H	2A-7
Hanlon, E M	7D-8	Johnson, D E	7F-9
Hanus, D	4A-2	Johnson, D L	4D-2
Harbinson, J	4B-1	Jones, H D	2B-3
Hardwick, N V	7E-2	Jongsma, M A	8C-1
Haritos, V S	7B-5	Jørgensen, L N	8B-3
Harrington, R	9B-3		
Harris, C A	5G-2	**K**	
Hart, A	3B-5	Kalorizou, H A	5I-8
Hatzfeld, Y	2B-4	Kang, K G	2A-7
Häusler, A	5B-9	Kappers, I F	8C-1
Head, G P	8A-1	Kapsalis, A V	5I-12
Heier, J	2A-1	Karimi, J	5A-3
Henry, C	9A-3	Kempenaar, C	4B-1
Herbst, A	3C-2	Kenyon, D M	7D-6, 7E-2
Hill, J H	2A-2	Khalid, H	7F-11
Hodsman, L V	7C-2	Khan, I	7D-5
Hofman, T W	5A-1	Kim, D S	2A-7, 4B-5, 7E-1
Holland, J	3B-5	Kim, D W	2A-6, 2A-7, 7B-2
Holm, R E	5G-3	Kim, J S	7B-2
Holmes, C A	7C-1	Kim, T J	2A-6, 7B-2
Hommel, B	8A-3	Kim, T Y	2A-7, 7E-1
Honek, A	5B-4	Kivuva, B M	7F-2
Hong, K S	7B-2	Kleter, G A	4C-4
Horia, I	7E-5	Ko, Y K	2A-6
Huber, B	4D-4	Kong, S	5I-6
Hughes, G R	6C-3	Konstantinovic, B	7A-2
Hunter, C	5G-3	Konstantinovic, Bo	7A-2
Hurle, K	7A-3, 7A-10	Koo, S J	2A-7, 7E-1
Hussaini, M A	7F-7	Kormawa, P M	7F-5, 7F-7
Hussey, D J	3A-4	Kropff, M J	4B-1
Hwang, I T	7B-2	Kuck, K H	7A-7
Hwang, K H	2A-7, 7E-1	Kudsk, P N	3C-4
Hwang, K S	2A-7	Kuechler, T	7E-3
Hyder, K	5D-2, 5G-1	Kuiper, H A	4C-4

Author	Paper
Kunkel, D L	5G-3
Kureh, I	7F-7
Kwon, O Y	2A-6
Kwon, Y W	4B-5

L

Author	Paper
Lamboll, R I	7F-6
Lane, A G	5C-3
Larelle, D	2A-5
Lazaraki, I	5B-7
Le Goff, T	8B-2
Leake, C R	4C-3
Lee, J N	2A-7, 7E-1
Leeds-Harrison, P B	8B-2
Lejeune, P	2B-4
Lemaitre, G	4A-2
Leontopoulos, S V	5I-7
Ley, G	7F-6
Li, B	2A-8
Li, B	5I-3
Li, Z CH	2A-8
Liégeois, E	2C-1
Lillford, P J	1A-2
Lole, M J	5B-5
Lovell, D J	8B-1
Lucas, J A	6A-2, 8C-3
Lücker, J	8C-1
Luckerhoff, L L P	8C-1
Lutman, P J W	3B-2, 3B-5, 4B-3

M

Author	Paper
Macdonald, O C	6A-4
MacLeod, A	9B-4
Macleod, I L	7D-8, 9C-3
Maestroni, B	4C-2
Magnusson, G	5F-2
Maina, J M	7F-2
Malik, R K	7F-13
Mann, R	2A-5
Marrs, R H	5C-1
Marshall, E J P	3B-2
Marshall, J E	4B-5
Martínez, M J	5H-2
Martinkova, Z	5B-4
Mashingaidze, A B	7F-4
Mason, P J	5H-1
Mathiassen, S	3C-4
Matola, T	7B-4

Author	Paper
Matthes, M	9C-4
Mavrotas, C	2A-5
May, M J	5E-2
Mayes, A	4B-3
Mazid, M	7F-8
Mburu, M W K	7F-2
Mbwaga, A M	7F-6
McCracken, A R	5B-6
McCubbin-Green, A	5B-8
McCurrie, K	7C-3
McEwen, A B	7C-3
McGrath, S P	4D-2
McKee, M J	8A-1
Mead, A	4B-4
Meakin, I	6A-4
Mehl, A	7A-7
Meseldzija, M	7A-2
Miller, A J	8B-2
Miller, P C H	3C-1, 3C-4, 4B-2
Milligan, A L	5C-1
Milne, A E	4B-3
Milner, L J	7B-7
Miura, I	2A-10
Miyake, Y	2A-10
Mol, H G J	5C-5
Moorcroft, D	3B-1
Moores, S R	6A-1
Morgan, D	9A-3
Morris, A J	3B-3
Mortimer, M	7F-8, 7F-9
Moss, S R	7A-8
Mudzunga, J	5C-2
Müller, M	2B-2
Murdoch, A J	5D-1, 5I-15, 7F-2
Muzenda, S	7F-4
Mwangi, D M	7F-2
Myung, E J	7B-2

N

Author	Paper
Nagayama, K	2A-10, 5A-1
Napier, J A	9C-4
Nauen, R	7A-6
Neustifter, J	4D-4
Nicholls, J W	3C-3
Nickson, T E	8A-1
Nicolai, M	7F-10
Nielsen, G C	8B-3
Nielsen, O K	7F-5

Author	Paper	Author	Paper
Ninkovic, V	8C-2	Powley, C R	5F-2
Njoroge, P M	7F-3	Press, M C	7F-6
Njuguna, J M	7F-2, 7F-3	Prijic, L	7E-4
North, M	5C-2	Putwain, P D	5C-1
Nuttyens, D	5C-4		

O

		R	
Oprea, M	7E-5	Rahman, A	5F-1
Or, A	7F-9	Reade, J P H	7B-3, 7B-7
Orr, A W	7F-8	Resseler, H	7E-3
Orson, J H	3C-4, 4A-2	Reuzeau, C	2B-4
Osuna, M D	7A-9, 7A-10	Rice, M E	2A-2, 2A-4
van Oudheusden, Z	5A-1	Richardson, D M	6A-4
		Riches, C R	7F-4, 7F-6, 7F-8
		Robinson, T H	3C-5
P		Rodríguez-Franco, A	7A-9
Pallutt, B	8A-3	Rose, S C	5H-1
Park, C H	2A-6	Rosenblom, J A	DS-3
Park, J R	5D-1	Rossall, S	5I-13, 5I-14
Parker, S R	8B-1	Rotteveel, A J W	3A-3
Parker, W E	4B-4	de Ruiter, H	5C-5
Parkin, C S	3C-3	Ryan, P	DS-1
Parsons, D J	4B-3	Rylott, P	6B-4
Parsons, R G	7C-3	Ryu, J W	2A-6
Pascoe, B	7D-7		
Paveley, N D	8B-1	**S**	
Peerbolte, R	2B-4	Sakai, J	2A-10
Peis, S	4D-4	Santiago, R	5H-2
Pekrun, C	8A-4	Sanz, A	2B-4
Peña, F	5H-2	Saunders, L	7D-2
Pepler, S	7E-7	Scheer, C E	7B-6
Perryman, S A M	7A-8	Schmitt, A	5B-7
Persson, T	5I-9	Scholes, J D	7F-6
Pettersson, J	8C-2	Schröder, P	4D-4, 7B-6
Pickett, J A	9C-4	Schulte, M	7E-3
Pidgeon, J	9A-2	Schulteis, D T	2A-1
Pierce, S	7F-6	Schulz, S	7F-7
Ping, L	9C-1	Scotford, I M	3C-6
Pingel, U	5G-4	Scrimshaw, J	7D-9
Plaza, G	7A-9	Seddon, B	5B-7
Ploss, H	5A-1	Semenov, M A	9B-1
Popovic, S	7A-2	Shaber, S H	2A-8
Popple, S C	3A-4	Shewry, P R	2B-3
Poppy, G M	9A-1	Shibata, M	2A-10
Port, G R	7D-4	Shirley, M D F	7D-4
Potts, G R	1A-4	Shock, C	7D-2
Powell, E S	3C-4	Simko, B	7D-2
Powell, V	3A-3	Singh, G	7F-9
Power, J D	3C-5, 7F-5	Singh, M	7F-12, 7F-13

Author	Paper		Author	Paper
Singh, P	7F-9		**W**	
Singh, R K	7F-9		Wade, L	7F-8
Singh, S	7F-12		Wagner, J	7A-10
Singh, S	7F-13		Walker, R	9C-3
Singh, V P	7F-9		Walklate, P J	3C-3
Singh, Y	7F-9		Wang, J	2A-8
Smeets, L	3A-1		Ward, R L	7D-1
Smith, D A	5I-2		Watson, C A	5B-1
Sohm, R H	DS-3		Watson, S J	5D-1
Sonck, B	5C-4		Watts, A J	4B-2
SonnewaldU	2B-2		Webb, D A	3C-6
Sparks, C	2B-3		Weekes, R	9A-3
Spencer, C	6C-2		Weinert, T	7D-3
Spiteller, D	9C-1		Wells, D M	8B-2
Srebric, M	7E-4		Western, R D	6C-3
Stefan, A L	7E-5		Whalley, W R	8B-2
Stefan, S	7E-5		White, R	7F-4
Storer, R	7D-3		Whittle, E B	7C-3
Sun, K	2A-8		Wilcox, A	5E-1
Sutherland, K G	5B-8		Wilkinson, D J	4B-3
Suty-Heinze, A	7A-7		Williams, D P E	2C-3
Symondson, W O C	7D-4		Williamson, M S	6A-1
			Wilson, F E A	4D-3
T			Wiltshire, C W	7D-3
Talei, D	5A-3		Wimbush, J M	5F-4
Tarawali, G	7F-5, 7F-7		Windey, S	5C-4
Taylor, M C	7E-2		Wise, C J C	6B-3
Thacker, J R M	7D-5, 7F-1		Woodcock, C M	9C-4
Thomas, J E	7D-6, 7E-2		Woodward, S	5B-7
Thompson, A R	6A-3		Wooldridge, J	5C-2
Tomiya, K	2A-9		Wren, J	7A-4
Tooby, T E	8C-4		Wright, D	6C-3
Townley, D	5I-10		Wu, H	2B-3
Travis, K Z	5D-2, 5G-1			
Turley, D B	6C-4, 7C-2		**Y**	
			Yadav, A	7F-13
U			Yanase, Y	2A-9
Udensi, U E	7F-5		Yang, H Z	5I-3
V			**Z**	
Vagelas, I K	5A-2, 5I-7		van de Zande, J C	5C-5
Van Camp, W	2B-4		Zhan, F K	2A-8
Vellini, E D	7F-10		Zhang, L	2A-8
Vencill, W K	5F-3, 7B-1		Zhang, Z	2A-8
Verschwele, A	5B-9, 5G-4			
Verstappen, F W A	8C-1			
de Vlieger, J J	5C-5			

ABBREVIATIONS

Where abbreviations are necessary the following are permitted without definition

acceptable daily intake	ADI		growth stage	GS
acetolactate synthase	ALS		hectare(s)	ha
acetyl CoA carboxylase	ACCase		high performance (or pressure)	
acid dissociation constant	pKa		liquid chromatography	hplc
acid equivalent	a.e.		high volume	HV
active ingredient	a.i.		hour	h
approximately	c.		infrared	i.r.
base pair	bp		inner diameter	id
becquerel	Bq		integrated crop management	ICM
body weight	b.w.		integrated pest management	IPM
boiling point	b.p.		International Organization for Standardization	ISO
British Standards Institution	BSI		in the journal last mentioned	*ibid.*
by the author last mentioned	*idem.*		Joules	J
centimetre(s)	cm		Kelvin	K
Chemical Abstracts Services Registry Number	CAS RN		kilobase pair	kb
coefficient of variance	CV		kilodalton	kD
colony-forming unit(s)	cfu		kilogram(s)	kg
compare	cf.		kilogram(s) per hectare	kg/ha
concentration x time product	ct		kilometres per hour	km/h
concentration required to kill 50% of test organisms	LC50		least significant difference	LSD
correlation coefficient	*r*		litre(s)	litre(s)
counts per minute	cpm		litres per hectare	litres/ha
cultivar	cv.		logarithm, common, base 10	log
cultivars	cvs.		logarithm, natural	ln
dalton	D		low volume	LV
day(s)	d		mass	*m*
days after treatment	DAT		mass per mass	*m/m*
degrees Celsius (centigrade)	°C		mass per volume	*m/V*
degrees of freedom	df		mass spectroscopy	ms
Department of Environment,			maximum	max.
Food & Rural Affairs	Defra		maximum residue level	MRL
disintegrations per minute	dpm		melting point	m.p.
dose required to kill 50% of test organisums	LD50		metre(s)	m
dry matter	d.m.		metres per second	m
Edition	Edn		milligram(s)	mg
editor	ed.		milligrams per litre	mg/litre
editors	eds		milligrams per kg	mg/kg
emulsifiable concentrate	EC		millilitre(s)	ml
enzyme-linked immuno-sorbant assay	ELISA		millimetre(s)	mm
fast-protein liquid chromatography	FPLC		minimum	min.
Food and Drugs Administration	FDA		minimum harvest interval	MHI
for example	e.g.		Ministry of Agriculture, Fisheries and Food	
freezing point	f.p.		(England & Wales) (now Defra)	MAFF
gas chromatography-mass spectrometry	gc-ms		minute (time unit)	min
gas-liquid chromatography	glc		moisture content	M.C.
genetically modified	GM		molar concentration	M
genetically modified organism	GMO		mole	mol
gram(s)	g		molecular weight (relative)	*Mr*
gravity	g		no observed adverse effect level	NOAEL

ABBREVIATIONS continued

no observed effect concentration	NOEC	technical grade	tech.
no observed effect level	NOEL	temperature	temp.
no significant difference	NSD	that is	*i.e.*
nuclear magnetic resonance	nmr	thin-layer chromatography	tlc
number average diameter	n.a.d.	time for 50% loss; half life	DT_{50}
number median diameter	n.m.d.	tonne(s)	t
octanol/water partition coefficient	K_{ow}	tonne(s) per hectare	t/ha
organic matter	o.m.	ultra low volume	ULV
page	p.	ultraviolet	u.v.
pages	pp.	United Kingdom	UK
parts per billion	ppb	United States	US
parts per million	ppm	United States Department of Agriculture	USDA
parts per trillion	ppt	vapour pressure	v.p.
pascal	Pa	variety (wild plant use)	var.
percentage	%	volume	V
polyacrylamide gel electrophoresis	PAGE	volume median diameter	v.m.d.
polymerase chain reaction	PCR	water dispersible granule	WG
post-emergence	post-em.	weight	*wt*
power take off	p.t.o.	weight by volume	*wt/v*
pre-emergence	pre-em.	(mass by volume is more correct)	(m/V)
pre-plant incorporated	ppi	weight by weight	*wt/wt*
probability (statistical)	*P*	(mass by mass is more correct)	(m/m)
relative humidity	r.h.	wettable powder	WP
revolutions per minute	rev/min		
second (time unit)	s		
standard error	SE		
standard error of the difference	SED	less than	<
standard error of the mean	SEM	more than	>
soluble powder	SP	not less than	≮
species (singular)	sp.	not more than	≯
species (plural)	spp.	Multiplying symbols-	Prefixes
square metre	m^2	mega	$(x\ 10^6)$	M
subspecies	ssp.	kilo	$(x\ 10^3)$	k
surface mean diameter	s.m.d.	milli	$(x\ 10^{-3})$	m
suspension concentrate	SC	micro	$(x\ 10^{-6})$	μ
systemic acquired resistance	SAR	nano	$(x\ 10^{-9})$	n
tandem mass spectrometry	MS-MS	pico	$(x\ 10^{-12})$	p

SESSION 6A

RESISTANCE: SCIENCE INTO PRACTICE

Chairman: Dr Ian Denholm
                       Rothamsted Research, Harpenden, UK

Session Organiser: Dr Geoff L Bateman
                       Rothamsted Research, Harpenden, UK

Papers: 6A-1 to 6A-4

Insecticide resistance: from science to practice

M S Williamson, J A Anstead, G J Devine, A L Devonshire, L M Field, S P Foster,
G D Moores, I Denholm
Rothamsted Research, Harpenden, Hertfordshire, AL5 2JQ, UK
Email: martin.williamson@bbsrc.ac.uk

ABSTRACT

In this paper we review how rapid advances in understanding the biochemical and
molecular nature of insecticide resistance is contributing or might contribute to
combating resistance in practice. Knowledge of the different enzyme systems that
degrade insecticides and the specific target site mutations that selectively neutralise
particular classes or types of insecticide has progressed dramatically over the past
decade, and this in turn has enabled the development of highly sensitive
mechanism-specific diagnostic assays for resistance monitoring. These tools can be
used for analysing the incidence, dynamics and practical importance of resistance,
and for exploring the influence of both operational (e.g. pesticide use patterns) and
biological (e.g. insect dispersal and fitness costs) factors on the frequency of
resistance genes. Such techniques are particularly valuable for species (e.g. the
peach-potato aphid, *Myzus persicae*) that possess multiple resistance mechanisms,
each with distinct but sometimes over-lapping cross-resistance spectra. Frequent
similarities between mechanisms in different species also mean that the techniques
developed for one species can often be transferred to others with little additional
developmental research.

INTRODUCTION

Few areas of applied entomology have advanced as rapidly or received such widespread
attention in recent years as that of insecticide resistance. This reflects both the increasingly
severe impact of resistance on pest and disease management programmes, and the exciting
contributions that resistance is making to fundamental knowledge of insect genetics,
biochemistry and physiology. Without doubt, some of the most significant recent progress with
understanding resistance has resulted from the application of molecular biology to resistance
research. Depending on the mechanism involved, resistance has been shown to arise through
structural alterations of genes encoding target-site proteins or detoxifying enzymes, or through
processes (e.g. amplification or altered transcription) affecting gene expression (ffrench-
Constant, 1999; Hemingway, 2000). Despite this diversity of origin, genetic options available
to insects can also be very limited, especially for mechanisms based on a decreased sensitivity
of the insecticide target site. For example, the primary mechanism of cyclodiene resistance in
insects, based on a modification of the GABA-gated chloride channel in nerve membranes, has
been attributed to a single point mutation in several species of diverse taxonomic origin
(Thompson *et al.*, 1993). Work on two other target-site mechanisms - altered
acetylcholinesterase (AChE), conferring resistance to organophosphates (OPs) and carbamates,
and knockdown resistance or kdr (conferring resistance to DDT and pyrethroids) - has also
shown striking parallels between species but has proved more complicated due the occurrence
of multiple resistance alleles at the same loci (see below).

This paper explores the extent to which research on resistance mechanisms is contributing or may contribute to managing resistance in practice, through both the development of *in vitro* diagnostics for specific genes and gene products, enabling more precise studies of factors affecting the evolution and dynamics of resistance mechanisms, and an improved understanding of factors affecting cross-resistance between molecules potentially available for use in strategies aimed at diversifying the selection pressures imposed on pest populations.

MECHANISMS OF RESISTANCE IN *MYZUS PERSICAE*

The extent to which an improved knowledge of mechanisms can contribute to resistance management is exemplified well by work on the peach-potato aphid, *Myzus persicae* Sulzer. This species attacks and can transmit disease to several arable and horticultural crops including brassicas, potatoes, sugar beet and lettuce. *M. persicae* possesses three distinct mechanisms that collectively confer strong resistance to organophosphate, carbamate and pyrethroid insecticides. The first, discovered at Rothamsted 30 years ago, is based on the overproduction of one of two closely related carboxyesterase enzymes (E4 and FE4) that inactivate organophosphates, and to a lesser extent carbamates and pyrethroids before they reach their target sites in the insect's nervous system. Depending on the amount of carboxylesterase present, individuals of *M. persicae* are broadly classified into one of four categories: S-susceptible; R_1 – moderately resistant; R_2 – highly resistant or R_3 – extremely resistant (Devonshire & Moores, 1982). This elevated esterase results from the presence of amplified genes (Field *et al.*, 1993) and detailed molecular studies have shown that amplified E4 genes are on 24 kb units of DNA present as a tandem array of head-to-tail repeats, usually at a single chromosomal location associated with a translocation (Field & Devonshire, 1997). However, amplified FE4 genes can be present at multiple loci and there are no visible chromosomal abnormalities (Blackman *et al.*, 1999). An immunoassay that quantifies the amount of E4/FE4 in single aphids (see next section) has shown that there are approximately 4-fold increases in the amount of enzyme present in S, R_1, R_2 and R_3 aphids and this reflects a proportionate increase in gene copy number rising to around 80 copies in R_3 aphids (Field *et al.*, 1999).

The second mechanism, termed MACE (Modified AcetylCholinEsterase) is due to a modification to the insecticide target enzyme, acetylcholinesterase (AChE), which renders it insensitive to attack by the dimethyl carbamates, pirimicarb and triazamate (Moores *et al.*, 1994). MACE resistance was first seen in the UK in 1995 in aphids caught in Rothamsted's suction trap network, caused severe control failures in eastern England in 1996, and has been present at varying frequencies thereafter. Analogous MACE-type resistance mechanisms have been reported in a wide range of agricultural pest insect species, though generally these tend to be less selective, conferring a much broader resistance to OPs and/or carbamates. Although molecular cloning and sequencing studies of *Ace* genes from the 'model' insects, *Drosophila melanogaster* Meigen and *Musca domestica* L., have revealed several point mutations within the active site of the enzyme that disrupt insecticide binding to cause resistance (Mutero *et al.*, 1994; Walsh *et al.*, 2001), exploiting this information to identify the corresponding *Ace* mutations in other insects has proven unexpectedly difficult. It now seems that this is because most insects (other than *Drosophila* and *Musca*) possess two distinct *Ace* genes, with the structural mutations associated with resistance being located within the second, more divergent *Ace* gene sequence (Weill *et al.*, 2003). Recent cloning and analysis of this second gene from *M persicae* has indeed now identified a single point mutation, a serine to phenylalanine substitution (S331F) deep within the active site of the enzyme, that is likely to confer the highly selective resistance to dimethyl carbamates which is characteristic of the *M. persicae* MACE mechanism (Andrews *et al.*, 2003; Nabeshima *et al.*, 2003). Further studies are in progress to confirm the functionality of this mutation and to understand better how it selectively affects binding and inhibition of only the dimethyl carbamates.

In the last few years, we have also identified a third resistance mechanism, termed knockdown resistance or kdr, which is associated specifically with resistance to DDT and pyrethroids. Kdr involves a modification to the voltage-gated sodium channel protein in nerve membranes, which are vital for the normal transmission of nerve impulses and are the primary target site of these insecticides (Narahashi, 1992). There has been considerable progress in characterising the sodium channel mutations that are responsible for resistance, initially from work on *M. domestica* where two point mutations, leucine to phenylalanine (L1014F) and methionine to threonine (M918T) within the domain II region of the channel protein, were found to correlate with kdr (moderate resistance) and super-kdr (enhanced resistance) phenotypes respectively (Williamson *et al.*, 1996). The L1014F mutation has since been shown to occur in a range of insect species where it seems to confer a 'basal' kdr phenotype of 10-20 fold resistance to most pyrethroids. The enhanced super-kdr phenotype, that can give over 1000 fold resistance, is however less well conserved and several secondary mutations have been found that differ between species (Liu *et al.*, 2000; Pittendrigh *et al.*, 1997; Schuler *et al.*, 1998). In the case of *M persicae*, however, the same two point mutations originally described for houseflies (L1014F and M918T) have also been found and shown to correlate with DDT and pyrethroid resistance (Martinez-Torres *et al.*, 1999; Eleftherianos *et al.*, submitted). Consistent with their previous classification, *M. persicae* strains carrying the kdr mutation show generally moderate levels of resistance, whilst those with the M918T super-kdr mutation are virtually immune to the effects of even the most potent pyrethroids. The identification of these two point mutations within the *M. persicae* sodium channel (a large and complex membrane protein comprising over 2000 amino acids) has presented exciting new opportunities for the rapid diagnosis of this resistance mechanism in individual, field-collected aphids (see next section).

DIAGNOSIS OF MULTIPLE RESISTANCE IN *MYZUS PERSICAE*

These three mechanisms – overproduced carboxylesterase, MACE and kdr – can be present in different combinations that have different implications for which insecticides are likely to be effective or not. An ability to diagnose them individually and rapidly, ideally in single aphids, is therefore invaluable for anticipating and combating resistance problems. Biochemical assays for diagnosing overproduced carboxylesterase and MACE in single aphids have been developed at Rothamsted and are now used widely in many countries with resistance monitoring programmes for *M. persicae*. In most cases, the level of carboxylesterase (E4 or FE4) is measured using a sensitive immunoassay technique in 96-well microplates (Devonshire *et al.*, 1986) that can accurately score the esterase phenotype (S, R_1, R_2, R_3) of a small aliquot (1/20) of a single aphid homogenate. An additional polymerase chain reaction (PCR)-based technique is also available for scoring the esterase genotype (E4 or FE4) of the aphid where this is desirable (Field *et al.*, 1996). MACE phenotypes (susceptible, resistant homozygote and partially resistant heterozygote) are measured using a kinetic assay of AChE activity over time in the absence and presence of a low concentration of pirimicarb (Moores *et al.*, 1994). This assay is also very sensitive, using a further 1/8 aliquot of the same aphid homogenate and is run in 96-well format with a Tmax plate reader (Molecular Devices).

Kdr has proved more challenging in this respect since it is not readily accessible to biochemical tests based on electrophoresis, immunodiagnosis or kinetic measurements of target site inhibition. We have therefore concentrated on developing *in vitro* assays (as opposed to whole-organism bioassays, which are time-consuming and not mechanism-specific) based on the kdr (L1014F) and super-kdr (M918T) sodium channel mutations that cause the resistance phenotypes (see previous section). Several sequence-based approaches have been attempted, the most successful being the recent development of 5' nuclease allelic discrimination PCR assays specific to each of the two mutations (Anstead *et al.*, submitted) using fluorescent Taqman® MGB probes (PE Applied Biosystems). The main advantage of fluorogenic probe assays is that they enable PCR amplification and product detection to be combined in a single step, thereby greatly increasing the speed and efficiency of the assay and removing the requirement for time-consuming post-PCR manipulations (e.g. gel electrophoresis of PCR products). The 5' nuclease assay (Livak, 1999) uses short oligonucleotide probes that are matched against either the wild-type (susceptible) or kdr/super-kdr (resistant) sodium channel sequences (i.e. they are allele specific). These probes are each labelled with two fluorescent dyes; a reporter dye at one end and a quencher dye at the other and are added to PCR reactions of aphid DNA that are designed to amplify across the kdr and super-kdr sites within the sodium channel gene. In the intact probe, the fluorescence of the reporter dye is quenched by the close proximity of the quencher dye. However, during the PCR reaction, the probe is broken down if it anneals to its matching sequence in the sodium channel gene of the aphid that is being tested. Thus, an increase in fluorescence during the PCR indicates that the allele for the probe being tested is present in the aphid, and by testing small aliquots of individual aphids with each probe the exact susceptible/kdr/super-kdr genotype can be determined. Using this method, the three possible genotypes (resistant homozygote RR, heterozygote RS, susceptible homozygote SS) are easily distinguished for each of the two resistance alleles. The fluorescence output data for each probe is fed into an analysis programme that gives automated calling of the full genotype of each aphid. These assays are also very sensitive, each probe reaction requiring only 1/50 of a single aphid homogenate, and are designed to run alongside existing ones for overproduced carboxylesterase and MACE. This suite of tools collectively enables a single aphid to be assigned to one of 108 possible genotypes encompassing all three resistance mechanisms, providing accurate predictions of resistance phenotype. To our knowledge, this level of precision is unprecedented for any multi-resistant insect pest.

APPLICATION OF RESISTANCE DIAGNOSTICS

The availability of such diagnostics has enabled us to track changes in the frequency of resistance mechanisms, relating these to the control measures adopted and the biological characteristics of *M. persicae*. Aphids for these surveys have come directly from field crops and from 12.2 m suction traps deployed around the UK as part of the Rothamsted Insect Survey (Woiwod & Harrington, 1994). Two distinct patterns have emerged from this research. The first is a long-term periodicity with resistance being most frequent in years such as 1996 with severe aphid outbreaks – and hence greatest insecticide use - followed by declines in frequency over years when aphids are less abundant. Secondly, resistance frequencies usually show a characteristic increase within seasons as insecticides are applied, but then often decline before the start of the following cropping season. This shorter-term periodicity, like patterns observed over a longer period, demonstrates that resistance levels can, under certain conditions, decrease as well as increase and prevent an overall, sustained increase in the severity of resistance problems. Declines can be due to a number of factors but appear attributable in part to side-effects that resistance mechanisms impose on aphid biology, which may adversely affect their survival (Foster *et al.*, 1996) and/or reproduction (Foster *et al.*, 2000) in the absence of exposure to insecticides. Detailed work at Rothamsted has shown that resistant individuals of *M. persicae* tend to overwinter less successfully than their susceptible counterparts, be less fecund, and be less responsive to important environmental stimuli including the aphid alarm pheromone (E)-β-farnesene (Foster *et al.*, 1999; Foster *et al.*, 2003a). This compound is released from cornicle secretions exuded by aphids when they are physically disturbed, for example by foraging predators and parasitoids. Neighbouring aphids respond to the pheromone by withdrawing their stylets from the plant and dispersing away from the pheromone source. The intriguing possibility that decreased responsiveness to (E)-β-farnesene could render resistant aphids more vulnerable than susceptible ones to parasitism or predation is currently being investigated.

IMPLICATIONS FOR RESISTANCE MANAGEMENT

M. persicae poses a number of challenges for resistance management due to dramatic and often unpredictable changes in the severity of aphid attack from year to year, its large number of host plants, and the occurrence of multiple resistance mechanisms that collectively compromise the majority of compounds available for aphid control. However, increased knowledge of the incidence of these mechanisms, their cross-resistance characteristics, and of factors influencing the frequency of resistance genes has led to a series of recommendations based on alternating chemical groups, optimising the efficacy of individual treatments, and avoidance of tactics such as insecticide mixtures likely to result in the rapid accumulation of resistance mechanisms. These recommendations have been publicised through a number of organisations and publications, and are downloadable from the website for the UK Insecticide Resistance Action Group (IRAG) (www.pesticides.gov.uk/committees/Resistance). These guidelines also encompass newly-introduced insecticides available for inclusion in management strategies. Neonicotinoids (with imidacloprid as the commercial forerunner) and pymetrozine (a pyridine azomethane) represent newer insecticide groups available for use on some crops attacked by *M. persicae*, and which are unaffected by resistance mechanisms already present (Foster *et al.*, 2002a; Foster *et al.*, 2003b). However, their unrestrained use can unquestionably lead to selection of additional mechanisms, compounding the problem still further. Clones of *M. persicae* have been identified from southern Europe showing up to 18-fold resistance to imidacloprid, and individuals with lower resistance levels have been isolated from UK samples over the last three years. The commercialisation of neonicotinoids on an increasing number of crops harbouring *M. persicae* must therefore represent a significant new resistance risk requiring extensive co-operation between scientists, grower groups and agrochemical producers to address effectively.

Continuing access to new tools in molecular biology offers very exciting insights of processes governing the origin and spread of resistance, especially by combining markers for selected traits such as resistance with ones (e.g. microsatellites) with no obvious adaptive significance (Sunnucks, 2000). The reasons that some aphids such as *M. persicae* evolve resistance so rapidly whilst others (e.g. cereal aphids) do not, despite receiving insecticide treatments, should therefore become more tractable and provide greater scientific support for resistance management strategies, and risk assessment schemes built into pesticide approval procedures. Since the same resistance mechanisms often evolve in parallel in different species, diagnostic techniques developed for *M. persicae* may be transferred across species with little or no extra work. For example, a mechanism of resistance based on elevated esterase activity in the potato aphid, *Macrosiphum euphorbiae* Thompson, has many parallels with the equivalent mechanism of overproduced carboxylesterase in *M. persicae* (Foster *et al.*, 2002b).

ACKNOWLEDGEMENTS

We thank BBRO, Defra and BBSRC for support of work reported in this paper, and Barbara Hackett, Diana Cox and Kevin Gorman for technical assistance. Rothamsted Research receives grant-aided support from the Biotechnology and Biological Sciences Research Council of the United Kingdom.

REFERENCES

Andrews M C; Williamson M S; Callaghan A; Field L M; Moores G D (2003). A single amino acid substitution found in pirimicarb-insensitive acetylcholinesterase (AChE) of the peach-potato aphid, *Myzus persicae*. In: *Cholinergic Mechanisms,* ed. I Silman. Taylor & Francis (in press).

Blackman R L; Spence J M; Field L M; Devonshire A L (1999). Variation in the chromosomal distribution of amplified esterase (FE4) genes in Greek field populations of *Myzus persicae* (Sulzer). *Heredity* **82**, 180-186.

Devonshire A L; Moores G D (1982). A carboxylesterase with broad substrate-specificity causes organo-phosphorus, carbamate and pyrethroid resistance in peach-potato aphids (*Myzus persicae*). *Pesticide Biochemistry and Physiology* **18**, 235-246.

Devonshire A L; Moores G D; ffrench-Constant R H (1986). Detection of insecticide resistance by immunological estimation of carboxylesterase activity in *Myzus persicae* (Sulzer) and cross reaction of the antiserum with *Phorodon humuli* (Schrank) (Hemiptera, Aphididae). *Bulletin of Entomological Research* **76**, 97-107.

ffrench-Constant R H (1999). Target site mediated insecticide resistance: what questions remain? *Insect Biochemistry and Molecular Biology* **29**, 397-403.

Field L M; Blackman R L; Tyler Smith C; Devonshire A L (1999). Relationship between amount of esterase and gene copy number in insecticide-resistant *Myzus persicae* (Sulzer). *Biochemical Journal* **339**, 737-742.

Field L M; Crick S E; Devonshire A L (1996). Polymerase chain reaction-based identification of insecticide resistance genes and DNA methylation in the aphid *Myzus persicae* (Sulzer). *Insect Molecular Biology* **5**, 197-202.

Field L M; Devonshire A L (1997). Structure and organization of amplicons containing the E4 esterase genes responsible for insecticide resistance in the aphid *Myzus persicae* (Sulzer). *Biochemical Journal* **322**, 867-871.

Field L M; Williamson M S; Moores G D; Devonshire A L (1993). Cloning and analysis of the esterase genes conferring insecticide resistance in the peach-potato aphid, *Myzus persicae* (Sulzer). *Biochemical Journal* **294**, 569-574.

Foster S P; Denholm I; Devonshire A L (2000). The ups and downs of insecticide resistance in peach-potato aphids (*Myzus persicae*) in the UK. *Crop Protection* **19**, 873-879.

Foster S P; Denholm I; Thompson R (2002a). Bioassay and field-simulator studies of the efficacy of pymetrozine against peach-potato aphids, *Myzus persicae* (Hemiptera: Aphididae), possessing different mechanisms of insecticide resistance. *Pest Management Science* **58**, 805-810.

Foster S P; Denholm I; Thompson R (2003b). Variation in response to neonicotinoid insecticides in peach-potato aphids, *Myzus persicae* (Hemiptera: Aphididae). *Pest Management Science* **59**, 166-173.

Foster S P; Hackett B; Mason N; Moores G D; Cox D; Campbell J; Denholm I (2002b). Resistance to carbamate, organophosphate and pyrethroid insecticides in the potato aphid (*Macrosiphum euphorbiae*). *Proceedings of the BCPC Conference – Pests and Diseases 2002*, **2**, 811-816.

Foster S P; Harrington R; Devonshire A L; Denholm I; Devine G J; Kenward M G; Bale J S (1996). Comparative survival of insecticide-susceptible and resistant peach-potato aphids, *Myzus persicae* (Sulzer) (Hemiptera: Aphididae), in low temperature field trials. *Bulletin of Entomological Research* **86**, 17-27.

Foster S P; Woodcock C M; Williamson M S; Devonshire A L; Denholm I; Thompson R (1999). Reduced alarm response for peach-potato aphids (*Myzus persicae*) with knock-down resistance to insecticides (*kdr*) may impose a fitness cost through increased vulnerability to natural enemies. *Bulletin of Entomological Research* **89**, 133-138.

Foster S P; Young S; Williamson M S; Duce I; Denholm I; Devine G J (2003a). Analogous pleiotropic effects of insecticide resistance genotypes in peach-potato aphids and houseflies. *Heredity* **91**, 98-106.

Hemingway J (2000). The molecular basis of two contrasting metabolic mechanisms of insecticide resistance. *Insect Biochemistry and Molecular Biology* **30**, 1009-1015.

Liu Z Q; Valles S M; Dong K (2000). Novel point mutations in the German cockroach para sodium channel gene are associated with knockdown resistance (kdr) to pyrethroid insecticides. *Insect Biochemistry and Molecular Biology* **30**, 991-997.

Livak K J (1999). Allelic discrimination using fluorogenic probes and the 5' nuclease assay. *Genetic Analysis* **14**, 143-9.

Martinez-Torres D; Foster S P; Field L M; Devonshire A L; Williamson M S (1999). A sodium channel point mutation is associated with resistance to DDT and pyrethroid insecticides in the peach-potato aphid, *Myzus persicae* (Sulzer) (Hemiptera: Aphididae). *Insect Molecular Biology* **8**, 339-346.

Moores G D; Devine G J; Devonshire A L (1994). Insecticide-insensitive acetylcholinesterase can enhance esterase-based resistance in *Myzus persicae* and *Myzus nicotianae*. *Pesticide Biochemistry and Physiology* **49**, 114-120.

Mutero A; Pralavorio M; Bride J M; Fournier D (1994). Resistance-associated point mutations in insecticide-insensitive acetylcholinesterase. *Proceedings of the National Academy of Sciences of the United States of America* **91**, 5922-5926.

Narahashi T (1992). Nerve Membrane Na+ Channels as Targets of Insecticides. *Trends in Pharmacological Sciences* **13**, 236-241.

Nabeshima T; Kozaki T; Tomita T; Kono Y (2003). An amino-acid substitution on the second acetylcholinesterase in the pirimicarb-resistant strains of the peach potato aphid, *Myzus persicae*. *Biochemical and Biophysical Research Communications* **307**, 15-22.

Pittendrigh B; Reenan R; ffrench-Constant R H; Ganetzky B (1997). Point mutations in the Drosophila sodium channel gene para associated with resistance to DDT and pyrethroid insecticides. *Molecular & General Genetics* **256**, 602-610.

Schuler T H; Martinez-Torres D; Thompson A J; Denholm I; Devonshire A L; Duce I R; Williamson M S (1998). Toxicological, electrophysiological, and molecular characterisation of knockdown resistance to pyrethroid insecticides in the diamondback moth, *Plutella xylostella* (L.). *Pesticide Biochemistry and Physiology* **59**, 169-182.

Sunnucks P (2000). Efficient genetic markers for population biology. *Trends in Ecology & Evolution* **15**, 199-203.

Thompson M; Steichen J C; ffrench-Constant R H (1993). Conservation of cyclodiene insecticide resistance-associated mutations in insects. *Insect Molecular Biology* **2**, 149-154.

Walsh S B; Dolden T A; Moores G D; Kristensen M; Lewis T; Devonshire A L; Williamson M S (2001). Identification and characterization of mutations in housefly (*Musca domestica*) acetylcholinesterase involved in insecticide resistance. *Biochemical Journal* **359**, 175-181.

Weill M; Lutfalla G; Mogensen K; Chandre F; Berthomieu A; Berticat C; Pasteur N; Philips A; Fort P; Raymond M (2003). Insecticide resistance in mosquito vectors. *Nature* **423**, 136-137.

Williamson M S; Martinez-Torres D; Hick C A; Devonshire A L (1996). Identification of mutations in the housefly para-type sodium channel gene associated with knockdown resistance (kdr) to pyrethroid insecticides. *Molecular & General Genetics* **252**, 51-60.

Woiwod I P; Harrington R (1994). Flying in the face of change – The Rothamsted Insect Survey. In: *Long Term Research in Agricultural and Ecological Sciences*, eds R A Leigh & A E Johnson, pp. 321-342. CABI: Wallingford, UK.

QoI resistance development in populations of cereal pathogens in the UK

B A Fraaije, J A Lucas
Rothamsted Research, Harpenden, Hertfordshire, AL5 2JQ, UK
Email: bart.fraaije@bbsrc.ac.uk

W S Clark,
ADAS Boxworth, Boxworth, Cambridge, CB3 8NN, UK

F J Burnett,
Scottish Agricultural College, West Main Road, Edinburgh, EH9 3JG, UK

ABSTRACT

The effectiveness of strategies aiming to retard the development of resistance to Qo inhibitor fungicides in barley powdery mildew populations was determined with PCR by measuring the frequency of the G143A mutation in cytochrome *b*. Preliminary results from field trials show that the frequency of the G143A mutation increases with higher doses and increasing number of sprays. Mixtures of fungicides with different modes of action appeared to slow down the increase in the frequency of the mutation. For most locations sampled in the UK, high frequencies of G143A were detected in *Septoria tritici* populations during spring 2003. Studies are now in progress to establish the significance of G143A in QoI resistance development in populations of *S. tritici*, and to evaluate anti-resistance strategies for this pathogen.

INTRODUCTION

Strobilurins and related compounds inhibit mitochondrial respiration by binding to the ubiquinol oxidation (Qo) site formed by domains of cytochrome *b* and the iron-sulphur protein within the cytochrome bc_1 complex. Because ATP production is compromised, energy-demanding stages of fungal development, such as spore germination, are particularly affected. The Qo inhibitors (QoIs) have become a key component of disease control strategies on cereals in NW-Europe due to their persistent broad-spectrum disease control and potential extra yield benefits through increased green canopy duration. In 1998, within two years of commercial use, field resistance to QoIs was found in wheat powdery mildew (*Blumeria graminis* f. sp. *tritici*) populations in North Germany. In all resistant isolates, a single point mutation leading to a change from glycine to alanine at amino-acid position 143 (G143A) was found in the cytochrome *b* gene (Heaney *et al.*, 2000). This mutation was also found in a single resistant isolate of *B. graminis* f. sp. *hordei* (barley powdery mildew) in N-Germany in 1999. By 2001, resistance in cereal powdery mildews was widespread in NW-Europe. In 2002, G143A was detected in resistant field isolates of *Septoria tritici* (teleomorph *Mycosphaerella graminicola*) in the UK (Fraaije *et al.*, unpublished). Up to 11 different amino-acid exchanges have been found to confer resistance to QoIs in other organisms, but only mutations at codons 129 and 143 have been reported for plant pathogens (Gisi *et al.*, 2002). Besides alteration of the target site, induction of alternative respiration (Ziogas *et al.*, 1997) and an unknown mechanism in *Venturia inaequalis* (Steinfeld *et al.*, 2001) have been reported to confer resistance to QoIs.

Practical disease control failures have only been linked with the occurrence of the G143A mutation in plant pathogen populations. This evolution can be explained by the high resistance levels and/or low fitness costs often associated with this mutation. Because of the importance of G143A as a predictive marker for QoI resistance, different real-time PCR-based diagnostics have been developed to monitor this mutation in pathogen populations (Gisi et al., 2002). For wheat powdery mildew, the prevalence and dynamics of G143A in field populations before and after application of fungicides have been studied (Fraaije et al., 2002). This paper presents preliminary results from the Sustainable Arable LINK programme 'Providing a scientific basis for the avoidance of fungicide resistance in plant pathogens'. Using QoI resistance in barley powdery mildew as a model, bioassays and PCR diagnostics were used to test the effects of different anti-resistance strategies. Similar techniques were also used to monitor the current status of resistance to QoIs in field populations of S. *tritici* throughout the UK.

MATERIALS AND METHODS

During 2002-2003, the spring barley cultivar Golden Promise was grown in three replicated field plots (17 m x 24 m) in three different locations in the UK. This paper presents the results of location Findon Mains, near Inverness, Scotland. One plot remained untreated throughout the season and other plots were treated three or four times at 14-day intervals with fungicides. Fungicides were applied to test the three factors likely to influence the evolution of resistance and to be amenable to manipulation in an anti-resistance strategy, i.e. dose, number of sprays and alternation/mixing of fungicides with different modes of action (see Table 1). A key aspect of the experimental design is the use of fungicide doses that give similar levels of disease control to minimise the confounding effects of pathogen population size on selection.

Table 1. Overview of barley powdery mildew field trials

Experiment 1: Effects of dose rate and number of sprays

Treatment	Number of sprays	Dose per spray (litres ha^{-1} Amistar)	Anticipated level of disease control (%)
1	Nil	Nil	0
2	1	1.0	80
3	1	2.0	95
4	1	3.0	99
5	2	0.5	80
6	2	1.0	95
7	2	1.5	99
8	3	0.3	80
9	3	0.6	95
10	3	1.0	99

Experiment 2: Mixtures and alternations

Treatment	Sequence and treatment[1]			
11	A	B	A	B
12	B	A	B	A
13	A	A	A	A
14	B	B	B	B
15	A+B	A+B	A+B	A+B

[1] A = 0.5 litre ha^{-1} Amistar; B = 0.25 litre ha^{-1} Corbel

For each plot, 25 leaves with fresh pustules were collected from the middle leaf layers of the canopy just before each spray and 14 days after the final spray between GS31 and GS65. DNA was extracted from leaf samples and tested for the presence of G143A. Mildew was assessed visually on 25 shoots per plot at different growth stages. Mildew strains isolated from leaves were tested for sensitivity to QoIs in bioassays and their genotype determined by PCR.

To detect QoI sensitive (G143) and resistant (A143) alleles, a 5'-nuclease-based real-time PCR assay was developed using allele-specific minor groove binder (MGB)-conjugated TaqMan probes labelled with different reporter dyes (Figure 1). For each DNA sample, the ratio of the VIC and FAM signals, measured five cycles after detection, was used to calculate the A143 allele frequency. This was done by reference to a calibration curve generated by DNA standards containing different proportions of A143 and G143 alleles.

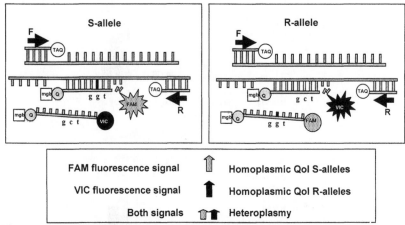

Figure 1. Detection of G143A using MGB-TaqMan probes.

Septoria tritici strains were isolated from samples consisting of 25 leaves showing symptoms (pycnidium-bearing lesions). Samples from commercial and trial crops were collected in different locations in the UK before GS31. Single-spore isolates were cultured and genotyped for the presence of G143A using real-time PCR. A number of isolates were also tested for sensitivity to QoIs by growing them in liquid medium in the absence and presence of fungicides. For a few isolates, the *in vivo* sensitivity to QoIs was also determined in the glasshouse by inoculation of untreated and fungicide-treated plants.

RESULTS

Barley powdery mildew

Heavy rain reduced mildew levels at Findon Mains and late infection meant that, for experiment 2 (see Table 1), only three out of the four anticipated sprays could be applied. The bioassays detected resistance levels between 0.5 and 13% before spraying, in agreement with the low resistance levels detected with real-time PCR using G143A as a marker (Figure 2). Calibration curve samples containing less than 5% R-alleles were not detected in PCR. Only a few pustules sampled after spraying were viable, making later comparisons using the bioassay impossible.

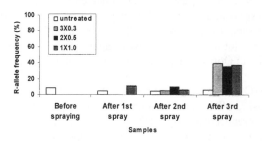

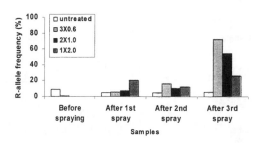

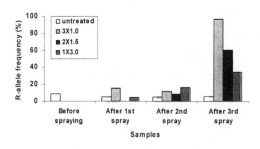

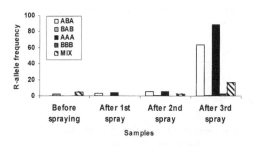

Figure 2. Effects of different fungicide applications on the development of QoI-resistance using G143A as a marker. See Table 1 for description of treatments. Leaf 3 was sampled before spraying at GS26-31 and after the first spray at GS41-43, leaf 2 after the second spray at GS70 and the flag after the third spray at GS90. Average values of three replicated plots are presented.

The R-allele frequency only increased under selection pressure from QoI fungicides. The selection was most pronounced after three sprays and increased with dose and number of sprays. With the lowest total fungicide input (1 litre ha^{-1} Amistar) no clear difference in selection for G143A was observed with spray frequency, but the single high-dose spray provided best disease control. Higher doses generally improved disease control (Figure 3), but because of low mildew infection levels, results were not always consistent and large variations between replicated plots were observed, especially after the third spray (data not shown). Experiment 2 showed fungicide mixtures can slow down the development of resistance. Because the fourth spray could not be applied, the effects of alternation could not be measured.

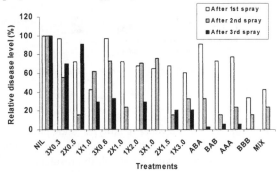

Figure 3.Efficacy of treatments to control barley powdery mildew. Disease levels of untreated plots (regarded as 100%) were, respectively, 9.3, 6.3 and 3.3% of infected leaf area after the first (L3 at GS41-43), second (L2 at GS70) and third spray (flag at GS85). Average values of three replicated plots are presented.

Septoria tritici

Sample test results (Table 2) revealed that the G143A mutation was common and widespread in populations of *Septoria tritici* throughout the UK during spring 2003.

Table 2. The occurrence of G143A in populations of *Septoria tritici* in spring 2003.

Sample	Number of isolates tested	Location	Cultivar	Number of isolates with G143A
1	38	Bedfordshire	Option	26 (68%)
2	35	Buckinghamshire	Consort	12 (34%)
3	36	Carlow, Ireland	Madrigal	20 (56%)
4	36	Dorset	Option	5 (14%)
5	94	Hertfordshire	Savannah	30 (32%)
6	52	North Somerset	Claire	15 (29%)
7	53	North Yorkshire	Consort	20 (38%)
8	16	North Yorkshire	Napier	0 (0%)
9	59	Warwickshire	Claire	19 (32%)
10	24	Wiltshire	?	14 (58%)

For 80 strains, isolated in Hertfordshire in 2002, ED$_{50}$ values for azoxystrobin were determined *in vitro* (Figure 4). Isolates with G143A showed high resistance levels and were cross-resistant to kresoxim-methyl, trifloxystrobin and pyraclostrobin. *In vivo* studies showed that resistant isolates were not controlled, even at full rate, when azoxystrobin was applied 7 days after inoculation. For some isolates, increased disease levels were recorded when a quarter dose was used. However, when azoxystrobin was applied 7 days prior to inoculation, resistant isolates were partially controlled at full dose rate (Lovell *et al.*, unpublished).

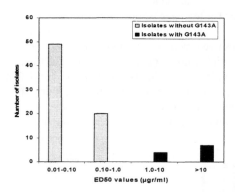

Figure 4. Azoxystrobin sensitivity testing of *Septoria tritici* isolates.

DISCUSSION

Provided a clear relationship exists between genotype and phenotype, real-time PCR diagnostics is a powerful tool that can be used to monitor the effects of anti-resistance strategies by directly monitoring the genotype. Although the results are preliminary and more trials are needed to validate them, it is clear that the effects of dose, spray frequency and alternation/mixing of fungicides with different modes of action on QoI resistance development in mildew populations can be measured. Similar studies are now in progress with *S. tritici* and other pathogens at risk in order to help prolong the practical use of QoI fungicides.

ACKNOWLEDGEMENTS

We thank colleagues from Defra, HGCA, BASF, Bayer CropScience, DuPont and Syngenta for contributions to this LINK project LK0920 supported by Defra through the Sustainable Arable LINK Programme. Rothamsted Research receives grant-aided support from BBSRC.

REFERENCES

Fraaije B A; Butters J A; Coelho J M; Jones D R; Hollomon D W (2002). Following the dynamics of strobilurin resistance in *Blumeria graminis* f. sp. *tritici* using quantitative allele-specific real-time PCR measurements with the fluorescent dye SYBR Green I. *Plant Pathology* **51**, 45-54.

Gisi U; Sierotski H; Cook A; McCaffery A (2002). Mechanisms influencing the evolution of resistance to Qo inhibitor fungicides. *Pest Management Science* **58**, 859-867.

Heaney S P; Hall A A; Davies S A; Olaya G (2000). Resistance to fungicides in the QoI-STAR cross-resistance group: current perspectives. *Proceedings of the BCPC Conference – Pests & Diseases 2000*, **2**, 755-762.

Steinfeld U; Sierotski H; Parisi S; Poirey S, Gisi U (2001). Sensitivity of mitochondrial respiration to different inhibitors in *Venturia inaequalis*. *Pest Management Science* **57**, 787-796.

Ziogas B N; Baldwin B C; Young J E (1997). Alternative respiration: a biochemical mechanism of resistance to azoxystrobin (ICIA 5504) in *Septoria tritici*. *Pesticide Science* **50**, 28-34.

The issues facing Industry in the management of resistance in Europe

A R Thompson
Dow AgroSciences, Latchmore Court, Brand Street, Hitchin, Herts SG5 1NH, UK
Email: anthompson@dow.com

ABSTRACT

The issues facing Industry in the management of resistance in Europe continue to increase. Resistance risk analysis is now a component of the registration process within the EU and guidance on how to implement the requirements became available with the publication of EPPO guideline PP1/213 (1). This paper examines the guidelines and approaches by industry to assess the risk of practical resistance and the difficulties in monitoring for resistance. The use of modelling and its value in predicting resistance are discussed with comparisons made across the disciplines. A brief description of the testing methods available to screen new compounds for their potential vulnerability to the development of resistance is made. The role of the various Resistance Action Groups which act at global, European and country levels and their role in providing guidance on both testing and management strategies is described and a proposal is made for better communication across the disciplines.

INTRODUCTION

Resistance is not a new phenomenon but it is increasing, however. The problem was recognised as far back as 1910 and the first resistance to synthetic chemicals was noted in 1947 when DDT resistance was observed in houseflies (*Musca domestica*). Fungicide resistance was first noted in *Pyrenophora avenae*, which was observed to be resistant to organomercurials in 1964, and then in 1970 resistance to benzimidazoles was found in *Venturia inaequalis* and *Botrytis cinerea*. Organomercurials were used for 40 years before resistance appeared but resistance to the benzimidazoles appeared in *B. cinerea* after two years of use.

A classic graph by Georghiou showing the time line of species developing resistance to one insecticide, fungicide or herbicide from the 1930s through to 1985 showed that, by 1985, the number of species showing resistance to an insecticide was about 450, for plant pathogens it was between 100 and 150 species and for weeds <50. (Georghiou, 1986). Since that time, the number of cases of herbicide resistance has soared with, today, 276 resistant biotypes and 166 species (99 dicots and 67 monocots) recorded on the HRAC website (Heap, 2003). Insect pests began to develop resistance before disease pathogens and weeds but now weeds are catching up. One reason for this rise in resistance is that the vast majority of early pesticides were multi-site and development of resistance was slow. During the last 30 years, however, discovery goals were more likely to result in finding chemicals with single sites of action and high activity. As a result, for all disciplines, resistance to pesticides is growing and resulting in a significant economic impact. This paper looks at the current situation regarding the regulatory requirements in Europe and the various approaches from industry and the wider crop protection industry to evaluating and managing resistance.

EPPO GUIDELINE

The European Union Commission Directive 93/71/EEC amending Council Directive 91/414/EEC concerning the placing of plant protection products on the market requires that applicants evaluate the risk of resistance developing and propose management strategies to address such risks. An EPPO guideline was first published in 1999 (OEPP/EPPO, 1999) and a revised guideline in April 2003 (OEPP/EPPO, 2003). The specific scope of the guideline is to describe how risk of resistance to plant protection products can be assessed and, if appropriate, how systems for risk management can be proposed in the context of official registration of plant protection products.

Practical Resistance

An important aspect of the guideline is that it focuses on "practical resistance". Resistance is defined as the "naturally occurring inheritable adjustment in the ability of individuals in a population to survive a plant protection product treatment that would normally give effective control". Practical resistance is the term used for loss of field control due to a shift in sensitivity.

The guideline divides risk assessment into two parts: resistance risk assessment, in which the probability of resistance development and its likely impact are evaluated and, if necessary, resistance risk management, in which strategies to avoid or delay the development of resistance are proposed.

The risk analysis considers the inherent risk, that is the risk to the target organism and the mode of action of the chemical and the agronomic risk for the area in which the product will be used. There are many ways of conducting these and tools have been developed within companies to assess resistance. For example, for insecticides Dow AgroSciences developed the Practical Resistance Assessment Tool in Table 1.

The biological factors change for the other disciplines but the principles of the tool may be used for any discipline. For example, for weeds the important "Biological Factors" to consider are high inherent genetic variability, high fecundity, outcrossing versus selfing and the number of generations per year. For diseases, the biological factors to consider are incubation time, number of spores, spore mobility, ability to overwinter, fitness and sexual recombination.

This type of tool can be used across all disciplines after defining the parameters involved and can be used at a very local level to assess the risk of resistance occurring.

Table 1. Practical Resistance Assessment Tool

Attributes	Risk score	Low Risk: Score = 1	Moderate Risk: Score = 3	High Risk: Score = 5
Biological Factors		NOTE: Intermediate scores are permissible; score 5 if unknown		
# generations/year	3	< 2	2 to 5	> 5
Migration/population mixing	3	High (black cutworm)	Moderate (corn rootworm)	Low (houseflies in a chicken house)
Host range	3	Broad (cotton bollworm, beet armyworm)	Moderate (diamondback moth, tobacco budworm)	Narrow (rootworm, boll weevil, Colorado potato beetle)
Reproduction capacity	3	10	50	100
Reproduction style	3		Sexual	Parthenogensis
Operational Factors				
Life stages treated	1	One stage		Multiple stages
Residual activity	3	Low (methyl parathion, chlorpyrifos methyl)	Moderate (pyrethroids)	Long (chlorinated hydrocarbons, soil insecticides, transgenics)
Resistance history	3	None	Resistant to < 2 classes of insecticides	Resistant to >2 classes of insecticides
Systemicity	3	Not systemic	Moderately mobile	Highly mobile
% refugia	3	High	Moderate	Low
Alternative control options	3	Many, effective as rotation partners		None or Few
Expected market share	3	< 25%	25-50%	> 50%
Crop cycles	1	Seasonal		Overlapping/ continuous
Market place receptive to IRM practices	3	Yes, good infrastructure		No, poor infrastructure
Cross-resistance with other control options	3	None; novel mode of action		Extensive; widely used mode of action
# insecticide applications	3	1 per year	3 per year	>5 per year
Dose (% killed per application)	3	<30%	30-90% or >99%	90-99%

Total

Total score	Risk
<40	Low
40-60	Moderate
>60	High

Management strategies

If the risk is acceptable, then no further analysis or provision of data are needed. If there is risk, then modifiers must be proposed to reduce the risk. These include the following:
- Frequency of application – limiting the number of applications against a pest in a season will reduce the selection pressure
- Timing of application – applications should be made at times of the year, crop growth stage or pest stage critical to optimum control
- Mixtures - the active substance may be applied in mixture with one or more substances with similar or complimentary activity but with different modes of action.
- Alternation - alternating pesticides from different resistance groups
- Cultural control

Monitoring

As part of the monitoring strategy for products whose unmodified risk of resistance has been evaluated as unacceptable, a programme must be instigated to monitor the continued efficacy of the products on the target pest. This programme comprises observations of field performance from efficacy trials and commercial use. Random monitoring is generally not feasible to detect major gene mutants in samples from field populations until frequencies of 1% are reached. At 1% frequency, >300 samples are needed to have a 95% chance of detecting resistance. In this area it is worth noting that it is easier to work on a large number of fungal samples than of insects or plants.

At this stage there continues to be considerable confusion between authorities regarding the requirements especially in the area of monitoring.

MODELLING

To date, modelling has been more successful in comparing alternative resistance management strategies than in the prediction of resistance. Various types of models have played an essential role in building a framework for resistance management. Cavan *et al.* (1999) compared different cultivation strategies and cultivation techniques for their effects on herbicide resistance. Significant differences were found in the speed of resistance development when the use of ploughing was compared with tine cultivation and when alternation of herbicides with different modes of action was tested. Studying the models across the disciplines, there are a number of common themes. Alternating or mixtures of chemistries with different modes of action and use of integrated crop management are common methods to slow the build up of resistance. The details vary within the disciplines, with cultivation techniques having a major impact on weed resistance and the use of beneficial insects in insect resistance.

Predicting resistance using models has had limited success across the disciplines, especially in weed science. Some of the predictions resulting from the use of herbicide resistance development models have proved unrealistic (Friesen *et al.*, 2000). The reason for this is a lack of information on plant characteristics, such as initial frequencies of resistance, rates of random mutation, relative fitness of resistant plants and the importance of gene flow, which are largely unknown. To be really successful, we need more information than is currently available. The use of models for the prediction of insect resistance looks more hopeful. In recent years, agriculture has seen the commercialisation and widespread adoption of transgenic crops based on the insecticidal toxins from the bacteria *Bacillus thuringiensis* (Bt). These Bt crops can be valuable pest management tools and preserving their efficacy has become a high priority for entomologists. As a result, significant resources are aimed at understanding pest biology, the roles of agronomic operations, pest population dynamics and genetics in resistance evolution and our ability to product accurate prediction models will improve (Storer *et al.*, 1996).

For new pesticides, advances in molecular genetics and biochemistry will help to determine the mode of action of new compounds and to select for resistant biotypes. Also, researchers can look at crop selectivity to determine possible methods of detoxification. This information can be used to predict what mechanisms of resistance may develop but can not predict how quickly practical resistance will occur in the field.

MANAGING RESISTANCE ON FARMS

The awareness of the possibility of resistance developing is not enough to alter the short-term decisions that farmers make on a yearly basis. The difficulty in screening for resistance on a large scale means that farmers become aware after it occurs. Once resistance has occurred, then farmers are prepared to adopt management strategies. These strategies often cause an increase in cost in the short term. Continuous autumn cropping and using a range of selective herbicides, annual ploughing, and sowing a significant proportion of winter wheat in early October will increase costs in the short term. However, if it delays the build up of resistance in *Alopecurus myosuroides* (blackgrass), it will offer a sustainable long term solution (Orson & Harris, 1997).

Today, labels advise not to use single modes of action continuously. North America and Australia have adopted a mode of action labelling to aid farmers in decision making. This can be beneficial for managing target site resistance but has little advantage where detoxification processes exist (with some exceptions where a specific mode of action is not susceptible to that particular detoxification mechanism). More education is needed at farmer level and resistance management strategies developed at a local level to take account of the economic, environmental and agronomic needs. The most successful programmes have been those that have involved scientists and producers working together such as Arizona's extension-based resistance management programme. A coalition of farmers, a commodity organisation, members of the crop protection industry, university research and extension personnel researched and communicated a successful plan to combat white fly, *Bemisia argentifolia*. This programme has been successful for six years and continues. It is clear that communication between industry, researchers and farmers is essential and the Resistance Action Groups are fundamental to that communication.

RESISTANCE ACTION GROUPS

In the early 1980s, the threat of resistance was recognised but there was no collective forum for addressing the problems within the crop protection industry. Today the situation is very different with industry, farmers and academics working together. This is due in the main to the formation of action committees which bring together people with the common objective of resistance management. Three Specialist Technical Groups were formed as committees of Crop Life International (previously GIFAP). These Action Committees were established in the 1980s and dedicated to prolonging the effectiveness of pesticides by identifying, devising and implementing the management of strategies. These were the Insecticide Resistance Action Committee (IRAC, 2003) the Fungicide Resistance Action Committee (FRAC, 2003) and the Herbicide Resistance Action Committee (HRAC, 2003). All have individual web sites and are recognised as advisory bodies by organisations such as the European Commission, the Food and Agriculture organisation (FAO) and the World Health Organisation (WHO) of the United Nations.

There are some fundamental aims shared across these committees:

1. To promote a better understanding of the causes and results of resistance.
2. To foster a responsible attitude to pesticide use.
3. To support work to identify the technical basis of resistance.
4. To identify the magnitude of resistance through surveys.
5. To communicate resistance management strategies.
6. To facilitate communication between industry and academics by the establishment of workshops.

IRAC

IRAC was formed in 1984 to provide a co-ordinated crop protection industry response to the development of resistance in insect and mite pests. During the last decade, IRAC has formed several international working groups to provide practical solutions to mite and insect resistance problems within major crops and pesticide groups. IRAC has achieved success in a number of areas:
1. Surveys. By surveying member-companies about documented cases of resistance, IRAC has been able to identify and classify resistance problems. Identifying and concentrating on problem areas allows IRAC to work with individual farmers to manage resistance problems. Comprehensive surveys - including more than 50 countries, 70 species of insects and mites, and more than 30 crops - are conducted periodically to assist the industry.
2. Monitoring methods. IRAC has developed and published several methods for monitoring resistance under a variety of field settings. Many methods have become the basis of wide-reaching monitoring programmes around the world. IRAC Method No. VII, for leaf-eating *Lepidoptera* and *Coleoptera*, for example, has been validated in the laboratory and in the field.
3. Resistance mechanisms and management. IRAC was instrumental in the discovery that a change in the mode of action is not always necessary to reduce resistance. IRAC discovered in Italy, for example, that apple leaf miner (*Leucoptera scitella*) resistance to diflubenzuron may not always be conferred to a whole class of insecticides, even if they all have the same mode of action.
4. Member companies agreed to limit applications of mitochondrial electron transport inhibitors (METI) to one application per year and published the strategy at the Brighton Crop Protection Conference in 1994.

FRAC

FRAC was formed in 1981 and is comprised of a Central Steering Committee and six Working Groups. Each Working Group consists of specialist technical representatives from two or more manufacturing companies with fungicides of a similar mode of action or cross resistance potential. Companies with a compound in the market or in late development are encouraged to participate. The working groups are

- Anilinopyrimidines
- Benzimidazoles
- Dicarboximides
- Phenylamides
- SBI Fungicides
- QoI Fungicides

FRAC working groups have made achievements in the following areas:
1. Recommending procedures for use in fungicide resistance studies.
2. Providing guidelines and advice on the use of fungicides to reduce the risk of resistance. developing, and to manage it should it occur.
3. Identifying existing and potential resistance problems.
4. Collating information and distributing it to those involved in fungicide research, distribution, registration and use.
5. Stimulating open liason and collaboration with universities, government agencies, advisors, extension workers, distributors and farmers.

HRAC

HRAC was formed in 1989 with three working groups
- Acetolactase synthase inhibitor
- Triazine
- Grass herbicide

Since that time the committee has amalgamated to one group but with very strong regional working groups. Thus the European Herbicide Resistance Working Group has supported and participated in research, conferences and seminars, which serve to increase the understanding of herbicide resistance. The North American group is extremely active and other working groups exist in the Pacific and Asia.

Accomplishments:
1. Financial support to research on a range of activities including the survey and gene flow in *Kochia scoparia* and *Salsola iberica* in the USA, management of urea-resistant *Phalaris* in India and, more recently, the technical and financial impact of herbicide-resistant *Alopecurus myosuroides* on individual farm businesses in the UK.
2. Open meetings with academic and governmental research.
3. Publication of resistance monographs to review specific areas of resistance.
4. Collaborative testing programmes - such as the *Alopecurus myosuroides* testing kit ring-tested via the group.
5. Monitoring.

To date, the disciplines have worked in isolation but it is clear that the three committees would benefit from closer collaboration to produce a joint strategy on common issues. The difficulties facing each discipline and the potential solutions are the same and at a time when resources are reducing we must cooperate to ensure maximum influence.

REFERENCES

Cavan G; Cussans J; Moss S R (1999). Modelling different cultivation and herbicide strategies for their effect on herbicide resistance in *Alopecurus myosuroides*. *Proceedings of the 1999 Brighton Crop Protection Conference - Weeds*, **3**, pp.778-782.

FRAC (2003). website www.frac.info/links.htm.

Friesen S J L; Ferguson G; Hall J C (2000). Management strategies for attenuating herbicide resistance: untoward consequences of their promotion. *Crop Protection* **19**, 891-895.

Georghiou G P (1986). *The magnitude of the resistance problem. Pesticide resistance strategies and tactics for management*. National Academy of Science Press: Washington, DC.

Heap I. (2003) The International survey of herbicide resistant weeds. Online. Internet July 01,2003. Available www.weedscience.com.

HRAC (2003). website www.plantprotection.org/HRAC.

IRAC (2003). website www.plantprotection.org/IRAC.

OEPP/EPPO (1999). EPPO standard PP 1/213(1) Resistance risk analysis. *Bulletin OEPP/EPPO Bulletin* **29**, 325-347.

OEPP/EPPO (2003). EPPO standard PP 1/213(2) Resistance risk analysis. Bulletin *OEPP/EPPO Bulletin* **33**, 37-63.

Orson J H; Harris D (1997). The technical and financial impact of herbicide resistant blackgrass (*Alopecurus myosuroides*) on individual farm businesses in England. *Proceedings of the 1997 Brighton Crop Protection Conference – Weeds,* **3**, 1127-1132.

Storer N P; Peck S L; Gould F; Van Duyn J W; Kennedy G G (2003). Sensitivity analysis of spatially–explicit stochastic simulation model of the evolution of resistance in *Helicoverpa zea* to Bt transgenic corn and cotton. *Journal of Economic Entomology* **26,** 173-187.

The role and impact of the regulator in resistance management

O C Macdonald, I Meakin, D M Richardson

DEFRA, Pesticide Safety Directorate, Mallard House, Kings Pool, York, YO1 7PX, UK

ABSTRACT

Resistance risk analysis and the implementation of resistance management strategies are an integral part of the pesticide registration process in Europe. They also play a vital role in ensuring sustainable agricultural production. To be effective, resistance management strategies must be consistent across products and must be communicated to and implemented by end users. Using the examples of the ALS herbicides and QoI fungicides this paper explores the difficulties in ensuring that resistance management strategies are effective and how the regulatory authorities in the UK play an active role in their development and implementation.

INTRODUCTION

Resistance to pesticides is a widespread problem that limits the effectiveness of many existing products and reduces the options for controlling a range of target organisms. It is financially costly to growers and the agrochemical industry, and these costs are likely to be passed on to consumers. There may also be environmental costs if growers are forced to use additional pesticide or substitute products with less environmentally friendly ones. For growers of minor crops, where the range of approved chemicals is often limited, the loss of effective products can be particularly serious. Resistance management is therefore an integral component of sustainable crop production.

The European pesticide registration process, driven by directive 91/414, recognises the importance of resistance and requires applicants to address the risk of resistance development as part of dossiers submitted for EU registration (Anon., 1993). However, the withdrawal of active substances and products as a result of the re-registration requirements within Europe also poses a threat to resistance management as the diversity of active substances is reduced, and makes it more important to protect those that remain.

As with other areas of efficacy evaluation, guidance on the conduct of resistance risk analysis and development of resistance management strategies is given in an EPPO guideline (Anon., 2003). Although this includes some well known examples of chemical groups or target organisms that present a high risk of developing resistance, it essentially only provides an outline of the processes involved and each case will inevitably require specialist consideration. Assessing resistance sections of dossiers submitted to support product registration generates a unique challenge for regulatory scientists. The available knowledge is often limited and the best approach to resistance management in a given situation will be conjectural. Different applicants may therefore legitimately propose very different resistance management strategies for similar situations.

SUPPORTING EFFECTIVE RESISTANCE MANAGEMENT STRATEGIES

The regulatory system must be uniformly applied, unbiased and evidence-based. Inconsistencies in approach could result both in unfair restrictions on some products and may also confuse the user, with the result that resistance management messages are not effectively communicated. There is also a potential conflict of interest between the desire for profit and the goal of preventing resistance to support the long term sustainability of crop production. As Russell (2001) pointed out, identifying effective strategies is, however, problematic. If a strategy is implemented and resistance does not develop we are still left with a dilemma. Has resistance failed to develop because the resistance management strategy *per se* is effective or is it because of some other factor in the original hypothesis relating to the target organism or chemical was incorrect? The regulator has to tread a narrow line between acting reasonably in restricting the use of products and ensuring both that resistance management strategies are consistent and effective and that suitable crop protection products remain available. Defining that line can be extremely difficult, particularly where new chemistry is concerned and there is limited information on resistance development. Furthermore, if a strategy appears to be failing, there must be a mechanism to reconsider the management strategy and communicate changes to users. The 10-year rolling review process for products approved under European legislation is clearly not appropriate when dealing with rapidly changing resistance problems.

For established chemistry the implementation of effective resistance management strategies is helped by the publication of guidelines by the international resistance action committees (FRAC, HRAC, IRAC and RRAC). In the past the UK Pesticides Safety Directorate (PSD) has generally accepted strategies proposed as part of the registration package provided they were in line with those produced by the RACs. However, the UK Advisory Committee on Pesticides (ACP) has expressed concern that the RACs, being composed solely of agrochemical industry representatives, may not be sufficiently independent. RAC guidelines also take a global view and may not always be applicable to local conditions. Within the UK, national Resistance Action Groups (FRAG-UK, IRAG, WRAG and RRAG), which have a wider membership, provide a more independent and local view and are more appropriate bodies for generating guidance. However, as they are voluntary bodies with no financial support their resources are limited.

Research coordination

R&D to support the understanding of pesticide resistance is a key business priority for PSD. It improves our ability to undertake resistance risk assessments and to evaluate proposed resistance management strategies. Without the adoption of effective resistance management strategies, production of some crops or on some sites may become unsustainable. Work funded in recent years has included projects, some conducted in partnership with industry, looking at the effectiveness of both fungicide and herbicide resistance management strategies.

PSD also influences the research conducted by industry. As part of the resistance management strategy put forward in registration packages, companies are increasingly making commitments to undertake ongoing resistance monitoring programmes, which must be agreed by the regulator. Additionally, if changes in sensitivity do occur, PSD will encourage the collaboration of all relevant parties to develop suitable research and monitoring programmes to support the ongoing resistance management needs. Of course, a pragmatic approach must be taken and the cost of research and monitoring by approval holders needs to be offset against the profits from a given use of a product. While monitoring programmes are financially justifiable for broad-acre crops, the returns on sales for use on minor crops are unlikely to cover the cost of extensive monitoring. Equally, the limited range of products available for minor crops means that resistance cannot be ignored in this area and other sources of funding must therefore be identified.

Getting the message across

European pesticide labels must be approved by the regulatory authorities. Thus regulators can ensure that product labels include statements relating to resistance management and that those statements are consistent between similar products. PSD has introduced a number of standard insecticide resistance statements over the years that have been agreed with industry and the ACP. Specific wording has also been agreed for phenylamide fungicides, annual grass-weed herbicides and, most recently, QoI fungicides.

With the exception of restrictions on the number of applications, however, resistance management information is generally considered to be advisory information and falls within the 'directions for use' section of labels. The full implementation of a resistance management strategy is therefore at the discretion of the user. Growers may therefore ignore resistance management advice, as was seen with the QoI fungicides (see below), particularly if they perceive it to adversely affect the economics of immediate crop production. Grower education may help and PSD has in the past supported the production of leaflets for distribution to growers advising on resistance management. There are options for further action, however, as seen in recent statutory restrictions introduced for QoIs in the UK and Ireland. Similar action has also been taken in the past with some insecticides.

THE QoI STORY

Azoxystrobin was first registered in the UK in 1997. Several other compounds with similar modes of action, now classed as the QoIs, have since been registered. In 2000 azoxystrobin was the most extensively used fungicide in UK barley production and ranked second in wheat (Garthwaite & Thomas, 2000). Azoxystrobin was also the first compound to be placed on Annex 1 of directive 91/414 and thus receive European listing. As such a resistance risk assessment was considered as part of the registration package. In view of subsequent resistance development (Russell, 1999), it is arguable that a stronger resistance management strategy should have been imposed from the start. At the time, however, there was no guidance on the issue available from EPPO and both the regulatory authorities and applicants were still developing their understanding of the European registration process.

Resistance to wheat mildew, and some diseases in other crops, appeared very quickly and prompted a flurry of research, from both the original approval holder and other companies with similar compounds in development. The industry, working together through a specialist forum of FRAC, introduced global resistance management guidelines. These were adopted for all the QoIs in the UK, although there was some variation in the specific resistance management recommendations on labels depending on the guidelines adopted by FRAC at the time the product was approved.

In late 2002 resistance surveys started to find isolates of *Septoria tritici*, the pathogen causing the most widespread disease of wheat in the UK, which carried a gene responsible for disruptive resistance to the QoIs. Additionally, analysis of pesticide usage data showed that despite advice on the labels of most QoI fungicides to apply no than two applications to a crop and to use solo products in mixture, around 20% of UK cereal crops received three or more foliar sprays of a QoI containing product, and at least 10% of growers applied solo QoI products alone (M Thomas pers. comm.).

Due to the significance of septoria disease and the importance of this group of fungicides, action was clearly needed. Working with industry, independent researchers and agronomists, and with the help of FRAG-UK, a package of measures to reinforce the resistance management strategy was agreed and implemented in April this year (2003). The statutory conditions of use for all QoI products on cereals were changed to limit the number of applications to two and standard resistance management phrases were introduced onto labels. The story is, of course, ongoing. By the time this is published further data should be available from the 2003 survey and ongoing research projects. It is to be hoped that the situation will have stabilised but, if not, further steps may have to be taken. What these will be will depend on further findings, but actions that were discussed previously have included restricting QoIs to only a single application and withdrawing approvals for all solo products.

THE ALS INHIBITOR STORY

Weed resistance presents somewhat different problems, with less potential for rapid changes in resistance across a wide area but an increasing reliance on a single group of herbicides likely to result in widespread problems over time. The development of acetolactate synthase (ALS) inhibitors and, specifically, sulfonyl ureas (SUs) provided farmers with a new class of highly active and effective herbicides. The first ALS inhibitors were approved in the UK in the early 1980s. Since then, a further 13 SUs have been approved in the UK for use on a wide range of crops and weeds and six other non SU ALS inhibitors, four of which are cereal herbicides.

World-wide there are very many weed species resistant to ALS inhibitors and, while most are broad-leaved weeds, resistance does occur in some grass-weeds. In the UK, enhanced metabolism resistance in black-grass is widespread and reduces the effectiveness of many cereal herbicides, including the ALS inhibitors, although cross-resistance patterns are by no means straightforward. In broad-leaved weeds there have been few cases of herbicide resistance in the UK but resistance to the SUs has been identified in both common chickweed and poppy. In 2000/1 there were six cases of resistance confirmed in chickweed and three cases in poppy (Moss & Orson, 2003).

In the past there was always the hope that a new herbicide would be developed to combat resistance problems. The reality is that most of the new herbicides seeking registration in the UK for the foreseeable future will be ALS inhibitors and, for these, the risk of rapid resistance development will be high. It is also unclear to what extent the SU herbicides approved for control of broad-leaved weeds may be exerting an additional selection pressure on grass weeds. Together with this, in the EU review of pesticides several active substances have not been supported and will therefore be withdrawn from use. These include terbutryn, flamprop-M-isopropyl, difenzoquat and sethoxydim, from three separate herbicide mode of action groups. The future of some of the other non-ALS inhibitor active substances is also uncertain. Economic considerations could further encourage the move towards simplified crop management in terms of rotations, cultivations, and crop monitoring. All of these factors could put additional pressure on the remaining active substances and potentially increase selection for resistance not only in cereals but across a range of UK crops. To date there have been no UK cases of target-site resistance to the ALS inhibitors in black-grass. However, there is a concern that, with increasingly limited opportunities to use products with different modes of action and with use of ALS inhibitors on different crops in a rotation, this could occur. Alternatively, the increasing reliance on herbicides as yet little or unaffected by resistance could lead to resistance development to these modes of action.

Clearly, regulatory authorities have a key role to play along with industry in the prevention and management of resistance. For many years a standard warning phrase has been placed on the labels of all products with grass weed control recommendations and this initiative could be expanded to include broad-leaved weeds. There has been a great deal of activity in trying to get key messages across to growers. This has included the publication of a revised set of WRAG guidelines on managing and preventing herbicide resistance in both grass and broad-leaved weeds (Moss & Orson, 2003).

FUTURE REQUIREMENTS AND ACTION

PSD has previously outlined how it interprets EC Directive 91/414/EEC (e.g. Slawson & Furk, 1995 and Godson et al., 1996). The publication of the EPPO guidance on resistance risk analysis has provided an additional steer to both industry and regulators on how this might be achieved in practice. The two-stage process consists of resistance risk assessment, where the probability of resistance development is evaluated, and resistance risk management where, if necessary, strategies for avoiding or delaying the development of resistance are considered and implemented. This process, whilst logical and intuitive, presents several challenges for both regulators and the industry. For example, one component of risk assessment is baseline sensitivity testing. For weeds, the guidelines outlined by Moss (2001) could provide the methodological framework to approaching this. However, critical to monitoring any shift in the sensitivity of populations is the maintenance of susceptible populations as standards. While this has become commonplace for black-grass in the UK with the use of the Rothamsted strain, other weed species present more of a challenge, particularly those species where there is inherently greater variability in sensitivity.

We may reasonably expect approval holders to support resistance management strategies, including, if necessary, the maintenance of susceptible standards for major 'on label' uses through their own ongoing research. However, the responsibility for minor uses, particularly off label ones, is less obvious but no less important and we must ensure that the area is not neglected.

The regulatory authorities also need to be responsive and to have the necessary procedures in place to enable resistance management strategies to be modified when required. The recent changes to the approvals for QoI fungicides show that this is not only possible but can be done relatively quickly. However, this was largely a fire-fighting action and may still turn out to be too little too late. If we are to ensure the continued availability of effective products for all sectors of crop production we need a better understanding of resistance in general so that we can focus our efforts and better identify both what action to take and when best to take it.

An important aspect of any strategy is to monitor its success. Approval holders must accept responsibility to monitor and review resistance management strategies after product registration. Likewise the regulator must keep approvals under review and it is thus important that survey results are made available to them. Better product stewardship, including more regular and pro-active monitoring to provide feedback as soon as possible on resistance development and the impact of resistance management strategies in the field are likely to be required. The development of suitable diagnostic tools and appropriate monitoring plans are an integral part of this and, in some cases, could become a requirement for registration. PSD would also encourage wider dissemination of baseline and survey information to allow the greater participation by independent researchers and a broader debate of the issues.

We must also avoid becoming too focused on the chemistry. Resistance management has traditionally concentrated on pesticide usage and not fully explored the range of cultural practices that may be important in managing or preventing resistance in an integrated system. Current guidelines from both WRAG and FRAG-UK promote good practice but more sophisticated strategies that effectively incorporate cultural control methods are required to manage resistance in the long term, for example with weeds, where farms may have several resistant weeds occurring in mixed populations. Greater emphasis must be placed on the promotion of integrated pest management programmes that incorporate cultural approaches alongside chemical ones.

PSD does not wish to place unnecessary restrictions on the use of products but resistance management strategies must be effective and we must be prepared to take action where required. Finding the right balance of approaches can only be achieved through the industry and the regulator working together. The RAGs provide an ideal forum for this, but closer links between the individual groups may be required, and the issue needs to be given greater prominence in their agenda. We need to be able to prioritise areas for consideration, identify where action is required, and be prepared to support it and ensure that it is implemented.

REFERENCES

Anon. (1993). Commission Directive (93/71/EEC) amending Council Directive 91/414/EEC concerning the placing of plant protection products on the market. *Official Journal of the European Community*, **L221**, 31 August 1993, 27-36.

Anon. (2003). Efficacy evaluation of plant protection products; PP1/213(2) Resistance risk analysis. *EPPO Bulletin* **33**, 37-63.

Garthwaite D G; Thomas M R (2000). *Pesticide Usage Survey Report 171: Arable Crops in Great Britain 2000*. DEFRA; London.

Godson T G; Furk C; Slawson D D (1996). Herbicide resistance and the registration of plant protection products under the EC Authorisations Directive. *Proceedings of the 10th International Conference on Weed Biology, Dijon - 1996*, pp. 247-252

Moss S R (2001). Baseline sensitivity to herbicides: a guideline to methodologies. *Proceedings of the BCPC Conference – Weeds 2000*, **2**, 769-774.

Moss S R; Orson J (2003) Managing and preventing herbicide resistance in weeds. *Home Grown Cereals Authority. UK/ Weed Resistance Action Group*. January 2003.

Russell P (1999). Fungicide resistance management: Into the next millennium. *Pesticide Outlook*, October 2001, pp. 213-215.

Russell P (2001). Fungicide Resistance Action Group (FRAC). *Pesticide Outlook*, August 2001, 165-167.

Slawson D D; Furk C (1995). Registration requirements and fungicide resistance. In: *A Vital Role for Fungicides in Cereal Production*, eds H G Hewitt, D Tyson, D W Hollomon, J M Smith W P Davies & K R Dixon, pp. 149-154. Bios Scientific Publishers Ltd: Oxford.

SESSION 6B

PESTICIDE RESIDUES IN FOOD

Chairman: Professor David Atkinson
                       SAC, Edinburgh, UK

Session Organiser: Dr Fiona Burnett
                       SAC, Edinburgh, UK

Papers: 6B-1 to 6B-4

Pesticide residues – better early than never?

G N Foster
SAC, Auchincruive, Ayr, KA6 5HW, UK
Email: g.foster@au.sac.ac.uk

D Atkinson, F J Burnett
SAC, West Mains Road, Edinburgh EH9 3JG, UK

ABSTRACT

Some supermarkets are leading the drive for zero-tolerance of pesticide residues in food, acknowledging the concerns of the average consumer. The Food Standards Agency recently instituted a review of literature in the public domain concerning pesticide residues and the potential for their minimisation. A review of UK research initiatives indicated that the concern to reduce environmental impact has outweighed the main - and often conflicting - demands of the consumer for food that is both cheap and "chemical"-free. Any attempt to reduce residues in food must inevitably focus on late season and storage practices rather than earlier prophylactic treatments that may have more environmental impact. Procedures can be cited that do or could promote additional pesticide near to or after harvest. These include the long-term storage of fruit and potatoes, the use of strobilurin fungicides, and the introduction of crops with herbicide insensitivity.

INTRODUCTION

The Food Standards Agency recently instituted a review on the crop protection of UK food commodities, particularly fresh fruit and vegetables, as a preliminary to developing a strategy on the minimisation of pesticide residues. This arose from clear evidence that the public do not favour any "chemical" residues occurring in food and from the zero-tolerance response of some supermarket chains. This zero option may have environmental consequences.

THE DOMINANCE OF PESTICIDES

Pesticides are used in food production to control the effects of fungal diseases and pests on crop development, to reduce competition with the crop by other plants, and to protect harvested food from pest and disease attack, and to control development of stored products. Pesticides may not provide the only means of crop protection but their effectiveness and simplicity of use have made them the method of choice for global agriculture. The use of pesticides became the norm after the Second World War, with more than 800 active ingredients in use across the European Union by the 1990s. Agricultural systems have developed in response to the availability of pesticides to prevent most previously intractable problems. Concern about pesticide use has been voiced since shortly after their inception, with counter arguments based on the need to combat crop losses, put conservatively at 35% of potential crop production, with a further 20% loss post-harvest. Holm (1976) showed that yield reductions ranged from zero to 90% due to weed competition, with means in the range

17-51%. Pimentel (1992) estimated that pesticides, with sales of 2.5 million tons per annum, had saved about 10% of the world's food supply, but contended that the damage caused by pesticides exceeded their benefits. Pretty *et al.* (2000) expanded this contention, reckoning that the total external costs of UK pesticide-based production was £2.3 billion per year, or £208 per hectare, of which the presence of pesticides in drinking water required £120 million treatment per annum.

Public concern

This dominance of pesticides has led to concern over pesticide residues in food, and this has repeatedly been endorsed in surveys of public concern. *The Guardian* published 81 articles on pesticide residues in 1999-2002. Recent press coverage is based on pesticides being an ever present contaminant of food, with the word chemical frequently being substituted. It would be difficult to find a report from the public media that endorsed the use of pesticides, unless it was perhaps associated with an issue of immediate concern for public health. Thus, whilst the first reality is our dependence on pesticides the second has come to be the control exerted over the public consciousness by media and pressure groups such that pesticide residues in food are unacceptable, and the belief that they are to be found only in conventionally produced food.

Sources of residues data

The principal sources of data within the UK are the surveillance reports of the Pesticide Residues Committee (PRC), established in 2000 to replace the Working Party on Pesticide Residues (PRC 2002). PRC oversees the monitoring of the UK's food and drink in a three part programme of checks:- that no unexpected residues occur; that residues do not exceed *Codex Alimentarius* Maximum Residue Levels (MRL); and that human dietary intakes are within acceptable levels. MRL are usually measured in mg/kg or parts per million, but in some cases are based on current Limits of Detection (LOD, hence LOD-MRL). PRC's reports are directed at an informed public, and use every opportunity to explain that MRL are not safety limits, i.e. they can be exceeded without implying a risk to health, and that their role is to demonstrate pursuit of Good Agricultural Practice (GAP), thus facilitating international trade. Nevertheless the very nature of the expression *maximum residue level* gives the wrong steer to even an informed public, and brings us back to the second reality, the fact that the public's perception of pesticides is utterly negative. The third of PRC's checks, the acceptable levels, derive from exposures primarily established in short and longer term studies of pesticides in mammals, generating the Acceptable Daily Intake (ADI), the Acute Reference Dose (ARfD), and the Acceptable Operator Exposure Level (AOEL). In addition to PRC's monitoring the Pesticides Safety Directorate operates an enforcement programme, dedicated for example to winter lettuce in 2001; its results are included in PRC publications. Other sources of data on products in the UK are generated by the food industry and consumers' associations, with some results being published, or at least the subject of some publicity. The European Commission publishes an annual compilation including UK data.

Residue results

The third reality concerns the actual levels of contamination observed in foodstuffs. For example, 29% of the 4,003 samples tested by PRC in 2001 were free from pesticide residue (Table 1). PRC (2002), in reporting these results, noted that "desirable safety margins" had been eroded by 0.25% for the 0.7% of samples exceeding MRL. Figures for nine supermarket chains, as measured on behalf of Friends of the Earth (2002), were 29 to 63% of fruit and vegetables with pesticide residues.

Table 1. Pesticide Residues in UK Food Samples (source: Pesticide Residues Committee)

| | Year | | |
	1999	2000	2001
No of Samples Analysed	2,300	2,304	4,003
% with measurable residues	27	28	29
% with residues exceeding MRL	1.6	1	0.7
% of samples of with measurable residues			
Bread	6	44*	38
Milk	0	0	2
Potato	51	48	33

* Residues of chlormequat assessed for first time and found in 41% of samples.

Table 2. Pesticide residues detected in a selection of vegetables and fruit 1991-2002 (source: Pesticide Residues Committee)

Crop	No. samples tested	% with residues	% > MRL	No. pesticides found
Carrot	369	64	0.8	12
Celery	276	66	4.0	30
Lettuce	803	58	3.7	37
Mushroom	255	11	0.8	5
Onion	146	48	0	1
Potato	1,722	37	0.3	15
Tomato	359	23	0.3	26
Apple	396	44	0	25
Banana	181	65	2.8	7
Grapes	382	44	2.1	46
Orange	303	95	2.0	30
Strawberry	383	67	0.3	12

Residue occurrence is generally in fruit and vegetables among products sold in the UK (Table 2), with rather lower levels of occurrence in potatoes offset by the importance of this crop to the national diet. The residues detected are primarily fungicides, but sprout suppressants dominated the residues found in potato, as again in 2002, when chlorpropham was found in 23 out of 138 samples. Chlorpropham does not have an MRL set, but the highest level found was 6.6 mg/kg (PRC 2003).

The origins and potential impact of the result

PRC (2002) note that the outcome of MRL exceedance in 2001, on worst case scenario, would be a few upset stomachs. The calculation of ADI, expressed in mg active ingredient per kg body weight, is based on a complex model of risk factors coupled to the "no observed adverse effect level" in animal experiments, but multiplied up by an uncertainty factor, usually one hundredfold. It is not clear the extent to which ADI as a risk assessment takes into account residue losses during processing, and residue gains associated with, for example, the use of spices and the treatment of food premises (Singh & Singh, 1990). It is relevant to note that the passage of the Food Quality Protection Act in the USA in 1996 resulted in a major, US-wide risk assessment of human exposure to organophosphorous (OP) insecticides as a whole (Miller, 2002). Its main finding was that exposure was largely associated with the use of dichlorvos (DDVP) for domestic pest control rather than with dietary exposure. Dichlorvos was withdrawn from the UK domestic market in 2002 (Department for Environment, Food and Rural Affairs, 2002). However, the assumption is still that the main source of pesticide residues overall is by consumption of treated crops or through the consumption of milk and meat products from animals fed on crops containing residues. The herbicides 2,4-D, 2,4,5-T and MCPA regularly occur in milk. The residues derived from persistent organochlorine pesticides are easily absorbed into fats, resulting in animals constantly recycling them and causing contamination of milk and meat. It is possible to derive a signature from the degradation products of DDT to indicate exposure to recent use, historical use, or metabolism via animals or micro-organisms (Working Party on Pesticide Residues, 2000).

There may be misconceptions about the importance of conventional production relative to other systems. Baker *et al.* (2002) compared pesticide residues in fruit and vegetables originating from conventional and organic production systems, and from crops subject to integrated pesticide management (IPM). They found that 23% of organically produced samples contained one or more residues, compared to 73% of conventional samples and 47% of IPM-derived samples. Forty per cent of the residues in organic samples were derived from persistent organochlorine pesticides banned in western Europe.

A consideration of the routes of pesticide residues to the plate must take into account the relative importance of products derived from the UK and those coming from abroad. PRC reports differentiate, where possible, between UK-derived products and those from abroad. The level of pesticide detection and MRL exceedance are higher for imported products than for those of UK origin (PRC, 2002). The level of pesticides in foodstuffs must normally decline from the moment of their use through continued crop growth, harvest, storage, to the cleaning and cooking of the food. Exotic raw spices and dried food or preserves may add pesticide residues to the plate, to which must be added those from animal products and finally non-dietary exposures at work or in domestic pest control. The human body immediately takes on the task of excreting or degrading any ingested residues.

Data that track the passage of pesticides from application to human excretion are limited. The only accurate and copious figures are those at the shop counter. Figures are also available for pesticide sales, their actual usage and levels on crops when the pesticide is undergoing evaluation. The actual point of consumption of residues, i.e. the meal as a whole, is only analysed for foods eaten whole – bread, some fruit and prepared foods such as preserves and instant meals, and for ADI and ArfD, usually in the event of concern about a particular residue finding. There are few studies of the movement within the human body of modern pesticides; those that have been done concerning breast milk, blood and urine typically concern residues of the largely banned persistent organochlorine insecticides. Thus our knowledge of the "life-cycle analysis" of a pesticide within the food chain is incomplete, with possibly more information available about its leaving that system, i.e. entering the environment.

The market response

Attempts to explain that exceedance of maximum residue levels does not constitute a health risk have failed. Attempts to explain that even lower levels of residue are of no concern have failed. Telling the public that everything they eat is a chemical have failed to convince them. Stating that some naturally occurring chemicals are more toxic pesticides than those applied to the crop probably adds to the confusion. It is unlikely that the hormetic benefits of such exposure (Calabrese & Baldwin, 2002) will be accepted by the general public.

The reality has become that the public require food to be free from any trace of pesticides. The toxicology of the residue is largely irrelevant. The argument for dominance of an alternative reality, that consumers require cheap and blemish-free food, is being eroded by systems less dependent on pesticides, i.e. organic production, and pesticide-free food, i.e. infant food products. The supermarkets respond by setting requirements well below MRL, and most are developing sales policies based on zero tolerance. It is pertinent to assess the impacts of this policy, given that we are still working with production systems that evolved in response to the availability of synthetic pesticides.

The negative impact of zero tolerance

The benefit of zero tolerance must foremost be the satisfaction of the consumer. A longer term benefit might be a realisation by consumers and their advisors that there is more to health than avoidance of xenobiotics.

Some high-yielding modern cultivars can survive only if protected from pests and pathogens to which they are susceptible either by the use of pesticides or by intensified breeding to introduce resistance factors. A classic example would be the potato cv Maris Piper, resistant to some cyst nematodes, but susceptible to aphids, the viruses they transmit, and to slugs. Taking this to extremes some crop species cannot survive unless protected, e.g. potato affected by late blight, *Phytophthora infestans*.

The "better the devil you know" syndrome applies here, whereby well established pesticides are associated with well established methods of detecting their residues. The substitution of an easily detected existing pesticide by a seemingly residue-free pesticide may prove unsustainable as analytical technology catches up.

And then there is the problem of minimising pesticide use around harvest time. Earlier concerns about insecticides were largely associated with their persistence or their direct effect on the human nervous system. The replacement of these materials by synthetic pyrethroids shifted the focus towards the pesticides on which we are more heavily dependent, the fungicides and herbicides. The more recent concern about pesticide residues *per se* has highlighted the use of growth regulators. The emphasis now is surely on those pesticides that generate residues at harvest or in store irrespective of the hazards associated with them – and these are largely fungicides, desiccants and growth regulators.

Knock-on effects of treatments

If late season treatments are more likely to generate residues than those applied earlier, a solution to one crop problem that requires a further treatment for another must also give cause for concern. There are a number of examples, actual and potential, of this knock-on effect.

1. Mushrooms. PRC (2001) reported seven samples of mushrooms containing chlormequat in 2000. These residues probably arose from use of straw-based growing media from treated cereal crops.

2. Fruit storage rots and maturation control. The amount of rotting during storage of apples is mainly determined by the growing conditions. Different varieties also have greater susceptibility and each has its own storage requirements in terms of temperature, carbon dioxide and oxygen concentration. Thus a risk assessment on a crop as it arrives at store may restrict the need to apply a fungicide drench. Post harvest fungicides are not essential – they are banned in some EU countries – but rotting levels may be doubled by failure to treat. A fast turnaround at harvest is rarely possible, owing to the need to obtain the best market price for the produce, and so it is the market that largely dictates the need for post-harvest treatment. Harvest damage of pears is responsible for post-harvest infection by *Botrytis*. This is largely because the fruit stalks do not absciss naturally, as in apples, leading to sharp-ended stalks ("snags") that inflict damage on other fruit when moved into store. Pears are stored at sub-zero temperatures, and then ripened over 6-8 days once out of store, again in contrast to the slow maturation process of apples. Iprodione has an off-label approved usage for this problem, and its residues are frequently detected on pears.

One major food outlet has experienced difficulty in meeting its zero tolerance declaration with lemons. Citrus fruits are generally picked green and then 'degreened' prior to marketing using ethylene at high humidities. The raised humidity increases the risk of infection with *Penicillium* and *Botrytis*, requiring late pre-storage treatments with fungicides. The public are not aware that skin colour in citrus is not an indicator of ripeness, green produce being wholesome but nevertheless unacceptable. Incidentally, waxing of fruits, in particular citrus, is essentially cosmetic but is claimed to have added value in terms of reduced water loss and some protectant action against fungal infections, but not enough to guarantee freedom from risk. Thus the withholding of products to maximise their economic impact on the market results in additional fungicide use because of increased risk of attack.

3. The need for desiccants following effective fungicide action. The introduction of strobilurin fungicides to a range of crops can reduce senescence of aerial parts such that desiccants may be required at the end of the season. This may explain the occurrence of glyphosate residues in 7% of bread samples analysed on behalf of the Pesticide Residues Committee in 2000 (PRC 2001).

4. Crops genetically modified to facilitate the use of selective herbicides. Irrespective of the outcome of current trials concerning the environmental impacts of herbicide-tolerant crops, the delay in application of pesticides associated with herbicide-insensitive crops may be expected to increase the risk of residues at the end of the season.

Environmental consequences of zero tolerance

The greatest threat of adopting a zero tolerance policy in association with the continued use of pesticides will be to push back treatments as far as possible within the growth season. Integrated pest management depends on accurate scouting of the crop to minimise unnecessary treatments and to validate those that are undertaken. The latter is an expectation under the Pesticide Voluntary Initiative. Thus there should be more reliance on "intervention" treatments based on eradicant fungicides and fast-acting, selective and non-persistent insecticides to address detected problems rather than prophylactic treatments such as seed coatings, nematicidal granules applied at planting and protectant fungicides. The widespread and indiscriminate protection conferred by the latter types of treatment has caused environmental concern, but their deployment at the beginning of the growing season rather than near its end minimises their potential to generate residues (Figure 1). Thus a demand for zero tolerance may result in increased use of less targeted, broad spectrum pesticides likely to have a greater environmental effect than treatments pinpointing problems.

Figure 1.The pesticide timetable in relation to crop growth, emphasising the increasing likelihood of residues with age of the crop.

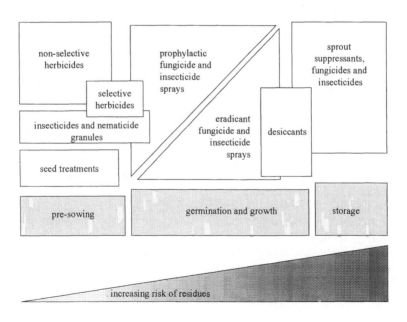

ACKNOWLEDGEMENTS

The authors are grateful to Dr Elizabeth Stockdale, whilst on secondment from Rothamsted Research to the Food Standards Agency, for facilitating this project, and to the FSA for funding it; however the views presented here are not necessarily shared by FSA. We should like to thank Marilyn Mullay, SAC Library, Edinburgh, for undertaking much of the literature search on which the survey was based. Also, Drs David Johnson and Angela Berrie, of Horticulture Research International, East Malling, are thanked for helpful discussions.

REFERENCES

Baker B P; Benbrook C M; Groth E; Benbrook K L (2002). Pesticide residues in conventional, integrated pest management (IPM) – grown and organic foods : insights from three US data sets. *Food additives and contaminates* **19**, 427-446.

Calabrese E J; Baldwin L A (2002). Applications of hormesis in toxicology, risk assessment and chemotherapeutics. *Trends in Pharmacological Sciences* **23**, 331-337.

Department for Environment, Food and Rural Affairs (2002). Ministers act against a range of insecticides containing the chemical dichlorvos. *HSE/FERA/DH/DTLR News Release* 157/02 .

Friends of the Earth (2002). Pesticides in food: latest results. Press Release, 12 November 2002, Friends of the Earth: London.

Holm L (1976). The importance of weeds in world food production. *Proceedings of the BCPC Conference – Weeds 1976*, 753-769.

Miller D (2002). Probabilistic acute dietary risk assessment for pesticides: the U.S. EPA perspective. *Proceedings 1ˢᵗ International Fresenius Conference Food Safety and Dietary Risk Assessment*: Mainz.

Pesticide Residues Committee (2001). *Annual report of the Pesticide Residues Committee 2000*. Defra: London

Pesticide Residues Committee (2002). *Annual report of the Pesticide Residues Committee 2001*. Defra: London

Pesticide Residues Committee (2003). *Pesticide residues monitoring report. Fourth quarter results 2002. October- December 2002*. Defra: London

Pimentel D (1992). Pesticides and the world food supply. In: *The science of global change: the impact of human activities on the environment*, eds D A Dunnette & R J O'Brien, pp. 309-323. American Chemical Society: Washington.

Pretty J N; Brett C; Gee D; Hine R E; Mason C F; Morison J I L; Raven H; Rayment M D; van der Bijl G (2000). An assessment of the total external costs of UK agriculture. *Agricultural Systems* **65**, 113-136.

Singh P P; Singh B (1990). Food contamination with insecticide residues from nonagricultural environmental sources. *Advances in Environmental Science and Technology* **1990**, 295-320

Working Party on Pesticide Residues (2000). Annual report of the Working Party on Pesticide Residues 1999. Supplement to the Pesticides Monitor 2000. Ministry of Agriculture, Fishers & Food: London.

Removing hazardous products from the food chain

K Barker

The Co-operative Group (CWS) Ltd, PO Box 53, New Century House, Manchester, M60 4ES, UK

Email: Kevin.Barker@co-op.co.uk

ABSTRACT

A survey of consumers in 2000 identified widespread public concern over the potential health and environmental impact of pesticides and also a general distrust of the framework surrounding food safety issues. To restore consumer confidence the Co-op developed controls that avoid or restrict the use of certain pesticides by suppliers worldwide. Pesticides are selected on the basis of comparative assessments for efficacy, environmental impact and known health issues. The Co-op promotes a three step approach to the control of pests by encouraging the use of preventative measures, cultural and biological control rather than relying on pesticide use. During the past few years the Co-op has banned and restricted the use of 50 pesticides and is continuing it's work to develop it's policy and position. The Co-op take a proactive stance with growers and issues data sheets allowing growers to compare the relative hazards and benefits of products. It is necessary to continue to develop alternative strategies that reduce the reliance on pesticides and promote the use of more benign alternatives. Quality assured food schemes have the potential to help with this. Regulation is essential to maintain the safety of registered products but the addition of a comparative assessment of risk when evaluating new products would be welcomed. Co-operation between all parties in the food industry is essential to reduce residues, improve food safety and restore consumer trust.

INTRODUCTION

Providing safe, wholesome food was one of the founding principles of the Co-op movement some 150 years ago. Company policy-makers and managers believe that new work on pesticides simply brings those principles into practice.

A survey of Co-op customers, described in their recent report (2001), reveals that, whilst they are generally happy with the product choice and quality they now see on supermarket shelves, they are increasingly concerned about health scares, environmental concerns and animal welfare outrages which have created an atmosphere of mistrust, not just of the retail industry, but of the whole framework that surrounds food safety and quality. The survey also showed that after BSE and genetic modification, pesticides were an important area of concern, ahead of emotive subjects such as battery chickens and animal welfare. There is a general belief that pesticides are a risk to health, and that they permeate the food chain as residues. Consumers have very little ability to control their exposure to pesticides, other than through choosing to buy organic food, which may not be available to everybody. They have concerns about the effect of pesticides on health, the environment, and occupational health. Overall, two thirds of consumers gave pesticides a thumbs down, with 'concerned' and 'very concerned' responses accounting for over two thirds in the survey.

The Co-op reflected this level of concern, tempered with a pragmatic approach, in a new programme of work on pesticides that they have developed over a number of years. The Co-operative Group in the UK, through Farmcare, is the largest farmer in the UK, and has a strong ethos of integrated crop management, using many techniques derived from organic farming. In conjunction with Farmcare they have developed controls that involve avoiding certain pesticides and restricting others, applied to all their growers worldwide.

MANAGING PESICIDE RISK

The starting point for the Co-op was a risk assessment of a number of pesticides, taking into account all the available information, although they observe that this was in some cases minimal. Working in partnership with Farmcare, they considered the toxicology of each substance, its bioaccumulation and persistency within the environment. A resulting list of banned pesticides was instituted (Anon, 2001).

Co-op restricted pesticides can only be used by specific agreement with the Co-op, and where a supplier or grower requests approval for use they have to provide supporting evidence that other alternatives are not viable. The Co-op then encourages the grower first to consider other control measures including cultural or biological controls, or more benign chemical alternatives, before approval is granted. Because of the work done with Farmcare, and developing knowledge, the Co-op have been able to suggest to other suppliers viable alternatives, confident that they would perform at an economic as well as at a control level. Farmcare has shown over a number of years that an integrated crop management approach can deliver improved overall results with less reliance on chemical intervention, and thus a reduction in the overall pesticide costs.

These controls form part of a Code of Practice, which the Co-op developed for all suppliers almost three years ago and which is applied to the worldwide production of all fresh produce, and produce for frozen, dried and canned goods. Where problems are identified, for example the use of a pesticide without approval, then steps can and have been taken to stop supplies from a particular grower until matters are resolved to the Co-op's satisfaction. This involves working with growers to find alternatives, and information is provided to assist this process.

Pro-active approaches

The Co-op publicises all of their pesticide results on their website (www.co-op.co.uk) so that all consumers, including their members can access the data. The Co-op was the first retailer to do this and believes that this transparency is vital to reinstating consumer trust. The Co-op would welcome initiatives from other retailers to follow suit: this would provide opportunities to share data more broadly, and allow collaborations on research into alternatives, and how to make practical improvements.

The Co-op believes that it is extremely important that they do not just apply more restrictions to the agricultural industry, but that they help to provide solutions. This applies equally to large and smaller growers worldwide: those in other countries have an equal, if not greater, need for information and assistance. Obtaining unbiased advisory information from agrochemical companies is not easy, especially in developing countries, and the Co-op believe it is fundamental in allowing growers to make informed decisions on crop management. The industry has produced Environmental Information Sheets, but these have a UK focus, do not yet cover all pesticides, and do not offer comparative information, so this is not accessible unless a whole collection of Environmental Information Sheets is available.

As an alternative and to provide improved support for growers, the Co-op has produced a series of Product Advisory Sheets. These aim to share information with growers on the possible control methods for pests in the particular crop so they can make an informed decision on the controls best suited to their needs. They include details of preventative measures, and cultural and biological controls. Information on the approved pesticides includes details on their potential environmental and health effects, potentially enabling a comparative risk assessment to be made, and the more benign products to be selected, if used at all. The Co-op has produced Product Advisory Sheets for a growing range of crops, including carrots, potatoes, avocadoes and pineapples, demonstrating their equal commitment to growers in the UK and further afield. They have been very well received by growers, and remove reliance on agrochemical sales sources for information on products.

The role of quality assured schemes

The Co-op has begun to progress this idea with the Assured Produce Scheme. Unfortunately due to the disparate nature of the scheme progress, to date, has been slow. The Co-op believes schemes such as the Assured Produce Scheme (APS) and the Euro-Retailer Produce Working Group (EUREP) can help to deliver small steps in improvements and practices, both in terms of effectiveness and efficiency of control, whilst supporting a change in how people think about farming and growing controls. However, such development is not inherent within the APS and rarely exhibited by EUREP Good Agricultural Practice (GAP). It is clear that the long term aim should be to support a more sustainable scheme.

The role of the regulator

The Co-op would like to see the Pesticides Safety Directorate (PSD) supporting comparative data as part of the approvals process. It will prove valuable when the first pesticides are removed from the market by the European Union this year, and more information on alternatives is needed.

For the Co-op, working with growers has identified difficulties for UK producers, particularly in relatively small crop and usage areas, for example, in apple growing. UK approvals are not being sought by manufacturers for actives that would be advantageous for UK growers and are already approved on the continent. There are also products approved for limited applications in the UK that have, in some cases, wider approval on the continent. They may offer more effective and yet more benign control. Such restrictions create a disadvantage for UK growers and potentially increasing dependence on older chemistry. The Co-op would like to see improved ways of looking at the way 'mutual recognition' is applied by PSD.

They would also like the Advisory Committee on Pesticides (ACP) to consider methods for the registration of alternative forms of pest control, with an appropriate regulatory hurdle. However the Co-op are in no way advocating deregulation of the approvals process, which is still critical in maintaining safety.

Developing the Co-op pesticide control programme

As the Co-op continue to develop their programme of control over pesticides, they regard the way they regulate the selection of pesticides as the most important aspect. They have developed a new advisory panel of eminent scientists (including two who also sit on the ACP), chaired by Christopher Stopes, a consultant in food and farming, who also sits on the ACP. The panel reviews the pesticides against a hazard framework based closely on the work of the ACP. It does not supersede the regulatory approach but provides a parallel model for development.

Currently the Co-op are reviewing their list of restricted pesticides, focusing on, for example the most commonly found residues, and those actives with potential for endocrine disruption. This may lead to more restrictions, and the development of alternatives. For example, there is an urgent need for an alternative to carbendazim. It is the most common residue found in Co-op testing programmes, though always below the Maximum Residue Limit (MRL). There is also a need for more research into alternatives, led perhaps by government and industry.

Specific research work is required within the pesticide area to investigate the efficacy at lower rates and degradation curves for all pesticides, with the overall aim of reducing residues within products. In addition there is a need to further examine the impact of chemical mixtures (cocktail effect) on human health.

In developing countries there is a need help find alternatives to pesticides where the MRL has been reduced to the limit of detection. Food production is a global process and, as such, the Co-op believes that the needs of growers must be considered. There is scope for collaboration between government departments, potentially including The Department for International Development (DfID), to generate sustainable solutions, and access to the market for small growers abroad.

CONCLUSIONS

With customers continuing to raise concerns regarding the use of pesticides and residues within products, it remains necessary to continue with the work to develop alternative strategies that reduce the reliance on pesticides and promote the use of more benign or non-chemical alternatives. In achieving these aims, the Co-op urges all parties, both directly and indirectly connected to the food industry, to work closely together.

REFERENCES

Anon. (2001). Retailer bans suspect pesticides, *Pesticide News* **53**, September 2001, p3.
Co-op (2001). *Green and Pleasant Land*, 2 July 2001, Co-op, Manchester, UK.

The growers' perspective on strategies for the minimisation of pesticide residues in food

C J C Wise
National Farmers' Union, 164 Shaftesbury Avenue, London, WC2H 8HL
Email: christopher.wise@nfu.org.uk

A Findlay
Bedfordshire Growers Ltd., Potton Road, Biggleswade, Bedfordshire, SG18 OER

ABSTRACT

Current crop protection is largely based on the use of pesticides. Although the scale of use results in the occurrence of measurable residues in about a third of food products, only a very small proportion of residues detected exceed maximum residue levels (MRL) and there is no substantive evidence that current residues represent a health issue. On the other hand there are significant health risks in insufficient consumption of roughage, fruit and vegetables. At the present time, in both the EU and the UK, the application of pesticides in agriculture is decreasing. Growers' maintain that pesticide residues should not be seen in isolation within the debate about food quality, and minimising pesticide residues through reduced use or alternative practices must be seen in the context of consumer demands for products with high visual impact, and the need for available and affordable produce. The balance of perspective for consumers regarding relative risks must be maintained.

INTRODUCTION

There is now overwhelming evidence that the lack of fruit and vegetables in our diet is a major factor in the ill health issues facing the developed world. Many informed commentators submit that pesticide residues, provided they are strictly within maximum residue levels (MRLs) industry guidelines, are not a risk of any consequence in comparison to faulty diet, i.e. excessive consumption of fats, sugar, salt and over manufactured food and insufficient consumption of roughage, fruit and vegetables. Nevertheless, at a recent Food Standards Agency (FSA) stakeholders' meeting (30/04/02) Prof. David Coggon, Chair of Advisory Committee on Pesticides, stated "In advising ministers, we must base our advice on scientific advice but also the need to reflect public concerns over pesticide residues". Growers' appreciate the pressures on the FSA to compromise on this issue but urge very careful consideration of any advice to Government on changes, which are not fully justified, and to evaluate the likely repercussions such a compromise would send in several directions. To keep matters in perspective it should be remembered that any synthetic pesticide residues are only a tiny fraction of total ingested pesticide. Prof. Bruce Ames, Director of the National Institute of Environmental Health Sciences Centre, UC Berkeley has calculated that naturally occurring pesticides in food constitute 99.99% of ingested pesticides. He estimates we ingest more carcinogens in one cup of coffee than we get from the residues of synthetic pesticides on all the fruits and vegetables we eat in a year (Ames, 1997).

FARMERS' AND GROWERS' INITIAL PERCEPTIONS

Every pesticide application cost is straight off the grower's potential profit margin. The pressure to minimise pesticide application is already heavy, but a producer also has to meet consumer and buyer expectations and failure to do so can be catastrophic with margins at their current level. One occasional aphid per sprout is just acceptable but two aphids means the probable rejection of the entire crop. Rejection by the market results in major investment loss. The risk always resides with the producer and can easily result in total financial failure. Often the decision of whether or not to spray is akin to walking a tight rope with customer demands of appearance and cleanliness on the one side and demands of minimal residue on the other, not to mention the invidious Governmental policy to 'name and shame' retailers with supplier problems.

To reduce MRLs purely as a concession and not on a sound scientific basis will send a host of messages. What message will it send to embattled producers and their evaluation of risk? What message will it also send to the host of pressure groups who may seize on any such 'concession' as positive proof that MRLs were not safe in the first place and renew pressure for further reductions? What message will it send to those supermarkets who recognise the scientifically based safety margins built into MRLs are so amply extensive and have had the courage to stand by this line?

If Government is not prepared to use scientific evidence as the basis of risk assessment and scientific evidence alone, public and parliamentary confidence will be shaken. When so much evidence from organisations like the Food Research Institute and National Centre for Policy Analysis is so uncompromisingly positive about the benefits to health from the inclusion of fruit and vegetables in the national diet, why is it that an entire nation's common sense seems to have been 'high jacked' by a movement which started out with such laudable objectives.

So why is fresh produce consumption so unfashionable? Three reasons come to mind:

1. The attractiveness and convenience of manufactured snacks and fast food. The whole basis of this industry is for the product to be desirable with little or no concern that excessive consumption will eventually harm the consumer. Fast food is now an integral part of our society's culture but the cost to the National Health Services has yet to be fully revealed. Perhaps the UK and EU governments should be considering a tax on fats and sugars rather than pesticides!

2. The association of fruit and vegetables with pesticide residues. We need to recognise the benefit the media have derived from this issue, it has 'sold a lot of copy' and entrenched consumers perception that all fruit and vegetables must be potentially harmful; this line is also regrettably promoted by scientists anxious for research funding.

3. The cost of fruit and vegetables. Actually the fact is that strictly controlled use of herbicides, fungicides and insecticides all makes fruit and vegetables remarkably freely available and affordable to the consumer. Losses of essential chemicals or reductions of MRLs for political expediency could deprive many, and in particular those of lower income, of their choice of a healthy diet with a subsequent deleterious effect on general health of considerable magnitude.

ARE THERE VIABLE OPPORTUNITIES AT FIELD LEVEL?

Nevertheless, farmers and growers are responsive to their markets and they constantly review the number of options not related to current pesticide application practices and technologies, which could influence the quantity of residues or the frequency with which such residues are found. Both biotechnology enhanced production systems and organic farming have as part of their basic rationale the reduction of pesticide use to low or no levels. Both approaches individually and as part of a whole UK strategy have a potential role to play in reducing residues in food.

Organic farming has been successful in reducing the frequency and levels of pesticide residues in produce from this sector (Baker *et al.*, 2002). In many cases this means of production results in a yield penalty. It is a fallacy to present organic production as the panacea. Already, the evidence in several EU Member States, notably France and the UK, indicates that organic production is increasingly unprofitable (up to 40% of UK organically produced milk is currently sold in the mainstream commodity market). Moreover, organic producers may use a number of pesticides authorised under the framework of Directive 91/414 as well as certain traditional elemental substances such as copper and sulphur, which are known to have a negative environmental impact. The producers of minor crops who will suffer profoundly under the 91/414 revocations are very concerned over the lack of research into, and promotion of, alternative pest control strategies, which will soon be key to the continuation of any production within the EU of certain fresh produce.

However, many of the crop protection practices developed for organic farming seem likely to have value to conventional agriculture, especially integrated crop management (ICM) systems. Introducing appropriate methods from this sector may therefore reduce both pesticide use and recovery as residues e.g. selection of varieties, timing of operations, but some organic techniques adopted by conventional production e.g. use of fleece to deter insect pests, bring higher costs and there are waste disposal issues. There needs to be joined-up thinking from Government - alternative technologies can sometimes fall foul of other regulations.

The use of genetically modified (GM) crops in crop production in USA has resulted in some reductions in pesticide use. Total reductions seem less than had been anticipated. Varieties engineered to be resistant to insect pests, *Bacillus thuringiensis* (Bt) varieties, have reduced the use of insecticides but currently, no commercial GM varieties seem to have been rendered resistant to fungal infection. Conventional plant breeding can reduce the need for fungicides and insecticides but is likely to have little impact on herbicide use.

The adoption of alternative pest control methods and a reduction of farmers' dependence on pesticides is desirable but the sustainable use of pesticides can only be delivered by ensuring better training of the people who use pesticides. This has been recognised within the industry and considerable progress made in training, record keeping and crop assurance scheme uptake. Enforcement, by monitoring for MRLs or measures of environmental impact, is flawed as some pesticides leave little or no detectable residues. In addition some active substances occur naturally and traces may not result from agriculture.

Mandatory EU requirements would be impractical and unworkable because they would be unenforceable. The use of EUREP (a produce assurance scheme in Europe), which involves the whole food chain from producer to consumer, is more likely to result in positive action because commercial expediency drives up production standards. The adoption of the Assured Produce Scheme in the UK, which is funded by the producers, has raised standards of management and awareness throughout the food chain in a remarkably short time. Since there are no agreed or comparable protocols of ICM/IPM/IFM across member states, how can compliance be linked to subsidy without introducing the real risk of distorting production costs for produce grown in more than one member state? At the moment adherence to good agricultural practice (GAP) is the only criteria that could be used but the mechanisms for demonstrating compliance vary markedly between member states. It seems logical to standardise inspection mechanisms before lifting standards.

CONCLUSION

No decision should be taken without proper evaluation of possible side effects. Vegetable producers know at first hand the enormous pressures that have been placed on production to conform to an avalanche of legislation, withdrawal of many established pesticides, costly directives and margin reductions from supermarkets and now an erosion of confidence from their bankers after some spectacular business failures. Confidence is low, even amongst the most efficient in the UK production, but the current strength of sterling ensures the retailers' shelves are full. But one would indeed be foolish in the extreme to say they will always be full. Governments need to weigh up most carefully the effect of a message that reducing the permitted levels of pesticide residues to almost an unsustainable degree will have on the confidence of growers and particularly if there is no scientific or statistical basis for such changes. Fruit and vegetables are, without question, essential to the national diet and the nations health. A solid core of domestic production is essential as a basic national insurance (witness this year's drought in central, southern and eastern Europe), but if production becomes uneconomic because 'the hurdles are set too high', for whatever reason, many producers will reduce their commercial exposure and simply exit production.

REFERENCES

Ames B (1997) Misconceptions about the causes of cancer lead to skewed priorities and wasted money. www.berkeley.edu/news/media/releases/97legacy/11_01_97a.html
Baker B P; Benbrook C M; Groth E; Benbrook K L (2002). Pesticide residues in conventional, integrated pest management (IPM) – grown and organic foods: insights from three US data sets. *Food additives and contaminates*, **19**, 427-446.

The role of biotechnology in the management of pesticide residues

P Rylott

Agricultural Biotechnology Council, PO Box 38 589, London, SW1A 1WE, UK
Email: paul.rylott@bayercropscience.com

ABSTRACT

Despite the fact that 70% of food eaten in the UK in 2000 had no detectable pesticide residue, this subject, whether it has a real or perceived risk, is on the consumer agenda. The issue must therefore be managed in a responsible manner if the industry is to gain support. If we are to learn from the GM debate, it is clear that we must all recognise that there is no such thing as one solution to the needs of agriculture and so by default recognise that choice is necessary. However, as industry, we must be bold enough to say that this choice applies in all directions. The current generation of GM crops with herbicide tolerance or insect resistance are, in reality, unlikely to significantly affect the levels of pesticide residues in food. In the future, genetic fungal resistance has the capacity to have a more fundamental effect, but again, genetic resistance will not obviate the need for chemical protection. As such therefore, GM crops may be able to play a role, and indeed can help in sensible pesticide residue management strategies, but they are not a silver bullet. They are, and should be seen as, part of a range of modern R&D based solutions. However, if they are to play a role, then we must continue to ensure that sound science in both research and development and regulation, and not populist reaction, is the foundation stone on which to build. We must also demonstrate and ensure that this foundation is enhanced with quality stewardship of our products to ensure they are used in a responsible manner and offer consumer and grower choice – no matter where in the world they are used. This is where global companies, such as those represented by the Agricultural Biotechnology Council, have a major, significant and possibly unique role to play

INTRODUCTION

During the 'GM Nation?' debate, I remember talking to one lady who said she was concerned about GM and food safety. There have been no tests at all she insisted. I took the time to explain in great detail the safety of the PAT protein and the feeding studies and toxicological tests we had carried out, which lead to us being able to define the No Observable Effect Level. I then ended by saying that, for the average human (70kg), this means that you could eat the equivalent of 24,000 tonnes of oilseed rape seed (a heap the size of a row of terraced houses), every day of your life for the rest of your life and there would not be any effect due to the ingestion of the PAT protein. She thought about this for a little while, then said in all seriousness, what would happen if I ate 25,000 tonnes a day?

I use this not to make fun but as an example of those who, having suddenly realised that they did not really know where their food came from, feel disenfranchised, worried or both. Pressure groups and a media hungry for a "scare" story, have added to and perpetuated this feeling by undermining and questioning everything. The result is that in the absence of "acceptable" answers, people yearn for a utopian era where all food was "good for us". Such an era of course has never existed, but in reality if it did we are probably closer to it now than was ever the case in this never-defined bygone time.

The lady at the meeting was not given comfort by the fact that we could quantify the food safety levels of this crop, she just felt that it was "wrong". Of course she should have the right to choose, but it was also clear that she was unable to assess the risk to herself as an individual in any real or helpful way. The mere fact that we had measured it at all meant that she assumed the worst. Her reaction of "I just want to go back to the good old days," may of course have been a desire to go back to a time when worries and concerns were not constantly in the headlines, regulators were trusted, and she did not have to try and weigh up the risks and benefits for herself.

Pesticide residues create exactly the same dilemma. Industry and regulators alike have to try to get risk into perspective whilst accepting that moral or ethical considerations will play a part in consumer choice.

The challenge for politicians is perhaps more acute. They should rise above the "knee-jerk" populist reaction to tabloid headlines that are constantly calling for this or that to be banned or for him or her to resign. They must also weigh up the needs of the many against the demands of the few or the noisy. The question with GM crops as with pesticide residues is will they?

Whatever the outcome of their deliberations, industry will have to comply with the regulatory requirements. Clearance of, and adherence to, these regulatory requirements is of course not the same as trying to convince others of our product's benefits. If we are to learn anything from the GM debate, it is clear that all must recognise that there is no such thing as one solution to the needs of agriculture and so must recognise that choice is necessary. However, we must be bold enough to say that this choice applies in all directions. We must base our messages on sound science, and try to communicate in clearly understandable terms. Finally we must be honest and open and not fall into the trap of selling "jam tomorrow", but tell it like it is.

That is what I hope I will be able to do in this paper on the role of biotechnology in pesticide residue management.

Pesticide Residues

Despite the fact that 70% of food eaten in the UK in 2000 had no detectable pesticide residue (Pesticide Residues Committee, 2001), this subject, whether it has a real or perceived risk is on the consumer agenda (though not at the high levels that some pressure groups would have us believe). The issue must therefore be managed in a responsible manner if the industry is to gain support.

Foods most likely to contain pesticide residues are typically those that have had a crop protection product applied later on in the growth stage of the crop or indeed during storage. The persistence or systemic nature of the product also defines residue levels and so they tend to be insecticides or fungicide rather than herbicides. Finally there is a tendency that food produced in countries with high pest pressures (e.g. warmer climates), have a higher potential for pesticide residues due to the nature of the spray programme needed e.g. in exotic fruits.

The role of GM crops in pesticide residue management

Since their commercial introduction in the mid 1990s, GM crops are being chosen by more and more farmers each year and grown on more and more acres (Table 1). They are now grown in 16 countries by nearly 6 million growers, three quarters of which are resource-poor farmers (James, 2002). The main crops grown remain the commodity crops of soya, maize, cotton and canola and of course the main traits are herbicide tolerance and insect resistance (Table 2).

Table 1: Global area of GM crops in 2002 (James, 2002)

Year	Hectares (millions)
1996	1.7
1997	11.0
1998	27.8
1999	39.9
2000	44.2
2001	52.6
2002	58.7

Table 2: Dominant GM crops in 2002 (James, 2002)

Crop	Hectares (millions)	% GM Area
Herbicide tolerant soyabean	36.5	62
Bt Maize	7.7	13
Herbicide tolerant canola	3.0	5
Herbicide tolerant maize	2.5	4
Bt Cotton	2.4	4
Herbicide tolerant cotton	2.2	4
Bt / Herbicide tolerant cotton	2.2	4
Bt/Herbicide tolerant maize	2.2	4
Total	58.7	100

It is clear from 20 years of research and commercial experience that herbicide tolerant (HT) crops enable farmers to produce high yielding, high quality crops. In addition, according to the Prime Minister's Strategy Unit's assessment of the costs and benefits of GM crops, they offer convenience and cost savings. It is also clear that with appropriate stewardship and management guidelines that all of these benefits can be achieved in a way that is environmentally benign or even beneficial compared to some farming techniques.

Recent research carried out at Brooms Barn in Suffolk, UK (May, 2003) for example, demonstrated that different application timings and application methods meant that the weeds within a crop of GM sugar beet could be managed in various ways which could be tailored to different wildlife needs. Thus the crop could be managed to be more skylark or stone curlew friendly.

Research at Scottish Agricultural Colleges (Booth *et al.*, 2002, Walker *et al.*, 2003) has shown that the introduction of GM herbicide tolerant oilseed rape could facilitate uptake of minimal cultivation techniques in the UK. With GM, it is possible to produce high quality crops without the concomitant reductions in yield that often currently occur. The switch from current establishment and husbandry techniques, to one based on GM HT and minimal cultivation, could save over 16 million litres of fuel per annum. Such a decrease in fuel use would not only reduce the amount of greenhouse gas emissions by 57,000 tonnes per annum, but increase the "fuel out to fuel in" efficiency ratio from 12:1 to 19:1. This in turn could provide the much needed stimulus for the bio-diesel market (Agricultural Biotechnology Council, 2003).

As with any crop protection product, the companion herbicides to GM HT crops follow the usual regulatory assessments, which include safety and likely residue levels. Good stewardship ensures that the rates of application and timings, defined by the regulatory process, are adhered to, and also balance need, due to weed incidence and efficacy, with cost efficiency.

There is some debate about whether the use of GM HT crops reduces herbicide application (usually due to definition of a.i.). In reality, however, because of the nature of the products and the growth stage of the crop at application, the net effect of GM HT crops on pesticide residues in food will be minimal / neutral.

It is well documented that the introduction of insect tolerant (IT) crops, particularly cotton has resulted in a big decrease in the amount of insecticide needed to be applied. The often-quoted example is that less insecticide is used in Alabama now than at any time since the 1940s. James (2002) estimates that Bt cotton could reduce the use of insecticides by 33,000 tonnes. The technology can clearly also improve the yields (by up to 80% (Qaim and Zilberman, 2003)) and quality of crops. In addition, the use of insect resistant maize for example can reduce secondary infection levels with a consequent reduction in mycotoxins such as aflatoxin and so lead to a general increase in food quality and or safety (Miller, 1999).

Whilst GM IT crops have reduced the need for insecticides, they have not negated them. Depending on the incidence of pest levels and the need to ensure a sensible pest resistance management scheme, insecticides are applied at various application rates. Once again application of these insecticides to the current commercial crops is made at a growth stage of the crop where residues do not generally become an issue. Thus with the use of GM IT, even though there has been a documented reduction in the use of chemical control methods, it is unlikely to have a major effect on pesticide residues in food.

Future potentials

At the risk of selling jam tomorrow, future traits such as disease resistance (potato blight, *Phytophthora infestans,* for example) could have a more significant effect on pesticide residues in food. Clearly in such examples, where products are applied at a growth stage where residues are more likely to appear in the harvested product, then the use of genetic resistance rather than chemical control can play a more significant role in residue management. In this example however, it should be stressed that absolute control is probably unlikely and this coupled to the need for a resistance management strategy is likely to require some chemical control. In addition of course the blight fungicide is only one of the crop protection products applied; thus the genetic fungal resistance would have no effect on the residues that may appear from application of storage products for example.

Other future GM crops such as increased protein wheat, increased vitamin rice or enhanced starch potatoes are not necessarily going to have any effect on pesticide residue management as they may need to be treated exactly the same as non-GM crops. If they are introduced to the market with stacked genes for pest and disease management then this may have an effect. However, as for all of the other examples, this will always be dependent on pest incidence and resistance management strategies, which will define the levels and timing of pesticide applications. It is this in turn therefore, that may have the greater effect on pesticide residues.

Finally within this section, one of the biggest contributors to the pesticide residue register is exotic fruit. Given the nature of the returns from these crops and the current low level of commercial GM developments in these crops, it is unlikely that we will see widespread growing of GM disease or pest resistant pineapples in the foreseeable future.

CONCLUSIONS

The goal of today's food industry is to balance the consumer needs of, quality, safety, continuity of supply and convenience with those of animal welfare, environmental issues and of course the biggest driver, price.

As part of that industry, the goal of today's research and development based crop production companies must be to help farmers around the world to supply these foods efficiently and in a way that has as little negative environmental impact as possible. Clearly we must also take pesticide residue management into account.

This remit holds true whether we are producing products for sale in the developed or developing world countries. However, we must remain cognisant of consumer and grower choice, and adopt sensible pragmatic and responsible approaches to the needs of agriculture and food supply, and not try to impose prescriptive solutions. Without such an approach, the long-term benefits of which we are convinced may not be achieved.

Within this overall goal, GM crops have the potential to play a significant role by producing high quality, safe, affordable foods in a way that is sympathetic to the environment. They may also be able to play a role, and indeed can help in pesticide residue management strategies, but in all of this, they are not a silver bullet.

Europe), then we must continue to ensure that sound science not populist reaction continues to be the foundation stone on which to build.

We must then demonstrate and ensure that this foundation is enhanced with quality stewardship of our products to ensure they are used in a responsible manner and offer consumer and grower choice – no matter where in the world they are used. This is where global companies such as those represented by the Agricultural Biotechnology Council, (contrary to pressure group spin), have a major, significant and possibly unique role to play.

REFERENCES

Agricultural Biotechnology Council (2003). Evidence submitted to the Environment, Food and Rural Affairs Select Committee enquiry on biofuels. www.parliament.uk/parliamentary_committees/environment__food_and_rural_affairs/e fra_biofuels.cfm

Booth E J; Walker R L; Walker K C (2002). The use of herbicide tolerant oilseed rape with minimal cultivation techniques. *Proceedings Crop Protection in Northern Britain 2002*, 109-114.

James C (2002). Global status of commercialised transgenic crops. ISAAA Brief No. 27. www.isaaa.org

May M J (2003). Economic consequences for UK farmers of growing GM herbicide tolerant sugar beet. *Annals of Applied Biology* **142**, 41-48.

Miller J (1999). Factors affecting the occurrence of fumosin in corn. *ILSI North America International Conference on the toxicology of Fumosin*: 1-2.

Pesticide Residues Committee (2001). *Annual report of the Pesticide Residues Committee 2000*. Defra: London.

Qaim M; Zilberman D (2003). Yield effects of genetically modified crops in developing countries. *Science* **299**, 900-902.

Walker R L; Wightman P S; Booth E J; Walker K C (2003). Energy balance evaluation of minimal cultivation techniques for establishing oilseed rape comparing herbicide tolerant and conventional systems. *Proceedings of GCRIC Congress*, July 2003, 435-538.

SESSION 6C

NOVEL AND INDUSTRIAL CROPS: REALISING THEIR POTENTIAL

Chairman:	Melvyn Askew
	Central Science Laboratory, York, UK
Session Organiser:	David Turley
	Central Science Laboratory, York, UK
Papers:	6C-1 to 6C-4

An overview of opportunities and factors affecting exploitation of crops for industrial use

M F Askew

Central Science Laboratory, York, North Yorkshire, YO41 1LZ, UK
Email: m.askew@csl.gov.uk

ABSTRACT

The exploitation of products from plants is not new but went into decline as synthetic materials were developed from coal and oil and technological development meant that animals were outclassed as primary sources of traction. The recognition of the need for true sustainability, led by concerns over the impacts of current farming practices and the impacts of our industrialised society on pollution and global climate change, has caused a revision of views. Significant markets for sustainable biorenewable raw materials now exist, created by legislative change or by technical or economic advantage. Nonetheless progress in uptake has been slow for a number of reasons and aspirations to achieve targets for increased use of renewable raw materials may prove difficult to fulfil. Some of the reasons for this are discussed.

INTRODUCTION

The production of non-food products from plants and animals is not new but has changed due to introduction of novel technologies, availability of raw materials/feedstocks and public demand. Examples occur in the energy, oils and fibres sectors. Prior to the introduction of internal combustion engines most power came from draught horses or oxen which were fed biorenewable energy as oats, other cereals, forages or proteins like Faba beans. Similarly the utilisation of fibres from plants like hemp, flax and jute provided ropes, canvases and a range of other products, whilst animal and vegetable oils and fats provided lubrication and a basis for lighting. Most of these non-food crop uses were superseded by the exploitation of fossil coal and oil resources. With a move towards a demand for use of more sustainable raw materials (in terms of their economic impact, environmental performance/impact and cultural/ social acceptance) the pendulum is moving back again to biobased materials. There have been considerable technological developments in the biofeedstocks sector such that many sustainable products can have as good a technical performance as synthetic materials and in some recent cases (e.g. in-car composite panels) could be superior to existing synthetically derived products.

For the successful development of such opportunities there is a need to link raw material markets with processing and production industries and to provide appropriate underpinning support. This can be characterised as shown in Figure 1, taken from a recent United States roadmap for the planed future development of the US non-food crop sector.

Realistically, for the continued and desirable exploitation of sustainable biorenewable feedstocks and products four fundamental questions have to be asked. In tackling responses to these questions it has to be recognised that a fundamentally new appreciation of the crops or animal species in question may be essential to fully exploit all possible opportunities.

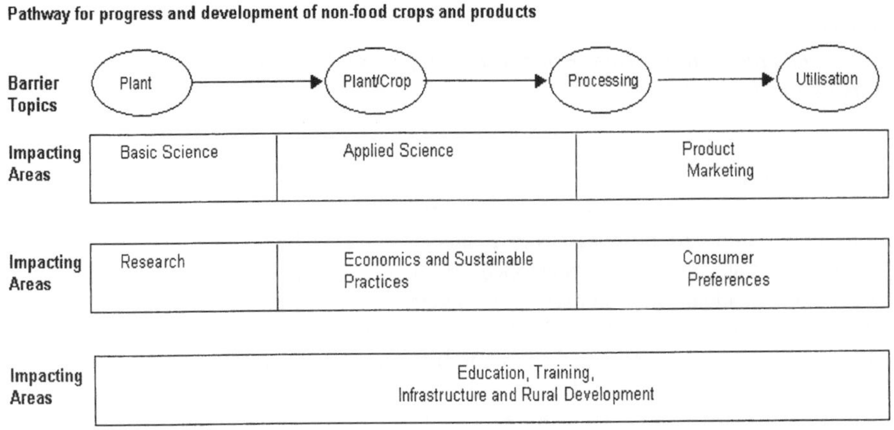

Pathway for progress and development of non-food crops and products

Barrier Topics	Plant → Plant/Crop → Processing → Utilisation

Impacting Areas	Basic Science	Applied Science	Product Marketing

Impacting Areas	Research	Economics and Sustainable Practices	Consumer Preferences

Impacting Areas	Education, Training, Infrastructure and Rural Development

Figure 1. Pathway for progress and development of non-food crops and products.

The fundamental questions are:

Is there an awareness of the potential for land-based industries to produce diverse biorenewable products?

Is there a strategic view on how biorenewables should be developed? If so why is progress slow?

How should sustainability be considered?

How can the diverse needs of individual production/utilisation chains be identified, characterised & integrated?

Considerable markets for products from plants or at least some of their components already exist, as exploited on a large scale in the food sector. But a fundamental re-appraisal of potential plant products reveals a much wider range of opportunities especially in the non-food sector. An example of the potential range of products that could be derived from wheat via a number of, and in some cases complimentary, pathways is shown in Figure 2.

Similar opportunities have been identified in the fibre and oleaginous plant sectors. Good examples include hemp, which has numerous realised and unrealised market outlets for both vegetative and oil based plant components, and castor bean, where a wide range of materials can be derived from modification and further processing of this valuable tropical oil. For long term sustainability the way forward must be to exploit such opportunities concurrently, using a whole plant products approach.

Drivers for Change

A number of diverse drivers stimulating change to renewable raw materials exist. Some are inter-related and complementary although this is not always the case. These include:

736

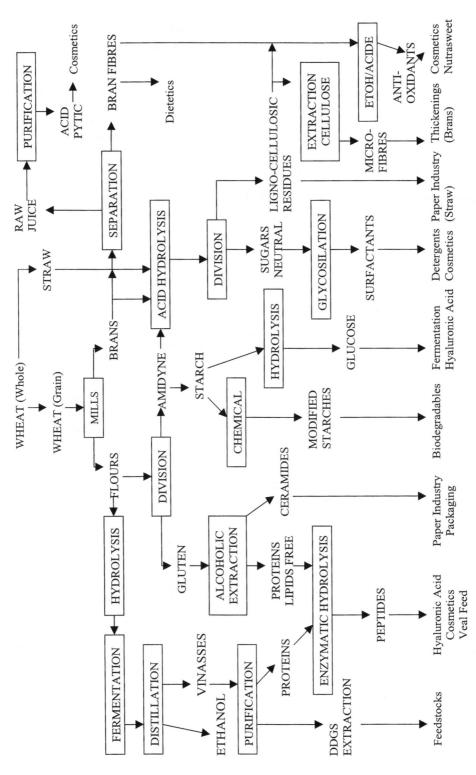

Figure 2. Potential range of products and feedstocks that can be derived from Wheat

- sustainability of agriculture, the rural economy and industry at large
- environmental protection and mitigation of global warming
- legislation and cost of non-compliance for industry
- public opinion
- international agreements of various types but with the common resolution of demanding renewable sustainable feedstocks e.g. Kyoto; WTO discussions

One major area needing radical action is that of global warming and the need to reduce green house gas (GHG) emissions. One means of tackling this is through the development of, and change to, carbon-sequestering and CO_2-neutral technologies.

Examples are shown in Table 1 of the extent of diminution in GHG accumulation that could occur through the exploitation of sustainable biorenewable resources in a number of market sectors.

Table 1. Examples of potential primary savings in greenhouse gas emissions (CO_2 equivalents) that could be achieved through substitution by renewable raw materials.

	Current market penetration (%)	Current savings in GHG emissions ('000 tonnes)	Approx. total potential market penetration (%)	Approx. total potential saving in GHG emissions ('000 tonnes)
Polymers	0.15	100	1	600
Lubricants	2	200	20	2000
Solvents	1.5		12.5	1000
Surfactants	20*	1700	50-100***	2000
Total GHG savings:		2000		5600**

* Of which 16% derived from vegetable oils and 4% from animal oils and fats.

** Corresponds to approx 1.5% of the EU Kyoto commitments.

*** This is an over-estimation of today's technical potential, but represents what possibly could be achieved over a longer time perspective (for GHG savings, a more conservative market penetration potential has been used).

Other drivers stimulating uptake of renewable raw materials and feedstocks include EU Directives (e.g. the banning of volatile organic carbons (volatile solvents) under health and safety legislation; the banning of inclusion of used vegetable oils in animal feedstuffs; moves to reduce packaging and encourage use of more biodegradable degradable packaging through the EU packaging directive; development of EU energy policies for renewable energy sources and targets for renewable energy generation).

Given recognition of the need to re-develop sustainable biorenewable feedstocks, and the various direct and indirect political and legislative procedures that exist as drivers, the slow rates of change and uptake by industry is disappointing.

Change and Future Progress

It is now generally recognised, especially in EC circles, that rate of change needs to be accelerated. Despite the EC having funded R&D to the extent of 160 millions of euros over the last 10 years, the current "technology push" has not secured an adequate rate of progress. A number of issues have been identified as hampering the rate of uptake of sustainable biorenewables. These include; lack of awareness of opportunities within industry, lack of financial need or incentive to change, investment in current technologies and lack of capital to re-tool, lack of clarity in the development of the non-food renewables market in political and environmental sectors, lack of market organisation and guaranteed supply of primary products in the quantities and quality required.

Markets

One fundamental question is that of markets: do real markets exist for sustainable biorenewables and if so what are the opportunities and the potential for growth and development ?

Markets exist in two types; the large commodity market, where the feedstock supplier has little control over price, and the small, high value market. In the latter, the primary producer can add value through exclusive contracts and partial or total vertical integration of the business into the sector. At a basic level, added value can be achieved by undertaking primary processing etc or by cooperating to co-ordinate supply and oversee quality etc.

The IENICA project, funded by DG Research of EC undertook ground breaking studies of potential markets for sustainable biorenewables for EU 15 during the period 1997-2000. Current work is assessing the potential of Eastern European and other markets. Considerable market opportunity was identified. Markets for renewable raw materials were divided into several broad groups: oils, fibres, carbohydrates and speciality products. For the sake of brevity a résumé of the key findings only is given below; full details are available on the world wide web at www.ienica.net. Based on industrial applications, further groupings can be made e.g. lubricants, solvents, surfactants etc. The diversity of renewable raw material sources and products can in itself be a barrier to development by hampering focussed attention within the sector.

Oils

Overall usage of vegetable oils and animal fats in the non-food sector of EU-15 is estimated at approximately 3 million tonnes per annum (excluding biofuels). Key potential EU market volumes for substitution by renewables are: bio-lubricants (370,000 tonnes/annum), bio-printing inks (in excess of 120,000 tonnes/annum) and bio-solvents (approximately 0.5 million tonnes/annum). Only a fraction of these potential markets have been realised to date. There are also opportunities to expand use in the polymer sector, particularly for erucamide derived from High Erucic Acid Rape and Crambe.

Fibres

There are opportunities for EU produced fibres to substitute for imported natural fibres (e.g. jute and kenaf). There are limited opportunities for use in the textile market and most of these will be small niche areas. There are significant opportunities in the technical fibre market. The car and aircraft industry is currently driving demand for fibres for bio-composite production and the potential European market could be as high as 350,000 tonnes per annum of fibre, which represents a demand for 1 million tonnes of raw product. There could be further opportunities in the building industry and for insulation but theses markets will need further development.

Carbohydrates

Starch markets in the EU and elsewhere are well developed and organised. 3.7 million tonnes is used in the non-food sector; 1.4 million tonnes in paper and cardboard making, 1.1 million tonnes in plastics and detergents and 1.2 million tonnes in fermentation and other technical uses. There are also opportunities for small high value niche markets such as cosmetics and pharmaceuticals.

Speciality Products

These offer considerable potential for high value, low volume products. However such markets are volatile and subject to commercial sensitivity. Essential oils markets world-wide ammount to approximately 45,000 tonnes per annum and aromatic plants have a world market of greater than 50,000 tonnes per annum. The European herbal supplements market is valued in excess of €7 billion per annum.

Energy

EC/EU energy policies for development of renewable sources of energy are now in place and being developed in practice. The UK Government Policy White Paper "Our Energy Future – Creating a Low Carbon Economy" was published during February 2003 and states the UK's aim of tackling global warming and increasing fuel security while maintaining affordable energy for all. The UK plans to achieve a 60% reduction in its carbon dioxide emissions by 2050, this will have a significant impact on the uptake of renewable raw materials.

CONCLUSION

Without doubt, scientific and technological developments have progressed to an extent which currently permits the widescale exploitation of biorenewable products. However, some key areas are still hampering exploitation including;
- Lack of political and administrative co-ordination of effort
- Lack of awareness of opportunities in all sectors of industry
- Full assessment of environmental benefits compared to fossil-derived alternatives
- Focussed technology transfer to stimulate development
- Market structuring to support development

Issues affecting development of non-food crops – an industry view

C Spencer

Springdale Crop Synergies Ltd, Springdale Farm, Rudston, Driffield, East Yorkshire, YO25 4DJ, UK
Email: info@springdale-group.com

ABSTRACT

In recent years there has been significant and growing interest in the production of non food crops and their derivatives; examples include specialist oilseeds, fibre crops, natural dyes and energy crops. To date, the commercial uptake of such crops has been relatively limited and this paper aims to provide an insight into why this is and how such obstacles have been overcome in a number of cases to create a dynamic and expanding range of commercial non-food crops. Commercialization of crambe (*Crambe abyssinica*) otherwise known as Abyssinian mustard in the UK, is used as an example case study, building from initial research and development through to field production of over 3500 ha within 3 years, with plans for a significant increase in 2004 and beyond. The contents of this paper are derived from both practical and commercial first hand experiences in developing a wide range of oilseed, fibre and energy crops from initial conception through to full establishment of viable markets.

INTRODUCTION

For a variety of reasons discussed below, there has been increasing interest amongst primary producers in moving away from food crop production and towards production of non-food and industrial raw materials.

Commodity prices

The recent significant reductions in commodity prices, for example the price of UK feed wheat falling from approximately £120/tonne ex farm in 1996 to approximately £80/tonne ex farm in September 2003, with no corresponding reduction in input costs has resulted in declining farm incomes (Figure 1). There is a desperate need to find means of boosting farm profitability and of diversifying sources of income.

Legislation

There is a strengthening "green" environmental lobby, plus other EU legislation affecting areas such as use of volatile organic carbon compounds and control of emission of 'greenhouse gases', which is stimulating industry interest in use of renewable raw materials. Both growers and manufacturing industry are subject to close scrutiny regarding justification for use of inputs and for any environmental impacts associated with output. International agreements such as those agreed under the Kyoto protocol to reduce greenhouse gas emissions have a significant effect on government policy and its impact on stimulation of renewable raw materials for industry and energy production.

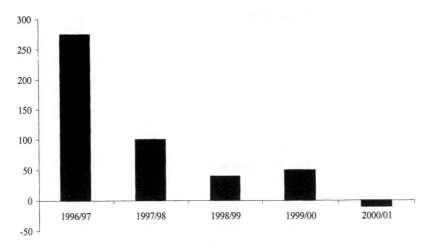

Source: Auborn, Deloitte & Touche, HGCA

Figure 1. Falling farm incomes in the UK, 1996 – 2001 (£/ha)

Energy

It is increasingly recognized that fossil fuel supplies are limited. At current levels of demand, conventional oil supplies are expected to last up until around 2040. The UK will become a net importer of gas and oil by 2010 according to industry estimates. There is a need to develop renewable energy supplies to ease pressure on fossil fuel stocks and secure energy supplies. The recent Iraq conflict highlights the UK's susceptibility to severe fluctuations in price and its reliance on other countries. Home grown sources of liquid biofuels include biodiesel and bioethanol and biomass crops can be used for electricity generation.

Consumer demand

There is an increasing awareness of health issues and an associated increasing consumer demand for products derived from plants particularly in areas such as 'nutraceuticals' where the availability of encapsulated products has increased acceptance and use of such products. There is also increasing demand for mild, biodegradable, vegetable based materials in cosmetic and personal care markets and an increasing public awareness of issues of sustainability associated with production of crops for both industrial and food use.

Key areas to consider when introducing a new crop

To introduce a successful, long term new crop to a country there are a number of key issues that must be tackled and overcome.

Continuous research and development is required to ensure the crop will grow satisfactorily under a range of soil types and husbandry programmes. If not, at least the limits to production must be known.

Markets must be defined to assess what aspects of the crop (oil/fibre content etc) are most useful commercially, to ensure that the new crop is at least as good as or better than current raw materials sources.

End users need to be identified before embarking on significant production, to gauge reaction and information on possible material requirements. Crops should never be produced without knowing that there is demand, and preferably long term secure contracts should be in place with end users and processors before crops are released onto farm, making sure that sufficient seed supply is available.

After using initial landrace varieties, breeding programmes need to be initiated or restarted, with close liaison between all parties in the chain (Figure 2).

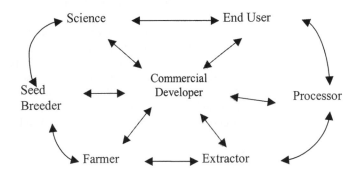

Figure 2. The non-food crop dependency chain.

Numerous trials and development work may be required to develop crop husbandry, from work on seed rates, fertiliser requirements, fungicide and insecticides to desiccants and harvesting studies.

Expansion in the use of co-products ensures improved returns and greater competitiveness against other sources of raw material.

To overcome obstacles, practical aspects of production need to be revisited and improved through persistence and enthusiasm. Growers and end users need to be kept satisfied and it is important to never under-perform.

BARRIERS TO OVERCOME

Developing end user markets

End users need a continuous supply of raw materials. No plant based products can be manufactured and delivered to requirements without sufficient lead-in time. There may also be a seasonal lead-in time, new crops need to be planned for and grown.

Manufacturers need a homogenous product. The delivered material must meet agreed specifications. In depth evaluation of causes of variation due to seasonal factors or inputs for example may be required before agreeing to any quality criteria.

Research and development is expensive and end users need to see potential returns on investment to justify investment.

The costs of changing practices can be significant. New equipment, new procedures, marketing and labelling may be required when end users switch to the use of a new product.

End users need to see a cost benefit or environmental or working practice benefit to encourage change to a new product. Industry needs to see tangible results to assess the benefits that could be obtained and all areas of the business need to agree on a benefit. There can be a conflict between technical advancement and costs involved in adoption.

Barriers to development can be overcome by providing obvious benefits to the consumer or industry such as improvements in technical efficiency, provision of a premium product, or a unique background to aid marketing, a positive environmental profile, reduced cost or improved efficiency. Development can be stimulated by supplying small quantities and building up production in a steady, controlled manner. Producers need to ensure industry satisfaction with raw materials by meeting or exceeding quality requirements. Increased interest in the industry grows on success and this stimulates both demand and competition.

Crop advancement and breeding

In the early stages of crop development there can be limited availability of germplasm (which is often derived from wild types) with poor technical specifications, poor field performance, low yield of key metabolites (oil or fibre etc) and there is restricted income to fund breeding programmes. This creates a limiting cycle that inhibits development of novel crop breeding initiatives.

This situation can be improved by developing long term markets with end users, which provides security to breeders. Ensuring that seed royalty payments get back to the breeders can also stimulate further development. In other cases, breeding programmes may need to be restarted or initiated with key aims to improve oil/fibre content and to develop and understand the basic agronomic factors affecting traits such as yield, maturity and standing power.

Crop husbandry

There is a limited range of agrochemicals available and approved for use on novel crops which can potentially create problems, particularly with weed control. In some cases specialist equipment may be required, particularly for planting or harvesting. Production of small initial quantities can also provide difficulties in handling and processing. Seed lots from early breeding programmes can be variable in terms of quality which can affect drilling operations. Care needs to be taken over land preparation. In general, development can be hampered by the limited availability of agronomic knowledge.

These problems can be overcome by agrochemical testing but those growing novel crops need greater flexibility with respect to applications and off-label uses, particularly where final products are not consumed. There is also a need for chemical manufacturers to maintain older products or to evaluate new products on a greater range of crops.

Equipment

Novel crops can provide new uses for older machines, e.g. inter row hoes etc. However, work is required to determine appropriate settings for drills with novel seeds and combine settings to optimise seed retention and cleaning. In addition, moisture meters are likely to need calibrating to deal with novel crops. Novel crops can also put pressure on the use of swathers, seed cleaners and driers at busy times.

Partnerships can be used to jointly develop crop protocols. There is often a mind set that the effort required is not worth it, however, assessment of the potential acreages that could be developed can encourage initial scoping studies.

Technical development

Agronomy is the key to novel crop development. Developed knowledge needs to be transferred throughout the on-farm advisory network by way of agronomists and supply networks. Training days and technical updates for growers and advisors help disseminate knowledge and assist with new product development. It is crucially important to counter any lack of knowledge or mis-information circulating amongst agronomists to ensure that this does not dissuade potential growers.

Improving grower uptake

There is a need to reassure growers by developing tried and tested crops. Growers are also looking for security through well defined end markets. Crop agronomy must fit with their current capabilities and they must be given access to the best available varieties. Growers are risk averse and crop prices need to be set to stimulate development. Growers respond well to the success stories of other growers.

Current problems in the grower sector include a "look see" mentality. Often growers will only try a small acreage of a new crop, which is commonly grown on the worst land to see how it fares, which does not give the crop a fair chance. Growers may also reduce on the recommended inputs in an attempt to make cost savings. Spray timings may be missed through prioritising for other mainstream crops. Harvest timings can be missed and combines may be set up poorly. In addition small seed lots may cause post harvest handling difficulties, which can jeopardise quality and the integrity of samples.

The above problems can be minimised by ensuring regular agronomic updates for growers in relation to crop timings, information on what to look out for and initiatives such as 'pestwatches'. Regular contact with staff provides reassurance. Growers seeing the product destination is beneficial and this encourages growers to feel part of the supply chain. Field trials and open days and promotion of successful results also helps overcome grower fears and misconceptions.

Price – an essential component

Crops need to be price competitive with end users but also produce sufficient margin to garner grower interest. After time, economies of scale related to haulage, storage, crushing, extraction and processing meal and use of co-products can be exploited as volumes increase. There is commonly a 'chicken and egg' situation, where a high price is required to stimulate interest, yet economies of scale only appear once the crop is grown on a significant acreage.

Government support

Many novel and industrial crops are not supported under current IACS schemes, and until recently received no underpinning support. Growers perceived this situation as a risk with crops with which they had limited experience or where there was risk of crop loss. The extension of support for non-food crops under the recent review of Agenda 2000 provides a welcome boost for the sector.

Funding

Support funding for research is essential and it is also necessary to bring interested parties together from research, academia, industry and commercial backgrounds to link developments.

CASE STUDY

Crambe (*Crambe abyssinica*) – an example of a successful introduction.

Within the UK, Springdale Crop Synergies Ltd has been working with crambe for over 10 years and after developing the husbandry and the potential of the crop and speaking to specific end users has now commercialized the crop. After over 7 years of research the company is now in its third year of commercial production, supplying a large end user with a high quality vegetable oil rich in erucic acid. The unique fatty acid profile of the crop is shown in Table 1.

Table 1. Fatty acid composition of crambe seed oil

Fatty Acid	Content in oil (%)
Erucic	58
Oleic	16
Linoleic	8
Linolenic	5
Eicosanoic	4
Palmitic	2
Others	7
Oil content = 35%	

Crambe oil has a number of uses (Table 2) and demand for the crop is growing rapidly. The potential markets allow the crop to be utilised in a number of areas, which offers security of supply and demand to growers who may be concerned about the long term potential of such crops. Careful management of the supply chain ensures that there is no overproduction and prices are maintained at sensible levels for producers.

Table 2. Major uses for erucic acid and its derivatives

	Commercial use
erucamide	polymer additive
behenyl fumarate vinyl copolymer	oil field chemical
behenyl ketone dimer	textile auxiliary
stearyl erucamide	polymer additive
behenyl trimethylammonium chloride	personal care product
brassidolide	perfumery
glyceryl trierucate	pharmaceutical
erucyl erucate	cosmetics

The main use of crambe oil is in the production of erucamide, which is used as a slip agent within the plastics industry. The fact that the resulting oil is vegetable based, fully traceable and at present non-GM is seen as a benefit by consumers.

As well as being grown for a known market, the crop confers a number of benefits to growers, a summary of which are outlined below.

Crambe is spring sown which allows growers to tidy-up problem weeds such as perennials or resistant grasses prior to sowing.

It offers opportunities for increased profitability. The crop can be grown as an industrial crop on set aside land. From 2005 it will be possible to grow the crop on both set-aside and main regime land without loss of income.

It allows farming costs to be spread over a wider acreage. Industrial cropping on set-aside allows growers to spread their fixed costs over a larger area.

Crambe is relatively drought tolerant once established and performs well on lighter soils.

There is a substantial breeding programme in progress to develop new cultivars and improve pest and disease resistance. A totally new variety will be released in 2005.

The crop shows excellent standing power. Crambe has not yet lodged in the UK.

Crambe can be harvested relatively early in the season and the likely harvest slot can be predicted and manipulated according to sowing date to optimise harvest efficiency on the farm. The crop is easy to harvest and may be swathed, desiccated or direct cut.

There are currently no GM varieties of crambe and so no issues associated with contamination.

It is an excellent break crop. Crambe has a deep tap root which may help improve the soil structure

The crop is in demand and all production is on a fixed price buy back contract.

ACKNOWLEDGEMENTS

Thanks go to the entire team at Springdale with regards to the effort put into making crambe and other non-food crop developments a reality.

Development of flax and hemp agronomy for industrial fibre production

J P R E Dimmock, G R Hughes, R D Western, D Wright
*School of Agricultural and Forest Sciences, University of Wales Bangor, Henfaes Research
Centre, Abergwyngregyn, Llanfairfechan LL33 0LB, UK*
Email: j.p.dimmock@bangor.ac.uk

ABSTRACT

The agronomy, history and politics of fibre production from flax and hemp are
discussed, together with an overview of potential future market developments.
Results from ongoing experiments in north Wales are presented, showing good
potential for large improvements in productivity and reliability for flax, but less
initial promise for hemp due to poor growth, weed problems and damage from
pathogens. Gross margins available for flax and hemp production are shown to be
competitive with those of major arable crops without additional price support.

INTRODUCTION

Temperate bast (i.e. stem) fibre crops, mainly flax (*Linum usitatissimum*) and hemp (*Cannabis
sativa*) have historically been essential sources of raw materials for industry. Their importance
has been greatly diminished over the course of the 20th century by synthetic substitutes and
tropical or subtropical sources of competitor fibres, particularly cotton, but also jute, sisal,
kenaf, etc. The continued supply of synthetic fibres is, however, largely dependent on supplies
of petroleum, as is the long-distance transportation of materials such as jute or cotton. Political
and public interest in increasing sustainability, together with the development of new products
and markets has renewed interest in these potentially highly productive and versatile crops
(Smeder & Liljedahl, 1996). This paper seeks firstly to describe the crops, then outline the
political and commercial environment in which they are grown and finally to report some of
the advances towards exploiting their potential that have recently been made at Bangor.

Flax

Flax has been cultivated since prehistoric times for the production of its fibres, which are fine
and soft to the touch whilst also strong and highly durable; characteristics ideally suited to high
quality textile production. Flax is an annual with a thin, erect and wiry stem that can be grown
for both fibre and seed. Fibre cultivars may grow to about 1.2 m, and through sowing at high
rates, typically between 800–2000 seeds/m², field-grown crops show little branching except at
the top of the stems where a number of flowers form. Cellulose fibres develop around each
group of vascular bundles in the stem cortex, bound together with pectin. The growing period
is short. Seeds are drilled from late March to early May, and after rapid development the crop
is desiccated in July shortly after the onset of flowering and harvested after a period of retting
(Langer & Hill, 1991). Retting is a process that allows microorganisms to decompose pectins
in the vascular bundles, easing release and removal of cellulose fibres from the woody core of
the plant (shive) during the process of decortication or scutching (Easson & Molloy, 1996).
Traditionally bundles of flax were retted in rivers or in open pools, but this practice is no
longer accepted in Europe due to environmental pollution and it has been replaced by in-field

dew-retting, where rain and dew usually produce the intended effect.

Hemp

Hemp also has a long history of production, with cultivation recorded some 4500 years ago in China (Langer & Hill, 1991). The plant is annual and herbaceous, and grows up to 4 m in height. Again, the degree of branching of individual stems is reduced by using high sowing rates, typically 100–300 plants/m^2 for fibre production. Fibres are produced in the stem in much the same way as flax. Hemp is sown from late April to mid-May as development is slow below 10°C. Following establishment the crop grows rapidly, typically reaching 2–3 m by mid-August. Harvesting usually involves swathing the crop and dew-retting in the swath. This takes from 3 to 5 weeks and necessitates frequent turning to ensure even retting. Hemp fibres are coarser than those of flax as a result of greater lignification, so the crop is more suited to rope and heavy-duty textile production.

Political and commercial pressures on fibre production

Use of both hemp and flax declined in western Europe for a variety of reasons. These include pollution resulting from water-retting techniques causing a change to the less reliable and lower quality alternative of dew-retting; increased production costs from traditional fibre scutching and hackling methods and availability of cheaper alternative products such as synthetic fibres and cotton. However, with increasing emphasis now being placed on the sustainability and carbon-neutrality of industrial feedstocks, there has been renewed interest in these crops. For a number of reasons, alternative materials are now being sought to replace those derived from petroleum, i.e. most synthetic fibres, or crops such as cotton that require high inputs of pesticides. A wide range of end uses have been identified that offer clear benefits both to the environment and to customers from using flax and hemp fibres. Examples include insulation products to replace mineral wools, providing reduced respiratory and handling hazards and also lower decommissioning costs through composting rather than landfill. Another high profile use for flax and hemp fibres is in moulded biocomposite panels for the automotive industry, which give numerous advantages over synthetic products in terms of weight reduction, better acoustic performance, non-toxic fumes on combustion, ease of disposal at end-of-life and reduced risks to workers during production.

Unfortunately market confidence in industrial fibres has been damaged by the dramatic changes in subsidies available under the Common Agricultural Policy (CAP). During the 1990s, high aid levels (typically around £570/ha) enabled the development of a model for fibre production based on simple agronomic practices and minimal specialist machinery on farms, feeding low-cost straw into high throughput factories producing short fibres for the emerging markets described above. Rapid expansion of production occurred, leading to the establishment of crop processing plants throughout Europe. These developments, however, took place in a market where average flax yields were only 1.5–3.0 t/ha and worth £20/t (Nix, 1997). Straw sales therefore represented only 5% of the value of the subsidy for growing the crop, meaning that no motivation existed for developing agronomy or commercialising natural fibre products, as the crop could be grown profitably for the subsidy alone. Following CAP reforms in 2001 where fibre crop aid was cut to the same rate as for cereal production, this lack of commercialisation resulted in a rapid decline in the industry, to the extent that of the seven processing plants operational in the UK in 2000, only one is now trading at a significant level.

In order to provide for an industry that is market rather than subsidy-driven, weaknesses in fibre crop production and productivity must be fully addressed. The first of these issues is low productivity, particularly that of flax. Without price support, yields of around 2 t/ha mean flax straw has to be worth around three times the value of barley grain to make planting worthwhile for farmers. The second issue is whether a crop of sufficient quality can reliably be produced for technical market outlets, as the degree and evenness of retting is crucial to the further processing of the straw. The importance of this is seen through crop rejection rates during the 1990s, which were typically around 40% (BioFibre Europe Ltd., personal communication). A genuine market cannot sustain failures of this magnitude, as growers will be unwilling to take risks without a large price premium. Irregular supply of fibre will also fail manufacturers who need consistent supplies of quality raw materials.

Research at Bangor

Our work seeks to enable a consistent supply of fibre of sufficient quantity and quality to facilitate market development whilst advancing crop productivity to a point where it presents a worthwhile commercial proposition for farmers. We began from a low knowledge base, as relatively little material is available in the scientific press about flax and particularly hemp production, and of the existing research material, much is concerned with long fibre production for linen. In addition, whilst 29 cultivars of flax and 26 of hemp are eligible for financial support under the EU Arable Area Payment Scheme in 2003, there is no guidance available as to the comparative characteristics of these cultivars.

Research began in 2001 with a series of pilot plot-scale experiments at Henfaes, alongside commercial scale grower-participative research in which farmers cultivated substantial quantities of flax and hemp crops applying variations on previously used short fibre cultivation practices such as different sowing rates (40 or 80 kg/ha), drilling times between April and early June and the use of different chemical desiccants. From this work it was determined that for 2002, plot-scale replicated field experimentation investigating the performance of a wide range of genetic material was necessary, so flax and hemp cultivars from throughout Europe were obtained. In addition, on the basis of experiences during the pilot trials and on work by Easson & Cooper (2002), stand-retting was adopted for all experiments. This method produces a slower, more controlled ret than where the crop is swathed, and is likely to reduce crop failures in the wet climate of west Wales, where excessive decay in wet straw can markedly reduce fibre yields. In addition to producing a slower and more homogeneous ret, this technique can reduce losses through enabling baling after a shorter drying period than is necessary for a swathed crop. Stand-retting offers further advantages, as dew-retted straw swath needs frequent turning and can be difficult to mechanically bale, leading to yield losses. Additionally, dew-retted straw is often contaminated with stones and soil, increasing the likelihood of crop rejection and damage to processing equipment.

Straw and fibre yields from both flax and hemp in our 2002 experiments are presented below together with a breakdown of the current value of fibre crop outputs. Potential gross margins are also compared with those available from cereal production.

METHODS AND MATERIALS

Flax was drilled on 9 April 2002 in 10 m × 1.8 m plots with 12 cm between rows following conventional ploughing and cultivation, using randomised blocks with four replicates. Seeds were drilled to 15 mm at a rate of 1000/m^2. Fertiliser was applied to the seedbed before final cultivation at the rate of 40 kg each of N, P & K as NH_4NO_3, P_2O_5 and K_2O respectively. Bentazone (Basagran; BASF UK Ltd.) herbicide was applied at 1.44 kg a.i./ha in mid-May, and the crop was desiccated with glyphosate trimesium (Touchdown; Syngenta) at 4 litres/ha on 29 July at 35 days past mean mid-flowering point (MPF). This is the time defined by Easson & Cooper (2002) as the point where 50% of buds present have opened. Plots were harvested with a pedestrian-operated finger bar mower during October 2002. Sub-samples were oven-dried for dry matter determination and to allow yields to be corrected to 16% moisture content. A further sub-sample was also rippled (i.e. seed capsules were removed by combing) to assess the proportions of straw and seed to calculate overall straw yields. Fibre contents were then determined in accordance with Long *et al.* (1988).

Hemp was drilled on 24 April 2002 using the same equipment and experimental design, using seed rates of 150 and 300 seeds/m^2. A fertiliser application of 80 kg N, 80 kg P & 160 kg K as NH_4NO_3, P_2O_5 and K_2O respectively was made to the seedbed immediately after drilling, followed by a further application of 80 kg N when five pairs of leaves were visible. The crop was desiccated with glyphosate trimesium, applied at 4 litres/ha on 15 August 2002 and harvested by hand in the week beginning 16 September 2002. Straw was weighed and sub-samples taken for drying to correct for dry matter content.

RESULTS AND DISCUSSION

Flax straw and fibre yields from replicated field experiments are shown in Table 1 together with mean yields attained by growers in 2001 for comparative purposes. Table 2 shows hemp straw yields obtained from field experiments.

Flax yields from the cultivar trials were substantially in excess of those returned by growers in 2001. The best-yielding group of cultivars produced over 7 t/ha of straw, reflecting a potential for improvement in commercial production systems of 300%. Laura, the cultivar used by commercial growers in 2001, possibly performed better in our experiments due to earlier sowing, as many commercial crops in 2001 were not drilled before early May. Following fibre determination, even greater increases in performance were seen over 2001, with the leading cultivars yielding a five-fold increase in fibre production over that of the commercial growers in 2001. It is also significant that Alice, a dual-purpose cultivar intended to produce worthwhile quantities of both fibre and seed performed poorly both in terms of straw yield and in fibre percentage, reflecting the difficulties reported by Foster *et al.* (1997) in breeding such a desirable cultivar. The applicability of stand-retting techniques to this high-yielding group of flax cultivars is currently being investigated with promising results in terms of standing ability and ease of decortication. The commercial use of glyphosate-mediated stand-retting has already paid dividends, having reduced crop rejections due to over-retting from 45% in 2001 to zero in 2002.

Table 1.   Straw and fibre yields of flax cultivars in 2002 experiments compared with mean straw yield from growers in 2001 (primarily cv. Laura); SED is provided for between-cultivar comparisons in 2002.

Cultivar	Straw yield (t/ha; 16% mc)	Fibre %	Fibre yield (t/ha; 16% mc)
2001 mean	*2.65*	*17.0*	*0.45*
Alice	5.55	17.8	0.96
Aurore	7.36	33.0	2.45
Diane	7.52	28.9	2.14
Electra	7.93	32.3	2.70
Elise	6.82	28.1	1.65
Laura	5.48	22.2	1.20
Liviola	7.35	28.8	2.04
SED	0.60 (160 d.f.)	3.5 (154 d.f.)	0.30 (152 d.f.)

Table 2.   Mean straw and fibre yields of hemp cultivars in 2002 field experiments.

Cultivar	Straw yield (t/ha ; 16% mc)	Fibre %	Fibre yield (t/ha ; 16% mc)
Beniko	5.94	36.7	2.19
Bialobrzeski	5.91	40.4	2.53
Fasamo	1.43	29.4	0.52
Fedora 17	6.71	31.2	2.06
Felina 34	6.57	24.9	1.61
Ferimon 12	5.44	21.0	1.13
Futura 75	7.17	35.3	2.44
USO 31	2.42	32.6	1.13
SED	0.55 (24 d.f.)	5.5 (23 d.f.)	0.42 (24 d.f.)

Hemp yields were lower than expected, with the best being just under 7 t/ha, in contrast to the 10 t/ha reported by Cromack (1998) in southern England. Performance of cvs. Fasamo and USO 31 was particularly poor, probably because of excessive weed competition reducing growth in early stages, and due to the fact that both are early-maturing cultivars. This has impacts on both fibre yield and quality, as metabolism of the mature hemp plant favours seed production over fibre production, and existing fibre becomes increasingly lignified and therefore of lower quality. Weed problems also limited growth in the other cultivars, but their longer vegetative phase allowed greater straw yields to be obtained. There are currently no herbicides available to control weeds in hemp. Despite the successful use of stand-retting in our plot-scale experiments, dew-retting with its associated high risk of crop rejection is still commonly used in commercial hemp-growing. This is because the height of the crop, often exceeding 2.5 m, prevents the use of conventional sprayers. Substantial levels of *Botrytis* infection within the crops also caused fibre losses through reduction in stem strength, resulting in breakage. Whilst fungicides may control this problem, the expense and difficulty of application may prevent commercial usage.

Having shown that substantial yield improvements can be obtained over previously reported levels, the question remains as to whether flax and hemp can compete against major arable crops without additional support. A measure of the viability of commercial fibre crop production can be gained through comparing gross margins (GM) expected from standard arable cropping with average productivity and costs (Nix, 2002) with yields and variable costs derived from our own experiments (Table 3). It is shown that GM parity with major crops is currently obtainable at a straw price of £60–70/t. Since Hemcore are currently offering in excess of £100/t for hemp straw, it appears that attractive gross margins are already available to growers. Evidence that such returns are sustainable and also applicable to flax is provided in Table 4, where proportions and value of the straw components (i.e. fibre, shive and dust) are given together with a calculation of processing costs as provided by BioFibre Europe Ltd. (personal communication). It is shown that the value of the shive (as horse-bedding) effectively covers the cost of processing, enabling the value of the fibre to provide a competitive return to both grower and processor. Furthermore, as demand for novel products from industrial fibre that are currently in development grows, returns are likely to become even more competitive.

Having demonstrated that fibre crops have the clear potential to provide worthwhile returns to growers without further subsidy, their broad range of potential environmental benefits will only be realised if adequate provision of processing facilities is made available, and as such, the success of these crops is dependent on substantial investment either from the public or private sectors in this essential role.

Table 3. Average gross margins (GM) from arable crops (Nix 2002) with fibre crop straw prices given in italics required to match the GM currently available from winter barley. Variable costs for flax and hemp include £50/ha for straw haulage.

Crop	Yield (t/ha)	Value (£/t)	Area Payment (£/ha)	Variable costs (£/ha)	GM (£/ha)
Winter wheat	8.0	62.50	225	225	500
Winter barley	6.4	60.00	225	185	425
Winter oilseed rape	3.2	135.00	225	210	445
Hemp	7.0	*68.60*	225	280	425
Flax	7.0	*57.14*	225	200	425

Table 4. Proportions of flax and hemp straw components, market value and processing costs

Component	Fibre	Shive	Dust	Processing cost	Total value
Market value (£/t)	400	160	0	77	-
Proportion of straw (%)	30	50	20	-	-
Product value (£/t)	120	80	0	77	123

ACKNOWLEDGEMENTS

We would like to thank the European Union, The National Assembly for Wales Agricultural Department and the Welsh Development Agency for funding this work.

REFERENCES

Cromack H T H (1998). The effect of cultivar and seed density on the production and fibre content of *Cannabis sativa* in southern England. *Industrial Crops and Products* **7**, 205-210.

Easson D L; Cooper K (2002). A study of the use of the trimesium salt of glyphosate to desiccate and ret flax and linseed (*Linum usitatissimum*) and of its effects on the yield of straw, seed and fibre. *Journal of Agricultural Science, Cambridge* **138**, 29-37.

Easson D L; Molloy R M (1996). Retting – a key process in production of high value fibre from flax. *Outlook on Agriculture* **25**, 235-242.

Foster R; Pooni H S; Mackay I J (1997). Quantitative evaluation of *Linum usitatissimum* varieties for dual-purpose traits. *Journal of Agricultural Science, Cambridge* **129**, 179-185.

Langer R H M; Hill G D (1991). *Agricultural Plants* (2nd ed.). Cambridge University Press.

Long F N J; Easson D L; Frost J P (1988). The laboratory determination of fibre content and quality and content in flax. *Record of Agricultural Research* (Department of Agriculture for Northern Ireland) **36**, 27-36.

Nix J (1997). *Farm Management Pocketbook* (28th ed). Wye College, University of London.

Nix J (2002). *Farm Management Pocketbook* (33rd ed). Imperial College at Wye.

Smeder B; Liljedahl S (1996). Market oriented identification of important properties in developing flax fibres for technical uses. *Industrial Crops and Products* **5**, 149-162.

Liquid biofuels – an opportunity for UK agriculture ?

D B Turley
Agricultural and Rural Strategy Group, Central Science Laboratory, Sand Hutton, York, YO41 1LZ, UK
Email: d.turley@csl.gov.uk

ABSTRACT

The UK has taken a leading position in seeking means to reduce greenhouse gas emissions. Liquid biofuels derived from agricultural crops, crop residues and novel biomass crops offer a means of reducing greenhouse gas emissions from the transport sector, a key contributor to UK CO_2 emissions. However, incentives to date have failed to stimulate significant production in the UK. Indicative targets for substitution of fossil fuels have been proposed by the EU. Meeting these targets is likely to have significant impacts on UK cropping patterns and UK agriculture. Is it likely that significant benefits will flow to the agricultural sector as a result of liquid biofuel cropping and are liquid biofuels the most cost effective means of mitigating CO_2 emissions ? These and other issues are discussed in the paper.

INTRODUCTION

The UN Framework Convention on Climate Change (UNCCC) commits signatories to the Kyoto Protocol to tackle the effects of climate change at an international level by taking steps to significantly reduce greenhouse gas emissions. Real progress towards a 5% global reduction (against a 1990 baseline) is expected by 2008-2012. The UK is committed to reducing greenhouse gas emissions by 12.5% in this period. The UK Government recently outlined its aim of creating a low carbon economy, which includes investment in 'clean' low carbon transport (DTI, 2003). Transport accounts for around 25% of UK greenhouse gas emissions, the majority (85%) derived from road transport. Biofuels derived from agricultural materials have significantly lower carbon lifecycle emissions than fossil derived fuels and could play a significant role in helping the UK to meet its targets. The EU has proposed indicative targets for biofuel substitution of 2% by 2005, rising by 0.75% per annum to 5.75% by 2010. In response, the UK will shortly have to confirm and ratify its own targets.

Biofuel feedstocks

In international markets, biodiesel, derived commercially from trans-esterification of plant oils and animal wastes (typically oilseed rape and sunflower as well as waste vegetable oils, animal fats, grease and tallow) and bioethanol (derived from fermentation of starch or sugar crops) dominate as the most technically feasible and commercialised biofuel sources. Most car and truck manufacturer warranties currently allow inclusion of appropriate biofuels in blends of up to at least 5% with fossil diesel or petrol. Production of bioethanol by fermentation of starch and sugar feedstocks has been undertaken for many years in Brazil (from sugar cane) and the US (from corn), and more recently in the EU from wheat and sugar beet (France, Spain and Sweden). These represent relatively expensive feedstocks and research is ongoing to commercialise the production of bioethanol from lignocellulosic sources, i.e. paper and plant wastes (such as straw residues) and wood. More complex physiochemical or enzymic processing is required to release the sugars for fermentation. This technology is some 5-10 years away from commercialisation, but offers the potential to diversify feedstocks and reduce costs of production. The potential biofuel yields obtainable from UK produced feedstocks are shown in Table 1.

Table 1. Biofuel production potential of UK agricultural feedstocks. ([a] Derived from Marrow, Coombs and Lees 1987, [b] derived from Marrow and Coombs, 1990. [c] Derived from industry estimates (Cargill and North East Biodiesel)).

Biofuel feedstock (typical field yield)	Feedstock requirement (tonnes) per tonne of biofuel produced	Potential biofuel yield (tonnes/ha/yr)
Bioethanol		
Wheat (8 t/ha)	2.5-3.0 [a]	2.6 – 3.2
Sugar beet (53 t/ha)	11-12.5 [a]	4.24- 4.82
Coppice/forestry waste	5.5-7.5 [b]	1.2-1.65
Straw residues	4.25-6.25 [b]	0.75-1.05
Biodiesel		
Oilseed rape (3.5 t/ha)	2.4 [c]	1.45

Targets for substitution and current levels of production

UK fuel demand is predicted to reach 40.3 M tonnes by 2005 and 44.5 M tonnes by 2010. Based on the EC indicative targets, this gives a target for substitution of 0.8 million tonnes in 2005, rising to 2.56 million tonnes in 2010.

The cost of production of crop-derived biofuels is 2-3 times that of mineral fuels. Figures from Cargill (who produce biodiesel in Germany) indicate that over the past 3 years biodiesel cost between 22 and 33 p/litre more to produce than fossil diesel (which cost between 12 - 14p/litre over the same period). This differential is reduced at the point of sale by reductions in, or (as in some other EU member states) by exemption from fuel duty payments. Current UK fuel duty rates provide for a 20p/l reduction for biodiesel over conventional Ultra-Low Sulphur Diesel (ULSD). A similar duty cut for bioethanol will come into force from January 2005. This duty rebate has incentivised commercial UK production of biodiesel from waste oil, but little production from fresh rapeseed oil. Current production is running at just under 800 tonnes per month (May 2003) around one quarter of which is sold as a blended diesel product. There is currently no bioethanol production in the UK.

A problem for feedstock producers is that, raw material costs (ex duty) account for between 62% (North East Biodiesel) and 78% (Cargill) of biodiesel costs and 60-70% (Ballesteros, 2002) of bioethanol production costs (from wheat). This results in pressure to keep feedstock costs as low as possible, as variation in such costs has a significant effect on the point of sale price (Figure 1). In the 1992/93 season, oilseed rape prices ranged from a low of £135 up to £180/tonne which had a significant impact on competitiveness of any UK produced biodiesel with fossil diesel trading around 0.78p/litre. Since biodiesel and bioethanol can be made from a wide range of feedstocks the cost of competitor oils (e.g. soya), starch and sugar (e.g. corn starch and cane sugar) sources also keeps prices competitive. Increasing support to the industry through further cuts in rates of duty would risk increasing import of biofuels from other countries with more liberal support measures and lower costs of production, though, with the exception of Brazilian ethanol, domestic demands mean there is currently little international trade in biofuels.

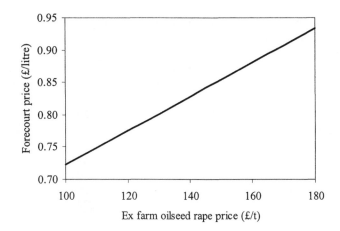

Figure 1. Effect of oilseed rape cost on final cost of biodiesel at the pump, based on current conversion efficiencies and at prevailing rates of biodiesel fuel duty (25.82 pence/litre).

Meeting the EU biofuel substitution targets

In the short term it is likely that only production of biodiesel will be sufficiently well developed commercially in the UK to contribute significantly to meeting the biofuel substitution targets for 2005. Biodiesel production from waste oils and fats will only meet a fraction of demand, limited to around 0.1 million tonnes (Ecotec, 2002). A further 0.2 million hectares of oilseed rape would be required to meet targets for substitution of road diesel alone and just under 0.5 million hectares to substitute for 2% of all transport fuel requirement in 2005. This would represent a significant increase in the oilseed rape area of between 45 and 108% (assuming the existing area is retained for current market outlets). Meeting the target for 5.75% substitution will require a much broader range of biofuel feedstocks.

For a number of reasons, including rotational limits on production of OSR in traditional growing areas, it is unlikely that biodiesel derived from UK oilseed crops will be able to significantly exceed 2% of UK transport fuel demand. Other feedstocks will be required to meet the demand. The UK produces a significant exportable cereal surplus of around 2.9 million tonnes, but it is unlikely that all of this would be available for bioethanol production. In addition, forthcoming reform of the EU sugar regime and opening up of the sugar market to imports from developing countries is likely to significantly affect profitability of UK sugar beet production and the industry is predicted to contract over the next 10 years. For illustrative purposes it is assumed that around half of the exportable wheat surplus could be made available for bioethanol production and that at least half of the current area of sugar beet is retained and used for bioethanol production in 2010. Even with this level of supply directed towards biofuels, there would still be a requirement for a further 1 million tonnes of bioethanol production to meet the 2010 substitution target. This demand would have to be met from novel sources such as lignocellulosics. A possible breakdown for supply from these sources is given in Table 2, which indicates that up to 1.2 million hectares of land in the UK would need to be directed towards biofuel production to meet the indicative targets for 2010.

Table 2. Possible scenario for biofuel feedstock cropping to meet the 2010 target for biofuel substitution.

Feedstock	Fuel required (million tonnes)	Feedstock area (thousand ha)	% of current crop area
Waste fats/oils	0.10		
Rape oil (RME)	0.70	459	102
Wheat grain	0.40	173	11
Sugar beet	0.40	98	55
Wheat straw	0.25	164	10
Miscanthus	0.20	100	-
Short rotation coppice	0.50	229	-
Total:		1,222	

An outcome of the recent mid-term review of the common agricultural policy (CAP) was that it will still be possible to grow crops for industrial use on set-aside. In the last three years between 560-800 thousand hectares have been set-aside and a significant proportion of this area could be devoted to biofuel cropping, which would ease competition with crops for food markets. It is by utilising this 'additional' land resource that the greatest financial and employment benefits will flow back to the agricultural sector. The alternative approach is that crops would just be diverted from food to industrial use, or would substitute for other crops in the rotation with little net benefit to producers. To meet the proposed biofuel targets there would need to be a mix of approaches. There would be consequences for the environment associated with any increase in winter over spring cropping and reduction in the area of naturally regenerated set-aside, favoured by some key farmland bird species. Pesticide and fertiliser use would increase where set-aside is used for biofuel cropping. However, development of lignocellulosic technologies would help stem such increases by increasing the efficiency of biofuel production per unit area of arable feedstock crop by utilising 'waste' biomass (e.g. straw). Similarly, short rotation coppice and miscanthus biomass crops have a relatively low demand for agrochemical and fertiliser inputs. In general, except for the noted possible effects on set-aside, production of biofuels from a broad mix of arable crops should have a neutral effect on the farmed environment. Environmental mitigation measures may be required where biofuel feedstock crops are produced on set-aside land. These could include features such a grass field margins.

Impacts on the rural and wider economy

As part of the mid term review of CAP, it has been agreed that an Energy Crop Payment of €45/ha/year (currently worth £32) would be made available to support biofuel energy crops up up to a maximum guaranteed area (MGA) of 1.5 million hectares across the EU, with a proportionate scale back where this is exceeded. The scale of production required to meet the biofuel targets combined with better incentives in other EU countries, as well as competition with solid biofuels for electricity generation, means that the MGA will be rapidly overshot. Assuming UK oilseed rape producers could access the full payment rate, at current yield levels this would provide some compensation (i.e. £9/tonne for a 3.5 t/ha rape crop) where low prices are being offered on contracts for biodiesel production. Prices being discussed within the biodiesel industry are currently around of £8-12/tonne less than those currently available for conventional oilseed rape market outlets. Those wishing to procure feedstocks hope that the offer of long-term supply contracts will encourage production of biofuel crops. The best returns to growers are likely to arise from expansion of cereal and oilseed biofuel cropping onto set-aside which could improve returns to growers by up to £120-£300/ha.

A UK biofuel industry will create employment opportunities but these are likely to be limited. Turley, *et al.* (2002), calculated that around 2 jobs were created in the rural economy and associated industries per 1000 tonnes of biodiesel production where rape feedstocks were grown on set-aside, this would be negligible where biofuel crops replaced crops grown for feed markets. Recent work by Bullard, *et al.* (2003) estimated that bioethanol production from wheat and sugar beet could create 5.5 jobs/1000 tonnes of production. Very few additional jobs are created in processing. A 100,000 tonne biodiesel plant would employ in the region of 62 staff and a similar sized bioethanol plant around 75 jobs in production, blending and transport (Bullard, *et al.*, 2003). Impacts on the wider economy are difficult to calculate but Bullard, *et al.* (2003) estimate that UK bioethanol production could return around 6.5 pence to the Exchequer for every litre sold, though savings in job seeker allowance (created by increased employment) and taxation revenues arising from growth in ancillary industries.

Carbon savings

There has been considerable debate over the carbon savings derived from biofuels. Latest figures indicate greenhouse gas savings of between 51 and 65% for bioethanol (v Ultra Low Sulphur Petrol), 56-80% for Rape Methyl Ester and 84% for biodiesel derived from waste oil (v ULSD) (Mortimer, *et al.*, 2002, Woods and Bauden, 2003). Meeting the biofuel substitution targets would result in carbon savings of around 0.5 M tonnes by 2005 rising to 1.5 to 2 million tonnes by 2010, costing the Exchequer £197 million in 2005, rising to £630 million by 2010. The cost of greenhouse gas abatement achieved by biofuels (CO_2 saving per £ subsidy expended) gives CO_2 abatement costs ranging from £91-£143/tonne for bioethanol derived from wheat and £110-£178/tonne for biodiesel derived from rapeseed (£76/tonne from waste oil). The equivalent cost of CO_2 savings generated by electricity generation from short rotation coppice is around £51/tonne (Mortimer *et al.*, 2003). When lignocellulosic technologies are commercially developed, the cost of CO_2 abatement for biofuels is likely to improve as the CO_2 savings associated with these feedstocks are likely to be greater.

CONCLUSIONS

Biofuel cropping offers an opportunity to diversify market outlets for UK growers and to derive added value from crop production on set-aside land. However, at current levels of industrial efficiency and cost, returns to growers for feedstocks grown outside set-aside are likely to be similar to, or less than, those of traditional market outlets, though with some security derived from the offer of long term contracts. Extensive biofuel cropping is likely to result in loss of natural regeneration set-aside and could result in intensification of some crops, in particular oilseed rape for biodiesel production. This could result in agronomic difficulties in achieving timely crop establishment where rape starts to occur more than once in the rotation, but these difficulties are not insurmountable.

The costs of carbon savings achieved by adoption of current biofuel technologies and supported by fuel duty cuts, appear uncompetitive compared with other possible CO_2 mitigation measures (i.e. renewable energy generation and investment in energy saving technologies) and this may hamper provision of additional Government support. However this could prevent development of technologies and initiatives that could quickly deliver real benefits in terms of reduction in greenhouse gas emissions on a wide scale. Other lower-cost incentives which could be adopted to stimulate the industry, without increasing the risk of imports, includes introduction of mandatory targets for biofuel blends, which would pass costs to consumers, or support with grants to cover capital costs, which would reduce costs to the Exchequer in the long term. Technologies could be developed to produce bioethanol much more cheaply from lignocellulosic raw materials while providing greater reductions in CO_2 than are possible with current technologies, but this step will not occur in the UK without investment and development in current technologies as a stepping stone. Given the political will to support the industry, in the medium to long term, novel biomass feedstocks are likely to be the key industrial crops required for UK liquid biofuel production.

REFERENCES

Ballesteros M (2002). Desarrollos en Tecnología y aplicaciones industrials de biocombustibles líquidos, CIEMAT. 6 pages. (www.istas.net/portada/bio06m.pdf).

Bullard M; Martin D; van den Broek R; Tijmensen M; Bradshaw C; Garstang J; Boeke J; Blake J; Vertooren M (2003). *The Impacts of Creating A Domestic UK Bioethanol Industry.* Report For the East of England Development Agency. 226 pages.

DTI (2003). DTI Energy White Paper. *Our energy future creating a low carbon economy.* HMSO: London, 138 pages.

ECOTEC (2002). *Analysis of costs and benefits of biofuels compared to other transport fuels.* British Association for Biofuels and Oils: Sutton Bridge, Lincolnshire UK. 27 pages.

Marrow J E; Coombs J (1990). An assessment of bio-ethanol as a transport fuel in the UK, Volume 2. (ETSU-R-55) HMSO: London. 159 pages.

Marrow J E; Coombs J; Lees E W (1987). An assessment of bioethanol as a transport fuel in the UK. HMSO: London.

Mortimer, N D; Cormack P; Elsayed M A; Horne R E (2003). Evaluation of the comparative energy, environmental and socio-economic costs and benefits of biodiesel. Report for Defra. Sheffield Hallam University - project CSA 5982/NF0422 (www.shu.ac.uk/rru/reports.html).

Woods J; Bauden A (2003). Technology Status review and Carbon Abatement Potential of Renewable Transport Fuels (RTF) in the UK. Research Report for DTI by Imperial College, Centre for Energy Policy and Technology, London.

Turley D B; Boatman N D; Ceddia G; Barker D; Watola, G (2002). Liquid biofuels – prospects and potential impacts on UK agriculture, the farmed environment, landscape and rural economy. Report for DEFRA OFIC Division, Sept 2002. 60 pages.

POSTER SESSION 7A

RESISTANCE: SCIENCE INTO PRACTICE

Session Organiser: Dr Geoff Bateman
Rothamsted Research, Harpenden, UK

Poster Papers: 7A-1 to 7A-10

Gene flow from Bt transgenic corn to nonBt corn: can refuges speed the evolution of pest resistance?

C F Chilcutt

Department of Entomology, Texas A&M University System, 10345 Agnes St., Corpus Christi, TX 78406 USA
Email: c-chilcutt@tamu.edu

ABSTRACT

Bacillus thuringiensis transgenic corn kills several pest species, but its usefulness is dependent on the prevention of pest resistance. To slow resistance to toxins in Bt crops, they are supposed to have high expression levels and nonBt refuges planted near the Bt crops. However, pollen from Bt crops such as corn can fertilize nonBt plants, causing toxin expression in the seeds or kernels of the nonBt plants. This paper examines how gene flow from Bt to nonBt corn affected toxin expression in nonBt refuges. Cry1Ab genes from Bt hybrids were spread for up to 32 m across nonBt refuge plots with moderate to low toxin levels throughout the nonBt refuge. These findings were used in a simulation model to determine the effects of Bt toxin expression in refuges on the development of resistance to Bt toxins by pests. Results indicate that refuges must be located at a distance, dependent on wind speed and pollen movement, from Bt plantings, in order to act as a refuge or they may actually increase the rate of resistance evolution in pests.

INTRODUCTION

Toxins produced by *Bacillus thuringiensis* transgenic corn hybrids kill several pest species, reducing injury to whorls, ears, and stalks. Their continued usefulness, however, is dependent on the prevention of pest resistance (Shelton *et al.*, 2002). Populations of all major pest species have evolved resistance to insecticides and several have evolved resistance to Bt sprays (McGaughey, 1985; Tabashnik *et al.*, 1990). To slow resistance to Cry toxins in Bt crops, nonBt refuges are planted with the Bt crops (Tabashnik, 1994). The strategy is to use highly toxic Bt plants to kill homozygous susceptible and heterozygous insects (Denholm & Rowland, 1992). Any surviving resistant homozygotes will mate with susceptible insects from refuges producing susceptible individuals that will be killed by Bt toxins (Roush & McKenzie, 1987). The strategy assumes that toxin expression is high enough to kill heterozygous insects, resistant allele frequencies are low, and random mating occurs between adults of different genotypes from Bt and nonBt plots (Gould, 1998).

Because corn is wind-pollinated, nonBt refuge plants near Bt corn can be pollinated with Bt pollen and will express Bt toxins. In theory, moderate to low doses could actually speed the evolution of resistance by allowing the survival of partially resistant heterozygotes. In planning refuge structure and placement in resistance management for insects in Bt crops, inter-mating of insects from Bt plantings and nonBt refuges has been stressed while the effects of gene flow to nonBt refuges has been ignored.

Toxin expression that only occurs in corn kernels will mainly affect ear-feeding pests such as corn earworm, *Helicoverpa zea* and fall armyworm, *Spodoptera frugiperda*. However, larvae of most species of borers, such as European corn borer, *Ostrinia nubilalis*, and southwestern corn borer, *Diatraea grandiosella*, the main targets of Bt transgenic maize, feed on ear tissues during their second (or later) seasonal generation. Because all target pests will come into contact with the Bt toxins in refuge plants that are within the halo of pollen from Bt plantings, nonBt plantings of small width will not act as refuges. Actually, for any refuge close to the Bt planting there will be a wide range of concentrations found throughout nonBt plantings rather than the high concentration of toxins required for the high dose strategy.

In this study, I measured the expression of Cry1Ab toxins in nonBt corn refuges, then used these measurements in a computer model to simulate the development of resistance to Bt transgenic corn by *H. zea*. Although *H. zea* is used as an example, any lepidopterous pest that Bt transgenic plants target will be affected in a similar manner. The effects of Bt gene flow on supposed nonBt refuges and on the development of pest resistance are then discussed.

MATERIALS AND METHODS

Six isogenic Bt/nonBt hybrid corn pairs were used in each of two replicate plots. Hybrids were from four different companies and included four Bt11 insertion event and two Mon810 insertion event hybrids, all genetically engineered with Bt genes to express the Cry1Ab protein toxin. Each of the two replicates was divided into six test plots. The first eight rows of each test plot were planted with one of the six Bt hybrids, then 36 adjacent rows were planted with its nonBt counterpart.

Ears were harvested when all hybrids were below 15% moisture and then dried to approximately 10% moisture. Samples were harvested from two rows of each Bt subplot, and rows 1-4, 8, 16, 24, and 32 of each nonBt subplot, (with row 1 being 0.965 m from the adjacent row of the Bt subplot and row 32 being 30.88 m from the Bt subplot). For all samples, kernels were removed from each ear and then ground to a fine powder.

Cry1Ab in each ground sample was quantified using EnviroLogix Inc. (Portland, Maine, USA) plate kits to perform Enzyme Linked Immunosorbent Assay (ELISA). Ground samples were placed in an extraction/dilution buffer for 24 h and then the extracts were added to the test wells of the ELISA plate. Test wells had been coated with antibodies raised against Cry1Ab toxin to which residues would bind and were then detected by the addition of horseradish peroxidase–labeled Cry1Ab antibody.

A single quadratic regression equation was fitted to a plot of Cry1Ab concentrations by distance from the Bt subplot for all nonBt hybrids. Distances for 1 to 76 rows were then inserted into the equation to obtain predicted Cry1Ab concentrations for each of these 76 rows.

A stochastic, generation-specific, simulation model as described by Chilcutt & Tabashnik (1999) was developed that included a population model and a Cry1Ab resistance evolution model for *Helicoverpa zea*. Three genotypes were included in the model, a homozygous susceptible genotype (SS), a homozygous resistant genotype (RR), and a heterozygote (RS). Mortality was varied in the model with values of 99, 90, and 60% for the SS genotype, 90, 60, and 30 % for the RS genotype, and a constant 1% mortality for the RR genotype.

To determine the effects of Bt toxin expression in refuge plants on resistance evolution, five *H. zea* larval subpopulations were included in the model, with one subpopulation feeding within the Bt planting and four subpopulations feeding within a 20% nonBt refuge. Each of the nonBt subpopulations was located within 1 to 19 rows of corn. For a 4-row refuge each subpopulation would be one row wide, whereas for a 76-row refuge each would be 19 rows wide.

The concentration used in the Bt subpopulation was a single value, an average for all Bt hybrid samples, whereas the Cry1Ab concentration in each of the four nonBt subpopulations was an average for all rows in that subpopulation and, therefore, changed depending on the number of rows in each subpopulation. At the end of each generation, all genotypes from all subpopulations mated randomly.

The model was then run with 10 different Bt plot and nonBt refuge plot sizes (number of rows) all with the refuge occupying 20% of the planting. The model was also run once with no refuge. For each of the 10 planting size values and the zero refuge, the model was run once for each of the set of SS/RS/RR genotype % mortality values, including 99/90/1, 99/60/1, 90/60/1, and 60/30/1. For each simulation, the model was run until the resistance allele frequency (R) at the end of a generation was above 0.5. This generation was considered to be the generation in which the population became resistant to Cry1Ab.

RESULTS

Cry1Ab toxin levels in nonBt plots of all hybrids decreased exponentially with increasing distance from Bt plots (Figure 1). This pattern was similar for all hybrid pairs, with some small row to row variations. Cry1Ab concentrations in Bt plots varied from 80 to 300 ng/g of dry kernel depending on the hybrid. In nonBt plots, Cry1Ab concentrations ranged from 88 to 307 ng/g at one row distance from the Bt plot (0.97 m), 1 to 7 ng/g at 16 rows distance (15.4 m) and 1 to 9 ng/g at 32 rows distance (30.9 m). This indicates that in the nonBt row adjacent to the Bt plot, Bt toxin levels are actually higher than in some Bt plots.

The model demonstrated that Bt gene flow to nonBt refuge plants will, in most cases, speed the evolution of resistance to Cry1Ab by *H. zea* (Figure 2). All values in Figure 2 are the number of generations to resistance in the presence of gene flow divided by the number of generations to resistance in the absence of gene flow (uniformly nontoxic refuges). Therefore, values less than one indicate that resistance occurs faster when Bt gene flow to refuges occurs than when refuges are uniformly nontoxic.

The results demonstrate that, except when susceptible homozygote and heterozygote mortality is low and the refuge physical size is large, resistance always occurs faster when gene flow occurs than when no gene flow occurs. Also, if the refuge is small in physical size (although always 20% of the corn planting) and if heterozygote mortality is nearly as high as for susceptible homozygotes, then resistance evolution will actually be faster than if there were no refuge.

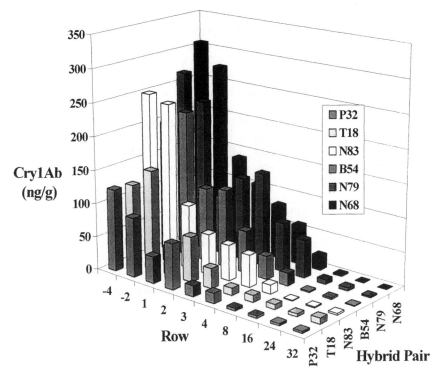

Figure 1.   Average Bt toxin levels in corn kernels from two rows of Bt plots (-2,-4) and eight rows of an adjacent nonBt refuge at increasing distance from the Bt plot. Row spacing is 0.97 m.

DISCUSSION

The results indicate that pollen from Bt transgenic corn will produce moderate to low levels of Cry1Ab toxins in refuge plants for at least 30 m. The extent of these effects throughout a refuge depends on a number of factors including refuge size, shape, distance from the Bt crop, and wind speed and direction as well as similarity in planting times, and maturation times between Bt and nonBt corn hybrids.

The movement of Bt genes into nonBt refuges is extremely important to resistance management. The production of a range of levels of Bt toxins in nonBt corn ears within refuges is in direct contrast to the goals of a high dose-refuge strategy for controlling resistance. Not only is the refuge compromised by gene flow, but there is also no possibility of the uniform, high toxin concentrations required for the high dose strategy. Of course, even in a uniform planting of Bt corn, there is a wide range of toxin levels produced in leaves, silks, shanks, and kernels, as well as plant-to-plant variation throughout a field. These variations already call into question the probability that major corn pests always receive a high toxin dose when feeding on Bt corn. The addition of gene flow into refuges just increases the range of toxin concentrations throughout a planting, including very low concentrations that might not be present in uniform Bt corn plantings.

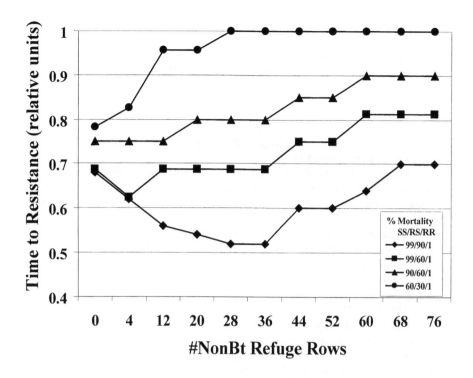

Figure 2.   Amount of time it takes *Helicoverpa zea* to develop resistance to Cry1Ab toxins in the presence of toxic plants in a nonBt refuge. Time values are generations relative to a 20% nontoxic refuge (no gene flow). Lines represent different mortality values for susceptible homozygotes and heterozygotes, with resistant homozygotes always having 1% mortality.

I have shown here that the expression of Bt toxins in refuges will increase the rate of resistance development in ear-feeding pests over nontoxic refuges and could even increase resistance development faster than if a high dose were used with no refuge. The latter would only be possible if there were a population of a pest species that actually consumed high toxin doses throughout Bt plantings within the range of the population, a condition that is questionable at this point in time, but may be a factor in the future as hybrids with higher toxin expression are produced.

Several possible solutions to the problem of Bt gene flow into refuges include planting refuges in a manner that limits cross-pollination by Bt plants (Morris *et al.*, 1994), or planting refuges at different times than Bt plots, which Alstad & Andow (1995) have shown may slow resistance for other reasons. More information is needed to assess these tactics and their effects on mating between insects from refuges and Bt plots. Also, as with all current resistance management strategies, field tests of the effects of gene flow on resistance in pest populations is needed.

ACKNOWLEDGEMENTS

I thank Gary Odvody and Bruce Tabashnik for their helpful suggestions. I also thank Carlos Correa and Leo Sanfilipo for their technical assistance.

REFERENCES

Alstad D N; Andow D A (1995). Managing the evolution of insect resistance to transgenic plants. *Science* **268**, 1894-1896.

Chilcutt C F; Tabashnik B E (1999). Simulation of integration of *Bacillus thuringiensis* and the parasitoid *Cotesia plutellae* (Hymenoptera: Braconidae) for control of susceptible and resistant diamondback moth (Lepidoptera: Plutellidae). *Environmental Entomology* **28**, 505-512.

Denholm I; Rowland M W (1992). Tactics for managing pesticide resistance in arthropods: theory and practice. *Annual Review of Entomology* **37**, 91-112.

Gould F (1998). Sustainability of transgenic insecticidal cultivars: integrating pest genetics and ecology. *Annual Review of Entomology* **43**, 701-726.

McGaughey W H (1985). Insect resistance to the biological insecticide *Bacillus thuringiensis*. *Science* **229**, 193-195.

Morris W F; Kareiva P M; Raymer P L (1994). Do barren zones and pollen traps reduce gene escape from transgenic crops? *Ecological Applications* **4**, 157-165.

Roush R T; McKenzie J A (1987). Ecological genetics of insecticide and acaracide resistance. *Annual Review of Entomology* **32**, 361-380.

Shelton A M; Zhao J-Z; Roush R T (2002). Economic, ecological, food safety, and social consequences of the deployment of Bt transgenic plants. *Annual Review of Entomology* **47**, 845-881.

Tabashnik B E (1994). Evolution of resistance to *Bacillus thuringiensis*. *Annual Review of Entomology* **39**, 47-79.

Tabashnik B E; Cushing N L; Finson N; Johnson M W (1990). Field development of resistance to *Bacillus thuringiensis* in diamondback moth (Lepidoptera: Plutellidae). *Journal of Economic Entomology* **83**, 1671-1676.

Study of resistance to ALS inhibitors in the weed species *Echinochloa crus-galli*

B Konstantinovic, M Meseldzija, S Popovic, Bo Konstantinovic
Faculty of Agriculture, Department for Environmental and Plant Protection, Novi Sad, Serbia and Monte Negro
Email: brankok@polj.ns.ac.yu

ABSTRACT

The aim of the study was the determination of whether resistance to ALS inhibitors occurred in the weed species *Echinochloa crus-galli*. Herbicide resistance represents an adaptive phenomenon resulting from repeated use of herbicides with the same mode of action. Resistance determination studies were performed in 2002, and material for the study was collected from different localities in the region of Vojvodina (Serbia), specifically Kamendin, Backi Maglic and Becej. Repeated use of the ALS-inhibiting herbicides, which are used very successfully against dicotyledonous and monocotyledonous weeds, has resulted in the occurrence of resistant biotypes of *E. crus-galli*. Results obtained from biological studies, whole plant tests and Petri dish bioassays, confirmed the presence of resistant *E. crus-galli*.

INTRODUCTION

The potential for adaptation by weed species to herbicides by single applications is weak. It becomes expressed after repeated use over a long period. Resistance development in some biotypes then becomes a major constraint on the use of herbicides that were previously efficient. The resistance phenomenon can not be recognized by visual assessment until it occurs in 1-10% of individuals in a field population, but in less than 0.1% of resistant individuals in laboratory conditions. Where only one weed species is present, it can usually be considered to have become resistant (Konstantinovic, unpublished).

The most frequently used ALS-inhibiting herbicides in our country are sulphonylureas and imidazolinones, of which imazethapyr was used in our studies. *Amaranthus retroflexus* was the first weed in Israel to develop resistance to ALS inhibitors (Sibony & Rubin, 2003). Our studies on resistance of the weed species *Echinochloa crus-galli* to ALS inhibitors are the first of this kind in our country. Up to now, there have been 80 reports of resistant of weed species to this mode of action and only one case in the genus *Echinochloa (E. colona)*, which was identified in Costa Rica in 1988 (HRAC, 2003).

MATERIALS AND METHODS

Seeds were collected from the localities Kamendin, Backi Maglic and Becej, which had a long history of imidazolinone and sulphonilurea herbicide use (over the last 10 years). A susceptible population collected from an area where no herbicides had been used was used as a reference population. Imazethapyr was used since it was one of the most frequently applied ALS inhibitors in the localities studied.

The most important individual factor for the initial determination of resistance is the level of non-susceptibility in the field. Consequently, we have used a method of visual assessment of imazethapyr efficiency to detect possible resistance.

There are several factors that can indicate possibility of resistance occurrence in field, such as:
i)   level of control of other susceptible species,
ii) presence of live plants alongside dead ones,
iii) past experiences, i.e. previously successful control by the same treatment,
iv) herbicide history, i.e. repetition of the same herbicide treatment, or herbicide with the same mode of action,
v)   resistance occurrence in the region,
vi) harvest,
vii) cultivation history, i.e. monoculture and minimum tillage (Moss,1995).

Studies were made on whole plants (Thurwachter, 1998) and Petri dishes bioassays (Clay & Underwood, 1990). Assays were performed in four replications and plants were treated with various doses of imazethapyr, representing. 40, 80, 100, 150 and 200 g a.i. ha^{-1}.

In whole plant studies, plants were grown in controlled conditions in pots from seed which was suspected to be imazethapyr resistant. There were 10 seeds per plot and the trial was set on chernozem, with 3.5% humus, in four replications, and assessments were done 3 – 4 weeks after treatment (pre emrgence herbicide application). In whole plant studies, efficacy was evaluated by measuring foliage fresh weight, as well as by counting emerged plants and assessing their vigour.

In the Petri dish assays, 10 seeds per dish were spread evenly over filter paper and 5 ml of imazethapyr solution added to saturate, but not flood, the filter paper (pre emergence herbicide application). There were four replications of each treatment. Dishes were kept at room temperature, out of direct sunlight. Germination and seedling condition were recorded at intervals up to 25 days from the start, with visual assessment of number of healthy and damaged seedlings in each dish. In Petri dishes bioassays, the lengths of epicotyls and hypocotyls of shoots were measured.

RESULTS AND DISCUSSION

Pot tests

At doses equivalent to 100 g ha^{-1} and above, none of plants from the Backi Maglic locality or the susceptible standard survived (Table 1), suggesting that the Backi Maglic population remains susceptible to imazethapyr. In contrast, some plants from both the Becej and Kamendin populations survived this herbicide dose, which resulted in 73% and 24% decreases in fresh weight for the two populations, respectively. Only a 44% reduction in fresh weight of plants from the Kamendin population was achieved by imazethapyr at the highest dose of 200 g ha^{-1}. This suggests that there may be some resistance in this population.

Table 1. Effects of doses of imazethapyr on foliage fresh weight and number of emerged plants of *Echinochloa crus-galli* in pot tests

	Imazethapyr dose (g a.i. ha^{-1})											
	0		40		80		100		150		200	
Locality	a	b	a	b	a	b	a	b	a	b	a	b
Becej	54.6	23	43.5	17	17.4	6	14.5	5	0	0	0	0
SED	3.0	-	2.2	-	1.5	-	1.3	-	-	-	-	-
Kamendin	52.1	29	46.8	27	40.2	19	39.8	12	31.2	8	29.4	6
SED	5.2	-	3.4	-	1.2	-	2.3	-	0.8	-	0.2	-
Backi Maglic	45.3	28	38.4	17	15.9	2	0	0	0	0	0	0
SED	4.1	-	2.7	-	0.2	-	0	-	-	-	-	-
Susceptible standard	49.6	27	31.5	19	12.5	1	0	0	0	0	0	0
SED	3.5	-	2.4	-	0.3	-	0	-	-	-	-	-

a, foliage fresh weight (mg per plant); b, total number of emerged plants.

Petri dish bioassays

After 25 d in Petri dishes, damage to emerged plants occurred at some imazethapyr concentrations. At 0.15 and 0.2 mg l^{-1}, there were no undamaged plants in the Becej population (Table 2). There was 30-45% damage to plants from Backi Maglic, depending on the concentration used. Only plants from Kamendin were less susceptible than the standard susceptible plants. This decrease in susceptibility of the Kamendin population was confirmed by hypocotyl lengths (Figure 1) and epicotyl lengths (Figure 2), which were greater in plants from this population, after treatment at 2.0 mg l^{-1}, than in those from other populations, including the standard susceptible.

The Petri dish bioassays provide some confirmation of the whole-plant data, suggesting that biotypes from the Backi Maglic locality are still susceptible to imazethapyr at field doses of 80 and 100 g ha^{-1} but that there is some resistance in the population at the Kamendin locality. The situation at Becej is less clear, since the Petri dish bioassay indicated good susceptibility although there was some plant survival at 100 g ha^{-1} in the whole-plant tests.

The decreased susceptibility in the *E. crus-galli* population from Kamendin is a result of more intensive use of ALS-inhibiting herbicides in that locality. Data from other studies support the suggestion that repeated use of herbicides with this mode of action increases the risk of resistance development.

Table 2. Effects of imazethapyr concentration on percentage of damaged plants 25 days after emergence in Petri-dish assays

Locality	Imazethapyr dose (mg litre⁻¹)											
	0		0.04		0.08		0.1		0.15		0.2	
	%	SED	%	SED	%	SED	%	SED	%	SED	%	SED
Becej	0	0	14.7	1.5	13.5	1.8	28.8	2.4	100	0	100	0
Kamendin	0	0	13.3	3.8	9.3	3.2	10.0	1.4	13.3	23	20.0	2.4
Backi Maglic	0	0	36.6	4.7	30.0	3.7	40.0	2.1	43.3	1.7	40.0	1.4
Susceptible standard	0	0	20.0	1.3	23.3	2.6	23.3	1.8	30.0	1.2	33.3	1.5

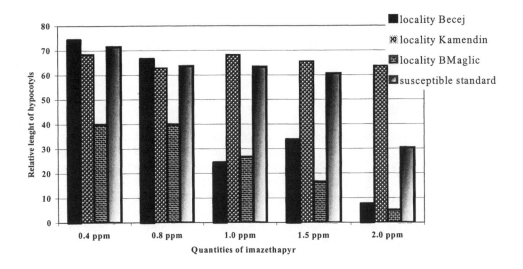

Figure 1. Effects of imazethapyr concentration on lengths of hypocotyls of seedlings of *Echinochloa crus-galli* from different localities in Petri-dish bioassays.

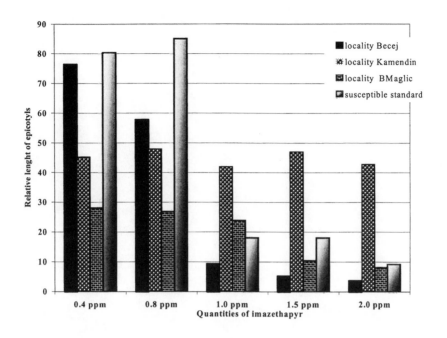

Figure 2.   Effects of imazethapyr concentration on lengths of epicotyls of seedlings of *Echinochloa crus-galli* from different localities in Petri-dish bioassays.

REFERENCES

Clay D V; Underwood C (1990). The identification of triazine- and paraquat-resistant weed biotypes and their response to other herbicides. *Importance and perspectives on herbicide-resistant weeds*. Report of the Commission of the European Communities: Luxembourg, pp. 47-55.

HRAC (2003). Available at http:// www.weedscience.org

Sibony M; Rubin B (2003). The ecological fitness of ALS-resistant *Amaranthus retroflexus* and multiple-resistant *Amaranthus blitoides*. *Weed Research* **43**, 40-47.

Thurwachter D (1998). The identification of triazine and paraquat-resistant weed biotypes and their response to other herbicides. *Importance and perspectives on herbicide-resistant weeds*. Report of the Commission of the European Communities: Luxembourg, pp. 67-81.

Moss S R (1995). Techniques for determining herbicide resistance. *Proceedings of the Brighton Crop Protection Conference-Weeds 1995* **2**, 547-556.

Differential sensitivity of Jordanian *Amaranthus retroflexus* populations to post-emergence herbicides

H Z Ghosheh
Department of Plant Production, Jordan University of Science & Technology, P.O. Box 3030, Irbid 22100, Jordan
Email: ghosheh@just.edu.jo

K Hurle
Department of Weed Science, Institute of Phytomedicine, University of Hohenheim, Stuttgart, D-70599, Germany

ABSTRACT

The differential sensitivity of three Jordanian *A. retroflexus* populations to 2,4-D, glyphosate, and paraquat was examined in three greenhouse experiments. Herbicides were applied at rates that enclosed estimated ED_{50} doses for a control population in preliminary experiments. Results indicated that one population had a higher tolerance of 2,4-D. This population was very sensitive to glyphosate applications. The three populations were very sensitive to paraquat, but their responses to this herbicide were different. These experiments revealed the presence of diversified responses to commonly used herbicides in *A. retroflexus* populations, a fact that should be considered if site-specific herbicides are utilized more often in the future.

INTRODUCTION

Amaranthus retroflexus (redroot pigweed) is one of the most widely distributed weeds in arable crops worldwide. The species is present in more than 60 crops in 70 countries (Holm *et al.*, 1997). *A. retoflexus* is present in almost all parts and environments of Jordan (Abu-Irmaileh, 2000). Ghorbani *et al.* (1999) reported that *A. retroflexus* seeds germinate over a wide range of temperatures, water potentials, and burial depths. Interest in the biology of *A. retroflexus* increased dramatically after triazine resistance was confirmed in many biotypes of the species (Holm *et al.*, 1997). *A. retroflexus* populations have shown resistance to photosystem II inhibitors, acetolactate synthase (ALS) inhibitors, ureas and amides (Heap, 2003).

Despite the relatively small area of Jordan, the country is characterized by diverse topography and environmental conditions. This has created a diversity in agricultural systems. Jordanian agricultural systems are characterized by limited reliance on chemical weed control. Nevertheless, 2,4-D, glyphosate and paraquat were used frequently over the past 20 years. No resistance of *A. retroflexus* to any of these herbicides has been documented (Heap, 2003).

The repeated use of herbicides with similar modes of action on the same weed population imposes selection for increased resistance within species that had been susceptible. Therefore, recognition, prevention, and management of herbicide resistance in all agricultural situations is imperative (Holt & LeBaron, 1990). In that regard, the differential response of *A. retroflexus* populations from different Jordanian locations to herbicides is not well defined. Our objective in this research was to determine the sensitivity of three Jordanian *A. retroflexus* populations to 2,4-D, glyphosate, and paraquat herbicides through dose-response relationships and to diagnose any progression of herbicide resistance.

MATERIALS AND METHODS

Individual *A. retroflexus* inflorescences were collected in summer 2002 from three locations in Jordan, which are briefly described in Table 1. Seeds were stored for 7 months in paper bags at room temperature before use in experiments. Seeds from 10 random plants per location were combined to represent a population for the designated location.

Table 1.   Geographical, environmental, and agricultural systems prevailing in Jordanian collection sites

Location	Latitude	Longitude	Altitude (m)	Average annual rainfall (mm)	Average upper & lower temperatures (°C)	Cropping system
Jordan University of Science & Technology (JUST)	32° 34'	36° 01'	560	235	23.7, 10.7	Barley-Fallow
Mushaqer Agricultural Reserach Center (MUSR)	31° 43'	35° 48 '	85	358	22.9, 10.2	Wheat-Legumes
Faisal nursery (FAIS)	32° 12'	35° 53 '	260	350	24.8, 11.1	Orchard and Nursery

Source: Jordanian Meteorological Department.

Experiments were conducted in spring 2003 at the Institute of Phytomedicine, University of Hohenheim, Germany. Seeds from the three populations were sown 0.5 cm deep in boxes (20 cm x 10 cm x 3 cm deep) containing compost. Boxes were placed in a dark cold chamber (4°C, 48 h) and then transferred to a greenhouse (24/18°C day/night). Individual seedlings were transplanted at the cotyledon stage to 10-cm pots filled with sterilized compost. Mercury halogen lamps were used to provide 300 µE m^{-2} s^{-1} for a 16-h photoperiod.

A. retroflexus seedlings from the three populations were subjected to herbicide applications at the 4 or 5-leaf stages in three separate experiments. The dose causing 50% reduction in dry weight, referred to as the ED_{50}, was approximated for the three herbicides by conducting preliminary experiments on a control *A. retroflexus* population from Germany. Approximate ED_{50} rates were 155 and 4 g a.i. ha^{-1} for 2,4-D and paraquat, respectively, and was 86 g a.e. ha^{-1} for glyphosate. Therefore, we decided to apply 2,4-D (U 46® D-Flud) at 0, 8.75, 17.5, 35, 70,

140, 280, 560, 1120, 2240, 4480 and 35840 g a.i ha^{-1}. Glyphosate (Roundup Ultra$^{®}$) was applied at 0, 13.125, 26.25, 52.5, 70, 105, 157.5, 210, 420, 840 and 1680 g a.e. ha^{-1}. Paraquat (Gramaxon Extra$^{®}$) was applied at 0, 1.0937, 2.1875, 2.9166, 4.375, 8.75, 17.5, 35, 70, 280, 2240 and 4480 g a.i. ha^{-1}.

A spraying chamber equipped with a flat-fan nozzle (8004) calibrated to deliver 400 l ha^{-1} at 250 kPa was utilized. Treated plants were arranged in a completely randomized design with six replicates and monitored closely in the greenhouse. A very rapid response was observed in all three herbicide applications. The experiments were terminated when necrosis appeared with the low-dose treatments, approximately 24, 72, or 96 h after applications in experiments on paraquat, glyphosate, and 2,4-D, respectively. Plant foliage was harvested and their dry weights (48 h at 80° C) were recorded.

Statistical analysis followed procedures described by Seefeldt *et al.* (1995). The log-logistic curve was adopted to describe the response y to herbicide dose x by the mathematical expression of

$$y=f(x)=C +((D - C)/ (1 + exp[b(log(x) - log(ED_{50}))])) \dots\dots\dots\dots\dots\dots\dots\dots\text{Eq.1}$$

where C = lower limit, D = upper limit, b = slope, and ED_{50} = dose giving 50% response. Dry weight was analysed as a percentage of the average untreated control for the particular population. Thus, 100 was considered the upper limit for all equations.

The first non-linear analysis developed equations to predict the fit of three different dose-response curves, one for each population. The curves were allowed to differ in their lower limits, slopes and ED_{50} values. Then, three non-parallel curves that have a common lower limit were developed to fit dose-response data. To test whether the dose-response curves were parallel (i.e., had a common slope), another non-linear routine was performed that forced dose-response curves to have a common slope and variable ED_{50} values. Lack-of-fit tests were performed to make comparisons between any two models as described by Seefeldt *et al.* (1995).

RESULTS

2,4-D

Lack-of-fit tests indicated that it is not reasonable to assume equal lower limits for the response of the populations to 2,4-D applications. FAIS and MUSR populations were better described by the log-logistic model than was the JUST population (Figure 1). The estimated ED_{50} for the FAIS population was 510 g a.i. ha^{-1}, which is much higher than the estimated value in the preliminary experiment or the estimated values for the other two populations in this experiment. The log-logistic curve does not describe the data of the JUST population adequately due to high variability.

Glyphosate

Populations collected from JUST and MUSR were better described by the log-logistic equation than from the FAIS population. The FAIS population experienced approximately 40%

reduction in shoot dry weight in response to low doses of glyphosate. Thus, the log-logistic equation was considered unsuitable to describe the data for this population. Lack-of-fit tests indicated common lower limits and slopes, but not equal ED_{50} values for the JUST and MUSR populations (Figure 2). The estimated ED_{50} value for the MUSR population was greater than that estimated for the JUST population.

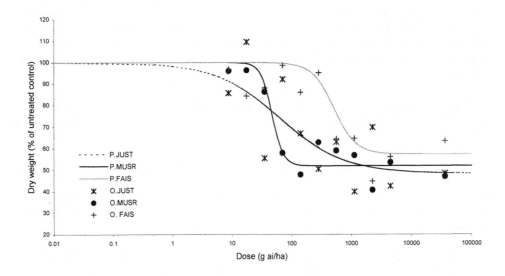

Figure 1. The log-logistic dose-response curves corresponding to differential sensitivity of three Jordanian *A. retroflexus* populations to 2,4-D applications. Parameters of Eq.1: for JUST population, D = 100, C = 48.3, ED_{50} = 63.4, and b = 0.80; for MUSR population, D = 100, C = 51.99, ED_{50} = 46.7, and b = 4.56; for FAIS population, D = 100, C = 57.4, ED_{50} = 510, and b = 2.36. (Abbreviations: O. = Observed; P. = Predicted).

Paraquat

Lack-of-fit tests between individual non-linear equation and a non-linear model that considered the lower limits common for the response of the populations to paraquat indicated that it is possible to assume equal lower limits. A further non-linear regression routine and lack-of-fit tests indicated that assuming equal slopes for the three populations is not appropriate (Figure 3). Estimated ED_{50} values ranged from 6.22 to 2.32 g a.i. ha^{-1}, which is very much less than the minimum recommended rate of 280 g a.i. ha^{-1} (Vencill, 2002).

DISCUSSION

Results of these experiments indicate variations in the responses of the three populations to herbicides commonly used in Jordan. However, the differences in response varied among herbicides and populations. The FAIS population had greater tolerance of 2,4-D, which can be attributed to the genetic make-up rather than herbicidal response. Use of 2,4-D is very limited in nurseries and orchards and so shifts in tolerance would not have been expected.

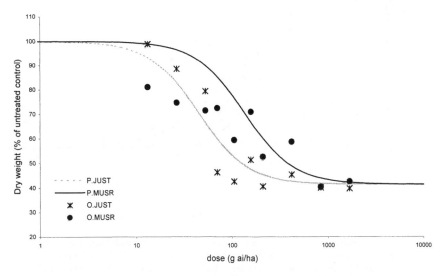

Figure 2.   The log-logistic dose-response curves corresponding to differential sensitivity of two Jordanian *A. retroflexus* populations to glyphosate applications. Parameters of Eq.1: for JUST population, D = 100, C = 41.38, ED_{50} = 44.2, and b = 1.68; for MUSR, D = 100, C = 41.38, ED_{50} = 133.9, and b = 1.68. (Abbreviations: O. = Observed; P. = Predicted).

Results of the glyphosate experiment suggest that the three populations had somewhat different responses to this herbicide. This variation is also believed to be related to the genetics of the populations. The FAIS population, which was the most sensitive to glyphosate applications, as indicated by major dry weight reduction at low rates, was collected from a site where glyphosate applications are common. On the other hand, the relatively high ED_{50} value estimated for glyphosate in the MUSR population is thought not to be related to glyphosate application, which is uncommon in cereal-legume cropping systems.

For paraquat, the very high sensitivity observed in all three populations is more related to the experimental conditions and is not expected to be observed in field conditions. The growing conditions in our experiments apparently created plants that were very sensitive to this herbicide. Although variations in the estimated ED_{50} values for the three populations were minor, these values corresponded to different herbicide application rates in the experiment. This indicates that differential responses exist among the three populations to paraquat. Because associations between cropping systems and ED_{50} values could not be established, judging whether this variation is related to the frequency of paraquat use or not is not possible.

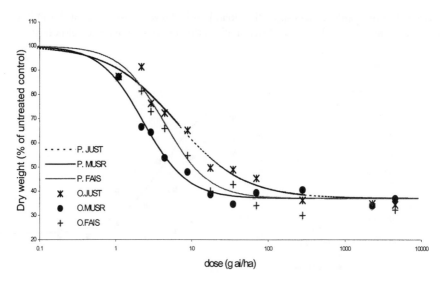

Figure 3.   The log-logistic dose-response curves corresponding to differential sensitivity of three Jordanian *A. retroflexus* populations to paraquat applications. Parameters of Eq.1: for JUST population, D =100, C = 37.05, ED_{50} = 6.22, and b = 0.98; for MUSR population, D = 100, C = 37.05, ED_{50} = 2.32, and b = 1.53; and for FAIS population, D = 100, C = 37.05, ED_{50} = 4.29, and b = 1.49. (Abbreviations: O. = Observed; P. = Predicted).

ACKNOWLEDGEMENTS

We acknowledge the Fellowship of the Alexander von Humboldt Foundation to H Z Ghosheh. We thank Mr Jean Wagner for his technical assistance.

REFERENCES

Abu-Irmaileh B E (2000). *Weeds of cultivated fields*. University of Jordan Press: Amman, Jordan.

Ghorbani R; Seel W; Leifert C (1999). Effects of environmental factors on germination and emergence of *Amaranthus retroflexus*. *Weed Science* **40**, 441-447.

Heap I (2003). The international Survey of Herbicide Resistant Weeds. Online Internet. July 05, 2003. Available www.weedscience.com.

Holm L; Doll J, Holm E; Pancho J; Herberger J (1997). *World Weeds: Natural Histories and Distribution*. John Wiley & Sons: New York.

Holt J S; LeBaron H M (1990). Significance and distribution of herbicide resistance. *Weed Technology* **4**,141-149.

Seefeldt S S; Jensen J E; Fuerst E P (1995). Log-logistic analysis of herbicide dose-response relationships. *Weed Technology* **9**, 218-227.

Vencill W K, ed. (2002). *Herbicide Handbook (8th edition)*. Weed Science Society of America: Kansas, USA.

Characterisation of neonicotinoid resistance in *Bemisia tabaci* from Spain

K Gorman, J Wren, G Devine, I Denholm
Rothamsted Research, Harpenden, Hertfordshire, AL5 2JQ, UK
Email: kevin.gorman@bbsrc.ac.uk

ABSTRACT

Three strains of the 'Q' biotype of the whitefly, *Bemisia tabaci*, from tomatoes in the Almeria region of southern Spain were tested for resistance to three neonicotinoid insecticides (imidacloprid, thiamethoxam and acetamiprid), two insect growth regulators (buprofezin and pyriproxyfen), as well as abamectin and diafenthiuron. Compared to a strain collected in 1994, two strains obtained in 2000 showed strong resistance to all three neonicotinoids. The more recent strains also resisted buprofezin and pyriproxyfen, through mechanisms considered genetically distinct from that conferring neonicotinoid resistance. All strains retained full susceptibility to abamectin and diafenthiuron. The response to imidacloprid of F_1 female progeny of reciprocal crosses between neonicotinoid-susceptible and -resistant strains was intermediate to those of females of the parental strains.

INTRODUCTION

The commercial introduction of neonicotinoid insecticides has provided agriculture with valuable new tools for controlling some of the world's most damaging crop pests. Many of the major pest species targeted by neonicotinoids, including aphids, whiteflies, planthoppers and Colorado potato beetle, have a long history of developing resistance to older insecticides. In most cases, neonicotinoids have proved to be unaffected by compounds used previously (Cahill & Denholm, 1999; Denholm *et al.*, 2002), and are therefore ideally suited as components of integrated pest management (IPM) and insecticide resistance management (IRM) strategies. However, the speed and scale with which neonicotinoids (especially imidacloprid) were taken up by growers have also led to concerns over the prospects and implications of selecting for resistance to neonicotinoids themselves (e.g. Cahill & Denholm, 1999).

In general, neonicotinoids have proved relatively resilient to resistance, with still very few cases of pests acquiring levels of resistance capable of compromising field efficacy. One of the most notable exceptions relates to the cotton or tobacco whitefly, *Bemisia tabaci* Gennadius, a highly polyphagous pest causing direct damage through feeding and by transmitting virus diseases to a wide range of arable and horticultural crops. Resistance of *B. tabaci* to imidacloprid was first reported in the intensive horticultural production system occupying over 40,000 ha near Almeria in southern Spain. A number of strains collected from Almeria in 1994 and 1995, and tested using a systemic leaf-dip bioassay, showed significantly reduced mortality at a diagnostic concentration of imidacloprid (Cahill *et al.*, 1996a). At the time there was no evidence of this impairing the performance of imidacloprid in the field. More recently, resistance has increased in potency with strains exhibiting cross-resistance to other neonicotinoids (Nauen *et al.*, 2002).

Developments in the Almeria region constitute a significant problem in their own right, but also highlight the importance of developing control strategies to reduce reliance on neonicotinoids and to exploit a greater diversity of insecticide classes. In this paper we report on the responses of two imidacloprid-resistant strains *B. tabaci* from Spain to a range of neonicotinoid and non-neonicotinoid molecules, and provide preliminary results of experiments investigating the genetic characteristics of resistance to imidacloprid.

MATERIALS AND METHODS

Insect strains and rearing method

All whitefly strains were reared at Rothamsted on cotton (*Gossypium hirsutum*; cv. 'Deltapine 16') under a 16 h photoperiod at 27°C and without exposure to insecticides. Adults used in bioassays were between 2 and 8 days old.

The three strains of *B. tabaci* for which results are reported were as follows: ALM-1 – collected in the vicinity of Almeria from a tomato crop in 1994; SPAN-R1 and SPAN-R2 – two strains collected near Almeria from tomatoes in 2000. Based on native polyacrylamide gel electrophoresis of non-specific esterases, all three strains conformed to the 'Q' biotype of *B. tabaci*, which predominates on the Iberian Peninsula and occurs through the Mediterranean Basin including the Middle East (Horowitz *et al.*, 2003a).

Insecticides

All insecticides were applied as formulated products diluted to the required concentrations in an aqueous solution of 0.01% of the non-ionic wetter 'Agral' (Zeneca, UK). Compounds tested were imidacloprid (SL formulation, 20% a.i., 'Confidor'), thiamethoxam (WG formulation 25% a.i., 'Actara'), acetamiprid (SG formulation, 20% a.i., 'Mospilan'), pyriproxyfen (EC formulation, 0.86% a.i., 'Knack'), buprofezin (SC formulation, 25% a.i., 'Applaud'), abamectin (EC formulation, 0.18% a.i., 'Vertimec') and diafenthiuron (EC formulation, 25% a.i., 'Polo').

Bioassays

Leaf-dip assays for imidacloprid, thiamethoxam, acetamiprid, abamectin and diafenthiuron against adult whiteflies were based on the method published by Cahill *et al.* (1995), with leaf discs being dipped in insecticide solutions and adults being confined to these treated surfaces in ventilated Petri-dishes. Mortality was assessed after 48 h exposure for imidacloprid, thiamethoxam and abamectin. Mortality for acetamiprid and diafenthiuron was scored after 72 h. Bioassays for assessing the response of nymphs to buprofezin followed the method of Cahill *et al.* (1996b). Adults were confined in clip cages to cotton leaves trimmed into rectangles of approximately 40 mm x 50 mm, thereby providing a synchronised cohort of eggs. Leaves were dipped 11 days later (when whiteflies were at the 2nd nymphal instar) into either the required concentration of insecticide or into a control solution, and mortality was assessed when surviving insects had reached late fourth instar, 22-25 days after oviposition. The ovicidal activity of pyriproxyfen was determined following the method of Ishaaya & Horowitz (1995). Adult females were again confined on cotton leaves for 24 h in clip-cages and removed 24 h later. Leaves with eggs were dipped for 20 s into the required concentrations of formulated pyriproxyfen or in deionized water as a control. Eggs were counted one day after treatment and egg-hatch was determined 10 days later. All bioassays had 2-3 replicates per concentration, and each bioassay was repeated at least 3 times. Data from repeat bioassays were pooled for probit analysis to estimate dose-response lines and LC_{50} values.

Crossing experiments

Since different biotypes of *B. tabaci* often show partial or complete reproductive incompatibility, genetic crosses to investigate the inheritance of traits such as resistance should be performed on strains of the same biotype (Horowitz *et al.*, 2003b). For this work, we established reciprocal crosses between the ALM-1 (imidacloprid-susceptible) and SPAN-R1 (imidacloprid-resistant) strains, both of the Q biotype. Virgin adults were obtained by placing individual pupae with leaf material into individual wells of 96-well microplates until emergence (Horowitz *et al.*, 2003b). Males and females were then placed on cotton leaves in perspex leaf-boxes until the emergence of F_1 adult progeny. Due to the haplodiploid genetics of *B. tabaci* (Denholm *et al.*, 1998), females produced from reciprocal crosses were heterozygous for alleles from each parent, whereas male progeny were hemizygous for one of the maternal alleles. Responses of F_1 female progeny relative to those of their parents therefore provided a preliminary indication of the dominance of the gene or genes conferring resistance in the SPAN-R1 strain.

RESULTS AND DISCUSSION

Bioassays with neonicotinoids

LC_{50} values for ALM-1 (Table 1), collected from Almeria in 1994, were close to those obtained separately at Rothamsted for a standard susceptible strain (SUD-S) of *B. tabaci* that has been maintained in laboratory culture since 1978. Thus, although ALM-1 showed low levels of imidacloprid resistance at the time of collection (Cahill *et al.*, 1996a), it appeared to have reverted towards susceptibility in the intervening years. Both SPAN-R1 and SPAN-R2 showed strong (200-fold or greater) resistance to imidacloprid, which was also evident for the other two neonicotinoids tested, thiamethoxam and acetamiprid. This finding of cross-resistance encompassing several neonicotinoids is consistent with other studies on contemporary Spanish populations (Nauen *et al.*, 2002). The primary mechanism of resistance in Spain appears to be one of enhanced detoxification based on cytochrome P-450 dependent monooxygenases (Nauen *et al.*, 2002), which evidently show sufficiently broad substrate specificity to affect a range of molecules within the neonicotinoid class of chemistry.

Bioassays with other insecticides

LC_{50} values for the other four insecticides tested against ALM-1 (Table 1) were again an accurate reflection of baseline responses for these compounds. The two insect growth regulators (IGRs), buprofezin and pyriproxyfen, were both resisted by SPAN-R1 and SPAN-R2, with resistance levels for pyriproxyfen being 100-fold or more. These two compounds are, however, structurally and functionally very distinct from each other, buprofezin inhibiting chitin formation and pyriproxyfen being a juvenile hormone mimic affecting hormonal balance and disrupting embryogenesis (Ishaaya, 2001). The level of pyriproxyfen resistance, in SPAN-R2 especially, was similar to those reported in *B. tabaci* on cotton in some areas of Israel, where it occurs independently of responses to buprofezin and neonicotinoids (Horowitz *et al.*, 1999; A R Horowitz, pers. comm. 2002). Thus, although IGR resistance occurred alongside neonicotinoid resistance in SPAN-R1 and SPAN-R2, it seems certain that the mechanisms involved are genetically independent and have evolved separately under selection with the respective control agents. LC_{50} values for abamectin and diafenthiuron were consistent across all three strains, disclosing no evidence of resistance and demonstrating that these compounds remain fully effective against neonicotinoid-resistant populations.

Table 1. Response of three Spanish strains of *B. tabaci* to neonicotinoid and non-neonicotinoid insecticides (Figures shown are LC_{50} values computed by probit analysis and expressed as ppm a.i.)

Insecticide	ALM-1	SPAN-RI	SPAN-R2
Imidacloprid	10	2200	>5000
Thiamethoxam	15	800	1400
Acetamiprid	3.5	60	210
Buprofezin	0.3	1.2	4.0
Pyriproxyfen	0.001	0.1	0.7
Abamectin	0.02	0.01	0.007
Diafenthiuron	52	53	68

Crossing experiments

Both reciprocal crosses between ALM-1 and SPAN-R1 produced substantial numbers of female progeny, proving that successful mating had taken place. Dose-response relationships for imidacloprid against females of both parental strains are shown in Figure 1. Mortality data for SPAN-R1 above 1000 ppm were erratic and implied important pharmo-kinetic constraints on bioassays that exceed this concentration. Mortality data for F_1 progeny of the reciprocal crosses were similar, and therefore pooled for presentation in Figure 1. These F_1 responses, although intermediate to those of the parental strains, appeared closer to those of ALM-1.

Further work is required to validate this result for a larger number of strains, and for neonicotinoids other than imidacloprid. The implications of heterozygote expression for the speed of resistance selection must also be interpreted with care, given that a primary consequence of haplodiploidy is that resistance genes arising by mutation are exposed to selection from the outset in hemizygous males, irrespective of intrinsic dominance or recessiveness (Denholm *et al.*, 1998).

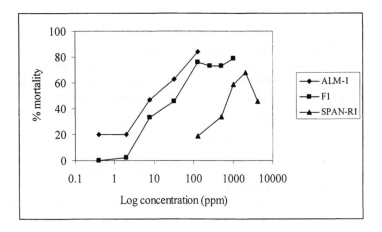

Figure 1. Response of parental females and F_1 female progeny to imidacloprid.

CONCLUSIONS

Although cases of neonicotinoid resistance in insects are still rare and relatively localised (Denholm *et al.*, 2002), developments with *B. tabaci* in Spain have highlighted the potential of pests to adapt and withstand exposure to this important group of insecticides. The status of whitefly resistance to neonicotinoids in other countries is less well documented, abut there are recent confirmed reports from Israel (A R Horowitz, pers. comm. 2003), Australia (R Gunning, pers. comm. 2002), Cyprus (M Hadjistylii, unpublished data), and isolated cases from greenhouses elsewhere in Europe (Nauen *et al.*, 2002). The homology of the underlying mechanism(s) to that present in Spain is largely unknown, as are the implications for cross-resistance between neonicotinoids and to unrelated molecules. Studies to compare the genetic and toxicological characteristics of resistance in strains from different parts of the world are clearly a priority, as is work to exploit lessons from regions such as the south-western USA where neonicotinoid resistance has so far been combated successfully (Denholm *et al.*, 1998, 2002; Li *et al.*, 2000). Management strategies based on the restriction and co-ordination of neonicotinoid use, coupled with alternation of chemical groups, currently offer greatest scope for sustaining the efficacy of neonicotinoids against *B. tabaci* and other target pest species (Denholm *et al.*, 2002).

ACKNOWLEDGEMENTS

We thank Syngenta for financial support. Rothamsted Research receives grant-aided support from the Biotechnology and Biological Sciences Research Council of the United Kingdom.

REFERENCES

Cahill M; Byrne F J; Gorman K; Denholm I; Devonshire A L (1995). Pyrethroid and organophosphate resistance in the tobacco whitefly *Bemisia tabaci* (Homoptera, Aleyrodidae). *Bulletin of Entomological Research* **85,** 181-187.

Cahill M; Denholm I (1999). Managing resistance to the chloronicotinyl insecticides – rhetoric or reality? In: *Nicotinoid insecticides and the nicotinic acetylcholinesterase receptor*, eds I Yamamoto & J E Casida, pp. 253-270. Springer-Verlag: Tokyo.

Cahill M; Gorman K; Day S; Denholm I; Elbert A; Nauen R (1996a). Baseline determination and detection of resistance to imidacloprid in *Bemisia tabaci* (Homoptera: Aleyrodidae). *Bulletin of Entomological Research* **86**, 343-349.

Cahill M; Jarvis W; Gorman K; Denholm I (1996b). Resolution of baseline responses and documentation of resistance to buprofezin in *Bemisia tabaci* (Homoptera: Aleyrodidae). *Bulletin of Entomological Research* **86,** 117-122.

Denholm I; Cahill M; Dennehy T J; Horowitz A R (1998). Challenges with managing insecticide resistance in agricultural pests, exemplified by the whitefly *Bemisia tabaci*. *Philosphical Transactions of the Royal Society Series B* **353**, 1757-1767.

Denholm I; Devine G; Foster S; Gorman K; Nauen R (2002). Incidence and management of insect resistance to neonicotinoids. *Proceedings of the BCPC Conference – Pests and Diseases 2002*, **1**, 161-168.

Horowitz A R; Denholm I; Gorman K; Cenis J L; Kontsedalov S; Ishaaya I (2003a). Biotype Q of *Bemisia tabaci* identified in Israel. *Phytoparasitica* **31**, 1-5.

Horowitz A R; Mendelson Z; Cahill M; Denholm I; Ishaaya I (1999). Managing resistance to the insect growth regulator, pyriproxyfen, in *Bemisia tabaci*. *Pesticide Science* **55**, 272-276.

Horowitz A R; Gorman K; Ross G; Denholm I (2003b). Inheritance of pyriproxyfen resistance in the whitefly, *Bemisia tabaci*. *Archives of Insect Biochemistry and Physiology* (*in press*).

Ishaaya I (2001). Biochemical processes related to insecticide action: an overview. In: *Biochemical sites of insecticide action and resistance*, ed. I Ishaaya, pp. 1-16. Springer-Verlag: Berlin.

Ishaaya I; Horowitz A R (1995). Pyriproxyfen, a novel insect growth regulator for controlling whiteflies: mechanism and resistance management. *Pesticide Science* **43**, 227-232.

Li Y; Dennehy T J; Li X; Wigert M E (2000). Susceptibility of Arizona whiteflies to chloronicotinyl insecticides and IGRs: new developments in the 1999 season. *Proceedings Beltwide Cotton Conferences, San Antonio, TX, USA,* **2**, 1325-1330.

Nauen R; Stumpf N; Elbert A (2002). Toxicological and mechanistic studies on neonicotinoid cross resistance in Q-type *Bemisia tabaci* (Hemiptera: Aleyrodidae). *Pest Management Science* **58**, 868-874.

Negative cross-resistance between indoxacarb and pyrethroids in the cotton bollworm, *Helicoverpa armigera*, in Australia: a tool for resistance management

R V Gunning
NSW Agriculture, RMB 944 Calala Lane, Tamworth, NSW, Australia 2340
Email: robin.gunning@agric.nsw.gov.au

A L Devonshire
Rothamsted Research, Harpenden, Hertfordshire, AL5 2JQ, UK

ABSTRACT

Helicoverpa armigera is Australia's most important agricultural pest, especially on cotton. Insecticide resistance in *H. armigera* is, however, an enduring threat to the economic production of cotton in Australia and pyrethroid resistance has been of particular concern. Insecticide use against *H. armigera* on cotton is subject to an insecticide resistance management strategy and new insecticides such as indoxacarb are particularly important. Indoxacarb requires bio-activation to a toxic metabolite. Our studies show that, in Australian *H. armigera*, this is performed by esterase isoenzymes with conversion to the active metabolite of indoxacarb being correlated with esterase titre. Pyrethroid-resistant *H. armigera* has overproduced esterases and our results show greater indoxacarb conversion compared to susceptible strains. Indoxacarb had significantly better efficacy against more highly pyrethroid-resistant strains of *H. armigera*. Negative cross-resistance between indoxacarb and pyrethroid resistance should prove a valuable tool for the management of pyrethroid resistance in Australian *H. armigera*.

INTRODUCTION

The cotton bolloworm, *Helicoverpa armigera*, is arguably Australia's most important agricultural pest, especially on cotton and other summer crops. *H. armigera* has a long history of insecticide resistance in Australia (involving DDT, pyrethroids, carbamates, organophosphates and endosulfan), and resistance is an enduring threat to the economic production of cotton. Pyrethroid resistance in *H. armigera* has been of particular concern and has become fixed in some *H. armigera* populations. Pyrethroid resistance is mediated by overproduced esterase isoenzymes that metabolise and sequester pyrethroids (Gunning *et al.*, 1996)

Since the early 1980s, the use of insecticides against *H. armigera* on cotton has been regulated by a resistance management strategy to manage old chemistry such as the pyrethroids and the registration and deployment of new insecticides with novel modes of action such as indoxacarb. Indoxacarb is a potent sodium channel blocker with broad-spectrum efficacy against Lepidopteran larvae (Wing *et al.*, 1998). It requires bio-activation to an active, toxic metabolite, a decarbomethoxylated indoxacarb (DCJW). Studies indicate that indoxacarb conversion can be prevented by esterase inhibitors (Wing *et al.*, 1998). This paper describes how, in Australian *H. armigera*, indoxacarb is activated by esterase isoenzymes and how, as a consequence, there is negative cross-resistance between pyrethroids and indoxacarb in the species.

MATERIALS AND METHODS

Insects and bioassay

A laboratory susceptible strain of *H. armigera* was used in these studies, as well as pyrethroid-resistant strains (obtained by selecting with fenvalerate). Third-instar contact-toxicity bioassays were used. Technical grade fenvalerate [(*RS*) -α-cyano-3-phenoxybenzyl (*RS*)-2-(4-chlorophenyl)-3-methylbutyreate] and technical indoxacarb [(*S*)-7-chloro-2,5-dihydro-2-[(methoxycarbonyl)indeno[1,2,-e]=[1,3,4]oxadiazin-2-ylcarbonyl]-´4-(trifluromethoxy) carbanilate] were dissolved in acetone and serially diluted concentrations prepared. Larvae were treated with 1 μl of solution. After dosage, the test larvae were held at 25° C with adequate food. Mortality was assessed 2 (fenvalerate) and 4 (indoxacarb) days after treatment. The data were analysed by probit analysis. Resistance factors were calculated as the ratio of the resistant LD_{50} / susceptible LD_{50}.

Esterase activity

Total esterase activity of pyrethroid-susceptible and resistant larval homogenates were detected using 1-naphthyl acetate as a substrate and kinetic assays (Gunning *et al.*, 1996). Larvae (3 – 4 mg) were homogenised in 2M phosphate buffer (pH 7.0) with 0.01% Triton X-100 (50 μl per 4 mg/insect tissue). Aliquots (10 μl) were transferred to a microplate and 240 μl of phosphate buffer (pH 6) containing 0.6% fast blue salt RR and 1.86% 1-naphthyl acetate added. Assays were run immediately on a BioRad 3550 microplate reader in kinetic mode at 450 nm.

Metabolism experiments

Larvae were homogenised in Tris buffer (pH 8, 0.05% Triton X-100). Indoxacarb was added to a final concentration of 10^{-4}M, total volume 200 μl. The homogenates were incubated for 140 min at 25°C. The reaction was stopped by the addition of 200 μl of very cold (-20°C) acetone. 200 μl of samples were loaded onto reverse phase, fluorescent, silica gel, thin layer chromatography plates. The running solvent was methanol:water (9:1) made up to 1% formic acid. Samples were co-chromatographed with indoxacarb and DCJW standards. Indoxacarb and DCJW were visualised under UV light and quantified by density scanning.

Similar experiments were performed with purified *H. armigera* esterase (from pyrethroid-resistant strains). Purified esterase was diluted in Tris buffer to concentrations of 1740, 870, 435, 218 and 109 mOD/min per 5 μl aliquot. A buffer only control was included.

RESULTS

Bioassay data

Bioassays showed a strong correlation between the toxicity of indoxacarb and pyrethroid resistance factor in the *H. armigera* strains tested (Figure 1). Negative cross-resistance between indoxacarb susceptibility and pyrethroids was therefore indicated. Indoxacarb had significantly greater toxicity against the more highly pyrethroid-resistant strains. There was an approximately 10-fold difference in the toxicity of indoxacarb between *H. armigera* strains and 150-fold resistance to fenvalerate.

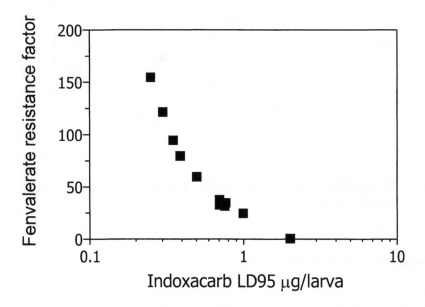

Figure 1.   Toxicity of indoxacarb to strains of pyrethroid-resistant Australian *H. armigera*.

Esterase analysis

The mean esterase activity in each pyrethroid-resistant strain was determined and plotted against indoxacarb toxicity. Increasing esterase activity in the pyrethroid-resistant strains of *H. armigera*, gave rise to greater susceptibility to indoxacarb (Figure 2). Increasing esterase activity is correlated with increasing pyrethroid resistance factor (Gunning *et al*., 1996).

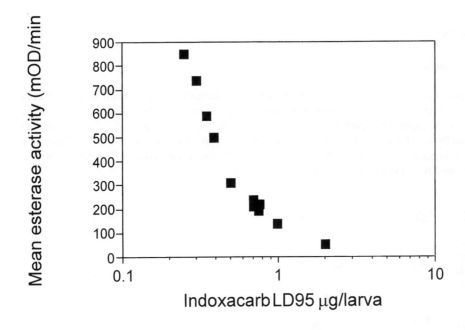

Figure 2.   Relationship between total esterase and indoxacarb toxicity in pyrethroid-resistant strains of Australian *H. armigera.*

Bioactivation of indoxacarb by *H. armigera*

A good separation of indoxacarb and the metabolite DCJW was achieved by the thin layer chromatography solvent system and RF values for were 0.64 and 0.55 respectively.

When indoxacarb was incubated with *H. armigera* homogenate there was clear evidence of the formation of DCJW and that conversion was related to esterase concentration (Figure 3). Increasing esterase activity resulted in increased activation of indoxacarb to DCJW.

Indoxacarb was also incubated for 24 h with varying concentrations of purified esterase associated with resistance in *H. armigera*. Conversion to DCJW was directly proportional to esterase concentration and complete conversion could be achieved at higher esterase concentrations (Figure 4)

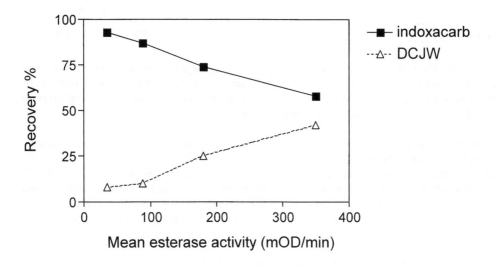

Figure 3.   *In-vitro* activation of indoxacarb by *H. armigera* homogenates with
             varying concentrations of pyrethroid resistance-related esterase.

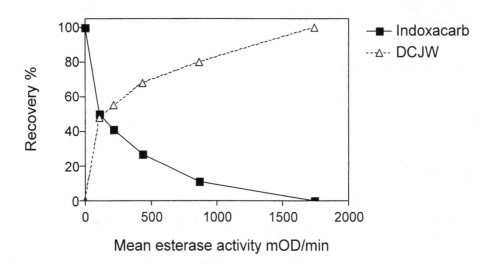

Figure 4.   *In-vitro* activation of indoxacarb to DCJW by varying concentrations
             of purified *H. armigera* pyrethroid resistance-related esterase.

CONCLUSIONS

Our results show that, in Australian *H. armigera*, indoxacarb is bio-activated to the toxic metabolite after topical application of indoxacarb.   *In-vitro* studies showed that in *H. armigera* indoxacarb was activated to DCJW by pyrethroid resistance associated esterase enzymes.   Activation rates were proportional to the esterase titre.

Bioassays of strains of pyrethroid-resistant *H. armigera* showed that indoxacarb toxicity increased with an increasing pyrethroid resistance factor.   The increased indoxacarb toxicity was correlated with increased titres of esterase associated with pyrethroid resistance in the *H. armigera* strains.   Clearly, the negative cross-resistance exhibited between pyrethroid and indoxacarb in Australian *H. armigera* results from increased conversion of indoxacarb to the active metabolite by esterases also involved in the hydrolysis or sequestration of pyrethroids in resistant strains.

Despite resistance problems, pyrethroids have remained a valuable, low cost insecticide group for controlling *H. armigera* on cotton in Australia.   However, pyrethroid performance has declined markedly in recent years.   While indoxacarb is an excellent insecticide in its own right, negative cross-resistance to pyrethroids gives us an exciting tool to restore some measure of pyrethroid susceptibility.   Indoxacarb has significantly greater toxicity to highly pyrethroid-resistant *H. armigera* and could be applied to reduce pyrethroid resistance levels. As indoxacarb is reliant on esterase for bio-activation in *H. armigera*, we should be cautious, however, in tank-mixing with other esterase-inhibiting insecticides such as organophosphates and pyrethroids.

ACKNOWLEDGEMENTS

This work was partially funded by the Cotton Research and Development Corporation, Australia. Rothamsted Research receives grant-aided support from the BBSRC.

REFERENCES

Gunning R V; Moores G D; Devonshire A L (1996). Esterases and es-fenvalarate resistance in Australian *Helicoverpa armigera* (Hubner) (Lepidoptera: Noctuidae). *Pesticide Biochemistry and Physiology* **54,** 12-23.

Wing K D; Schnee M E; Sacher M; Connair M (1988). A novel oxidiazine insecticide is bioactivated in Lepidopteran larvae. *Archives of Insect Biochemistry and Physiology* **37**, 91-103.

Biological evaluation of spiromesifen against *Bemisia tabaci* and an assessment of resistance risks

F Guthrie, I Denholm, G J Devine
Rothamsted Research, Harpenden, Hertfordshire, AL5 2JQ, UK
Email: greg.devine@bbsrc.ac.uk

R Nauen
Bayer CropScience, Leverkusen, D-5136, Germany

ABSTRACT

The efficacy of spiromesifen was evaluated against insecticide-resistant 'Q' biotypes of *Bemisia tabaci* from Israel and Spain. The compound was extremely effective against early instars (LC_{50}s of $0.1 - 6.2$ ppm for 12-d-old nymphs). One Spanish 'Q' type was significantly less susceptible (15-fold). Further selection of that strain with spiromesifen however, did not select for increasing resistance. Spiromesifen was highly effective against pyriproxyfen- and imidacloprid-resistant whitefly. It also had pronounced transovariole effects on oviposition and egg hatch. Given the current difficulties experienced in the control of 'Q' biotype *B. tabaci* around the Mediterranean, it is likely that spiromesifen will be a valuable addition to the available chemical options. We consider that the efficacy of this compound is unlikely to be compromised by existing resistance mechanisms.

INTRODUCTION

Over the past ten years, the whitefly *Bemisia tabaci* (Homoptera: Aleyrodidae) has become a devastating insect pest of horticultural crops (especially tomatoes, curcubits and peppers) in southern Europe, North Africa and the Middle East, and it remains a considerable threat to protected horticulture in northern Europe. It can cause serious crop losses by direct feeding, but its pest status has increased dramatically due to the widespread occurrence of several whitefly-transmitted plant viruses (e.g. *tomato yellows leaf curl virus*; TYLCV).

The effective management of *B. tabaci* and its associated plant viruses poses a severe challenge to scientists and the horticultural and pest management industries. Although much work is being conducted to formulate management tactics, including cultural, physical and biological control methods, these are proving difficult to implement on a large scale. This is due in part to the fact that *B. tabaci* is an extremely efficient vector of some viruses (e.g TYLCV; Mehta *et al.*, 1994) and growers can tolerate only very low thresholds of insects. Insecticides therefore remain an integral component of *B. tabaci* control.

There is however, in this species, an alarming increase in resistance not only to more conventional insecticides but to novel and environmentally compatible compounds such as buprofezin, pyriproxyfen and the neonicotinoids (Horowitz & Ishaaya, 1992; Elbert & Nauen, 2000; Ishaaya & Horowitz, 1995), all of which are highly relevant to Southern European horticulture.

The current study was conducted to ascertain whether the novel compound spiromesifen (Nauen *et al.*, 2002) might be a useful addition and / or alternative to the chemical tools already available for whitefly control in the Mediterranean region. The test populations used were predominantly of the 'Q' biotype, as this is the biotype that is currently perceived as being the most problematic in the Mediterranean basin.

MATERIALS AND METHODS

All assays were conducted using formulated spiromesifen supplied by Bayer CropScience on strains of *B. tabaci* listed in Table 1.

Table 1. Biotype and response of strains of *Bemisia tabaci* to imidacloprid and pyriproxyfen

Strain	Year collected	Origin	Biotype	Imidacloprid / pyriproxyfen resistance[a]
SUDS	1978	Sudan	-	None
ALM1	1994	Spain	Q	Slight /none
ESP99	1999	Spain	Q	Medium/none
EL EJIDO	2000	Spain	Q	High/medium
HOF CARMEL	1998	Israel	Q	Medium/medium
PYRI-R	Lab. selected	Israel	Q	None/high

[a]unpublished data (Rothamsted Research)

Effects on second instars (12-d-old nymphs)

All larval-dip bioassay protocols were similar to those published by Cahill *et al.* (1996). All except three true leaves of a cotton plant were removed. The remaining three were cut to a size of c. 20 cm². Plants were infested with adult whiteflies in clip cages at c. 20 mass-reared females per leaf for 48 h. Afterwards the whiteflies were removed and, at the appropriate point (when the desired stage was predominant), the infested leaves were dipped in serial dilutions of insecticide for 10 s. Percentage mortality was scored by counting all dead, live, hatched or unhatched eggs and nymphs at day 21, once all survivors had progressed through to the pupal instars.

Selection experiments

On three occasions the population most tolerant of the spiromesifen compounds (ESP99) was further selected by dipping 12-d-old nymphs in 10 ppm spiromesifen solutions and assaying the F1 progeny of the survivors.

Transovariole effects on egg-hatch

Adults were exposed to different concentrations of material on leaf boxes for 72 h. Survivors were then clip-caged to whole plants for a further 48 h. Subsequent hatch of the resulting eggs was monitored at day 10. This method is analogous to that used by Ishaaya & Horowitz (1992) for assessing the transovariole effects of pyriproxyfen.

Larger scale illustrations of spiromesifen efficacy against resistant *B. tabaci*

In order to illustrate the efficacy of spiromesifen on large, insecticide-resistant populations of mixed life stages under 'field conditions', sizable populations of *B. tabaci* were established on cotton plants in large population chambers (Rowland *et al.*, 1990).

Effect of spiromesifen on a pyriproxyfen-resistant population

An Israeli 'Q' biotype strain, resistant to imidacloprid and pyriproxyfen (Hof Carmel) was used for this illustration. Thirty-one days after infestation, with populations of >2000 insects spread over six cotton plants (5 – 6 node stage), these simulators were sprayed to near run-off with the recommended rates of spiromesifen (Bayer CropScience, 150 ppm a.i.) or pyriproxyfen (Sumitomo, Sumilarv; 40 ppm a.i.).

Effect of spiromesifen on an imidacloprid-resistant population

A Spanish, imidacloprid-resistant 'Q' biotype (ESP99) was used for this illustration. Pots containing cotton plants were treated with the recommended field rate of imidacloprid (Scotts, Intercept 70WG, 0.02 g/l of compost) or were left untreated. Two days after the treatment date all plants, whether imidacloprid-treated or not, were infested with whitefly. On day 12, when large numbers of nymphs were present on the plants, untreated plants were sprayed with the recommended rate of spiromesifen.

RESULTS AND DISCUSSION

Bioassays

The LC_{50}s for 12-d-old (2nd instar) nymphs varied between 0.10 ppm (Pyri-R) and 6.16 ppm (ESP99) (Table 2). ESP99 was significantly more tolerant than the SUDS standard (15-fold), but this tolerance could not be further selected for. None of the tolerance patterns seen correlated with imidacloprid or pyriproxyfen resistance.

Effects on egg-lay and egg-hatch

The effects of pre-exposing adults to spiromesifen residues for 72 h were consistent (Fig. 1). At concentrations of 10 - 100 ppm, the mean number of eggs laid by females over a 72-h period was reduced dramatically. Moreover, the numbers of these eggs hatching was also affected. The combined effects of spiromesifen on egg-lay and egg-hatch clearly have the potential to severely limit fecundity in *B. tabaci*.

Figure 1.　Effect of exposing adults of *Bemisia tabaci* to spiromesifen for 72 h on subsequent egg-lay over the next 72 h on a fresh, untreated surface (means and SEs).

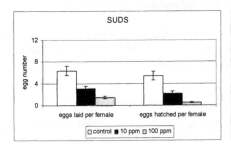

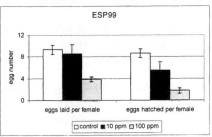

Table 2.　Mortality of 12-d-old *Bemisia tabaci* nymphs, in response to spiromesifen treatment

Strain	n	LC$_{50}$ (ppm)[a]	95% CLs	Slope	RF
SUDS	20528	0.42 b	0.25 to 0.64	0.96 ±0.02	-
PYRI-R	898	0.10 a	0.02 to 0.22	0.99 ±0.10	0.2
EL EJIDO	4744	0.36 ab	0.17 to 0.70	0.68 ±0.02	0.8
Hof Carmel	3385	0.90 bc	0.25 to 2.44	0.68 ±0.03	2.1
ALM1	3830	1.24 bc	0.56 to 2.35	0.92 ±0.04	3.0
ESP99[b]	7067	6.16 d	3.12 to 10.87	0.84 ±0.03	14.7
ESP99-sel (x2)[b]	3266	2.59 cd	1.05 to 5.03	1.00 ±0.05	6.2
ESP99-sel (x3)[b]	878	3.26 cd	2.30 to 4.32	1.62 ±0.20	7.7

[a] Limits followed by different letters denote significant differences (p<0.05).
[b] Sub-populations of ESP99 were further selected by spiromesifen (10 ppm) to ascertain whether the variation in tolerance could be increased.

Laboratory bioassays, in which insects are treated topically or confined to treated leaf surfaces for prescribed periods, are convenient for screening the intrinsic toxicity of insecticides against different life stages. They are not necessarily very informative about efficacy under field conditions where deposition is usually non-uniform and where some stages may avoid exposure by inhabiting parts of the plants not reached by insecticide. Additional illustrations of the efficacy of the spiromesifen compound, on large populations of insecticide-resistant whitefly, were therefore considered desirable.

The compound was very effective against imidacloprid-resistant whitefly (Figure 2a). At 48 d (40 d after soil application of imidacloprid and 37 d after spraying with spiromesifen the full rate of spiromesifen had reduced numbers to just 5% of those that had been treated with the full rate of imidacloprid.

Spiromesifen was also extremely effective against pyriproxyfen-resistant whitefly (Figure 2b). Twenty-five days after spraying, the population sprayed with spiromesifen was still in decline (numbering < 500 individuals) whilst that sprayed with pyriproxyfen had returned to pre-spray levels (numbering > 4000 individuals).

Figure 2.   The effect of spiromesifen on imidacloprid –resistant whitefly (a) and on pyriproxyfen-resistant whitefly (b).

a.   b.

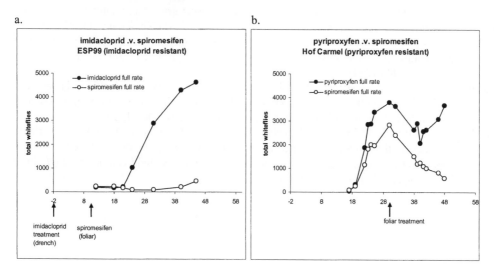

CONCLUSION

Spiromesifen is clearly highly effective against *B. tabaci*. It is lethal to young instars at low concentrations and has additional effects on oviposition and on egg hatch. Its efficacy is unaffected by imidacloprid or pyriproxyfen resistance. It has considerable potential as a chemical control tool for this pest.

ACKNOWLEDGEMENTS

Rothamsted Research receives grant-aided support from the Biotechnology and Biological Sciences Research Council of the United Kingdom

REFERENCES

Cahill M; Jarvis W; Gorman K; Denholm I (1996). Resolution of baseline responses and documentation of resistance to buprofezin in *Bemisia tabaci* (Homoptera: Aleyrodidae). *Bulletin of Entomological Research* **86,** 117-122.

Elbert A; Nauen R (2000). Resistance of *Bemisia tabaci* (Homoptera: Aleyrodidae) to insecticides in southern Spain with Special Reference to Neonicotinoids. *Pesticide Science* **56,** 60-64.

Horowitz A R; Ishaaya I (1992). Susceptibility of the sweet-potato whitefly (Homoptera, Aleyrodidae) to buprofezin during the cotton season. *Journal of Economic Entomology* **85,** 318-324.

Ishaaya I.; Horowitz A R (1992). Novel phenoxy juvenile hormone analog (pyriproxyfen) suppresses embryogenesis and adult emergence of sweetpotato whitefly (Homoptera: Aleyrodidae). *Journal of Economic Entomology* **85,** 2113-2117.

Ishaaya I; Horowitz A R (1995). Pyriproxyfen, a novel insect growth-regulator for controlling whiteflies – mechanisms and resistance management. *Pesticide Science* **43,** 227-232

Mehta P; Wyman J A; Nakhla M K; Maxwell D P (1994). Transmission of tomato yellow leaf curl geminivirus by *Bemisia tabaci* (Homoptera: Aleyrodidae). *Journal of Economic Entomology* **87,** 1291-1297.

Nauen R; Bretschneider T; Brueck E; Elbert A; Reckmann U; Wachendorff U; Tiemann R (2002). BSN 2060 - A novel compound for whitefly and spider mite control. *Proceedings of the BCPC Conference - Pests & Diseases 2002,* **1,** 39-44

Rowland M W; Pye B; Stribley M; Hackett B; Denholm I; Sawicki R M (1990). Insecticide resistance in the whitefly, *Bemisia tabaci* Gennadius. I. Apparatus and techniques for rearing and treating insect with insecticide under simulated field conditions. *Bulletin of Entomological Research* **80,** 209-216.

Fluoxastrobin: risk assessment and anti-resistance management strategy for seed treatment application in winter wheat

I Haeuser-Hahn, K H Kuck, A Suty-Heinze, A Mehl, P Evans
Bayer CropScience, Alfred-Nobel Str. 50, D-40789 Monheim, Germany
Email: Isolde.Haeuser-Hahn@bayercropscience.com

ABSTRACT

Fluoxastrobin is a novel broad-spectrum strobilurin (QoI) fungicide from the chemical class of dihydro-dioxazines. Applied as a seed treatment, fluoxastrobin shows very good efficacy at 5-10 g a.i./100 kg seed against seed- and soil-borne pathogens such as *Microdochium nivale* and *Tilletia caries* but no activity against wind-borne diseases. In the case of strobilurins, strains of several pathogens targeted by foliar application have developed field resistance to the QoI fungicides. As fluoxastrobin is the first QoI fungicide expected to be registered for application to cereal seeds in Europe, a very detailed risk assessment has been undertaken. Additionally, extensive base-line sensitivity studies and investigations on the chemodynamic behaviour have been carried out. This assessment identified a somewhat enhanced risk only in the case of *M. nivale* as this pathogen may be targeted by QoIs and by fluoxastrobin from both seed and foliar application within a crop/season. A robust resistance management strategy will therefore be implemented and fluoxastrobin will be marketed for both seed and foliar use only in combination with DMI-fungicides, particularly prothioconazole (which is also effective against *M. nivale*), providing a product with complementary and excellent efficacy against economically important seed- and soil-borne diseases whilst providing an appropriate anti-resistance management strategy in line with FRAC guidelines.

INTRODUCTION

Fluoxastrobin (code name: HEC 5725) belongs to the chemical class of the methoxyimino-dihydro-dioxazines. This fungicide is a strobilurin analogue and binds to the Q_o–ubiqinone binding-site of the cytochrome bc_1 subunit of complex III (Becker *et al.*, 1981). Fluoxastrobin shows cross-resistance to other QoI fungicides. Fluoxastrobin controls economically important pathogens from all fungal classes by inhibition of mitochondrial respiration. Targeted as foliar application in combination with a DMI (prothioconazole), diseases controlled by fluoxastrobin include: septoria leaf spot and glume blotch, brown and stripe rust, tan spot, scald and net blotch (Dutzmann *et al.*, 2002). As fluoxastrobin is the first QoI fungicide expected to be registered not only for foliar application but also for treatment of winter wheat seeds in Europe, an extensive risk assessment has been undertaken. This analysis was based on studies including field trials, base-line sensitivity assessment, chemodynamic behaviour and quantification of residues.

MATERIALS AND METHODS

Assessment of spectrum of efficacy under field conditions

Numerous field trials were carried out in compliance with approved guidelines from 1997 to 2001 in order to establish the optimum use pattern for fluoxastrobin and to characterize the effect of a seed treatment containing fluoxastrobin on wind–borne diseases such as powdery mildew or septoria leaf spot (*Septoria tritici*). As wheat is normally sown relatively late in autumn, the incidence of mildew infection tends to be low. Furthermore, the appearance of resistance to QoI fungicides in winter wheat since 1999 did not allow a trial series to be made over several years. For this reason, characterization of activity on powdery mildew was performed on barley, as barley is sown some weeks earlier and is more regularly prone to mildew infections.

Sensitivity profile of *Microdochium nivale* populations

To obtain isolates of *Microdochium nivale*, kernels originating from grain samples taken from different cereal-growing areas in Europe were surface-sterilized with sodium hypochlorite immediately after harvest and placed in Petri dishes on potato dextrose agar. After incubation under near-UV radiation at 18°C for 6 days, mycelia and conidiospores could be microscopically identified and single spore isolates generated on the same media. For determination of baseline sensitivity, a microtitre test system was used. For this, potato dextrose broth was treated with different concentrations of fluoxastrobin a.i. (0.0003, 0.001, 0.003, 0.01, 0.03, 0.1 and 0.3 mg/l) and used to fill wells of a 96-well microtitre plate (two wells per concentration). Then, each well was inoculated with 200 conidiospores of a single-spore isolate and incubated for 6 days at 20°C and 150 rpm in darkness. Two untreated wells inoculated with the same isolate served as a control. After incubation, the mycelial growth was measured photometrically and EC_{50} values were calculated on the basis of different light transmission depending on mycelial density.

Systemicity studies with radio-labeled active ingredients

In controlled systemicity studies, wheat seeds (cv. Kanzler) were treated with ^{14}C-labelled fluoxastrobin, as FS-formulation, at 15 g a.i./100 kg of seed. Seeds were planted into an artificial substrate (LECA) and maintained at 18°C and 70% relative humidity under hydroponic cultivation conditions. Artificial light was given for 12 h/day. At the end of the experiment, plants were harvested and dried. The distribution of radioactivity was determined with the aid of an image analyser (Fuji X BAS 2000); illumination period, 24 h. The false colour processing was done with the software TINA.

Determination of fungicide concentrations in the second and third leaf

To investigate residue levels in the growing crop, green-mass samples (untreated, fluoxastrobin 10 g a.i./dt seed, fluoxastrobin + azole 7.5 + 7.5 g a.i./dt seed) were taken from a field trial at the 2-leaf and 3-leaf stages. With standard residue methods (method 00649), the concentration of fungicidally active ingredients in the whole shoot was determined.

RESULTS AND DISCUSSION

Field efficacy of fluoxastrobin

Results of field trials show that fluoxastrobin, when applied as a seed treatment at the proposed dosage of <5-10 g/dt seed, had no significant systemic effect on the leaf pathogens *Blumeria graminis* (barley powdery mildew) or *Septoria tritici* (Table 1). Therefore, seed treatment is not expected to cause significant selection pressure on leaf, stem and ear pathogens such as *Blumeria graminis* or *Septoria tritici*.

According to the efficacy spectrum (Table 2), *Microdochium nivale* is the only important pathogen which may be targeted by QoI fungicides and by fluoxastrobin from both seed and foliar application within a crop/season. Therefore, *M. nivale* is the only important pathogen for which, theoretically, there could be an enhanced risk of resistance.

Table 1.   *In-vivo* activity of fluoxastrobin against wind-borne fungi after seed treatment in trials in Germany

Pathogen	Dose of fluoxastrobin (g a.i./dt)	% disease control[a]	
		Trial 1	Trial 2
Blumeria graminis f.sp. *hordei*	untreated	(26.7%)	(5.7%)
	10	0	7[ab]
Septoria tritici	untreated	(7%)	(7%)
	5	0	0
	10	0	0
	15	0	0

[a] % infection in untreated wheat is shown in brackets.
[b] Statistically not significant using t-test at $p < 0.05$.

Table 2.   Summary of *in-vivo* spectrum of activity of fluoxastrobin against different fungi after seed and foliar application in wheat

Pathogen (disease)	Efficacy level of fluoxastrobin under field conditions	
	Seed treatment ($\leq$ 10 g/dt seed)	Foliar application (recommended rate)
Blumeria graminis f.sp. *tritici* (barley mildew)	-	+/+++
Septoria tritici (septoria leaf spot)	-	+++
Ustilago spp. (rusts)	++	-
Tilletia caries (bunt)	+++	-
Fusarium culmorum; F. avenaceum; *Gibberella zeae* (fusarium ear blight)	+	-/+
Microdochium nivale (seedling blight; snow mould)	+++	++/+++
Pseudocercosporella herpotrichoides (eyespot)	-	+/++

-, no activity; +, low activity; ++, moderate activity; +++, high activity.

Base-line sensitivity monitoring of *Microdochium nivale* towards fluoxastrobin

The sensitivity profile of *Microdochium nivale*, established on the basis of 308 single spore isolates originating from France, Great Britain, Germany and the Netherlands shows that mean EC_{50} values (in mg/l) varied between 0.0016 and 0.0049 at the maximum over all regions, indicating very small differences in sensitivity towards fluoxastrobin (Table 3). Moreover, the standard deviation in all regions was low and the factor $mEC_{50}max$ / mEC_{50} min over all tested isolates is very small (value: 3.1). This narrow sensitivity profile shows that the population of *M. nivale* is very homogeneous and allows the assumption that this fungal population has, up to now, not been exposed to a significant selection pressure by QoI fungicides.

Table 3. Sensitivity base-line of *Microdochium nivale* towards fluoxastrobin (EC_{50} in mg/l) from different regions of Europe in the year 2000

Country: region or department	n	mEC_{50} value	Standard deviation
France:			
Nord Pas de Calais, Picardie	77	0.0023	0.0011
Bretagne. Loire Atlantique	11	0.0020	0.0006
Bourgogne	2	0.0024	0.0012
Centre	13	0.0020	0.0009
Pays de la Loire. Poitou-Charentes	3	0.0027	0.0011
Cher. Nievre	7	0.0022	0.0004
Aude. Bouches du Rhone	2	0.0026	0.0004
Gers	6	0.0017	0.0006
Indre et Loire. Sarthe	10	0.0022	0.0007
Alsace	11	0.0021	0.0008
Champagne-Ardennes	14	0.0022	0.0006
Haute Garonne	4	0.0019	0.0003
Aisne. Alpes maritimes	6	0.0021	0.0004
Maignelay	3	0.0020	0.0005
Aube. Yonne	10	0.0021	0.0006
Haute Normandie	1	0.0049	
Ile de France	3	0.0016	0.0006
Rougemontier	8	0.0025	0.0007
others	15	0.0020	0.0005
UK:			
Weymouth	2	0.0016	0.0004
Germany:			
Burscheid	7	0.0017	0.0004
Weikersheim	18	0.0020	0.0006
Haidenhofen	2	0.0018	0.0002
Netherlands:			
Moerstraten. Fijnaart	32	0.0022	0.0009
Others	41	0.0024	0.0008
Mean		0.0022	0.0006
Total	308		

Systemicity studies with radio-labelled active ingredients

It is a general experience that uptake rates in hydroponic systems are significantly greater than under practical conditions in the field. Therefore, the relative distribution of a fungicide within the plant can be determined, but not the absolute uptake rate.

In these systemicity studies, 84% of the applied label stayed within the kernel 8 days after sowing (Table 4). About 16% of the applied radioactivity was detected in the coleoptile and roots, whereas no measurable radioactivity was found in the first emerging leaf. After 11 days, about 3% and after 15 d about 4% of the total applied radioactivity per kernel was in the first leaf. In the second emerging leaf, less than 1% of the total radioactivity was found after 15 d and, in the third emerging leaf, the translocated amount of fluoxastrobin was below quantitative measurement. Fluoxastrobin showed low systemicity in seed-treated wheat plants but demonstrated good properties against seed and soil-borne diseases from its strong presence in the kernel.

Table 4. Distribution of ^{14}C fluoxastrobin in wheat plants after seed treatment

Period after planting (d)	% of applied activity in kernels	% of applied activity in root and coleoptile	% of applied activity first leaf	% of applied activity second leaf	% of applied activity third leaf
8	84	16	0	-	-
11	73	23	3	0	-
15	70	>25	4	<1	0

Determination of fungicide concentrations in the second and third emerging leaves

Table 5. Concentrations in young wheat leaves after seed treatment with fluoxastrobin (field trial)

Growth stage at analysis	Treatment [g a.i./dt]	Residue (mg/kg)		
		fluoxastrobin (E-)	fluoxastrobin (Z-)	total fluoxastrobin
	untreated	<0.045	<0.005	<0.05
2 leaf stage	fluoxastrobin (10 g)	<0.045	<0.005	<0.05
	fluoxastrobin & azole (7.5 g & 7.5 g)	<0.045	<0.005	<0.05
	untreated	<0.045	<0.005	<0.05
3 leaf stage	fluoxastrobin (10 g)	<0.045	<0.005	<0.05
	fluoxastrobin & azole (7.5 & 7.5 g)	<0.045	<0.005	<0.05

Method used:
fluoxastrobin: method 00649. LoQ = 0.05 mg/kg (total); 0.045 mg/kg (E-isomer); 0.005 mg/kg (Z-isomer).

Results of the field residue study (Table 5) show that, within the detection limits, no measurable residues of fluoxastrobin applied at 10 g a.i./dt could be detected in wheat plants harvested at the 2- or the 3-leaf stages. In addition, the combination with an azole did not modify the systemic behaviour of fluoxastrobin as again no measurable residues could be detected. These findings strongly support the results that have been observed in the biological studies, showing that fluoxastrobin does not generate a significant selection pressure on wind-borne diseases.

CONCLUSIONS

Biological field trial results, supported by controlled systemicity studies and field residue analysis, showed that fluoxastrobin applied as a seed treatment at low doses ($\leq$ 10 g a.i./100 kg seeds) does not cause a significant selection pressure on wind-borne diseases such as powdery mildew and septoria leaf spot.

The risk assessment identified a somewhat enhanced risk in the case of *Microdochium nivale* since this pathogen may be targeted by QoIs and by fluoxastrobin from both seed and foliar application within a crop/season. Therefore, a preventive anti-resistance strategy is desirable in order to minimise this risk. In order to lower the resistance risk of the QoI fungicide fluoxastrobin as a seed treatment, it will be marketed exclusively in mixture with an effective DMI partner such as prothioconazole (Products: ®Bariton, ®Scenic), which shows, at the application rates used, a good activity against seed- and soil-borne *M. nivale*. Although no likely risk can be identified, this mixture concept will also help to decrease any resistance risk for the DMI partner. Moreover, monitoring studies will continue after commercialization of the product.

In conclusion, extensive studies have demonstrated that the use of fluoxastrobin as a seed treatment in wheat will not lead to significant selection pressure for any wind-borne diseases. Furthermore, commercial use will only be in mixture with a robust and effective disease control partner, thus further minimising any potential resistance risk concerns for seed/soil borne diseases.

REFERENCES

Becker W.F; von Jagow G; Anke T; Steglich W (1981). Ouedemansin, strobilurin A, strobilurin B and myxothiazol: new inhibitors of the bc$_1$ segment of the respiratory chain with an E-ß-methoxyacrylate system as common structural element. *FEBS Letters* **132**, 329-333.

Dutzmann S; Mauler-Machnik A; Kerz-Moehlendick F; Applegate J; Heinemann U (2002) HEC 5725: A novel leaf systemic strobilurin fungicide. *Proceedings of the BCPC Conference - Pests and Diseases 2002*, **1**, 365-370.

The response of *Echinochloa colona* populations from Nigeria to oxadiazon, propanil and pendimethalin

F B Jafun
Biological Sciences, Abubakar Tafawa Balewa University, P.M.B. 0248, Bauchi, Nigeria

S A M Perryman, S R Moss
Rothamsted Research, Harpenden, Hertfordshire, AL5 2JQ , UK
Email: sarah.perryman@bbsrc.ac.uk

ABSTRACT

The responses of suspected resistant populations of jungle rice (*Echinochloa colona*) from Nigeria were compared with susceptible and resistant reference populations in glasshouse dose-response and field simulation experiments using oxadiazon, propanil and pendimethalin. Results indicated that some Nigerian populations (from Miri, Gubi and Inkil) showed varying degrees of partial tolerance of oxadiazon and one (Miri) of pendimethalin. However, all the Nigerian populations were susceptible to propanil. The level of control achieved with pendimethalin, usually a pre-emergence herbicide, was generally lower than that of oxadiazon or propanil. If the results obtained are indicative of what is occurring in Nigeria, then the evolution of herbicide resistance to oxadiazon and pendimethalin may be occurring and could be a threat. This threat is more acute if current control practices remain unchanged.

INTRODUCTION

The development of herbicide resistant weeds is a serious worldwide threat to agricultural production. Since its first detection in the 1960s, herbicide resistance has been reported in 276 weed biotypes in 59 countries (Heap, 2003). Jungle rice *(Echinochloa colona* (L.) Link) is one of the serious grass weeds of the tropical world and its resistance to different classes of herbicides has been reported in several countries including, in Central and South America, Mexico, Costa Rica, Colombia and Venezuela (Heap, 2003). *E. colona* is also the most important grass weed in the rice (*Oryza sativa*)-growing areas of the scrub savannah region of Nigeria where rice weed management now largely depends on the use of herbicides.

Oxadiazon, propanil and pendimethalin are amongst the most widely and most frequently used herbicides for the control of grass weeds in rice, including *E. colona* (Akobundu, 1987). When introduced in the early 1980s, these herbicides provided adequate control of *E. colona* and other grasses. Recently, however, farmers in Nigeria have reported cases of poor control such that higher doses and more frequent applications together with hand weeding are required for adequate management of *E. colona*. Repeated use of herbicides could result in the build up of herbicide-resistant biotypes and resistance was suspected as the possible cause of the recent observed herbicide failures. Determination of the herbicide resistance status of *E. colona* in the rice growing areas of Nigeria is required for developing appropriate management strategies. Thus, this study was conducted at Rothamsted

Research to determine if selection for resistance to oxadiazon, propanil and pendimethalin has occurred in the *E. colona* populations from rice fields of Nigeria.

MATERIALS AND METHODS

Seeds

Seeds were collected in October and November 2000, from four rice fields (at Miri, Gubi, Inkil and Fulani) in Nigeria in which farmers had reported cases of herbicide control problems. Three standard populations were used in addition, for reference purposes: two susceptibles, Herbiseed-S (from UK) and LARS-S (susceptible to propanil, originating from Columbia) and one resistant LARS-R (resistant to propanil, originating from Costa Rica).

Glasshouse dose-response experiment

Seeds of all seven populations were pre-germinated in 9 cm Petri dishes containing four filter papers moistened with 7 ml of 2 g/l KNO_3 under a 14 h photoperiod at 30°C/20°C (day/night) controlled environment regime. Seedlings were then transplanted into 5 cm square pots containing Kettering loam (4% organic matter) at one seedling per pot. All plants were kept in glasshouse conditions of 14 h photoperiod of 300 μm m^{-2} s^{-1} light intensity at 30°C/20°C (day/night) and 80% relative humidity for 2 weeks until they attained the four-leaf stage. Plants were sprayed with commercial formulations of oxadiazon (an inhibitor of protoporphyrinogen oxidase) (250 g/l), propanil (an inhibitor of Hill's reaction at photosystem II) (800 g/kg) and pendimethalin (an inhibitor of microtubules assembly) (400 g/l), each with eight different doses in a set of serial dilutions in the range: 62.5 – 8,000 g oxadiazon a.i./ha; 240 – 30,400 g propanil a.i./ha and 82.5 – 10,560 g pendimethalin a.i./ha. Treatments were applied using a laboratory sprayer equipped with a flat-fan nozzle ('Teejet' 110015VK) delivering 262 litres spray solution/ha at a spray pressure of 210 kPa. Sprayed plants were returned to the glasshouse and, after 24 h, watered from above as necessary. The experiment was a complete randomised design with 12 replicate plants per herbicide dose. There were 40 untreated pots per population. Plants were harvested 14 d after spraying and foliage fresh weights determined per pot as a measure of herbicide activity.

Container experiment (field simulation conditions)

An experiment was set up to validate the response of three populations of *E. colona* (LARS-R, Miri and LARS-S) from the glasshouse dose-response assay. Seeds were pre-germinated as in the previous experiment. Seedlings were then transplanted into plastic containers (27 x 18 x 10 cm deep) containing Kettering loam at 12 plants per container. All plants were kept in glasshouse conditions of 14 h photoperiod of 300 μm m^{-2} s^{-1} light intensity at 30°C/20°C (day/night) and 80% relative humidity for 2 weeks until they attained the three-leaf stage. Herbicide treatments comprised the recommended and double the recommended rates of oxadiazon (1 and 2 kg a.i./ha), propanil (4.8 and 9.6 kg a.i./ha) and pendimethalin (3.3 and 6.6 kg a.i./ha). Treatments were applied 3 weeks after transplanting, at the four-leaf stage, using a laboratory sprayer with a single flat-fan nozzle ('Teejet' 110015VK) delivering 271 litres spray solution/ha at 210kPa. The experiment was a randomised complete block design with three replicates per treatment. There were three untreated containers for each population. Plants were returned to the same glasshouse conditions. Herbicide activity was determined by assessing reduction in foliage fresh weight 4 weeks after spraying.

Statistical analysis

Foliage fresh weight data from the glasshouse dose-response experiment were analysed using Maximum Likelihood Programme (Ross, 1987). The concentration of each herbicide required to reduce foliage fresh weight by 50 % relative to untreated controls (ED_{50}) and log_{10} ED_{50} was calculated for each population. Foliage fresh weight data from the container experiment underwent an analysis of variance using Genstat Version 5.0 (Payne *et al.*, 1997) to determine SEDs.

RESULTS

Glasshouse dose-response experiment

Foliage fresh weight of all populations was reduced with increasing doses of oxadiazon up to 8000 g a.i./ha, but mainly at doses in excess of 500 g a.i./ha. The ED_{50} values (concentration of herbicide required to reduce foliage fresh weight by 50%) for oxadiazon treatments ranged from 821to1521 g a.i./ha (Table 1). These values were high, with only the susceptible standard (Herbiseed-S) and one Nigerian population (Fulani) recording ED_{50} values below the recommended rate of oxadiazon (1000 g a.i./ha). The Miri population from Nigeria had the highest ED_{50} value (1521 g a.i./ha) and those of Gubi and Inkil were also significantly higher than the susceptible standard Herbiseed-S. Resistance indices ranged from 1.0 to 1.9, with the population Miri recording the highest value, indicating that all populations except Fulani showed slight tolerance of oxadiazon. No populations showed a high degree of resistance to oxadiazon.

Table 1.   Responses of seven populations of *Echinochloa colona* to oxadiazon, propanil and pendimethalin in a glasshouse dose-response experiment

Population	Oxadiazon			Propanil			Pendimethalin		
	ED_{50}	RI	Log_{10} ED_{50}	ED_{50}	RI	Log_{10} ED_{50}	ED_{50}	RI	Log_{10} ED_{50}
Herbiseed-S	821	1.0	2.91	5283	1.0	3.72	1622	1.0	3.21
LARS-S	1162	1.4	3.07	6302	1.2	3.80	2031	1.3	3.31
LARS-R	1340	1.6	3.13	43981	8.3	4.64	4275	2.6	3.63
Inkil	1227	1.5	3.09	3160	0.6	3.50	2439	1.5	3.39
Fulani	942	1.1	2.97	2942	0.6	3.47	1183	0.7	3.07
Gubi	1320	1.6	3.12	3803	0.7	3.58	2100	1.3	3.32
Miri	1521	1.9	3.18	3019	0.6	3.48	4409	2.7	3.64
SED			0.068			0.108			0.121

ED_{50} is the dose required (g/ai/ha) to reduce foliage fresh weight by 50% relative to untreated controls of the same population. Resistance index (RI) is the ratio of ED_{50} value relative to that of the susceptible standard, Herbiseed-S

The standard resistant population, LARS-R, demonstrated a high level of resistance to propanil, with over 70 % of plants surviving 38,400 g a.i./ha, eight times the recommended rate. The four populations from Nigeria and two susceptible standards did not vary greatly in their sensitivity to propanil. The values for ED_{50} and for RI were significantly higher in LARS-R (ED_{50}= 43981 g a.i./ha, RI= 8.3) (Table 1). Other populations recorded ED_{50} and RI ranging from 2942 to 6302 kg a.i./ha and 0.6 to 1.2 respectively. All populations from Nigeria had ED_{50} values below the recommended rate of propanil and RI below 1, indicating they were susceptible to propanil.

Two populations (LARS-R and Miri) showed some evidence of tolerance of pendimethalin. Reductions in foliage fresh weight (%) with increase in pendimethalin dose for these populations were slightly less than those for the other five populations at the three highest doses. The ED_{50} values for these two populations were significantly ($P<0.05$) higher than both the Herbiseed and LARS-S standards (Miri, 4409 g a.i./ha; LARS-R, 4275 g a.i./ha; Herbiseed 1622 g a.i./ha) (Table 1) The highest level of pendimethalin sensitivity was recorded in the Fulani population, with the lowest ED_{50} of 1183 g a.i./ha. Resistance indices ranged from 0.7 to 2.7, with the Fulani and Miri populations recording the lowest and highest values, respectively. Of the Nigerian populations, Miri showed the greatest tolerance of pendimethalin. Comparing the three herbicides, the results indicate a degree of cross-tolerance of oxadiazon and pendimethalin in the Miri population, which was the least sensitive to both herbicides. The Inkil and Gubi showed slightly reduced sensitivity to oxadiazon.

Container experiment

Results confirm that the susceptible standard population LARS-S was sensitive to oxadiazon at the recommended rate of 1 kg a.i./ha, while LARS-R and Miri showed slightly reduced susceptibility at this rate (Table 2). However, all three populations were effectively controlled with 2 kg oxadiazon/ha.

Table 2. Percentage reduction in foliage fresh weight in three populations of *Echinochloa colona*, relative to untreated controls of the same populations, by two doses of oxadiazon, propanil and pendimethalin in a container experiment.

Population	Oxadiazon (kg a.i./ha)		Propanil (kg a.i./ha)		Pendimethalin (kg a.i./ha)	
	1	2	4.8	9.6	1.32	2.64
LARS-S	87.9	96.7	73.8	87.9	51.9	76.7
LARS-R	77.5	95.4	-21.9	7.4	35.0	77.3
MIRI	74.2	91.5	82.0	96.8	22.6	62.1
SED			5.22			

Neither rate of propanil gave control of the resistant LARS-R population, confirming its high resistance status. Moderate control of Miri and LARS-S was achieved at the recommended rate (4.8 kg a.i./ha) and good control at the higher rate (9.6 kg a.i./ha), confirming susceptibility. The overall level of control achieved with pendimethalin was generally lower than that of oxadiazon and propanil. All populations were poorly controlled at the recommended rate of 1.32 kg a.i./ha and control at the higher rate of 2.64 kg a.i./ha was mediocre (62 - 77%).

DISCUSSION

This study indicated that three populations of *E. colona* from Nigeria (Inkil, Gubi and Miri) showed slight insensitivity to oxadiazon and one population (Miri) showed tolerance of pendimethalin, but all were susceptible to propanil. In the glasshouse experiment, most populations had ED_{50} values above the recommended rate of oxadiazon (1000 g a.i./ha). Oxadiazon is the most widely used herbicide in this region because of its past history of effectiveness. Selection pressure through continuous use may have shifted the three *E. colona* populations, especially the Miri population, from susceptibility to partial tolerance, thus potentially creating a resistance threat. Studies have shown that continuous use of a given herbicide or chemically related herbicides promotes the build-up of resistance in *Echinochloa* spp. However, differences between populations in terms of resistance indices were too low to demonstrate categorically that any of the Nigerian populations were resistant to oxadiazon. As a general rule, tested populations can be considered resistant only when resistance indices (RI) values are greater than two (Valverde *et al.,* 2000). Resistance can not be assigned purely on the basis of resistance indices and interpreting RI values below three in terms of the impact of herbicide performance in the field should be done with caution.

The low levels of resistance in these experiments do not accord with reports of poor control from the field in Nigeria. Therefore, factors other than herbicide resistance may have contributed to the reported high cases of oxadiazon failures in this region. Herbicide choice, dose, timing, adverse environmental conditions, inaccurate calibration, incorrect mixing, worn out equipment and failure to read and understand the product label are all possible causes of herbicide failure.

There was good agreement between the results for the glasshouse and container experiments with all three herbicides at the recommended doses. The marginal difference between the oxadiazon and pendimethalin responses in the Miri population from Nigeria recorded for in the dose-response studies was supported by the container experiment. Miri was sensitive to propanil in the dose-response experiment, and was the best-controlled population in containers. These results indicate that glasshouse dose-response assays and the container experiments are capable of detecting marginal differences in tolerance between populations. The advantage of containers, compared with field trials, is that they allow comparison of herbicide performance on several populations under identical soil and environmental conditions.

Multiple mechanisms of resistance to propanil and some graminicides are known to have evolved in *E. colona* around the world (Heap, 2003; Gressel, 2000). The levels of herbicide tolerance, albeit slight, exhibited by populations from the scrub savannah region of Nigeria in this study indicate that resistance may be a risk. The experiments conducted here cannot confirm whether the small differences in tolerance recorded in the Nigerian populations are a consequence of selection pressure by herbicides, or merely reflect innate inter-population variation. Hence, there is a need to monitor the response to herbicides in Nigerian populations such as Miri, to determine whether resistance is developing and, if so, how fast and what mechanisms are responsible. To achieve effective control of these populations in the field, alternative herbicides with better efficacy may have to be introduced. These results agree with findings of Valverde *et al.* (2000), which suggested that herbicide alternation regimes may serve as a useful tool in controlling herbicide-resistant *E colona* biotypes. It will also be important to determine which other factors, unrelated to resistance, are responsible for poor control by herbicides, and to develop weed management strategies based on rotation, cultural and biological methods as a means of reducing the dependence on herbicides.

ACKNOWLEDGEMENTS

This research was funded through the Rothamsted International Fellowship scheme. Rothamsted Research receives grant-aided support from the Biotechnology and Biological Sciences Research Council. The authors thank Herbiseed and Hortichem Ltd for the supply of seeds and herbicide, respectively. Thanks also go to Drs Charlie Riches and Bernal Valverde for the donation of seeds and herbicides.

REFERENCES

Akobundu I O (1987). *Weed Science in the Tropics: Principles and Practices.* 522 pp., John Wiley and Sons: Chichester, New York, Brisbane, Toronto, Singapore.

Gressel J (2000). More non-target site herbicide cross-resistance in *Echinochloa spp.*in rice. *Resistant Pest Management* **11**, 6-7.

Heap I (2003). International survey of herbicide resistant weeds. Online, http://www.weedscience.com.

Payne R W; Lane P W; Baird D B;Gilmour A R; Harding S A; Morgan G W; Murray D A; Thompson R; Todd A D; Tunnicliffe Wilson G; Webster R; Wellham S J (1997). *Genstat 5 release 4.1.* Reference summary, 156 pp. Numerical Algorithm Group: Oxford, UK.

Ross G J S (1987). *Maximum Likelihood Programme User Manual*, version 3.08. Numerical Algorithm Group Ltd: Oxford, UK.

Valverde B E; Riches C R; Caseley J C (2000). *Prevention and Management of Herbicide Resistant Weeds in Rice: Experiences from Central America with Echinochloa colona.* Camara de Insumos Agropecuarios de Costa Rica, 123 pp.

A mutation in the C domain of the acetolactate synthase (ALS) gene of *Bidens pilosa* confers resistance to imazethapyr

M Duran
Departamento de Bioquímica y Biología Molecular, Universidad de Córdoba, 14071, Spain. Actual address: Dpto. Biología Celular e Inmunología. Universidad de Córdoba. Campus de Rabanales. Edificio Severo Ochoa. 14071 Córdoba

G Plaza
Departamento de Agronomía, Universidad Nacional de Colombia, AA-14490. Bogotá, Colombia

M D Osuna, R De Prado
Departamento de Química Agrícola y Edafología, Universidad de Córdoba, Campus de Rabanales. Edificio Marie Curie. 14071 Córdoba, Spain

A Rodríguez-Franco
Departamento de Bioquímica y Biología Molecular, Universidad de Córdoba, Campus de Rabanales. Edificio Severo Ochoa. 14071, Spain
Email: bb1rofra@uco.es

ABSTRACT

A biotype of *Bidens pilosa* resistant to imazethapyr has been isolated and characterized. A preliminary set of whole plant and *in vitro* ALS assays in the presence of this herbicide strongly suggested that resistance was due to an alteration in target site by mutation. This was confirmed when the C, A, D, B and E conserved domains of the ALS were amplified. This was done by PCR using a set of universal and degenerate oligonucleotides useful for the cloning of these sequences in all plants tested to date. Several amino acid replacements were found. Some of them are either out of the five conserved domains from where mutations can confer resistance to herbicides, or are located in non-conserved regions of the gene. This suggests that these substitutions are not responsible for the observed resistance. However, a M_{18} to T substitution, located in the D domain, was found in the resistant plants. This mutation has only been reported in resistant plants isolated in the laboratory. This is the first case of a resistant plant isolated from the wild with this same mutation.

INTRODUCTION

Acetolactate synthase (ALS), which catalyses the first common step in the biosynthesis of the branched-chain amino acids, is the target of five herbicide groups: sulfonylurea, imidazolinone, triazolopyrimidine, pyrimidinylthiobenzoate, and sulfonylamino-carbonyl-triazolinone. Resistance to ALS-inhibiting herbicides was first described in 1987, 5 years after the commercial introduction of chlorsulfuron (Mallory-Smith *et al.*, 1990). Since then, the number of ALS-resistant weed populations has been increasing at an exponential rate, and over 80 cases have been reported by June 2003 (Heap, 2003).

Most cases of resistance are due to the presence of nuclear-inherited dominant mutations in the DNA sequence coding for this enzyme (Devine & Shukla, 2001). These mutations have been found to be located in at least five different conserved domains where the herbicides bind to the enzyme (Tranel & Wright, 2002). One of these cases is *Bidens pilosa*. This weed is a parasite of soybean crops, and was the first to develop resistance to acetolactate synthase herbicides in Brazil in 1993. No previous molecular studies have been done on *B. pilosa*, making it difficult to clone the ALS gene.

The aims of this study were to determine the molecular basis conferring resistance of the *B. pilosa* biotype, and to study the degree of resistance to the herbicide imazethapyr.

MATERIALS AND METHODS

Plant material

Resistant (R) and susceptible (S) biotypes of *B. pilosa* were collected from infested soybean fields in Mato Grosso do Sul, Brazil. Seeds from the resistant population were from fields that had been treated with imidazolinones and sulfonylurea herbicides for 8 years before they were collected.

Seeds were germinated in Petri dishes in a growth chamber under controlled conditions (28/25°C day/night temperature, with a 16 h photoperiod of 350 μmol/m radiation and 70% relative humidity). Plants of uniform size were selected when the cotyledon leaves had emerged and expanded and were then transplanted to plastic pots containing a 50% perlite-turf mixture. Plants were grown in a greenhouse under controlled conditions.

For the molecular studies, seeds were surface-sterilized for 5 min in a 30% hypochlorite solution and then washed twice with sterile water. Sterilized seeds were sown in Petri dishes with 1.5% agar supplemented with 0.02% KNO_3 and 0.02% gibberellin GA3 under the same conditions described above. DNA was isolated from individual resistant plants germinated in selective medium containing 10^{-4} M of technical grade imazethapyr.

Chemicals

Technical grade and commercially formulated imazethapyr (Pursuit ®) were provided by BASF.

Whole plant assays

The herbicide was sprayed once at the four- to five-leaf stage of development using a laboratory track sprayer delivering 200 l/ha at 200 kPa. Two plants per pot were sprayed. Plants were harvested and analysed 21 d after treatment in the dose-response experiment. The dose experiment had a randomized block design with three replications per dose. The imazethapyr doses were 100, 200, 400, 800, 1000, 1600 and 2000 g a.i./ha. The herbicide dose that caused 50% reduction of shoot fresh weight (ED_{50}) was calculated for imazethapyr as previously described (Menendez *et al.*, 1994). The R/S ratio was calculated as $ED_{50}(R)/ED_{50}(S)$.

ALS activity assay

The ALS response to herbicide was determined *in vitro* using crude extracts. ALS enzyme was isolated from R and S seedlings. The extraction and assay methods have been described elsewhere (Osuna & De Prado, 2003). The herbicide concentration that caused 50% reduction in ALS activity (I_{50}) was calculated for imazethapyr and the R/S ratio was calculated as $I_{50}(R)/I_{50}(S)$.

DNA extraction

DNA was extracted from plants at the four-leaf stage using a CTAB-based extraction method with a Macherey–Nagel kit using 250 mg of plant material and following the kit's instructions.

PCR amplification of conserved domains

Two sets of degenerated universal primer pairs were used to amplify the regions containing the conserved domains C, A and D (primers ALS-U-295 and ALS-L1170) and domains B and E (primers ALS-U-1580 and ALS-L-2160), according to the method developed previously (Duran, unpublished).

Cloning and sequencing of PCR products

PCR products were visualized in agarose gels and purified using GeneClean. Extracted bands were treated with 2 U of Klenow, adding 5 µl of dNTPs 0.125 mM and incubating for 15 min at 37°C and were cloned into the *Eco*RV site of pBluescript KS II+. Recombinant plasmids were introduced into competent *E. coli* DH5α. Plasmids with inserts were isolated using a Macherey Nagel Plasmid Isolation Kit, according the manufacturer's protocol. Inserts were sequenced by the central services at the University of Cordoba using M13 forward and M13 reverse primers with an ABI PRISM^{TM} 310 sequencer and ABI PRISM^{TM} Dye Terminator Cycle Sequencing Ready Reaction Kit.

RESULTS AND DISCUSSION

Dose-response assays

Putative resistant and susceptible populations were treated with imazethapyr. The ED_{50} value for the R biotype was 13 times greater than the susceptible biotype (Table 1).

Table 1. ED_{50}, resistance factor [ED_{50} (R) / ED_{50} (S)], I_{50}, and resistance factor [I_{50} (R) / I_{50} (S)] values for ALS from resistant and susceptible *B. pilosa* biotypes

Biotype	ED_{50} (g a i ha^{-1})	Resistance Factor [ED_{50} (R) / ED_{50} (S)]	I_{50} (M)	Resistance Factor [I_{50} (R) / I_{50} (S)]
R	1365	> 13	> 100	> 21
S	< 100	-	4.68	-

ALS activity assays

The imazethapyr concentration required to reduce the ALS activity by 50% (I_{50}) was greater than 100 µM when extracts were obtained from the biotype R, and 4.68 µM for the S biotype (Table 1). These ALS assays are consistent with resistance to imazethapyr of *B. pilosa* being mediated by a target-site modification, and are similar to other resistance reports such as in *Amaranthus quitensis* (Tuesca & Nisensohn, 2001), *Amaranthus rudis* (Hinz & Owen, 1997) and *Bidens pilosa* (Christoffoleti & Foloni, 1999). In all these cases, the ALS enzyme changed its structure, diminishing or even preventing the binding of the herbicides without loss of enzymatic activity (Saari *et al.*, 1994).

Molecular studies

PCR reactions were performed using the degenerated and universal oligo primers previously described (Duran, unpublished). Two different PCR fragments were obtained. The first one, coding for 237 amino acids, contained the conserved C, A and D domains of the ALS. The second one coded for a 71 amino acid fragments containing the B and E conserved domains. No differences were observed in the nucleotide sequences coding the B and E domains among resistant and susceptible plants. However, a detailed comparison of the sequence coding the C, A and D domains first revealed the presence of two different ALS isoenzymes. The first one, called isoenzyme 1, has 76% similarity to *Arabidopsis thaliana* sequence, while the second, called isoenzyme 2, has 81% similarity (Figure 1).

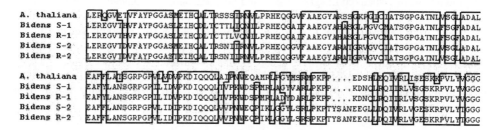

Figure 1.   Partial alignment of the sequences coding for the C, A and D conserved ALS domains. Conserved regions are in boxes. S stands for susceptible plants, and R for resistant biotypes. The numbers stand for the two types of ALS isoenzymes found. Notice the gap found in sequence of isoenzyme 1 that helps in recognizing these two isoenzymes.

Both isoenzymes were found in resistant and susceptible plants. This means that resistance is not due to the presence of a particular isoenzyme in the resistant plant. The comparison revealed several changes in the amino acid sequences. The first one is an I_{30} to V substitution in isoenzyme 1 (Figure 2). We also noticed a G_{169} to D and a V_{171} to D substitutions. Although all these residues are conserved in most ALS cloned to date, they are not located in any of the five described conserved domains, presumably involved in the binding of the herbicide to the enzyme. Their involvement in resistance could therefore initially be ruled out. These amino acid changes can be due to the existence of a natural polymorphism in this plant. It is also consistent with the tetraploid nature of this plant.

```
Bidens S-1  LEREGVTHVFAYPGGASLEIHQDLTCTTLIQNILPRHEQGAIFAAEGYAHASGLPGVCMATSGPGATNLFSGFADALL
Bidens R-1  LEREGVTHVFAYPGGASLEIHQDLTCTTLMQNILPRHEQGAIFAAEGYAHASGLPGVCMATSGPGATNLFSGFADALL

Bidens S-1  EAFYLANSGRPGPILIDVPKDIQQQLTVPKWDSPMRLAGYMARLPKPPKDNQLRQIIRLVSGSKRPVLYVGGGCLNSG
Bidens R-1  EAFYLANSGRPGPILIDVPKDIQQQLTVPKWDSPMRLADYDARLPKPPKDNQLRQIIRLVSGSKRPVLYVGGGCLNSG
```

Figure 2.   Partial alignment of the *B. pilosa* fragment of isoenzyme 1. The letter S stands for susceptible and R for imazethapyr resistant biotypes. The number stands for the type of isoenzyme considered in the alignment.

In the isoenzyme 2 (Figure 3), also two more changes are found between susceptible and resistant sequences. The first and the most important is a M_{18} to T substitution located in the D domain.

```
Bidens S-2  LEREGVTDVFAYPGGASMEIHQALTRSNIIRNVLPRHEQGGVFAAEGYARATGRVGVCIATSGPGATNLVSGLADALL
Bidens R-2  LEREGVTDVFAYPGGASTEIHQALTRSNIIRNVLPRHEQGGVFAAEGYARATGRVGVCIATSGPGATNLVSGLADALL

Bidens S-2  EAFFLANSGRPGPVLIDIPKDIQQQLVVPNWEQPIKLGGYLSRLPKPTYSANEEGLLDQIVRLVGESKRPVLYTGGGC
Bidens R-2  EAFFLANSGRPGPVLIDIPKDIQQQLVVPNWEQPIKLGGYLSRSPKPTYSANEEGLLDQIVRLVGESKRPVLYTGGGC
```

Figure 3.   Partial alignment of the isoenzyme 2 fragment of *B. pilosa*. The letter S stands for susceptible and R for imazethapyr resistant biotypes.

This mutation has been described previously only in mutants isolated in the laboratory (Ott *et al.*, 1996). This is the first case reported of a resistant plant isolated from the wild with this mutation. This suggests that the fitness of this resistant plant in nature is adequate enough to allow the plants to survive, and that a decreased fitness does not explain the lack of plants isolated with this particular mutation from nature. In this isoenzyme, a L_{174} to S replacement has also occurred. This portion of the sequence, however, is not conserved at all among the acetolactate synthase and so it remains unlikely that this mutation could be involved in the observed resistance. This work represents our attempt to develop a rapid and universal method for the molecular diagnostic of the resistance to herbicides in weeds.

ACKNOWLEDGEMENTS

The authors gratefully acknowledge Dr Pedro Chrisofolleti who provided the seeds used in this work. This work was financed by grants AGL2000-1713-C03-02 and AGL2001-2420 from CYCIT (Ministerio de Ciencia y Tecnología, Spain).

REFERENCES

Christoffoleti P J; Foloni L (1999). Dose response curves of resistant and susceptible *Bidens pilosa* to ALS inhibitor herbicides. *Proceedings of the 1999 Brighton Conference - Weeds*, **1**, 159-162.

Devine M D; Shukla A (2001). Altered target sites as a mechanism of herbicide resistance. *Crop Protection* **19**, 881-889.

Heap I M (2003). International Survey of Herbicide-Resistant Weeds. Herbicide Resistance Action Committee and Weed Science Society of America. Available at htpp://www.weedscience.com.

Hinz J R R; Owen M D K (1997). Acetolactate synthase resistance in a common waterhemp (*Amaranthus rudis*) population. *Weed Technology* **11**, 13-18.

Mallory-Smith C A D; Thill D C; Dial M J (1990). Identification of Sulfonilurea Herbicide-Resistant Prickly Lettuce (*Lactuca serriola*). *Weed Technology* **4**, 163-168.

Menendez J; Jorrin J; Romera E; De Prado R (1994). Resistance to cholotoluron of a slender foxtail (*Alopecurus myosuroides*) biotype. *Weed Science* **42**, 340-347.

Osuna M D; De Prado R (2003). *Conyza albida*: a new biotype with ALS inhibitor resistance. *Weed Research* **43**, 221-226.

Ott K H; Kwagh J G; Stockton G W; Sidorov V; Kakefuda G (1996). Rational molecular design and genetic engeneering of herbicide resistant crops by structure modeling and site-directed mutagenesis of acetohydroxiacid synthase. *Journal of Molecular Biology* **263**, 359-368.

Saari L L; Cotterman C; Thill D C (1994). Resistance to acetolactate synthase inhibiting herbicides. In: *Herbicide Resistance in Plants: Biology and Biochemistry*, eds S B Powles & J A M Holtum, pp. 83-139. CRC Press: Boca Raton, FL, USA.

Tranel P J; Wright T R (2002). Resistance of weeds to ALS-inhibiting herbicides: What have we learned? *Weed Science* **50**, 700-712.

Tuesca D; Nisensohn L (2001). Resistance of *Amaranthus quitensis* H.B.K. to Imazethapyr and Clorimuron-ethyl. *Pesquisa Agropecuaria Brasileira* **36**, 601-606.

A new mutation site in the acetolactate synthase (ALS) gene in *Amaranthus quitensis* resistant to imazethapyr

M D Osuna, C Casado, R De Prado
Departamento de Química Agrícola y Edafología, University of Córdoba , 14071 Córdoba, Spain
Email:bq2osrum@uco.es

J Wagner, K Hurle
Weed Science Department, Institute of Phytomedicine, University of Hohenheim, D70593 Stuttgart, Germany

ABSTRACT

An *Amaranthus quitensis* population (R7) resistant to imazethapyr was found in a soybean field in Cordoba, Argentina. Greenhouse and laboratory experiments determined resistance to imazethapyr and imazapyr in this population. Based on whole-plant experiments, the resistant population required over 10 times more imazethapyr than a susceptible population to reduce growth by 50%. Cross-resistance to several imidazolinones was also detected. Based on *in-vitro* enzyme activity assays, ALS in the R7 population was 12-fold less sensitive than ALS in those susceptible to imazethapyr. Polymerase chain reaction amplification and sequencing of two regions of the ALS gene containing the domains B/E and C/A/D, respectively, were performed. The resistant population had a mutation that caused a Gly by Cys substitution in the domain E, adjacent to one where mutations in the ALS gene have been documented in other resistant weed species.

INTRODUCTION

Pigweed [*Amaranthus quitensis* (HBK)] is one of the most important weeds of soybean crops in Argentina causing important losses in yield (Leguizamon *et al.*, 1994). Weed control is largely based on herbicide use, since *A. quitensis* is susceptible to many selective herbicides. Herbicides belonging to the ALS inhibitor group have usually been used in soybean fields in Argentina. The first ALS inhibitor-resistant *A. quitensis* population was reported in 2001 in Argentina (Tuesca & Nisensohn, 2001).

Resistance to ALS-inhibiting herbicides is mostly conferred by alterations of the ALS enzyme (Saari *et al.*, 1994; Devine & Eberlein, 1997). Target-site resistance to ALS inhibitors in all weed biotypes thus far has been due to a substitution of one of five conserved amino acids (Tranel & Wright, 2002). Three of these amino acids (Ala_{122}, Pro_{197} and Ala_{205}) are located near the amino-terminal end of ALS and the other two (Trp_{574} and Ser_{653}) are located near the carboxy-terminal end. In domain E, a mutation coding for Ser_{653} Thr substitution has recently been described in several *Amaranthus* populations (McNaughton *et al.*, 2001; Patzoldt & Tranel, 2002; Diebold *et al.*, 2003). It usually results in imidazolinone, but not sulfonylurea, resistance. An *A. quitensis* population resistant to imazethapyr was identified in a soybean field in Cordoba, Argentina. The objectives of this research were to asses the magnitude of resistance in this *A. quitensis* population to imazethapyr both at the whole plant level and by ALS assays *in vitro*, and to determine the molecular basis for this resistance.

MATERIALS AND METHODS

Plant material

Seeds from a resistant *A. quitensis* population (named R7) were collected from different soybean fields in the province of Cordoba (Argentina) that had been intensively treated for several years with imazethapyr. Seeds from the susceptible population were collected from nearby areas never treated with herbicides.

Seeds of both populations were placed in a tray with a peat+soil mixture (1+1) and allowed to germinate in a growth chamber (28/25°C day/night 16-h photoperiod photon-fluxdensity $m^{-2} s^{-1}$ under 350 μmol $m^{-2} s^{-1}$ and 80% relative humidity). Pre-germinated seeds were then transplanted (four plants per pot) into 7 x 7 cm pots filled with a peat+soil mixture (1+1) and grown under the above conditions.

Whole plant assays

R7 and sensitive (S) *A. quitensis* plants were treated with imazethapyr at the three- to four- leaf stage. The herbicide application rates ranged from 0 to 10 g a.i./ha for the S population and from 0 to 30 g a.i./ha for the R7 population. Herbicide applications were made using a laboratory track sprayer delivering 200 l/ha at 200 kPa. Treatments were replicated three times and shoot fresh weight per plant was determined 21 days after treatment and expressed as percent of the untreated control. Dose-response curves were plotted and herbicide rate that caused 50% shoot growth inhibition (ED_{50}) was established for each population (Osuna *et al.*, 2002).

ALS activity assays

ALS extraction and activity was carried out following the protocol described in Osuna & De Prado (2003). Three experiments, each with a separate tissue extract from different plant material, were conducted per population and each sample at each herbicide concentration was assayed per triplicate. Imazethapyr and imazapyr concentrations that caused 50% ALS activity reduction (I_{50}) were established for each population.

DNA analysis

Genomic DNA was extracted from young leaves of each sampled plant from the different populations. The extraction procedure was performed according the recommendations of the kit used (Dneasy plant mini kit, Qiagen GmbH, Hilden, Germany). DNA content and quality after extraction was checked by gel electrophoresis.

Based on the published sequence of the ALS gene from *Amaranthus* sp. (Woodworth *et al.*, 1996), the following primers were designed to amplify the region containing the domains B and E: primers UpDomB (5′GGGGCTATGGGGTTTGGTCTA3′) and Low Dom E (5′GCCCTTCTTCCATCACCCTCTG3′). A second set of primers, Amfl

(5'TACCGATGTTTTTGCTTACC3') and Amr1 (5'TGCTTATTCTTCCGGATTTCA3'), were designed according to Michel (2000) to amplify the region containing the domains C, A and D. The primers were synthesized using the software DNAstar. The PCR-purified products were sequenced using the Thermo Sequenase^{TM} Cy5^{TM} Dye terminator kit (Amersham Pharmacia Biotech Europe GmbH, Freiburg, Germany). The sequences of the resistant and susceptible populations were compared for the identification of mutations.

RESULTS

Whole plant assays

Dose response analysis confirmed that population R7 had a high level of imazethapyr resistance. For the R7 population 21.1 g a.i./ha imazethapyr was required to achieve 50% growth reduction; the ED$_{50}$ of the standard susceptible population was 2 g a.i./ha, being the resistance factor 10.8. (Table 1)

The R7 population of *A. quitensis* was cross-resistant to imazapyr (Table 1) as well as imazamethabenz and imazaquin but not to imazamox (data not shown).

Table 1.   ED$_{50}$ and I$_{50}$ values of imazethapyr-resistant and –susceptible biotypes of *Amaranthus quitensis* populations

	Whole plant assay		Enzyme assay	
	ED$_{50}$ (g a.i./ha)	Resistance factor [ED$_{50}$(R)/ ED$_{50}$(S)]	I$_{50}$ (µM)	Resistance factor [I$_{50}$(R)/ I$_{50}$(S)]
Imazethapyr				
S	2.0 ± 0.11		0.9 ± 0.12	
R7	21.7 ± 1.98	10.80	11.7 ± 1.68	12.48
Imazapyr				
S	2.7 ± 0.24		1.3 ± 0.95	
R7	18.3 ± 0.99	6.78	11.7 ± 1.68	9.38

ALS activity assays

In order to elucidate the mechanism of resistance, *in-vitro* studies were carried out using a crude extract of the ALS enzyme. The resistance level of ALS isolated from the R7 population was more than 12-fold higher for the imazethapyr than that found in the S population (Table 1). The same pattern of cross resistance was found as at the whole plant level. These data are consistent with the results found for the whole-plant studies and support the hypothesis that the resistance mechanism is based on an altered target site.

DNA analysis

In order to elucidate the molecular basis of the observed target site, PCR amplification of the ALS gene with the primers pairs Up DomB/Low DomE, as well as Amf1/Amr1, was conducted. A single band of the expected length of 476 bp for the region containing the domains B and E and 894 bp for the region containig the domains C, A and D was produced. Sequencing of both fragments and comparison of the sequences enabled the identification of the mutations.

No mutations were identified in population R7 that coded for amino acid substitutions in the domains A, B, C and D (data not shown). There was, however, a G to T mutation in domain E of ALS gene resulting in a glycine by cysteine substitution (Figure 1).

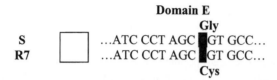

Figure 1. Nucleotide and deduced amino acid sequences in domain E region of R7 and S populations of *Amaranthus quitensis*. The shaded box indicates the nucleotide and substituted amino acid.

DISCUSSION

These results confirmed resistance to imazethapyr in the R7 population of *A. quitensis* at the whole plant as well as ALS enzyme activity level. The ED_{50} for most populations was less than the field-recommended doses (1500 and 100 g a.i./ha for imazapyr and imazethapyr, respectively); previous studies in *A. quitensis* showed that the effective doses for the control of this weed with imazethapyr were less than the field-recommended dose (Vita *et al.*, 2000). Cross-resistance to several imidazolinones was found in the R7 population, but not to imazamox (unpublished data). Cross-resistance to ALS-inhibiting herbicides is a common phenomenon but the pattern of cross-resistance is unpredictable (Saari *et al.*, 1994). The wide variation in target-site cross-resistance between biotypes and among diffferent ALS inhibitors results from a number of different functional mutations of the ALS gene. In studies on *Amaranthus hybridus,* Manley *et al.* (1999) found cross-resistance both to imazethapyr and imazaquin but not to the sulfonylureas studied. Lack of cross-resistance to some imidazolinones but not to others, as found in the present study, has been reported previously (Kudsk *et al.*, 1995).

Sequencing of the ALS gene enabled the identification of a point mutation leading to substitution of Gly in domain E by Cys. Because no other mutation was found in the ALS of population R7, we conclude that the $Gly_{654}Cys$ substitution is the most likely cause of resistance to imazethapyr in this population. To our knowledge, this is the first report of a weed species developing resistance due to this mutation after selection in field. It has not been described in laboratory selections either. The only mutation identified in domain E conferring resistance to ALS inhibitor codes for a Ser_{653} Thr change in the ALS protein in several *Amaranthus* populations. In each case it conferred resistance to imidazolinones but not to sulfonylureas (Diebold *et al.*, 2003). The mutation described in this work is located adjacent to that in which mutations in the ALS gene has been documented in other resistant weed species.

Here, cross resistance to some other imidazolinones was found, but studies on sulfonylurea have been not performed.

Futher studies need to be carried out in order to confirm that the $Gly_{654}Cys$ substitution is responsible for the resistance to ALS-inhibiting herbicides found in the R7 population of *A. quitensis*. DNA sequences changes associated with resistance can be characterized in some mutants by using mutagenesis, tissue culture selection, transformation and/or back crossing (Devine & Eberlein, 1997).

ACKNOWLEDGEMENTS

Financial support was provided in project AGL2001-2420 by the Ministerio de Educación, Cultura y Deportes (Spain).

REFERENCES

Devine M D; Eberlein C V (1997). Physiological, biochemical and molecular aspects of herbicide resistance based on altered target sites. In: *Herbicide Activity: Toxicology, Biochemistry and Molecular Biology,* eds R M Roe, J D Burton & R J Kuhr, pp. 159-185. IOS Press: Amsterdam, The Netherlands.

Diebold R S; McNaughton K E; Lee E A; Tardif F J (2003). Multiple resistance to imazethapyr and atrazine in Powell amaranth (*Amaranthus powellii*). *Weed Science* **51,** 312-318.

Kudsk P; Mathiassen S K; Cotterman J C (1995). Sulfonylurea resistance in *Stellaria media* (L.) Vill.*Weed Research* **35,** 19-24.

Leguizamon E; Faccini D; Nisensohn L; Puricelli E; Mitidieri A; Lopez J; Rainero H; Papa J; Rossi R; Cepeda S; Ponsa J; Moreno R; Falla L (1994). Funciones de daño y cálculo de pérdidas por malezas en el cultivo de soja. *Instituto Nacional de Tecnología Agropecuaria (INTA: Informe Técnico),* 1-19.

Manley B S; Hatzios K K; Wilson H P (1999). Absorption, translocation, and metabolism of chlorimuron and nicosulfuron in imidazolinone-resistant and -susceptible smooth pigweed (*Amaranthus hybridus*). *Weed Technology* **13,** 759-764.

McNaughton K E; Lee E A; Tardif F J (2001). Mutations in the ALS gene conferring resistance to group II herbicides in redroot pigweed (*Amaranthus retroflexus*) and green pigweed (*A. powelli*). *Weed Science Society American Abstracts* **41,** 97.

Michel A (2000). Untersuchungen von *Amaranthus* spp und *Conyza canadensis* (L) Cronq gegen verschiedene ALS-Inhibitoren. PhD Thesis, University of Hohenheim, Stuttgart, Germany.

Osuna M D; Vidotto F; Fischer A J; Bayer D E; De Prado R; Ferrero A (2002). Cross-resistance to bispyribac-sodium and bensulfuron-methyl in *Echinochloa phyllopogon* and *Cyperus difformis*. *Pesticide Biochemistry and Physiology* **73,** 9-17.

Osuna M D; De Prado R (2003). *Conyza albida*: a new biotype with ALS inhibitor resistance. *Weed Research* **43,** 221-226.

Patzoldt W L; Tranel P J (2002). Molecular analysis of cloransulam resistance in a population of giant ragweed. *Weed Science* **50,** 299-305.

Saari L L; Cotteman J C; Thill D C (1994). Resistance to acetolactate synthase inhibiting herbicides. In: *Herbicide Resistance in Plants,* eds S B Powles & J A M Holtum, pp. 83-140: CRC Press: Boca Raton.

Tranel P J; Wright T R (2002). Resistance of weeds to ALS-inhibiting herbicides: What have we learned? *Weed Science* **50**, 700-712.

Tuesca D; Nisensohn L A (2001). Resistencia de *Amaranthus quitensis* H.B.K a imazetapir y clorimuron-etil. *Pesquisa Agropecuaria Brasileira* **36**, 601-606.

Vita J I; Faccini D E; Nisensohn L A (2000). Control of *Amaranthus quitensis* in soybean crop in Argentina: an alternative to reduce herbicide use. *Crop Protection* **19**, 511-513.

Woodworth A R; Rosen B A; Bernasconi P (1996). Broad range resistance to herbicides targeting acetolactate synthase (ALS) in field isolate *Amaranthus* sp. is conferred by a Trp to Leu mutation in the ALS gene. *Plant Physiology* **111**, 1153-1159.

POSTER SESSION 7B

MODE OF ACTION AND METABOLISM

Session Organiser: Dr Fergus Earley
                      Syngenta, Bracknell, UK

Poster Papers: 7B-1 to 7B-7

Duration of yellow nutsedge (*Cyperus esculentus*) competitiveness after treatment with various herbicides.

J A Ferrell, W K Vencill and H J Earl
Department of Crop and Soil Sciences, University of Georgia, Athens, GA 30602
Email: wvencill@uga.edu

ABSTRACT

Experiments were initiated to determine the amount of time required for POST herbicides to render yellow nutsedge physiologically non-competitive. The rate of net CO_2 assimilation (A_N) was chosen as the response variable to describe competitiveness. When A_N of treated plants declined below 50% (A_{N50}) of the untreated control, the plants were no longer considered competitive. The time to reach A_{N50} for halosulfuron, imazapic, glyphosate and MSMA were 2.6, 3.1, 4.2, and 4.3 days, respectively. An A_{N50} value was not calculated for bentazon since A_N rapidly decreased below 50%, but recovered to >50% by 10 DAT. Stomatal conductance (g_s), a measure highly correlated with transpiration, declined similarly with A_N over time for halosulfuron, imazapic, and glyphosate treatments. However, stomatal conductance rates for MSMA treated plants was near 95% of the untreated control while A_N was near 35% 12 DAT. MSMA reduced carbon assimilation one day after treatment and by 5 days after treatment, respiration exceeded carbon assimilation during the photoperiod for MSMA. MSMA rapidly and completely eliminated carbon assimilation, but had almost no effect on plant water use. Halosulfuron and MSMA reduced shoot regrowth to between 0 and 5% of the control. Mesotrione treatment allowed some 58% regrowth. In the field, these three treatments would likely have both quantitatively and qualitatively different effects on the competitive ability of yellow nutsedge.

INTRODUCTION

Yellow nutsedge is a C_4 perennial that infests 21 crops in as many as 30 countries (Holm *et al.*, 1991). It has been shown to be competitively superior to many crop species due to its higher photosynthetic rate, fast sprouting and early growth rate (Holt and Orcutt, 1991).

The highly competitive nature of yellow nutsedge has raised questions concerning the amount of time required for various postemergence herbicides to render the plant non-competitive. Since some enzyme inhibiting herbicides, such as glyphosate and halosulfuron, often do not cause visual injury symptoms for 7-10 days after application (Vencill, 2002), it was questioned whether the yellow nutsedge plants were remaining competitive during that period (Ferrell *et al.*, 2003).

Little work has focused on the physiological response of yellow nutsedge after herbicide treatment. The objective of this study was to compare the time required for several herbicides to render yellow nutsedge physiologically non-competitive. A second objective was to compare MSMA with halosulfuron and mesotrione, for effects on both whole plant carbon assimilation and water use.

MATERIALS AND METHODS

Tubers were planted into 4 litre pots containing a 2:1 sand: sandy loam soil mix and placed in the greenhouse. The tubers sprouted and grew for 5 weeks before treatment. The plants were watered daily and fertilized weekly.

Study 1

Herbicide treatments consisted of halosulfuron (70 g ai ha^{-1}), imazapic (70 kg ai ha^{-1}), glyphosate (840 kg ai ha^{-1}), bentazon (840 kg ai ha^{-1}), and MSMA (2.2 kg ai ha^{-1}), with an untreated control. Non-ionic surfactant was included with each herbicide (0.25% v/v), except bentazon, which received crop oil concentrate (1% v/v). Herbicides were applied in a spray cabinet calibrated to deliver 187 litre/ha with an operating pressure of 270 kPa. Each plant had one mature leaf tagged prior to herbicide application. This leaf was used exclusively throughout the experiment for data collection. Data was collected for 12 days after herbicide application. Measurements on day 1 occurred 4 hours after herbicide application.

Photosynthesis was measured using a portable, open-flow gas exchange system (Ferrell *et al.,* 2003). For each measuring day, rate of CO_2 assimilation (A_N) and stomatal conductance (g_s) data were expressed as a percent of the control, to adjust for daily variations not associated with the herbicide treatment. From these data, the time required for 50% reduction in A_N and g_s for each treatment and replicate was obtained via linear interpolation. Analysis of variance (ANOVA) was employed and means were separated by Fisher's Protected LSD test (P=0.05).

Study 2

Before transfer from the greenhouse, each pot was watered to excess, and then allowed to drain to constant weight in the dark. This was taken as the saturated weight + plant fresh weight ($W_{SAT + P}$). The saturated weight was also determined for a pot containing the same amount of soil but no plant (W_{SAT}), and the weight of water in the soil at 100% water holding capacity (W_{water}) was calculated as the difference between W_{SAT} and the weight of just the pot and dry soil. Then, the weight of each pot at 80% water holding capacity was calculated as $W_{SAT+P} - 0.2W_{water}$.

Each pot was transferred to a different chamber of an eight-chamber open flow CO_2 exchange measurement system (van Iersel and Bugbee, 2000) at 28 ± 2 °C and approximately 350 µmol m^{-2} s^{-1} during the 16-h photoperiod (20 mol m^{-2} d^{-1}). Net carbon dioxide assimilation was recorded for each chamber once every five minutes during the experiment, and average net assimilation rates were determined for each chamber during each photoperiod and each dark period. Soil and plant respiration rates were assumed to be the same for both the photoperiod and dark period, and so mean gross CO_2 assimilation rates were calculated for each day as the mean daily net assimilation rate, minus the mean respiration rate measured during the following dark period. Temperature and relative humidity of each chamber were also recorded to calculate the average daily vapor pressure deficit for each day of the experiment.

After spending three days in the chambers (one acclimation day, then two normalization days), each plant was removed at the end of the photoperiod and received one of four herbicide treatments: MSMA (2.2 kg ai ha^{-1}), halosulfuron (63 g ai ha^{-1}), mesotrione (110 g ai ha^{-1}), and untreated. MSMA and halosulfuron were applied with non-ionic surfactant at a concentration of 0.25% v v^{-1} while mesotrione was applied with crop oil concentrate at 1% v v^{-1}. After returning the plants to the chambers, CO_2 assimilation and plant water use were recorded for an additional 11 days.

To determine plant transpiration from daily measurements of pot weights, it was necessary to adjust for the amount of water that evaporated directly from the soil surface. The daily soil water loss had a strong linear relationship to daily mean vapour pressure deficit. This function along with the vapor pressure deficit data from the main experiment was then used to estimate water lost to soil evaporation for each day of the experiment. This was subtracted from individual pot weight loss on each day to estimate the amount of water transpired by the plants.

Net CO_2 assimilation rates and daily water use were normalized for differences in plant size that existed at the beginning of the experiment. This expression of plant water use rate is mathematically equivalent to the "normalized transpiration ratio" (Ray and Sinclair, 1997). Net assimilation and water use data were analyzed separately for each day of the experiment using ANOVA, and means separations were via a protected LSD test (P = 0.05).

To determine the effects of the herbicide treatments on regrowth, all plant foliage was removed and pots were returned to the greenhouse, where water and fertilizer routines continued. After two weeks, shoot regrowth from each pot was harvested, dried and weighed. The data were analyzed by ANOVA, and protected LSD test (P = 0.05).

Statistical Analysis. Experimental design consisted of a randomized complete block with five replications. The experiment was conducted twice.

RESULTS AND DISCUSSION

Study 1

The most commonly used parameter to measure weed/crop competition is weed biomass accumulation. Biomass accumulation is, in essence, an integrated value of the rate of CO_2 assimilation (A_N) and stomatal conductance (g_s). This experiment measured both of these parameters at the leaf level. It was our assumption that plants possessing high rates of A_N and g_s were the most competitive and would likely have the highest rates of biomass accumulation. Likewise, a reduction in A_N and g_s can be related to a loss in competitive ability.

Figure 1 describes the response of yellow nutsedge to three herbicides that inhibit amino acid biosynthesis. These data demonstrate that halosulfuron and imazapic reduced A_N to 50% after 2.6 and 3.1 d, respectively. The lack of differences between these herbicides was expected, considering their similar mechanism of action as well as their comparably high levels of yellow nutsedge control (Grichar and Nester, 1997). Glyphosate, although displaying a similar response over 12 d to halosulfuron and imazapic, acted more slowly, taking 4.2 d to reach A_{N50}.

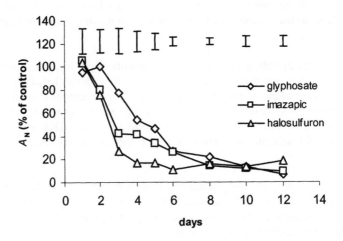

Figure 1. Photosynthetic response of yellow nutsedge to glyphosate, imazapic, and halosulfuron for 12 days after treatment. Bars indicate $LSD_{0.05}$ values.

Reduction of A_N with MSMA (Figure 2) was slower than for the herbicide treatments displayed in Figure 1. Although the pattern of A_N reduction was dissimilar, the time to reach A_{N50} was similar to that of glyphosate at 4.3 d. Conversely, bentazon displayed a trend that was dissimilar to all other treatments observed. The bentazon treatment displayed a reduction in A_N to 60% of the control after only 4 hours of exposure. A_N continued to decline until negative values were recorded on days 2-4. Negative A_N values denote that cellular respiration, on days 2-4, was greater than total CO_2 fixation by the dark reactions. However, recovery began to occur at 5 d and continued until A_N was at 60% of the control by 12 d.

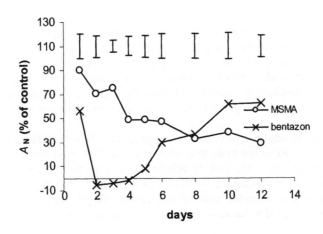

Figure 2. Photosynthetic response of yellow nutsedge to MSMA and bentazon for 12 days after treatment. Bars indicate $LSD_{0.05}$ values.

Competition for water is often considered the most important source of weed/crop competition. Therefore, g_s was monitored for each treatment, relative to the control (Figure 3). For glyphosate, imazapic, and halosulfuron, declines in g_s were highly correlated to reduction in A_N. Reduction in A_N increases leaf internal CO_2 concentrations, which signals stomata to close (Jones, 1992). However, the MSMA treatment displayed a quite different pattern between A_N and g_s. The initial decline in g_s for the MSMA treatment was similar to that of A_N. However, recovery occurred after 12 d and g_s was near 95% of the untreated control while A_N was near 35%. Therefore, MSMA treated sedge plants were transpiring water at near full capacity while A_N was reduced by 70%.

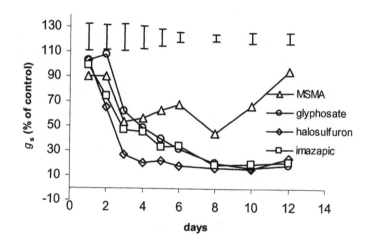

Figure 3. Yellow nutsedge stomatal conductance response to glyphosate, imazapic, halosulfuron, and MSMA treatment. Bars indicate $LSD_{0.05}$ values.

Foliar regrowth was examined after each herbicide treatment. Halosulfuron, imazapic, glyphosate, and MSMA treatments allowed between 0 and 5% regrowth, relative to the control. The bentazon treatment allowed 44% regrowth, relative to the control.

Taken together, these data suggest that application of halosulfuron or imazapic would reduce, or eliminate, yellow nutsedge competition with desirable plants more quickly than glyphosate, MSMA, or bentazon. Application of bentazon was shown to be insufficient to alleviate yellow nutsedge competition due to photosynthetic recovery after 6 d. Moreover, bentazon treatment allowed regrowth to 44% of the untreated control. MSMA did little to reduce competition for water, although reducing A_N by 70% after 12 d.

Study 2

Daytime gross carbon assimilation rates stayed fairly constant for untreated plants over the course of the experiment, dropping from 111% to 90% of the average rate during the normalization days. All three herbicide treatments significantly reduced the daytime carbon assimilation relative to the control over time, but this reduction was greater and occurred more quickly with MSMA than with mesotrione. Halosulfuron was intermediate in its effect (Figure 4). The effect of MSMA was significant even one day after treatment (DAT), and by 5 DAT respiration exceeded carbon assimilation during the photoperiod (i.e., net carbon assimilation rate was negative) (data not shown). Halosulfuron reduced gross carbon assimilation to 30% of the pre-treatment rate by the end of the experiment, while mesotrione never reduced carbon assimilation below 59% of the pre-treatment rate (Figure 4). Night-time respiration rates were also significantly reduced by MSMA treatment by 6 DAT.

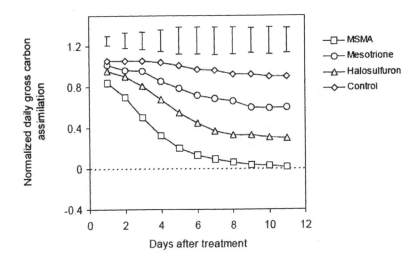

Figure 4. Effects of three herbicide treatments on daytime net carbon assimilation of yellow nutsedge plants.

The effects of the herbicide treatments on whole plant water use contrasted sharply with the effects on photosynthetic carbon assimilation. MSMA treatment resulted in small, but statistically significant, reductions in whole plant water use at 2 and 4 DAT, but otherwise had normalized transpiration rates very close to 1.0 (i.e., no indication of transpiration being reduced relative to control plants). Water use by halosulfuron treated plants declined steadily over the first 7 DAT, and was significantly lower than water use of MSMA treated plants from 6 DAT until the end of the experiment. Similar to MSMA, yellow nutsedge treated with mesotrione showed no discernible reduction in whole plant water use over the course of the experiment.

Halosulfuron and MSMA reduced shoot regrowth to between 0 and 5% of the control (Table 1). Halosulfuron effectively reduces yellow nutsedge shoot number, shoot weight, and root-tuber production (Vencill et al., 1995). Conversely, the mesotrione treatment allowed some 58% regrowth. The ineffectiveness of mesotrione for yellow nutsedge rhizome control was expected, considering that yellow nutsedge does not appear on the product label as a weed that is controlled by postemergence applications.

Table 1. Regrowth of above ground phytomass occurring after treatment with herbicides. Means followed by the same letter do not differ according to a protected LSD test (P < 0.05). n = 4.

Herbicide	Rate (g/ha)	Dry Weight of Regrowth (g)
Untreated		9.5 a
Mesotrione	110	5.5 b
MSMA	2200	0.5 c
Halosulfuron	63	0.0 c
LSD (0.05)		0.8

In study 1, the application of halosulfuron or imazapic reduced, or eliminated yellow nutsedge competition with desirable plants more quickly than glyphosate, MSMA, or bentazon. However, the MSMA treatment displayed a quite different pattern between A_N and g_s. The initial decline in g_s for the MSMA treatment was similar to that of A_N. However, recovery occurred after 12 d and g_s was near 95% of the untreated control while A_N was near 35%. MSMA treated sedge plants were transpiring water at near full capacity while A_N was reduced by 70%. Study 2 was initiated to examine this phenomenon and confirmed the effect. MSMA rapidly and completely eliminated carbon assimilation, but had almost no effect on plant water use. The mechanism of action for MSMA is not well understood (Vencill 2002). However, there has been evidence to suggest that MSMA inhibits the malic enzyme in C_4 plants (Knowles and Benson 1983). The accumulation of malic acid could then lead to cessation of carbon fixation and photooxidative damage. This hypothesis is supported by the visual symptomology present after MSMA application to susceptible plants. Photooxidative damage generally results in cellular disintegration or leakage. Therefore, we suggest that application of MSMA to yellow nutsedge results in destruction of the guard cells, which would lead to unregulated water loss through the stomata.

REFERENCES

Ferrell J A; Earl H J; Vencill W K (2003). The effect of selected herbicides on CO_2 assimilation, chlorophyll fluorescence, and stomatal conductance in johnsongrass. *Weed Science* **51**, 28-31.

Grichar W J; Nester P R (1997). Nutsedge control in peanut with AC 263,222 and imazethapyr. *Weed Technology* **11**, 714-719.

Holm, L G; Plucknett D L; Pancho J V; Herberger J P (1991). *The World's Worst Weeds. Distribution and Biology*. Univ. Press:Hawaii.

Holt J S; Orcutt D R (1991). Functional relationships of growth and competitiveness in perennial weeds in and cotton. *Weed Science* **39**, 575-584.

Jones H G (1992). *Plants and microclimate*. Cambridge University Press: Cambridge, England.

Knowles F C; Benson A A (1983). The mode of action of a herbicide. Johnsongrass and methanearsonic acid. *Plant Physiology* **71**, 235-240.

Ray J D; Sinclair T R (1997). Stomatal closure of maize hybrids in response to drying soil. *Crop Science* **37**, 803-807.

van Iersel M W; Bugbee B (2000). A multiple chamber, semicontinuous, crop carbon dioxide exchange system: Design, calibration, and data interpretation. *Journal of the American Society of Horticultural Science* **125**, 86-92.

Vencill W K; Richburg III J S; Wilcut J W; Hawf L R (1995). Effect of MON-12037 on purple (Cyperus rotundus) and yellow (Cyperus esculentus) nutsedge. *Weed Technology* **9**, 148-152.

Vencill W K (2002). *Herbicide Handbook 8th edition*. Weed Science Society of America: Lawrence, KS, USA.

Metamifop: mechanism of herbicidal activity and selectivity in rice and barnyardgrass

T J Kim, H S Chang, J S Kim, I T Hwang, K S Hong, D W Kim, K Y Cho
Korea Research Institute of Chemical Technology, P. O. Box 107, Daejeon 305-600, Korea
Email: tjkim@krict.re.kr

E J Myung, B J Chung
Dongbu Hannong Chemical Co., Ltd., Hwasung, Gyeonggi 445-960, Korea

ABSTRACT

Metamifop (coded DBH129, ISO proposed) is a new aryloxyphenoxypropionate (AOPP) post-emergence herbicide developed by Dongbu Hannong Chemical Co Ltd, Korea. One of the most outstanding features of metamifop is that it shows an exclusive whole plant safety to rice with a high control efficacy to annual grass weeds, especially barnyardgrass. To determine the reason for the selectivity of metamifop, we examined ACCase sensitivity, absorption and translocation of [^{14}C] metamifop in both rice (tolerant) and barnyardgrass (susceptible). The I_{50} values for inhibition of ACCase by metamifop was >10 μM in rice and 0.5 μM in barnyardgrass. This differential sensitivity is consistent with whole plant sensitivity under greenhouse conditions. More [^{14}C] metamifop was absorbed through the leaf surface in barnyardgrass than in rice, with about 83% and 56% of the total applied [^{14}C] penetrating 72 hrs after application respectively. Translocation was not significantly different between the two species. These data demonstrated that the selectivity of metamifop between rice and barnyardgrass could be due to both differential foliar absorption rate and differential ACCase sensitivity.

INTRODUCTION

Metamifop [coded DBH-129, (*R*)-2-[4-(6-chloro-1,3-benzoxazol-2-yloxy)phenoxy]-2'-fluoro-*N*-methylpropionanilide] (Figure 1), is a new post-emergence herbicide discovered first by the Korea Research Institute of Chemical Technology (KRICT). For a member of the AOPP class of herbicides, metamifop shows excellent whole plant selectivity between rice and barnyardgrass. Like other AOPP herbicides, metamifop is an inhibitor of ACCase which catalyses the first committed step in fatty acid biosynthesis in plants. Metamifop strongly inhibits plant ACCase, with an I_{50} value of approximately 0.6 μM for the partially purified ACCase from barnyardgrass (Kim *et al.*, 2002 & 2003). This is the first report of the selectivity of metamifop within grass species. In this study, we confirm the primary target site of metamifop and determine the fundamental mechanisms involved in the robust rice safety.

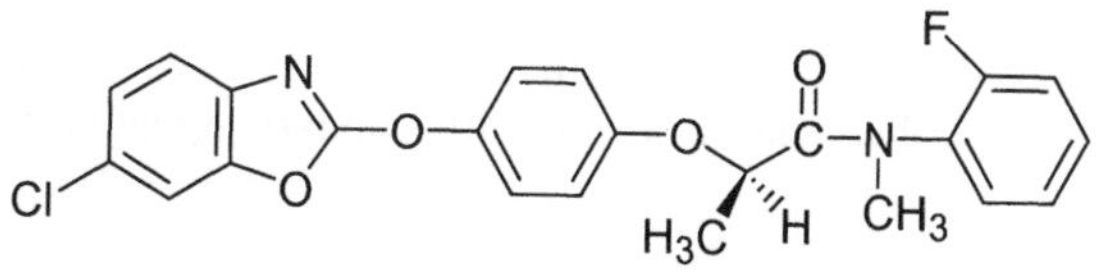

Figure 1. Chemical structure of metamifop

MATERIALS AND METHODS

Chemicals

Two stereoisomers of (R) and (S) metamifop with > 97% purity were prepared by KRICT. The [^{14}C] metamifop (specific activity 1,620 MBq mmol^{-1}) was provided from Korea Radiochemical Center, Suwon, Korea. The (S) metamifop was separated by HPLC using a chiral column.

Preparation of ACCase and assay of activity

ACCase was assayed as described previously (Kim *et al.*, 2000), and all procedures were carried out in a cold chamber at 4°C. Meristematic tissues of the 2-leaf stage grown under greenhouse conditions were harvested and stored in a deep freezer at −70°C until used. The leaf tissues (10 g) were ground with a 30 ml of 100 mM Tris buffer (pH 8.5) containing 1 mM EDTA, 10 % (v/v) glycerol, 2 mM D-isoascorbic acid, 1 mM phenylmethylsulfonyl fluoride, 0.5 % (w/v) polyvinylpolypyrrolidone 40, and 20 mM DL-dithiothreitol. The homogenates were then filtered through a layer of Miracloth (Calbiochem, USA) and centrifuged (J2-21M/E, Beckman) at 27,000 g for 10 min. To obtain an adequate reaction in barnyardgrass, the decanted supernatant was adjusted to 20% ammonium sulfate for 30 min. After centrifugation for 30 min at 27,000 g, the protein in the supernatant was precipitated by adding ammonium sulfate to 40% saturation. The final pellet was then resuspended in an elution buffer (2.5 ml) of 50 mM Tricine (pH 8.5) containing 2.5 mM MgCl$_2$6H$_2$O, 1.0 mM DTT and 50 mM KCl. The enzyme extracts were desalted through a PD-10 (Amersham Pharmarcia Biotech, Sweden) column that had been equilibrated with the elution buffer.

ACCase activity was measured by the incorporation of [^{14}C] into heat-stable products following incubation with H^{14}CO$_3$. A 30 µl of enzyme preparation was pre-incubated for 2 min in a water bath at 32°C in a medium of 20 mM Tris (pH 8.5) containing 10 mM KCl, 5 mM ATP, 2 mM MgCl$_2$, 2.5 mM DTT, 0.15 mM NaH^{14}CO$_3$ (Dupont-NEN, specific activity 251.6 MBq mole^{-1}). A 10 µl aliquot of various concentrations up to 2.5 µM of (R) metamifop dissolved in dimethyl sulfoxide (DMSO) was applied in the reaction. The final volume of reaction mixture was adjusted to 200 µl, and 100 µg protein was used in each reaction. The enzyme activity was initiated by adding 10 µl of 16 mM acetyl-CoA, allowed to proceed for 10 min at 32°C and stopped by adding 20 µl of 12 N HCl. The samples were then dried under a stream of air in a water bath at 90°C for 1 hr and dissolved with 0.5 ml ethanol and 4 ml scintillation cocktail solution. The amount of radioactive products generated during the reaction interval was quantified by a liquid scintillation counting (LS6500, Beckman). Background [^{14}C] fixation was determined by substituting water for acetyl-CoA, and background counts were commonly less than 5% of ^{14}C-fixation in no-herbicide controls. The protein content in enzyme preparations was determined by the method of Bradford using bovine serum albumin as a standard.

All experiments were conducted at least twice, with 3 replicates for each experiment. The data from all experiments were pooled, and the means with standard deviation are presented.

Foliar uptake and translocation

Solutions of [^{14}C] metamifop were prepared in 50% aqueous acetone containing 0.1% Tween 20 so that each 10 μl included approximately 6.4 KBq (440,000 dpm). Using a micropipette, the 10 μl solution was applied as 10 microdroplets to middle of the fully expanded 3rd leaves in rice and barnyardgrass. At various time of intervals, the treated parts were excised, and unabsorbed [^{14}C] metamifop was washed out of the leaf surface by shaking 40 times by hand with 10 ml of 50% aqueous methanol containing 0.1% Tween 20. The amount of [^{14}C] in 1 ml of each wash was determined by liquid scintillation counting.

For the translocation study, the treated leaves were separated from the remainder of shoot 72 hrs after application. The treated leaf was subdivided into the treated area, the upper portion (toward the leaf tip), and the lower portion. The plant tissues were then dried in an oven at 50°C for a week and combusted in a biological sample oxidizer (Packard 306). The evolved [^{14}C] in 15 ml of carbosob/Permafluor E$^+$ (5/10, v/v) was determined by liquid scintillation counting. The amount of [^{14}C] metamifop absorbed through the leaf surface was calculated as the total amount of radioactivity recovered in the treated plant and expressed as a percentage of the total applied. The translocation amount was expressed as a percentage of the total radioactivity absorbed by the plants.

RESULTS AND DISCUSSION

Although the chemical structure of metamifop is grouped in the AOPPs, the most prominent feature of this new herbicide is the remarkable whole plant selectivity shown between rice and barnyardgrass (Kim *et al.*, 2003). Under greenhouse conditions, whole plant dose-responses to metamifop were remarkably different in rice and barnyardgrass. Barnyardgrass was completely controlled with a rate of 8 g a.i./ha, while rice survived even at a rate of 2,000 g a.i./ha metamifop (Table 1). It has been reported (Kim *et al.*, 2003) that the primary target site

Table 1.   Whole plant dose response of metamifop on rice and barnyardgrass under greenhouse conditions

Treatment	Rate	Rice	Barnyardgrass
	(g a.i./ha)	(% of injury)	(% of control)
(R) metamifop	2,000	21	100
	1,000	0	100
	500	0	100
	250	0	100
	125	0	100
	63	0	100
	32	0	100
	16	0	98
	8	0	99
	4	0	63

of metamifop is ACCase, which is known as the first committed step in fatty acid biosynthesis in plants. In that report, the I_{50} value for metamifop against the partially purified barnyardgrass ACCase was about 0.6 μM. Metamifop showed steroselectivity both in whole plant and *in vitro* ACCase assays, the (S) isomer being much less active than the (R) isomer (data not shown). These results confirmed that the primary target site of metamifop in plants is ACCase.

Selectivity was also seen between rice and barnyardgrass in the sensitivity of ACCase to metamifop. The *in vitro* I_{50} values for ACCase inhibition were >10.0 μM in rice and 0.5 μM in barnyardgrass, demonstrating that rice ACCase is at least 20 times less sensitive to metamifop than that of barnyardgrass (Figure 2). This differential *in vitro* ACCase sensitivity mirrors the whole plant sensitivity shown in Table 1. This result suggests that the binding sites of metamifop on rice and barnyardgrass ACCase are different, and that this could be a major contributor to the whole plant selectivity.

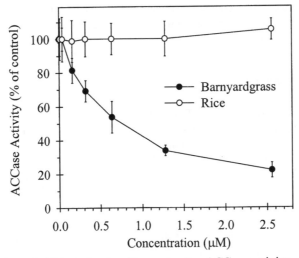

Figure 2. Effect of metamifop on *in vitro* ACCase activity in rice and barnyardgrass.

Foliar absorption of [^{14}C] metamifop through the leaf surface of rice and barnyardgrass was almost complete within 24 hrs after treatment, and was not significantly changed afterward (Figure 3). Rice showed a lower foliar uptake than barnyardgrass 72 hrs after application, values being about 85% and 50% of total applied [^{14}C] metamifop, respectively (Figure 3).

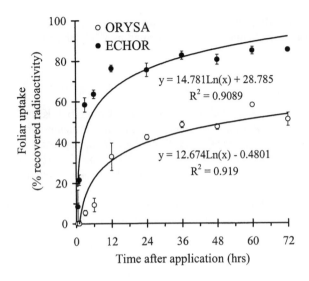

Figure 3. Foliar absorption of [^{14}C] metamifop into rice (ORYSA)
and barnyardgrass (ECHOR).

Translocation was very similar between rice and barnyardgrass 72 hrs after application, with about 75% of absorbed [^{14}C] remaining in the treated zone and about 25% exported from the treated zone in both species (Table 2). Of the exported [^{14}C] amounts, around 19% moved to the upper part of treated zone while less than 1% was recovered in the lower part, suggesting that metamifop moves mainly through xylem rather than through phloem. Only small [^{14}C] amounts, 0.8% in rice and 1.0% in barnyardgrass, were recovered from the remaining parts of the plant.

Table 2. Distribution of [^{14}C] in rice and barnyardgrass 72 hrs after treatment

Species	[^{14}C] content (% of absorbed)				Recovery rate
	Treated zone	Upper leaf	Lower leaf	Remainder of plant	
Rice	74.2	18.3	0.7	0.8	0.94
Barnyardgrass	75.4	19.5	1.0	1.0	0.97

In conclusion, the different levels of foliar absorption could contribute to the selectivity between rice and barnyardgrass; however, the differential ACCase sensitivity is fundamental in explaining the robust rice safety of metamifop.

ACKNOWLEDGEMENTS

The authors would like to thank Mr. Shin and Mr. Song for their excellent technical assistance. We also acknowledge Korea Radiochemical Center for providing [^{14}C] labeled metamifop.

REFERENCES

Kim T J; Chang H S; Ryu J W; Ko Y K; Park C H; Kwon O Y; Chung B J; Kim D W; Cho K Y (2003). Metamifop: a new post-emergence grasskilling herbicide for use in rice. *Proceedings of the BCPC – Crop Science and Technology 2003,* in press.

Kim T J; Song J E; Kim J S; Chang H S; Chung B J; Kim D W; Cho K Y (2002). The target site and its selectivity of metamifop, a new rice herbicide. *Korean Society of Pesticide Science Abstract* (fall), p 69.

Kim T J; Shin H J; Kim J S; Chung B J; Cho K Y (2000). *In vitro* acetyl-coenzyme A carboxylase assay for rice and barnyardgrass. *Korean Journal of Weed Science* **3**, 208-216.

Herbicide resistance in *Lolium multiflorum* Lam. (Italian rye-grass): involvement of glutathione *S*-transferases

J P H Reade, A H Cobb
Crop and Environment Research Centre, Harper Adams University College, Newport, Shropshire, TF10 8NB, UK
Email: jreade@harper-adams.ac.uk

ABSTRACT

Italian rye-grass (*Lolium multiflorum* Lam.) is a major weed of arable crops in the UK. The extent of herbicide resistance in this species is now second only to that of black-grass and hinders the effective control of this grass weed. Elucidation of the mechanisms underpinning this resistance is vital in the battle to control rye-grass. Glutathione *S*-transferases (GSTs) have been implicated in herbicide resistance in many species, enabling resistant individuals to detoxify herbicides at an enhanced rate. Data is presented from glasshouse trials on a number of rye-grass biotypes that have previously been shown to be poorly controlled by herbicides in the field. GST activity and abundance data is presented for these biotypes, demonstrating that this important enzyme family may be implicated in herbicide resistance in the biotypes studied. These findings will be discussed in relation to both herbicide resistance and GST activity in other UK grasses.

INTRODUCTION

Lolium multiflorum Lam. (Italian Rye-grass) is a major weed of arable crops, especially cereals, in the UK and Northern Europe. Its presence results in significant yield losses, poor quality product and increased lodging of crops.

Herbicide resistance is the inheritable ability of a weed biotype to survive the application of a dose of herbicide that would be lethal to a susceptible population of the weed. Resistance in *Lolium multiflorum* in the UK was first reported in 1993 to the herbicides diclofop-methyl, fenoxaprop-ethyl and fluazifop-P-butyl (Moss *et al.*, 1993). Since then, incidents of resistance have increased and the number of reports of resistance in UK rye-grass populations is now only second to that of *Alopecurus myosuroides* (black-grass). By 2003 over 100 cases of resistance have been reported from 21 UK counties (WRAG, 2003). Herbicide resistant populations of rye-grass result in chemical control being less effective, more expensive and less predictable.

Glutathione *S*-transferases (GSTs) are a family of enzymes that catalyse the conjugation of a variety of xenobiotic chemicals, including some herbicides, to the tripeptide glutathione. This often results in both increased solubility and decreased toxicity of the xenobiotic (Marrs, 1996). GSTs have been implicated as being involved in enhanced metabolism-based resistance in *A. myosuroides* (Reade and Cobb, 1999; 2002). Resistant biotypes of this weed possessed constitutively higher GST activities and GST polypeptide abundance than susceptible biotypes. Investigation of resistance mechanisms in *L. multiflorum* have also suggested a role for GSTs in this species (Cocker *et al.*, 2001). The role of GSTs in herbicide resistance in grasses has recently been reviewed (Reade and Cobb 2003).

This study presents findings from glasshouse-based herbicide trials and measurements of GST activities and abundance for *L. multiflorum* biotypes that have previously proved to be poorly controlled in the field. Results are discussed in comparison to herbicide resistance in *A. myosuroides*, population plasticity and the possibility of correlations between GSTs and herbicide resistance.

MATERIALS AND METHODS

Materials

L. multiflorum seeds from a susceptible standard and from biotypes demonstrating poor control in the field were provided by Syngenta Crop Protection UK. All herbicides were commercial grade. Propaquizafop was provided by Makhteshim-Agan.

Glasshouse Trial

Plants were grown as previously described for *A. myosuroides* (Reade and Cobb, 1999) using John Innes No 2 compost, under glasshouse conditions. Herbicide treatments were delivered at GS 12/13, as detailed in Table 1, using a patent pot sprayer with 03 F110 nozzles delivering a medium quality spray at a volume of 200 litres ha^{-1}, 45cm above the plants. Fresh weights of individual plants were determined three weeks after herbicide treatment.

Table 1.   Rate of application (g a.i./ha) of herbicides in glasshouse trials

Active Ingredient	Fenoxaprop-ethyl	Clodinafop-propargyl	Isoproturon	Propaquizafop	Sethoxydim
Rate Applied	70g/ha	60g/ha	1500g/ha	120g/ha	338g/ha

Protein extraction and GST assay

Proteins were extracted as described by Reade and Cobb (1999). GST activities were assayed against the artificial substrate 1-chloro-2,4-dinitrobenzene (CDNB) using the micro GST assay described by Reade and Cobb (2002). Protein concentration of extracts were determined using a modification of the Bradford dye-binding assay (Bradford, 1976), as previously described (Milner *et al*, 2001). GST activity data is expressed as nmoles CDNB min^{-1} mg^{-1} total protein.

Determination of GST polypeptide abundance

GST polypeptide abundance was determined by enzyme-linked immunosorbent assay (ELISA) using monoclonal antiserum raised against the 30-kD GST subunit purified from *A.myosuroides* biotype Peldon (Reade and Cobb, 2002).

Data analysis

Fresh weight data from herbicide trials were converted to a resistance classification as described by Moss *et al.* (1999). GST activity data are expressed as the ratio of activity to that extracted from susceptible biotype. GST abundance data are expressed as normalised data, taking biotype B1 as 1.0. Three replications were used in all experimentation and analyses.

RESULTS

The results of the glasshouse herbicide trial are shown in Table 2. All biotypes, except the susceptible standard (B1), demonstrated resistance to clodinafop. Cross-resistance to fenoxaprop was detected in 3 biotypes and resistance to propaquizafop in only one biotype (B11). No biotype demonstrated resistance to sethoxydim. Two biotypes, B9 and B12, also showed resistance to isoproturon.

Table 2. Glasshouse-based herbicide trials of five *L. multiflorum* biotypes. Resistance classifications (S, R, RR) were calculated as described by Moss *et al.,* (1999)

Biotype	B1	B9	B10	B11	B12
Isoproturon	S	RR	S	S	RR
Fenoxaprop	S	RR	S	RR	RR
Clodinafop	S	R	R	RR	RR
Propaquizafop	S	S	S	RR	S
Sethoxydim	S	S	S	S	S

GST activities are shown in Figure 1. All biotypes identified as possessing resistance to at least one of the herbicides studied had extractable GST activities greater than that of the susceptible biotype. These ranged from 1.9 to 4.3 times the activity in the susceptible biotype (Table 3). GST abundance was greater in three of the four biotypes displaying resistance to at least one of the herbicides studied, ranging from 2.74 to 5.91. In biotype B11 a relative abundance of 0.37 was obtained.

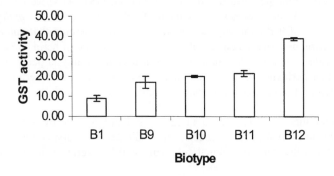

Figure 1.   GST activities (nmoles min^{-1} mg^{-1} total protein ± standard error) for five *L. multiflorum* biotypes

Table 3.   GST activities and abundance for five *L. multiflorum* biotypes expressed as ratios to those of biotype B1

Biotype	B1	B9	B10	B11	B12
GST activity (ratio to biotype B1)	1.0	1.9	2.3	2.4	4.3
GST Abundance (ratio to biotype B1)	1.0	2.74	5.91	0.37	5.76

DISCUSSION

Herbicides from two mode of action classes were used in the glasshouse trials, namely inhibition of photosynthesis at PS II (IPU) and inhibition of ACCase ('fops' and 'dims'). Biotypes B9 and B12 demonstrated resistance against herbicides from both of these classes, indicating the presence of multiple resistance in these biotypes. The other resistant biotypes (B10 and B11) were susceptible to IPU, but possessed different susceptibilities to the 'fops' used. Absence of resistance to sethoxydim suggests that target site resistance in the form of herbicide-insensitive ACCase is not present in any of the biotypes studied (Moss *et al.*, 2003), indicating that resistance in these biotypes to 'fops' is due to enhanced metabolism of these herbicides.

GST activities were lowest in the susceptible biotype (B1), with resistant biotypes possessing between 1.9 and 4.3 times the extractable GST activity against CDNB (Table 3). GST abundance was greater in three of the four resistant biotypes compared to the susceptible biotype B1. A high degree of correlation between activity and abundance was not observed. However, CDNB is not a substrate for all GSTs and antiserum was raised against an individual GST polypeptide, so correlation between GST activity and abundance may not always be seen. In this respect the *L. multiflorum* biotypes studied show similarities to *A. myosuroides*, where resistant biotype Peldon contains approximately double the GST activity and greater GST polypeptide abundance than susceptible biotype Herbiseed (Reade and Cobb, 1999). Other resistant *A. myosuroides* biotypes also demonstrate enhanced GST activities and abundance (Reade and Cobb, 2002). In addition, the enhanced GST activity in *L. multiflorum* is constitutive, not a result of herbicide application. It is therefore possible that enhanced GST activity in *L. multiflorum* biotypes is responsible for an enhanced rate of herbicide conjugation and therefore herbicide resistance. Alternatively, GSTs may be acting as peroxidases in the detoxification of either herbicides or active oxygen species resulting from herbicide activity, as previously reported in *A. myosuroides* (Cummins *et al.*, 1999).

It is interesting to note that antiserum raised against a GST polypeptide from *A. myosuroides* detected polypeptides in *L. multiflorum* extracts. This indicates that polypeptides with similar epitopes are present and that the monoclonal antiserum will be useful in future studies in *L. multiflorum*.

The complex patterns of cross-resistance shown in the biotypes studied suggests that GSTs are not the only factor imparting resistance in *L. multiflorum*, as if this were the case then more consistency between GST activities/abundance and resistance to individual herbicides might be expected. It is postulated that increased GST activities play a role in resistance, as in *A. myosuroides*, but that they are involved alongside other stress-related enzymes in detoxification of herbicides and protection from herbicide damage.

The large variation in GST activities and abundance between biotypes suggests that there may be a high degree of plasticity in this species with respect to GSTs. This has been observed in field populations of *A. myosuroides* (Reade and Cobb, 2002) and it has been postulated that herbicide application to such populations results in selection of those individuals possessing greater GST activity/abundance. The observed variation in GST activity and abundance in *L. multiflorum* biotypes suggests that the same could be happening in this species.

CONCLUSIONS

The *L. multiflorum* biotypes studied demonstrate individual, complex, cross-resistance patterns to the herbicides studied. They are unlikely to possess target site resistance due to their sensitivity to sethoxydim. All demonstrated enhanced GST activity and three of the four possessed greater abundance of a polypeptide recognised by antiserum raised against a 30kDa GST polypeptide from *A. myosuroides*. It is postulated that GSTs may play an important role in enhanced metabolism-based herbicide resistance in *L. multiflorum*.

ACKNOWLEDGEMENTS

We would like to thank Syngenta Crop Protection UK for provision of *L. multiflorum* biotypes and Makhteshim-Agan for supplying propaquizafop.

REFERENCES

Bradford M M (1976). A rapid and sensitive method for the quantification of microgram quantities of protein utilising the principle of protein-dye binding. *Analytical Biochemistry* **72,** 248-254.

Cocker K M; Northcroft D S; Coleman J O D; Moss S R (2001). Resistance to ACCase-inhibiting herbicides and isoproturon in UK populations of *Lolium multiflorum*: mechanisms of resistance and implications for control. *Pest Management Science* **57,** 587-597.

Cummins I; Cole D J; Edwards R (1999). A role for glutathione transferases functioning as glutathione peroxidases in resistance to multiple herbicides in black-grass. *The Plant Journal* **51,** 244-250.

Marrs K A (1996). The functions and regulation of glutathione S-transferases in plants. *Annual Review of Plant Physiology and Plant Molecular Biology* **47,** 127-158.

Milner L J; Reade J P H; Cobb A H (2001). Developmental changes in glutathione *S*-transferase activity in *Alopecurus myosuroides* Huds (black-grass) in the field. *Pest Management Science* **57,** 1100-1106.

Moss S R; Horswell J; Froud-Williams R J; Ndoping M M (1993). Implications of herbicide resistant *Lolium multiflorum* (Italian rye-grass). *Aspects of Applied Biology* **35**, 53-60.

Moss S R; Cocker K M; Brown A C; Hall L; Field L M (2003). Characterisation of target-site resistance to ACCase-inhibiting herbicides in the weed *Alopecurus myosuroides* (black-grass). *Pest Management Science* **59**, 190-201.

Reade J P H; Cobb A H (1999). Purification, characterisation and comparison of glutathione *S*-transferases from black-grass (*Alopecurus myosuroides* Huds) biotypes. *Pesticide Science* **55**, 993-999.

Reade J P H; Cobb A H (2002). New, quick tests for herbicide resistance in black-grass (*Alopecurus myosuroides* Huds) based on increased glutathione *S*-transferase activity and abundance. *Pest Management Science* **58**, 26-32.

Reade J P H; Cobb A H (2003). A role for glutathione *S*-transferases in resistance to herbicides in grasses. *Weed Science* (in press)

WRAG (2003). Managing and preventing herbicide resistance in weeds. Weed Resistance Action Group/HGCA.

Structure of dichloromethyl-ketal safeners affects the expression of glutathione S-transferase isoforms

T Matola, I Jablonkai
Institute of Chemistry, Chemical Research Center, Hungarian Academy of Sciences, H-1525 Budapest, Hungary.
E-mail: jabi@chemres.hu

D Dixon, I Cummins, R Edwards
Department of Biological Sciences, University of Durham, Durham DH1 3LE, UK

ABSTRACT

The herbicide safener MG-191 and its acetal and ketal analogues as well as mono- and dichloroacetamides were tested for their ability to alleviate toxicity of acetochlor to maize and differentially enhance the glutathione (GSH) content and the expression of glutathione transferase (GST) isoforms in maize. Our results demonstrate that the safener structure affects the specific expression of GSTs mediating the detoxication of acetochlor. No correlation was found between the degree of induction of GSH and GSTs and the safening activity.

INTRODUCTION

Safeners are chemical agents that increase the tolerance of crop plants to herbicides without affecting the weed control efficacy. They appear to induce a set of genes that encode enzymes and the biosynthesis of cofactors involved in herbicide detoxication (Gatz, 1997). Glutathione S-transferase isoenzymes (GSTs) and endogenous glutathione (GSH) play a vital role in chloroacetamide herbicide detoxication by GSH conjugation. Safeners of various chemical classes were found to induce the activity of GSTs and the level of GSH in the protected plants (Davies & Caseley, 1999).

The highly active dichloromethyl ketal MG-191 (2-dichloromethyl-2-methyl-1,3-dioxolane) is used in the safening of maize against thiocarbamate and to a lesser extent chloroacetamide herbicides. MG-191 has been found to induce *Zm*GSTU1-2, a tau (U) class GST isoform of maize (Jablonkai, *et al.*, 2001). In order to further clarify the significance of GST and GSH enhancement in safening maize against the herbicide acetochlor (**Ac,** 2-chloro-N-(ethoxymethyl)-N-(2-ethyl-6-methylphenyl) acetamide) for this safener class, the relationship of structure to safening efficacy, GSH and GST inducibility was examined using halogenated acetals (**1a-l**), ketals (**2a-k**) and acetamides (**3a-d**).

1a-l   2a-k   3a-d

METHODS AND MATERIALS

Chemicals

Open-chain dichloromethyl acetals and ketals were synthesized from dichloroacetaldehyde, 1,1-dichloroacetone, and 1,1-dichloroacetophenone (Dutka, 1991). Cyclic acetals and ketals were prepared from diethyl acetal and ketal of dichloroacetaldehyde and 1,1-dichloroacetone by transacetalisation. Acetamides were synthesised by haloacetylation of amines using standard Schotten-Baumann conditions. Crude reaction products were purified by either distillation or silica gel column chromatography. Acetochlor was purified by column chromatography from the commercial product. [Carbonyl-^{14}C] acetochlor (sp. act. 37 MBq /mmol) was a sample prepared previously (Jablonkai & Hatzios, 1991). Purity for all compounds was greater than 95 %. All other chemicals were purchased from Aldrich (Sigma-Aldrich Kft., Budapest, Hungary)

Safener activity of experimental molecules

Seeds of maize (Gazda MV) were soaked in water and planted in plastic cups (6 cm diameter, 9 cm deep, 3 seeds/cup) containing air-dried foundry sand (250 g, OH-4 type). Treatment solutions (50 ml) containing safener (50 M) and/or acetochlor (50 M) were applied to each cup. Seeds were placed 2 cm deep. The plants were grown in a growth room (temperature: 23 $\pm$ 1 °C; relative humidity: 60 $\pm$ 5 %; light intensity: 10 klux; light period: 16 h per day). The plants were watered three times a week to bring the weight of cups to 300 g. Plants were harvested two weeks after the treatment and shoot lengths measured. The experiment was carried out twice with four replicates.

Plant material and enzyme isolation

For GST activity analyses seeds (25) of maize were placed in Petri dishes (18.5 cm in diameter) on two layers of filter paper wetted by aqueous solution (20 ml, 50 M) of chemicals studied. The dishes were placed in a germination thermostat. The seedlings were grown in the dark for 5 days at 27 °C. Five-day-old seedlings were thoroughly washed with tap water and separated shoots were homogenized in a mortar and pestle using quartz sand then extracted with 5 volumes of cold Tris-HCl buffer (100 mM, pH 7.5) containing 2 mM EDTA, 1 mM dithiothreitol and 5 % (w/v) polyvinyl polypirrolidone. The homogenates were filtered through two layers of Miracloth and the filtrates were centrifuged at 10,000 x g for 20 min at 4 °C. The supernatants were brought to 80% $(NH_4)_2SO_4$ saturation and centrifuged at 10,000 x g for 20 min at 4 °C. Aliquots of the protein precipitates were resuspended in potassium phosphate buffer (20 mM pH 6.5) and desalted by gel filtration (Sephadex G25, medium) before use for enzymatic studies.

For Western blot experiments shoot and root enzyme extracts of maize (Cecilia) were prepared as reported previously (Jablonkai et al., 2001)

For determination of GSH contents, shoot tissues of etiolated seedlings were grown as described earlier. Tissues were frozen and homogenized in liquid nitrogen and extracted with 4 volumes of 70% ethanol. The homogenates were centrifuged at 10,000 x g for 20 min at 4 °C and the supernatants were collected.

Analysis of GSTs and GSH

Glutathione *S*-transferase activities of desalted enzymes were determined with CDNB (1-chloro-2,4-dinitrobenzene) and [carbonyl-^{14}C]acetochlor (Ac) substrates. GST(CDNB) activities were determined spectrophotometrically (340 nm) and expressed as nmol product formed per second (nkat) per mg protein (Dixon *et al.*, 1998a). GST(Ac) activities of the samples were determined by liquid scintillation counting of the conjugate formed in the reaction of [carbonyl-^{14}C]acetochlor (0.75 mM) and GSH (10.0 mM) mediated by the desalted enzymes at 37 °C in 30 min. The GST(Ac) activity was expressed as pmol conjugate per second (pkat) per mg protein. Protein contents of the extracts were determined spectrophotometrically using a Coomassie Brillant Blue reagent with bovine serum albumin as reference protein.

The polypeptide composition of the GST preparations were analyzed by sodium dodecylsulfate polyacrylamide gel electrophoresis (SDS-PAGE). Western blotting was carried out using antisera raised to *Zm*GSTF1-2 and *Zm*GSTU1-2 (Dixon *et al.*, 1998a).

Non-protein thiol (GSH) content of alcoholic supernatant was measured spectrophotometrically (412 nm) using DTNB reagent (Jablonkai & Hatzios, 1991).

RESULTS AND DISCUSSION

Safening experiments were carried out in sand at a relatively high pre-emergence acetochlor rate (2.4 kg/ha) and at high moisture content. Under these conditions the herbicide is extremely phytotoxic and no complete protection can be achieved. The bromoacetaldehyde diethyl acetal (**1b**) showed moderate safening effects while the monochloroacetal **1a** and the dichloroacetals (**1c-l**) exhibited poor or no safening activity (Table 1). Among dialkyl ketals having increasing alkyl chain length (**2a-d**) the highest safening activity was observed for the diethyl (**2a**) and dipropyl (**2b**) derivative. In general, cyclic ketals (**2e-k**) were effective safeners. Derivatives having 1,3-dioxolane (**2f**), dioxane (**2g**) and dioxepane (**2i**) ring in their stucture were the most active molecules. Interestingly, dioxacycloalkanes with 8- and 9-membered ring were still active. The safening activity of ketals also exceeded that of acetals against the thiocarbamate EPTC (Dutka, 1991). It seems that the hydrolytic cleavage of the acetals or ketals is likely not involved in their mode of safening action since both the dichloroacetaldehyde and the dichloroacetone, the products of the hydrolysis, were inactive safeners (Dutka, 1991). Among amides the marketed safener dichloroacetyl-diallylamide (dichlormid, **3a**) was highly protective. Decreasing the number of halogens and allyl groups yielded less active molecules. On the other hand, the monochloroacetamide **3c**, which is an alkylating agent with herbicidal activity, was protective against EPTC (Pallos *et al.*, 1975).

The GSH content of shoot tissues of safener-treated plants was significantly increased by treatment with monohalomethyl acetals (**1a-b**) and was not affected by the dihalo derivatives as compared to that of untreated control (Table 1). Among ketals only cyclic derivatives (**2e-k**) induced GSH biosynthesis while open-chain ketals (**2a-d**) were not inducers. Both mono- (**3b-c**) and dichloroacetamide (**3a**) pretreatment elevated the GSH levels. It appears that there is no direct correlation between the elevation of GSH content and the safening efficacy. While twofold increase was found with the moderately safening **2e** cyclic ketal only a low or no inducing effect was observed for the more active molecules **2a-b**. Elevation of GSH content has been observed for many safeners (Davies & Casely, 1999). However, safener efficacy is not well correlated with elevated GSH levels.

Table 1.   Safening activity and inducibility of shoot GSH content and GST activities by acetals, ketals and amides in maize

Code	R	X	Y	R^1	R^2	Protection[a] (%)	GSH[b]	GST(CDNB)[c]	GST (Ac)[d]
								treated/control	
Ac	-	-	-	-	-	-	1.11	1.48	3.74
1a	-	H	Cl	Et	Et	24	1.49	0.69	2.03
1b	-	H	Br	Et	Et	60	1.53	0.94	3.76
1c	-	Cl	Cl	Et	Et	8	0.69	1.42	1.83
1d	-	Cl	Cl	Pr	Pr	0	0.80	0.95	1.38
1e	-	Cl	Cl	Bu	Bu	-6	1.22	0.96	0.91
1f	-	Cl	Cl	i-Bu	i-Bu	-2	1.20	0.90	1.61
1g	-	Cl	Cl	-(CH$_2$)$_2$-		18	0.93	0.88	1.23
1h	-	Cl	Cl	-(CH$_2$)$_3$-		14	0.60	0.89	0.90
1i	-	Cl	Cl	-CH$_2$C(CH$_3$)$_2$CH$_2$-		-3	0.91	0.88	1.33
1j	-	Cl	Cl	-(CH$_2$)$_4$-		11	0.95	1.03	1.33
1k	-	Cl	Cl	-(CH$_2$)$_5$-		0	0.98	1.24	0.58
1l	-	Cl	Cl	-(CH$_2$)$_6$-		3	0.82	1.32	0.83
2a	Me	Cl	Cl	Et	Et	62	1.15	1.22	0.65
2b	Me	Cl	Cl	Pr	Pr	63	0.98	1.18	0.85
2c	Me	Cl	Cl	Bu	Bu	38	0.78	0.88	3.93
2d	Me	Cl	Cl	i-Bu	i-Bu	14	0.85	1.07	4.72
2e	Ph	Cl	Cl	-(CH$_2$)$_2$-		41	2.00	1.94	2.23
2f	Me	Cl	Cl	-(CH$_2$)$_2$-		64	1.18	1.83	3.93
2g	Me	Cl	Cl	-(CH$_2$)$_3$-		68	1.31	1.49	1.96
2h	Me	Cl	Cl	-CH$_2$C(CH$_3$)$_2$CH$_2$-		66	1.62	1.77	1.44
2i	Me	Cl	Cl	-(CH$_2$)$_4$-		70	1.71	1.48	0.92
2j	Me	Cl	Cl	-(CH$_2$)$_5$-		50	1.24	1.27	1.19
2k	Me	Cl	Cl	-(CH$_2$)$_6$-		60	1.38	1.39	1.14
3a	-	Cl	Cl	allyl	allyl	81	1.78	1.24	4.69
3b	-	H	Cl	H	allyl	48	2.25	1.25	3.60
3c	-	H	Cl	allyl	allyl	2	1.45	1.16	2.39
3d	-	H	Br	allyl	allyl	22	0.98	0.90	2.98

[a] based on shoot length; protection (%) = 100 x [(herbicide + safener)] / [control - herbicide];
shoot lengths 14 DAT: control, 27.9±5.3 cm, acetochlor, 3.1±0.3 cm
[b] GSH content relative to that of untreated control; GSH$_{contr.}$: 0.55±09 µmol/g fresh weight
[c] GST(CDNB) activity as compared to that of untreated control; GST$_{contr.}$: 3.87±0.33 nkat/mg protein
[d] GST(Ac) activity as compared to that of untreated control; GST$_{contr.}$: 8.26±1.68 pkat/mg protein

GST(CDNB) activity of shoot tissues was only slightly affected by pretreatment with safeners (Table 1). Acetals except for 1c and open-chain ketals (2a-d) did not influence GST(CDNB) activities. Cyclic ketals were all inducers of this GST isoform and derivatives having 1,3-dioxolane backbone (2e and 2f) exerted a twofold increase. Amides were less effective inducers than cyclic ketals. The herbicide acetochlor in itself also increased this isozyme activity by 50%. No correlation exists between GST(CDNB) enhancement and the safening activity of the experimental molecules. GST(CDNB) activity associated with the safener inducible ZmGSTF1-2 isozyme was increased by the dichlormid in both roots and shoots of maize (Dixon et al., 1997) and only slightly by the MG-191 (Jablonkai et al., 2001).

GST(Ac) activities were enhanced by both protective and less effective structures as compared to that of untreated control (Table 1). Among acetals pretreatment with the most active safener **1b** induced the highest (3.76-fold) increase in the enzyme activity. Safening activity of the ketals was not correlated with their effects on GST(Ac) activity. While a high increase (4.72-fold) was shown after treatment with the hardly active **2d**, there was no effect of the most active ketal **2i**. For the amides the degree of induction of the isoenzyme activity was parallel with their safening potential. Correlation between GST(Ac) induction and safening activity exists only for the amides. Pretreatment of maize seedlings with acetochlor resulted in a very high degree of induction of the enzyme activity indicating that the induction of GST isoforms by both chloroacetanilides and their safeners is based on a similar mechanism.

The polypeptide compositions of the GSTs in safener-treated and untreated control root and shoot tissues were examined by SDS-page and Western blotting experiments in order to understand which maize GSTs were induced by the safeners. In this study only the more active ketal derivatives were used. The resulting blots were probed using antisera raised to a phi class *Zm*GSTF1-2 and a tau class *Zm*GSTU1-2 (Dixon *et al.*, 1998a). A higher inducibility of these GST isoforms was observed in root tissues (Figure 1). In shoots, when the heterodimer *Zm*GSTF1-2 was used the expression of constitutive *Zm*GSTF1 and inducible *Zm*GSTF2 was enhanced only by **2f** (MG-191) and its analogue **2g** having a 6-membered ring (Figure 1b).

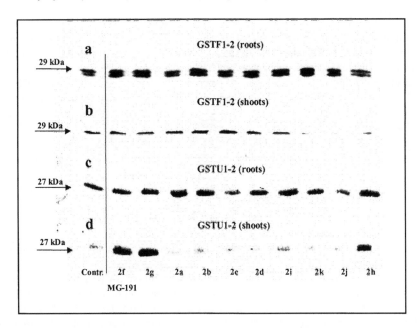

Figure 1. Western blots of crude GST extracts from maize roots and shoots; (a) and (b) analysis of GSTs using the anti-*Zm*GSTF1-2 serum from maize roots and shoots; (c) and (d) analysis of GSTs using the anti-*Zm*GSTU1-2 serum from maize roots and shoots.

These molecules and also **2h** were the most potent inducers of the expression of tau class ZmGSTU1 in shoot tissues (Figure 1c). ZmGSTU1 has previously been shown to play a key role in metabolism of nitrodiphenyl ether herbicides (Cole *et al.*, 1997). It seems that dichloromethyl ketal type safeners are more specific inducers ZmGSTU1-2 than other compounds commonly used to safen thiocarbamate and chloroacetanilide herbicides in maize (Jablonkai *et al.*, 2001).

The exact mechanism of the safener-mediated enhancement of GST activity is not completely understood. GSTs are induced by a diverse range of chemicals and accompanied by the production of active oxygen species. Thus the connection between safener-mediated protection of crops and oxidative stress tolerance has been suggested (Theodoulou *et al.*, 2003). Many GSTs are effective not only in conjugating electrophilic substrates but also function as glutathione peroxidases. Safeners may induce GST expression by mimicking oxidative insult (Dixon *et al.* 1998b). Our results indicate that safener structure plays a decisive role in specific expression of GSTs mediating the detoxication of chloroacetamide herbicides. Since no correlation between the degree of induction of levels of GSH and GST isoforms and the safener activity was found the mode of action of safeners is a more complex process than simply promoting the metabolism of herbicides.

REFERENCES

Cole D J; Cummins I; Hatton P J; Dixon D; Edwards R (1997). Glutathione transferases in crops and major weeds. In: *Regulation of enzymatic systems detoxifying xenobiotics in plants*, ed. K K Hatzios, pp. 139-154 Kluwer: Dordrecht.

Davis J; Caseley J C (1999). Herbicide safeners: a review. *Pesticide Science* **55**, 1043-1058.

Dixon D P; Cole D J; Edwards R (1997). Characterization of multiple glutathione S-transferases containing the GSTI subunit with activities toward herbicide substrates in maize (*Zea mays* L.). *Pesticide Science* **50,** 72-82.

Dixon D P; Cole D J; Edwards R (1998a). Purification, regulation and cloning of glutathione transferase (GST) from maize resembling the auxin-inducible type-III GSTs. *Plant Molecular Biology* **36,** 75-87.

Dixon D P; Cummins I; Cole D J; Edwards R (1998b). Glutathione-mediated detoxication system in plants. *Current Opinion in Plant Biology* **1**, 258-266.

Dutka F (1991). Bioactive chemical bond systems in safeners and prosafeners. *Zeitschrift für Naturforschung* **46c**, 805-809.

Gatz C (1997). Chemical control of gene expression. *Annual Review of Plant Physiology and Plant Molecular Biology* **48**, 89-108.

Jablonkai I; Hatzios K K (1991). Role of glutathione and glutathione-S-transferase in selectivity of acetochlor in maize and wheat. *Pesticide Biochemistry and Physiology* **41**, 221-231.

Jablonkai I; Hulesch A; Cummins I; Dixon D P; Edwards R (2001). The herbicide safener MG-191 enhances the expression of specific glutathione S-transferases in maize. *Proceedings of the BCPC Conference – Weeds 2001*, **2**, 527-532.

Pallos F M; Gray R A; Arneklev D R; Brokke M E (1975). Antidotes protect corn from thiocarbamate herbicide injury. *Journal of Agricultural and Food Chemistry* **23**, 821-822.

Theodoulou F L; Clark I M; He X L; Pallett K E; Cole D J; Hallahan D L (2003). Co-induction of glutathione S-transferases and multidrug resistant protein by xenobiotics in wheat. *Pesticide Management Science* **59**, 202-214.

Mode of action of the rediscovered fumigant - ethyl formate

G Dojchinov, V S Haritos

CSIRO Entomology, GPO Box 1700, Canberra, ACT 2601, Australia
Email: Greg.Dojchinov@csiro.au

ABSTRACT

Ethyl formate is a potential replacement for the ozone-depleting fumigant, methyl bromide. We have investigated the mode of toxic action of ethyl formate as part of an evaluation of its efficacy against insects. The acute toxicity of a range of alkyl esters, ethanol and formic acid were tested in the adult rice weevil, *Sitophilus oryzae* (L.) and adult grain borer, *Rhyzopertha dominica* (F.). All alkyl formates and formic acid were similarly toxic to *S. oryzae* and at least twice as potent as ethyl propionate, methyl acetate or ethanol. The order of potency was similar in *R. dominica* for the tested substances. Alkyl formates were rapidly metabolised *in vitro* to formic acid, when incubated with insect homogenates, presumably through the action of esterases. *S. oryzae* and *R. dominica* fumigated with a lethal dose of ethyl formate had 8 and 17-fold higher concentrations of formic acid, respectively, in their bodies than untreated controls. Cytochrome c oxidase activity from isolated insect mitochondria was unaffected by acetate and propionate esters or salts, ethanol or methanol but sodium formate was inhibitory. Toxicity of volatile formate esters to insects is much higher than related alkyl esters, due to hydrolysis of the formate esters to form formic acid and its inhibition of cytochrome c oxidase. From our knowledge of the mechanism of action, the development of insect resistance to ethyl formate is predicted to be slow.

INTRODUCTION

Ethyl formate is being re-evaluated as an alternative fumigant for methyl bromide, which is being phased out due to its contribution to depletion of stratospheric ozone (Bell, 2000). Alternatives to methyl bromide should be efficacious against a variety of insect pests and safe to consumer and workers, whilst not damaging either the stored product or the environment. Ethyl formate may satisfy these requirements. It is currently registered in Australia for protection of dried fruit but is being investigated for use as a horticultural and stored grain fumigant. Ethyl formate is similar to methyl bromide in killing all stages of insects within hours.

There is a range of volatile formate, acetate and propionate esters with similar physical and chemical characteristics to ethyl formate that could potentially be used as insecticidal fumigants of fresh and dried commodities, but little is known of their comparative toxicity to insects. Formate, or more probably, formic acid causes toxicity in mammals through its binding to cytochrome a_3 and inhibition of cytochrome c oxidase, the terminal oxidase of the electron transport chain (Nicholls, 1975). Therefore, it is reasonable to examine the inhibition of cytochrome c oxidase of insects by formate/formic acid in insects as a mechanism of ethyl formate toxicity, as formic acid may be generated in insects from hydrolysis of formate esters.

The relative toxicities of a range of alkyl esters and related compounds toward two pests of stored commodities, the rice weevil *Sitophilus oryzae* (L.) (Coleoptera; Curculionidae) and the lesser grain borer *Rhyzopertha dominica* (F.) (Coleoptera; Bostrichidae) were investigated through mortality bioassays and their inhibition of cytochrome *c* oxidase activity. The intention was to discover the toxic agent of the alkyl esters in insects; that is, to determine whether it is the intact ester or one or more of its components. The capacity of insects to convert ethyl formate to formic acid as a result of exposure was also examined.

MATERIALS AND METHODS

Insect culturing and mortality assessments

S. oryzae (L.) and *R. dominica* (F.) were obtained from laboratory strains cultured at CSIRO Entomology. Insects were cultured on soft wheat, which included some wholemeal flour for *R. dominica*, and were held at 25°C for *S. oryzae* and 30°C for *R. dominica* and 60% relative humidity.

Adult insects (100 per species) were exposed to one of a range of concentrations of volatile alkyl esters or related chemicals, having similar physical and chemical characteristics, in 2.7 litre sealed desiccators. The experiments were repeated at least twice to obtain sufficient data to determine lethal concentrations. The insects were exposed to the fumigants for 3 or 24 h at 25°C, then aired for 1 h, and placed on fresh medium in the culturing rooms for 4 d, after which they were assessed for mortality. LC_{50} and LC_{90} values were determined using a log concentration probit scale program (Finney, 1971). The confidence intervals for LC_{50} and LC_{90} values in *S. oryzae* exposed to methyl acetate could not be calculated, as the slope of the curve was too steep for sufficient points to be obtained.

Formic acid measurement in whole insect homogenate

Whole adult *S. oryzae* or *R. dominica* (3 g) were ground in a mortar and pestle at 4°C with 15 ml of 100 mM phosphate buffer pH 7.4 plus 1 mM disodium ethylene diamine tetraacetic acid (EDTA) and centrifuged at 9,000 g for 20 min at 4°C. The supernatant was removed and combined with ethyl formate at 20, 30 or 50 mM (final concentration) in sealed vials, in triplicate samples, and incubated for 10 min at 30°C. Formic acid, was detected and quantified by established method (Lang & Lang, 1972). Protein concentration of the supernatant was determined by the dye binding method (Bradford, 1976).

Insects (3 g each species, three replicates) were fumigated for 2 h with ethyl formate at 270 µmol litre^{-1} containing 10% carbon dioxide and then aired in a fume cupboard. The treated insects and untreated controls from the same culture were processed as described above and the total formic acid content of their bodies was quantified.

Isolation of mitochondria and cytochrome *c* oxidase measurement

Adult *S. oryzae* (5 g) were ground at 4°C in 50 mM Tris buffer pH 7.4 containing 250 mM sucrose, 1 mM EDTA, 5 mM $MgSO_4$ and 0.2% bovine serum albumin, filtered, then centrifuged at 300 g for 10 min. The supernatant was removed and centrifuged at 5000 g for

10 min. and the resulting mitochondrial pellet was resuspended in isolation medium and again centrifuged at 5000 g for 10 min. The mitochondrial pellet was finally resuspended into a volume of 1.5 ml.

Cytochrome c oxidase activity was measured by monitoring the oxidation of cytochrome c at 550 nm in the presence of detergent-solubilised mitochondria (Storrie & Madden, 1990). Intact mitochondria gave a background rate of cytochrome c oxidation of less than 5% of the solubilised rate.

The effect of formate, acetate and propionate esters and related compounds on mitochondrial cytochrome c oxidase was determined by addition, with mixing, of pure ester into the assay buffer just prior to addition of mitochondria and cytochrome c. Concentrated stocks of cyanide, formate, acetate, and propionate as their sodium salts, were prepared in assay buffer containing lauryl maltoside. The effect on cytochrome c oxidase activity due to the inhibitor was determined from the difference in rates between inhibited and control samples and tested in triplicate. The maximum final concentration tested was 100 mM.

RESULTS AND DISCUSSION

To explore the comparative toxicities of volatile esters, mortality bioassays were conducted with a range of alkyl formates, methyl acetate and ethyl propionate against $S.$ $oryzae$ and $R.$ $dominica$ after 24 h exposure. In Figure 1, the concentration required to kill 50% or 90% of the sample of insects (LC_{50} or LC_{90}) for each volatile ester or related chemical is shown graphically, along with the confidence intervals for those parameters. In both insect species LC_{50} and LC_{90} values for formate esters and formic acid are very close and always lower than those for ethyl propionate, methyl acetate and ethanol. In $S.$ $oryzae$ and $R.$ $dominica,$ the LC_{50} values for the formate esters show they are approximately 5- and 9-fold more toxic, respectively, than that of methyl acetate (Figure 1 A&C). The higher toxicity of substances able to generate formic acid directly by hydrolysis is especially marked in $R.$ $dominica$ (Figure 1 C & D).

To determine the approximate rates of ethyl formate hydrolysis to ethanol and formic acid in insects, homogenates were prepared from the whole bodies of $S.$ $oryzae$ and $R.$ $dominica$ and incubated with ethyl formate in sealed vials. The production of formic acid was determined in the incubation mixture. The rate of metabolism was fast in both insect species. Mean rate of formate production at 20, 30 and 50 mM ethyl formate was 96, 122, 166 and 42, 72, 111 $nmol.min^{-1}.mg^{-1}$ protein for $R.$ $dominica$ and $S.$ $oryzae$, respectively.

When live insects were exposed to ethyl formate at 270 µmol L^{-1} and 10% carbon dioxide, $S.$ $oryzae$ and $R.$ $dominica$ were killed within two hours. These conditions were chosen to ensure as little as possible degradation of metabolites in the insect bodies before analysis. The ethyl formate concentration in the desiccator containing insects decreased by a total of 219 µmol compared with an identically dosed but empty desiccator. Therefore, the theoretical maximum uptake of ethyl formate by the insects in the desiccator was 36 µmol.g^{-1} insect. Following the airing period, the insects were processed and the formic acid concentrations were compared with batches of unexposed insects from the same culture. The concentrations of formic acid in fumigated $S.$ $oryzae$ and $R.$ $dominica$ were 23 and 34 µmol g^{-1} and substantially higher than the unexposed controls (3 and 2 µmol g^{-1} insect, respectively). The higher concentration of formic acid in *R. dominica* is consistent with its higher rate of hydrolysis *in vitro* as described previously.

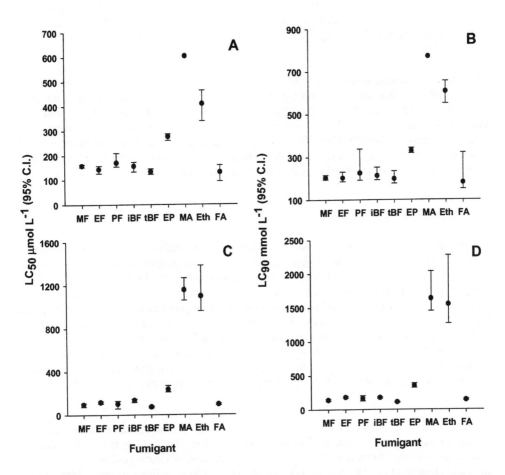

Figure 1. Comparative toxicity of volatile alkyl formate, acetate and propionate esters and related chemicals after a 24 h exposure. (A) LC_{50} with 95% confidence intervals (C.I.) for *S. oryzae* (B) LC_{90} *S. oryzae* (C) LC_{50} *R. dominica* (D) LC_{90} *R. dominica*. Key: Formate ester series: MF – methyl, EF – ethyl, PF – propyl, iBF – *iso*-butyl, tBF – *tert*-butyl; EP – ethyl propionate; MA – methyl acetate; Eth – ethanol; FA – Formic acid.

Cytochrome *c* oxidase activity in detergent solubilized mitochondria isolated from *S. oryzae* was 11 µmol cytochrome *c* oxidised.min⁻¹.mg⁻¹. The inhibitory potential of alkyl esters and related chemicals toward the terminal oxidase of the mitochondrial electron transport chain was determined (Figure 2). Sodium cyanide was used as a standard inhibitor of cytochrome *c* oxidase and to demonstrate the integrity of the system.

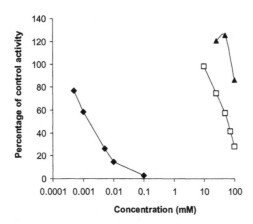

Figure 2. Inhibition of cytochrome *c* oxidase activity in mitochondria isolated from *S. oryzae* by sodium salts of cyanide (solid diamonds), formate (open squares) or acetate (solid triangles).

In comparison to cyanide, formate was a weaker inhibitor of cytochrome *c* oxidase, indicated by a shift in the inhibition curve of almost four magnitudes toward higher concentrations (Figure 2). Sodium acetate stimulated the activity of cytochrome *c* oxidase at 25 and 50 mM but was slightly inhibitory at 100 mM. The concentration to inhibit 50% of activity (IC$_{50}$) values calculated for cytochrome *c* oxidase inhibitors were 0.0015 and 57 mM for cyanide and formate respectively. Alkyl esters, methanol, ethanol and sodium propionate were tested at both 50 and 100 mM and none were found to be substantially inhibitory (data not shown).

In conclusion, the consistently higher toxicity of formate-containing compounds strongly suggests that formate is the main toxic component of these esters. This conclusion is supported by the >11-fold higher toxicity (based on LC50 values) of formic acid to *R. dominca* compared with ethanol, the two components of ethyl formate, and by the demonstration that formate esters are hydrolysed to produce formic acid in the insect. Thus, our experimental findings show that the toxicity of formate esters toward insects may be fully attributable to formic acid generated by enzyme-catalysed hydrolysis of the parent ester, once it has been absorbed by insects. The fast toxic action of ethyl formate is consistent with a mechanism of toxicity involving inhibition of cytochrome *c* oxidase, leading to a reduction in oxidative phosphorylation and depletion of cellular energy stores.

We argue that development of resistance in insects to the effects of alkyl formates via a loss of esterase activity would be unlikely to occur due to the presence of a plethora of esterases capable of hydrolysing short chain alkyl formates. Similarly, a resistance mechanism involving modification of cytochrome a to prevent binding by formic acid and hence inhibition of cytochrome c oxidase activity is improbable. However, other mechanisms of resistance could develop in insects under selection pressure.

ACKNOWLEDGMENTS

The Grains Research and Development Corporation (CSE164) and the Partners to the Stored Grain Research Laboratory Agreement are thanked for their financial support of this project.

REFERENCES

Bell C H (2000). Fumigation in the 21st century. *Crop Protection* **19**, 563-569.

Bradford M M (1976). A rapid and sensitive method for the quantitation of microgram quantities of protein utilizing the principle of protein-dye binding. *Analytical Biochemistry* **72**, 248-254.

Finney D J (1971). *Probit analysis*. 3rd edition. Cambridge University Press: Cambridge.

Lang E; Lang H (1972). Spezifische farbreaktion zum direkten nachweis der ameisensäure. *Fresenius' Zeitschrift fur analytische Chemie* **260**, 8-10.

Nicholls P (1975). Formate as an inhibitor of cytochrome *c* oxidase. *Biochemical and Biophysical Research Communications* **67**, 610-616.

Storrie B; Madden E A (1990). Isolation of subcellular organelles. *Methods in Enzymology* **182**, 203-225.

Two different vacuolar enzymes are responsible for degradation of glutathione-S-conjugates in barley (*Hordeum vulgare* L.)

P Schröder and C E Scheer
Institute of Soil Ecology, GSF-National Research Center for Environment and Health, D-85764 Neuherberg, Germany
Email: peter.schroeder@gsf.de

ABSTRACT

In plants, glutathione conjugation is a major pathway in the detoxification of organic xenobiotics with electrophilic sites. Glutathione S-conjugates (GS-X) are formed in the cytosol and postulated to be transported across the tonoplast into the vacuole for final storage. In recent studies with barley (*Hordeum vulgare* L.) we could show that GS-X undergo further degradation to a γ-glutamyl-cysteinyl-conjugate (γ-GC-X) catalysed by a vacuolar carboxypeptidase (CP). The high content of cysteine-conjugates (C-X) in vacuolar extracts measured with HPLC suggested a second enzyme catalysed step in the degradation of the conjugate. We were able to demonstrate the presence of two additional peptidolytic vacuolar enzyme activities in different fractions of a purified protein extract.

INTRODUCTION

Plants as sessile organisms are defencelessly exposed to pesticides and other hazardous foreign compounds in the environment. Numerous studies have investigated uptake and metabolic mechanisms of plant strategies in detoxification. The widely accepted "green liver"-concept describes a model derived from animal physiology but demonstrates in this case the co-evolutional development of biochemical detoxification pathways for the detoxification of organic xenobiotics (Sandermann, 1994). The concept consists of three phases. In the first phase the compounds are activated by P450 monooxygenases to yield primary metabolites of higher reactivity for the further reactions. The second phase is the detoxification phase in the strict sense of the word, as it comprises the conjugation of the xenobiotic with biomolecules like sugars or glutathione. These reactions are catalysed by glycosyltransferases and glutathione S-transferases (GST).

The third phase is often described in the literature as storage and sequestration and is usually initiated by export of the conjugate from the cytosol into the large central vacuole of the plant cell. This sequestration reaction might be of high importance, as glutathione conjugates have been shown to be inhibitory to glutathione reductase as well as to glutathione S-transferase (Schroeder *et al.*, 2001). The transport of GS-conjugates into the vacuole is mediated by tonoplast ATPases known as ABC-transporters. This concept of storage excretion is widely accepted in the literature.

However, in the past, metabolic studies with cell cultures have shown that glutathione conjugates generally undergo a rapid metabolism to a large number of intermediary metabolites within few days or weeks after application of the xenobiotic (Lamoureux *et al.*, 1989, 1991). It was the aim of our study to investigate the possible vacuolar degradation of xenobiotic glutathione conjugates in order to demonstrate that the vacuole is an active compartment in the metabolism of xenobiotics rather than a passive storage site. Our group has previously been able to demonstrate that the GS-conjugate of the chloroacetamide herbicide, Alachlor, (GS-X) undergoes cleavage in the vacuole of barley (Wolf *et al.*, 1996).

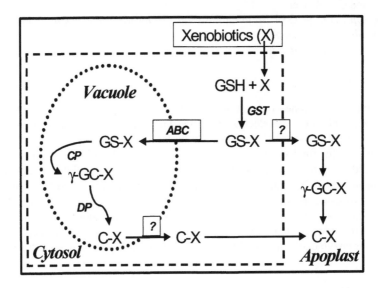

Fig. 1: Schematic overview of the working hypothesis underlying our study. Abbreviations: GSH: glutathione, GS-X: glutathionyl conjugate, γ-GC-X: γ-glutamylcysteinyl conjugate, C-X: cysteinyl conjugate, GST: glutathione S-transferase, CP: carboxypeptidase, DP: dipeptidase.

In a first step, glycine is hydrolysed from the GS-X and a γ-glutamylcysteine-conjugate is formed. This reaction is catalysed by a carboxypeptidase (Wolf *et al.*, 1996). The resulting conjugate is unstable and was assumed to be further metabolised to yield a cysteinyl conjugate or thiol containing metabolites. The degradation in the vacuole is assumed to be part of a complex cascade of reactions finally leading to soluble or bound residues in the cell wall (see Fig. 1).

MATERIALS AND METHODS
All experiments were carried out with 10 day old barley (*Hordeum vulgare* L, var. Cherie) seedlings grown in climate chambers at 17°C with 12 hr artificial light cycle. Plant leaves were frozen in liquid N_2 immediately after harvest.

Vacuoles were isolated from lower epidermal tissue of barley leaves as previously described (Wolf *et al.*, 1996). Protoplasts and vacuoles from the mesophyll of 5-day-old barley leaves were isolated as described by Rentsch and Martinoia (1991).

For the enzymatic studies, frozen barley leaves were ground with a mortar and pestle. The resulting powder was added to five volumes of MES extraction buffer (100 mM, pH 5) containing 5 mM EDTA and 5 mM pepstatin and allowed to stand for 10 min. Crude protein was precipitated from freshly ground leaves in two steps (35 and 80%) with $(NH_4)_2SO_4$. Pellets were resuspended in extraction buffer, and protein was desalted with PD-10 columns.

Further purification was performed by loading desalted protein on an FPLC cation exchange column (High S, BioRad). Protein was eluted within a linear gradient of NaCl (0-1M, flow rate: 1ml/min) and were collected in 1ml fractions which were concentrated 5-fold by lyophilisation and stored at $-80°C$ for further use.

GST activity was determined utilizing 1-chloro-2,4-dinitrobenzene (CDNB, e= 9.6 mM^{-1}cm^{-1}) as a model substrate (Habig et al., 1974). Alachlor conjugation was determined as previously described (Wolf et al., 1996).
Carboxypeptidase and dipeptidase activities were determined as follows: 60µl of the purified protein was incubated (4h, 25°C) with 80µl of 1mM GSH- and g-GC-CDNB conjugates which were synthezised in vitro. The reaction was stopped by adding 20% acetonitrile containing 0.1% tri-fluoroacetic acid (TFA). Protein concentration was determined using the dye binding method of Bradford (Bradford, 1976) with bovine serum albumin as standard. All enzyme and protein assays were performed in triplicate.

The samples were analyzed by HPLC on a RP C-18 column (Hypersil, Bischoff) using a linear gradient of acetonitrile from 20 to 100% in 30 min (flow rate 1 ml/min). Peaks were detected in an UV/VIS detector at 280 nm and co-chromatographed with commercially available reference compounds (Sigma).

RESULTS AND DISCUSSION

Crude protein extracts of barley leaves contained GST activity against several xenobiotic substrates, including alachlor and CDNB. In the same extracts, activity of carboxypeptidase (determined with S-dinitrobenzyl-glutathione) and dipeptidase (determined with γ-glutamyl-S-cysteinyl-dinitrobenzene) was observed.

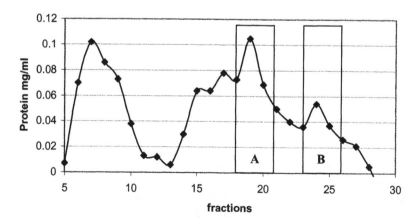

Fig. 2: Protein pattern obtained during cation exchange chromatography of an enzyme extract from barley leaves. Peaks A and B contain peptidolytic enzyme activity as explained in the text.

When the protein extracts were subjected to cation exchange chromatography on an FPLC system, three distinct peaks were resolved (Fig. 2). Of all fractions, activity for the cleavage of the dinitrobenzyl-glutathione was only observed in two peaks: A and B (Fig. 2). Dipeptidase activity for the cleavage of the γ-glutamylcysteinyl-conjugate was only detected in peak B, indicating that this activity represents a separate protein.

The purification factor for the carboxypeptidase after cation exchange chromatography was 160 fold as compared to crude extracts (Table 1). Longer incubation times or incubation of the CP-peak with γ-glutamylcysteinyl-DNB did not yield other reaction products. Hence, it is concluded that this peak does not contain other peptidolytic activtity. In contrast, the dipeptidase was purified 45fold by cation exchange chromatography (Tab. 2). The proposed product of this reaction, the cysteinyl-conjugate, was not further metabolised by any of the fractions.

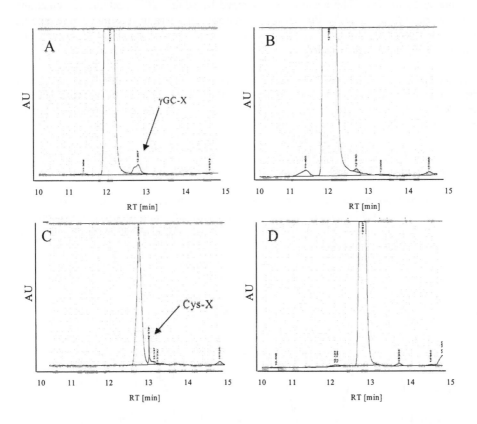

Fig. 3: HPLC chromatogram of the metabolites formed during the catabolism of glutathione conjugates in barley. In the presence of the first fraction (A) GS-X was degraded to γ-GC-X, indicating the presence of the known CP. When γ-GC-X conjugate was incubated with the second fraction (C) the respective cysteine conjugate C-X was formed. Control incubations of GS-X with the second (B) or of γ-GC-X with the first fraction (D) were negative.

Dipeptidase activity also seemed to be quite specific because incubation with the respective glutathionyl- or with the cysteinyl-metabolites did not result in the formation of products. Examples for the respective HPLC chromatograms of substrates and products are shown in Figure 3.

Table 1: Two-step purification of a carboxypeptidase from barley leaves by cation exchange chromatography. Barley leaves were precipitated in a two step ammonium sulfate precipitation and desalted via PD10 columns. The extract was further purified by cation exchange chromatography.

Purification step	Protein (mg/ml)	Total activity (μmol/min)	Specific activity (U/mg)	Purification factor
PD10-extract	2.85	0.016	0.005	1
FPLC-cation exchange peak	0.063	0.04	0.81	162

From the catalytic and biophysical properties and from inhibition studies (to be published elsewhere) it was concluded that the purified carboxypeptidase was of serine type and belongs to the class of endopeptidases previously detected in barley seedlings. Proteolytic activity during germination had been attributed to these CPs (Breddam et al., 1983). Contrary to this, the dipeptidase co-purified from the same barley protein extract has not been described before.

In animal metabolism, degradation of glutathione conjugates starts with the cleavage of the γ-glutamyl-moiety, thus producing a cysteinyl-glycine-conjugate. The latter is subsequently cleaved by a dipeptidase to yield the respective cysteinyl-conjugate (Schröder 2001).

Table 2: Two-step purification of a dipeptidase from barley leaves by cation exchange chromatography. Barley leaves were precipitated in a two step ammonium sulfate precipitation and desalted on PD10 columns. The extract was further purified by cation exchange chromatography.

Purification step	Protein (mg/ml)	Total activity (μmol/min)	Specific activity (U/mg)	Purification factor
PD10-extract	2.85	0.154	0.054	1
FPLC-cation exchange peak	0.02	0.048	2.44	45

Evidence that the identified peptidolytic enzymes were localized in the vacuole was obtained from pilot experiments with isolated barley mesophyll vacuoles. It could be clearly demonstrated that incubation of osmotically shocked vacuoles resulted in the same degradation products of the DNB-glutathione- and γ-glutamylcysteinyl-conjugates as with the isolated enzymes. Further studies will be performed to determine catalytic properties and inducibility of these proteins, as well as to elucidate the fate of the cysteinyl-conjugate formed as a product.

CONCLUSIONS

Glutathione conjugates of xenobiotics are frequently metabolized rather than stored in plants. Upon sequestration in the vacuole, glutathione conjugates are cleaved by carboxy-peptidases (CP). In plants, this CP-activity seems to be specific for glycine removal, and γ-glutamylcysteinyl conjugates are frequently found in the vacuole. Further degradation of the CP-product, γ-glutamyl-cysteinyl-X, is performed by a second peptidolytic enzyme, probably a dipeptidase so far not described. This work shows that in barley leaves these enzyme activities can be separated and are distinct form each other. The fate of the resulting cysteinyl conjugates in the vacuole and the cytosol remains to be elucidated.

ACKNOWLEDGEMENTS

The authors thank GSF for funding CES, and Sylvia Andres and Andreas Nuber for expert technical assistance.

REFERENCES

Bradford M M (1976). A rapid and sensitive method for the quantification of microgram quantities of protein utilizing the principle of protein dyebinding. *Analytical Biochemistry* **72**, 248-254.

Breddam K; Sorensen S B; Ottesen M (1983). Isolation of a carboxypeptidase from malted barley by affinity chromatography. *Carlsberg Research Communications* **48**, 217-230.

Habig WH; Pabst MJ; Jacoby WB (1974). Glutathione S-transferases. *Journal of Biological Chemistry* **249**, 7130-7139.

Lamoureux G L; Rusness D G (1989). The role of glutathione and glutathione S-transferase in pesticide metabolism, selectivity and mode of action in plants and insects. In: *Glutathione: Chemical, biochemical and medical aspects, series: Enzyme and Cofactors,* eds D Dolphin, R Poulson & O Avramovic, pp: 153-196. John Wiley & Sons: New York.

Lamoureux G L; Rusness D G; Schröder P; Rennenberg H (1991). Diphenyl ether herbicide metabolism in a spruce cell suspension culture: Identification of two novel metabolites derived from a glutathione conjugate. *Pesticide Biochemistry and Physiology* **39**, 291-301.

Rentsch D; Martinoia E (1991). Citrate transport into barley mesophyll vacuoles- comparison with malate-uptake activity. *Planta* **184**, 532-537.

Sandermann H (1994). Higher plant metabolism of xenobiotics: the 'green liver' concept. *Pharmacogenetics* **4**, 225-241.

Schröder P (2001). The role of glutathione and glutathione S-transferases in the adaptation of plants to xenobiotics. In: *Significance of glutathione in plant adaptation to the environment. Handbook Series of Plant Ecophysiology,* eds D Grill, M Tausz & LJ DeKok, pp. 157-182. Kluwer Academic Publishing: Boston, Dordrecht, London.

Schröder P; Scheer C; Belford E J D (2001). Metabolism of organic xenobiotics in plants: Conjugation enzymes and metabolic end points. *Minerva Biotechnology* **13**, 85-91.

Wolf A E; Dietz K J; Schröder P (1996). A carboxypeptidase degrades glutathione conjugates in the vacuoles of higher plants. *FEBS Letters* **384**, 31-34.

Can picoxystrobin protect winter wheat from environmental stress?

J P H Reade, L J Milner, A H Cobb

Crop and Environment Research Centre, Harper Adams University College, Newport, Shropshire, TF10 8NB, UK

Email: jreade@harper-adams.ac.uk

ABSTRACT

Strobilurin fungicides have been used in cereals in the UK for six years, and have activity against a number of important cereal fungal diseases. They have also been reported to affect crop physiology resulting in enhanced yield by prolonged greening and reduced appearance of stress symptoms. These effects may be a result of increased disease control or a direct interaction between the fungicide and the physiology of the crop plant. We investigated the physiological consequences of picoxystrobin treatment in the presence of environmental stressors. Drought, temperature, light, nitrogen and sulphur availability were investigated in winter wheat cv. Claire under experimental conditions in the glasshouse and in growth cabinets. Initial data suggest that physiological stress symptoms are ameliorated in picoxystrobin-treated plants. In the absence of any obvious crop disease, these observations indicate a direct interaction between picoxystrobin and crop physiology, especially with respect to chlorophyll content.

INTRODUCTION

The strobilurins are a family of fungicides based on naturally occurring compounds, such as strobilurins A and B (Anke *et al.*, 1977). Although structurally diverse they all act at a common site, inhibiting mitochondrial electron transport at the cytochrome bc_1 complex of the respiratory chain. Bartlett *et al.* (2002) have recently reviewed the history, chemistry, mode of action and biology of strobilurins. Picoxystrobin is a new systemic broad-spectrum fungicide with activity against a number of important cereal fungal diseases (Godwin *et al.*, 2000).

Strobilurins have been reported to affect crop physiology, resulting in enhanced or prolonged greening, reduced appearance of stress symptoms, yield enhancement and improved grain quality (Gooding *et al.*, 2000; Mercer & Ruddock, 1998; Ypema & Gold, 1999). These effects have been attributed to decreased ethylene production, reduced degradation of and/or increased endogenous concentrations of cytokinins (Grossmann & Retzlaff, 1997), increases in antioxidant defence systems (Wu & von Tiedemann, 2001) and increased nitrogen assimilation (Glaab & Kaiser, 1999). However, reduced senescence and delayed chlorosis may be a result of the broad spectrum disease control provided by this fungicide family (for example, Bayles, 1999).

We have investigated the effects of picoxystrobin on winter wheat cv. Claire grown under a variety of environmental conditions in the glasshouse or growth cabinet, and both morphological and physiological responses have been examined. Further experiments were performed in which plants were pre-treated with the fungicide quinoxyfen to assess the contribution of existing disease to physiological symptoms observed, thus testing the hypothesis that the enhanced appearance of picoxystrobin-treated plants was solely due to control of visible symptoms of disease. Water stress was imposed using polyethylene glycol (PEG), an osmotically active macromolecule that sequesters water, therefore making it unavailable to the plant.

MATERIALS AND METHODS

Plant growth

Winter wheat cv. Claire was sown in a Perlite medium (a naturally occurring silicaceous rock) saturated from below with modified Hoagland's growth medium and grown under glasshouse conditions (15°C/14 h day: 8°C/10h night ± 5°C).

Fungicide treatments

Picoxystrobin (250g a.i ha^{-1}; field rate) was applied at growth stage (GS) 21 (one tiller present) with a precision pot sprayer delivering the equivalent of 200 l ha^{-1} through 2 flat fan nozzles at 7 bar pressure at a height of 45cm above the pots. Where indicated, plants were pre-treated with quinoxyfen (Fortress™, 500g a.i l^{-1}; applied as 10 ppm a.i at 200 l ha^{-1}) at GS11/12 (one to two leaves emerged).

Stress conditions

Immediately after application, half the treated and half the untreated plants were grown under the following stress conditions; low light (10µmol m^{-2} sec^{-1}), low nitrogen (1/10th N Hoagland's, 1.025mM nitrogen), low sulphur (1/10th S Hoagland's, 0.16mM sulphur), high temperature (25°C), drought (imposed by 5% and 10% aqueous polyethylene glycol, PEG 8000). Individual experiments examined each environmental stress and monitoring was carried out from picoxystrobin treatment (0 days after treatment, DAT) to the end of the experiment (35 DAT).

Analyses

Non-invasive and invasive analyses were carried out at 0 DAT and at 7-day intervals to 35 DAT. Plant growth stage (GS), root and shoot fresh weight were recorded at each interval and both tip and whole-leaf senescence were assessed. Gas exchange by intact leaves was determined by infrared gas analysis (Cerius II, PP Systems, UK) and values for transpiration, stomatal conductance, carbon dioxide assimilation and sub-stomatal carbon dioxide concentration were calculated. Leaf thickness was measured at the midpoint of the leaf using a micrometer and leaf water potential was determined using a dew-point microvoltmeter (HR-33T, Wescor, UK). All measurements were carried out on the oldest fully expanded non-senesced leaf of each plant. Harvested tissue was frozen in liquid nitrogen and stored at -80°C until needed. Chlorophyll and carotenoid analyses were performed using an adaptation of the methods of Lichtenthaler & Wellburn (1983) and Hendry & Price (1993). Shoot tissue (0.5g) was extracted overnight in 40ml of 80% (v/v) aqueous acetone containing 1mg magnesium carbonate and 0.5mg sodium bisulfite. Extracts were clarified by centrifugation (15000g, 15 mins at 4°C) and their absorbance determined at 480, 645, 663 and 710nm.

RESULTS

Effect of picoxystrobin on stress symptoms

The effects of picoxystrobin on the development of stress symptoms in winter wheat are summarised in Table 1. Picoxystrobin treatment in the absence of stress consistently increased shoot and root fresh weight, increased root to shoot ratios and increased chlorophyll content. In addition, picoxystrobin-treated plants developed less leaf senescence than untreated plants. Similar patterns were noted in picoxystrobin-treated plants in the presence of stresses (Table 1). Treatment caused the amelioration of some stress symptoms in all conditions tested. The most common symptom of picoxystrobin treatment was the retardation of senescence. Under drought stress induced by PEG, treated plants demonstrated similar differences to treated plants in the absence of stress. The effects of picoxystrobin treatment were most pronounced in the drought-stressed plants.

Table 1. Effects of picoxystrobin on the development of stress symptoms in winter wheat.

↑, increased with treatment; ↓, decreased with treatment; X, not affected by treatment; NA , no data currently available. Results presented are from observations over the 35 DAT.

Environmental parameter	Shoot weight (g)	Root weight (g)	Root:Shoot ratio	Senescence	Chlorophyll content
Unstressed	↑	↑	↑	↓	↑
Low Light	X	X	X	X	↑
Low Nitrogen	X	↑	↑	↓	X
Low Sulphur	X	X	X	↓	NA
High Temperature	↑	↑	↑	X	NA
Drought	↑	↑	↑	↓	↑

Effects of drought stress and picoxystrobin on chlorophyll content

The effect of picoxystrobin on leaf chlorophyll content in drought stressed winter wheat plants is shown in Tables 2 and 3. In the presence of drought stress induced by PEG, picoxystrobin increased chlorophyll content by between 32 and 44% between day 0 and day 35. Under similar conditions, but in the absence of picoxystrobin, leaf chlorophyll content fell by between 5 and 34%. Picoxystrobin treatment also resulted in increased chlorophyll a and b content in the absence of drought stress.

Table 2. Total leaf chlorophylls (% change from day 0) for plants grown in the presence and absence of picoxystrobin and drought stress (5% PEG).

Growth conditions/treatment	Days after treatment	Total leaf chlorophylls (% change from day 0)
- PEG – picoxystrobin	28	+53
	35	+37
- PEG + picoxystrobin	28	-51
	35	+154
+ PEG – picoxystrobin	28	-25
	35	-5
+ PEG + picoxystrobin	28	+52
	35	+44

Table 3. Total leaf chlorophylls (% change from day 0) for plants grown in the presence and absence of picoxystrobin and drought stress (10% PEG).

Growth conditions/treatment	Days after treatment	Total leaf chlorophylls (% change from day 0)
- PEG – picoxystrobin	28	+40
	35	0
- PEG + picoxystrobin	28	+16
	35	+26
+ PEG – picoxystrobin	28	-16
	35	-34
+ PEG + picoxystrobin	28	+26
	35	+32

Pre-treatment with quinoxyfen

The effect of picoxystrobin on leaf chlorophyll content in drought stressed winter wheat plants pre-treated with quinoxyfen is shown in Tables 4 and 5.

Table 4. Total leaf chlorophylls (% change from day 0) for plants pre-treated with quinoxyfen and grown in the presence and absence of picoxystrobin and drought stress (5% PEG).

Growth conditions/treatment	Days after treatment	Total leaf chlorophylls (% change from day 0)
- PEG – picoxystrobin	28	-22
	35	-28
- PEG + picoxystrobin	28	-11
	35	-18
+ PEG – picoxystrobin	28	-11
	35	+5
+ PEG + picoxystrobin	28	+9
	35	+1

Table 5. Total leaf chlorophylls (% change from day 0) for plants pre-treated with quinoxyfen and grown in the presence and absence of picoxystrobin and drought stress (10% PEG).

Growth conditions/treatment	Days after treatment	Total leaf chlorophylls (% change from day 0)
- PEG – picoxystrobin	28	0
	35	-6
- PEG + picoxystrobin	28	+6
	35	+57
+ PEG – picoxystrobin	28	-4
	35	+16
+ PEG + picoxystrobin	28	-8
	35	+25

DISCUSSION

These preliminary studies have demonstrated that when winter wheat plants were treated with picoxystrobin less senescence was observed, as previously reported for both azoxystrobin (Bertelsen et al., 2001) and kresoxim-methyl (Grossman & Retzlaff, 1997). This response was enhanced when plants were grown under stress, especially drought induced by PEG. Under these conditions, picoxystrobin further reduced stress development to the extent that stressed treated plants appeared similar to unstressed plants. This may be due to a direct effect of picoxystrobin on the physiology of the plant or may be due to the broad spectrum of disease control provided by this fungicide. In the latter case, the reduction in disease burden may result in the plant being better equipped to combat external stresses, such as drought or reduced nutrient availability. To investigate this possibility, further experiments were carried out utilising plants that had been pre-treated with quinoxyfen to reduce disease interaction with the development of stress symptoms.

Pre-treatment with quinoxyfen resulted in a decrease in the differences between picoxystrobin-treated and untreated plants with respect to total chlorophyll content. However, plants treated with picoxystrobin still had more chlorophylls per g fresh weight than untreated plants grown under similar conditions. Even when all plants were treated with quinoxyfen to control existing disease, picoxystrobin treatment increased chlorophyll content, indicating a possible physiological role in either chlorophyll production or protection of chlorophyll from the damaging effects of active oxygen species.

It should be noted that these observations were carried out on plants grown under controlled conditions. Further study is now necessary to establish the mechanisms that explain picoxystrobin interacts with environmental stressors and with the development of senescence under field conditions.

ACKNOWLEDGEMENTS

This research was funded by Syngenta Crop Protection UK, and the authors wish to thank D Bartlett and S West for discussions and assistance.

REFERENCES

Anke T; Oberwinkler F; Steglich W; Schramm G (1977). The strobilurins – new antifungal antibiotics from the basidiomycete *Strobilurus tenacellus* (Pers. Ex Fr.) Sing. *Journal of Antibiotics,* **30**, 806-810.

Bartlett D W; Clough J M; Godwin J R; Hall A A; Hamer M; Parr-Dobrzanski B (2002). The strobilurin fungicides. *Pest Management Science* **58**, 649-662.

Bayles R (1999). The interaction of strobilurin fungicides with cereal varieties. *Plant varieties and seeds* **12**, 129-140.

Bertelsen J R; de Neergaard E; Smedegaard-Petersen V (2001). Fungicidal effects of azoxystrobin and epoxiconazole on phyllosphere fungi, senescence and yield of winter wheat. *Plant Pathology* **50**, 190-205.

Glaab J; Kaiser W M (1999). Increased nitrate reductase activity in leaf tissue after application of the fungicide kresoxim-methyl. *Planta* **207**, 442-448.

Godwin J R; Bartlet D W; Clough J M; Godfrey C R A; Harrison E G; Maund S (2000). Picoxystrobin: a new strobilurin fungicide for use on cereals. *Proceedings of the BCPC Conference – Pests & Diseases 2000,* **2**, 533-540.

Gooding M J; Dimmock J P R E; France J; Jones S A (2000). Green leaf area decline of wheat flag leaves: the influence of fungicides and relationships with mean grain weight and grain yield. *Annals of Applied Biology* **136**, 77-84.

Grossman K; Retzlaff G (1997). Bioregulatory effects of the fungicidal strobilurin kresoxim-methyl in wheat (*Triticum aestivum*). *Pesticide Science* **50**, 11-20.

Hendry G A F; Price A H (1993). Stress indicators: chlorophylls and carotenoids. In: *Methods of Comparative Study,* eds G A F Hendry & J P Grime, pp. 148-152. Chapman & Hall: London, UK.

Lichtenthaler H K; Wellburn A R (1983). Determination of total carotenoids and chlorophyll a and b of leaf extracts in different solvents. *Biochemical Society Tranactions* **603**, 591-592.

Mercer P C; Ruddock A (1998). Evaluation of azoxystrobin and a range of conventional fungicides on yield, *Septoria tritici* and senescence in winter wheat. *Tests of Agrochemicals and Cultivars,* **19**, 24.

Wu Y X; von Tiedemann A (2001).Physiological effects of azoxystrobin and epoxiconazole on senescence and the oxidative status of wheat. *Pesticide Biochemistry and Physiology* **71**, 1-10.

Ypema H L; Gold R E (1999). Kresoxim-methyl: Modification of a naturally occurring compound to produce a new fungicide. *Plant Disease,* **83**, 4-19.

POSTER SESSION 7C

NOVEL AND INDUSTRIAL CROPS: REALISING THEIR POTENTIAL

Session Organiser: David Turley
Central Science Laboratory, York, UK

Poster Papers: 7C-1 to 7C-3

IENICA – Interactive European Network for Industrial Crops and their Applications

C A Holmes
Central Science Laboratory, Sand Hutton, York YO41 1LZ, UK
Email: c.holmes@csl.gov.uk

ABSTRACT

Crop-derived materials can provide novel raw materials, as well as technical, environmental and waste disposal advantages over synthetic fossil-derived materials, whilst offering alternative options for agriculture. Uptake of 'renewable raw materials' is uneven and fragmented, however. In recognition of this, the EC in 1997 commissioned the 'IENICA' project. IENICA provides an overarching, pan-European facility, involving 26 countries, linking all EU industrial crop activities. Through a series of integrated activities, including the production of a novel crop agronomy booklet, market data sheets, national reports, newsletters and the organisation of a number of conferences and seminars, IENICA has identified significant potential for renewable raw materials in Europe. The project has also identified a number of barriers and constraints to the development of the industry which must be overcome before true market exploitation of renewable raw materials can occur.

INTRODUCTION

Although plant-based materials have been used for many thousands of years, the introduction of synthetic materials, which can be produced more cheaply, efficiently and reliably, has significantly reduced their use in industry. However, a number of key factors are driving the return to the use of natural materials and the non-food crop sector is once again seeing a resurgence in interest. These drivers include:

- Stringent environmental targets and regulations (e.g. emissions targets set by the Kyoto agreement to reduce climate change and VOC reduction targets) at regional, national and international levels, and increasing consumer demand for green products and environmental awareness;
- An increasing interest in alternative farm enterprises, led by decreasing farm incomes;
- An industrial 'pull' – where renewable materials offer either a reduction in price over the synthetic alternative (unlikely at present due to economies of scale) or superior technical performance. Industrial 'pull' is generally considered to be the key factor for the future of the non-food crop sector, as true sustainability will only come through market demands.

Currently the development and uptake of industrial crops throughout Europe and the rest of the world, is uneven. Development has been strongly supported and encouraged in some countries (such as Germany, France and the Netherlands) whilst in others it has occurred in a fragmented fashion. Uptake and development to date have been slow in the UK and while steps are being taken, the industry is someway behind counterparts in other EU countries.

This fragmented European approach led, in 1997, to DG Research of the European Commission to fund a group of researchers to form an 'Interactive European Network for Industrial Crops and Applications', under the FAIR programme. Fourteen countries participated in this three-year project (EU-15 except Luxembourg), with one partner institute in each country. Continuation funding was secured in 2000 from Framework Programme 5 of the EC to support the project for a further 3 years and to include a number of the EU accessing and associated states (EU project QLK5-CT-2000-00111). IENICA now involves 26 countries: Austria, Belgium, Bulgaria, Cyprus, the Czech Republic, Denmark, Estonia, Finland, France, Germany, Greece, Hungary, Ireland, Israel, Italy, Lithuania, the Netherlands, Poland, Portugal, Romania, Spain, Sweden, Switzerland, Canada, the USA and the UK.

The principle aim of IENICA is to "achieve enhanced technology transfer and market orientation in order to extend sustainable and economically viable non-food products from plants, through positive interaction and collaboration at all stages in the production-supply-processing-market chain". Towards this aim, the project's principle objectives are to:

- Create synergy within the EU industrial crops industry and facilitate interaction and interchange of information by developing an integrated network linking key individuals from industry, government and science in member states;
- Disseminate data by acting as a European Gateway facility for all data on non-food crops;
- Identify the strengths of the EC accessing and associate states and link this data into existing networks and market assessments;
- Allow an enhanced efficiency of use of limited RTD funding by identifying true market potential to focus funding for maximum value for money

METHODOLOGY

IENICA is based upon a series of independent 'workpackages' which integrate to meet the primary aim and key objectives of the project.

National reports

Produced by each of the original project states (EU-14) and currently being prepared by the participating accessing and associated states, the reports detail which non-food crops are grown, current levels of production, current and potential applications and markets plus barriers, constraints and opportunities to the development of the sector. Issues are considered in each of four market sectors: fibres, oils, carbohydrates and speciality crops. This data is essential to industry, policy-makers and scientists to help assess current and future trends as well as strengths and weaknesses in the sector. This helps identify where investment should be directed. An EU summary report will be prepared compiling the data and key issues from the national reports. An EU summary for the original fourteen partners was published in 2000 (IENICA, 2000)

Agronomy booklet

This will examine the agronomy of selected industrial crops, from a generic perspective, and will be published for use by farmers and growers. Information will be provided on a crop by crop basis covering issues such as climatic and soil requirements, recommended sowing dates and rates and likely pest and disease problems. A national expert contact in each partner state will also be provided for each crop.

Market data sheets

Four specialist market data sheets will be compiled by international experts within the network. These will contain market data and industry specifications for raw and processed materials in each market sector (oils, fibres, carbohydrates and speciality). These will supply much needed information to growers and processors and will provide a framework on which industry can build firm specifications for raw materials.

Conferences/seminars

IENICA organises a number of international conferences (e.g. BioPlastics and GreenTech, held in York and Amsterdam respectively, in 2002) and international regional seminars, which focus upon regional developments and opportunities for non-food crops. Seminars focussed on Southern Europe and the Mediterranean and Central and Eastern Europe have been held in 2003.

Monitor uptake

The final phase of the project will be to assess the success of the IENICA project by scrutinising the uptake of industrial crops and their products across Europe. At present uptake is sporadic and industry slow to invest where the supply chain is unreliable. This work will assess whether the introduction of a closely industry-focused approach has increased the natural momentum of the uptake of non-food crops in the EU.

Newsletters

Dissemination of information is a key element of the project and IENICA publishes a quarterly newsletter, which includes articles on new developments in non-food crops, results of scientific research and policy developments plus reports on the network activities.

Website

The IENICA website (www.ienica.net) is a key Gateway facility for non-food crop information. The website holds all project deliverables and a range of other information, including an extensive plant database with detailed information on over 100 plants with realised/potential industrial applications. A large contacts database has contact details and areas of interest for over 3000 contacts working in, or researching, industrial crops in 30 countries.

Activities are scrutinised by an Industry Advisory Group to ensure that the project remains well-focused on industrial needs and industrial uptake of non-food crop products.

DISCUSSION

The national reports have become a central resource for non-food crop information in Europe, and in many cases represent the first instance where the information has been collated and aggregated to provide and EU overview. Significant potential for increased growth in the markets for various crop-derived materials were identified (Table 1). Current work will bring this data up to date and extend it to include current and potential production and applications in the accessing and associated states.

Table 1. Production of crop derived raw materials for industrial use (million tonnes)

	EU Output 1998	EU Output 2003*	% Growth (Estimated)
Vegetable Oils	2.6	4.1	58
Starch	2.4	3.6	50
Non-Wood Fibres	0.5	0.6	21
TOTAL	5.5	7.64	38.9

Source: IENICA UK Report (Actin, 1999)   * Based on % growth

Some of the major findings and issues identified are detailed below.

Oil crops

European production of vegetable oils is dominated by oilseed rape and sunflower with some soya bean and linseed production. These oil crops have some non-food applications in the oleochemical, surfactant, soap, paint and surface coatings and lubricant sectors. EU markets are potentially significant but currently under-exploited: the potential EU market for biodegradable lubricants, for example, is estimated at 370,000 tonnes; current exploitation is just 35,000 tonnes. Market opportunities exist particularly where high environmental contamination occurs i.e. in 'total loss' oils such as chainsaw oils, hydraulic fluids and drilling oils where oil is 'lost' to the surrounding environment. European vegetable oil production is currently supplemented by considerable quantities of imported oils, particularly tropical oils such as palm and castor oil, and tallow of animal origin. These imports represent 80% of EU oil demand. There is considerable potential to expand EU-produced vegetable oil use on the basis of import substitution alone. Considerable activity is underway to develop new oil crop species and modify the oil composition of existing EU oil crops (e.g. high oleic sunflower).

Fibre crops

In 2000, flax and hemp were the only commercialised sources of European plant fibres, with investigations into *Arundo donax*, kenaf, fibre sorghum, miscanthus, nettle and reed canary grass. Applications for natural fibres include textiles, pulp and paper, fibre-reinforced composites, filters and absorbents and insulation materials. Market potential for high quality, high value textile products is limited and new uses for increased production are likely to focus upon high volume/lower value markets. Potential in the automotive industry is for up to 350,000 tonnes of raw material per year in Europe, with principal applications in door liners, boot liners and parcel shelves. Industry indicates a potential of up to around 10kg of raw material per vehicle.

Carbohydrate crops

Wheat, barley, maize, sugar beet and potatoes are the dominant carbohydrate sources in Europe. Estimates of the total EU starch market for the year 2000/2001 is 7.3 million tonnes/annum, of which 3.7 million tonnes is in the non-food sector: 1.4 million tonnes in paper and cardboard making, 1.1 million tonnes in plastics and detergents and 1.2 million tonnes in fermentation and other technical uses. Additionally, smaller markets exist in water purification, cosmetics, toiletries, pharmaceuticals, paints and agrochemicals. Several of these latter offer high potential for added value, but for limited tonnage. A significant quantity of the carbohydrate processed and used in Europe, particularly maize starch, is imported. However, European demand for carbohydrates is increasing and there is potential to replace imported products. All starch extraction processes produce by-products and whilst these are currently sold as animal feed, higher added-value applications (i.e. in cosmetics) are being developed.

Speciality crops

These generally represent high value/low volume markets and a very diverse range of species is grown in Europe. Applications are wide-ranging, for example, essential oils, pharmaceuticals, inks, dyes, perfumes and novel plant protection products. Markets are international and highly competitive and Intellectual Property Right protection and registration procedures can be confusing and prohibitively expensive. The quality and proportions of the desired plant-derived molecules vary in many species, which affects stability and quality of supply. Europe plays a major role in the international trade of medicinal and aromatic plants with typically around 120,000 tonnes imported annually from more than 120 countries. Between 1,200-1,300 species native to Europe are commercially traded and though some species are cultivated (10-15% of total volume), collection from the wild still plays a major role, causing problems for environmental sustainability and continuity of supply.

Factors affecting further development

IENICA has identified a number of barriers and constraints to the development of non-food crops. The natural-oil industry, for example, needs to improve the, currently slow, progress being made in the domestication of new oil species with useful fatty acid profiles. Likewise, in the natural fibres sector, little plant breeding of the most important crops (flax, hemp, miscanthus, reed canary grass) is taking place to meet the changing fibre-market requirements. Development of new crops (such as quinoa and sweet sorghum) is necessary within the carbohydrate sector to offer new crop options for European agriculture. Hand harvested speciality species have high production costs and crop production is generally high risk, with volatility of crop performance, quality and end product.

A number of generic issues were also identified across all sectors, including:
- Competition from cheap imports
- Price: European raw material prices are often not competitive compared with world market prices or fossil fuel and mineral oil derived synthetic materials
- Crops produced by gene transfer offer potential to meet industrial demands in all sectors, but are currently unacceptable to the general public
- The utilisation of by-products is necessary to improve the total income from all crops

- The environmental benefits of natural materials are poorly communicated to the general public. Education coupled with EU-wide labelling schemes (as already exist in some countries) would enhance consumer demand
- Communication between the main participants in the non-food industry needs improvement
- The industry is often based upon old technology and new environmentally sensitive and cost effective solutions are required. It is often difficult to introduce raw materials from new sources into production systems, where technology and practices are well established.

In terms of the UK market, the national report for the UK (ACTIN, 1999) identified a total of *circa*. 1400 organisations who are interested or involved in alternative crop development or utilisation – from academia through to industry. However, the industrial crop market in the UK was classed as "immature – industry lacks knowledge of, and links to, the supply chain and processes which can automatically utilise alternative crops cost-effectively". It was noted, however, that a strength of the UK is its diverse science base, with wide-ranging market expertise, academic support, an extensive research programme and skills ranging from basic agronomy through to economic and lifecycle assessment, which should support uptake and development.

An issue affecting all sectors is the lack of industrial specifications for raw materials. The market data sheets currently in preparation will go some way to addressing this issue and will, in association with the agronomy booklet, attempt to create linkages and communication within the supply chains.

Consumer and industry demand are, arguably, the major drivers of development in the industry and IENICA has taken significant steps towards raising greater awareness in both. The strong industrial focus has remained a key factor in all activities and industry has been keen to support IENICA. The non-food crop industry still has a long way to go to reach the potential identified by IENICA and momentum must be maintained.

ACKNOWLEDGEMENTS

I would like to thank all those who have contributed to the success of the IENICA project to date, particularly project members and collaborators.

REFERENCES

ACTIN (1999). Report from the State of the United Kingdom. IENICA project report (FAIR CT96-1495) (http://www.ienica.net/ienicareports.htm).

Askew M F (2000). Interactive European Network for Industrial Crops and their Applications (FAIR CT96-1495): Summary Report for European Union. European Commission Directorate General Research (http://www.ienica.net/ienicareports.htm).

Identification of opportunities for under-utilised crops in Wales – A novel approach

L V Hodsman, D B Turley, M G Ceddia
Central Science Laboratory, Sand Hutton, York, YO41 1LZ, UK
Email: l.hodsman@csl.gov.uk

ABSTRACT

This study was undertaken to identify opportunities for exploitation of under-utilised plant species to add value to agriculture and the wider rural economy in Wales. From lists of plants with known or documented uses 150 plant species were selected for further study, gathering information on potential markets, climatic and soil requirements, agronomy and any potential impacts on the local environment. Species were gradually eliminated based on climatic and other requirements, commercial viability, anticipated environmental impacts and estimated social, economic and cultural value arising from production and processing. Key species were mapped using GIS technology to identify areas of potential and marginal production. The location and extent of local processing facilities was also reviewed and the viability of local processing considered. The most promising opportunities were prioritised in a matrix that comprised likely time to fruition and potential limits to uptake. Information from the study will be utilised to encourage the development of new enterprises in Wales.

INTRODUCTION

Wales covers 2.1 million hectares; of this 81% is dedicated to agricultural use and 12% to forestry and woodland. The majority of agricultural land (84%) is permanent grass or rough grazing with only a small proportion (12%) dedicated to arable cropping, and this is dominated by rotational grassland (Welsh Institute of Rural Studies, 2002). The country remains dominated by livestock production, which has impacts on the available arable land for provision of feed and bedding supplies.

In the past 5 years there has been a dramatic and devastating fall in Welsh farm incomes, exacerbated by the outbreak of Foot and Mouth Disease during 2001. Total income from farming has declined by as much as 25% in recent years (MAFF, 2001), the greatest effect has been apparent in the designated Less Favoured Areas. Many farm businesses are currently unprofitable, in 2000, 15% of agricultural producers made a loss, the average loss being £5,500 although some were as high as £20,000.

There is a need to find additional ways of exploiting plants and animal products in new sectors to help add value to Welsh agriculture. Opportunities to develop new products from the rural economy which encourage local processing or primary manufacturing would also aid rural recovery in Wales and may offer opportunities for local branding to add value, or enhance tourism etc.

In July 2002 the Central Science Laboratory, in collaboration with the School of Agriculture and Forest Sciences at the University of Wales, Bangor (UWB) and the Centre for Ecology and Hydrology (CEH), also based at UWB were commissioned by the Welsh Development Agency to assess the economic potential of plants and animals not currently fully exploited by the Welsh agricultural sector. The aim was to identify food and non-food products to supply proven market opportunities, ideally where Wales and the Welsh Rural Economy has an advantageous position in the marketplace.

METHODOLOGY

The study was separated into two Phases; Phase I involved an evaluation of the agronomy and/or husbandry of the potential species, Phase II focused on a smaller range of species identified as having potential and involved a detailed evaluation of the commercial potential and potential added value for each identified opportunity.

Phase I

An initial list of over 150 plant species, with known or suggested potential for minor food or non-food use, was compiled by searching the internet, reviews of journals and through personal communications. Of the list of plant species identified with potential for commercial use 43 were identified as already growing in Wales (in the Atlas of British and Irish Flora) and a further 11 were identified, through The Postcode Plants Database, as native species. For each of the identified species a literature review was undertaken to identify potential uses, physical requirements (i.e. soil type and climate), nature of growth (e.g. annual, biennial, herb) and canopy characteristics, agronomy/husbandry, ability to cross pollinate or become a weed species, and value to insects and mammals. From the latter, it was possible to estimate the likely impacts on the landscape and related species. A website was created (http://safs.csl.gov.uk) to enable data to be searched by a wide audience.

Using the information gathered on each species, for those assessed as having the greatest commercial potential a number of mapping parameters were derived for use with a Geographic Information System (GIS) to illustrate potential and marginal areas for production. Table 1 illustrates the mapping parameters and includes details of the scale and sources of information.

Upon completion of Phase I a number of species were eliminated on the basis of their climatic and agronomic requirements. The number of species progressing to Phase II was reduced to 28.

Phase II

A more detailed market review was undertaken to assess current, potential and developed markets for renewable raw materials. For each species, information was collated regarding product value, potential market outlet, market size and likely timescale to commercialisation. A review of processing facilities was also undertaken, providing information on both the location and the extent of processing facilities already available in Wales or in nearby localities.

Table 1. Details of GIS mapping parameters, categorisation and sources of information.

Factor	Mapping parameters	Resolution	Source
Soil Type	1. Saltmarsh 2. Shallow acid peat over rock 3. Shallow soils over limestone 4. Sand dune soils 5. Slowly permeable clay over mudstone 6. Well drained loamy soils 7. Well drained sandy soils 8. Well drained soils in floodplains 9. Well drained acid loamy soils over rock 10. Well drained very acid loam and sand 11. Loamy acid soils with a wet peaty surface 12. Seasonally wet, loamy and clayey soils 13. Wet acid soils with a peaty surface 14. Stoneless loamy and clayey soils 15. Stoneless loamy and clayey coastal soils 16. Permeable sandy and loamy soils 17. Restored soils 18. Deep acid peat soils	$5km^2$	Simplified soil map from the National Soils Resources Institute (NSRI)
Rainfall bands	1. Up to 800mm 2. 800 – 1200mm 3. 1200 – 1600mm 4. >1600mm	$5km^2$	Met Office Rainfall data from GIServices
Days between first and last frost	1. 140 days 2. 155 days 3. 168 days 4. 185 days 5. 198 days 6. 213 days	$5km^2$	From Horticultural Website
Slope and altitude (for limits on mechanisation)	Option to exclude slopes greater than 15% Option to include/exclude upland or lowland areas	$50m^2$	Digital Elevation Model (held by CEH)
National Park Boundaries	Option to include/exclude National Park land	$100m^2$	Data held by CEH
Sites of Specific Scientific Interest	Option to include/exclude	$100m^2$	Data held by CEH

Detailed assessments were undertaken to allow the remaining species to be ranked in order of potential viability and success. The nature and magnitude of any likely environmental impacts were assessed, taking into account the following factors:

- Impacts on risk of soil erosion, loss of soil structure, and impacts on organic matter content
- Impacts on risk of flooding
- Odour, CO_2 emissions
- Anticipated inputs – fertiliser, herbicides, insecticides, fungicides
- Anticipated impacts on the farmed landscape
- Potential impacts on local biodiversity – risks to genetic resource, diversity and habitats

Species were considered for their social, economic and cultural value at the farm level and to the wider rural economy (by comparison with cereal production as a baseline). Each enterprise was allocated a total score (as in the example below for hemp and woad production). This was used as the basis for the final prioritisation.

Table 2. Scoring matrix to demonstrate the social, economic and cultural value of each enterprise (1-10 score for each item, where cereal production would typically receive an 'average' score of 5 in each category).

Class	Criterion	Hemp	Woad
Producer	Return/ha	5	6
Return	Demand	7	3
	Ease of access	4	4
	Total	16	13
Regional	Overall regional return	3	2
Economy	Jobs in production	4	1
	Quality of jobs in production	5	5
	Potential for post-production processing (A)	7	6
	Number of jobs in post-production (B)	6	1
	Quality of jobs in post-production (C)	7	5
	Total	32	20
Culture	Practicality	5	5
	Enhancement of Welsh agriculture	6	4
	Enhancement of Welsh tourism	5	5
	Total	16	14
TOTAL		64	47

On completion of Phase II an interactive workshop was held in North Wales, attended by around 70 key influences and related parties, to provide feedback and comment from a regional and practical perspective.

RESULTS

Table 3 shows the list of prioritised plant opportunities, the likely time to fruition and extent of perceived and actual limits to development.

The majority of the highlighted crop opportunities can be categorised as high value, low volume or high volume, low value. There is greatest potential for retaining added value locally with high value, low volume markets such as natural dyes and essential oils (e.g. Valerian, Peppermint, Woad, Madder). For relatively low value, high volume, commodity traded produce (e.g. oilseed crops) there is often little potential to add value to the local and wider rural economy.

Fibre crops appear to offer significant potential for added value processing in Wales, in part due to the expertise established at the Biocomposites Centre, Bangor. Other 'niche' crops such as echium (for healthcare), woad (as a dye) and peppermint also offer potential for adding value through the development of small-scale local or mobile processing facilities.

Table 3. Prioritised list of plant species and enterprises for further development in Wales.

Time to fruition	Few or no limits to uptake	Moderate limits to uptake	Major limits to uptake
0-3 years	Crambe (I)	Linola (F)	
	High Erucic Acid	Flax (I/T)	
	Rape (I)	St Johns Wort (H)	
	Hemp (I)	Valerian (H)	
		Borage (H)	
		Evening Primrose (H)	
		Echium (H)	
		Peppermint (E)	
		Foxglove (P)	
		Poppy (P)	
3-5 years		Meadowfoam (I/T)	Yarrow (Dye)
		Miscanthus (Fibre)	Madder (Dye)
		Calendula (Oils & food dye)	Native Grasses (Fibre)
		Woad (Dye)	Bog Myrtle (N)
		Gold of Pleasure (H)	
		Oats (H)	
		Mugwort (P)	
5-10 years		Spurge (Oils/polymer)	Giant Reed (Fibre)
		Nettle (Fibre)	Reed Canary Grass (Fibre)
			Sea Buckthorn (H)
			Henbane (P)

I – Industrial	H – Healthcare	P – Pharmaceutical	N-Novel
F – Food	T – Textile	E – Essential Oil	

There are no large scale commercial seed oil crushing or refining plants located in Wales; the nearest facility is located in Liverpool. Commodity-traded oilseeds therefore offer little opportunity for Wales in competition with the rest of the UK, despite the fact that there are few obstacles to production in low-lying areas of relatively moderate and low rainfall in Wales.

On the basis of all information gathered, 5 enterprises deemed the most promising for Wales in the short and medium term were identified (Table 4).

Table 4. Most promising opportunities for non-food crops in Wales.

Time to fruition	Plants	Application
0-3 years	Hemp and/or Flax	Fibre
	Miscanthus	Fibre
3-5 years	Nettle	Fibre
	Woad	Natural Dye
	Oats	Healthcare Products

Capitalising on existing Welsh experiences and knowledge in the area of fibres, fibre crops should receive high priority for research and development in Wales. Development of a generic fibre industry could capitalise on such markets and ensure that the added value obtained from processing remains in Wales.

Oats are widely grown in Wales and developments to commercialise novel products have been undertaken. Technical barriers have to be overcome but there is significant potential for Wales to capitalise on the industry in the mid to long term (3-5 years). In the interim, small scale markets exist for oat oils and starch.

Production of woad is not currently commercialised in the UK and therefore there is an opportunity to establish a small niche industry to counter imports. The indigo produced from woad is a valuable dye and could compliment the co-development of natural fibre industries. However, woad needs further research and development to commercialise its production.

The above represent opportunities with least barriers to adoption. Future work will focus on these to optimise returns to Welsh farmers and the wider Welsh economy. A similar methodology could easily be applied to other regions in the UK.

ACKNOWLEDGEMENTS

The authors would like to thank David Norris and Dr Bryan Reynolds of CEH for their expertise and assistance throughout the study and for provision of GIS support and Professor G Edwards-Jones, Ian Harris and David Wright of the University of North Wales, Bangor for general assistance and provision of advice from a regional perspective.

REFERENCES

MAFF (2001). *Agriculture in the United Kingdom, 2000*. London: Stationary Office.
Welsh Institute of Rural Studies (2002). *Farm business survey in Wales: statistical results for 2000/2001*. University of Wales: Aberystwyth.

[14C]-Glyphosate: Uptake into *Echium plantagineum* following pre-emergent application

A B McEwen, E B Whittle
BioDynamics Research Ltd., Rushden, Northamptonshire, NN10 6ER, UK
Email: andrew.mcewen@biodynamics.co.uk

R G Parsons, K McCurrie
Agrochemex, Manningtree, Essex, UK

ABSTRACT

Echium is a member of the borage family and like borage Echium grows rapidly and competes well with weeds. The seed oil is unusual in that it contains a unique ratio of omega-3 and omega-6 fatty acids. These lipids, previously obtained from other sources, have been used for many years in health supplements. Of particular interest when considering *Echium* as a health food supplement are the appreciable amounts of gamma-linolenic acid (GLA) as well as the unusual polyunsturated fatty acid stearidonic acid. These acids occupy similar positions in the biochemical pathway of essential fatty acids. *Echium* is currently the best agricultural source of this material. The seed oil is also valued for its moisturising and anti-inflammatory action.

Health food supplements are generally grown without the use of pesticides due to the limited range of products approved for use in this sector. In addition, there are consumer concerns over any possible contamination by agrochemical products. This paper presents information on the uptake of glyphosate, a widely used and well characterised herbicide, into *Echium* following pre-emergent application to soil.

INTRODUCTION

This work was undertaken to develop and demonstrate a novel approach to pesticide metabolism studies for horticultural crops grown for the healthfood market. A key aim was to show that *Echium* could be grown in a novel pot growing system and provide information on the uptake of glyphosate by *Echium* following application to soil prior to crop emergence. Another aim was to monitor soil characteristics over a 12 month period which included the growing season of *Echium*.

MATERIALS AND METHODS

Echium plantaginuem was obtained from an accredited supplier and sown in a 230 litre pot in May 2002 in accordance with the principles of current commercial practice (Figure 1). The pot was then buried within a larger area of 4 m^2 of crop. This gave a treated crop area of 0.5 m^2 which equated to approximately 50 plants. [14C]-Glyphosate was obtained from Sigma and the area in the pot was sprayed on the day of sowing at a nominal field rate of 1.44 kg/ha using a sprayer devised for applications of this sort (Figure 2). Soil cores (10 to a depth of 10 cm

c. 1 kg) were taken from inside and outside a control pot (sprayed with non-radiolabelled glyphosate as for the radiolabelled compound) planted with *Echium* in March, May, September and November (2002). Soil cores were analysed for organic carbon (dichromate digest method), pH (soil extracted into water) and microbial biomass (fumigation/extraction method).

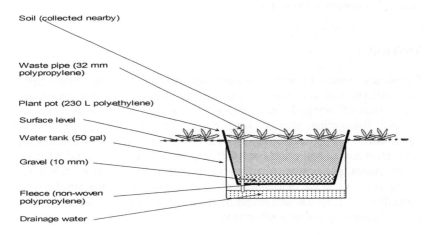

Soil (collected nearby)

Waste pipe (32 mm polypropylene)

Plant pot (230 L polyethylene)
Surface level
Water tank (50 gal)
Gravel (10 mm)

Fleece (non-woven polypropylene)
Drainage water

Figure 1.   Novel pot used for growing *Echium*.

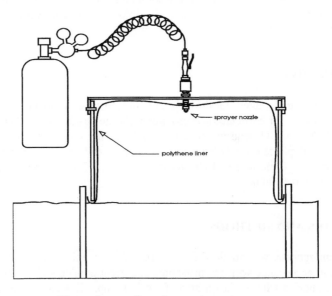

sprayer nozzle

polythene liner

Figure 2.   Spraying equipment.

Echium was harvested by cutting as close to the soil as possible approximately 110 days after sowing and was separated into seed and straw components. These were homogenised to a fine powder and aliquots (c. 0.2 g) taken for analysis. Soil was allowed to air-dry and then homogenised to a fine powder and aliquots (c. 0.2 g) taken for analysis. Radioactivity in the samples was determined after combustion in oxygen using an Automatic Sample Oxidiser (Model 307 MK2 Tri-Carb®, Packard Instruments Co. Ltd.).

RESULTS

Soil pH and microbial biomass in soil taken from inside the pot increased over the course of the growing season (May to September) whereas soil taken from outside the treated area showed no notable increase. Comparable growth of *Echium* was achieved in both the treated and non-treated areas. However, at the time of harvest (September) the microbial biomass in the treated area was approximately twice that measured in the untreated area.

Table 1. Soil parameters inside and outside the sprayed area.

Pot	Parameter	Month (2002)			
		March	May	September	November
Treated	Organic carbon (%)	1.6	1.4	1.5	1.6
(In)	pH	6.0	6.1	6.7	7.6
	Biomass (µg C/g)	173.4	194.3	303.3	298.6
Untreated	Organic carbon (%)	3.0	1.7	1.7	1.9
(Out)	pH	5.8	5.5	5.9	6.3
	Biomass (µg C/g)	28.4	185.1	142.8	212.5

The particle size distribution of the soil used in the pots was: 63µm – 2mm, 41.80%; 2µ - 63µm, 46.43% ; <2µm 11.77%.

No uptake of glyphosate was detected in *Echium* at harvest (all values were below the limit of detection) but traces of glyphosate residues were still present in soil 110 days after treatment (Table 2).

Table 2. Uptake of glyphosate at harvest.

Sample	Concentration (µg equiv./g)
Soil	1.888
Grain	BLQ
Straw	BLQ

(BLQ - Below limit of quantification (<0.02 µg equiv./g))

CONCLUSIONS

This study demonstrated the use of a new type of pot system for the conduct of pesticide metabolism studies in herbaceous crops. It also demonstrated that application of glyphosate as a pre-emergence spray to *Echium* does not result in detectable residues in seed or plant material at harvest.

POSTER SESSION 7D

ASPECTS OF HORTICULTURAL CROP PROTECTION

Session Organiser: Dr Jean Fitzgerald
                       Horticulture Research International,
                       East Malling, UK

Poster Papers: 7D-1 to 7D-9

Control of field thrips, *Thrips angusticeps*, in vining peas, Pisum sativum

R L Ward, A J Biddle

Processors and Growers Research Organisation, Thornhaugh, Peterborough, PE8 6HJ, UK
Email: becky@pgro.co.uk

ABSTRACT

The effects of insecticides on reducing leaf damage caused by field thrips in vining peas, were investigated in six field trials in the UK from 1999 to 2002. Seven products were used at different rates and compared to a standard treatment and an untreated control. The results showed varying levels of control within and between trials. In 1999 only one product, triazamate, showed a reduction of damage, and the standard treatment, fenitrothion, had no effect. Reduction of damage in 2000 was better, and fenitrothion, lambda-cyhalothrin CS and thiacloprid with a mineral oil adjuvant significantly reduced leaf damage. In 2001 experiments at both sites showed some level of control and all products were effective at one site. In 2002 a smaller trial was carried out and lambda-cyhalothrin CS and spinosad significantly reduced leaf damage. Overall, the most effective treatments were fenitrothion and lambda-cyhalothrin as a capsule suspension formulation. Thiacloprid at 250 ml per hectare with a mineral oil adjuvant showed good effects in some years but reduced damage less consistently.

INTRODUCTION

Field thrips cause damage in vining peas in most seasons, particularly during periods of slow growth and on stony soils. The plants are attacked as they emerge and leaves are damaged as the thrips feed, becoming pale and distorted. In many situations peas can outgrow this attack with no long term effects on the crop. Occasionally, however, when attack is severe, peas may develop multiple shoots and develop as stunted, bushy plants causing 'pea dwarfing syndrome', which may persist throughout the life of the plants. Thrips feed inside the enclosed shoots of peas as they emerge, and are therefore difficult to control using contact acting insecticides (Biddle *et al.*, 1992).

Until 2001 two organophosphate products, dimethoate and fenitrothion, were approved for use in peas, although the processing industry wished to reduce use of organophosphates in food crops. There became a need to evaluate alternative products for activity against field thrips in vining peas.

MATERIALS AND METHODS

Spray trials were carried out between 1999 and 2002 comparing pyrethroids and newly developed insecticides, using fenitrothion as a standard. In 1999 the trial was at Great Wakering in Essex and in 2000, trials were carried out at Appleby and Cadwell in Lincolnshire.

In 2001 trial sites were at Swallow and Hibaldstow in Lincolnshire, and in 2002 a trial was carried out at Thornhaugh in Cambridgeshire.

In 1999, 2000 and 2001 trials were carried out in commercial vining pea crops where plant density was 100 plants m^{-2}. In 2002 the trial was drilled at 100 plants m^{-2} using a two metre Nordsten plot drill.

Insecticides were applied to plots measuring 10m x 2m using an Azo plot sprayer with 02F/110 nozzles in 200 litres water/ha at 2.5 bar pressure using propane gas. Treatments were applied at early seedling emergence (growth stage 101) (Knott, 1987) before the leaves had fully expanded. Each treatment was replicated four times in a randomised block design.

Thrips damage assessments were carried out approximately two weeks after spray application (growth stage 104) (Knott, 1987) by assessing the percentage leaf area of the whole seedling which showed symptoms of attack. The plants were assessed using twenty five plants per plot. Mean damage per plant was calculated and analysis of variance carried out on the data using GENSTAT. The data were analysed before and after angular transformation of the percentage damage for each plot.

RESULTS

At Great Wakering thrip populations were low and at the time of application only two thrips per plant were present. Damage levels had increased by the time of assessment.

Table 1. Leaf damage and percentage control at Great Wakering 1999. Date of application: 15. 04.99. Air temperature: 10°C

Treatment rate ha^{-1}	% thrips damage	angular transformation	% control
1. untreated	16.4	23.6	0
2. fenitrothion 1400 ml	16.1	22.6	1.8
3. zeta-cypermethrin 150 ml	10.1	18.3	38.4
4. lambda-cyhalothrin EC 150 ml	10.9	18.8	33.5
5. triazamate 100 ml	8.0	16.1	51.2
6. thiacloprid 250 ml	33.4	35.1	0
7. thiacloprid 250 ml + mineral oil adjuvant	19.3	25.0	0
8. thiacloprid 500 ml	24.3	29.3	0
LSD	14.08	10.04	
Probability	0.021	0.014	

Damage levels were variable over the trial area and there were anomalies in the results. Damage appeared to be significantly higher than the untreated following the lower rate of thiacloprid, but at other rates no effects were recorded (Table 1). The only significant reduction in damage was recorded from the triazamate treatment.

In 2000, damage levels were very low at Appleby, but a significant reduction of damage was recorded following fenitrothion, lambda-cyhalothrin in the capsule suspension formula (CS) and thiacloprid with mineral oil adjuvant (Table 2).

Table 2. Leaf damage and percentage control at Appleby 2000. Date of application: 10.04.00 Air temperature: 11°C

Treatment rate ha^{-1}	% thrips damage	angular transformation	% control
1. untreated	9.85	18.26	0
2. fenitrothion 1400 ml	5.2	12.92	47.2
3. lambda-cyhalothrin CS 75 ml	5.1	12.89	48.2
4. thiacloprid 250 ml	7.85	15.9	20.3
5. thiacloprid 500 ml	5.35	12.94	45.7
6. thiacloprid 250 ml + mineral oil adjuvant 1000 ml	4.45	12.09	54.8
LSD	2.83	3.43	
Probability	0.007	0.011	

Table 3. Leaf damage and percentage control at Cadwell 2000. Date of application: 16.05.00 Air temperature: 12°C

Treatment rate ha^{-1}	% thrips damage	angular transformation	% control
1. untreated	7.34	14.97	0
2. fenitrothion 1400 ml	3.89	11.17	47.0
3. lambda-cyhalothrin CS 75 ml	4.73	11.82	35.6
4. thiacloprid 250 ml	5.93	13.89	19.2
5. thiacloprid 500 ml	6.45	14.69	12.1
6. thiacloprid 250 ml + mineral oil adjuvant 1000 ml	3.29	10.25	55.2
LSD	3.77	4.512	
Probability	0.231	0.184	

Table 4. Leaf damage and percentage control at Hibaldstow 2001. Date of spray application: 26.04.01. Air temperature: 15°C

Treatment rate ha[-1]	% thrips damage	angular transformation	% control
1. untreated	27.5	30.7	0
2. spinosad 75 ml	45.2	41.9	0
3. spinosad 100 ml	20.7	27.0	25
4. spinosad 150 ml	29.5	32.8	0
5. spinosad 200 ml	19.8	25.1	28
6. fenitrothion 1400 ml	5.2	13.0	81
7. lambda-cyhalothrin CS 75 ml	8.8	16.6	68
8. thiacloprid 250 ml	25.8	29.2	6
9. thiacloprid 500 ml	36.0	36.0	0
10. thiacloprid 250 ml + mineral oil adjuvant 1000 ml	27.3	30.7	0
LSD	21.7	14.7	
Probability	0.03	0.017	

Table 5. Leaf damage and percentage control at Swallow 2001. Date of spray application: 11.05.01. Air temperature: 24°C

Treatment rate ha[-1]	% thrips damage	angular transformation	% control
1. untreated	27.1	30.1	0
2. spinosad 75 ml	11.3	19.1	58
3. spinosad 100 ml	7.8	15.5	61
4. spinosad 150 ml	8.8	16.8	68
5. spinosad 200 ml	12.8	20.8	53
6. fenitrothion 1400 ml	5.6	13.4	79
7. lambda-cyhalothrin CS 75 ml	4.9	11.7	82
8. thiacloprid 250 ml	8.6	16.6	68
9. thiacloprid 500 ml	10.3	18.6	62
10. thiacloprid 250 ml + mineral oil adjuvant 1000 ml	11.6	18.8	57
LSD	11.7	9.7	
Probability	0.04	0.05	

At Cadwell damage was also low and no statistically significant differences were found between treatments (Table 3). The addition of a mineral oil adjuvant to thiacloprid gave the best overall reduction of leaf damage and the results compared very well with the standard fenitrothion. Lambda-cyhalothrin CS also reduced damage at both sites.

Variable levels of control were found at Hibaldstow (Table 4). Lambda-cyhalothrin in the capsule suspension formulation controlled thrips attack and a significantly lower percentage of damage was seen where this was applied.

All of the treatments at Swallow showed good control of thrips damage (Table 5). Lambda-cyhalothrin CS showed highest reduction of damage, even when compared to the standard fenitrothion.

Lambda-cyhalothrin CS significantly reduced damage levels at Thornhaugh in 2002 (Table 6).

Table 6. Leaf damage and percentage control at Thornhaugh 2002. Date of spray application: 02.04.02. Air temperature 16°C

Treatment rate ha[-1]	% thrips damage	angular transformation	% control
1. untreated	23.5	29.0	0
2. spinosad 150 ml	11.6	19.5	51
3. lambda-cyhalothrin CS 75 ml	5.7	13.8	76
4. thiacloprid 250 ml + mineral oil adjuvant 1000 ml	24.2	29.2	0
LSD	11.4	8.9	
Probability	0.02	0.013	

DISCUSSION

Thrips in vining peas are difficult to control using contact acting insecticides as they are found in the enclosed leaflets at early emergence. Insecticide applications need to be made at seedling emergence to be of any value. (Biddle et al., 1988)

Results for 1999 and 2000 showed variable levels of reduction of thrip damage at the three sites. Lambda-cyhalothrin CS showed promising levels of control compared to the EC, and also when compared with the standard fenitrothion. In 2000, thiacloprid also appeared to reduce damage levels and further work on this product was continued in 2001 and 2002.

In 2001 lambda-cyhalothrin CS gave the best reduction of leaf damage at both sites, with all products giving high levels of control at Swallow. The temperature at Swallow when sprays were applied was 24°C, considerably higher than at the other sites. Thrips may have been more active at this temperature and therefore more exposed, allowing better targeting of the pest.

In 2002 lambda-cyhalothrin again gave good control of damage. Overall it gave significantly better control than any of the other products used at the six sites. It also compared very well with fenitrothion and therefore is a useful replacement for organophosphate insecticides for thrips control in vining peas.

REFERENCES

Biddle A J; Gent G P; Knott C M (1988). *The Pea Growing Handbook,* pp. 149-150 Processors and Growers Research Organisation, Peterborough, UK.

Biddle A J; Hutchins S H; Wightman J A (1992). Pests of Leguminous Crops. *Vegetable Crop Pests*, ed. McKinlay R G, pg. 177. The Macmillan Press Ltd.

Knott C M (1987). A key for stages of development of the pea (*Pisum sativum*). *Annals of Applied Biology,* **111**, 233-244.

Alternative methods for controlling onion thrips

L Jensen, B Simko

Malheur County Extension Office, Oregon State University, 710 SW 5ᵗʰ Ave., Ontario, OR, 97914, USA

Email: lynn.jensen@oregonstate.edu

C Shock, L Saunders

Malheur Experiment Station, Oregon State University, 595 Onion Ave., Ontario, OR, 97914 USA

ABSTRACT

Onion thrips (*Thrips tabaci*) is the major insect pest for dry bulb onions grown in the arid production regions of the western United States. High thrips populations reduce yield and bulb size, decreasing the per cent of colossal sized bulbs (> 9.53 cm). Pesticide resistance to commonly used insecticides has increased substantially over the past eight years. The number of insecticide applications required to keep onion thrips controlled has also increased. The fairly recent development of a mechanical straw mulching machine coupled with the development of "soft" insecticides has led to new strategies to improve thrips control.

Straw mulch applied at layby was coupled with applications of spinosad and azadirachtin in an integrated pest management program designed to suppress onion thrips populations while allowing predator populations to increase to the level where they can give economic thrips control. Onion thrips populations and predator populations were monitored throughout the growing season. Yield and grade measurements were made to determine the impact of control measures. The alternative program of straw mulch, spinosad and azadirachtin gave significantly higher yields and gross return compared to standard grower practices.

INTRODUCTION

Onions are a major economic crop in the eastern Oregon and western Idaho regions of the United States. Annually about 8094 ha of onions are grown in the region. Typically the onions are Spanish hybrids and are grown for their large size, high yield and mild flavor. The value of the Idaho-Eastern Oregon onion industry for the 2001 production year was 85 million US dollars. Over the past 10 years the value of the industry has ranged from a high of 140 million dollars to a low of 75 million depending upon market fluctuations.

The principal onion pest in this region is the onion thrips (*Thrips tabaci*). It causes yield reductions by feeding on the epidermal cells of the plant, reducing the photosynthetic ability of the onion. Onion thrips can reduce total yields from 4 per cent to 27 per cent, depending on variety, but can reduce yields of colossal sized bulbs from 28 per cent to 73 per cent (Jensen, 1990). The larger sized colossal bulbs are difficult to grow and demand a premium in the marketplace. Growers typically spray 3 to 6 times per season to control onion thrips.

Treatments include the use of synthetic pyrethroid, organophosphate, and carbamate insecticides. The ability of these products to control thrips has gone from over 90 per cent control in 1995 (Jensen, 1996) to less than 70 per cent control in 2000 (Jensen, 2002). Onion growers are applying insecticides more frequently in order to keep thrips populations low.

Mechanical straw mulching was introduced in 1985 (Jensen & Hobson, 1991; Shock *et al.*, 1999) as a means of improving irrigation water infiltration and reducing sediment loss. Some growers using this technique reported having less onion thrips pressure. A possible explanation for decreased thrips pressure may be from enhanced habitat for predators.

New biological insecticides have been developed including neem tree extracts (azadirachtin) and bacterial fermentation products (spinosad). Both of these materials have previously been evaluated for thrips control (Jensen, 2000; 2002) and have performed poorly compared to conventional insecticides. It was decided to test these products in combination with straw mulch (to provide predator habitat) as an alternative program to the conventional insecticide program currently used by growers.

MATERIALS AND METHODS

A 0.73 ha field was planted to onions (cv. 'Vaquero', Sunseeds, Brooks, OR) on March 23, 2001 and a 0.8 ha field on March 12, 2002. The onions were planted as two double rows on a 1.1 m bed. The double rows were spaced 5 cm apart. The seeding rate was 380,000 seeds per hectare. Lorsban 15 G (chlorpyrifos) was applied in a 15 cm band over each row at planting at a rate of 105 g/305 m of row for onion maggot control. The field was divided into plots 12.5 m wide by 30.5 m long in 2001 and 11.2 m wide by 30.5 m long in 2002. There were three treatments with six replications in both years.

The three treatments were a grower standard treatment, an untreated check and the alternative treatment. The grower standard practice included Warrior (lambda-cyhalothrin) and Lannate (methomyl). The check did not receive any treatments for thrips control. The alternative treatment included straw mulch applied to the center of the bed plus Success (spinosad), and Ecozin or Aza Direct (azadirachtin).

Insecticide treatments were applied weekly or biweekly during the first half of the growing season. All insecticides were applied with water at 277.8 litres/ha in 2001 and 299.3 litres/ha in 2002. Straw was applied only between the irrigation furrows on top of the beds to avoid confounding irrigation effects with thrips effects. The straw was applied on May 23, 2001 at a rate of 1067 kg/ha and on May 28, 2002 at a rate of 1210 kg/ha.

Thrips populations were sampled by two methods. The first was by visually counting the number of thrips on five plants per plot in 2001 and 15 plants per plot in 2002. The second method was by cutting five plants in 2001 and 10 plants in 2002 at ground level and inserting the plants into a berlese funnel. Turpentine was applied to a sponge attached to the underside of the berlese funnel lid. The turpentine vapors dislodged the thrips from the plants. The thrips fell through the funnel into a jar containing 90% isopropyl alcohol. The collected thrips were then counted through a binocular microscope. Thrips populations were monitored weekly though the growing season.

The predator populations were monitored using pitfall traps (one per plot) that contained ethylene glycol. They were evaluated three times per week in 2001 and one time per week in 2002. The berlese funnel was also used to monitor predators foraging on the plants.

RESULTS AND DISCUSSION

The onions in the conventional treatment and the alternative control treatments looked similar throughout the growing season, with minimal thrips damage to the foliage. In contrast, the onions in the untreated check treatment had severe foliage damage due to thrips feeding.

The visual counts did not correlate well with the funnel counts in 2001 but were somewhat better in 2002 where more plants were counted. Thrips populations, whether by the visual plant counts or with the berlese funnel counts did not correlate well with visual thrips damage or with overall size and yield response, particularly in 2002. No other insect or disease pests were observed which might have impacted yield. There were statistical differences in thrips populations between treatments on some of the sample dates as shown in Tables 1 and 2.

Table 1. Weekly thrips population during the 2001-2002 growing season from visual counts beginning with the second week of June. Average number of thrips per plant. Malheur Experiment Station, 2001 & 2002.

Week	1	2	3	4	5	6	7
Check	10.9	10.4	17.1	19.4	20.6	14.1	23.0
Standard	10.3	15.4	20.7	25.4	20.8	7.4	21.0
Alternative	6.5	8.5	17.6	13.6	19.7	14.8	14.7
LSD (0.05)	3.2	3.9	NS	6.0	NS	5.6	NS

Table 2. Weekly thrips population from berlese funnel for the 2001-2002 growing season beginning with the second week of June. Average number of thrips per plant. Malheur Experiment Station, 2001 & 2002.

Week	1	2	3	4	5	6	7
Check	5.6	14.0	14.7	18.8	33.9	17.7	7.9
Standard	2.7	11.0	10.0	12.7	25.6	11.2	10.2
Alternative	4.5	11.0	7.3	7.3	14.9	18.9	6.2
LSD (0.05)	NS	NS	NS	5.9	NS	5.6	NS

Predator composition varied throughout the season but consisted mostly of spiders (*Araneae*), big-eyed bugs (*Geocoris* spp.), damsel bugs (*Nabis alternatus*) and minute pirate bugs (*Orius tristicolor*), with smaller populations of lacewings (*Chrysopa* spp.), ladybeetle (*Coccinella* spp.), and rove beetles. Spiders and big-eyed bugs were the dominant predators in June, but minute pirate bugs and damsel bug populations increased in July. Late in the season minute pirate bugs and spiders were the dominant predators.

The highest populations of predators were in the alternative control plots (Figure 1). The alternative control plots had significantly higher predator populations than did the standard treatments in both years. Predator populations increased in the unsprayed and conventionally sprayed plots in August, but decreased slightly in the alternative control plots, although the population was still well above that of the conventionally sprayed plots.

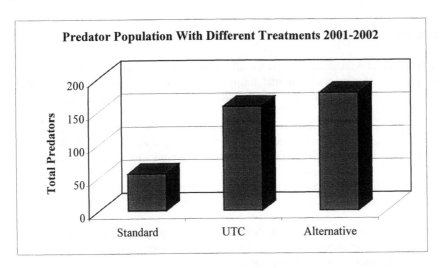

Figure 1. Treatment effect on predator populations. Total predators captured in pit fall traps and berlese funnel for the 2001-2002 growing seasons. Malheur Experiment station, Oregon State University, Ontario, Oregon, 2001 & 2002. (UTC is untreated check.)

The onions were harvested on September 13 and graded on September 14 and 17 in 2001 and harvested on September 11 and graded on September 12 in 2002. The alternative treatment gave the highest total marketable yield and the highest yield of colossal and super colossal bulbs in both years (Table 3). In 2001 there was a significant increase in super colossal size bulbs in the alternative treatment compared to the untreated check. There was also a significant difference in total yield between both alternative and standard treatments compared to the untreated check. There was a trend towards higher super colossals and total yield in the alternative control treatment compared to the standard control, but this was not statistically significant. In 2002 there was a significant increase in super colossals, colossals and total yield with the alternative treatment over any of the other treatments. The standard treatment had significantly higher yield of super colossals, colossals and total yield compared to the untreated check. The alternative and standard treatments had significantly reduced yield of jumbo onions compared to the untreated check as the yield shifted to the larger sized colossals and super colossals with decreased thrips injury.

Weekly FOB shipping prices were averaged for the 2001-2002 shipping season to determine gross returns to the grower for each treatment. These values are shown in Table 4. The alternative treatment averaged $951/ha more than the standard treatment and $2854/ha more than the untreated check over the two years and was significantly better than either of the other treatments. The standard treatment averaged $1903/ha, more than the untreated check.

Table 3. Onion grade and yield as influenced by commercial and alternative insecticide controls. Malheur Experiment Station, 2001 & 2002.

2001

Treatment	Super colossal > 10.8 cm	Colossal 10.2–10.8 cm	Jumbo 7.6-10.2 cm	Medium 5.7-7.6 cm	Total marketable yield
		-----kg/ha-----			
Untreated check	36.0	216.4	686.7	55.4	994.5
Standard	52.6	285.3	704.8	40.8	1083.4
Alternative Control	71.4	342.0	683.3	33.8	1130.5
LSD (0.05)	26.7	NS	NS	NS	71.7

2002

Treatment	Super colossal > 10.8 cm	Colossal 10.2-10.8 cm	Jumbo 7.6-10.2 cm	Medium 5.7-7.6 cm	Total marketable yield
		-----kg/ha-----			
Untreated check	10.6	172.0	811.6	40.1	1034.4
Standard	52.9	367.1	749.4	26.8	1196.2
Alternative Control	73.4	458.3	708.0	26.2	1266.0
LSD (0.05)	14.0	66.7	54.7	NS	66.4

Table 4. Market value of onions grown under different insecticides treatments – weekly shipping prices averaged over the 2001-2002 shipping seasons. Malheur Experiment Station, 2001& 2002.

Treatment	Avg. per ha value
Untreated Check	$11,335
Standard	$13,238
Alternative	$14,189
LSD (0.05)	$582

CONCLUSION

The alternative treatments worked better than standard grower practices. The test was not designed to determine the individual effects of spinosad or azadirachtin on yield and quality, but only to answer the question of whether these materials in combination with straw mulch might control thrips and give yield and quality similar to the conventional spray program.

Thrips control with the alternative program was not as good as the conventional program in 2001 but better than the conventional program in 2002. Yield and quality were improved with the alternative treatments. The next step will be to determine what each alternative product is contributing towards thrips control, yield and quality.

REFERENCES

Jensen, L B (1990). The effect of onion thrips (*Thrips tabaci* Lindeman) on sweet Spanish onions. *Special Report 682, Agricultural Experiment Station, Oregon State University.* June 1990. pp. 38-44.

Jensen, L B (1996). Strategies for controlling onion thrips (*Thrips tabaci*) in sweet Spanish onions. *Special Report 964, Agricultural Experiment Station, Oregon State University.* June 1996. pp. 26-33.

Jensen, L B (2000). Insecticide trials for onion thrips (*Thrips tabaci*) control. *Special Report 1015, Agricultural Experiment Station, Oregon State University.* July 2000. pp. 68-72.

Jensen, L B (2002). Insecticide trials for onion thrips (*Thrips tabaci*) control. *Special Report 1038, Agricultural Experiment Station, Oregon State University.* June 2002. pp. 100-103.

Jensen, L B and Hobson, J (1991). Straw mulch and wheel compaction effects on onion yields in the Treasure Valley. *Proceedings of the National Onion Research Conference, Savannah, GA.* pp. 88-90.

Shock, C C, Jensen, L B, Hobson, J, Seddigh, M, Shock, B M, Saunders, L D, and Stieber, T D (1999). Improving onion yield and market grade by mechanical straw application to irrigation furrows. *HortTech.* 9:251-253.

Slug control by molluscicide and herbicide application prior to planting iceberg lettuce

D M Glen
Styloma Research & Consulting, Phoebe, The Lippiatt, Cheddar, BS27 3QP, UK
Email: davidmglen@btopenworld.com

C W Wiltshire
Arion Ecology, The Brambles, Stinchcombe Hill, Dursley, Gloucestershire, GL11 6AQ, UK

D A Bohan
Rothamsted Research, Harpenden, Herts, AL5 2JQ, UK

R Storer, S Clarkson, T Weinert
Langmead Farms, Fishbourne, West Sussex, UK

ABSTRACT

Control of slug damage is difficult in lettuce, where the presence of slugs, faeces, damage or slug pellets is unacceptable in harvested produce. A replicated factorial field experiment is described where metaldehyde pellets and glyphosate herbicide were applied singly or together, in mid February 2002, to plots on land that had been ploughed in December 2001 prior to planting Iceberg lettuce in early May 2002. Mild wet weather through May and June permitted slug numbers and activity to increase as the crop matured, especially on untreated plots. Under these conditions, the treatments applied in mid February had valuable effects in significantly reducing slug damage close to harvest by 64% for molluscicide and 74% for herbicide used alone and by 91% for both used in combination. These benefits were achieved despite overall applications of molluscicide pellets to the lettuce crop. Slugs found in damaged lettuce heads were almost all small juvenile *Deroceras reticulatum*, which were probably eggs or neonates when the experimental treatments were applied. It is therefore thought that the treatments reduced the number of eggs laid by *D. reticulatum* adults and survival of juveniles present at or hatching shortly after the time of treatment. The juvenile slugs in lettuce heads had survived pellet application to the growing crop, probably because juveniles were unlikely to come into contact with pellets in this crop.

INTRODUCTION

Control of slug damage is difficult in lettuce, where the presence of slugs, faeces, damage or slug pellets is unacceptable in harvested produce (Port *et al.*, 2002; 2003a, b). Langmead Farms often plough land in autumn or early winter after cereals, then apply molluscicides (metaldehyde slug pellets) and herbicide (glyphosate) in winter in preparation for planting Iceberg lettuce in the following growing season. The herbicide treatment is of course important for weed control but it and the other practices described above are intended to reduce slug populations to low levels before the lettuce crops are planted. This is important because it is often difficult to achieve adequate control of slugs by applications of chemical molluscicides or the nematode biological control agent *Phasmarhabditis hermaphrodita* in the lettuce crop itself (Port *et al.*, 2003a, b).

It is well documented that ploughing usually results in substantial reductions in slug numbers (Glen & Symondson, 2003), so there is little question that winter ploughing prior to planting lettuce is a valuable component of integrated control of slug damage. A molluscicide application would be expected to kill ca. 50% of the population present at the time of treatment (Glen & Moens, 2002); glyphosate treatment would be expected to have no immediate effect but could deprive slugs of a future source of food and shelter. However, the effects of such pre-planting applications of molluscicide and herbicide have not been investigated in controlled experiments. It is possible that slug populations may have sufficient time to recover following treatment before the lettuce crop is planted. We investigated the impact of these treatments applied alone or in combination, on slug populations and damage to Iceberg lettuce, in comparison to untreated plots.

MATERIALS AND METHODS

The experiment site was Chequers Field, Langmead Farms, Fishbourne, West Sussex. The experiment design was two randomised Latin squares side-by-side, with a total of 32 plots. The individual plot size was 12 m × 12 m.

There were four treatments, as follows:

A	No molluscicide	no herbicide
B	Metaldehyde pellets	no herbicide
C	No molluscicide	glyphosate
D	Metaldehyde pellets	glyphosate

The field was ploughed in December 2001 and the experiment was marked out on 16 January 2002. Because of rain, we were unable to apply the experimental treatments, as intended, on that day. Furthermore, because of persistently wet weather in the following weeks, it was not possible to apply the treatments until 14 February.

Treatments applied

Metaldehyde slug pellets (Metarex, 6% a.i., De Sangosse) were broadcast by hand at the recommended rate of 8 kg/ha = 0.8 g/m^2 on 14 February 2002. Pellets were weighed out for each plot individually and 50% of the pellets for each plot were broadcast while walking in one direction, then 50% were broadcast while walking at right angles to the original direction. Glyphosate was applied on 14 February as Roundup Bioactive at 3 litres product/ha in a volume equivalent to 250 litres/ha (equivalent to 12 ml product per litre of spray). The total volume applied = 25 ml/m^2.

Metaldehyde pellets, followed by methiocarb slug pellets (Draza, 4% a.i., Bayer CropScience) were applied as an overall treatment to the whole experiment after lettuce planting.

Crop planting and harvest

Iceberg lettuce was planted on 3-9 May and harvested on 25 June 2002.

Assessments of slugs and slug damage

All assessments of slug numbers and plant damage were made in the central 4 x 4 m area of each plot.

On 18 January, we took one pre-treatment soil sample to assess slug populations in each of the 32 plots. Each soil sample was 25 cm x 25 cm x 10 cm deep and slugs were extracted from the soil samples by a process of slow flooding at the soil flooding unit at Long Ashton Research Station, as described by Glen *et al.* (2003). Slug populations were also assessed by soil sampling on each plot on 21 March and 16 April 2002 (approx. 5 and 9 weeks after treatment), up to the time just before beds were prepared for lettuce planting. By 16 April the whole field including the experimental area had been treated with herbicide and all weeds were dead or dying.

Slug damage to lettuce plants was first assessed on 27 May, when the plants were open with no hearts and bare soil was still visible between the plants. Damage was assessed once again on 20 June, when plants were close to harvest. Each 12 x 12 m plot contained six raised lettuce beds each 2 m wide, with four rows of plants per bed and a total of 39 plants per row in each 12 m row per plot. The central 13 plants in each of the 4 rows in a central bed were examined on each plot on each date (52 plants examined per plot).

RESULTS

Slug populations in soil

Initial, pre-treatment sampling on 16 January, after overnight frost when the soil was moist, gave a total of 11 slugs from the 32 plots ($5.5/m^2$), with no significant differences between the subsequent treatments. There were ten *Deroceras reticulatum* ranging in weight from 36 to 327 mg and one *Arion circumscriptus weighing 178 mg*. A total of 49 slugs (all *D. reticulatum*) were extracted from the soil samples taken on 21 March (5 weeks after treatments were applied on 14 February), The soil was moist on that date and ideal for soil sampling for slugs. Plots treated with metaldehyde pellets had fewer slugs (1.12 per sample) compared to untreated plots (1.94 per sample). This represents a 43% reduction in numbers (similar to the *ca.* 50% reduction normally expected from such treatment) but the effect was not statistically significant. Numbers on plots treated with glyphosate (1.56 per sample) were similar to those on untreated plots (1.50 per sample).

On 16 April, the soil was dryer and only 14 slugs were extracted from the 32 samples (0.4 slugs per sample) and there were no statistically significant differences between treatments.

Slug damage to lettuce and slug presence in lettuce plants

Damage assessments on 27 May revealed a mean of 0.5 damaged plants per plot (i.e. about 1% of the 52 plants examined per plot), with no significant differences between treatments. The soil surface was moist and suitable for slug activity. Methiocarb pellets and occasional poisoned slugs were visible on the soil between the plants.

Table 1. Mean number of lettuce plants (out of 52 examined per plot) recorded with damage by slugs, close to harvest on 20 June 2002, in a replicated field experiment where molluscicide (metaldehyde pellets) and herbicide (glyphosate) were applied to plots on 14 February.

Treatment	No. plants/plot damaged by slugs
No molluscicide	2.62
Metaldehyde pellets	0.94
SED (25 df)	0.75
No herbicide	2.81
Glyphosate	0.75
SED (25 df)	0.75

At the final damage assessment on 20 June, slug damage had increased and there was evidence that both pellet treatment ($P < 0.05$) and glyphosate treatment ($P = 0.01$) on 14 February had resulted in significant reductions in damage compared with untreated plots (Table 1). There was no evidence of any interaction between treatments, indicating that their effects were additive. Thus, plots with no molluscicide and no herbicide application had a mean of 4.1 damaged plants per plot, plots with molluscicide or herbicide alone had 1.5 and 1.1 damaged plants respectively, whilst plots with both molluscicide and herbicide had only 0.4 damaged plants per plot. Thus, the best result in terms of reduced slug damage was achieved with a combination of both pellets and glyphosate treatments applied on 14 February.

Table 2.   Individual weights of slugs (*Deroceras reticulatum*) found in lettuce plants collected on 20 June.

Slug no.	Body weight (mg)
1	9
2	13
3	16
4	23
5	29
6	38
7	56
8	57
9	81
10	91
11	109
Mean	47

The figure of 4.1 damaged plants per plot on untreated plots represents 8% of the plants examined. This is similar to the 10% loss recorded for the field as a whole.

On 20 June, a sample of 10 lettuce plants with visible slug damage was also collected in a walk through the crop. These were put in polythene bags, placed in a cold room on return to Long Ashton Research Station and examined the following day by removing leaves and recording damage and any slugs present. Eleven outer leaves showed slug damage, compared to 11 upper heart leaves and only 2 inner heart leaves. Slug faeces were present on 1, 3 and 2 leaves in each of these zones respectively. Eleven *D. reticulatum* were found in these ten lettuce plants with the number of slugs per lettuce head ranging from 0 to 3. Ten were found in the outer leaves and one in the heart. However, the slugs may have moved from their original resting positions during transport and overnight storage.

Individual slug weights are shown in Table 2. Almost all the slugs were relatively small juveniles with a mean weight of 47 mg and even the largest, at 109 mg, was only about pea-sized.

DISCUSSION

The lack of any statistically significant effects of the molluscicide or herbicide treatments on slug populations in March and April and on slug damage on May, contrasts with the significant effects of both treatments on slug damage close to harvest on 20 June. The lack of earlier effects could simply have resulted from the relatively low slug numbers recorded in March and April and the low incidence of damage in May. These low incidences could have obscured any underlying differences. Favourable weather through May and June evidently permitted slug numbers and/or activity to increase, especially on the untreated plots. The treatments applied in mid February had measurable and valuable effects in reducing slug damage close to harvest by 64% for molluscicide and 74% for herbicide used alone, and by 91% for both materials used in combination. It is particularly interesting that these benefits were visible despite the routine application of molluscicide pellets to the crop during its period of growth.

The slugs found in damaged lettuce heads were almost exclusively small juvenile *D. reticulatum*, which were probably eggs or neonates at the time when the experimental treatments were applied on 14 February. Some of the smallest slugs may have hatched from eggs laid after that date. It is likely that the treatments on 14 February had reduced the number of eggs subsequently laid and the survival of juveniles. The juvenile slugs found in lettuce heads had evidently survived pellet application to the growing crop, probably because juveniles were unlikely to come into contact with pellets in such a crop environment.

Cultivation to prepare the lettuce beds is likely to have killed substantial numbers of slugs. However, it is also likely that many of the surviving slugs would have been deep in the soil at the time of lettuce planting and would therefore not have come into contact with pellets broadcast on the surface at this time. In this context, it is interesting to note that, following ploughing prior to drilling winter wheat in autumn 2001, Glen *et al.* (2003) recorded that 40% of surviving slugs were in the lower, 10-20 cm layer of soil compared to 60% in the upper 10 cm. This comparison of slug numbers at two depths probably underestimates the effect of cultivation on slug surface activity and their likelihood of coming into contact with slug pellets, as it is likely that many of the slugs in the upper 10 cm would at that time not have been capable of reaching the soil surface. Later, when these buried slugs did reach the soil surface, it is likely that the lettuce plants provided a suitable shelter and source of food by that time, so that slugs did not forage on the soil surface and therefore did not come into contact with slug pellets applied after planting.

We conclude that the results of this experiment demonstrate a clear benefit from both molluscicide and herbicide treatments prior to planting Iceberg lettuce. It will be important for lettuce growers to assess slug populations, as described by Port *et al.* (2003a,b) during the period leading up to the time when such treatments could be applied in order to assess the need for such pre-planting treatments.

ACKNOWLEDGEMENTS

This work was supported by the Department for Environment, Food and Rural Affairs (Defra) (CSA5465, HL0160LFV) and the Horticultural Development Council (FV 225) under the HortLink Programme. We thank all our colleagues in this programme, especially the Chairman, David Piccaver and the Lead Scientist, Gordon Port.

REFERENCES

Glen D M; Green D; Oakley J; Wiltshire C W; Bohan D A; Port G R (2003). Progress in improving the prediction and integrated control of slug damage in arable crops. In: *Slugs & Snails: Agricultural, Veterinary & Environmental Perspectives*, ed. G Dussart, in press. British Crop Protection Council: Alton.

Glen D M; Moens R (2002). Agriolimacidae, Arionidae and Milacidae as pests in West European cereals. In *Molluscs as Crop Pests*, ed. G M Barker, pp. 271-300. CABI Publishing: Wallingford.

Glen D M; Symondson W O C (2003). Influence of soil tillage on slugs and their natural enemies. In: *Soil Tillage in Agroecosystems*, ed. A El Titi, pp 207-227. CRC Press, Boca Raton, Florida.

Port G R; Basil G; Bohan D; Brittain M; Weinert T; Collier R H; Hinds H; McCulloch J; Parker C; Piccaver, D; Reed I: Roberts A; Shapland M; Wallwork C (2002). Slugs in vegetable crops: Can control methods meet the needs of growers and consumers? *Proceedings of the BCPC Conference – Pests & Diseases 2002*, **1**, 485-490.

Port G R; Collier R H; Symondson W O C; Bohan D A; Glen D M (2003a). Progress in improving the prediction and integrated control of slug damage in horticultural crops. In: *Slugs & Snails: Agricultural, Veterinary & Environmental Perspectives*, ed. G Dussart, in press. British Crop Protection Council: Alton.

Port G R; Shirley M D F; Collier R H; Bohan D A; Symondson W O C; Glen D M (2003b). An IPM strategy for slugs in vegetable and salad crops. *Proceedings of the BCPC International Congress: Crop Science & Technology 2003*, in press.

An IPM strategy for slugs in vegetable and salad crops

G R Port, M D F Shirley,
School of Biology, University of Newcastle, Newcastle upon Tyne, NE1 7RU, UK
Email: Gordon.Port@ncl.ac.uk

R H Collier
Horticulture Research International, Wellesbourne, Warwick CV35 9EF, UK

D A Bohan
Rothamsted Research, Rothamsted, Harpenden, Hertfordshire AL5 2JQ, UK

W O C Symondson
Cardiff School of Biosciences, Cardiff University, PO Box 915 Cardiff CF10 3TL, UK

D M Glen
Styloma Research & Consulting, Phoebe, The Lippiatt, Cheddar, BS27 3QP, UK

ABSTRACT

The very low thresholds for slug damage in many vegetable crops mean that some growers use molluscicide pellets as a routine treatment. Despite these treatments some crops still sustain damage and, equally some treatments may be unwarranted. To minimise both the use of pellets and damage to crops we have investigated a number of control tactics in lettuce and Brussels sprout crops. These tactics form the components of an integrated pest management strategy for slugs and include; improved detection of slug problems, prediction of population changes, and rational timing of treatments including both cultivations and molluscicide applications. The integration of these tactics into a useable strategy and the relevance of the strategy for other horticultural crops are discussed.

INTRODUCTION

Many vegetable crops have very low thresholds for damage by slugs. In some cases the damage may be due to slug feeding, but in others it is due to contamination of the plant by slugs or slug products (mucus and faeces). Retailers and their customers are very sensitive to damage and contamination by slugs and strict quality controls are used. The relatively high value of crops such as lettuce and Brussels sprout means that crop rejection or downgrading by quality control assessors may cost the growers large amounts of money. In order to minimise the risks of financial losses, growers often use molluscicide pellets as a routine, prophylactic measure, but this introduces other risks, including that of contamination of the crop by molluscicide pellets. Routine use of molluscicide pellets also poses risks to non-target organisms and of environmental pollution.

An integrated approach to management of slugs is required so that the pests are maintained at population levels which minimise the risk of damage and also the risks to non-target organisms and the environment. As part of a Horticulture LINK project we have investigated ways to reduce slug damage and molluscicide use in horticultural crops. To do this we focussed on two contrasting crops; lettuce and Brussels sprout. Our research was not aimed at predicting the direct impact of the slugs on the crop, but at minimising economic losses.

APPROACH

The most obvious solution to the problem of managing slug populations would be the development of a product that minimised slug damage to crops, whilst being relatively cheap, easy to use and produced no unwarranted side effects. In our research we have investigated the potential of biological and novel chemical controls, but have not found anything that meets these criteria (Port *et al.*, 2003). There are a number of techniques which may control slugs in specific circumstances, e.g. horticultural mattings which act as barriers to slug movement in protected crops (Schüder *et al.*, 2003), but none of them are applicable to field vegetable or salad crops. Most growers will thus continue to rely on conventional molluscicide pellets to control slugs, but as a single application of pellets will only reduce the numbers of slugs by about 50% at best, guidance on rational use of molluscicides is required. We have focused on three specific areas where improved techniques may help minimise losses to slugs. These are 1) detection of slug populations, 2) prediction of population changes and 3) rational timing of treatments including both cultivations and pesticide applications.

Improved detection of slug populations

Growers often assess the risk of slug damage to a crop based on direct observations of slugs and/or damage to crop or other plants in the field. A more objective method is to use refuge traps with suitable bait. However, there has been little attempt to define a standard trap type. We found that traps made from upturned plant pot saucers baited with chicken food (layers mash) gave fairly consistent results at a range of sites. Furthermore, in other projects, we have shown that there is a good correlation between numbers of slugs collected from these traps and similar traps baited with molluscicide pellets (Glen *et al.*, 2003a). A major factor influencing the numbers of slugs recovered from refuge traps, whatever the population in the soil, is the extent of slug activity on the soil surface. Slug activity is strongly influenced by weather conditions, especially air temperature and soil surface moisture (Young *et al.*, 1993). We have produced a method to provide a short term forecast of when slugs will be active (Port *et al.*, 2002). When activity is predicted then it is advisable to trap (to assess the activity-density of the slug population). Managing the effort spent in monitoring slug populations based on the weather conditions, will reduce the time spent on this activity and increase the reliability of the data collected, allowing growers to use action thresholds to initiate pest control actions.

We have also investigated the possibility of using a novel slug detection method, based on ELISA (Port *et al.*, 2003). With this approach there is no need to trap or extract slugs from the soil. A series of soil samples are taken and eluted with a solution. Samples of the solution are then subjected to an ELISA using a slug specific monoclonal antibody. The ELISA gives an indication of the biomass of slugs in the soil and the results can be compared to standards to determine whether control action is required.

Predicting population changes

These improved techniques for detecting slugs in the soil will be of immediate use when a site is being used for cropping. They will also allow us to assess the slug population in advance of cropping so that we can make predictions of whether a potentially damaging slug population will be present in the future. This will allow growers to take action to minimise slug damage in advance of the crop, whether this be by attempting to control the slug population or by changing cropping plans so that less susceptible crops are grown on the infested land.

We have developed a framework for modelling the population dynamics of slugs in arable crops (Shirley *et al.*, 2001) and have modified this for horticultural crops. Using the model will allow growers to decide whether the slug problem predicted will require interventions and the scale on which these will be required. The output of the model is sensitive to seasonal changes and requires the user to enter the current date together with an estimate of slug numbers (for example obtained by trapping). The output shows both the numbers of slugs predicted to be active on particular dates throughout the simulation and the total numbers of slugs (active plus inactive) (Figure 1).

Number of slugs

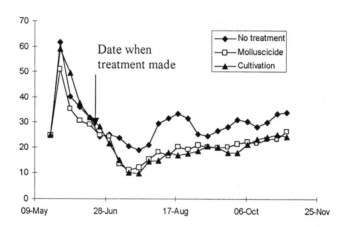

Figure 1:   Plot of data output from the slug population model with three different management techniques, no control, control with molluscicides and control with cultivations.

The model requires the duration of the simulation (maximum 24 weeks) to be specified and, as might be expected, the level of confidence in the predictions declines with increasing time from the start of the simulation.

Rational timing of treatments

There is no benefit in making an application of slug pellets to a site unless a substantial proportion of the slug population is likely to be active and hence able to consume the bait. Thus the same weather constraints that apply to the use of refuge traps for monitoring slug populations also apply to the use of control actions where the slug has to come into contact with the control agent. Molluscicide bait pellets are an obvious example of such a control action, but so too is use of the slug parasitic nematode *Phasmarhabditis hermaphrodita*. The short term forecast of when slugs will be active is also of use in deciding when to treat – the so called *trap or treat* forecast.

There is equally no benefit from applying molluscicides pellets when there are already viable pellets on the soil surface from a previous application. The simplest way of assessing this is by visual inspection, as the rate at which pellets disintegrate varies dramatically with their formulation and weather conditions. There is, unfortunately, no single, objective source of data available to compare the longevity of the different available pellet formulations.

Cultivations and other cultural activities are known to have a dramatic effect on the numbers of slugs in many circumstances (e.g. Glen *et al.,* 2003b) and contribute to any efforts to control slugs. Clearly they have usually to be used before the crop is planted. Where slugs have been detected in substantial numbers by trapping or other detection methods there should be careful attention to how well the soil is cultivated and, if necessary a double cultivation should be considered.

In addition to cultivations there are other cultural activities which will have an impact on slug populations. Anything that reduces the food available is likely to be beneficial, for example the use of herbicides to clean up a site prior to seedbed preparation. In one trial, at a site where lettuce was to be planted, the use of a herbicide in the early spring was as effective in reducing slug damage as a molluscicide application at the same time. The use of both a molluscicide and a herbicide before planting reduced damage to the subsequent crop to the greatest extent.

CONCLUSIONS

These tactics described in this paper have been integrated into strategies which are being tested in both lettuce and Brussels sprout crops in the current season (e.g. Figure 2). Whilst the options for slug control are limited, it is likely that these tactics will, with some modification, form the basis for integrated management of slug pests in other field-grown horticultural crops.

ACKNOWLEDGEMENTS

This work was supported by Department for Environment Food and Rural Affairs (HORT219, HL0160LFV) and the Horticultural Development Council (FV 225). We are grateful to our many colleagues who have contributed to this work including: Graham Basil, David Bolshaw, Martin Brittain, Alan Craig, Sarah Edwards, Matthew Ellison, James Harwood, Howard Hinds, Marie Keys, Jacqui Mair, John McCulloch, Andy McKemey, Sally Minns, Ed Okello, Caroline Parker, Kath Phelps, David Piccaver, Tim Pratt, Alec Roberts, Mick Sandall, Mike Shapland, Rhian Thomas, Chris Wallwork, Tom Weinert and Chris Wiltshire.

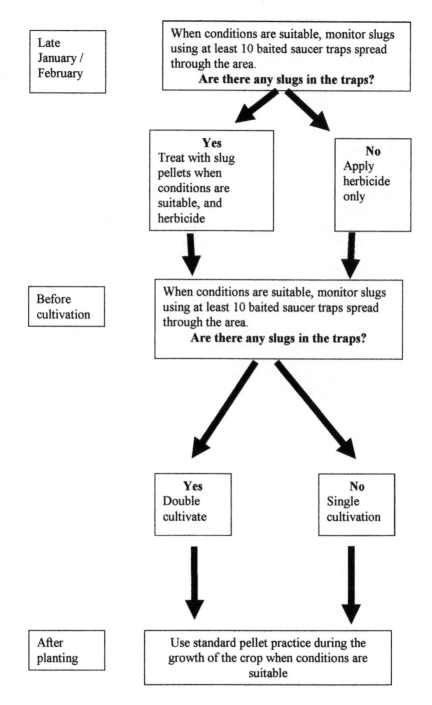

Figure 2   A strategy for slug management in lettuce crops. At all times application of pellets or trapping with refuge traps should only be done in conditions recommended by the trap or treat forecast.

REFERENCES

Glen D M; Green D; Oakley J; Wiltshire C W; Bohan D A; Port G R (2003a). Progress in improving the prediction and integrated control of slug damage in arable crops. In: *Slugs & Snails: Agricultural, Veterinary & Environmental Perspectives*, in press, British Crop Protection Council: Alton.

Glen D M, Wiltshire C W; Bohan D, Storer R, Clarkson S, Weinert T (2003b). Slug control by molluscicide and herbicide application prior to planting iceberg lettuce. *Proceedings of the BCPC International Congress: Crop Science & Technology 2003,* in press.

Port G R; Basil G; Bohan D; Brittain M; Weinert T; Collier R H; Hinds H; McCulloch J; Parker C; Piccaver, D; Reed I: Roberts A; Shapland M; Wallwork C (2002). Slugs in vegetable crops: Can control methods meet the needs of growers and consumers? *Proceedings of the BCPC Conference – Pests & Diseases 2002*, **1**, 485-490.

Port G R; Collier R H; Symondson W O C; Bohan D A; Glen D M (2003). Progress in improving the prediction and integrated control of slug damage in horticultural crops. In: *Slugs & Snails: Agricultural, Veterinary & Environmental Perspectives*, in press, British Crop Protection Council: Alton.

Schüder I; Port G; Bennison J; Maher H (2003). Integrated Management of slug and snail pests in ornamental plants. In: *Slugs & Snails: Agricultural, Veterinary & Environmental Perspectives*, in press, British Crop Protection Council: Alton.

Shirley M D F; Rushton S P; Young A G; Port G R (2001). Simulating the long-term dynamics of slug populations: a process-based modelling approach for pest control. *Journal of Applied Ecology* **38**, 401-411.

Young A G; Port G R; Green D B (1993). Development of a forecast of slug activity: validation of models to predict slug activity from meteorological conditions. *Crop Protection* **12**, 232-236.

Aggressiveness of cucumber isolates of *Pythium aphanidermatum* on tomato and pepper in the Sultanate of Oman, and the relationship between aggressiveness and resistance to the fungicide metalaxyl

A M Al-Saadi, M L Deadman, I Khan
Department of Crop Sciences, College of Agricultural and Marine Sciences, Sultan Qaboos University, PO Box 34, Al Khod 123, Sultanate of Oman
Email: saad2000@squ.edu.om

J R M Thacker
Pesticides Research Group, Biological Sciences, University of Paisley PA1 2BE, UK

ABSTRACT

Research to investigate the degree of aggressiveness of ten *Pythium* isolates from cucumber on ten tomato and ten pepper varieties and the relationship between their aggressiveness and sensitivity to the fungicide metalaxyl is described. All *Pythium* isolates were found to be pathogenic on cucumber and pepper, but significant differences were observed among isolates in their degree of aggressiveness. Twenty per cent of the isolates were highly aggressive on pepper, while 10% were highly aggressive on cucumber. The isolates varied in their sensitivity to metalaxyl but there was no correlation between aggressiveness and sensitivity to the fungicide. Significant differences were observed between tomato and pepper varieties in their resistance to *Pythium*. The tomato varieties CLN1555A and 076FARIDEH and pepper varieties 9955-27 and PBC344 were the most resistant to damping-off disease. The data are discussed in relation to control strategies for damping-off disease and in relation to cultivar selection in the Sultanate of Oman.

INTRODUCTION

Pythium is one of the most widespread soil-borne fungal pathogens, causing damping-off disease on a wide range of crops. In Oman, it can result in yield losses of up to 20% in greenhouse cucumber crops (Deadman *et al.*, 2002; Deadman *et al.*, 2003). Annual losses due to damping-off within the Sultanate have been high enough for farmers to resort to extreme methods of management such as complete exchange of greenhouse soil. In most situations however farmers use chemicals for disease suppression, often at very high levels. For example, some farmers have been recorded as making as many as 35 pesticide applications per season (Thacker *et al.*, 2000; Deadman, *et al.*, 2003). Within cucumber crops the fungicide of choice for control of damping-off disease is metalaxyl (Ridomil).

The predominant damping-off pathogen in Oman is *Pythium aphanidermatum*. This pathogen can attack members of the cucurbitaceae family, especially cucumber, as well as members of the solanaceae family, including tomato and pepper. Cucumber crops are among the top vegetables in production in Oman and specialist varieties have the potential to become high value greenhouse crops. At present, over 95% of greenhouses within the sultanate are used to cultivate cucumber crops (Deadman *et al.*, 2002). Typically, farmers who grow cucumbers protect their crop against pathogens using fungicides, as stated above. The results of research presented elsewhere indicated that the average number of fungicide applications in greenhouse cucumber crops was *ca.* 5 (Deadman *et al.*, 2002). To reduce fungicide applications in greenhouses however, other management practices, such as resistance management should be adopted.

Before making general recommendations for selected varieties regarding their innate resistance to pathogenic organisms screening against local isolates of the pathogen is necessary. At present, there is a paucity of published information concerning the level of aggressiveness of local *P. aphanidermatum* isolates, and no reports have been made concerning the cross aggressiveness of isolates from one crop on varieties of a second crop. Isolates of *P. aphanidermatum* are also known to differ in sensitivity to metalaxyl-based fungicides such as metalaxyl.

An understanding of resistance and aggressiveness, as well as the sensitivity of this fungus to fungicides may help in formulating management practices for *Pythium*. Within this context aggressiveness represents the ability of a pathogen isolate to cause disease relative to other isolates or strains. Resistance by contrast, refers to the ability of a pathogen isolate to resist the harmful effects of a fungicide, usually via a inherited mutation. The research described in this paper therefore aimed at investigating the aggressiveness of *Pythium* isolates from cucumber on pepper and tomato and their associated relationships with *in vitro* sensitivity tests to the fungicide metalaxyl.

MATERIALS AND METHODS

Isolation of *Pythium* from diseased plants

A collection of ten *Pythium* isolates was established from infected cucumber plants showing symptoms of damping-off disease in ten greenhouses on different farms across three regions of northern Oman. The infected tissues were washed with tap water, cut into 3- to 5-mm pieces and then placed in 1% sodium hypochlorite solution for 1 minute for surface sterilization. Plant material was subsequently rinsed twice in sterile distilled water. Surface-sterilized tissues were then placed on potato dextrose agar (PDA) and incubated at room temperature (25°C) for 2 days. *Pythium* coming out of the tissues was transferred to 2% water agar (WA) and incubated for 2 days. Hyphal tips were then taken from each isolate and grown on separate PDA in order to produce samples of single isolates.

Aggressiveness of *Pythium* isolates on cucumber and pepper

The degree of aggressiveness of *Pythium* isolates on the original host cucumber as well as pepper was investigated using the cucumber variety Luna and the pepper variety PBC535. *Pythium* isolates were transferred to PDA and incubated for 7 days in the dark. Each culture was homogenized and mixed with a sterilized soil mix in 250 ml pots. Three replicate pots were prepared for each isolate using ten seeds of each crop type per pot. The pots were incubated at 28°C and maintained in an incubator with a 8 hr:16 hr dark/light photoperiod for 4 weeks.

A modified disease index, adopted from Zhang & Yang (2000), was used to assess the aggressiveness of *Pythium* isolates. The rating scale was: 0 = no visible symptoms (good germination and growth); 1 = died after germination; 2 = died before germination. The following equation was used to summarize the disease index:

$$Y = \sum_{i=1}^{3} \chi_i / 20$$

where Y is disease index (scale 0 to 1), χ_i is disease rating of the *i*th replicate (i = 1 to 3) and 20 equals the number of replicates in each pot multiplied by the highest rating category.

Reaction of ten tomato and ten pepper varieties to *Pythium*

The level of resistance to *Pythium* in ten tomato and ten pepper varieties supplied by the Asian Vegetable Research and Development Center (AVRDC) was investigated using the P01 isolate of *Pythium*. Preparation for inoculation and the assessment procedures used were as described above. Assessments were made over a period of 4 weeks.

***In vitro* sensitivity of *Pythium* isolates to the fungicide metalaxyl**

Metalaxyl, the fungicide most commonly used in the greenhouses of Oman for the control of *Pythium*-induced damping-off was used to determine the level of fungicide resistance in a small sample of the *P. aphanidermatum* population in Oman. After autoclaving half strength PDA (19.5 g/litre) the fungicide was dissolved in sterile water, filter sterilized, and added to the PDA when it had cooled to 40°C. The media were prepared using metalaxyl concentrations of 0, 5, 10 and 50 mg a.i./litre. Six mm diameter discs were taken from the edge of 7-day old pure *P. aphanidermatum* cultures. One disc was placed at the center of each PDA plate. Four replicates were used for each fungicide concentration, including a control (i.e. 0 mg/litre metalaxyl). The radial growth of *Pythium* was recorded daily for 5 days using 4 measured diameters per PDA plate. The rate at which *Pythium* growth was reduced at increased fungicide concentrations was then determined.

RESULTS AND DISCUSSION

All *Pythium* isolates tested were found to be pathogenic, although to a varying extent, on both cucumber and pepper. The isolates varied significantly in aggressiveness ($P < 0.05$), some being highly aggressive while others displayed lower levels of aggressiveness (Table 1). Two isolates (P13 and P18) were found to have levels of aggressiveness above 0.5 on pepper. The other isolates showed lower levels of aggressiveness. The P01 isolate that was used in the assessments was highly aggressive on cucumber with a disease index value of 0.87. None of the other isolates showed levels of aggressiveness above 0.5.

Zhang & Yang (2000) reported similar results for a range of *Pythium* isolates tested for aggressiveness on corn and soybean. In that case *Pythium* isolates were shown to have varying degrees of aggressiveness on both crops. Based on their findings, 29% of the isolates were highly aggressive on both crops. Brantner & Windels (1989) using 21 isolates of *P. aphanidermatum* reported similarly varying degrees of aggressiveness on sugar beet.

There was a significant and negative correlation ($r = -0.76$; $P < 0.0114$) in aggressiveness between isolates on cucumber and pepper, with the isolates most aggressive on pepper being significantly less aggressive on cucumber, and vice versa. This may indicate the presence of specific host-pathogen interactions (Al-Saadi, 2002). However, other reports have indicated a high positive correlation in aggressiveness between two different crops, such as corn and soybean, for example Zhang & Yang (2000).

Increased concentrations of metalaxyl in the growth medium resulted in a reduction in the growth rate of *Pythium*. However, isolates varied significantly in their sensitivity to the fungicide as indicated by the significant differences in the rate of growth reduction (Table 1). No correlation was found between sensitivity to metalaxyl and the aggressiveness of the isolates on either pepper ($P = 0.1893$) or cucumber ($P = 0.2884$). These results suggest, for the first time, the possible presence, in Oman of *P. aphanidermatum* populations with some level of resistance to metalaxyl. The lack of a relationship between aggressiveness on either cucumber or pepper and sensitivity to metalaxyl concurs with the reports of Brantner & Windels (1989) who used *P. aphanidermatum* populations in bioassays of pathogen aggressiveness to sugar beet plants.

Table 1.   Aggressiveness of 10 *Pythium* isolates on pepper and cucumber and the rate of reduction of *Pythium* growth at increased metalaxyl concentrations. Different letters indicate significant differences within each category.

Isolate	Pepper Death Index	Cucumber Death Index	Rate of Reduction (relative to control)
Control	0.00a	0.07a	----
P01	0.07a	0.87b	-0.0318a
P02	0.17a	0.43ab	-0.0297abc
P05	0.33ab	0.33a	-0.0286abc
P07	0.43ab	0.23a	-0.0312ab
P09	0.20ab	0.37a	-0.0260abc
P10	0.30ab	0.47ab	-0.0259abc
P13	0.53ab	0.10a	-0.0229bc
P14	0.37ab	0.47ab	-0.0222c
P15	0.37ab	0.47ab	-0.0242abc
P18	0.67b	0.27a	-0.0264abc

The varieties of tomato and pepper differed in their reaction to the *Pythium* isolate P01. Significant differences were observed among varieties of both crops in the level of resistance to damping-off disease ($P < 0.05$) as indicated by different disease index values (Table 2). Tomato varieties CLN1555A (disease index value 0.45) and 076FARIDEH (0.50) appeared to be resistant to the disease, while varieties CLN1466P (0.83), CLN2070B (0.83), and CLN1462A (0.85) appeared to be highly susceptible. In the case of the pepper varieties assayed, 9955-27 (0.52) and PBC344 (0.53) showed some resistance, while varieties PBC577 (0.75) and 9852-149 (0.78) appeared to be significantly more susceptible. Villineuve *et al,.* (1997) have previously reported differences in resistance among carrot varieties to the related pathogen *P. violae*.

Table 2.   Variability in resistance among tomato and pepper varieties to damping off disease (varieties with low disease index value are more resistant). Different letters indicate significant differences within each category.

Tomato variety	Disease Index	Pepper varieties	Disease Index
CLN1555A	0.45a	9955-27	0.52a
076 FARIDEH	0.50ab	PBC344	0.53ab
CLN2037B	0.62ab	9852-170	0.58abc
CLN2116B	0.68ab	9852-100	0.62abc
CH154	0.72ab	9852-173	0.63abc
CLN2123A	0.77ab	PBC845	0.63abc
PT4664B	0.80ab	9852-115	0.68abc
CLN1466P	0.83b	9852-90	0.70abc
CLN2070B	0.83b	PBC577	0.75bc
CLN1462A	0.85b	9852-149	0.78c

CONCLUSIONS

The results detailed in this paper represent the first report of the extent of the variability in pathogenicity in the Omani population of the pathogen *P. aphanidermatum*. Furthermore, there appears to be significant differences in the levels of aggressiveness on related crops. The results will be of significant benefit for breeding programmes in the region where attention needs to be focused on alternative crops to cucumber that are also suitable for greenhouse cultivation. Subject to suitable agronomic traits being shown by those varieties exhibiting higher levels of resistance to damping-off, the results could be of immediate benefit to local growers by indicating potentially profitable varieties for use in crop production.

However, attention should also be paid to any specific isolate-variety interactions that may appear in Oman, similar to that recently reported for the wheat-barley-*Bipolaris sorokiniana* isolate-variety interactions as described by Al-Saadi (2002).

The demonstrated presence, for the first time in Oman, of isolates of *P. aphanidermatum* with some level of resistance to metalaxyl will require further and in-depth monitoring. In Oman, metalaxyl is the most widely used fungicide applied for the control of damping-off disease. Clearly, a wider selection of *P. aphanidermatum* isolates should be tested at regular intervals in order to determine whether a change in management recommendations, notably fungicide use, is necessary. This research is currently underway.

ACKNOWLEDGEMENTS

The authors would like to acknowledge technical support by Yousif Al-Maqbali, Ahmed Al-Azizi, Shaima Ahmed, Ali Al-Nabhani and Saad Al-Habsi. The authors are also grateful to AVRDC for the supply of the tomato and pepper seeds used in this research.

REFERENCES

Al-Saadi A M (2002). Variability in Natural Host-Pathogen Interactions; Characterization of *Cochliobolus sativus* (anamorph *Bipolaris sorokiniana*)-Wheat-Barley Pathosystem in Oman. *M.Sc. Thesis, Sultan Qaboos University, Sultanate of Oman.*

Brantner J R; Windels C E (1989). Variability in sensitivity to metalaxyl in vitro, phytopathogenicity, and control of *Pythium* spp. on sugar beet. *Plant Disease* **82**, 896-899.

Deadman M L; Al-Saadi A M; Al-Mahmuli I; Al-Maqbali Y M; Al-Subhi R; Al-Kiyoomi K; Al-Hasani; Thacker J R M (2002). Management of Pythium aphanidermatum in greenhouse cucumber production in the Sultanate of Oman. *Proceedings of the British Crop Protection Council Conference – Pests & Diseases 2002* **1**, 171-176.

Deadman M L; Al-Saadi AM; Al-Kiyoomi K; Al-Hasani H; Al-Maqbali Y; Al-Mahmuli I (2003). Management of *Pythium* induced damping off in greenhouse cucumber production in the Sultanate of Oman. *Proceedings of the 8th International Plant Pathology Congress New Zealand 2003* **2**, 328.

Thacker J R M; Ambusaidi Q; Al-Azri M; Al-Fahdi R; Al-Hashmi K; Al-Jabri R; Al-Makmhari S; Al-Mandheri I; Al-Shidi A; Al-Shidi R (2000). Assessment of pesticide use on farms in Al Batinah, Oman. *Agricultural Sciences* **5**, 79-84.

Villineuve F; Bosc J P; Rouxel F; Breton D (1997). Intra and Inter-specific variability of *Pythium* and possibility of varietal resistance improvement in carrot. Proceedings of the V Meeting of the EUCARPIA Carrot Working Group, Krakow, Poland, 1-5 September 1997. *Journal of Applied Genetics* **38A**, 71-80.

Zhang B Q; Yang X B (2000). Pathogenicity of *Pythium* populations from corn-soybean rotation fields. *Plant Disease* **84**, 94-99.

Forecasting and control of Alternaria blight in carrots

J E Thomas, D M Kenyon
NIAB, Huntingdon Road, Cambridge, CB3 OLE, UK
Email: jane.thomas@niab.com

D Martin
Plantsystems Ltd, 97 Hollycroft Road, Emneth, Wisbech, PE14 8BB, UK

ABSTRACT

Alternaria blight on carrots has increased in incidence and severity in recent years. Crops are often sprayed routinely to control the disease, but little is known about its effects on yield and quality in the UK. Experiments using inoculated field plots were carried out over three years to investigate potential losses in marketable yields, and the benefits of different spray programmes. Observations of disease in a number of commercial crops treated either according to growers' normal practice, or an Alternaria spray forecasting system, were made. In addition, the potential of cultivar resistance to reduce the rate of Alternaria development was investigated. Results showed that moderate and high levels of Alternaria had a significant impact on root yield. In moderate disease years, a forecasting system reduced the number of sprays applied compared to normal practice without affecting disease control. Cultivar had a significant effect on Alternaria severity, and partial resistance could be exploited in integrated control systems.

INTRODUCTION

Alternaria blight of carrots, caused by *Alternaria dauci*, is a common disease of carrot occurring in all major growing areas. Incidence and severity on UK carrot crops increased during the early 1990s. Fungicide application to control disease development has become more common, but there is little information on the effects of *A. dauci* infection on the yield and quality of crops. Foliage infection can increase rapidly, starting on the older leaves first, before spreading to cause a widespread blight. "Green top" lifting systems may be adversely affected, as well as root yield. A forecasting system for the disease is commercially available to growers in the UK, though the benefits that this may confer in terms of improving spray timing and reducing unnecessary sprays have not been quantified. There is evidence that carrot breeding material and cultivars vary in resistance to *A. dauci*, but no comparative information exists for cultivars commonly grown in the UK, and thus the extent to which cultivar resistance could contribute to reducing disease severity is unknown.

This work describes experiments undertaken to determine the effect of *A. dauci* on marketable yield of carrots, the value of a forecasting system for the disease, and the relative resistance of a range of carrot cultivars, in order to develop advice for UK growers on the need for Alternaria control.

MATERIALS AND METHODS

Effects of Alternaria on yield

Trials were established in each of three years from 2000 to 2002 at one site in Cambridgeshire with cv. Nairobi. In the third year, cvs. Maestro and Indiana were included in the trial. Plots (9 m long and four rows wide) in each trial were inoculated when plants met between the rows with a spore suspension of *A. dauci* at 10^4 spores/ml after a period of irrigation (12 mm rain equivalent) to create an initial disease risk. Disease was then allowed to develop without further irrigation. An Adcon meteorological data recording device (Adcon Telemetry AG) was erected within 500 m of the trial each year, and information on precipitation, temperature, humidity, wind direction and wind speed was recorded. Together with crop observations on growth stage, ground cover, and presence of senescent leaf and Alternaria lesions, the data were transmitted to a commercially available Alternaria forecasting system (PLANT Plus, from Dacom PLANT-service BV). In each year, a number of fungicide programmes were applied to the trial, using various sequences and dose rates of Amistar (azoxytrobin), Folicur (tebuconazole), and Compass (iprodione and thiophanate methyl) one day before the inoculation and then prior to disease risks predicted by the forecasting system. Sprays were applied in 400 litres water/ha using medium nozzles at 2.5 bar with an AZO compressed air sprayer. Azoxystrobin was used at 0.8 litre/ha in the first and second years, and 1 litre/ha in the third year. Tebuconazole was used at 1 litre/ha in the first and third years, and 0.5 litre/ha in the second year, and iprodione and thiophanate methyl was used at 2 litres/ha. Each treatment and an untreated control was replicated three times in a randomised block design. In the third year, cultivars and treatments were fully randomised. Disease was assessed as % leaf area infected over whole plots at ten to fourteen day intervals. The trials were harvested during November, and the yield of marketable roots assessed.

Use of a forecasting system in commercial crops

In each year, varying numbers of paired fields were selected in major carrot growing areas. One of each pair was sprayed with fungicides according to the normal practice of the grower concerned. The other was sprayed according to advice from the PLANT Plus forecasting system, and interpretation from a local agronomist. Weather data for each field was collected using an Adcon weather station and data as described above was transmitted every 15 min to a receiver base station, and extracted automatically every six hours by a land line link to a Dacom Ltd Databank server. Crop records taken by field scouts were combined with weather information to create the disease forecast. Each field contained an untreated area towards the centre. The treated and untreated areas of each field were recorded for growth and development and the presence of *A. dauci* infections throughout the growing season, and a final record from each site was obtained in October prior to harvest.

Evaluation of cultivar resistance

Small plots (4.5 m long and four rows wide) of carrot cultivars were established in each of three years at Cambridge. Some cultivars were common to all years, but new ones were also introduced. Each cultivar was replicated three times in a randomised block design. Plots were irrigated and then inoculated with *A. dauci* when plants had met between the rows with a spore suspension of 10^4 spores/ml, and further irrigation was applied for up to 10 min/day in dry

dry conditions. Alternaria was assessed at intervals throughout the season by estimating % foliage and petiole area infected on a per plot basis.

RESULTS

Effects of Alternaria on yield

Alternaria developed on untreated plots in the inoculated trials each year. In 2000, 3% leaf area cover was recorded on 14th September, increasing to 22% by 12th October, and 38% just before harvest on 2nd November. In 2001, disease level and progress were similar but in 2002, 3% disease was recorded on 9th August and this increased rapidly to 20% by 23rd August, and 80% by 18th October. All the forecast fungicide sequences (Table 1) reduced the level of Alternaria each year, and significant effects on marketable yield of roots were seen in the third year (Tables 2, 3 and 4).

Table 1.   Number of forecast applications, and spray sequences, applied to inoculated carrot trials 2000-2002

Year	Total number of forecast sprays	Spray sequences te = tebuconazole, az = azoxystrobin, ip = iprodione and thiophanate methyl				
2000	4	te	te	te	te	
	4	az	az	az	az	
	4	ip	ip	ip	ip	
2001	3	te	te	az		
	3	az	te	te		
	3	az	az	az		
	3	te	te	te		
2002	5	az	te	az	te	az
	5	te	az	te	az	te

Table 2.   Yield of marketable carrot roots (t/ha) in fungicide treated trials inoculated with *A.dauci* in 2000 cv. Nairobi, and levels of Alternaria (% leaf area infected before harvest

Treatment	Marketable roots t/ha	% Alternaria before harvest
Untreated	59.2	38.0
te/te/te/te	71.6	16.0
az/az/az/az	65.7	15.3
ip/ip/ip/ip	58.2	22.7
LSD (P=0.05)	ns	7.29

Table 3.   Yield of marketable carrot roots (t/ha) in fungicide treated trials inoculated
            with *A.dauci* in 2001, cv. Nairobi, and levels of Alternaria (% leaf area
            infected) before harvest

Treatment	Marketable roots t/ha	% Alternaria before harvest
Untreated	114.4	25.00
te/te/az	127.4	13.33
az/te/te	124.3	11.33
az/az/az	122.3	11.67
te/te/te	118.5	12.33
LSD (P=0.05)	ns	9.21

Table 4.   Yield of marketable carrot roots (t/ha) in fungicide treated trials inoculated
            with *A.dauci* in 2002, for cvs. Nairobi, Maestro and Indiana and levels of
            Alternaria (% leaf area infected) before harvest

Cultivar and treatment	Marketable roots t/ha	% Alternaria before harvest
cv. Nairobi		
Untreated	89.6	80.0
az/te/az/te/az	109.9	24.7
te/az/te/az/te	97.9	44.0
cv. Maestro		
Untreated	92.6	54.0
az/te/az/te/az	123.8	8.7
te/az/te/az/te	108.7	21.7
cv. Indiana		
Untreated	74.6	53.3
az/te/az/te/az	88.5	14.0
te/az/te/az/te	87.1	22.3
LSD (P=0.05)	9.35	8.01

Use of a forecasting system in commercial crops

There were fewer sprays applied in 2000 and 2001 through use of the forecasting system
compared to growers' normal practice, with no adverse effect on the level of disease control
recorded. However, in 2002, normal practice and forecasting resulted in about the same
number of applications on average over all the sites recorded (Table 5).

Table 5. Mean spray number for normal practice and forecast spray number in paired commercial carrot fields during 2000-2002, and mean level of Alternaria recorded on a 0-10 scale (10 = >10 % leaf area infected)

Year	Number of paired fields	Spray number		Alternaria level			
		Normal	Forecast	Normal	Untreated	Forecast	Untreated
2000	8	4.3	3.4	6.3	8.3	5.8	7.8
2001	9	5.1	2.5	5.1	6.5	5.1	6.7
2002	5	4.4	4.2	6.4	9.2	6.6	9.2

Evaluation of cultivar resistance

There were significant differences between levels of disease developing on cultivars in each year of testing, though none were completely resistant (Table 6, showing a sub-set of cultivars which were common to each year). Maestro and Indiana had consistently greater levels of partial resistance than Nairobi, and this was still apparent at the end of the season.

Table 6. Levels of Alternaria (% leaf area infected) developing on five carrot cultivars at early and late season scoring times in 2000, 2001 and 2002

Year and cultivar	Early season	Late season
2000	20th September	27th October
Maestro	0.4	23.3
Nerac	2.2	34.0
Nairobi	3.7	48.3
Nepal	1.9	23.3
Indiana	0.1	10.0
LSD (P=0.05)	3.70	21.21
2001	16th September	12th October
Maestro	0.0	23.3
Nerac	1.3	40.0
Nairobi	3.4	46.7
Nepal	0.2	28.3
Indiana	0.0	20.0
LSD (P=0.05)	3.10	18.56
2002	30th September	31st October
Maestro	5.0	41.7
Nerac	14.7	46.7
Nairobi	15.0	58.3
Nepal	13.3	46.7
Indiana	6.7	31.7
LSD (P=0.05)	9.31	16.54

DISCUSSION

Controlling Alternaria with forecast spray sequences gave significant yield benefits in 2002 when disease levels increased rapidly during the early part of August. A five spray sequence alternating between azoxystrobin and tebuconazole gave benefits of 20 t/ha marketable roots in Nairobi. The yield benefit was less when the sequence began with tebuconazole, and disease control was less effective. Fungicide treatments increased yield by up to 16 t/ha compared to untreated plots in 2001 as well, though this effect was not significant. Cvs. Maestro and Indiana showed partial resistance to Alternaria, and in the fungicide trial in 2002, it was evident that a combination of partial resistance and fungicide resulted in the most effective disease control. However, in the more susceptible cv. Nairobi, disease still reached relatively high levels even when fungicides were applied. Partial resistance to *A. dauci* has been identified in breeding material (Simon & Strandberg, 1998), but further results on cultivar resistance in the current study (data not shown) have indicated that only a few new cultivars have resistance levels comparable to that of Maestro and Indiana, and none has a greater level.

In commercial carrot fields, use of the forecasting system reduced spray application compared to growers' normal practice in two out of the three seasons studied. A mean reduction of 2.6 sprays was seen in 2001, when Alternaria severity in the untreated areas was relatively low, and there was little difference between the severity of disease developing in the forecast and normal practice treatment fields. In 2000, the mean reduction in spray number was lower, but levels of disease in the forecast spray fields were slightly less overall than those in the normal practice fields, suggesting more effective timing. Use of a forecasting system in Canada also reduced spraying by between one and three applications per season (Gillespie & Sutton, 1979). In 2002, when higher levels of Alternaria occurred, the number of forecast and normal practice sprays was similar. However, over a number of seasons, growers in the UK could have a reasonable chance of reducing spray number and decreasing costs, though the cost of subscribing to a forecasting system has to be taken into account.

Results from this work show that the yield of marketable roots is likely to be decreased by about 20 t/ha when Alternaria increases rapidly throughout August, but that disease developing later in the season, from mid to late Sepetmber onwards, is unlikely to have such a serious effect. Forecasting systems can help effective spray timing, and reduce unnecessary sprays in years when disease pressure is lower. Partial cultivar resistance can contribute to more effective disease control, though choice of resistant material is currently quite limited.

ACKNOWLEDGMENTS

This work was funded by the Horticultural Development Council (Project FV 234)

REFERENCES

Gillespie T J; Sutton J C (1979). A predictive scheme for timing fungicide applications to control Alternaria leaf blight in carrots. *Canadian Journal of Plant Pathology* **1**, 95-99.
Simon P W; Strandberg J O (1998). Diallel analysis of resistance in carrot to Alternaria leaf blight. *Journal of the American Society for Horticultural Science* **3**, 412-415.

Can crab shells protect roses from blackspot?

A M Hall, A Ali, B Pascoe
Department of Biosciences, University of Hertfordshire, Hatfield, AL10 9AB, UK
Email: A.M.Hall@herts.ac.uk

ABSTRACT

Roses treated with salicylic acid showed resistance to rose blackspot. The resistance lasted for twelve days from a single treatment. Roses planted in soil enhanced with chitin also showed good resistance to rose blackspot for three weeks and some resistance for three months. Rose leaflets held *in vitro* in agar containing chitin also showed resistance to blackspot.

INTRODUCTION

Roses are an important horticultural crop in the UK, and there is also a world wide trade in roses. However they are prone to a number of diseases of which blackspot, caused by *Diplocarpon rosae* Wolf is one of the most prevalent. In the UK growers spray fortnightly to control this disease (Ali & Hall, 2002). *Diplocarpon rosae* is a variable fungus (Ali *et al.*, 2000), and through there are some reports of resistant cultivars, resistance is not a high priority in the breeding programme and our work (unpublished) showed that all cultivars tested were susceptible to one or more isolates. There is a clear need for a control strategy that would provide long term, sustainable disease control with reduced use of fungicides.

The overall aim of the work reported here was to screen control methods which utilised Systemic Acquired Resistance (SAR) to give longer term sustainable disease control. SAR confers on the plant non-specific protection against a broad range of pathogens, which at best is comparable to good disease control using fungicides. SAR is induced by agents (including pathogens) that cause necrosis in the plant, which stimulate the production of Pathogenesis Related (PR) proteins that provide long lasting resistance. Two agents that are reported to confer SAR are salicylic acid (Malany *et al.*, 1990) and chitin (Spiegal *et al.*, 1987). Chitin is obtained from crab shells for laboratory experiments, though it also forms the exoskeleton of all insects. The objectives of the experiments reported here were a) to spray salicylic acid onto rose bushes and then challenge the leaves with *D. rosae*; b) to challenge leaves from plants grown in soil containing chitin with *D. rosae* and c) to place detached leaflets in agar containing chitin and then to challenge them with *D. rosae*.

MATERIALS AND METHODS

Salicylic acid (0.02 mM and 0.4 mM)was sprayed onto healthy leaves harvested from the cultivar Memento in the glasshouse and then after treatment the leaves were placed on tap water agar and inoculated with *D. rosae* 3, 4, 7, and 8 days after treatment. They were examined for disease development seven days after inoculation (objective a). For the *in vivo* chitin experiment, (objective b) roses of the cultivar Memento were grown in the glasshouse in pots containing John Innes number 3 compost, enhanced with chicken manure pellets and treated with 50 g or 100 g chitin incorporated into the compost.

Controls had no chitin incorporated into the growing medium. Lastly, *in vitro* experiments were carried out using leaflets detached from healthy, untreated roses (Memento)which were placed with the stalk embedded in 'chitin agar' containing 0.5 g chitin and 2 g agar in 400 ml tap water. These leaves were then challenged with inoculum of *D. rosae* (objective c). In all cases leaves were inoculated with spores taken directly from acervuli on infected rose leaves.

RESULTS

Figure 1 shows the results of spraying rose leaves with salicylic acid and then challenging them with *D. rosae in vitro*. The results recorded show that salicylic acid gives good control for 12 days, but that after that the effect fades. Similar levels of control were obtained with both 0.2 mM and 0.4 mM of salicylic acid. These leaflets had significantly less infection than the untreated $(P > 0.001)$.

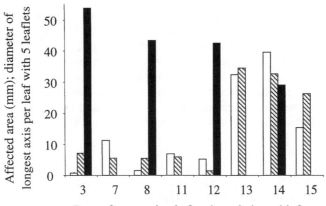

Figure 1. Comparison of the infected area of leaves sprayed with 0.2 and 0.4 mM of salicylic acid and untreated controls.

The results of growing roses in chitin enhanced soil, harvesting leaves and then challenging them with *D. rosae* are shown in Figure 2. The untreated controls show a typical epidemic curve but the curves for chitin treated plants show complete disease suppression for the first twelve days. Thereafter, 50 g chitin continues to give reasonable control for 60 days, though

100 g chitin has ceased to control the disease by 21 days. The leaflets from plants grown in soil enhanced by 50 g chitin had significantly less disease than the untreated controls (P = 0.001).

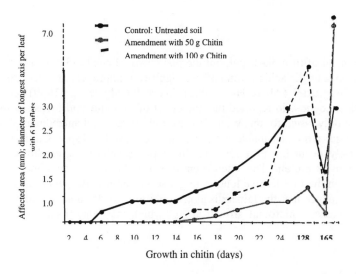

Figure 2. Effect of soil amendment with chitin on disease development.

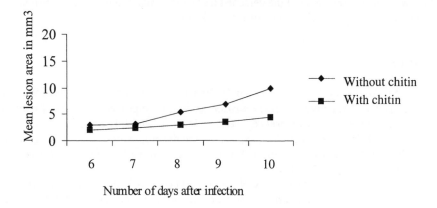

Figure 3. The effect of chitin on lesion area in leaflets stored *in vitro* 3 days prior to inoculation.

Tap water agar enhanced with salicylic acid was toxic to rose leaves and so the method could not be used. However incubating detached leaves in chitin agar with the stalk immersed in the agar gave disease control as seen in figure 3. In this experiment the detached leaves were allowed to equilibrate for 2, 3, 4, 5, or 6 days in the chitin agar before inoculation. These results also show that the presence of chitin in the agar gives good control. However unpublished results show that the longer the leaflet is left in the agar prior to inoculation (e.g. 6 days) the less the control effect.

DISCUSSION

Salicylic acid gave control of rose blackspot, but the plants would need to be re-sprayed at frequent intervals and so salicylic acid may not offer a significant improvement over existing control with regular fungicides (Ali & Hall, 2002). Work by Shi *et al.* (1999) on rice seedlings treated with salicylic acid reported that the effect of salicylic acid increases for 6 days after spraying but only lasted for one week. However chitin as a soil amendment shows some promise as a longer term sustainable disease control of rose blackspot. Chitin is the most abundant naturally occurring nitrogen containing polysaccharide and chitinase is produced by plants as a PR protein. The amendment of soil with chitin may stimulate the production of chitinase in the rose to give long lasting disease control (Brown *et al.*, 2000). Furthermore there is evidence that the mineralisation of chitin provides a source of carbon and nitrogen which enhances microbial growth in soil which may also result in disease suppression.

ACKNOWLEDGMENTS

The authors would like to thank Defra for funding for A. Ali and the British Society for Plant Pathology for funding B. Pascoe with a student bursary. In addition, thanks are also due to Jackie Chan who carried out some of the detached leaf work whilst funded by the Nuffield Science Bursary scheme at the University of Hertfordshire.

REFERENCES

Ali A; Hall A M; Aquino de Muro M; Cannon P (2000). The investigation of the biology of the rose blackspot fungus *Diplocarpon rosae* leading to improved methods of control. *Proceedings of the BCPC Conference - Pests & Diseases 2000*, 1, 251-256.

Ali A; Hall A M (2002). The effect of rain splash on the development of rose Blackspot and the implications for a disease control strategy. *Proceedings of the BCPC Conference - Pests & Diseases 2002*, **2**, 219-224.

Brown J A; Neville F J; Sarathchandra R N (2000). *Effects of chitin amendment on plant growth, microbial populations and nematodes in soil.* New Zealand pastoral research Institute: Hamilton, New Zealand.

Hall A M (2001). Report to Defra (MAFF) on Project no. HH1750THN.

Malamy J; Carr J P; Klessig D F (1990). Salicylic acid: a likely endogenous signal in the resistance response of tobacco to viral infection. *Science* **50**, 1002–1004.

Spiegal Y; Chet I; Cohn E (1987). Use of chitin for controlling parasitic nematodes. *Plant and Soil* **98**, 337- 345

Shi S; Pan M; Lu T (1999). Analysis of salicylic acid induced proteins in rice. *Natural Science Foundation of China* no 39780030.

Evaluation of oxadiargyl herbicide in various Australian horticultural crops

P R Frost, I L Macleod
Serve-Ag Research, PO Box 690, Devonport, Tasmania 7310, Australia
Email: imacleod@serve-ag.com.au

E M Hanlon
Serve-Ag Research, P O Box 4041, Gumdale, Queensland 4154, Australia

ABSTRACT

Oxadiargyl was screened for weed efficacy and crop safety in a range of annual horticultural crops in Australia. Oxadiargyl is a selective herbicide, which belongs to the oxadiazole chemical group. The product acts by inhibition of protoporphyrinogen oxidase and has both pre and early post emergent weed activity. Australian trial work has shown the product is active on a range of broadleaf and grass weeds at 400 g a.i./ha, applied pre weed emergence. Key weeds controlled include *Amaranthus powellii*, *Solanum nigrum*, *Chenopodium album*, *Nicandra physaloides*, *Echinchloa crus-gallii* and *Eleusine indica*. Oxadiargyl has been shown to have high levels of crop safety to transplanted crops including cauliflower, cabbage, broccoli, capsicums and potatoes.Continued availability and development of new crop protection products in horticultural crops in Australia continues to be a production issue. Oxadiargyl herbicide potentially offers a new class of herbicide chemistry for management of weeds in a range of horticultural crops in Australia. The product also has a number of characteristics that make it particularly suited to annual horticultural crops including short residual activity period, broad weed spectrum and use in a wide range of soil types.

INTRODUCTION

Oxadiargyl is a selective herbicide, which belongs to the oxadiazole chemical group and acts by the inhibition of protoporphyrinogen oxidase. The product acts on germinating weeds as the shoots come into contact with treated soil. Oxadiargyl acts principally via contact with only very limited translocation. Oxadiargyl has both pre and early post emergent weed activity, on a range of both grass and broadleaf weeds. A number of pre emergent herbicides are strongly affected by soil components such as clay and organic matter, which can greatly influence their efficacy and crop safety. The efficacy and crop safety of oxadiargyl is not affected by soil type as much as most other herbicides such as metolachlor or clomazone.

Globally, oxadiargyl was developed for rice and sugar cane, however the product is also being evaluated in sunflower, transplanted vegetables and perennial crops (Thomson, 1997).

MATERIALS AND METHODS

Oxadiargyl has been evaluated in replicated small plot trials for the past 5 years in Australia. Small plot trials were sprayed with flat fan nozzles, generally applying water rates of between 200 and 300 litres/ha at an application pressure of between 200 and 300 kPa. In all trials oxadiargyl was applied post plant pre crop emergence or pre plant in transplanted crops. A 400 g a.i./litre SC formulation of oxadiargyl was used in all trials. Plot sizes were between 10 and 30 m^2. Assessments were conducted as whole plot subjective ratings using the European Weed Research System (EWRS) scales for weed control efficacy (1 = total weed control, 9 = no effect on weeds) and crop tolerance (1 = healthy plant, 9 = crop killed) (Puntener, 1981). Oxadiargyl has been compared to a range of other herbicides used both alone and in combinations.

RESULTS

Trials conducted over a number of sites throughout Australia have shown oxadiargyl at 400 g a.i./ha effectively controls a range of broadleaf and grass weeds including *Amaranthus powellii, Solanum nigrum, Chenopodium album, Nicandra physaloides, Echinchloa crus-gallii and Eleusine indica* (Table 1).

Oxadiargyl showed some activity on both *Raphanus raphanistrum* and *Polygonum aviculare*. However, these weeds were not controlled effectively, with EWRS ratings of 4.7 and 6.3 respectively (Table 1).

Table 1.   Average EWRS weed control ratings for different weed species for oxadiargyl applied pre weed emergence at 400 g a.i./ha.

Weed	No Sites	Average EWRS Rating	Standard Error
Amaranthus powellii	3	2.7	0.2
Chenopodium album	6	2.1	0.5
Eleusine indica	3	1.3	0.1
Nicandra physaloides	4	1.9	0.9
Polygonum aviculare	1	6.3	-
Raphanus raphanistrum	4	4.7	1.3
Solanum nigrum	9	2.4	0.5

Transplanted vegetable crops including broccoli, cabbage, cauliflower, lettuce and capsicum showed high tolerance to oxadiargyl at between 200 and 400 g a.i./ha applied pre transplant (Table 2). The product was also safe when applied post plant pre emergence in potatoes. Oxadiargyl was not safe when applied post plant pre emergence at 400 g a.i./ha to carrots and cucurbit crops including pumpkins and squash (Table 2).

Despite the variation in soil types on which the trials were conducted the low standard error values for both the crop safety and weed efficacy ratings suggest that soil type is having minimal effect on the efficacy of this herbicide, which would support the findings of Dickmann *et al.* (1997).

Table 2. Average EWRS crop tolerance ratings for various crops with oxadiargyl applied pre transplant (PT) or post plant pre crop emergence (PE).

Crop	Application Timing	Rate (g a.i./ha)	No Sites	Average EWRS Rating	Standard Error
Broccoli	PT	400	4	1.9	0.3
Cabbage	PT	400	3	1.4	0.4
Capsicum	PT	400	3	1.6	0.5
Cauliflower	PT	400	1	1.0	-
Lettuce	PT	200	2	2.2	1.2
Carrots	PE	200	2	4.1	1.3
Carrots	PE	400	1	7.8	-
Potato	PE	400	3	2.0	0.6
Pumpkin	PE	400	1	4.0	-
Squash	PE	400	1	6.0	-

DISCUSSION

Continued availability and development of new crop protection products in horticultural crops in Australia continues to be a production issue. Oxadiargyl herbicide potentially offers a new class of herbicide chemistry for management of weeds in a range of horticultural crops.

Oxadiargyl is a potential herbicide in crops such as lettuce and capsicums, for which few effective herbicides are registered, and also offers a solution to industry problems such as control of Solanaceae weeds, such as *Solanum nigrum*, in crops such as potatoes and capsicums, which are from the same family.

The product also has a number of characteristics, which make it particularly suited to annual horticultural crops including short residual activity period, broad weed spectrum and high crop safety on a wide range of soil types.

ACKNOWLEDGEMENTS

Horticulture Australia Ltd provided funding for this project. We thank all growers who kindly provided trial sites. We also thank all researchers who undertook trials as part of this project. Researchers included, Lloyd Williams, Mark Sumner, Chris Monsour, Greg Barnes, Lauren O'Connor, Tim Hingston, Matthew Sherriff, Brendan Finch, Keith Lewis and David Kilpatrick.

REFERENCES

Dickmann R; Melgarejo J; Loubiere P; Montagnon M (1997). Oxadiargyl: A new novel herbicide for rice and sugar cane. *Proceedings of the BCPC Conference – Weeds 1997*, **1**, 51-57.

Puntener W (1981). Manual for Field Trials in Plant Protection. Second Edition. Ciba-Geigy Limited, Basle, Switzerland.

Thomson W (1997). Agricultural Chemicals Book II Herbicides. Thomson Publications, California.

Possible future herbicide options in green beans, *Phaseolus vulgaris*

J Scrimshaw

Processors and Growers Research Organisation, Peterborough PE8 6HJ, UK
Email: jim@pgro.co.uk

ABSTRACT

Four field experiments were carried out over two years to investigate the potential of chlorthal dimethyl and propachlor, alone and in mixtures, linuron and pendimethalin to provide an effective alternative to fomesafen for weed control in green beans. The most promising treatments were propachlor (9 litres/ha) with chlorthal dimethyl (6 litres/ha), and a pre-formulated propachlor/chlorthal dimethyl product (20 litres/ha). Linuron gave reasonable control of most weed species present although *Chenopodium album* control appeared variable between the two years. Pendimethalin was effective but crop phytotoxicity levels were unacceptable at one site in one year.

INTRODUCTION

Green beans occupy around 1762 ha in the UK (Defra, 2002) and can achieve gross margins of £900/ha (Nix, 2003). After the 2007 season growers will lose the use of Flex (fomesafen) an early post emergence herbicide, upon which there is a heavy reliance for effective weed control.

Green beans are a high value and high quality crop and must be kept weed free. Fomesafen controls a wide range of weeds and suppresses volunteer potato shoots, which can be an important contaminant in the harvested beans.

Without effective alternatives after 2007 weed competition could cause 48-87% yield loss (Knott, 2001). Harvesting would be less efficient and there would be additional cleaning required of the harvested crop. Processors may reject increasing numbers of crops because of stem and toxic berry contamination.

Other materials, such as trifluralin used as a pre-drilling herbicide, are still available for use but require incorporation. However this may result in loss of vital soil moisture, and an additional pass across the area to be drilled increases costs and increases the chances of soil compaction. Applications of trifluralin in wet conditions can affect emergence and it's limited weed spectrum does not include black nightshade (*Solanum nigrum*, SOLNI), the berries of which are a toxic contaminant in the produce. For these reasons the popularity of this material is declining.

Arresin (monolinuron), a pre-emergence material, could be used in conjunction with trifluralin and was used on around 60% of the crop but it was not supported in the first round of the EU pesticide review and is no longer available. Basagran (bentazone) is available post emergence but it has problems controlling speedwells (*Veronica* spp.), annual meadow grass (*Poa annua,* POAAN), knotgrass (*Polygonum aviculare,* POLAV) and fat hen (*Chenopodium album,* CHEAL). It is expensive and has temperature and varietal restrictions. Dacthal (chlorthal dimethyl) has off-label approval for pre-emergence use but weed control can be variable and again it is relatively expensive. All these factors emphasise the requirement for an effective weed control option after the loss of fomesafen in 2007.

MATERIALS AND METHODS

Over two seasons and at four sites, two at Thornhaugh, Cambridgeshire and two in commercial crops in Warwickshire, chlorthal dimethyl, and propachlor, alone and in mixtures, linuron and pendimethalin were applied pre-emergence to green bean crops using an Azo precision plot sprayer fitted with Lurmark flat fan nozzles delivering 200 litres/ha water volume at 1.9 bar pressure giving fine/medium spray quality. Treatments were replicated 4 times. The cultivars Masai, grown on a fine sandy loam, Roma, on a silt loam and Laguna and Nerina, on a sandy loam were studied over the two seasons.

After herbicide treatments were applied the green beans were assessed for any phytotoxicity. Counts of individual weed species were made in three random quadrats of $0.33m^2$ per plot and the results statistically analysed for variance (2 way ANOVA with replications within a complete block experimental design) using GENSTAT. An overall weed control score was given on a scale of 1 - 10 (1 = poor, 7 = acceptable, 10 = no weeds).

RESULTS AND DISCUSSION

The results of the weed counts for 2001 (plants per square metre) at each site are shown in Tables 1 and 2 and all weed species are referred to using Bayer codes (© Bayer Code System). At the bottom of weed count result tables the symbol ' * ' denotes a probability <0.001.

Table 1   Cultivar: Masai. Weed count - Thornhaugh - 2001

Treatment	CHEAL 16 DAT	CHEAL 35 DAT
untreated	8.75	9.25
propachlor (9 litres/ha)	4.5	5
propachlor + chlorthal dimethyl (9 litres/ha + 4 kg/ha)	2	3.25
chlorthal dimethyl (6 kg/ha)	4.25	7.5
propachlor + chlorthal dimethyl (9 litres/ha + 2 kg/ha)	3.75	6.5
propachlor + chlorthal dimethyl (5 litres/ha + 2 kg/ha)	8.75	12
pendimethalin (3.3 litres/ha)	1.5	5.5
linuron (0.5 litres/ha)	10.75	16.5
linuron (0.75 litres/ha)	9.75	14.75
linuron (1.0 litre/ha)	8.75	14
LSD	6.745	9.34
Probability	0.069	0.072

Table 2   Cultivar: Roma. Weed count at Luddington 2001.

Treatment		CHEAL		CAPBP		SENVU		MAT spp		POLPE	
	DAT	14	41	14	41	14	41	14	41	14	41
untreated		33	22	11	2	3.5	1.5	5	1	2.25	0
propachlor (9 litres/ha)		4.5	5.25	0	0	0	0	0	0	0	0
propachlor + chlorthal dimethyl (9 litres/ha + 4 kg/ha)		0.5	0.5	0	0	0	0	0	0	0	0.5
chlorthal dimethyl (6 kg/ha)		17	10	3	1	1	0.5	3	0	0	0
propachlor + chlorthal dimethyl (9 litres/ha + 2 kg/ha)		15	0.5	0	0	0	0	1	0	0	0
propachlor + chlorthal dimethyl (5 litres/ha + 2 kg/ha)		4.5	1.25	0	0	0	0	1	0	0	0
pendimethalin (3.3 litres/ha)		12	2.5	3	0	2	0	8	0.5	1	0
linuron (0.5 litres/ha)		10	14	0	1	0	1	1.5	0	1	1
linuron (0.75 litres/ha)		12	17	0	0	0	0	1	0	0	0
linuron (1.0 litres/ha)		14	10	0	0	0	0	0.5	0	1	0
LSD		28.7	9.1	11.2	1.25	2	1.13	1.95	0.75	1.7	0.8
Probability		0.6	*	0.16	0.15	0.02	0.15	*	0.46	0.12	0.17

In 2001 at Thornhaugh (Table 1) the most abundant weed was fat hen and the number of other weed species were very low. Propachlor (9 litres/ha) with chlorthal dimethyl (4 litres/ha) and pendimethalin (3.3 litres/ha) gave the best levels of control.

There was more variation in the weed species present at Luddington (Table 2) but again fat hen was present in greatest numbers. Similar treatments were most effective against the weed population present and again the propachlor chlorthal dimethyl mix exhibited good persistence. Although chlorthal dimethyl and propachlor alone significantly reduced fat hen populations 41 DAT a mix of the two together was more effective and the control achieved was comparable with pendimethalin used at 3.3 litres/ha. Linuron treatments had activity against most weed species present but did not significantly reduce the fat hen population.

The results for 2002 are shown in Tables 3, 4 and 5

In 2002 at Thornhaugh (Table 3) populations of black nightshade were initially reduced by all treatments except chlorthal dimethyl alone. The addition of propachlor to chlorthal dimethyl was the most effective treatment and the pre-formulated propachlor/chlorthal dimethyl showed increasing control with increasing rate. By 38 DAT, all treatments were giving 70-95% control with the linuron and low rate propachlor/chlorthal dimethyl formulation being the poorest treatments.

Satisfactory fat hen and field speedwell (*Veronica persica*, VERPE) control was achieved with all treatments. Annual meadow grass populations were not high but control appeared satisfactory with all treatments except chlorthal dimethyl and low rate pendimethalin.

Cleaver (*Galium aparine*, GALAP) control improved with increasing rates of the propachlor/chlorthal dimethyl formulation and the level of control achieved at 20 litres/ha was equivalent to the propachlor (9 litres/ha) and chlothal dimethyl (6 kg/ha) mix. Chlorthal dimethyl alone, linuron and pendimethalin were not effective.

Table 3   Cultivar: Laguna. Weed count at Thornhaugh 2002.

Treatment	SOLNI		VERPE		POAAN		CHEAL		GALAP		POLPE	
DAT	17	38	17	38	17	38	17	38	17	38	17	38
Untreated	18	19	3	6	3	6	13	18	4	4	14	4
propachlor + chlorthal dimethyl (10 litres/ha)	4	5.25	0	0	0	1	2	2	5	3	0	0.5
propachlor + chlorthal dimethyl (15 litres/ha)	3.25	2	0	0	0	0	0	0	3	4	1	1
propachlor + chlorthal dimethyl (20 litres/ha)	3	1	0	0	1	0	0	0	2	2	0	2.5
chlorthal dimethyl (6 kg/ha)	13.5	3	0	0	4	4	4	1	4	2	1	2
propachlor (9 litres/ha)	4	3	0	0	0	0	1	4	2	3	1.25	2
chlorthal dimethyl + propachlor (6 kg + 9 litres/ha)	2	2	0	0	0	0	0.5	0	2	1	0	0
linuron (0.75 litres/ha)	5	5	0.5	0.5	0.5	1	1.25	3	5	6	0	1
linuron (1.0 litre/ha)	4.5	6	0.5	1.5	0.5	2	0.75	3	4	4	0	1
pendimethalin (2.5 litres/ha)	8	1	1.75	0	1.75	4	1.25	0	9	7	0	0
pendimethalin (3.3 litres/ha)	5	2	0	0	0	1.5	1.5	0.5	6	6	0	0
LSD	8.3	7	1.1	1.6	2.8	3.4	2.0	4.0	4.3	4	1.9	1.3
Probability	*	*	*	*	0.09	0.01	*	*	0.03	0.07	0.87	0.04

Table 4   General weed control scores - Thornhaugh 32 DAT

Treatment	Replicate 1	Replicate 2	Replicate 3	Replicate 4	Ave
untreated	0	0	0	0	0
propachlor + chlorthal dimethyl (10 litres/ha)	8	7	4	5	6
propachlor + chlorthal dimethyl (15 litres/ha)	8	7	5	9	7.25
propachlor + chlorthal dimethyl (20 litres/ha)	8	8	9	8	8.25
chlorthal dimethyl (6 kg/ha)	7	5	6	4	5.5
propachlor (9 litres/ha)	6	8	6	7	6.75
chlorthal dimethyl + propachlor (6 kg + 9 litres/ha)	9	8	6	7	7.5
linuron (0.75 litres/ha)	9	6	5	7	6.75
linuron (1.0 litre/ha)	8	8	8	5	7.25
pendimethalin (2.5 litres/ha)	7	6	5	6	6
pendimethalin (3.3 litres/ha)	5	5	9	8	6.75

Table 4 shows the general weed control scores at Thornhaugh in 2002. Both the 15 and 20 litres/ha formulation of chlorthal dimethyl/propachlor gave acceptable levels of weed control as did linuron at 1.0 litre/ha.

Although pendimethalin gave excellent control of some species at Thornhaugh there was some phytotoxicity to green beans. After application there was frequent heavy rainfall within the first week and, though not apparent at the first assessment, by the time of the second, all 3.3 litres/ha pendimethalin treatments could be identified in all replications. As the trifoliate leaves began to open and expand they were chlorotic and the plants appeared stunted. These effects were apparent on the lower rate pendimethalin plots but not to the same degree. The crop did not grow away from these effects.

Table 5   Cultivar: Nerina. Weed counts - Hampton Lucy

Treatment		POAAN		STEME		CHEAL		General weed control 47 DAT
DAT		28	47	28	47	28	47	
untreated		8	4	5	6	7	10	0
propachlor + chlorthal dimethyl (10 litres/ha)		3	3	2	3	3	10	4.25
propachlor + chlorthal dimethyl (15 litres/ha)		3.5	1	2	1	2	6	5.5
propachlor + chlorthal dimethyl (20 litres/ha)		3	1	1	1	4	6	6.5
chlorthal dimethyl (6 kg/ha)		5.25	3	4	1	4	10	4
propachlor (9 litres/ha)		3	2	5	2	3	9	5.5
chlorthal dimethyl + propachlor (6 kg + 9 litres/ha)		3	1	2.5	0	3	6	6.25
linuron (0.75 litres/ha)		3.5	2	4	2	3	10	6
linuron (1.0 litre/ha)		2	2	7.5	3	2	9	4.75
pendimethalin (2.5 litres/ha)		4.5	3	4	1	4.5	9	6
pendimethalin (3.3 litres/ha)		3.5	5	4	1	4.25	8	6.75
LSD		3.61	2.3	3.28	2.9	2.47	5.57	
Probability		0.1	0.118	0.023	0.018	0.023	0.536	

At Hampton Lucy (Table 5) the control of the predominant annual meadow grass, chickweed (*Stellaria media,* STEME) and fat hen was initially disappointing; there were population reductions but control was far from complete. After 47 days control had improved, and annual meadow grass was effectively controlled by 15 litres/ha and 20 litres/ha propachlor/chlorthal dimethyl formulations together with the propachlor + chlorthal dimethyl mix.

Chickweed control was least effective with linuron and the lowest rate of the propachlor/chlorthal dimethyl formulation.

Fat hen control at this site was poor with all treatments and overall general weed control levels achieved were not as good as those at Thornhaugh. None achieved a satisfactory level of control i.e. a score of 7 or above. This was because the fat hen population was not controlled and at the time of the assessment plants had reached a significant size influencing the score achieved. Large fat hen plants can cause harvesting and contamination problems at harvest.

Overall the 20 litres/ha propachlor/chlorthal dimethyl formulation was effective along with the propachlor (9 litres/ha) with chlorthal dimethyl (6 kg/ha) as the mix. Propachlor and chlorthal dimethyl alone gave useful levels of control but activity was enhanced with the addition of the other material. Control with linuron was variable but it had some useful activity against many of the species present. The main concern was its inability to control fat hen populations consistently. Relative costs, however, may make this potentially a useful tool in some situations after 2007. Pendimethalin showed good activity on several species but there is a question mark concerning its crop safety, which could have been due to the rainfall following application, a specific varietal tolerance factor or a combination of the two.

Potentially there are materials that could provide alternative weed control when fomesafen is withdrawn from the market in 2007. On-label recommendations are unlikely because of the costs involved so off-label approvals will be pursued for some materials used in these trials. Some are more effective than others but there is also a price differential which may influence the product of choice.

REFERENCES

Defra (2002). *Vegetables and Salad by Region: June 2002 Census*. National Statistics Department: York

Knott C M (2001). Rearguard herbicides. *Grower (August 2001)*, pp. 22-23

Nix J (2003). *Farm Management Pocket Book, 33rd edition*, p.45. Imperial College: Wye.

POSTER SESSION 7E

ASPECTS OF PRODUCTION, PROTECTION AND REGULATION IN ARABLE CROPS

Session Organiser: Dr Anthony Biddle
Processors and Growers Research
Organisation, Peterborough, UK

Poster Papers: 7E-1 to 7E-8

Flucetosuluron: a new tool to control *Galium aparine* and broadleaf weeds in cereal crops

D S Kim, J N Lee, K H Hwang, K G Kang, T Y Kim, S J Koo
LG Life Sciences Ltd, 104-1, Yuseong-gu, Daejeon 305-380, Korea
Email: dosoonkim@lgls.co.kr

J C Caseley
Formerly IACR-Long Ashton Research Station, University of Bristol, Bristol BS41 3AF, UK

ABSTRACT

Flucetosulfuron is a novel post-emergence sulfonylurea herbicide providing excellent control of *Galium aparine* and other important broadleaf weeds with good safety to cereal crops, wheat and barley. The efficacy of flucetosulfuron was less influenced by low temperature than fluroxypyr and florasulam, showing that flucetosulfuron was as good as or better than these herbicides under all temperature regimes tested, particularly with its superior efficacy established under cool conditions. The addition of adjuvants improved significantly its herbicidal performance in controlling *G. aparine* and achieved improved rainfastness. Field evaluations also confirmed that flucetosulfuron performed excellently in controlling *G. aparine* and some important broadleaf weeds including *Matricaria*, *Papaver*, and *Stellaria* spp. Therefore, flucetosulfuron can be an alternative solution for broadleaf weed management including *G. aparine* in cereal crops.

INTRODUCTION

Flucetosulfuron (LGC-42153) is a new sulfonylurea herbicide discovered by LG Life Sciences Ltd for rice and cereal crops (Koo *et al.*, 2003; Kim *et al.*, 2003). This new herbicide controls *Echinochloa* spp. and most weed flora in rice, and shows good efficacy against *Galium aparine* and various other broadleaf weeds by foliar application. Recently we conducted various studies to evaluate factors influencing the performance of flucetosulfuron in controlling major broadleaf weeds including *G. aparine* in cereal crops. In this paper, we report the results of our studies including field evaluation, which demonstrates the possibility of flucetosulfuron as an alternative solution for control of *G. aparine* and broadleaf weeds in cereal crops.

MATERIALS AND METHODS

Pot experiments

Pot experiments were conducted using plants grown in 9 cm diameter plastic pots or 20 x 15 cm^2 square pots containing loam soil amended with 30% coarse grit and Osmocote slow-release fertiliser. Pots were placed in glasshouses maintained at 20/15 ± 4 °C (day/night) and plants were watered to maintain the soil close to field capacity by sub-irrigation. A laboratory track sprayer fitted with a Lurmark 01-F80 nozzle calibrated to deliver 200 or 300 litre ha^{-1} of herbicide at a pressure of 30 psi (2.1 bar) was used to treat weeds at appropriate growth stages.

Flucetosulfuron was tested at a range of doses in comparison with amidosulfuron (Eagle), florasulam (Boxer), fluroxypyr (Starane2) and metsulfuron-methyl (Ally). To evaluate effects of adjuvants on the performance of flucetosulfuron against *G. aparine*, seven different adjuvants were tested at three rates. After the adjuvant study, a rain experiment was conducted to evaluate the effect of rainfall and the interaction of rainfall and adjuvants. Rain was applied with the Long Ashton precision rain simulator at an intensity of 3 mm/hour for a period of one hour at 1, 2, or 4 hour intervals after herbicide application. In addition, a controlled environment cabinet experiment was also conducted to evaluate temperature effects on herbicide performance in controlling *G. aparine* by maintaining plants under three different temperature regimes, $7/5^{\circ}C$, $10/5^{\circ}C$ and $16/10^{\circ}C$ (day/night). All pot experiments consisted of three or four replicates of a randomised block design. Fresh weight of foliage was assessed at the times shown in figures and tables.

Field experiments

Field experiments were conducted at Long Ashton Research Station farm in 2001/02. Three replicates of plots containing sown broadleaf weed species were established and arranged in three fully randomised blocks. Flucetosulfuron was tested at 12~48 g a.i.ha[-1] in comparison with amidosulfuron, fluroxypyr, metsulfuron-methyl and isoproturon + diflufenican (IPU + DFF) at full and double rates of their recommended doses. Herbicide spray (containing Tween 20 at 0.2% of spray volume) was made with a knapsack sprayer fitted with Lurmark low pressure nozzles at a volume rate of 250 litres ha[-1] on the dates, March 4, March 27, April 9 in 2002. Visual assessments were made using a 0-5 score where 5 is as untreated plants and 0 is dead, which was then converted into % weed control.

RESULTS AND DISCUSSION

Weed control spectrum

Table 1. Shoot fresh weight (% of untreated control) of weeds at 29 days after treatment with flucetosulfuron and commercial herbicides.

Herbicide	Dose (g a.i./ha)	Grass weeds			Broadleaf weeds		
		ALOMY	BROST	LOLPE	GALAP	MATPR	STEME
Flucetosulfuron	12	71.3	97.5	38.7	3.0	6.6	8.1
	24	57.3	90.3	42.1	2.2	7.0	9.2
	48	60.1	93.1	12.1	2.4	5.9	8.6
	96	33.8	91.8	14.8	2.3	5.4	9.1
Amidosulfuron	30	85.7	85.7	66.6	4.4	12.3	13.5
Fluroxypyr	200	80.7	81.6	80.0	2.7	60.5	8.5
Metsulfuron-methyl	6	69.9	84.6	30.8	41.3	6.0	7.9
$LSD_{0.05}$		21.2	NS	31.2	9.4	7.4	4.1

Flucetosulfuron well controlled *G. aparine* and other broadleaf weeds, *Matricaria perforata* and *Stellaria media* (Table 1). The efficacy of flucetosulfuron against *G. aparine* was equivalent to amidosulfuron and fluroxypyr but superior to metsulfuron-methyl. Against *M. perforata*, flucetosulfuron was as effective as metsulfuron-methyl but superior to amidosulfuron and fluroxypyr. In addition, flucetosulfuron showed activity against *Alopecurus myosuroides* with greater effectiveness than the other herbicides tested, indicating that flucetosulfuron can provide extra benefits of managing some grass weed species.

Effects of adjuvant

It is well known that some adjuvants improve herbicide retention, absorption and penetration, often offering improved herbicidal efficacy. Our study also revealed that the addition of adjuvants in a spray solution improves very significantly the herbicidal efficacy of flucetosulfuron against *G. aparine* at the six whirl stages (Figure 1). The extent of improvement appeared to be increased with adjuvant rate but it was not statistically significant. Although all tested adjuvants significantly improved the efficacy of flucetosulfuron against *G. aparine*, penetrants Arma and Torpedo were the most effective and organo silicone Silwet L-77 was the least effective.

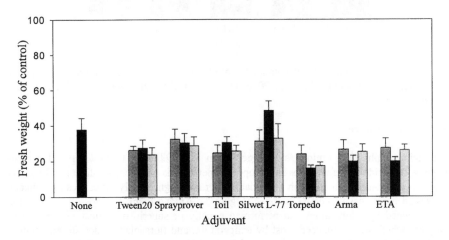

Figure 1. Shoot fresh weight (% of untreated control) of *G. aparine* at 31 days after treatment of flucetosulfuron at 24g a.i./ha without or with adjuvants at three different rates. Silwet L-77 at 0.05, 0.1 & 0.2% (from left), Sprayprover and Toil at 1, 2 & 4%, and the others at 0.1, 0.2, 0.4% of spray volume.

Effects of rain

The length of time required between herbicide application and the onset of rain for effective weed control is important for post-emergence herbicides, whose uptake by the foliage will be influenced by adjuvants. In our study, rain treatments clearly reduced the efficacy against *G. aparine* of flucetosulfuron but this was ameliorated by the addition of adjuvants (Figure 2).

Among tested adjuvants, rainfastness was best achieved with ETA and Arma whilst Torpedo was the least effective adjuvant for enhancing rapid uptake. To achieve the same level of *Galium* control with adjuvants in the absence of rain, 4 hours between herbicide application and rain appears to be not long enough, indicating that a slight increase of dose rate from 20 g a.i./ha is required to ensure good efficacy.

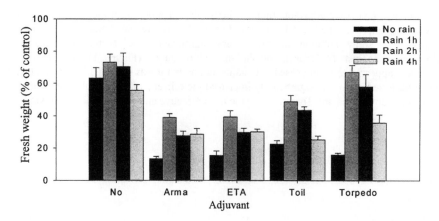

Figure 2. Shoot fresh weight (% of untreated control) of *G. aparine* measured at 22 days after treatment of flucetosulfuron at 20 g a.i./ha used with adjuvants and with four rain treatments.

Effects of temperature

As herbicide application timings are ranged from late February to mid April for post-emergence herbicide in cereal crops in Europe, temperature is an important factor influencing herbicide performance. Our study showed that temperature significantly influences the efficacy of the tested herbicides against *G. aparine* (Figure 3). Among them, flucetosulfuron was the least influenced by temperature and performed equally or superiorly against *G. aparine* to fluroxypyr, which was influenced most by temperature, and florasulam under all temperature regimes. In particular, the superior efficacy of flucetosulfuron was well established under cool conditions, indicating that flucetosulfuron can offer more consistent *Galium* control regardless of application timings from early spring to early summer in field conditions.

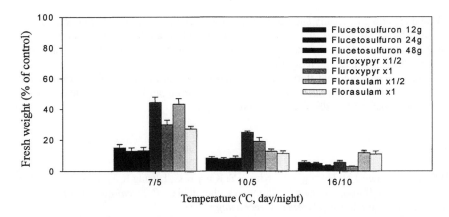

Figure 3. Shoot fresh weight (% of untreated control) of *Galium aparine* measured at 29 days after treatment of flucetosulfuron and other herbicides, and maintained under three different temperature regimes.

Field performance

Field experiments also clearly demonstrated that flucetosulfuron offers excellent levels of weed control, mainly broadleaf weeds including *G. aparine*, *M. perforata*, *P. rhoeas*, and *Raphanus raphanistrum* at less than 30 g a.i./ha (Table 2). Flucetosulfuron performed better than metsulfuron-methyl in controlling *G. aparine*. It also provided better efficacy against *M. perforata*, *P. rhoeas* and *S. media* than amidosulfuron and fluroxypyr.

Table 2. Weed control (%) by flucetosulfuron and commercial standard herbicides applied on March 4 (A), March 27 (B) and April 9 (C) in 2002.

Herbicide	Dose	G. aparine			M. perforata			P. rhoeas			R. raphanistrum		
		A	B	C	A	B	C	A	B	C	A	B	C
Flucetosulfuron	12	84	80	100	94	100	100	74	54	60	100	100	84
(g a.i./ha)	24	84	100	100	100	100	100	40	80	84	54	80	94
	48	100	100	100	100	100	100	64	100	84	64	84	100
Amidosulfuron	x 1	100	100	100	20	60	64	20	54	54	74	84	100
	x 2	100	100	100	24	40	94	60	44	84	100	100	100
Fluroxypyr	x 1	100	100	100	14	4	0	20	0	34	0	0	64
	x 2	100	100	100	14	34	14	20	0	24	34	34	44
Metsulfuron	x 1	0	4	20	100	94	100	100	100	100	100	80	100
	x 2	4	24	4	100	100	100	100	100	100	100	100	100
IPU+DFF	x 1	14	24	24	80	100	100	60	74	44	40	44	4
	x 2	54	74	44	100	100	100	100	100	84	94	64	54

CONCLUSIONS

Pot and field experiments clearly showed that flucetosulfuron provides excellent control of *G. aparine* and broadleaf weeds in cereal crops at 20~30 g a.i./ha. The performance of flucetosulfuron in controlling *G. aparine* was significantly improved by adjuvants, which also increased rainfastness. Although temperature influenced the performance, flucetosulfuron was least affected as compared with florasulam and fluroxypyr, indicating that flucetosulfuron is flexible in its application timings. Therefore, flucetosulfuron can be an alternative tool for control of *G. aparine* and broadleaf weeds in cereal crops.

REFERENCES

Kim D S; Koo S J; Lee J N; Hwang K H; Kim T Y; Kang K G; Hwang K S; Joe G H; Cho J H (2003) Flucetosulfuron: a new sulfonylurea herbicide. *Proceedings of the BCPC International Congress, Crop Science & Technology 2003.*

Koo S J; Kim D S; Kang K G, Kim T Y; Lee J N; Hwang K H; Joe G H; Kwon Y W; Kim D W (2003) LGC-42153: A new generation sulfonylurea herbicide. *Proceedings of the 19th Asian-Pacific Weed Science Society Conference 662-667.*

The effect of downy mildew (*Peronospora viciae*) on the yield of spring sown field beans (*Vicia fabae*) and its control

A J Biddle
Processors and Growers Research Organisation, Great North Road, Thornhaugh, Peterborough PE8 6HJ, UK
Email: anthony@pgro.co.uk

J Thomas, D Kenyon
NIAB, Huntingdon Road, Cambridge CB3 OLE, UK

N V Hardwick, M C Taylor
Central Science Laboratory, Sand Hutton, York YO41 1LZ, UK

ABSTRACT

Downy mildew in spring sown field beans has become an increasingly important disease in spring sown field beans. A series of experiments was undertaken between 2000 and 2002 at four sites across England to evaluate a range of fungicide timings to determine yield/disease loss relationships. Results indicated that a single fungicide spray applied seven days after the onset of flowering under conditions of high disease pressure can result in a yield response of 0.5 t/ha. However, because the occurrence of the disease is sporadic and cannot be predicted, routine spray applications are not justified. It is, therefore, important to identify those crops at risk. Collection of meteorological data at the experiment sites, together with disease monitoring, has indicated that disease is most likely to develop rapidly at temperature below 10°C in the seven days before the onset of flowering if leaves have been wet for long periods, that is longer that 12 h.

INTRODUCTION

Downy mildew first became a problem in spring-sown beans in 1988 when infected crops were mainly confined to the eastern half of the country, the main production area. Late-drilled crops appeared to be the worst affected. Troy was the main cultivar affected but others showed severe infection including Victor, whilst newer cultivars such as Maya and Quattro are also moderately susceptible, Maris Bead appears to remain relatively free from the disease. However, disease/yield interactions have not been quantified for bean downy mildew. Fungicides are applied prophylactically and, in the majority of cases, are not justified. This increases the costs of production and adds unnecessarily to the pesticide burden on the environment. A three year study on the control of downy mildew of spring beans (*Vicia fabae*) caused by the fungus *Peronospora viciae* was undertaken to determine the requirement for disease control in susceptible cultivars of spring beans and to identify the optimum timing for the application of fungicide in relation to disease development and growth stage by investigating the relationship of disease development and severity with local meteorological conditions. The germination and infection response of *P. viciae* sporangia to increasing temperature is not entirely known (Jellis *et al.*, 1998) but it was considered that empirical methods could be used to determine high-risk situations.

MATERIALS AND METHODS

Trials were established in growing crops of cv Victor at: Beeford near Driffield, East Yorkshire (2000); Stockbridge Technology Centre (STC) (2001, 2002, North Yorkshire; Pedlinge, Hythe, Kent (2000-2001); Harper Adams, Newport, Shropshire (2000-2002); Little Casterton, Stamford, Lincolnshire (2000) and Crowland, Spalding, Lincolnshire (2001, 2002). From all sites records of meteorological data including hourly temperature and relative humidity and daily rainfall data were taken automatically for April, May, June and July and stored in an Excel spreadsheet. Meteorological data were collected from the in-crop meteorological stations via cellphone analogue networks. The response curve methodology of Duthie (1997) was used to postulate curves of infection responses to temperature. Sequential applications of Folio (500 g/l chlorothalonil plus 75 g/l metalaxyl) at 2 l/ha in 200 litres water/ha at 2.5 bar with medium spray nozzles were made to provide variable disease epidemics. The first treatment (T1) was applied at GS 107/8 with subsequent applications made at regular intervals until 28 days after the onset of flowering (T7) (Thomas *et al.*, 1989). The development of infection was recorded at each of the treatment timings as the percentage of leaf area infected on 20 plants in each plot.

RESULTS

Disease/yield loss relationships

Disease severity varied considerably between trials with six of trials showing significant yield loss as a result of downy mildew (Tables 1 – 3). Maximum disease control was achieved in those plots that were treated on each occasion, whereas plots that received only a single treatment either at GS 107/8 (T1) or early flowering plus 28 days (T7) rarely showed any yield response. Where spray applications were sequentially started from T1 – T7, all programmes that were initiated at early flowering plus 14 days (T5) or earlier resulted in a significant yield response. Several of the trial programmes that started later than this timing still resulted in significant yield increases compared to the control. Inversely stopping fungicide applications at early flowering plus 14 days or later resulted in significant yield retention in all but Lincolnshire trial in 2002, were this was only achieved by continuing the programme for a further seven days. Comparison of the yield responses for the two sequential spray programmes at this site showed that, unlike other trials, there was no overlap in the point at which significant yield retention first occurred.

Forecasting

Using the response curve methodology of Duthie (1997) a postulated curve was defined based on unpublished observations (Figure 1).

Data from the in-field weather stations was summarised to find the mean temperature during periods of leaf wetness of greater than four hours duration, shorter periods were assumed to be of little or no significance. The temperature of the wet period was quantified for its significance using the temperature profile and multiplied by the number of hours that the sensors had recorded as being wet.

Table 1. Yields (t/ha) of spring bean cv. Victor in 2000 sprayed at different times with percentage leaf area infected with *Peronospora viciae* at T7.

Treatment combinations	Yorkshire Yield	Yorkshire Disease	Lincolnshire Yield	Lincolnshire Disease	Shropshire Yield	Shropshire Disease	Kent Yield	Kent Disease
Untreated (1)	6.40	14.2	7.84	3.5	5.12	9.5	5.61	1.1
T1 – T7 (1)	6.97	11.9	8.09	0.3	6.41	2.8	7.03	1.2
T2 - T7	6.83	10.2	8.18	0.5	6.19	2.2	7.00	0.0
T3 - T7	6.93	8.8	8.25	2.2	6.44	4.0	6.49	0.1
T4 -T7	7.17	9.6	8.10	2.8	6.03	7.2	6.14	0.2
T5 - T7	7.30	11.9	8.01	2.6	6.08	8.1	6.25	0.6
T6 -T7	7.03	8.8	7.43	3.2	5.99	10.5	6.12	0.5
T7	7.13	8.4	7.57	3.2	5.72	8.7	5.86	0.5
T1	6.37	10.8	7.50	2.6	5.24	9.9	5.66	1.4
T1 – T2	6.47	9.4	7.35	3.2	5.43	6.3	6.12	1.2
T1 – T3	6.37	10.9	7.50	1.0	5.48	4.1	6.16	1.1
T1 – T4	6.23	10.6	8.50	0.8	5.93	2.8	6.15	0.1
T1 – T5	7.17	11.9	8.17	0.5	6.11	2.3	6.51	0.1
T1 – T6	6.73	14.4	7.75	0.8	6.37	2.1	6.83	0.0
T1 – T7 (2)	6.57	11.2	7.34	3.3	6.24	3.2	6.64	0.1
Untreated (2)	-	-	-	-	-	-	5.90	1.1
LSD (*P*=0.05)	0.64	3.08	0.92	1.49	0.39	0.41	0.59	0.17

Table 2. Yields (t/ha) of spring bean cv. Victor in 2001 sprayed at different times with percentage leaf area infected with *Peronospora viciae* at T7.

Treatment combinations	Yorkshire Yield	Yorkshire Disease	Lincolnshire Yield	Lincolnshire Disease	Shropshire Yield	Shropshire Disease	Kent Yield	Kent Disease
Untreated (1)	4.09	0.0	3.89	7.7	2.95	1.7	6.09	0.0
T1 – T7 (1)	4.08	0.0	6.07	1.1	3.11	1.0	7.15	0.0
T2 - T7	4.08	0.0	5.82	2.3	3.10	0.8	6.90	0.0
T3 - T7	4.79	0.0	6.12	4.9	2.95	1.1	7.15	0.0
T4 -T7	3.89	0.0	5.60	2.8	2.99	1.1	6.90	0.0
T5 - T7	4.03	0.0	6.04	6.7	2.94	1.1	6.51	0.0
T6 -T7	4.23	0.0	5.61	6.3	2.93	1.2	6.69	0.0
T7	4.58	0.0	3.78	8.2	2.92	1.5	6.24	0.0
T1	3.99	0.0	3.78	6.8	3.06	1.2	5.78	0.0
T1 – T2	4.03	0.0	3.64	4.8	2.97	0.9	5.90	0.0
T1 – T3	3.67	0.0	4.44	9.0	3.01	1.0	6.17	0.0
T1 – T4	3.87	0.0	4.26	3.1	3.18	0.6	6.22	0.0
T1 – T5	4.21	0.0	5.72	4.3	3.03	0.8	6.54	0.0
T1 – T6	4.25	0.0	5.72	3.3	3.02	0.5	6.85	0.0
T1 – T7 (2)	4.87	0.0	6.16	2.0	2.97	0.6	6.57	0.0
Untreated (2)	3.86	0.0	3.62	5.0	2.89	1.9	5.89	0.0
LSD (*P*=0.05)	0.70	-	1.44	3.2	0.24	0.33	0.48	-

Table 3. Yields (t/ha) of spring bean cv. Victor in 2002 sprayed at different times with percentage leaf area infected with *Peronospora viciae* at T7.

Treatment combinations	Yorkshire Yield	Yorkshire Disease	Lincolnshire Yield	Lincolnshire Disease	Shropshire Yield	Shropshire Disease
Untreated (1)	5.11	0.0	4.11	15.9	3.59	7.9
T1 – T7 (1)	5.32	0.0	5.58	2.6	4.87	0.0
T2 - T7	5.50	0.0	4.97	2.0	4.55	0.0
T3 - T7	5.34	0.0	5.22	2.3	4.63	0.0
T4 -T7	5.60	0.0	5.17	2.5	4.60	0.0
T5 - T7	5.77	0.0	4.81	3.8	4.60	0.0
T6 -T7	5.48	0.0	4.91	6.8	3.51	4.8
T7	5.28	0.0	4.33	15.8	3.71	6.0
T1	5.19	0.0	4.32	14.0	3.48	3.9
T1 – T2	5.44	0.0	4.20	22.4	3.50	6.6
T1 – T3	5.29	0.0	4.16	18.2	3.94	0.8
T1 – T4	5.15	0.0	4.60	14.7	3.99	0.2
T1 – T5	5.48	0.0	4.48	10.8	4.73	0.0
T1 – T6	5.60	0.0	4.97	4.6	4.49	0.0
T1 – T7 (2)	5.16	0.0	5.30	2.1	4.66	0.0
Untreated (2)	5.00	0.0	4.55	10.5	3.38	5.6
LSD (*P*=0.05)	0.54	-	0.54	3.63	0.36	0.74

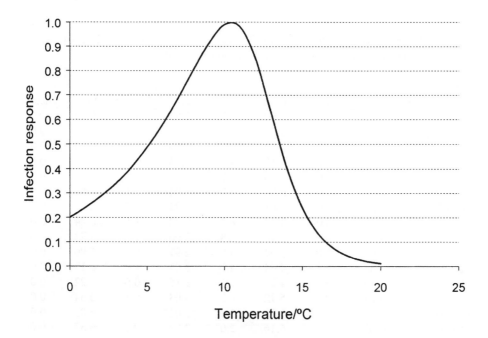

Figure 1. Possible temperature response of *P. viciae* sporangia during leaf wetness

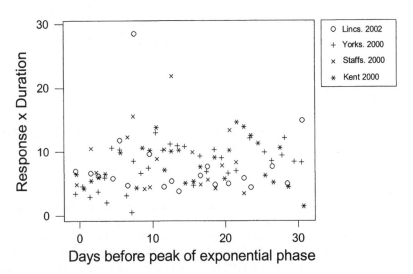

Figure 2. Significance of wet periods occurring prior to exponential phase of *P. viciae* growth curve.

The significance of the leaf wetness periods prior to infection or the onset of the exponential phase of the disease were characterised by cool periods (in line with the response curve) of more than 10 hours duration (Figure 2). The four locations illustrated suffered the most severe epidemics of downy mildew over the course of the experiment.

DISCUSSION

With the exception of the Lincolnshire trial 2002, in trials where significant levels of disease occurred, treatment programmes that included a spray at early flowering plus 14 days resulted in a significant yield response. Delaying the start of a spray programme beyond this timing, or stopping treatments prior to this growth stage, resulted in loss of disease control and a declining yield response. Yield responses for the Lincolnshire 2002 trial suggest that a two-spray programme, with applications both before and after early flowering plus 14 days, would be required to achieve significant yield increases. In two trials (Lincolnshire 2000 and Yorkshire 2001), where no significant yield response was recorded, low levels of downy mildew infection were seen early in the crops development. This initial infection failed to develop in the crop and indicated the need to be able to predict the development of epidemics within a crop environment. For practical monitoring of crops it would be possible to incorporate a trigger event if localised and preferably hourly weather information was available. Otherwise a less sophisticated warning period, comprising a maximum temperature during extended periods of damp conditions may serve equally well. So, to avoid spray applications when there is little risk of diseased spread, a high risk situation has been defined as conditions where the mean temperatures have been below 10°C when crops have been wet for more than 12 h combined with an observation that disease is obvious in the crop in the period seven days before the onset of flowering. A low risk situation would be at temperatures above 10°C when the weather had been dry during the same period and disease was absent. Although disease may be present at higher levels in the crop when the crop is in flower, it is considered that no benefit would accrue from spraying at this time. This work has successfully determined that downy mildew can impact on yield, that it can be controlled if sprays are timed accurately when conditions are favourable for disease development.

ACKNOWLEDGMENTS

The project was funded by the PGRO Pulse Levy and support from PGRO, NIAB and CSL colleagues is gratefully acknowledged.

REFERENCES

Duthie J A (1997). Models of the response of foliar parasites to the combined effects of temperature and duration of leaf wetness. *Phytopathology* **87**, 1088-1095.

Jellis G; Bond D; Boulton R (1998). Diseases of faba bean. In: *The pathology of food and pasture legumes*. Eds. Allen D, Lenné J, . Wallingford: CAB International, 371-422.

Thomas M R; Cook R J; King J E (1989). Factors affecting development of *Septoria tritici* in winter wheat and its effect on yield. *Plant Pathology* **38**, 246-257.

Terbuthylazine in maize - a model example of product stewardship and safe use

T Kuechler, B Duefer, H Resseler; M Schulte
Syngenta Agro GmbH, Am Technologiepark 1 – 5, D-63477 Maintal, Germany
Email: thoralf.kuechler@syngenta.com

D Cornes
Syngenta Crop Protection AG, Schwarzwaldallee 215, CH-4058 Basel, Switzerland

ABSTRACT

In Germany, the use of atrazine was banned in 1991 due to numerous detections of residues in groundwater above the European Community limit of 0.1 µg/l. These findings were mainly a consequence of the high number of uses, the high use rates and the uses outside agriculture (especially railway tracks). Syngenta reacted to this situation in two ways:

o   Introduction of terbuthylazine as follow-up product to be used at a substantially reduced use-pattern and
o   Pro-active product stewardship to accompany the new and sustainable use pattern from the very beginning.

In Germany, the use of terbuthylazine has been limited to maize since 1991. The maximum recommended use rate has been set to 750 g/ha and year. Furthermore, the use has been limited to mixtures with other active ingredients. Consequently, various ready-mix products have been developed, introduced and established in the market.
The efforts made by Syngenta to pro-actively protect the ground- and surface water have ensured the safe use of terbuthylazine. The successful enforcement of such pro-active product stewardship has been proven in Germany and has been recognized by the Regulatory Authorities, who in 2001 granted the first re-registration to terbuthylazine-containing plant protection products for another 10 years. Currently, the latest 10 years lasting re-registration of a terbuthylazine-containing plant protection product has been granted.

ACTIVE AND SUSTAINABLE USE MANAGEMENT

From the experience of the uses of atrazine, Syngenta Germany (at this time Ciba-Geigy) established a strategy for optimizing the uses of triazines while minimizing the risks for residues in water. This included for terbuthylazine a limitation to

- a use only in maize and a few perennial cultures,
- a use only in mixtures with other active ingredients,
- maximum recommended use rate of 750 g/ha and year and
- no use in vulnerable areas.

Various tank mixtures, twin-packs and new ready-formulated premixtures have been developed. Foliar-active combination partners such as pyridate, bromoxynil, bentazone and mesotrione ensure the efficacy necessary to control also triazine-resistant weed biotypes. By the development of these products in Germany the timing of application has been shifted to post-emergence when these foliar acting products are combined with modern soil-active partners such as S-metolachlor for residual control. In the course of this development direction, the application rate was minimized and the use conditions optimized. This specific German approach has led to proven environmentally safe uses with no entry into ground- or surface water. Because of their outstanding efficacy all these products are market leaders today.

Situations, where the groundwater table is shallow, the adsorption capacity of the upper soil is low or direct input into groundwater is possible (e.g. carstic soils), are considered vulnerable. To absolutely avoid entry of terbuthylazine into the groundwater in such areas, Syngenta actively recommends terbuthylazine-free solutions in these situations. Additionally, it is important to note that all stakeholders involved are required to ensure that this policy is enforced.

WEED CONTROL

Terbuthylazine can be effectively applied pre- or post-emergent to weeds and crop. It provides control of a wide range of annual dicotyledonous species and some grass weeds in maize, some of which are difficult to control using other herbicides. It offers excellent application flexibility because of its root and foliar uptake combined with superior residual activity which provides season long weed control across a wide application window.

Table 1.   Weeds susceptible to terbuthylazine (after pre- and post-emergent application at 750 g a.i./ha)

Amaranthus spp. (PC – partially controlled)	*Polygonum persicaria* (PC)
Anagallis arvensis	*Polygonum aviculare* (PC)
Atriplex spp.	*Portulaca oleracea* (PC)
Capsella bursa-pastoris	*Solanum nigrum*
Chenopodium spp.	*Stellaria media*
Galinsoga parviflora	*Urtica* spp. seedlings (PC)
Kickxia spuria	*Veronica persica* (PC)
Mercuralis annua	*Viola arvensis* (PC)
Poa annua	*Viola tricolor* (PC)

The use rate of 750 g a.i./ha was chosen in Germany as a sustainable rate from a groundwater perspective. At this rate the weed control spectrum of terbuthylazine comprises most of the annual key weeds in maize (Table 1). However, terbuthylazine should always be used in mixtures with herbicides offering another mode of action. Those mixtures can provide more than additive herbicidal activity on a much wider spectrum of weeds.

WEED CONTROL IN MIXTURES

Terbuthylazine is a very valuable mixture partner for a wide range of other herbicides. It can be used to fill gaps or weaknesses in the efficacy spectrum of other active ingredients, in particular on species difficult to control. In mixtures with HPPD inhibitors, such as mesotrione, terbuthylazine has been shown to be synergistic (Schulte *et al.*, 2002), giving more than additive activity from both pre- and post-emergent applications. Results from field trials in Europe during 2002 show the value of the combination across a wide range of important dicotyledonous weed species (figure 1). These trials even included triazine-resistant biotypes and whilst the activity of terbuthylazine is limited on these biotypes, a highly surprising synergism is still observed in mixture with mesotrione (Sutton *et al.*, 2002).

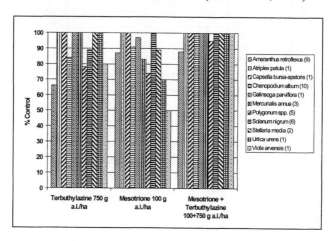

Figure 1.   Contribution of 750 g a.i./ha terbuthylazine to 100 g a.i./ha mesotrione on dicotyledonous weeds, post-emergent application, Europe 2001 (in brackets number of trials)

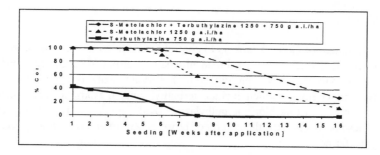

Figure 2.   Contribution of terbuthylazine to the residual grass weed activity of *S*-metolachlor measured by planting *Echinochloa crus-galli* and *Setaria viridis* at intervals after application

When terbuthylazine is used in mixture with chloroacetanilides, it results in improved grass weed activity and increased duration of control (figure 2). Even where *S*-metolachlor is used in combination with mesotrione, terbuthylazine significantly improves its performance on *Echinochloa crus-galli* (figure 3 from Schulte *et al.*, 2002).

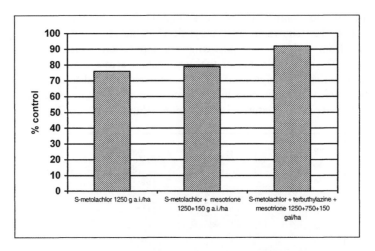

Figure 3.   Contribution of terbuthylazine to the activity of
S-metolachlor + mesotrione on *Echinochloa crus-galli* and *Setaria viridis* (Germany and Austria 2002, 6 trials)

CROP TOLERANCE

Selectivity in maize is one of the outstanding features of terbuthylazine. Studies at many times the registered use rate show excellent tolerance both pre- and post-emergence.

PRACTICAL USE

Due to the requirement of German farmers to control weeds in a one-pass application, usually early post-emergent, herbicides with a broad efficacy spectrum are required which provide enough residual activity to give season-long control. Terbuthylazine is an essential component of key products in Germany which include terbuthylazine, mesotrione and S-metolachlor, terbuthylazine and S-metolachlor, terbuthylazine and pyridate or terbuthylazine and bromoxynil. These products fulfil the criteria of broad-spectrum and season-long weed control demanded by the farmer.

Without terbuthylazine, the early post-emergent one-pass treatment would not be possible in many cases due to gaps in the spectrum of other herbicides or the lack of residual activity. Practical experience in areas of Germany where terbuthylazine use is not permitted has shown that species such a *Galium aparine, Geranium spp., Erodium spp., Viola spp. and Veronica spp.* have become problematic. Further investigations to confirm this by means of accurate data are underway in a comprehensive long-term weed monitoring programme all over the country. Weeds emerging after application are also problematic: due to those herbicides used having none or limited residual activity, applications would have to be delayed until all weeds have emerged, a time, by which significant weed competition will also have reduced the crop yield potential.

WATER QUALITY MONITORING & ELUCIDATION OF GROUNDWATER FINDINGS

In spite of the favourable leaching behaviour of terbuthylazine, in the last years some detections of terbuthylazine in groundwater have been published. In 1997, the LAWA (German working group water) published its latest report on groundwater quality. In 2000 and 2002, UBA (German EPA) reported findings until 1998 and 1999. Syngenta was required to elucidate the causes for these findings.

Table 2. Number of sampling sites analysed for terbuthylazine, and number of detections between 1990 and 1999 as issued by LAWA and UBA

Year	Number of sampling sites	Number of sampling sites with findings > LOQ		Number of sampling sites with findings > 0.1 µg/l	
		Number	Percentage	Number	Percentage
1990 – 1995	10,538	150	1.4	11	0.1
1996	8122	81	1.0	7	0.09
1997	4858	63	1.3	14	0.29
1998	3585	34	0.95	9	0.25
1999	4565	23	0.5	5	0.1

Therefore, a broad programme was started and 30 findings > 0.1 µg/l from 1996 - 2000 had to be clarified. The following causes were identified:

- direct entry into the sampling site (point sources),
- direct entry of drainage and ditch water into area of the sampling site,
- false analyses; contamination of samples,
- discharge of waste, one accident and
- writing mistakes.

It can be concluded that the use of terbuthylazine according to the label and the respective GAPs does not lead to any contamination of the groundwater. In cases where the detection of the a.i. was correct, the sampling site was flawed, i.e. no typical groundwater was sampled. It could be seen that it was either a surface water influenced site or surface water was directly sampled.

From these results it can be seen that terbuthylazine does not have substance-inherent properties leading to a higher leaching potential compared to other compounds. The respective GAPs ensure that residues in groundwater will not exceed the limit of 0.1 µg/l.

PROOF OF EFFICACY OF LABEL RESTRICTIONS

In the environmental fate studies carried out for registration purposes terbuthylazine was shown not to leach to groundwater under "realistic worst case" conditions. The German registration authorities took another pathway into consideration as possible cause for residues in groundwater: transport by run-off to surface water and entering groundwater via river bank filtration. The authorities therefore imposed a corresponding risk mitigation measure: 10 m vegetative buffer zone between maize field and surface water in locations where run-off might occur.

Syngenta started a 6 year monitoring programme with the objective to show that these risk mitigation measures work effectively. The efficacy of the label restriction of a 10 m broad vegetative buffer zone to prevent from an input of terbuthylazine via run-off could be proven by this monitoring. Even after 4 of 6 years, the results of this monitoring clearly demonstrate the safe use of terbuthylazine in maize fields susceptible to run-off adjacent to surface waters by observing the use restriction of a vegetative buffer zone of 10 m. Run-off (water and sediment) could be effectively retained. As a consequence, the width of the tested vegetative buffer zone was reduced to only 5 m beginning this year and will be continued in 2004.

Data show that in the recommended use pattern terbuthylazine is unlikely to leach directly to groundwater. Protecting surface water by vegetative buffer strips also prevents the alternative entry pathway via surface water and bank filtration into groundwater. Therefore, since no terbuthylazine enters the surface water, residues in groundwater above 0.1 µg/l are absolutely not probable.

REFERENCES

LAWA (1997). Bericht zur Grundwasserbeschaffenheit – Pflanzenschutzmittel. Kulturbuchverlag Berlin GmbH.

Schulte M; Rüegg W T; Sutton P B (2002). Synergie von Mesotrione, S-Metolachlor und Terbuthylazin in der Bekämpfungsstrategie von Maisunkräutern. *Zeitschrift für Pflanzenkrankheiten und Pflanzenschutz. Journal of Plant Diseases and Protection*, Sonderheft XVIII, 785-793.

Sutton PB, Richards C, Burren L, Glasgow L (2002). Activity of mesotrione on resistant weeds in maize. Pesticide Management Science **58**, 981-984

UBA (2002). Umweltdaten Deutschland 2002. Umweltbundesamt 31.05.2002. KOMAG Berlin-Brandenburg

Mixed maize and soya bean cropping as an effective fodder production method

L Prijic, G Cvijanovic, M Srebric
Maize Research Institute Zemun Polje, S Bajica 1, 11080 Belgrade-Zemun, SCG
E-mail: lprijic@mrizp.co.yu

D Glamoclija
Faculty of Agriculture, University of Belgrade, 11080 Belgrade-Zemun, SCG

ABSTRACT

The investigation was carried out with two maize hybrids, EPH2 and EPH7, and a soya bean cultivar, Nena, in three locations in Serbia, in 2002. Seed was sown in four-row strips of maize and soya bean, alternately. A combined fertiliser was applied. Data on maize plant height, number of ears per plant, fresh stalk and ear weight and percent dry matter, and soya bean fresh weight, stalk and pod dry matter and green fodder yield are presented in this paper.

INTRODUCTION

High quality home grown cattle feed production in moderate regions on farms with both cattle husbandry and arable crops can be achieved through mixed cropping. Improvement in cattle production in Serbia can be achieved through a better use of fodder and improvement in its quality. This can be done by increasing the proportion of legumes in fodder crop production and by greater usage of silage as conserved fodder for winter feeding (Dinic and Lazarevic 2000). Maize for silage is produced most effectively by means of mixed sowing with soya bean or some other legume. By this means, natural soil fertility is better utilised and a significantly higher yield and forage nutritional value can be obtained more economically. (Dolijanovic, 2002). In a balanced crop ratio in mixed crop production, higher yield components can be obtained, than by growing them separately (Kovacevic and Momirovic, 2000). Growing maize and soya bean in strips has the following advantages: maize obtains more light and produces more ears; soya bean in strips between maize is grown in a humid environment which is more favourable for growth. A higher proportion of maize kernels in silage fodder improves its quality, while soya bean, as a legume, provides proteins. Both maize and soya beans can be harvested together, simplifying silage fodder preparation.

MATERIALS AND METHODS

Mixed maize and soya bean cropping trials were carried out with two experimental maize hybrids, EPH2 and EPH7, and one soya bean cultivar, Nena, in three locations in Serbia: Loznica, Krusevac and Surduk in 2002. Seed obtained from Maize Research Institute Zemun Polje, was sown in 90m four-row strips of maize and soya bean, alternately. Row spacing was 70cm. The investigation included two fertiliser variants - fertilised and control without fertiliser, in three replicates. Maize border and internal row plant data were collected. Ecological Kemira Crop Care fertiliser, applied in this investigation, is very efficient because N, P, K nutrients and micronutrients are in the same granule and are readily available to the plant. The fertiliser was applied pre-sowing at 300 kg ha^{-1}, i.e. 36 kg N, 66 kg P, 24 kg K, on the basis of the soil analyses. Plant height, number of ears per plant ear weight and dry matter percent, fresh stalk weight and dry matter were calculated from 10 maize plant samples. Soya bean fresh above ground weight and stalk and pod dry matter percent were calculated on the basis of 20 soya bean plant samples. Maize and soya bean samples were taken when seeds on plants were in the immature milk stage. Maize and soya bean were harvested together across the rows, and silage fodder yield from 20 m^2 area was measured and expressed in tonnes per hectare, at the Krusevac location. Silage fodder was prepared for fermentation in 50 litre pots for further evaluation.

RESULTS AND DISCUSSION

Maize plant height

Data from the three sites were combined (Table 1). Plants in the internal rows were higher in both hybrids and all three locations, but the differences were not significant. Average maize plant height was 196.8 cm and 208.4 cm in border and internal rows, respectively. The differences between fertilised crop and control were also not significant and furthermore, plants were slightly taller in the control variant.

Number of maize ears per plant

Maize plants in the border rows, being under higher insolation, can produce more ears per plant. By growing maize in strips, the number of border plants is increased and thus grain yield. The results from these experiments confirmed that the average number of maize ears per plant in border rows was significantly higher than in internal rows (Table 1). The addition of fertiliser also significantly increased the number of ears per plant. An increase in the proportion of maize kernels in silage should improve quality.

Maize ears and stalk weight and dry matter per plant

Maize plants in border rows showed significantly higher fresh ear weight compared to internal row plants (Table 1). Higher yield in border rows was expected hence the reason for growing maize in strips. Fresh ear weight per maize plant in the fertilised crop was not significantly higher than the control. Where maize plants produced more than one ear, these were smaller, especially the second and third. This explains that although the difference between the numbers of ears was significant, the fresh ears yield difference between fertilised and the control was not significant. Ear dry matter percentage showed no significant difference between internal and border rows and between fertilised and the control. This indicated that maize in all treatments ripened at the same time. Average maize stalk weight and dry mass did not show significant differences between treatments.

Table 1. Average maize plant height, number of ears per plant/weight and dry matter per plant and stalk weight and dry matter.

	height cm	number	ears weight g	dry matter %	stalk weight g	stalk dry matter %
Border rows	196.8	1.75*	469.6*	60.8	564.6	40.9
Internal rows	208.4	1.47	379.6	62.2	525.8	39.9
Probability	0.2344	0.0006	0.0364	0.5333	0.4560	0.7064
With fertiliser	199.5	1.69*	435.7	60.1	580.1	39.8
Control	205.7	1.53	413.4	62.9	510.3	41.0
Probability	0.7226	0.0029	0.5053	0.4698	0.2807	0.5243

* significant differences at p = <0.05

Soya bean above ground biomass and stalk and pod dry matter

The soya bean data from the three sites were combined (Table 2). Both soya bean above ground biomass and green pod weight were higher in the fertilised crop, compared to the control, but only the above ground biomass differences were significant. Stalk dry matter percent in the fertilised crop was 52.1% and significantly higher than the control (44.7%). This agreed with the above ground data, showing that fertilising favours the vegetative growth of soya bean. The soya bean seed was not inoculated with Rhizobia strains, neither was soya bean previously grown in the fields. Soya bean plants used only soil nitrogen as atmospheric nitrogen fixation did not occur. Although the fertilised soya bean plants were more abundant in growth, they matured at the same time as the control plants, since there was no significant difference in the dry matter of the pods at the time of harvest.

Table 2. Soya bean plant and pods weight and dry matter

	above ground part plant weight (g)	green pods per plant weight (g)	dry matter % stalk	dry matter % pod
With fertiliser	94.70*	38.52	52.1*	39.8
Control	70.62	31.10	44.7	38.2
Probability	0.0190	0.3640	0.0208	0.5868

* significant differences at p = <0.05

Silage yield

The average yields in the mixed maize and soya bean crop from the Krusevac site were 17.281 and 15.367 tonnes per hectare in the fertilised and control variants, respectively (Table 3). The fertilising of the mixed crop contributed to a significant silage yield increase.

Furthermore, the silage dry matter percentage was higher in the fertilised crop, (39.8 %) than in control, (37.6 %). These results confirmed the benefits of the application of ecological fertiliser: i.e. to protect the environment, and to achieve a higher fodder silage yield.

Table 3. Silage yield and dry matter in Krusevac, 2002

	yield (t ha^{-1})	dry matter %
With fertiliser	17.281*	39.8*
Control	15.367	37.6
Probability	0.0035	0.0470

* significant differences at p = <0.05

ACKNOWLEDGEMENTS

Authors thank The Ministry of Science, Technology and Development of Republic of Serbia for financial support and Dr B Dinic, Institute of Forage Crops in Krusevac, for his suggestions and assistance in the trials work.

REFERENCES

Dinic B; Lazarevic D (2000). New technological procedures in conserving and fodder utilisation. *Proceedings of the First Meeting Science, Practice and Business in Agronomy*, V Banja 2002, 133-137.

Dolijanovic Z (2002). Influence of additive way of association and fertilisation on maize and soyabean productivity M.Sc. thesis, Faculty of Agriculture, Belgrade.

Kovacevic D; Momirovic N (2000). Integral weed control systems role in sustainable agriculture concept. *Proceedings of the Weed Congress*, 2000, B Koviljaca, 116-151.

Biological action of some herbicides on teluric microflora development from sugar beet cultivated soil

S Stefan, I Horia, M Oprea, E Bucur, A L Stefan
*Research and Development Institute for Plant Protection, Bd. Ion Ionescu de la Brad 8
Bucharest 71592, Romania*
Email: stefansorin@zappmobile.ro

L Ghinea
Research and Development Agricole Institute Fundulea, Romania

ABSTRACT

Research discussed in this paper, describes the evaluation of the biological action on the development of teluric microflora from sugar-beet cultivated soil of two herbicides from the ciclohexan dione class, clethodim and tepraloxidim. *In vitro*, tepraloxidim and clethodim (0.1 %), weakly inhibited the development of the teluric pathogens *Pythium debaryanum*, *Verticillium dahliae* and *Fusarium oxysporum* and of saprophytic fungi colonies with an antagonistic role, *Trichoderma viride*, *Trichotecium roseum* and *Cladosporium herbarum*. The development of *Sclerotinia sclerotiorum* colonies was inhibited to a larger percent. Herbicides clethodim and tepraloxidim did not negatively influence the development of the soil bacteria, this phenomenon being reflected by the number of colony forming units present in soil compared to the two controls (hoed and un-hoed).

INTRODUCTION

The development of some teluric fungi cultured from sugar beet cultivated soil on water-agar medium, was evaluated in the laboratory to determine the influence of the two ciclohexan dione herbicides, tepraloxidim 200 g/l (Aramo 50) and clethodim 120 g/l (Select Super). Saprophytic fungi *Alternaria*, *Scytalidium*, *Trichocladium*, *Poecylomyces*, *Humicola*, *Ulocladium*, *Mortierella*, *Mucor*, *Ciricinella*, together with saprophytic fungi with an antagonistic action *Cladosporium*, *Cephalosporium*, *Chaetomium* and pathogenic fungi such as *Fusarium*, *Verticillium*, *Stemphylium*, *Botrytis* and *Helminthosporium*, were predominant on sugar-beet cultivated soil. The development of some teluric fungi on water-agar medium was slightly inhibited *in vitro* by tepraloxidim and clethodim (Stefan, 2002).

MATERIALS AND METHODS

Laboratory studies were carried out to observe the effect of tepraloxidim and clethodim on teluric microflora development by using the following concentrations: 0.1; 0.05 and 0.025%. The soil was taken from the field at intervals of 1, 3, 7 and 28 days after treatment with herbicides and plated onto water-agar medium at 1:10 dilutions (Eliade *et al.*, 1975). The observations were made after 10 days of incubation and the number of fungi recorded. The results were compared with soil from an untreated and un-hoed variant from the commercial farm. The first step was observing the development of some teluric fungi on water agar to determine the influence of the two herbicides.

RESULTS AND DISCUSSION

The development of pathogenic fungi: *Verticillium dahliae, Pythium debaryanum, Fusarium oxysporum* was not greatly influenced, the inhibition percent being of 8-12 % for tepraloxidim (0.1 %) and 5-15 % for clethodim (0.1 %). Concentrations of 0.025 % did not inhibit the development of fungus colonies (Table 1). The inhibiting action of the two herbicides (0.1 %) was lower (6-15 %) upon the saprophytic fungi with an antagonistic role: *Trichoderma viride, Trichotecium roseum, Cladosporium herbarum*. The development of *Sclerotinia sclerotiorum* colonies was strongly inhibited by concentrations of 0.1 % for both of the herbicides. The inhibition percent for this concentration was 46 % for tepraloxidim and 37 % for clethodim. The inhibition percent was null (0) for both of the tested products when used at concentrations of 0.025 %. An analysis of the microflora structure of the sugar beet cultivated soil is shown in Tables 2 and 3. This soil was populated with microorganisms including bacteria, actinomycetes, micromycetes and nematodes. Saprophytic fungi: *Alternaria, Scytalidium, Trichocladium, Poecylomyces, Humicola, Ulocladium, Mortierella, Mucor, Ciricinella*, together with saprophytic fungi with antagonistic action *Cladosporium, Cephalosporium, Chaetomium* and pathogenic fungi like *Fusarium, Verticillium, Stemphylium, Botrytis, Helminthosporium* were predominant.

The number of colonies per 1 g of soil was higher in the un-hoed variant both at 0-10 cm deep and at10-20 cm deep. The number of colonies at the depth of 10-20 cm reached 482-490 colonies/g of soil.

For the hoed variant, the highest number of colonies was 335-370 at 0-10 cm deep. After hoeing the number of colonies/g of soil was higher at the depth of 0-10 cm than the un-hoed variant, where the most micromycetes colonies were found in the 10-20 cm layer.

When applied to the sugar-beet culture clethodim at 2 litres/ha resulted in a quality increase of the microfloral components (Table 4).

Table 1. Biological action of tepraloxidim and clethodim herbicides on teluric microflora development

| Fungus | Inhibition % of fungus colonies | | | | | |
| | Tepraloxidim concentration % | | | clethodim concentration % | | |
	0.1	0.05	0.025	0.1	0.05	0.025
Pythium debaryanum	10	6	0	15	9	9
Verticillium dahliae	8	2	0	5	2	0
Fusarium oxysporum	15	8	0	12	6	0
Trichoderma viride	10	5	0	10	4	0
Trichotecium roseum	12	7	0	11	5	0
Cladosporium herbarum	6	2	0	11	5	0
Sclerotinia sclerotiorum	46	12	0	37	10	0

The number of micromycetes genera increased comparing to the untreated, un-hoed control. Pathogenic and saprophytic teluric fungi, with an antagonistic role, were observed. The number of fungi, bacteria and actinomycetes/g of soil did not decrease. There were no differences between the first day and the 28th day after the application of the herbicide

Table 2. Teluric microflora on soils cultivated with sugar beet - un-hoed

| Microorganisms | Number colonies after n days, at the depth of d cm | | | | | | | |
| | (1st day) | | (3 days) | | (7 days) | | (28 days) | |
	0-10	10-20	0-10	10-20	0-10	10-20	0-10	10-20
Bispora	0	0	0	34	52	0	0	0
Alternaria	52	42	54	48	37	28	29	23
Cladosporium	14	39	47	59	48	41	17	23
Fusarium	12	34	23	47	29	22	25	54
Verticillium	0	0	0	24	29	29	45	0
Aleuria	0	0	0	29	23	0	0	0
Cephalosporium	12	0	21	0	0	0	0	25
Scytalidium	0	23	0	27	09	32	0	38
Acromoniella	22	32	21	0	0	0	23	0
Stemphylium	0	28	0	21	0	37	0	49
Trichocladium	0	0	0	0	14	36	0	0
Chaetomium	32	0	35	0	0	0	45	0
Paecylomyces	12	0	15	0	0	0	0	0
Mortierella	0	19	0	15	0	25	23	45
Mucor	24	32	0	25	0	36	0	23
Humicola	25	19	27	36	25	46	25	42
Botrytis	0	0	0	0	0	0	24	12
Scopulariopsis	24	0	0	25	0	16	0	25
Circinella	0	29	0	29	0	12	0	36
Arthrobotrys	0	14	0	15	0	10	12	0
Bacteria	54	63	49	41	29	34	45	48
Actinomycetes	32	29	27	24	31	28	23	39
Nematodes	0	+	0	+	0	+	+	0
TOTAL COLONIES	239	249	289	479	309	482	313	490

Tepraloxidim (1.5 %) had a stronger inhibiting action (Table 5). The total number of colonies decreased after the first day, but after 28 days the number of colonies almost doubled but did not exceed the number of colonies in the clethodim treated variant (2 l/ha).

The bacteria and actinomycetes could be observed beginning with the first day after treatment and ending with the 28th day. Especially in the 0-10 cm layer a decrease in quantity could be noticed after the first day of treatment applications. After 28 days, the number of microorganisms was almost equal in both of the layers (0-10 cm and 10-20 cm).

The influence of tepraloxidim 1.5 litres/ha (Table 5) determined a decrease in the micromycetes genera in the soil, but a quantity increase of fungi, bacteria and actinomycetes in both the layers (0-10 cm and 10-20 cm).

Table 3. The teluric microflora on soils cultivated with sugar beet - hoed

| Microorganisms | Number of colonies after n days, at the depth d cm | | | | | | | |
| | (1st day) | | (3 days) | | (7 days) | | (28 days) | |
	0-10	10-20	0-10	10-20	0-10	10-20	0-10	10-20
Helminthosporium	0	0	47	0	39	0	0	0
Alternaria	36	0	42	0	0	42	0	56
Cladosporium	0	0	0	0	42	25	0	0
Fusarium	36	38	0	24	49	47	0	36
Verticillium	0	0	0	0	54	0	0	0
Aspergillus	0	0	0	0	24	0	0	0
Cephalosporium	0	0	0	0	0	0	32	0
Scytalidium	0	0	42	24	0	0	12	10
Trichocladium	0	0	0	0	18	0	0	0
Stemphylium	14	22	13	0	25	19	12	10
Sepedonium	0	0	0	0	0	0	28	12
Chaetomium	0	0	0	0	0	0	47	10
Paecylomyces	11	27	0	0	0	0	12	10
Mortierella	16	11	24	12	0	0	25	12
Mucor	23	18	29	32	0	0	0	0
Humicola	0	0	0	24	19	14	0	0
Ulocladium	32	0	27	0	0	0	24	0
Circinella	0	0	0	22	0	0	32	0
Scopulariopsis	0	14	23	28	27	0	14	0
Oidiodenron	0	0	24	0	17	0	0	0
Bacteria	32	30	37	38	35	36	35	35
Actinomycetes	26	24	27	32	21	22	24	20
Nematodes	+	0	0	0	0	0	0	0
TOTAL COLONIES	226	184	335	236	370	205	297	215

Table 4. The influence of clethodim 0.2 % on teluric microorganisms development from sugar beet - cultivated soil

| Microorganisms | Number of colonies after n days, at the depth of d cm | | | | | | | |
| | (1st day) | | (3 days) | | (7 days) | | (28 days) | |
	0-10	10-20	0-10	10-20	0-10	10-20	0-10	10-20
Alternaria	48	47	43	39	49	31	44	40
Cladosporium	56	23	49	27	39	23	41	25
Fusarium	54	32	49	31	44	21	51	22
Verticillium	0	24	0	32	0	19	0	21
Scytalidium	15	0	12	0	0	0	0	12
Phythophthora	0	0	13	0	11	0	0	0
Scopulariopsis	0	0	0	0	10	0	19	0
Penicillium	0	0	0	0	0	0	22	12
Cephalosporium	14	17	0	0	9	21	10	16
Oidiodenron	0	17	0	14	0	0	0	0
Radiomyces	0	0	6	0	0	0	0	0
Botrytis	24	0	0	0	0	0	0	0
Paecylomyces	15	0	0	0	0	0	19	0
Periconia	0	0	0	0	0	0	0	29
Helminthosporium	0	0	17	0	12	0	9	0
Humicola	0	0	21	15	17	0	0	0
Bispora	24	0	0	0	0	0	0	0
Rhodotorula	0	24	0	0	0	0	0	18
Cryptoccochus	0	0	0	9	7	18	0	0
Trichophyton	0	0	0	0	17	0	0	0
Gonatobotrys	0	0	0	0	0	0	0	23
Aspergillus	0	0	14	0	11	0	14	0
Gymnoascus	0	0	14	0	0	0	0	0
Monodisctis	0	0	0	0	0	0	0	18
Mucor	0	0	25	18	0	0	20	18
Cunningamella	21	0	12	0	0	0	0	0
Mortierella	9	12	10	0	0	0	0	0
Rhizopus	10	0	0	10	0	10	0	0
Trichoderma	20	0	10	0	15	0	10	0
Bacteria	46	50	52	39	48	37	50	49
Actinomycetes	39	37	42	38	47	35	48	41
Nematodes	0	0	+	+	+	+	+	+
TOTAL COLONIES	379	273	389	270	312	215	331	351

Table 5. Influence of tepraloxidim 1.5 % on teluric microorganisms development from sugar beet - cultivated soil

Microorganisms	Number of colonies after n days, at the depth of d cm							
	(1st day)		(3 days)		(7 days)		(28 days)	
	0-10	10-20	0-10	10-20	0-10	10-20	0-10	10-20
Helminthosporium	0	0	0	24	19	0	0	0
Alternaria	11	24	28	24	21	28	20	10
Cladosporium	0	0	0	24	0	32	12	0
Fusarium	0	24	0	12	0	14	0	28
Verticilium	0	10	0	8	0	7	0	10
Scytalidium	32	38	0	0	0	0	35	31
Acremoniella	0	19	0	22	0	0	12	20
Stemphylium	0	21	0	0	0	0	10	23
Penicillium	16	0	14	0	0	0	22	26
Hormiactis	12	0	0	0	0	0	0	0
Paecylomyces	18	0	0	0	0	0	0	0
Mortierella	14	19	12	21	5	8	12	10
Mucor	17	21	0	0	0	0	24	28
Humicola	12	0	22	0	21	0	12	0
Ulocladium	0	0	12	0	23	22	21	20
Bacteria	25	28	21	20	25	20	29	22
Actinomycete	0	22	24	23	10	22	18	27
Nematodes	+	0	0	0	0	0	0	0
TOTAL COLONIES	157	226	133	186	124	145	227	246

CONCLUSIONS

In vitro, tepraloxidim and clethodim (0.1%) weakly inhibited the development of teluric pathogens, *Pythium debaryanum, Verticillium dahliae* and *Fusarium oxisporum* and of the saprophytic fungi colonies with an antagonistic role: *Trichoderma viride, Trichotecium roseum* and *Cladosporium herbarum*. The development of *Sclerotinia sclerotiorum* colonies was also inhibited to a larger percent. The fungi were predominant from the quality and quantity point of view, being represented by species of *Mucorales, Hyphales (Deuteromycetes)*, from the following families: *Moniliaceae, Dematiaceae, Tuberculariaceae*.

The presence of clethodim applied at 2 litres/ha in both soils from sugar beet, gave an increase in the number of the microorganism colonies and the microflora was richer in species compared to the untreated and un-hoed variant. Tepraloxidim, when applied to sugar beet soils produced a stronger effect in decreasing the number of colonies during the first days, which partially repaired after 28 days. The microfloral structure was poorer in species.

REFERENCES

Eliade G H; Ghinea L; Stefanic G H (1975). *Soil microbiology* Ed. Ceres; Bucharest.
Stefan S (2002). Relationships between ciclohexan-dionic herbicides and soil micropopulation. Doctoral thesis, 99-106, Timisoara University.

Influence of calcium ion on the efficacy of selected herbicides

C Gauvrit

UMR Biologie et Gestion des Adventices, INRA BP 86510, F-21065 DIJON Cedex, France
Email : gauvrit@dijon.inra.fr

ABSTRACT

200 ppm $CaCl_2$ had no influence on the efficacy of clethodim and cycloxydim on barley, of flupyrsulfuron-methyl on ryegrass and of metsulfuron-methyl on rapeseed. Bentazone efficacy on rapeseed was increased. $CaCl_2$ may affect glufosinate efficay on barley but anionic surfactants present in the formulation seem to counteract calcium antagonism.

INTRODUCTION

Several herbicides have been reported to be less efficacious in the presence of calcium ion, and some advisers to farmers tend to consider that this can be generalized to all herbicides (Pilche, 2003). Glyphosate is the most often cited and the best documented (Sandberg *et al.*, 1978 ; Nalewaja & Matysiak, 1993b). Acifluorfen, bentazone, dicamba and nicosulfuron were also affected by calcium (Nalewaja & Matysiak, 1993a ; Nalewaja *et al.*, 1995). However, the calcium concentrations used in these experiments were rather high (20 mM). A survey made in France showed that farmers rarely use water with calcium concentration higher than 5 mM (= 200 ppm) ; it was indeed most of the time around 2.5 mM (Blondlot *et al.*, 1999). We examined the influence of calcium at these moderate concentrations, on the efficacy of herbicides bearing a negative charge when dissolved in water. The following herbicides (pKa) were chosen : bentazone (3.3), clethodim (3.1), cycloxydim (4.2), flupyrsulfuron-methyl (4.9), glufosinate (<2 and 2.9), metsulfuron-methyl (3.3). In some experiments, the influence of magnesium ion was also studied.

MATERIALS AND METHODS

Chemicals

The origin of the chemicals were : bentazone (Basagran SG, 87%) and cycloxydim (Stratos Ultra, 100 g litre^{-1}), BASF ; clethodim (Centurion 240EC, 240 g litre^{-1}), Sipcam Phyteurop ; flupyrsulfuron-methyl (Lexus, 50 %) and metsulfuron-methyl (Allié, 20 %), DuPont de Nemours ; glufosinate (Basta F$_1$, 150 g litre^{-1} and Liberty, 200 g litre^{-1}, abbreviated as Formulations A and B, respectively), ethoxylated fatty acid sulphate (FAEOS) and glyphosate acid, Aventis ; ethoxylated nonylphenol (Agral 90, abbreviated as NPE), Syngenta. Trend 90 (ethoxylated alcohol, DuPont de Nemours) was present (0.2 %) when metsulfuron-methyl was applied on rapeseed. Glyphosate isopropylamine salt was prepared by neutralizing a 400 ml litre^{-1} isopropylamine solution with glyphosate. Glyphosate was then formulated with NPE as surfactant (glyphosate + NPE, 2 + 1, *m/m*).

Bio-assays

Barley (cv. Plaisant), ryegrass (cv. EF486) and rapeseed (cv. Lirajet) were grown under controlled conditions (17/12 °C, 60/80 % relative humidity, light/dark, fluorescent lamps delivering 220 µmole photon m^{-2} s^{-1} PAR during a 16-h photoperiod). Plants (ten per pot) were treated at the two-leaf stage using an indoor track sprayer with a movable boom equipped with two flat-fan 11004 nozzles. It delivered 200 litre/ha at 300 kPa. Three replicates were used for the treated plants and six for the control group. Treated plants and controls were randomized in the growth chamber. All plants were harvested 14 d after treatment. An observation corresponded to the dry biomass of ten plants per pot. The results were analyzed using non-linear regression. After variance stabilization all the observed data were simultaneously fitted using the log-logistic model :

$$W_{ij} = C + \frac{D-C}{1+\left(\dfrac{x_{ij}}{ED_{50_i}}\right)^{b_i}} \qquad [1]$$

where W_{ij} denotes the dry matter at the jth dose of glyphosate in treatment i ; D and C denote the upper and lower limits of dry matter at zero and at very large doses of glyphosate ; ED_{50i} denotes the dose of herbicide required to reduce dry matter by 50 between the upper and lower limits in treatment i ; and b_i is proportional to the slope of the curve around ED_{50i}. Lack-of-fit F-tests at the 0.05 % level of significance indicated that in all experiments presented the model was acceptable. F-tests were also used to compare parameters ; common b or common b and ED_{50} values indicated paralellism or similarity of the response curves, respectively.

RESULTS AND DISCUSSION

Bentazone

The influence of two calcium concentrations (5 and 10 mM) was studied. In both cases the response curves obtained with or without calcium were parallel (P = 0.48 and 0.54, respectively). $CaCl_2$ significantly decreased ED_{50} values (Table 1, Figure 1), indicating an increase in bentazone efficacy ; 36 to 38 % less bentazone allowed to obtain the same ED_{50} level. These experiments were repeated and gave similar results (not shown).

Table 1. Estimated parameters (SE) for the response curves of rapeseed plants treated with bentazone.

Treatment	C (mg)	D (mg)	b	ED_{50} (g ha^{-1})
Bentazone	702 (27)	4768 (220)	1.9 (0.16)	207 (17.9)
Bentazone + 5 mM Ca^{2+}	idem	idem	idem	128 (11.9)
Bentazone	457 (13)	3328 (59)	2.9 (0.23)	130 (5.7)
Bentazone + 10 mM Ca^{2+}	idem	idem	idem	83 (4.1)

These observations contradict the view that the influence of calcium ion on herbicide efficacy can only be negative (Pilche, 2003). They are also at deviance with Nalewaja & Matysiak (1993a), who found a decrease in bentazone efficacy against *Kochia scoparia* in the presence of Ca^{2+}. Apart from the differences between plant species, bentazone formulations and calcium concentrations, we have no other explanation to offer for this disagreement.

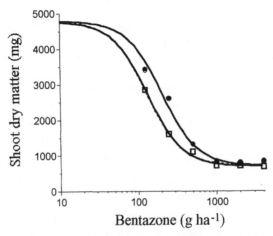

Figure 1. Observed means (symbols) and fitted curves (lines) of rapeseed plants treated with bentazone. ● , no calcium ; ❑ , 5 mM Ca^{2+}.

Cyclohexanediones and sulfonylureas

The response curves of barley to clethodim applied alone or in the presence of 5 mM $CaCl_2$ were similar ($P = 0.14$) with ED_{50} (SE) = 23.2 (1.47) g ha^{-1}. The same was observed with cycloxydim ($P = 0.65$, ED_{50} (SE) = 0.4 (0.03) g ha^{-1}). Hence, no influence of 5 mM calcium was found , in agreement with field experiments on the same species (Blondlot *et al.*, 1999).

The response curves of rapeseed to metsulfuron-methyl applied alone or in the presence of 5 mM $CaCl_2$ or $MgCl_2$ were similar ($P = 0.48$) with ED_{50} (SE) = 0.74 (0.06) g ha^{-1}. The same was true of ryegrass treated with flupyrsulfuron-methyl in the presence or not of 5 mM $CaCl_2$ ($P = 0.31$, ED_{50} (SE) = 32.7 (3.53) g ha^{-1}). These experiments were repeated with similar results (not shown). Hence, no influence of 5 mM calcium was detected on the efficacy of metsulfuron-methyl and of flupyrsulfuron-methyl. The effect of calcium ion on the efficacy of sulfonylureas herbicides has received little attention. To our knowledge, no data have been published concerning metsulfuron-methyl and flupyrsulfuron-methyl. Nicosulfuron was studied in the presence of 40 mM calcium. A 20 % decrease in efficacy against *Digitaria sanguinalis* was observed when calcium was brought as a nitrate or a chloride (Nalewaja *et al.*, 1995). However, no clear-cut effect was detected with calcium carbonate, phosphate or sulphate. As between this study and ours there are differences in herbicides, calcium concentrations and plant species, it is difficult to compare them further.

Glufosinate

The response curves of barley to glufosinate applied alone or in the presence of 5 mM $MgCl_2$ were similar (Table 2 ; $P = 0.07$ and 0.16 for formulations A and B, respectively). However, erratic results were obtained with $CaCl_2$, of which Table 2 shows typical examples. $CaCl_2$ could decrease the efficacy of formulation A but also increase it ; it could be without effect on formulation B in some cases but decrease its efficacy in others (Table 2).

Table 2. Estimated parameters (SE) for the response curves of barley plants treated with glufosinate. $[Ca^{2+}] = 5$ mM, $[Mg^{2+}] = 5$ mM.

Treatment	C (mg)	D (mg)	b	ED_{50} (g ha^{-1})
Formulation A	475 (10.7)	1608 (19.6)	2.4 (0.13)	246 (15.5)
Formulation A + Ca^{2+}	idem	idem	idem	191 (11.7)
Formulation A	354 (11.1)	1332 (24.9)	2.6 (0.24)	297 (10.0)
Formulation A + Mg^{2+}	idem	idem	idem	idem
Formulation B	231 (fixed)	1098 (13.8)	2.3 (0.12)	594 (10.7)
Formulation B + Ca^{2+}	idem	idem	idem	idem
Formulation B	495 (18.7)	1542 (26.2)	3.1 (0.36)	285 (14.6)
Formulation B + Ca^{2+}	idem	idem	idem	448 (38)
Formulation B	253 (27.1)	1361 (31.3)	1.5 (0.12)	367 (17.5)
Formulation B + Mg^{2+}	idem	idem	idem	idem

This was at deviance with field assays, that showed a decrease in glufosinate efficacy (Blondot et al., 1999). However, higher calcium and magnesium concentrations were used and these trials also showed unexpected variability (P. Boyer, personal communication). These observations led us to suspect an interaction between calcium and a formulant of glufosinate. Indeed, glufosinate formulations contain an anionic surfactant of the FAEOS type (Köcher & Kocur, 1995), which bears a sulphate moeity. In the case of glyphosate, the protective action of ammonium sulphate against calcium is thought to result from the low water solubility of calcium sulphate, allowing it to precipitate before calcium-glyphosate during droplet drying (Nalewaja & Matysiak 1993c). A similar mechanism may operate with a sulphated surfactant. To detect an interaction between FAEOS and Ca^{2+}, we used a herbicide well known for its sensitivity to Ca^{2+}, namely glyphosate (Sandberg et al., 1978). Experiments with a commercial glyphosate formulation (Roundup, Monsanto) failed because of strong antagonism from FAEOS (not shown). It was presumably due to the presence of a cationic surfactant in the glyphosate formulation (Franz et al., 1997).

To avoid such interaction, we formulated the isopropylamine salt of glyphosate with a non-ionic surfactant, namely NPE. Under these conditions, glyphosate efficacy was expectedly diminished by $CaCl_2$, as shown in Table 3. In the absence of $CaCl_2$, FAEOS decreased glyphosate efficacy. However, in the presence of $CaCl_2$, FAEOS overcame the antagonistic effects of calcium on glyphosate activity, to bring it back to the level observed in the presence of FAEOS alone (Table 3).

Table 3. Estimated parameters (SE) for the response curves of barley plants treated with glyphosate + NPE (2 + 1, *m/m*). $[Ca^{2+}] = 5$ mM, [FAEOS] = 0.6 %.

Treatment	C (mg)	D (mg)	b	ED_{50} (g ha^{-1})
Glyphosate	413 (16.5)	1632 (21.0)	1.5 (0.12)	228 (12.3)
Glyphosate + Ca^{2+}	idem	idem	2.7 (0.22)	501 (16.7)
Glyphosate + FAEOS	idem	idem	1.6 (0.11)	331 (15.4)
Glyphosate + FAEOS + Ca^{2+}	idem	idem	1.5 (0.12)	360 (18.7)

The response curves "Glyphosate", "Glyphosate + FAEOS" and "Glyphosate + FAEOS + Ca^{2+}" accepted a common b value (1.6±0.17) (P=0.94) and could thus be considered as parallel. Moreover, the response curves "Glyphosate + FAEOS" and "Glyphosate + FAEOS + Ca^{2+}" accepted a comm on ED_{50} value (343±13.2 g ha^{-1}) (P=0.34) and were therefore similar. The resulting fitted curves are shown in Figure 2. It can thus be hypothesized that anionic surfactants present in glufosinate formulations (Köcher & Kocur, 1995) prevent Ca^{2+} from antagonizing glufosinate.

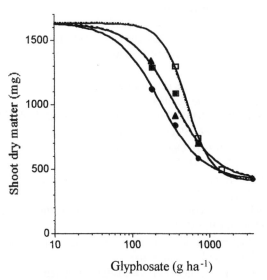

Figure 2. Observed means (symbols) and fitted curves (lines) of barley plants treated with glyphosate in the presence of various additions. ● , None ; ❑ , 5 mM Ca^{2+} ; ▲ , FAEOS ; ■ , 200 ppm Ca^{2+} + FAEOS.

CONCLUSION

These results show that at moderate calcium concentration (5 mM) in the spray water, the antagonism observed in the case of glyphosate (Gauvrit *et al.*, 2001) cannot be generalized to all other herbicides. Indeed, field experiments failed to detect any influence of 5 mM calcium on the efficacy of clopyralid, clodinafop-propargyl, diclofop-methyl, fenoxaprop-ethyl, quizalofop-ethyl and isoproturon (Blondlot *et al.*, 1999). This study also indicates that observations made under conditions of high water hardness should not be indiscriminately generalized to situations where spray water has a moderate hardness.

AKNOWLEDGEMENTS
The expert technical assistance of J-C Gaudry is gratefully aknowledged.

REFERENCES

Blondlot A; Bouclet G; Boyer P; Citron G; Davies K; Desroches B; Gaudry J.-C; Gauvrit C; Lucotte T; Pressoir A; Sauvage E; Terrier J (1999). Dureté de l'eau et efficacité herbicide. *Perspectives Agricoles* **251**, 60-66.

Franz J E; Mao M K; Sikorski J A (1997). General properties of glyphosate and glyphosate salts. In: *Glyphosate : a unique and global herbicide*, eds J E Franz, M K Mao & J A Sikorski, p. 192. American Chemical Society: Washington DC, USA.

Gauvrit C; Gaudry J-C; Lucotte T; Cabanne F (2001). Biological evidences for a 1:1-Ca^{2+}:glyphosate association in deposit residuals on the leaf surface of barley. *Weed Research* **41**, 433-445.

Köcher H; Kocur J; 1995. Influence of wetting agents on the foliar uptake and herbicidal activity of glufosinate. *Pesticide Science* **37**, 155-158.

Nalewaja J D; Matysiak R (1993a). Spray carrier salts affect herbicide toxicity to Kochia (*Kochia scoparia*). *Weed Technology* **7**, 154-158.

Nalewaja J D; Matysiak R (1993b). Optimizing adjuvants to overcome glyphosate antagonistic salts. *Weed Technology* **7**, 337-342.

Nalewaja J D; Matysiak R (1993c). Influence of diammonium sulfate and other salts on glyphosate phytotoxicity. *Pesticide Science* **38**, 77-84.

Nalewaja J D; Praczyk T; Matysiak R (1995). Salts and surfactants influence nicosulfuron activity. *Weed Technology* **9**, 587-593.

Pilche P (2003). La réduction des doses d'emploi des produits phytosanitaires. L'eau adoucie. pilche@oreka.com.http://agril.virtualave.net.

Sandberg C L ; Meggitt W F ; Penner D (1978). Effect of diluent volume and calcium on glyphosate phytotoxicity. *Weed Science* **26**, 476-479.

The effects of fungicides on grain water and dry matter contents during maturation of winter wheat

S Pepler, M J Gooding, R H Ellis
Department of Agriculture, The University of Reading, Earley Gate, PO Box 237, Reading, RG6 6AR, UK
Email: s.pepler@reading.ac.uk

ABSTRACT

Two field experiments were carried out comparing a range of fungicide treatments. Medial and apical grains were repeatedly extracted from 10 ears per plot during grain maturation. Grain dry weight and moisture content were determined, modelled using a 'broken stick' method and parameters of the models compared. Fungicide increased final grain weight and duration of grain filling. In medial grains maximum water content during the linear phase of grain filling with dry matter was highly correlated with maximum grain weight (g dm), whereas, in apical grains maximum grain weight was correlated with water content at the end of grain filling with dry matter.

INTRODUCTION

Final mean grain weight is an important determinant of yield. Fungicide applications at and after flag leaf emergence maintain wheat yields and grain weights. These effects have been associated with an extension in the life of the canopy, particularly the flag leaf (Gooding *et al.*, 2000). However, Dimmock and Gooding (2002) reported that such applications can sometimes increase the green area duration of the flag leaf without having a large effect on yield. Brocklehurst (1977) found that final grain weight is related to endosperm cell number, which increases until about 2 weeks after anthesis. This coincides with a period of net water deposition into the grain (Nicolas *et al.*, 1985). This raises the question of whether the extension of flag leaf life is relevant if the effect on the canopy is after the period of net water deposition. By applying a range of fungicide treatments to produce a range of green flag leaf area durations this experiment aims to determine when and how fungicides affect water content and final weight of wheat grains.

MATERIALS AND METHODS

Two field experiments were grown at the Crops Research Unit, The University of Reading, UK (51°29'N, 0°56'W). Experiment 1 was sown on 17th October and Experiment 2 on 19th November 2001. Both experiments were sown with cultivar Malacca in 4 randomised blocks.

Table 1. Fungicide treatments (g a.i./ha)

Treatment	GS 31	GS 39	GS 59	GS 67
	Epoxiconazole	Epoxiconazole/ Azoxystrobin	Epoxiconazole	Azoxystrobin
1	0	0/0	0	0
2	63	0/0	0	0
3	63	63/125	0	0
4	63	63/125	125	0
5	63	63/125	125	125

Five fungicide treatments were each applied to 10 x 2m plots (Table 1). All other fertiliser and pesticide applications were as per standard agronomic practice. Ten ears per plot were removed weekly from 13th June in Experiment 1 and 25th June in Experiment 2. One medial and one apical grain were extracted from each of the ears – the medial grain from the basal floret in the fourth spikelet from the base of one side of the ear, and the apical grain from the basal floret from the penultimate spikelet. The moisture contents and dry weights were then determined gravimetrically after drying at 80°C for a minimum of 48 h. 'Broken stick' models were applied to the grain filling and water content data (Figure 1 a & b) plotted against thermal time (base temperature = 0°C). The thermal time to m_2 was fitted simultaneously for both the grain filling and water content models as results from Schnyder and Baum (1992) and Sofield *et al.* (1977) suggested that the start of rapid net water loss coincided with the end of grain filling. Correlation analyses were then performed on the model parameters. Experiments 1 and 2 were combine harvested on 14th and 20th August, respectively.

RESULTS AND DISCUSSION

Fungicides caused a significant (P<0.001) increase in final grain weight (*maxgf*) in the medial and apical grains in both experiments. The largest increases were between treatments 1 and 2 and 2 and 3, with no significant differences being found between treatments 3, 4 and 5.

Table 2. Effect of fungicide treatment on model parameters (for explanation of parameters, see Figure 1)

	Treatment	*maxgf* (g)	*bgf* (g °C day^{-1})	m_1 (°C day)	m_2 (°C day)	wm_1 (g)	wm_2 (g)
Experiment 1							
Medial grains	1	0.0405	0.000079	315	608	0.0392	0.0329
	2	0.0454	0.000088	337	631	0.0417	0.0356
	3	0.0531	0.000083	388	744	0.0434	0.0339
	4	0.0542	0.000078	351	788	0.0425	0.0323
	5	0.0539	0.000089	351	720	0.0423	0.0381
	SED	0.00126	0.0000059	32.1	36.2	0.00196	0.00328
Apical grains	1	0.0297	0.000065	329	584	0.0282	0.0229
	2	0.0344	0.000059	351	651	0.0308	0.0226
	3	0.0406	0.000069	355	708	0.0309	0.0261
	4	0.0419	0.000052	359	732	0.0308	0.0270
	5	0.0396	0.000074	352	671	0.0301	0.0273
	SED	0.00150	0.0000011	12.1	30.7	0.00131	0.00281
Experiment 2							
Medial grains	1	0.0484	0.000086	360	722	0.0404	0.0397
	2	0.0510	0.000083	366	727	0.0423	0.0409
	3	0.0570	0.000089	429	798	0.0489	0.0390
	4	0.0568	0.000080	380	766	0.0441	0.0466
	5	0.0582	0.000088	452	781	0.0466	0.0411
	SED	0.00183	0.0000039	44.4	27.7	0.00190	0.00210
Apical grains	1	0.0358	0.000062	394	696	0.0306	0.0257
	2	0.0380	0.000068	370	693	0.0308	0.0295
	3	0.0407	0.000074	387	702	0.0307	0.0315
	4	0.0412	0.000069	412	723	0.0326	0.0291
	5	0.0422	0.000077	398	708	0.0300	0.0314
	SED	0.00180	0.0000032	79.3	31.1	0.00279	0.00211

Figure 1c shows the difference in *maxgf* between treatments 1 and 5 in the medial grains of Experiment 1, where the increase in weight was 0.013g (SED = 0.0013). The increase in *maxgf* can be seen to have come from a significant (P<0.01) increase in duration (m_2) of grain filling. There was no effect of rate (*bgf*).

In the medial grains, *maxgf* was highly correlated (P<0.05) with wm_1 in both experiments (Table 3). This suggests that the weight of medial grains may be determined early in grain development, i.e. medial grains may be sink limited and fungicides may be affecting sink size. This is consistent with results above showing later fungicides have little effect on final grain weight and also with work showing that environmental treatments imposed early on in grain filling have had a greater effect on grain filling than those applied later (Gooding *et al.*, 2002).

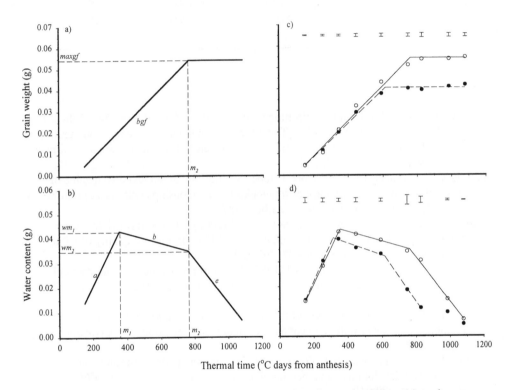

Figure 1. The 'broken stick' models used to describe grain filling (a) and water content changes (b) where *bgf* is rate of grain filling, *maxgf* is maximum grain weight, m_1 is time to 1st break in water content model, m_2 is both the break in the grain filling model and 2nd break in the water content model, wm_1 and wm_2 are water contents at m_1 and m_2 respectively, and *a*, *b*, and *e* are rates of water content increase and decline. Figures 1c) and 1d) show the models fitted to the grain filling and water content results for treatments 1 and 5 in the medial grains of Experiment 1.

Unlike the medial grains, in the apical grains there was no significant correlation between wm_1 and *maxgf*, but a significant correlation between wm_2 and *maxgf* in both experiments (Table 3). This suggests that the final weight of these grains may not be determined until late in grain filling, i.e. these grains could possibly be source limited.

Although there is a possible association between endosperm cell numbers and final grain weight due to the correlation between wm_1 and $maxgf$ this cannot be confirmed as endosperm cell numbers have not been measured in this experiment. However, work is ongoing to measure endosperm cell numbers in grains from different fungicide treatments.

Table 3. Correlation coefficients (df= 3) between maximum grain weight ($maxgf$) and water contents at m_1 and m_2 (wm_1 and wm_2) in the medial and apical grains of Experiment 1 and 2.

			wm_1	wm_2
$maxgf$	Experiment 1	Medial grains	0.89	0.76
		Apical grains	0.51	0.92
	Experiment 2	Medial grains	0.86	0.15
		Apical grains	-0.24	0.94

REFERENCES

Brocklehurst P A (1977). Factors controlling grain weight in wheat. *Nature* **266**, 348-349.

Dimmock J P R E; Gooding M J (2002). The effects of fungicides on the rate and duration of grain filling in winter wheat in relation to maintenance of flag leaf green area. *Journal of Agricultural Science* **138**, 1-16.

Gooding M J; Dimmock J P R E; France J; Jones S A (2000). Green leaf area decline of wheat flag leaves: the influence of fungicides and relationships with mean grain weight and yield. *Annals of Applied Biology* **136**, 77-87.

Gooding M J; Ellis R H; Shewry P R; Schofield, J D (2002). Effects of restricted water availability and increased temperature on grain filling, drying and quality of winter wheat. *Journal of Cereal Science* **37**, 295-309.

Nicolas M E; Gleadow R M; Dalling M J (1985). Effect of post-anthesis drought on cell division and starch accumulation in developing wheat grains. *Annals of Botany* **55**, 433-444.

Schnyder H; Baum U (1992). Growth of the grain of wheat (*Triticum aestivum L.*). The relationship between water content and dry matter accumulation. *European Journal of Agronomy* **1**, 51-57.

Sofield I; Wardlaw I F; Evans L T; Zee S Y (1977). Nitrogen, phosphorus and water contents during grain development and maturation in wheat. *Australian Journal of Plant Physiology* **4**, 799-810.

Optimising the benefits of fluquinconazole seed treatment in sequences of winter wheat crops

G L Bateman, J F Jenkyn, R J Gutteridge
Rothamsted Research, Harpenden, Hertfordshire, AL5 2JQ, UK
Email: geoff.bateman@bbsrc.ac.uk

ABSTRACT

A series of field experiments, each with a minimum of five consecutively grown crops of winter wheat, was used to study responses to fluquinconazole seed treatment applied at different stages in the development of take-all epidemics, including take-all decline. The results form the basis of recommendations for using fluquinconazole seed treatment for managing take-all in sequences of wheat crops.

INTRODUCTION

Take-all epidemics, caused by the root-infecting fungus *Gaeumannomyces graminis* var. *tritici*, develop characteristically from year to year in sequences of susceptible cereals. Typically, the disease increases to a peak of severity over 2-4 years before becoming less severe as a consequence of take-all decline, a form of natural biological control. A well-managed first cereal (typically wheat) has almost no take-all but, in present circumstances, many arable rotations include at least two cereal crops grown in succession. Until relatively recently, the most severe take-all usually occurred in third or fourth cereals. However, severe take-all has now become more frequent in second wheat crops. Seed treatment for take-all control can potentially contribute to the economic viability of growing successive wheat crops, but treatment currently increases the cost of seed by up to about 40%. This represents a significant extra cost with wheat grain at its present low price. It is therefore necessary to determine which crops in a sequence should be treated to ensure the best economic return from the whole sequence.

MATERIALS AND METHODS

Five field experiments tested the effects of fluquinconazole seed treatment (Jockey F), applied at 75 g a.i./100 kg seed, in sequences of winter wheat crops, cv. Hereward (except 1997, see below). The seed was treated using a small-scale Rotostat. Three of the experiments were on silty clay loam with flints at Rothamsted Experimental Farm; the others were on sandy loam in north Norfolk (East Winch) and on limestone brash in Cambridgeshire (Sacrewell). One of the experiments at Rothamsted (coded CS/476) tested fluquinconazole seed treatment against no treatment in all combinations of years from first wheats (cv. Brigadier), grown in 1997 (harvest year), to sixth wheats. This experiment was designed as four fully randomised blocks of eight plots (10 m x 3 m) to test effects of treatment in each of 3 years (i.e. 2^3). When the experiment was continued into the fourth and fifth years, it became, first, two blocks of 16 plots and then a single replicate. In the sixth year, the treatments repeated those applied in the first year, which were assumed to be no longer having an effect and were ignored in the analysis of the data. Other experiments, at East Winch, Rothamsted (coded CS/508) and Sacrewell, tested seed treatment against no treatment in all combinations of years from second wheats (in 1999) to fifth wheats. Four fully randomised blocks of 16 (2^4) plots (10 m x 6 m at Rothamsted, 12 m x 3 m at East Winch and 14 m x 4 m at Sacrewell) were used. An additional experiment at Rothamsted (coded CS/323) was used to test the effects of fluquinconazole in sequences of wheat crops in a take-all decline situation. CS/323 is a long-running crop-sequence experiment that had been used to test sequences of different cereal species from 1988-1995. Winter wheat was sown in all plots (10 m x 3 m), in three randomised blocks, from 1996, except in 1997 when the field was in set-aside. Fluquinconazole seed treatment was tested against no treatment in all combinations of years from 1999 to 2001.

The main plant samples to assess take-all were taken from all experiments in late June or early July (GS 69-73). Ten 20 cm row-lengths were dug from each plot along two parallel zig-zag transects. Take-all was assessed on each plant and scored on a 0-5 scale: 0 = no disease; 1 = slight take-all, less than 10% of the root system affected; 2 = slight take-all, 11-25% of the root system affected; 3 = moderate take-all, 26-50% of the root system affected; 4 = moderate take-all, 51-75% of the root system affected; 5 = severe take-all, 76-100% of the root system affected. We consider this more realistic than the widely used system in which category 5 has the range 61-100% (e.g. Schoeny et al., 1998). This is because, in UK conditions, yield losses tend to relate best to the upper part of this range in samples taken at this time (Gutteridge et al., 2003). From these scores, a mean take-all index (TAI) per plot (maximum 100) was calculated by summing the products of the percentages of plants in each score category multiplied by the corresponding score value, and dividing the total by 5. Grain yields were adjusted to 85% dry matter after combine-harvesting the plots and measuring the percentage dry matter in sub-samples from all plots.

RESULTS

Results from selected sequences of treatments in Rothamsted experiments CS/508 (2nd to 5th wheats) and CS/323 are presented as examples to show effects that occurred during the early years of a take-all epidemic and during take-all decline, respectively. These examples were chosen to indicate how recommendations for using fluquinconazole in sequences of wheat crops have been reached.

Effects of treatment of one crop in a sequence of wheat crops

Seed treatment applied to only one crop in a sequence of wheats almost always decreased take-all (assessed as take-all index) significantly in the year of treatment when the disease was moderate or severe (as in the 3rd and 4th wheats in the example shown, Table 1) but not when take-all was slight (2nd wheat in example shown). The poor response to seed treatment in the 5th wheat in this example was exceptional. Yield increases generally reflected the extent of take-all control, being proportionally greatest when amounts of disease and of disease control were greatest. In the example shown, however, a statistically significant yield increase occurred only in the 4th wheat (Table 2). Over all experiments, excluding CS/323, the average response to fluquinconazole applied to 2nd wheats was 0.37 t/ha (on a mean untreated yield of 8.23 t/ha), ranging from 0.02 t/ha (in CS/508, where take-all was slight) to 0.77 t/ha (at East Winch, in the same year and where take-all was much more severe; results not shown). The average response to fluquinconazole applied to 4th wheats was larger (0.50 t/ha) but this was on a non-treated mean yield of only 4.11 t/ha.

Effects of withholding treatment, after treatment of the previous crop

Take-all in non-treated crops in plots that grew treated crops in the preceding year was increased to the same level as in repeatedly non-treated crops until the take-all peak was reached in the non-treated plots (3rd and 4th wheats in the example shown, Table 1). With the onset of apparent take-all decline in the non-treated plots (5th wheat), take-all was greater in the plots with non-treated crops in which treated crops had been grown in the preceding year. The previous treatment had apparently delayed progress into take-all decline, and this was reflected in the effects on yield (Table 2). In the other experiments, however, there was no convincing evidence of the establishment of take-all decline.

Table 1. Effects on take-all index (0-100) of fluquinconazole seed treatment applied to all crops or selected crops of winter wheat grown successively on the same site (expt CS/508)

Crop(s) treated	Harvest year (no. wheat crops in sequence)			
	1999 (2nd)	2000 (3rd)	2001 (4th)	2002 (5th)
None	24.2	69.5	50.9	45.8
Harvest year only	20.6	50.0	22.0	43.6
Preceding year only	-	65.9	47.4	73.9
All years	-	47.6	38.2	56.8
Harvest and preceding year only	-	47.6	33.0	53.5
SED (df)	3.23 (59)	5.95 (57)	8.96 (53)	7.89 (45)

Table 2. Effects on grain yield (t ha^{-1}) of fluquinconazole seed treatment applied to all crops or selected crops of winter wheat grown successively on the same site (expt CS/508)

Crop(s) treated	Harvest year (no. wheat crops in sequence)			
	1999 (2nd)	2000 (3rd)	2001 (4th)	2002 (5th)
None	9.72	6.40	5.33	6.88
Harvest year only	9.74	6.69	6.50	7.10
Preceding year only	-	6.06	5.29	5.60
All years	-	6.53	5.27	5.81
Harvest and preceding year only	-	6.53	5.97	6.50
SED (df)	0.149 (59)	0.375 (57)	0.546 (53)	0.460 (45)

Effects of treatment of successive wheat crops

Treatment of all crops, or all crops with significant take-all (i.e. excluding the first wheat), in a sequence often resulted in poorer control than occurred with treatment of a single crop, as was the case in the 4th and 5th crops in the example shown (Table 1). This was because there was often more take-all in crops following treated crops than in those following non-treated crops (whether or not the following crops were themselves treated). Effects were mostly small, and seldom significant, but they were often associated with significant decreases in yield. Third, fourth and fifth wheats after second, third and fourth wheats, respectively, that had been treated gave significantly smaller yields than those after otherwise similar crops that were non-treated in five out of 11 comparisons. This yield penalty was usually larger than would have been expected from the associated increase in severity of take-all.

Effects of treatment of wheat crops grown on a take-all decline site

A once-only application of seed treatment on the take-all decline site decreased take-all (Table 3) and increased yield, often significantly (Table 4), in the year of treatment. There was, again, evidence of an increase in take-all, and a decrease in yield, in crops following a treated crop compared to crops following non-treated crops. Treatment of successive crops resulted in take-all control but effects on disease and on yield were smaller than from once-only treatments, especially in 2000.

Table 3. Effects on take-all index (0-100) of fluquinconazole seed treatment applied to all crops or selected crops of winter wheat grown successively on the same take-all decline site (expt CS/323)

| | Harvest year | | |
Crop(s) treated	1999	2000	2001
None	63.4	35.7	37.5
Harvest year only	40.7	22.3	22.8
Preceding year only	-	39.9	44.3
All years	-	29.3	23.7
Harvest and preceding year only	-	29.3	24.9
SED (df)	2.33 (64)	2.77 (58)	5.42 (51)

Table 4. Effects on grain yield (t ha^{-1}) of fluquinconazole seed treatment applied to all crops or selected crops of winter wheat grown successively on the same take-all decline site (expt CS/323)

| | Harvest year | | |
Crop(s) treated	1999	2000	2001
None	9.18	9.10	6.02
Harvest year only	9.82	9.40	6.73
Preceding year only	-	8.82	6.13
All years	-	8.89	6.56
Harvest and preceding year only	-	8.89	6.59
SED (df)	0.131 (64)	0.163 (58)	0.204 (46)

Economics of seed treatment

The margins over costs of different treatment regimes (assuming seed treatment costs of £132 t^{-1} and a grain value of £55 t^{-1}) were calculated for Rothamsted experiment CS/508. No account was taken of the decreases in quality as take-all became more severe or of possible improvements in quality as a consequence of applying fluquinconazole. The cost benefits, therefore, reflect the effects of treatment on grain yields. In this experiment, substantial cost benefits occurred only in the fourth wheat crop, after the take-all peak, when disease and yield responded best to seed treatment. The reason for the poor yield response in the third wheat, at the take-all peak, is unclear but is probably untypical. In the other experiments, the greatest proportional yield responses from once-only treatments occurred consistently where take-all was most severe. The greatest cost benefit of treatment was in plots growing a treated crop for the first time, or a treated crop after a non-treated crop. Plots growing successive treated crops showed less benefit.

DISCUSSION

The combined results of five field experiments, selected results from only two of which are described as examples, led to a series of recommendations for using fluquinconazole seed treatment to control take-all in sequences of winter wheat crops.

- Fluquinconazole should not be applied to a first wheat, since, if the break crop was properly managed, e.g. to control volunteers and grass weeds, there will be negligible take-all. A residual beneficial effect in the following wheat crop is possible (and occurred on the one occasion we tested treatment of a first wheat, in expt CS/476; results not shown) but is unlikely to repay the cost of treatment at current prices. If a sequence of wheat crops is planned, the first crop should be managed to minimise take-all development, e.g. by avoiding very early sowing.
- Fluquinconazole can be expected to be effective and economic when applied to a second or third wheat, when take-all is building up.
- Very severe take-all, which usually occurs at the peak of the epidemic, will also be decreased by fluquinconazole. This will usually be accompanied by a large proportional yield response, but the total yield and quality are likely to be poor and the crop unprofitable (as occurred in three of our experiments; results not shown).
- A break crop should follow a treated, diseased crop. A non-treated wheat crop should not be grown, since take-all will continue to build up when the treatment is withheld.
- If growing a wheat crop after a treated, diseased crop is unavoidable, seed for the new crop should also be treated. Although treatment will be effective, the yield benefit may not be commensurate with the amount of disease control.
- During the take-all decline phase, treatment is effective and economic where sufficient take-all is present, but decline may be less effective in the following year.
- Normal progress to take-all decline may be delayed by treatment and so there is no advantage in using the fungicide where the intention is to exploit the benefits of take-all decline.

The cost benefits of seed treatment, assuming a marketable crop and that all other costs were equal, were calculated for experiment CS/508. They reflect yield responses and confirm that, at current prices, optimum benefit results from treatment of only one crop in a sequence. The aim should, therefore, be to target the fungicide and treat that crop in a sequence that is expected to have significant take-all, and can thus be expected to repay the cost of treatment, but not have such severe disease that yield and quality are so poor that the crop as a whole loses money. As stated above, a treated crop should not be followed by another take-all-susceptible cereal but, if that is unavoidable, then the following crop should also be treated. A decrease in the cost of treatment would alter the economic arguments but would not eliminate the risk of a yield penalty where a treated crop with significant take-all is followed by another heat. However, because such a crop is likely to give only small yields of poor-quality grain, a reduction in the price of fluquinconazole is, perhaps, more likely to encourage its use on first wheats to exploit its activity against foliar diseases such as septoria and rusts (Wenz *et al.*, 1998). Treatment of a first wheat without take-all (experiment CS/476 at Rothamsted), indicated a residual benefit, presumably reflecting a reduction in inoculum available to infect the second wheat that followed it. If first wheats have more take-all, perhaps because cereal volunteers in the preceding break were not adequately controlled or because they follow set-aside (after a cereal), it is possible that the following, second, wheats will incur similar penalties to those that were often detected in third and subsequent wheats grown after treated crops. Research to test the effects on take-all of using fluquinconazole to control foliar diseases on first wheats, and the consequent effects on second wheats, is needed.

The results relate to only one of the fungicides available for controlling take-all. Recommendations for the other seed treatment, silthiofam (Beale *et al.*, 1998), or for foliar treatment with the strobilurin fungicide azoxystrobin (Jenkyn *et al.*, 2000), may be different. It is possible that the relative inefficacy of treating successive wheat crops with fluquinconazole may not occur with the other fungicides, or if more than one fungicide is used in the same crop sequence. Different recommendations may be needed for controlling take-all in sequences of cereals that include barley. These issues are being addressed in continuing research.

ACKNOWLEDGEMENTS

This research was sponsored by DEFRA in the Sustainable Arable LINK programme, with support from the Home-Grown Cereals Authority and Aventis CropScience. Rothamsted Research receives grant-aided support from the BBSRC.

REFERENCES

Beale R E; Phillion D P; Headrick J M; O'Reilly P; Cox J (1998). MON 65500: A unique fungicide for the control of take-all in wheat. *Proceedings of the 1998 Brighton Conference – Pests & Diseases*, **2**, 343-350.

Gutteridge R J; Bateman G L; Todd A D (2003). Variation in the effects of take-all disease on grain yield and quality of winter cereals in field experiments. *Pest Management Science* **59**, 215-224.

Jenkyn J F; Bateman G L; Gutteridge R J; Edwards S G (2000). Effects of foliar sprays of azoxystrobin on take-all in wheat. *Annals of Applied Biology* **137**, 99-106.

Schoeny A; Lucas P; Jeuffroy M-H (1998). Influence of the incidence and severity of take-all of winter wheat on yield losses and responses to different nitrogen fertilisations. *Proceedings of the 1998 Brighton Conference - Pests & Diseases*, **1**, 83-88.

Wenz M; Russell P E; Löchel A M; Buschhaus H; Evans P H; Bardsley E; Petit F; Puhl T (1998). Seed treatment with fluquinconazole for control of cereal take-all, foliar and seed-borne diseases. *Proceedings of the 1998 Brighton Conference - Pests & Diseases*, **3**, 907-912.

POSTER SESSION 7F

CROP PRODUCTION AND PROTECTION IN TROPICAL CROPS

Session Organisers: Dr Charlie Riches
                      Natural Resources Institute,
                      University of Greenwich, UK
                      and
                      Dr David Johnson
                      International Rice Research Institute,
                      Metro Manila, Philippines

Poster Papers: 7F-1 to 7F-13

Population dynamics and control of the dubas bug *Ommatissus lybicus* in the Sultanate of Oman

J R M Thacker

Pesticides Research Group, Biological Sciences, University of Paisley, Paisley PA1 2BE, UK
Email: thac-bs0@paisley.ac.uk

I H S Al-Mahmooli, M L Deadman

Department of Crop Sciences, College of Agriculture, Sultan Qaboos University, PO Box 34, Al-Khod 123, Sultanate of Oman

ABSTRACT

The dubas bug *Ommatissus lybicus* population was monitored over a 12-month period from May 1999 until May 2000 in a date palm plantation at the village of Al-Habra in Northern Oman. Direct measurements of the size of the pest population were made by using water traps to record the number of adults and nymphs. Indirect assessments of the size of the pest population were made by using water sensitive papers to measure feeding activity. Pesticide applications to control the pest population were undertaken by the Ministry of Agriculture during October 1999 and during April 2000. The organophosphate pesticide fenitrothion was applied by using either ground-based mistblowers (October 1999) or by using helicopters fitted with micronair spraying heads (April 2000). The data indicated that the aerial applications were much more effective than those applied from the ground. Analysis of the water sensitive papers indicated a rapid rise in feeding activity following the emergence of 1st instar nymphs. This rapid rise in feeding activity could be used to predict the most appropriate time to apply control measures for this pest species.

INTRODUCTION

Approximately 60% of the land that is cultivated in the Sultanate of Oman is planted with date palm *Phoenix dactylifera*. In total, approximately 35,000 hectares support over 10 million trees. The annual yield from these trees was approximately 250,000 metric tonnes of dates in 2002, a figure that represents an overall doubling in production since the start of the renaissance that occurred in 1970 following the accession of Sultan Qaboos bin Said. In Oman dates are not only important for historical and cultural reasons, but they also now make an important contribution to non-oil export income (Ministry of Information Oman, 2003).

At present, the biggest constraint to date production in Oman comprises the arthropod pest the dubas bug *Ommatissus lybicus* (Figure 1). This is a homopterous pest that damages plants as nymphs and adults, both directly and indirectly. Direct damage is caused by sap-sucking and very severe infestations can severely weaken trees which can result in their death. Indirect damage is caused by the production of honeydew that acts as trophic resource for opportunistic saprophytic fungi, especially sooty moulds. Under very severe conditions sooty moulds can have a substantial negative impact on photosynthetic activity and therefore upon yield.

To control the dubas bug the Ministry of Agriculture in Oman annually spends between RO 150,000 – 200,000 (US$ 390,00 – 520,000) on an aerial programme using helicopters fitted with micronair spraying heads (Ministry of Information Oman, 2003). In addition, the ministry also pays for extension workers who undertake regular surveys of dubas bug populations at a range of locations throughout the Sultanate. The control programme is therefore completely subsidised by the government. The chemicals that have been used to control this pest are all products with contact and stomach activity that are applied as Ultra Low Volume (ULV) spray applications. Historically, malathion and dichlorvos were used, but in recent years their has been a move to use fenitrothion.

In order to target pesticide applications effectively routine monitoring of dubas bug populations is undertaken by extension workers. Such monitoring typically involves recording the number of nymphs found on date palm shoots (suckers) that are located around the bases of trees. Although a major proportion of the pest population is known to feed in the upper canopy it is uneconomic as well as impractical to sample leaves that exist at a heights of 3 – 4 metres. In recent years there has also been a move to supplement direct count data by using Water Sensitive Papers (WSPs) to monitor feeding activity (Mokhtar & Al-Mjeini, 1999). These papers record honeydew droplets that fall from bugs feeding in the upper canopy. It has been argued that WSPs give a better estimate of pest population size than direct counting of nymphs on suckers because bugs are easily disturbed and disperse rapidly from the leaves that are sampled at the base of a tree.

Observations made by the authors indicate that there is a substantial flux in the pest population between the upper canopy (where most feeding occurs) and the soil surface at the base of trees. In heavily infested plantations dubas bug nymphs can be seen to walk and jump continuously up the trunks of trees. This process has been previously described for cereal aphids in wheat crops (Winder *et al.*, 1994) but the magnitude of its significance in date palm plantations is still unknown. That this flux occurs however suggests that the potential for monitoring dubas bug numbers in water traps should exist. If this were possible, it may be a better method for sampling population numbers because different instars could be easily identified (because sampled insects would be dead). The aim of the experiment that is described in this paper therefore was to assess the value of using water traps to sample dubas bug populations in date palm plantations. Sampling was undertaken over a continuous 12 month period that covered the two annual peaks in pest population activity. The data collected were supplemented with measurements of feeding activity using WSPs. Farm activities (including crop protection measures) were not manipulated in any way. The aim was to collect pest population data. The data collected are discussed in relation to control strategies for this pest.

MATERIALS AND METHODS

All experimental work was carried out in a date palm plantation at the village of Al-Habra. This village is located *c.* 40 km in from the coastal town of Barka on the Batinah coast. The date palm plantation at Al-Habra is shared by families from the village and is irrigated by a falaj. The site was located with assistance of extension workers from the Barka office, the Ministry of Agriculture.

Dubas bug numbers were sampled over a twelve month period from May 1999 until June 2000. Data were collected weekly. Direct counts of the dubas bug population size were made using water traps of dimensions 50cm * 50cm * 10cm. Water traps were filled to a depth of 6cm with water and 0.1% detergent. Four replicate water traps were placed on the soil surface under trees in a square grid, with each trap separated by a distance of 10m. Trees within the area sampled were *ca.* 3 – 4 metres high. Indirect measurements of the pest population were made using WSPs that were placed beside each water trap. The WSPs were 6cm * 2cm. Water traps and WSPs were left in the plantation for a 24hr period. Following collection of WSPs the number of droplets recorded was counted by eye. The dubas bugs that were collected in the water traps were then counted and separated by instar.

Ultra Low Volume (ULV) applications of the contact, organophosphate pesticide fenitrothion, were made during October 1999 and April 2000 by the Ministry of Agriculture (fenitrothion S-100 ULV at 2 litres/ha). The application carried out in 1999 was made by extension workers using motorised mistblowers at ground level. These mistblowers direct a spray of fine droplets up into the date palm canopy. The application carried out during 2000 was made using helicopters that were fitted with micronair spraying heads. The rates of application were in accordance with ministry guidelines for control of the pest. Decisions to apply pesticides were made on the basis of counts of nymphs on suckers (Mokhtar & Al-Mjeini, 1999).

The data are presented as the mean number of bugs recorded in traps for each week over the whole twelve month period. In addition, the data for 2000 are broken down to show the approximate durational time for each instar. Data collected on WSPs are presented as the mean number of droplets recorded on each sampling occasion.

Figure 1.   Third instar dubas bug *Ommatissus lybicus* on date palm

RESULTS

The results of the water trap catches and the WSP data are presented in Figure 2. Figure 3 shows the dubas bug data for 2000, as individual instars. Overall, there were two peaks in pest population activity, one in September – October, the other in March – April. These data are therefore consistent with what is known about this pest. Prior to each outbreak there was a rapid rise in density of droplets that were recorded on WSPs. In 1999, the pesticide application to control the pest was made *c.* 1 month after the indicated rise in feeding activity. In 2000, the pesticide application was made *c.* 2 months after the rise in feeding activity. In 2000 therefore the nymphal population developed to a far greater extent than in 1999. The 1999 data indicate that the pesticide applications were only partially effective in controlling the pest. Although the population of nymphs did not reach as high a level as in 2000, a significant number of individuals were able to complete their development and become adults. The data show that the adult population may exist for a protracted time period since in 1999 the first adults were detected towards the end of October. However, adults were recorded in the water traps continuously from the end of October 1999 until mid-February 2000, i.e. over a 4-month time period. No nymphs or adults were recorded during the months of June, July or August.

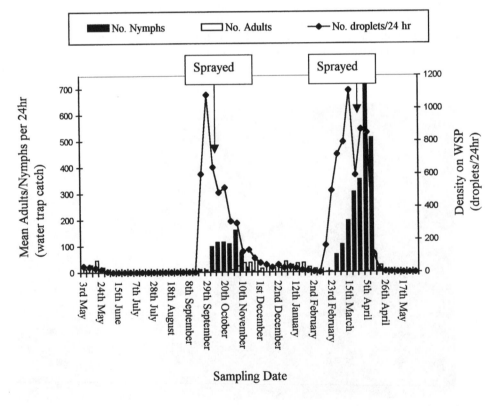

Figure 2.   Dubas bug population dynamics at Al-Habra 1999 – 2000. The Data show the number of adults and nymphs collected in water traps and the number of feeding droplets recorded on water sensitive papers.

The data shown in Figure 2 indicate that the developmental time of the nymphal population during February, March and April 2000 is *ca.* 4 – 8 weeks. The first nymph was detected on 16th February and the first new adult was detected on 10th April (Figure 2). Figure 3 shows, that as the nymphal population developed, that an increasing number of nymphs of older instars were detected in the water traps. This may reflect the functional efficiency of the water traps for different instars and is discussed in the conclusions. The approximate time period over which each instar developed was 4 – 6 weeks. During the middle of March all 5 instars existed in the pest population, together with adults from the preceding pest population.

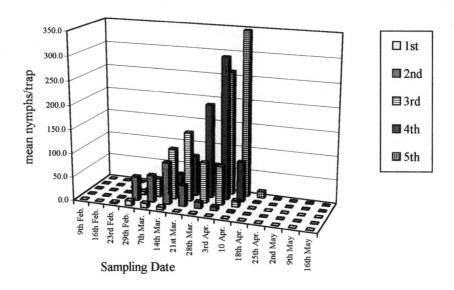

Figure 3.   Number of nymphs collected in water traps during 2000 by instar

DISCUSSION

The data presented in this paper represent the first attempt to continuously sample dubas bug numbers at one location over a protracted period of time. The results show two peaks of pest population activity, as has been reported before (e.g. Mokhtar & Al-Mjeini, 1999). The results show that water traps may be used to monitor numbers of this pest and this technique may therefore be useful for extension workers. Water traps are simple and cheap to operate and it is relatively easy to identify the pests from other arthropods that are caught in the traps. The results indicate that the traps become increasingly efficient with instar, i.e. early instars are not trapped as efficiently as older instars. This may be because early instars are able to escape the traps, because traps are less prone to catch early instars, or because the flux in the pest population between the upper canopy and the soil surface is greatest for later instars. To resolve this requires further investigation. Overall though, the data show that water traps can be used to monitor numbers of this pest.

The pest control measures that were used during the course of the sampling programme indicate that aerial spraying is more effective for pest control than ground based spraying. This results is not surprising since the limit for effective operation of ground-based mistblowers is 3 – 4m. The surface terrain in date palm plantations also makes ground-based spraying a difficult option. Studies are required on canopy coverage of the spray from a ground-based system in comparison to an aerial application. Aerial applications, while effective, are far more expensive than ground-based pesticide applications.

The pest population data indicate that the adult population, that develops during November, can survive and feed on date palm through to spring of the next year when new eggs that are laid, begin to hatch. The adult population that is produced in May does not survive through the summer months. During the summer the pest population survives as eggs, that are in diapause until favourable climatic conditions develop. This bottleneck in the dynamics of the pest population may proffer a point for effective pest control, i.e. if measures could be developed that target diapausing eggs. At present, control measures are directly at nymphal populations. The problem with this is that, if control is not complete, then adults will survive and produce eggs for the next generation. This was the case in the study undertaken here.

In conclusion, the data presented in this paper show that water traps can be used to sample dubas bug populations in date palm plantations. Further studies, using water trap catches as the basis for application decisions, are now required. The data also indicate a possible bottleneck in the dynamics of this pest species. Finally, further studies are required on biological control agents in date palm plantations. Observations by the authors indicate that numerous parasitoids can be found in date palm plantations. Whether these species feed on dubas bug is not yet known but is certainly worthy of further research, especially if egg parasitoids exist. Fenitrothion is a broad-spectrum compound and it is highly likely that, when it is used for dubas bug control, that is also impacts negatively on beneficial species that also inhabit the date palm ecosystem.

ACKNOWLEDGEMENTS

The authors would like to acknowledge the help provided by the Barka office, Ministry of Agriculture. The work described in this paper was supported by funds allocated to the authors by the Research Committee, College of Agriculture, Sultan Qaboos University.

REFERENCES

Mokhtar A M; Al-Mjeini A M (1999). A novel approach to determine the efficacy of control measures against dubas bug, *Ommatissus lybicus* de Berg, on date palms. *Agricultural Sciences* **4**, 1 - 4.

Ministry of Information Oman (2003). *http://www.omanet.com*

Thacker J R M; Ambusaidi Q; Al-Azri M; Al-Fahdi R; Al-Hashmi K; Al-Jabri R; Al -Makhmari S; Al-Mandheri I; Al-Shidi A; Al-Shidi R (2000). A preliminary assessement of pesticide use on farms in Oman. *Agricultural Sciences* **5**, 79-84.

Winder L; Hirst D J; Carter N; Wratten S D; Sopp P I (1994). Estimating predation of the grain aphid *Sitobion avenae* by polyphagous predators. *Journal of Applied Ecology* **31**, 1 – 12.

Weed management options for resource poor maize-dairy farmers in Central Kenya

J M Maina
Kenya Agricultural Research Institute, National Agricultural Research Laboratories, P O Box 14733, Nairobi, Kenya
Email: jedidahmaina@yahoo.com

B M Kivuva, M W K Mburu
Department of Crop Science, University of Nairobi, P O Box 30197, Nairobi Kenya

A J Murdoch
School of Agriculture, Policy and Development, The University of Reading, P O Box 237, Earley Gate, Reading RG6 6AR, UK

J M Njuguna, D M Mwangi
National Agricultural Research Centre, Muguga, Kenya Agricultural Research Institute, P O Box 30148, Nairobi, Kenya

ABSTRACT

The effects of weeding regimes on maize and edible weed forage were evaluated for three seasons in the Central Highlands of Kenya. Weeding regimes were weed free (W1), weedy (W2), pre-emergence herbicide (W3) and hand weeding twice (W4). Edible weeds had a dry matter digestibility of 65% and 19.9% crude protein (CP). The weedy regime (W2) reduced CP in maize stover and thinnings but increased the CP in edible weeds. Total weed biomass was higher in W4 than in W3. The residual effects of applying the weeding regimes were quantified in the third season when all plots were weeded by hand. Fourteen days after crop emergence (DAE), W1, W3 and W4 had low weed biomass whereas the W2 regime had the highest weed biomass (266.5 kg/ha). At 42 DAE, W2 again had the highest weed biomass (9.14 kg/ha) compared to 3.24 and 3.32 kg/ha for W1 and W4, respectively. The weedy regime (W2) used more man-days and was thus more expensive (81.1 man-days/ha) than W1 (67.2 man-days/ha), W3 (62.8 man-days/ha) and W4 (62.5 man-days/ha), which were similar. Although weeds provide a measurable source of forage, they directly reduce grain yield and the quality and quantity of maize forage. Failure to control weeds also results in more labour being needed to hand-weed subsequent crops.

INTRODUCTION

Mixed dairy farming is becoming increasingly popular among small-scale farmers in high potential areas of Central Kenya (Omore *et al.*, 1999). In these areas land for forage is becoming increasingly scarce, such that forage is a factor limiting dairy production (Kinuthia, 1998). Dairy animals are kept in "zero-grazed" and "semi-zero grazed systems". In a recent survey in the Kiambu district, thinnings, green stover, dry stover and weeds from the maize crop respectively comprised 6%, 10%, 8% and 5% of the total forage (McLeod *et al.*, 2001). Producing enough forage is difficult especially during the January to March dry season

(McLeod *et al.*, 2001) and farmers may sacrifice some of their maize grain yield by dense planting the maize and then thinning as late as tasselling to provide forage for their cattle.

The smallholder dairy sector in central Kenya produces about 80% of the total marketed milk (Omore *et al.*, 1999). In this farming system, therefore, crop protection to increase maize yields will not only improve grain yields but may also maintain milk production by ensuring a better supply of quality forage throughout the dry season.

Agronomic maize research in Kenya has however generally ignored the use of thinnings, leaf stripping, stover and edible weeds as sources of forage for livestock production. One aim of this paper is therefore to investigate the effects of weeds on forage yields and quality from maize. While weeds compete for plant resources and cause 15 – 90% loss in maize yields in Kenya (Maina, 1997), it should also be recognised that weeds infesting maize are a source of animal forage (Onim *et al.*, 1992) and their use as forage is also studied here.

Most resource poor farming households in Kenya face an acute labour constraint. The labour is scarce and expensive which affects the timeliness of weed control in the initial crop growth stages (Maina *et al.*, 2001). This leads to late and poor weed control. A further aim of this paper is to explore consequences of poor weed control on future weed infestations as well as the use of herbicides in reducing this labour requirement.

MATERIALS AND METHODS

The study was carried out at the National Agricultural Research Centre, Muguga 27 km NW of Nairobi, latitude 1° 13' South, longitude 36° 38' East, altitude 2096 meters above sea level. This sub-humid area receives on average 900 - 1000 mm rainfall annually. There are two distinct seasons: - long rains (mid March to June) with an average precipitation of 550 mm and the short rains (mid-October to December) with an average of 400 mm. Temperature ranges are, minimum 7°C maximum 24°C, mean 15°C. The soil is a well drained, very deep, dark reddish brown to dark red, friable clay classified as humic nitisols. The experiment commenced during 2001/2 short rains.

The plots were ploughed and harrowed to produce a good tilth for maize. The experiment was laid out as a randomised complete block design replicated four times with a plot size of 4 m x 4 m. Soil samples were taken before sowing in each plot and analysed for pH, organic C, N, and available P and K (Okalebo *et al.*, 1993). The treatments included four weeding regimes: weed free (W1), weedy (W2), pre-emergence herbicide (W3) and hand weeding twice (W4), two and six weeks after emergence. Two maize planting densities were also tested for all weeding regimes, that is, D1: 9 plants/m^2 (2 plants/hill) and D2: 18 plants/m^2 (4 plants/hill). Maize (cultivar H511) was planted in furrows spaced at 75 cm x 30 cm. Beans (GLP2; rose coco) were planted between maize rows, in all plots at 2 plants/hill and also at a spacing of 75 cm x 30 cm. Double Ammonium Phosphate (DAP: 18:46:0, N: P: K) fertiliser was applied before sowing at a rate of 25 kg/ha. Immediately after sowing beans and maize, pre-emergence herbicides (Alachlor 48 EC at 1.2 kg a.i./ha and Linuron at 0.6 kg a.i./ha) were applied using a knapsack sprayer in W3.

Ninety-six days after emergence (DAE) at 100% tasselling when the crop has reached maximum vegetative growth, the maize was thinned to 1 plant/hill. Total fresh weight of thinnings in each plot was determined. At maturity, (132 DAE), maize stover was harvested and its fresh weight determined. The fresh weight of shelled maize grain was taken. Ten plants per plot of thinnings and stover were sampled. These were separated into the vegetative (leaves and stems) and reproductive parts (cobs and husks), and oven dried at 60°C to constant weight to determine dry weights. The dried thinnings and stover samples were ground for quality analyses. The digestibility was determined using Pressure Transducer Technique (PTT). The crude protein was determined using Kjeldahl technique (Anderson & Ingram, 1989).

Weed species identification and quantification was done 14 and 42 DAE using three quadrats (0.5 m x 0.5 m) per plot. Fresh and oven dried (at 60°C) weights were determined. At the end of the season the weeds in the experimental area were harvested, sorted into edible and non-edible species and their fresh weights taken. A sample of 500 g of each of the main edible species was taken, dried at 60°C prior to determining dry matter and forage quality (crude protein and digestibility as described above). Times taken to weed each plot ($16/m^2$) were assessed and converted to man-days/ha (1 man-day = 8 hours) and the cost of weeding per hectare estimated assuming a payment of 158 Kenyan Shillings (KSh) per man-day. The cost of chemical weed control was KSh 5000/ha.

The experimental treatments were repeated on exactly the same plots for a second season (the 2002 long rains). In the third season (the 2002/3 short rains) the same plots were used again but all plots were hand-weeded to quantify residual benefits from the previous two seasons' weeding regimes in terms of weed infestations and hand-weeding times. Plots were irrigated in the first season but not in the second or third. Results from the second season and for the two planting densities are not presented in this paper. Analysis of variance was done using GENSTAT (Genstat 5 Release 3.2 Lawes Agricultural Trust, Rothamsted Experimental Station, 1995). Significantly different means ($P = 0.05$) were separated using SED values.

RESULTS

Maize grain yield and forage dry matter

Weed control (W1, W3, and W4) increased grain, thinnings, stover and total forage yields. Hand weeding (W4), increased grain yield compared to herbicide use (W3) (Table 1).

Table 1. The effect of weeding regimes on maize grain forage yields in tonnes/ha

Treatment	Grain	Thinnings	Stover	Forage (stover + thinnings)
2001/2 short rains				
Weed free (W1)	3.4	12.9	16.4	29.3
Weedy (W2)	1.6	8.1	10.2	18.3
Herbicide use (W3)	2.9	13.8	15.6	29.4
Two hand weedings (W4)	4.4	13.1	19.4	32.4
SED ($P = 0.05$, df = 21)	0.5	1.5	0.5	3.2

Hand weeding (W4) was, however, three times (KSh 15015/ha) more expensive than using herbicides (W3) (KSh 5000/ha) The area left weedy over two seasons had the highest weed biomass during the third season (Table 2).

Table 2. The timing of hand weeding and cost of the weed control during the 2001/2 short rains and 2002/3 short rains in Central Kenya

Weeding regime	Weed biomass, kg/ha		Man-days ha	Weeding cost, (KSh/ha)
	14 DAE	42 DAE		
2001/2 short rains				
Weed free (W1)	130	10	115.1	18188
Weedy (W2)	200	2400	0.0	0
Herbicide use (W3)	17	130	-	5000
Two hand weedings (W4)	170	250	95.0	15015
SED (P = 0.05, df = 21)	14	81	-	-
2002/3 short rains	All plots weeded by hand			
Weed free (W1)	154	3	67.2	10618
Weedy (W2)	267	9	81.1	12814
Herbicide use (W3)	145	7	62.8	9922
Two hand weedings (W4)	157	3	62.5	9875
SED (P = 0.05, df = 21)	26	2.3	5.3	844

Table 3.   Percentage dry matter digestibility (DMD) and crude protein (CP) of edible weeds 126 DAE and maize stover and thinnings in the 2001/2 short rains

Weed type	DMD (%)	CP (%)
Amaranthus spp	52	8.5
Emex australis	55	27.9
Galinsoga parviflora	64	19.7
Erlangea cordifolia,	65	16.4
Ageratum conyzoides	66	17.7
Erucastrum arabicum	66	32.1
Commelina benghalensis	68	13.0
Bidens pilosa	68	16.5
Leonotis mollissima	68	22.7
Sonchus oleraceus	73	27.1
Digitaria abyssinica	74	16.9
Weeds mean	65	19.2
Maize stover mean	62.5	4.3
Maize thinnings mean	76.5	7.3

Forage quality analysis

The most dominant and widespread weeds that were of value to farmers as forage were *Galinsoga parviflora, Bidens pilosa, Commelina benghalencis* and *Amaranthus* spp. Digestibility of the edible weeds ranged from 52 to 74% and the crude protein ranged 8.5 to

32% (Table 3). *Amaranthus* spp had the lowest CP (8.5%) and was also the least digestible (52%). On the other hand *Digitaria abyssinica* had the highest digestibility while its crude protein was about average. Thus digestibility increased with increase of crude protein to a point and then started decreasing (Table 3). The mean DMD and CP of the edible weeds were 65% and 19% respectively. Maize forage dry matter digestibility and crude protein were high in the thinnings and low in the stover (Table 4). The weedy regime (W2) reduced the CP and increased the DMD in stover, thinnings and total forage but increased CP and DMD in edible weeds (Table 4).

Table 4. The effect of weeding regime on the quantity of digestible dry matter and crude protein of maize and edible weeds forage in the 2001/2 short rains

Treatment	Crude Protein, t/ha				Digestible Dry Matter, t/ha			
	Stover	Thinnings	Weeds	Forage	Stover	Thinnings	Weeds	Forage
Weed free W1	0.7	0.9	0.0	1.6	10.3	9.9	0.1	20.2
Weedy W2	0.4	0.6	0.8	1.0	6.5	6.2	3.3	12.7
Herbicide W3	0.6	1.0	0.0	1.6	9.8	10.6	0.1	20.5
Hand weed W4	0.8	0.9	0.3	1.7	12.2	10.1	0.9	22.3
SED ($P = 0.05$, df = 21)	0.12	0.1	0.06	0.15	1.9	1.1	0.2	2.1

DISCUSSION AND CONCLUSION

Bhushaan *et al.* (1984) reported that three weeks after sowing, weeds from the weedy crops had taken up to four times as much nutrient (N, P, K and Mg) as was taken up by corresponding weed free crops. The competition for nutrients helps to explain why grain and fodder yields were reduced in the unweeded plots relative to where weeds were controlled. Weeds reduced maize biomass by 39 %, which compares well with findings of Maina (1997), who found out that weeds reduced yields by 15-90 %.

Weeding twice by hand (W4) proved more expensive than using herbicides (W3) because of the high cost of manual labour (Table 2). Maina *et al.* (2001) similarly found that chemical weeding was about 82% cheaper compared to two hand-weedings. In this experiment chemical weeding was one third of the cost of two hand-weedings. Herbicides controlled weeds faster and earlier than manual weeding and, were also highly efficient. Failure to control weeds in two previous seasons increased the cost of hand-weeding by between 17–31 % (Table 2). It is presumed that failure to control weeds will lead to an increase the soil weed seedbank and hence in weed emergence and the time taken to weed in the third season (Table 2). Work is currently in progress to quantify how the extra time taken corresponds with the soil seedbank and its changes with time.

Percentage digestibility and crude protein of maize forage was lower for the stover than for thinnings because at the time of thinning (96 DAE), the crop was investing its resources on the chlorophyll to maximise photosynthesis. However after seed set the crop switched the priority of N allocation to seeds neglecting the vegetative parts of the crop. Some of the N was probably re-translocated from the leaves and stems to the developing grains since N is mobile. This accounts for the lower CP in stover compared to the thinnings. Low crude protein content of maize stover was reported in central Kenya by Methu (1998). Leaving the crop unweeded increased %CP and digestibility of the stover because the weeds out-competed the crop that therefore invested very little on seed production. Thus the maize in the weedy plots might translocate less N to reproductive parts leaving the available N mainly in the stems and leaves. This is evident in the experiment since grain yields were very low in W2. Weeds (at 126 DAE) had higher %CP than maize while %DMD was similar to stover (Table 3). This may be because most of the edible weed species were leguminous and broad-leaved species and thus the conversion rate of photosynthates to protein may have been higher than in maize. However digestibility was similar to the maize stover probably because the fibre content was the same.

The cost of chemical weed control was much lower than hand weeding. Due to ignorance farmers are, however, reluctant to use herbicides until absence of residues is demonstrated in forage. They also may not want to risk buying herbicide in case their crop fails. Hand weeding two and six weeks after emergence gave the highest grain yields (Table 1) and so where labour is available or farming is "organic", it is a satisfactory control method. It is also advisable that weeds, whether edible or not, should be removed before flowering to minimise weeding times in subsequent crops.

ACKNOWLEDGEMENTS

This paper is an output from research project R7955, IPM of maize forage dairying, funded by DFID Renewable Natural Resources Knowledge Strategy Livestock Production (LPP) and Crop Protection (CPP) programmes for the benefit of developing countries. The views expressed are not necessarily those of DFID. Our sincere thanks to, the Director of KARI, Centre Director and the staff of KARI-NARC-Muguga, KARI-NARL and the University of Nairobi for their support.

REFERENCES

Anderson J M; Ingram J S (1989). *Tropical soil biology and fertility: A handbook of methods*, pp 40-42. CAB International: Wallingford, UK.

Bhushan L S; Chuvhau R S; Chand S (1979). Influence of tillage and simazine on weed growth, loss of nutrients and yield of rain fed maize. *Journal of Indian Society of Soil Science* 20, 158- 160.

Kinuthia M N (1998). *Performance of cross-bred dairy goats in small holdings in central Kenya.* MSc thesis. University of Nairobi, Kenya.

Maina J M (1997). *The effect of intercropping on weeds and weeds management in maize growing in Kenya.* Ph.D. thesis. The University of Reading,UK.

Maina J M; Kibata G N; Musembi F J; Muthamia J G N; Overfield D; Terry P J (2001). Participatory development of weed management strategies in maize based copping systems in Kenya. *Proceedings of the BCPC conference – Weeds 2001*, 1, 199-204.

McLeod A; Njuguna J; Musembi F; Maina J; Miano D (2001). *Farmers strategies for maize growing, maize streak virus control and feeding of small holder dairy cattle in Kiambu district, Kenya. Results of a rapid rural appraisal held in April and May 2001.* First technical report of DFID project R7955/ZC0180. University of Reading, Reading, UK.

Methu J N (1998). *Strategies for utilisation of maize stover and thinning as dry season feed for dairy cows in Kenya,* pp180-198. Ph.D. thesis, The University of Reading, UK.

Okalebo J R; Gathua K W; Woomer P L (1993). *Laboratory methods for soil analysis. A working manual.* T.S.B.F., UNESCO. ROSTA: Nairobi.

Omore H; Muruki M; Owango M; Staal S (1999). The Kenyan dairy sub sector, a rapid appraisal, January 1999.

Onim J F M; Fitzhugh H A; Getz W R (1992). Developing and using forages. In: *On-farm research and technology for dual purpose goats,* eds P Semenye & T Hutchcroft, pp. 47-70. Small ruminant collaborative research programme: Nairobi.

Epidemiology and maize crop resistance to head smut disease with reference to small-scale maize-dairy farmers in Central Kenya

J G M Njuguna, P G Njoroge

Kenya Agricultural Research Institute, National Agricultural Research Centre - Muguga, P. O. Box 30148, Nairobi, Kenya
E-mail: jgmnjuguna@yahoo.com

A N Jama

Department of Agriculture, The University of Reading, Earley Gate, P. O. Box 237, Reading, UK

ABSTRACT

Maize head smut, caused by *Sporisorium reilianum* was found in ten of the seventeen districts of Kenya surveyed between 1986-1987. Disease incidence was highest in the Central and Rift Valley Provinces where incidence of 2.6% and 2% respectively was recorded in some districts. Strategies of control investigated include resistant cultivars and a better understanding of disease epidemiology in the small-scale maize forage dairy farming systems of Central Kenya. Seventeen maize genotypes were among those identified and classified as immune to *S. reilianum* and three genotypes were classified as being highly resistant. Some of the resistant maize types have now been used in maize breeding programmes in East Africa. Experiments were conducted to determine if cattle manure disseminates head smut teliospores. Results indicated that smut teliospores passed through the gut of steers intact. A susceptible maize genotype was infected when grown in either fresh or dried dung from steers fed a ration containing smut spores. However, no infection was observed in plants manured with dung made from smutted ration that had been composted for 3 months. Implications for use of cattle manure in the epidemiology of head smut in central Kenya is discussed

INTRODUCTION

Head smut of maize is caused by *Sporisorium reilianum* (Kuhn) Langdon & Fullerton (syn. *Sphacelotheca reiliana* ((Kuhn) Clinton). The disease has a wide geographical distribution and occurs on maize throughout sub-Saharan Africa (Tarr, 1962) including Kenya. The disease is sporadic and incidences of 50% or more have been reported from some countries, but in general, this is rare. In maize *S. reilianum* can be responsible for a variety of symptoms and both tassel (male inflorescence) and cobs (female inflorescence) may be partially or completely smutted. In the tassel, only individual flowers may be attacked whilst in the cob, smut is usually a single large spore mass with a transient enclosing membrane replacing the whole cob. Since no grain is formed in the smutted cob, disease incidence of 10% translates to 10% yield loss. Head smut first appears when cobs and tassels are formed. Head smut is most common in sites where soil fertility is low and nitrogen fertiliser is not used (Shurtleff, 1980). Sporulation occurs mostly in the cob, frequently in the tassel and occasionally on the leaf. Vascular bundles of the host usually appear in the sori as threadlike strands often producing a phyllode in the flora parts. In Kenya, head smut was reported in 1925 (McDonald, 1925) and disease incidence of 70% was reported in some farmers' fields in parts of the Rift Valley (McDonald, 1928). Although seed treatment containing the fungicides triadimenol and carboxin has been recommended, the most economic management of head smut is through host resistance. Concerted efforts between Kenyan maize breeders and pathologists started in the mid 1980's to screen for head smut resistance at KARI-NARC-Muguga. This paper is a continuation of that research.

MATERIALS AND METHODS

Field surveys

Systematic field surveys were conducted between 1986 and 1987 to determine disease incidence in farmers' fields. In each district surveyed, five fields were picked at random along the main highway. At least two hundred maize plants were examined at the edge of the field and a further two hundred at the centre of each field. Disease incidence was expressed as the percentage of the two thousand plants examined in each district. Wherever possible during the survey farmers were interviewed using a questionnaire to find out if they recognized head smut as a disease, and what they did with smutted maize plants.

Maize germplasm evaluation

Germplasm screening was carried out in field plots at KARI-NARC-Muguga during short and long rainy seasons of the period 1985-1987 and 1996-2002. Head smut infected tassels and ears were collected. The smut infected plant parts were dried in a glasshouse by spreading the materials on newspapers and leaving them for 1-2 weeks. The dried smutted cobs were then crushed and teliospores separated from the plant's vascular tissue by a sieve. Inoculations were conducted using teliospores thus prepared at planting time. The field plots usually consisted of 1-2 rows 5 m long depending on the amount of seed available. Spacing was 75 cm between rows and 30 cm within rows. A randomised complete block design was used with three or four blocks again depending on seed availability. Phosphate fertilizer (P_2O_5) was applied at the rate of 50 kg ha^{-1} at planting and nitrogen (calcium ammonium nitrate) at the rate of 50 kg ha^{-1} as a top dressing six weeks post-emergence. 30 mg teliospores inoculum was layered on to every two seed kernels placed in a single hole at planting time using calibrated scoop before covering seed with soil as described by Njuguna & Odhiambo (1989). Records were made of head smut incidence after flowering by examining both the tassel and ear for signs of the disease. Disease incidence was expressed as a percentage of smutted plants in the total population inoculated in each entry. Maize hybrid 511 was initially used as a check in the 80s but later we found a more susceptible genotype ZM607 #bF37sr-2-3sr-3-3-x/[EP44SR]-BO-l-2sr-l]5-4-x-l-B-B from CIMMYT Zimbabwe. The screened entries were classified as immune, highly resistant, moderately resistant, susceptible and very susceptible as follows:-

0% smutted	-	Immune
1-9% smutted	-	Highly resistant
10-29%	-	Moderately resistant
30-49%	-	Susceptible
50-100%	-	Very susceptible

Passage of smut spores through dairy animals and manure management strategies

During the 2002/3 short rains season, experiments were conducted to determine if smut spores are dispersed through cow manure and if composting the dung would be a feasible option to eliminate these fungal spores. The experiment was conducted using three Friesian steers each weighing approximately 700 kg. The animals were fed on Napier grass for one week before being put on the ration containing smut spores. The dung collected before this smut spore ration was administered served as a control. 250 g of smut teliospores were mixed with 400 g mixture of maize germ, bran and molasses. This ration was given to each of the three steers daily for a period of 3 weeks. Additionally the animals were fed on 100 kg of chopped Napier grass. Dung was collected daily from the three steers and pooled and then split into two portions. One portion was put into a compost pile and composted for three months. The compost heap was mixed with chopped dried maize stover to facilitate aeration. The volume of maize stover was about 5% of the total. The second portion was spread on the floor to dry for use as dry manure. An additional batch of smut spores contained in a small polythene bag was incubated in the centre of compost heap at a depth of 30 cm. Survival of teliospores in the compost and dried manure was assessed in the glasshouse by planting seeds of susceptible maize cultivars in pots containing steam-sterilised soil mixed with various manure treatments. This experiment was a completely randomised design with five replicates each of 20 maize plants per pot of each of the following treatments:
1. Fresh cow dung from smutted ration.
2. Dried cow dung from smutted ration.
3. Composted cow dung from smutted ration.
4. Smut teliospores incubated in compost for three months.
5. Fresh teliospores stored in refrigerator (positive control).
6. Steam-sterilised soil alone (negative control).
7. Dried cow dung before treatment (spore free dung - negative control).

RESULTS

Head smut was recorded in 10 of 17 districts surveyed (Table 1). The highest disease incidence was reported in Central Kenya followed by the Rift Valley Province.

Farmers perception

Most farmers recognised head smut as a problem but did not perceive it as a disease. Most farmers fed smutted maize plants to their livestock. A few farmers did not use smutted stover as cattle feed but instead uprooted the smutted plants and left them in the field. In so doing the farmers were unconsciously spreading the inoculum all over the field. When asked if they had a local name for smut, farmers in central Kenya called head smut `ndutu` while those in the eastern province called it `tutu`. Most farmers had no knowledge of the disease cycle.

Screening for head smut resistance

Sources of resistance identified during the study of maize germplasm from CIMMYT (Zimbabwe), IITA (Nigeria), CIRAD (France), Pannar Seed Company, Summer Grains Institute South Africa and local are listed in Table 2. Over 600 maize entries including inbred lines, populations, land races and hybrids were evaluated.

Table 1: Occurrence of head smut of maize in Kenya 1986-1987

Province		District	Percentage of Crop Smutted
Central	1.	Kiambu	1.5
	2.	Muranga	2.6
	3.	Kirinyaga	0.1
	4.	Nyandarua	0.2
	5.	Nyeri	0.1
Eastern	6.	Embu	0.1
	7.	Meru	0.2
	8.	Machakos	0
Rift Valley	9.	Nakuru	2.0
	10.	Uasin Gishu	0.75
	11.	Trans Nzoia	0
	12.	Nandi	0
Western	13.	Bungoma	0
	14.	Kakamega	0
Coast	15.	Taita	0
	16.	Kilifi	0
Nairobi	17.	Nairobi	0.1

Table 2: Maize genotypes identified to have immunity (I) or high resistance (HR) to *S. reilianum* over the period from 1986 to 2003

Genotype/Pedigree	Source/Country	Classification
SR 52	Al Manwiller , Zimbabwe	(HR)
PAN 67	Pannar Seed Co., South Africa	(HR)
Embu 11	KARI, Kenya	(HR)
Tzi35	IITA, Nigeria	(I)
TZEMSR-W-F	IITA, Nigeria	(I)
[INTA-2-1-3/INTA-155-2-2]-x-3-1-2-B-B	CIMMYT, Zimbabwe	(I)
[N3/CML205/N3]-x-3-1-B-B	CIMMYT, Zimbabwe	(I)
INTA-F2-192-1-1-1-B-B-B	CIMMYT, Zimbabwe	(I)
LATA-26-1-1-1-1-6-B-B	CIMMYT, Zimbabwe	(I)
ZM605C2F1-142-2-B-2-B-B	CIMMYT, Zimbabwe	(I)
LATA-26-1-1-2-1-1-2-1-1-B-B	CIMMYT, Zimbabwe	(I)
[CML 202/K64R//FR812]-x-13-2-1-B-B]	CIMMYT, Zimbabwe	(I)
Pannar A241	Pannar Seed Co., South Africa	(I)
VHCY	Summer Grains, South Africa	(I)
LATA-26-1-2-BB	CIMMYT, Zimbabwe	(I)
ZM 605CF1-53-4-B-BB	CIMMYT, Zimbabwe	(I)
[CML 197/N311FR808]-x-8-3-B	CIMMYT, Zimbabwe	(I)
[DRB-F2-174-1-Y/DRB-39-2-2]-x-5-1-B	CIMMYT, Zimbabwe	(I)

Information on maize germplasm resistant to head smut has been shared among scientist participating in the regional nursery in Eastern and southern Africa. In Kenya some of the identified germplasm was used to make 16 synthetics which will be evaluated on-farm with farmers.

Transmission of *S. reilianum* through animal manure

The glasshouse experiment demonstrated that viable *S. reilianum* teliospores are transmitted through manure when dairy animals consume head smut infected stover (Table 3). It is, however, encouraging that composting the manure for three months before use kills the teliospores. Table 3 summarises the data on the incidence of maize head smut in the seven treatments confirming the absence of smut spores in the main negative control treatment. It appears that steam sterilisation does not eliminate smut teliospores in the soil.

Table 3. Transmission of *S. reilianum* teliospores through manure monitored as smut infection in susceptible maize genotype ZM607 #bF37sr-2-3sr-3-3-x/[EP44SR]-BO-l-2sr-l]5-4-x-l-B-B

Treatment	Number smutted	Total	% smutted
Fresh cow dung	24	55	43%
Dried cow dung	14	100	14%
Composted cow dung	0	101	0%
Fresh smut spores incubated in compost	0	67	0%
Freshly harvested teliospores (positive control)	32	60	53%
Steam-sterilised soil (negative control)	2	80	2.5%
Dried cow dung before treatment (negative control)	0	104	0%

DISCUSSION

Losses of grain and forage due to head smut of maize, which is widely distributed in Kenya, are widespread but have not as yet been quantified. Surveys reported in this study indicate the problem to be particularly acute in the central and Rift valley provinces. Our observations of the disease expression in nearly all the 600 maize types screened for resistance are very similar to those of Stromberg *et al.* (1984). Stunted maize plants were encountered in many maize genotypes as a result of *S. reilianum* infection. The stunting of maize plants caused reduction in maize stover biomass. Maize forage in the form of thinnings, green stover and dry stover is estimated to contribute 25% of the total forage fed to smallholder dairy animals in Kiambu district in Central Kenya (McLeod *et al.* 2001). Most of the farmers interviewed during the disease survey, said that they used smutted maize plants as cattle feed, and that they collected manure from their dairy animals and used it to plant subsequent maize crops. Our observations confirm that *S. reilianum* teliospores survive passage through the gut of cattle as reported by Kruger (1962). Composting dung from animals fed on smutted plants for three months kills the spores. In central Kenya where the size of the farms is becoming smaller every year because of population pressure, crop rotation is not a likely cultural practice but cow dung may be composted. The use of cattle manure is on the increase among smallholder dairy farmers because of the popularity of zero grazing. Farmers need to be made aware of the dangers of feeding smut infected plants and provided information on composting to avoid increasing the incidence of head smut disease, however, the best option for the farmers in the area is to use maize genotypes that are resistant to *S. reilianum*. Work to evaluate a range of synthetics derived from immune and highly resistant parents is continuing.

ACKNOWLEDGEMENTS

The technical assistance of Mr. Robert O. Odhiambo and David N. Kamau are gratefully acknowledged. The authors are grateful to Rockefeller Foundation and the United Kingdom Department for International Development (DFID) for financial support on varietal screening and smut transmission, respectively. This paper is an output from a research project funded by DFID for the benefit of developing countries. The views expressed are not necessarily those of DFID. Project R7955, IPM of maize forage dairying: Renewable Natural Resources Knowledge Strategy Livestock Production (LPP) and Crop Protection (CPP) programmes.

REFERENCES

Kruger W (1962). *Sphacelotheca reiliana* on maize. (1) Infection and control studies. *South Africa Journal of Agricultural Science* **5**, 43-55.

McDonald J (1925). *Report of the mycologist,1925-1927*. Kenya Department of Agriculture: Nairobi, Kenya.

McDonald J (1928). *Report of the mycologist, 1928-30*. Kenya Department of Agriculture: Nairobi, Kenya.

McLeod A; Njuguna J; Musembi F; Maina J; Miano D (2001). Farmers' strategies for maize growing, maize streak virus control and feeding of small holder dairy cattle in Kiambu district, Kenya. Results of a rapid rural appraisal held in April and May 2001. *First technical report of DFID project R7955/ZC0180*. University of Reading: Reading, UK.

Njuguna J G M (1998) Potential for control of head smut caused by *Sphacelotheca reiliana* in CIMMYT maize germplasm In: *Maize production for the future challenges: and opportunities: Proceedings of the Sixth Eastern and Southern Africa Regional Maize Conference, 21-25 September 1998*. pp. 67-68 Addis Ababa, Ethiopia:CIMMYT and EARO.

Njuguna J G M; Odhiambo R (1989) Head smut distribution, expression and genetics of resistance of maize to *Sphacelotheca reiliana* in Kenya. *East African Agricultural and Forestry Journal* **55**, 81-83.

Shurtleff C M (1980) *Compendium of corn diseases*. American Phytopathological Society, St Paul, Minnesota ,USA.

Stromberg E L; Stienstra W C; Kommedahl T; Maytac C A; Windels C E; Geadelmann J L (1984) Smut expression and resistance of corn to *Sphacelotheca reiliana* in Minnesota. *Plant Disease* **68**, 880-884.

Tarr S A J (1962) *Diseases of Sorghum, Sudan grass and broom corn*. The Commonwealth Mycological Institute: Kew, UK.

Solving weed management problems in maize-rice wetland production systems in semi-arid Zimbabwe

A B Mashingaidze, O C Chivinge, S Muzenda
Faculty of Agriculture, University of Zimbabwe, Mount Pleasant, MP167, Harare, Zimbabwe

A P Barton, J Ellis-Jones, R White
Silsoe Research Institute, Wrest Park, Silsoe, Bedfordshire MK45 4HS, UK

C R Riches
Natural Resources Institute, University of Greenwich, Chatham, Kent ME4 4TB, UK

ABSTRACT

Wetland cultivation can contribute to improved food security, poverty alleviation and improved livelihoods in semi-arid areas, but weeds, waterlogging and labour shortages are major constraints in this environment. Crop and weed management options identified in discussion with farmers were tested on-farm for two seasons (2000-01 and 2001-02). Weeding treatments used in sole crops of maize or rice and inter-crops, included hand hoeing, herbicides or combinations of the two. The two seasons were very different in terms of the rainfall distribution, the first favouring maize while the second favoured rice. Farmers showed particular interest in herbicides, particularly in sole maize, but were concerned about increasing cost, availability and their lack of knowledge regarding effective and safe application.

INTRODUCTION

V*leis*, or wetlands, in semi-arid areas of Zimbabwe are recognised as a valuable resource that contributes to rural livelihoods, particularly in times of drought (Kundlande *et al.*, 1992). The agricultural potential of *vleis* derives from the fact that they remain wet far into the dry season, allowing 2-3 crops to be grown per year, supplementing, dryland agriculture (Kundlande *et al.*, 1992), providing water for people, livestock and irrigation (Rattray *et al.*, 1953). Farmers utilising *vleis* identified weed infestation and water-logging as the principal constraints to production of maize and rice in the summer rainy season. In particularly wet years, these problems can lead to *vlei* fields being abandoned (Chivinge *et al.*, 2000). Weeding in *vleis* is predominantly by hand using a hoe, as conditions limit the opportunity to use draught animals. This highlights the additional problem of inaccessibility faced by many farmers in *vleis* once the rainy season commences. Alleviating the weeding constraints in *vlei* areas should contribute to stabilising yields, reducing pressures for cropping on the drier, often more fragile topland areas of the soil catena.

METHODOLOGY

Four areas in Masvingo Province were identified for on-farm trials, namely Mashagashe (small-scale commercial farms), Chatsworth (a resettlement area), Zimuto and Chikwanda (small holders in communal areas). All areas comprise granitic soils, experience low rainfall (450 - 650 mm per year) and are subject to severe periodic between- and in-season droughts. Farmers in these areas recognise two main types of *vleis* based on hydrology and soil type. Dry *vleis* are composed of light textured soils located on the valley sides and receive run-off from topland areas, while wet *vleis* are composed of heavier textured soils found on the lower end of the catena close to the valley bottoms. These remain waterlogged for much of the year.

Trials of weeding practices were implemented on farmers' fields across the four areas, encompassing both wet and dry *vleis* weeding treatments were tested in each area, four in dry *vleis* and five in wet *vleis* (Table 1), comprising maize, rice and maize-rice inter-crops. The treatments were replicated at three farms in each of the four areas and tested during two seasons, 2000-01 and 2001-02. Maize (*cv.* SC 513, at 37,000 plants/ha) and rice (*Muchecheni*, local variety) were planted in September before the onset of rains, germinating on residual moisture. Compound fertiliser (8%N, 14%P and 7%K) was applied at planting at a rate of 150 kg/ha, while a top dressing of ammonium nitrate (34.5% N) was applied (100 kg/ha) at six weeks after crop emergence (wace). Herbicides were applied three wace when most of the weeds were at the 2-3 leaf stage. Weeds were counted by species in three randomly placed 30 cm x 30 cm quadrats in each treatment at 6-7 and 12-13 wace. Counted weeds were cut at ground level and oven dried to constant weight to determine total weed biomass. Farmers' perceptions of the advantages and disadvantages of the practices tested were provided at group meetings in each area following a tour of representative sites before harvest.

Table 1.   Weeding treatments in wet and dry *vleis*

Treatment	Crop	Herbicide (g a.i./ha)	Other weeding
Dry *vlei*	T1 Maize	atrazine 1250 + halosulfuron-methyl 33.75	Hoe as required
	T2 Maize	Nil	Hoe
	T3 Maize + rice* in same row (FP)	Nil	Hoe from 3 weeks after planting
	T4 Maize + rice in rows between maize rows	Nil	Hoe as required
Wet *vlei*	T1 Rice broadcast (120 kg/ha)	bentazon 1440	Hoe as required
	T2 Maize + rice in same row (FP)	Nil	Hoe from 3 weeks after planting
	T3 Maize + rice broadcast	bentazon 1440	Hoe as required
	T4 Rice in rows (120 kg/ha)	bentazon 1440	Hoe as required
	T5 Maize	atrazine 1250 + halosulfuron-methyl 33.75	Hoe as required

*Rice seed rate was 60 kg/ha unless stated, FP=Farmer Practice

RESULTS

Total rainfall averaged across the four areas, was 669 and 793 mm in 2000-01 and 2001-02, respectively. However, distribution of rainfall between the two seasons was markedly different. Maize yields were lower in 2001/2002 (Table 2) because of a prolonged mid-season drought experienced from January onwards, which exacerbated moisture stress across all sites. Furthermore, heavy rainfall experienced early in the same season adversely affected much of the maize crop on the trials, particularly on the wet *vleis*, with many stands suffering losses due to waterlogging. The rice crop was better able to withstand the uneven rainfall distribution in the 2001/02 season. In contrast, the rains started much later in the 2000-01, but continued through to April, resulting in higher maize yields than in the following season.

Table 2. Mean maize and rice yields (kg/ha) on dry and wet *vleis*, based on 12 sites (9 for maize in 2001-02)

| | | 2000-01 | | 2001-02 | |
	Treatments	Maize	Rice	Maize	Rice
Dry *vleis*	T1 Maize, atrazine + halosulfuron	3699		1451	
	T2 Maize, hand weed	3328		2330	
	T3 Maize-rice (same row), hand weed	2617	577	1573	861
	T4 Maize-rice (alt. Rows), hand weed	2453	552	2040	939
Significance		***	NS	***	NS
S.E.D.		158	52	193	89
Wet *vleis*	T1 Rice broadcast, bentazon		1148		1201
	T2 Maize-rice (same row), hand weed	3244	816	1119	912
	T3 Maize-rice broadcast, bentazon	2439	875	1278	1102
	T4 Rice in rows, bentazon		1058		1351
	T5 Maize, atrazine + halosulfuron	4035		1123	
Significance		***	*	NS	*
S E D		253	107	259	129

*** Significant at P< 0.001; * Significant at P<0.05; NS = not significant

Significant treatment effects on maize yield occurred in the first season on both the wet and the dry *vleis*. Highest maize yields were recorded in sole maize where atrazine + halosulfuron-methyl was applied, while the lowest yields were recorded when maize was intercropped with rice between the maize rows. The significantly reduced weed pressure in the early part of the season in the sole maize with atrazine + halosulfuron-methyl is likely to have contributed to this increased yield compared to both the hand weeded and bentazon-treated plots (Table 3). This treatment was also the one chosen by farmers during mid-season evaluation days as being the best option from weed control and crop vigour perspectives (Riches, 2001). Halosulfuron-methyl proved particularly effective against *Cyperus esculentus*. Bentazon treatments were not as effective, and only caused a temporary setback to the perennial sedges in both *vleis* types. Halosulfuron-methyl is selective to both maize and rice and therefore was more effective against the predominant sedge population in *vleis*.

During the 2001/2002 season, there was no significant difference in maize yields from the wet *vleis*, which is thought to have been due primarily to the unfavourable conditions (waterlogging) for maize production, negating any treatment effects. On the dry *vleis*, there was no significant difference in intercropped rice yields in either year, therefore it made no difference whether the rice was planted in the same row with the maize or in alternate rows. On the wet *vleis* in the first year, although the sole rice crops produced higher yields, there was no difference whether the rice was broadcast or sown in rows, and similarly, weed control practice did not affect rice yield in the intercropped plots. In the second year a significantly higher rice yield was harvested from sole rice crops planted in rows and treated with bentazon compared to sole rice established by broadcasting.

Key variables in determining the highest returns are crop yields, market prices, herbicide and labour costs. Average yields from each of the treatments were adjusted according to statistical significance and the gross value of the crops determined using average farm-gate prices in August 2002. Labour inputs were based on measurements taken in the field during operations. Labour costs for each weed management treatment have been determined, as have the costs of purchasing and applying herbicide. In each case, comparison is made with farmer practice (FP) using partial budget analyses (Tables 4a and 4b).

Table 3. Mean weed density (number/m^2) 6-7 weeks after crop establishment in dry and wet *vleis* across 12 field sites.

Treatment	Dry *vleis*	
	2000-01	2001-02
T1 Maize, atrazine + halosulfuron	346 (16.60)	115.8 (10.76)
T2 Maize, hand weed	816 (27.49)	137.0 (11.7)
T3 Maize-rice in row, hand weed	697 (25.71)	115.3 (8.27)
T4 Maize-rice alternate rows, hand weed	705 (25.60)	124.9 (9.12)
Significance	***	ns
SED	(1.44)	(0.52)
	Wet *vleis*	
T1 Rice broadcast, bentazon	608 (22.85)	55.7 (6.64)
T2 Maize-rice in row, hand weed	781 (25.91)	65.3 (7.29)
T3 Maize-rice broadcast, bentazon	641 (23.72)	68.5(7.02)
T4 Rice in rows, bentazon	504 (20.24)	58.4 (6.96)
T5 Maize, atrazine + halosulfuron	305 (15.58)	42.6 (5.81)
Significance	***	*
SED	(2.02)	(0.46)

NB. Figures in brackets show the square root transformed data. SEDs are valid for comparisons on square root scale
*** Significant at P< 0.001; * Significant at P< 0.05; ns = not significant

In year 1, on the dry *vlei* greatest productivity in terms of gross crop value was achieved by growing sole maize and controlling weeds with herbicides, while on the wet *vlei* productivity was greatest when maize and rice was planted in the same row and hand weeded. In year 2, on the dry *vleis*, maize and rice in alternate rows, and in the wet *vleis* maize and rice in the same row, both hand weeded gave highest productivity. Labour for weeding is often a serious constraint. Indeed highest returns to labour were obtained in both years from herbicide treatments. In year 1 on both *vlei* types sole cropping maize with herbicide provided the greatest returns and in year 2, on the wet *vlei*, maize with rice broadcast with herbicide provided the highest return to labour. Clearly, as the price of labour increases, the herbicide options with sole crop maize become increasingly attractive. However, the importance of inter-cropping for food security must be stressed. Sensitivity analysis indicates that the price (and hence the availability) of labour is key. When labour is readily available (or is not valued) traditional farmer practices are the most productive. However, as the labour price increases, due to unavailability or opportunity elsewhere, the new systems may become more attractive. This will however depend on the resources available to farmers and their production objectives.

Table 4a. Partial budget analysis of the weeding treatments, indicating increase/decrease in productivity compared to farmer practice, 2000‑ 01. (US $/ha)

	Treatment	Benefits	Increased costs			Benefit less cost	Margins		Returns to labour
		Gross crop value	Herbicide	Labour	Total costs		Increase over FP	% increase over FP	$ per hour
Dry *vleis*	T1 Maize, atrazine + halosulfuron	617	61	42	104	513	36	8%	2.43
	T2 Maize, hand weed	555	0	60	60	495	18	4%	1.54
	T3 (FP) Maize-rice (same row), hand weed	549	0	72	72	477	0	0%	1.27
	T4 Maize-rice (alternate rows), hand weed	522	0	66	66	456	-21	-4%	1.33
Wet *vleis*	T1 Rice broadcast, bentazon	221	34	60	94	127	-508	-80%	0.61
	T2 (FP) Maize-rice (same row), hand weed	710	0	75	75	635	0	0%	1.57
	T3 Maize-rice broadcast, bentazon	574	34	48	82	492	-142	-22%	2.01
	T4 Rice in rows, bentazon	221	34	51	85	136	-499	-79%	0.72
	T5 Maize, atrazine + halosulfuron	673	61	44	105	567	-67	-11%	2.55

Farmer practice (FP).
Key assumptions: Maize price: $ 0.17 per kg, Rice price: $ 0.20 per kg, Labour price: $ 1 per day. Herbicide costs include cost of herbicide and knapsack sprayer (spread over 5 years, used over 5 ha each year).
US$1=Z$300 (August 2002)

Table 4b. Partial budget analysis of the weeding treatments, indicating increase/decrease in productivity compared to farmer practice, 2001-02. (US $/ha)

	Treatment	Benefits	Increased costs			Benefit less cost	Margins		Returns to labour
		Gross crop value	Herbicide	Labour	Total costs		Increase over FP	% increase over FP	$ per hour
Dry *vleis*	T1 Maize, atrazine + halosulfuron	252	61	42	104	148	-212	-59%	0.99
	T2 Maize, hand weed	388	0	60	60	328	-32	-9%	1.08
	T3 (FP) Maize-rice (same row), hand weed	432	0	72	72	360	0	0%	1.00
	T4 Maize-rice (alternate rows), hand weed	520	0	66	66	455	95	26%	1.32
Wet *vleis*	T1 Rice broadcast, bentazon	230	33	60	93	137	-89	-39%	0.64
	T2 (FP) Maize-rice (same row), hand weed	302	0	75	75	227	0	0%	0.67
	T3 Maize-rice broadcast, bentazon	302	33	48	80	222	-5	-2%	1.06
	T4 Rice in rows, bentazon	230	33	51	84	147	-80	-35%	0.75
	T5 Maize, atrazine + halosulfuron	140	61	44	105	35	-192	-85%	0.53

(FP) Farmer practice.
Key assumptions: Maize price: $ 0.17 per kg, Rice price: $ 0.20 per kg, Labour price: $ 1 per day Herbicide costs include cost of herbicide and knapsack sprayer (spread over 5 years, used over 5 ha each year).
US$1=Z$300 (August 2002)

DISCUSSION AND CONCLUSIONS

Timely weeding was undertaken in the trials, which does not reflect the scarcity of labour, as in many seasons entire crops are lost to weeds. The opportunity cost of not controlling weeds can therefore be the loss of the total crop as well as the costs incurred in producing it. The inability to control weeds by hand, declining labour availability due to HIV/AIDS, food shortages due to the current drought and the drudgery involved in weeding in wet conditions means that the use of herbicides is going to be increasingly justified. However, the deteriorating economic circumstances in Zimbabwe are dramatically increasing local costs of imported commodities and making them increasingly unavailable. Under such circumstances it is essential that the search for low cost safe herbicides continue. There is also a need for herbicide use and safety training to be carried out for extension personnel and farmers. Although farmers indicated a strong desire to use the successful herbicide combination of atrazine + halosulfuron-methyl to reduce weeding at the beginning of the season, their knowledge of herbicide technology is limited.

ACKNOWLEDGEMENTS

This study was funded by the United Kingdom Department for International Development (DFID), Crop Protection Programme (Project R7474). However, DFID cannot be held responsible for any views expressed.

REFERENCES

Chivinge O; Ellis-Jones J; Mutambikwa A; Muzenda S; Riches C; Twomlow S (2000). *Participatory Evaluation of Vleis Utilisation and Weeding Problems in Communal, Resettlement and Small Scale Commercial Farming Systems of Masvingo and Gutu Districts.* Institute Report IDG/00/8. Silsoe Research Institute: Silsoe, UK.

Kundlande G; Govere J; Muchena O (1992). *Socio-economic constraints to increased utilisation of dambos in selected communal areas.* In: *Dambo Farming in Zimbabwe: Water management, cropping and soil potential for small-holder farming in the wetlands. Proceedings of a conference held in Harare, September 1992,* eds Owen R; Verbeek K; Jackson J; and T Steenhuis pp. 87-96. University of Zimbabwe Publications: Harare, Zimbabwe.

Rattray J. M; Cormack R M; Staples R R (1953) The *vlei* areas of Southern Rhodesia and their uses. *Rhodesia Agriculture Journal* **50**, 465–483.

Riches C R (2001) *Mid-season evaluation of vlei weed management trials in Masvingo Province, Zimbabwe.* Institute Report IDG/03/01. Silsoe Research Institute: Silsoe, UK.

Scaling-up the use of improved *Imperata* Management Practices in the sub-humid Savannah of Nigeria

J Ellis-Jones, J Power
Silsoe Research Institute, Wrest Park, Silsoe, Bedford MK45 4HS, UK
Email: jim.ellis-jones@bbsrc.ac.uk

D Chikoye, O K Nielsen, P M Kormawa, S Ibana, G Tarawali, U E Udensi
International Institute of Tropical Agriculture, P.M.B. 5320, Ibadan, Nigeria

T Avav
Federal University of Agriculture, Makurdi, Nigeria

ABSTRACT

One of the most invasive weeds in sub-humid Savannahs of West Africa is *Imperata cylindrica*. Increasing spread threatens the sustainability of the natural resource base and rural livelihoods. Although farmers achieve some control through hand weeding, fallow, burning and limited use of chemicals, *Imperata* remains a serious problem. A participatory approach involved stakeholders in problem diagnosis, action planning, with farmer-led monitoring and evaluation of control methods. Major determinants for farmer choice of control technique were identified as cost, labour requirement, effectiveness, input availability, yield increases, knowledge and long-term sustainability. Farmers ranked herbicide as the most effective method of controlling *Imperata* particularly in maize, cassava and soya-bean, second was a combination of *Mucuna* and herbicide, third *Mucuna* and hand-weeding and fourth hand-weeding only with noticeable gender and age differences between farmers. Although herbicides increase cash needs, they reduce labour requirement, contribute to higher income, food security, and sustainability. Action is now taking place to scale up results of this approach through expanding extension, NGO, private sector and farmer involvement in problem diagnosis, farmer-led evaluation, improving input availability, providing access to credit and increasing farmer knowledge of chemical use. Improving public/private partnerships is seen as key to achieving this goal.

INTRODUCTION

One of the chronic weeds of the humid savannah of sub-Saharan Africa is the perennial rhizomatous weed, *Imperata cylindrica* causing crop yield loss, land abandonment, deforestation, land degradation, food insecurity, and severe rural poverty. Its control takes considerable labour resources, particularly of women and children, constituting a major constraint to crop production. Unfortunately, poverty, unequal distribution of resources, population growth, and continuous cultivation have created the conditions for unsustainable cultivation and weed management (including *Imperata* control) practices (Weber *et al.*, 1995).

Pilot research on the use of herbicides and cover crops to control the weed has shown some success, but adoption by farmers has been low (Chikoye *et al.*, 1999, 2000). Conventional extension approaches have not had significant impact. Since farmers often rely on advice from input suppliers and other (often wealthier) farmers, it became clear that participation of all stakeholders (researchers, extension agents, farmers, and input suppliers) in the design and implementation of sustainable management was required to improve *Imperata* control. This paper reports on work undertaken to identify currently used technologies, opportunities and constraints for controlling *Imperata* in communities in Benue, Cross River and Kogi States in Nigeria, where *Imperata* is a serious problem.

MATERIALS AND METHODS

Participatory technology development

A participatory research and extension approach (PREA), involving stakeholders was used for community analysis, problem diagnosis, action planning, experimentation, monitoring and evaluation (Hagmann *et al.*, 1998). Meetings with three communities provided information on livelihoods, household resources, crops, natural resource problems and their prioritisation, methods of controlling *Imperata*, trends of *Imperata* infestation, and identification of criteria for evaluating control practices. Community participants included traditional leaders, men, women and young people with discussions taking place in group sessions, with feed back, further discussion and modification during plenary. This provided a basis for agreeing a programme of "mother", "daughter", and "grand daughter" trials designed to improve *Imperata* control.

Research trials and demonstrations

As a result of these community consultations, trial treatments included hand weeding (farmer practice), use of glyphosate applied either pre-tillage or after crop establishment, glyphosate with *Mucuna* planted just after first weeding in cassava, yam and maize and fluazifop-p-butyl applied after crop establishment in cassava and soya-bean. Since only some communities already had some experience of improving *Imperata* control using researcher-developed technologies, trial design varied in each area and included "mother", "daughter" and "grand daughter" trials, which all played a role in testing and demonstrating new practices (Table 1).

Table 1: Trial types and treatments[1] in each State (Local Government Area) (2002)

Crop	Benue (Tarka) Mother trials (3)	Cross River (Ogoja) Daughter (3) and Grand daughter trials (72)	Kogi (Ankpa) Mother trials (8)
Cassava	HW, Gl, Gl+Mc, Fs		HW, Gl, Gl+Mc, Fs
Soya-bean	HW, Gl, Fs		
Maize			HW, Gl, Gl+Mc
Mixed crops[2]		HW, Gl, Gl+Mc	

[1]HW=Hand weed only, Gl=Glyphosate only, applied before tillage or after crop establishment, Gl+Mc= Glyphosate applied pre-tillage with *Mucuna* planted after HW, Fs=Fusilade applied after crop establishment
[2]Mixed crops = Cassava, yam, maize and palm.

In Benue State, replicated researcher-managed (mother) trials were established on farmers' fields, that had been under fallow for two years, and were infested with *Imperata* at densities of over 160 shoots /m². The area was initially burnt and *Imperata* foliage left to grow to 25-30 cm high before a pre-tillage application of glyphosate. The treatments comprised two inter-row spacings of soya-beans (75 cm and 50 cm, with an intra-row spacing of 10 cm). Three weed control options were tested: 1) pre-tillage glyphosate (applied as Sarosate, 2.16 kg a.i. /ha, (manufactured by Saro Agrochemicals-Nigeria) limited with one hoe-weeding (HW) at 6 weeks after planting (WAP); 2) post-emergence fluazifop-p-butyl, (applied as Fusilade super 125EC, 0.25 kg a.i./ha (manufactured by Zeneca Agrochemicals). Herbicides were applied by knapsack sprayer with a deflector-type impact nozzle and spray volume of 200 litres/ha at 2.5 bars, 3 WAP with one HW at 6 WAP; and 3) farmers' practice being two hoe weedings at 3 and 6 WAP. The trial was laid out in a split-plot design with four replications. Row spacing was the main plot (36 m ×12 m) with weed control options being sub-plots (12 m × 12 m). All plots were ridged by hoe, with management simulating farmers' practices. The soya-bean cultivar was TGX 1448-2E. Phosphorus was applied as single super phosphate at 40 kg/ha at 3 WAP. Data collected included grain yield, *Imperata* density before treatment and at harvest (12 WAP) and *Imperata* biomass at harvest.

In Kogi State, a researcher-managed maize "mother" trial was established on land abandoned due to severe *Imperata* infestation with densities above 100 plants/m^2. Treatments were maize inter-row spacings (0.75 m and 1 m) with three weed management options: 1) pre-planting glyphosate as before followed 10 days later by direct planting of maize without tillage, followed by two hoe weedings; 2) a similar treatment but with *Mucuna cochinchinensis* planted at 20,000 plants/ha just after first weeding and 3) farmers practice (hoe ridging before planting followed by two hoe weedings). Each treatment was replicated four times on a 15 m x 15 m plot, in a randomised complete block design. Each block was located on a different farm, each selected by the community. The data collected was yield at harvest, density and species of all weeds at harvest.

In Cross River State, where farmers were more aware of herbicide and *Mucuna* options for *Imperata* control, farmers formed groups each with a Lead Farmer (LF) appointed by the group. Each LF had 2-3 treatments (a daughter trial) with each member of the group having 1-2 treatments (grand daughter trials). Crops included palm, yam, cassava often intercropped with maize. IITA and extension agents provided support to LFs, who in turn supported others in the Group. It should be noted that "daughter" and "granddaughter" trials are presently being encouraged in both Benue and Kogi States.

Mid and end of season evaluations

Mid-season evaluation of the trials was undertaken in each area by farmers using pairwise ranking to compare treatments. During this process farmers' main evaluation criteria were identified and in order to identify different perspectives, groups of elders, youth and women undertook the evaluations separately. In addition, farmers' and local contractors' sprayers were inspected, with details of their use and condition recorded to assess their efficiency.

End of season results are only reported from the soya-bean and maize trials in Benue and Kogi at this stage, as cassava and yam, taking over 18 months before maturity remain to be harvested. Weed, maize and soya-bean data were analysed using SAS (Littell *et al.*, 1996). Means were separated using the standard errors of the mean. Economic analysis has been based on quantifying benefits (advantages) and costs (disadvantages) of each control method from a farmers' perspective using criteria identified during mid season evaluations.

RESULTS AND DISCUSSION

Natural resource problems, livelihood and resource ranking

Discussions in the three communities indicated that over 80% of households derive the major part of their livelihood from crop production, although this is decreasing due to high *Imperata* infestation rates. The main natural resource problems were weed infestation, notably *Imperata*, low soil fertility, and attack by pests and diseases. Although views differed slightly between the 'youth' and adult members of the communities, they both acknowledged weeds as the main farming problem. Hunting involving bush burning was increasing to meet family needs for food and income, exacerbating the spread of *Imperata*, and posing serious threat to bio-diversity due to destruction of forest. Crops mostly affected by *Imperata*, were yam, cassava, soya-beans, maize, bambara nut, cowpea, and oil palm. Existing control methods in order of importance included hand pulling, burning, deep hoe tillage, slashing and fallowing. Other methods recently introduced in Cross River and Kogi included herbicides and, cover crops (notably *Mucuna* sp). Farmers indicated that herbicides, slashing and burning ensured quick control, at least in the short term. However, farmers were aware that burning stimulates rapid growth of *Imperata*, decreases soil fertility, and could injure people or livestock. Although fallowing and cover crops were seen to suppress the weed and enhance soil fertility, length of fallow was decreasing due to population increase and farmers who had tried cover crops considered them to be labour-intensive. At the same time there was resistance to use of herbicides because of high cost, non-availability, and sometimes, ineffectiveness due to poor application skills and sometimes adulteration of herbicides.

Trials and demonstrations

Mid season evaluation

Criteria identified by farmers for evaluating the weed control methods included cost, labour requirement, effectiveness, effect on soil fertility, availability of inputs (seed, sprayers and chemicals), knowledge and skills requirement and yield benefits. Herbicides were favoured in all areas, glyphosate for pre-tillage control on all crops and fluazifop-p-butyl as a post emergent on soya-beans and cassava. Interestingly many older men preferred traditional hand weeding, as they were able to rely on family labour with no cash implications. Most women and youth preferred herbicides. Glyphosate with *Mucuna* was favoured by women in Cross River as having potential for soil fertility improvement but in other areas *Mucuna* was perceived as being competitive with the crop, labour intensive to incorporate into the soil and with little economic use. However farmers had not yet experienced the potential for increasing productivity of the following crop. In most areas the condition of many local sprayers is likely to lead to poor spray deposition with off target contamination in mixing areas and on operators.

End of season evaluations

Benue State. In Tarka, soya-bean grain yields were significantly higher in plots that received glyphosate followed by hand weeding and lowest in plots treated with fluazifop-p-butyl (Table 2). *Imperata* density and biomass were lower in glyphosate than in fluazifop-p-butyl and hoe weeding treatments.

Kogi State. In Ankpa, there was no significant treatment effect on maize grain yield (Table 2). Wide maize spacing reduced *Imperata* density from above 100 to 22 plants/m². Narrower spacing reduced the density from above 100 to less than 10 plants/m². There were no significant differences between the effects of the different weed management systems on *Imperata* density. However there was a shift in weed composition over the growing season. At the time of establishing the trial, the site was dominated by *Imperata* but by harvest weed composition had shifted to annual herbs dominated by *Oldenlandia* spp., *Cephalostigma* spp., and annual grasses such as *Digitaria horizontalis* and sedges. These weeds were however perceived by farmers to be easier to control than *Imperata*.

Table 2: Effect of control measures on soya-bean and maize grain yields, *Imperata* shoot density and biomass ± SE; weeding cost, crop value and margins over weeding cost (Benue and Kogi States, 2002)

Control option	Grain Yield (kg/ha)	*Imperata* density shoots/m²)	*Imperata* biomass (g/m²)	Weed control Costs ($/ha)[1]	Crop value ($/ha)	Margin over weeding cost ($/ha)[5]
Benue state (Soya-bean)						
Fluazifop-p-butyl	794 ± 55	3 ±1.3	33 ±4.1	39	254	215
Glyphosate	1031 ± 55	1 ±1.3	16 ±4.1	61	330	269
Farmer practice[2]	870 ± 55	6 ±1.3	36 ±4.1	60	279	219
Kogi state (Maize)						
Narrow spacing	854 ±138	6 ± 8.2	-		273	
Wide spacing	854 ±138	22 ± 7.4	-		273	
Glyphosate	854 ±138	ns	-	61	273	212
Glyphosate + Mucuna³	854 ±138	ns	-	78	273	204
Farmer practice[4]	854 ±138	ns		80	273	193

[1] *Imperata* control costs comprised the cost of herbicide and its application, hoe weeding, *Mucuna* seed and its planting
[2] First weeding cost $40/ha and the second hoe weeding half this amount
[3] *Mucuna* seed was estimated to cost the same as soya-bean seed although there is presently no market for *Mucuna*
[4] The costs of farmer practice was based on $40 for tillage and $20 for hand weeding
[5] Crop grain value was based on 2003 market prices of soya-bean and maize both being $0.32/kg
ns=no significant difference between treatments, - data not collected. Exchange rate: US $1=Naira 125

Farmer's practice of hand weeding twice, costs as much as glyphosate and glyphosate and *Mucuna* options in maize, and more than fluazifop-p-butyl in soya-beans. Although glyphosate costs more than hand weeding in soya-beans it gave the highest yields. As a result the highest margins over weeding costs were obtained with glyphosate in both soya-beans and maize. This was followed by hoe weeding only, then fluazifop-p-butyl in soya-beans, and glyphosate and *Mucuna*, then hoe weeding only in maize. High opportunity costs and non-availability of labour in Benue and Kogi make hoe weeding less viable as an *Imperata* control measure.

CONCLUSIONS

This work has shown that the community-based PREA is an important component of technology research. In the communities where *Imperata* was a priority problem, local control measures were failing and further options were identified and tested through joint consultations and agreement between stakeholders. Although this process is on going, farmers evaluation criteria based on the advantages and disadvantages of each control method were identified and used to evaluate the trials. Results to date indicate that herbicides have considerable potential for controlling *Imperata* with respect to both efficacy and profitability. Farmers' choice of glyphosate and fluazifop-p-butyl over hoe-weeding during the mid-season participatory evaluation was confirmed. Unfortunately although *Mucuna* also has potential, lack of short term economic benefit make it unattractive to farmers. However ongoing "daughter" and "granddaughter" trials and demonstrations should encourage wider adoption and farmer adaptation of an integrated approach to *Imperata* control using herbicides, *Mucuna* and handweeding This will assist in ensuring alternative control options are available for farmers with different access to resources. However it is essential that input supply systems are improved to ensure ready access to chemicals and sprayers, as well as improving farmer skills in their effective use.

ACKNOWLEDGEMENTS

This study is partially funded by the United Kingdom Department for International Development (DFID), (Project R7864C). However, DFID cannot be held responsible for any views expressed.

REFERENCES

Chikoye D; Manyong V M; Ekeleme F (2000). Characteristics of speargrass (*Imperata cylindrica*) dominated fields in West Africa: crops, soil properties, farmer perceptions and management strategies. *Crop Protection* **19**, 481-487.

Chikoye D; Ekeleme F; Ambe J T (1999). Survey of distribution and farmers' perceptions of speargrass (*Imperata cylindrica* (L.) Raeuschel] in cassava-based systems in West Africa. *International Journal of Pest Management* **44**, 1-7.

Hagmann J; Chuma E; Murwira K; Connelly M (1998). *Learning together through participatory extension. A guide to an Approach developed in Zimbabwe.* AGRITEX: Harare, Zimbabwe.

Littell R C; Milliken G A; Stroup W W; Wolfinger R D (1996). *A setting for Mixed Models Applications: Randomized Blocks Designs.* In *SAS*® System for Mixed Models, pp. 1-29. SAS® Institute Inc.: Cary, NC, USA.

Weber G; Elemo K; Lagoke S (1995). Weed communities in intensified cereal-based cropping systems of the Northern Guinea Savannah. *Weed Research*, **35**, 167-178.

Farmers, farms and physiology: an integrated approach to *Striga* research

S Pierce
Università degli Studi dell'Insubrica, Dipartimento di Biologia Strutturale e Funzionale, via J H Dunant, 21100, Varese, Italy
Email: dr_simon_pierce@hotmail.com

G Ley
Mlingano Agricultural Research Institute, Tanga, Tanzania

A M Mbwaga
Ilonga Agricultural Research Institute, PO Kilosa, Tanzania

R I Lamboll, C R Riches
Natural Resources Institute, University of Greenwich, Chatham Maritime, Kent ME4 4TB, UK

M C Press, J D Scholes
Department of Animal and Plant Sciences, University of Sheffield, Sheffield S10 2TN, UK.

ABSTRACT

Sorghum cultivar development in semi-arid Tanzania has understated the importance of heterogeneity in the farm environment. A new approach, combining farmer knowledge and on-farm involvement with field-station and controlled-environment quantification of sorghum growth, has provided baseline data on the response of cultivars to parasitic *Striga* species when different soil resources are available. Involving farmers and creating recommendations for the local use of the different cultivars represents a step towards empowering farmers to make informed choices in the selection of appropriate sorghums for diverse situations.

INTRODUCTION

Agricultural soils in semi-arid Tanzania are generally of low to moderate fertility. Low nitrogen (N) conditions favour the growth of witchweed (*Striga* spp.: Scrophulariaceae); root hemiparasites devastating to yields of cereal crops. Farmers recognise local soil types based on criteria including suitability for different crops, ease of cultivation, moisture retention and drainage (Lamboll *et al.*, 2001a). This study combined on-farm trials with fully replicated field-station trials and controlled-environment experiments (in which infection by *Striga* could be controlled) to assess the suitability of sorghums for a range of local soils. The effects of fertiliser on the host/parasite relationship were also evaluated. Investigated sorghums include P9405 and P9406 (registered in Tanzania as Hakika and Wahi, respectively) bred for resistance to *Striga* at Purdue University (Indiana, USA) and the released cultivars Macia and Pato (the latter a *Striga*-susceptible check). Decision trees were produced to facilitate understanding of sorghum cultivar choice in relation to local soils and fertility enhancement options.

MATERIALS AND METHODS

Participating farmers from Itope and Mwagala villages (Misungwi District, north west

Table 1. Summary of characteristics of the major soil types used for sorghum in Tanzania (names of soil types are the regional kisukuma (NW) and kigogo (Central) names). Data represent the mean ± 1 SE of nine replicates (n=6 for *nkuluhi* soil), with samples taken from farmers' fields in North West and Central Tanzania in October 2000. CEC = Cation exchange capacity. For more detailed farmers' descriptions see Lamboll *et al.* (2001a).

Soil type	Descriptions of soils	Chemical characteristics					
		pH (in KCl)	Org. C (%)	Total N (%)	C:N	Avail. P (mg/kg)	CEC (meq/kg)
NW Tanzania							
Ibushi	Clay loams to clay, grey/black. Moderate productivity. Friable when dry, becomes hard if left fallow. Retains water and is prone to waterlogging in lowlands, but is not prone to erosion.	5.8 ±0.06	1.5 ±0.04	0.11 ±0.002	13.3 ±0.32	6.2 ±0.64	21.2 ±2.40
Itogolo	Dark or light sandy clay loam. Moderate/poor productivity. Hard if dry, difficult to cultivate. Poor infiltration rate; water may stand on surface.	5.6 ±0.05	1.1 ±0.04	0.09 ±0.002	11.6 ±0.24	1.0 ±0.03	11.7 ±0.45
Luseni	Sandy, Red in lowlands, white in uplands. Easy to cultivate but unproductive.	5.1 ±0.02	0.4 ±0.01	0.04 ±0.001	11.9 ±0.28	4.2 ±0.60	1.6 ±0.05
Mbuga	Dark grey/brown, clay or sandy clay at valley floor. Very productive. Hard and difficult to cultivate unless moist for substantial period, but then more prone to erosion and waterlogging.	5.1 ±0.06	2.1 ±0.06	0.17 ±0.005	13.3 ±0.34	10.8 ±1.10	71.6 ±0.60
Central Tanzania							
Isanga	Coarse loam, sandy, grey-yellowish/brown. Very easy to dig.	5.6 ±0.07	1.5 ±0.05	0.13 ±0.002	11.2 ±0.33	18.4 ±2.16	6.6 ±0.27
Isanga chitope	Sandy clay. Productive.	5.3 ±0.03	0.5 ±0.03	0.05 ±0.003	11.6 ±0.30	14.9 ±0.98	4.8 ±0.23
Ngogomba	Grey clay soil. Hard when dry, very difficult to dig. Prone to surface runoff.	6.6 ±0.03	0.9 ±0.04	0.10 ±0.003	9.4 ±0.21	22.1 ±0.46	1.1 ±0.14
Nkuluhi	Red sandy clay loam. Easy to dig. Sticky when wet.	5.3 ±0.10	0.8 ±0.02	0.09 ±0.003	8.2 ±0.13	10.3 ±0.96	6.4 ±0.22

Tanzania, where soils are infested by *S. asiatica* and *S. hermonthica*) and Chipanga and Mvumi Makulu villages (Dodoma Rural District, Central Tanzania where *S. asiatica* is a problem) grew plots of sorghum cultivars Hakika, Macia, Pato and Wahi on a range of soil types (detailed in Table 1) from 2000 to 2002. Additional rows of these cultivars were fertilised using farmyard manure (FYM from cattle), with 0.25 or 0.5 kg (dry weight) applied to the base of each plant at planting. Farmers' perceptions of sorghum qualities (29 criteria were mentioned, about half being post-harvest, but yield, early maturity and drought tolerance were important to men and women everywhere) were recorded at group meetings in each village (see Lamboll *et al.*, 2001b), with information on local soils. Analysis of soil chemical characteristics and sorghum leaf tissue N and P contents are detailed in Pierce *et al.* (2003).

Fully replicated randomised-block experiments were implemented at Ukiriguru (*luseni* soil in NW Tanzania) and Hombolo field-stations (nkuluhi soil in Central Tanzania). At Hombolo manure was applied at rates of 0, 0.25 or 0.5 kg to the base of each plant following planting or urea at a rate of 50 kg/ha. At harvest, *Striga* numbers were counted, yields recorded, and soil and sorghum chemical constituents determined. During controlled-environment studies, the sorghum cultivars were grown in sand culture, and each plant infected with ~3000 pre-conditioned seeds of *S. hermonthica* (collected from Kibos, Kenya, in August 1997), with controls remaining uninfected. A day/night temperature of 28/22 °C was maintained, with 70/50 % r.h., a light intensity of ~500 µmol Q m^{-2}/s with a 12 h photoperiod. Following infection, pots were supplied with 40 % Long Ashton nutrient solution modified to provide nitrogen at 0.25, 0.5 or 1 mM N as NH_4NO_3, *via* an automatic irrigation system. After 85 days, sorghum plants were divided into root, pseudostem (true stem together with leaf sheaths), dead/senescent leaf material and green leaf material, and dry mass was determined.

RESULTS AND DISCUSSION

Characteristics of the soils sampled are shown in Table 1. On these soils, manure suppresses *Striga* when applied early in the growth season, with urea also effective (for example data for *nkuluhi* soil see Tables 2 and 3). However, urea application resulted in negligible yield increases on *nkuluhi* soil at Hombolo, with a lack of extra N in the soil/plant system at harvest. This sandy soil has a high infiltration rate (Ngalesoni, 2001), whereas clayey soils with higher organic matter content retain urea, also evident as enhanced yields for maize (Kwacha, 2001). Heavy rainfall occurred at Hombolo early in the trial, suggesting that urea was leached beyond the reach of sorghum roots. In contrast manure is rich in organic matter, retained N and other nutrients during the trial, so its use resulted in the highest yields and least *S. asiatica* numbers.

Table 2. An example of the effect of farmyard manure (FYM) addition on numbers of emerged *S. asiatica* at harvest and grain yield of different sorghum cultivars, in a 25 m^2 plot of *nkuluhi* soil (Mvumi Makulu village, Central Tanzania).

Cultivar	FYM application (kg/plant)	*Striga* count	Yield (kg)
Hakika	0	948	3.4
	0.5	325	4.5
Macia	0	2378	2.5
	0.5	1485	3.5
Pato	0	545	0.8
	0.5	892	1.1
Wahi	0	1204	3.1
	0.5	537	3.5

Table 3. An example of soil, leaf and grain characteristics of four cultivars of sorghum at Hombolo research station (Central Tanzania) grown with 0.25, 0.5 kg FYM per plant or 50 kg/ha N as urea, or no fertiliser treatment (control) on *nkaluhi* soil infested with *S. asiatica*. Data represent the mean ± SE of four replicates.

Cultivar	Fertiliser treatment	Striga count (plants/m²)	Soil pH (in KCl)	Total N (g/kg)	C:N	Avail. P (mg/kg)	Leaf N (mg/g)	Leaf P (mg/g)	Grain N (mg/g)	Grain P (mg/g)	Yield (t/ha)
Hakika	Control	5.7 ±4.17	4.7 ±0.06	0.5 ±0.17	12.4 ±1.95	4.7 ±2.97	16.0 ±2.42	1.2 ±0.23	18.6 ±1.34	2.5 ±0.36	1.8 ±0.30
	0.25 kg FYM	3.0 ±2.42	5.4 ±0.15	0.9 ±0.01	10.8 ±1.02	13.9 ±1.18	19.2 ±1.87	1.6 ±0.24	17.3 ±0.35	3.8 ±0.39	1.8 ±0.21
	0.5 kg FYM	1.0 ±0.41	5.6 ±0.11	0.9 ±0.13	12.8 ±0.84	23.3 ±6.68	24.4 ±1.58	2.1 ±0.47	16.5 ±0.87	3.3 ±0.37	2.1 ±0.09
	Urea	4.3 ±4.33	4.3 ±0.10	0.4 ±0.12	13.9 ±1.39	2.6 ±0.62	15.6 ±0.95	1.4 ±0.40	16.8 ±0.40	2.6 ±0.13	2.0 ±0.22
Macia	Control	42.5 ±30.71	4.6 ±0.13	0.7 ±0.16	12.1 ±1.97	2.2 ±0.19	16.6 ±0.80	0.9 ±0.10	17.0 ±0.08	2.1 ±0.11	0.9 ±0.36
	0.25 kg FYM	13.0 ±4.27	5.3 ±0.12	0.8 ±0.17	10.5 ±1.61	9.4 ±1.17	19.0 ±1.08	1.2 ±0.08	18.4 ±0.81	3.0 ±0.23	1.9 ±0.21
	0.5 kg FYM	7.1 ±3.23	5.3 ±0.17	0.9 ±0.07	12.0 ±0.69	16.6 ±6.82	20.1 ±1.56	1.2 ±0.08	16.0 ±0.67	2.8 ±0.23	1.6 ±0.19
	Urea	7.4 ±5.88	4.3 ±0.07	0.5 ±0.07	13.5 ±1.10	2.4 ±1.03	16.2 ±2.04	1.1 ±0.21	20.6 ±0.72	2.6 ±0.16	1.5 ±0.41
Pato	Control	49.0 ±29.23	4.7 ±0.19	0.5 ±0.18	12.1 ±1.51	5.3 ±1.66	12.1 ±2.42	0.8 ±0.04	15.8 ±1.32	1.9 ±0.11	1.0 ±0.30
	0.25 kg FYM	38.9 ±28.15	5.4 ±0.22	0.8 ±0.13	11.1 ±1.50	10.6 ±2.59	9.8 ±1.14	0.8 ±0.12	16.5 ±0.86	2.5 ±0.24	2.4 ±0.50
	0.5 kg FYM	11.1 ±4.34	5.5 ±0.21	1.0 ±0.16	11.1 ±0.57	16.4 ±7.77	15.0 ±1.37	1.1 ±0.22	13.9 ±0.77	2.9 ±0.29	2.5 ±0.07
	Urea	6.5 ±5.84	4.5 ±0.04	0.7 ±0.18	10.9 ±1.95	3.5 ±0.50	10.7 ±1.28	0.7 ±0.06	19.2 ±1.69	2.5 ±0.17	1.3 ±0.40
Wahi	Control	11.6 ±6.63	4.7 ±0.11	0.6 ±0.19	13.3 ±1.84	2.9 ±0.86	19.0 ±1.62	1.2 ±0.21	17.9 ±0.79	2.7 ±0.41	1.7 ±0.27
	0.25 kg FYM	14.3 ±12.59	5.3 ±0.14	1.0 ±0.00	9.1 ±0.53	12.4 ±2.38	11.9 ±1.56	0.9 ±0.17	18.7 ±1.12	3.4 ±0.31	2.3 ±0.40
	0.5 kg FYM	6.3 ±3.51	5.5 ±0.14	1.0 ±0.05	10.8 ±0.29	22.8 ±5.19	19.5 ±1.43	1.2 ±0.12	17.9 ±1.08	2.9 ±0.09	2.1 ±0.26
	Urea	7.0 ±6.78	4.3 ±0.09	0.5 ±0.08	13.0 ±1.01	2.8 ±0.20	17.1 ±1.83	1.1 ±0.15	18.3 ±1.44	2.8 ±0.26	1.8 ±0.20

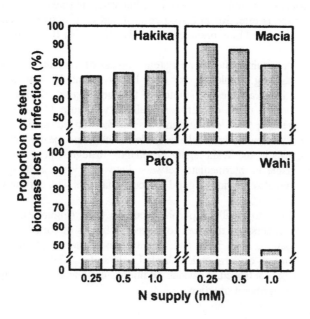

Figure 1. The proportion of sorghum stem biomass lost on infection with *Striga hermonthica*, under differing nitrogen supply (0.25, 0.5 or 1.0 mM N as ammonium nitrate) in controlled-environment conditions. Sorghum cultivars were Hakika, Macia, Pato and Wahi. Data represent the mean of six replicates.

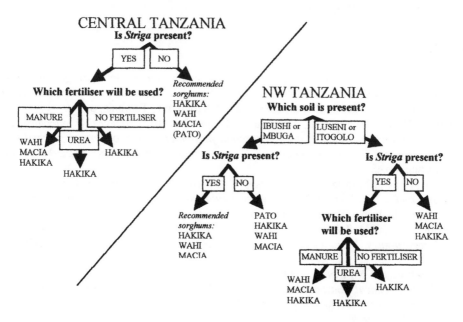

Figure 2. Decision trees outlining the choices of sorghum cultivars recommended for growth on soils in North West and Central Tanzania (N.B. Central soils were all either poor or extremely inconsistent, and so are not differentiated between in this scheme).

Data from *in situ* trials were subject to variability, but when all trials are considered together it is apparent that manure is effective in *Striga* control and crop nutrition, and upper-limits for application will be constrained by economics and availability rather than N-toxicity.

With sufficient N, Pato attained the greatest stem biomass of the cultivars tested, and typically had the highest yields (e.g. Table 3), but was heavily stunted when infected with *Striga* (Figure 1). Wahi and Hakika were not stunted to the same extent. Hakika retained the same degree of tolerance over a range of nitrogen availability (Figure 1). In the field Hakika and Wahi had yields surpassing those of Pato and Macia when no nutrients were applied (Tables 2 and 3). Thus, Hakika is particularly reliable (indeed, the name means 'certain'), and farmers also ranked Hakika, Macia and Wahi highly for *Striga*-, drought-, pest- and disease-resistance (data not shown). Macia is intermediate between Pato and Wahi in its growth response to *Striga* and fertiliser, and also provides a good choice for farmers who currently grow Pato.

Data has been distilled into locally applicable decision trees (Figure 2). These can facilitate extension workers to understand the need to consider choices of sorghums appropriate to the level of *Striga* infestation, local soils and fertility enhancement options. This approach to *Striga* research, integrating on-farm and replicated field-station trials with pot studies in which *Striga* infection can be controlled, provides additional confidence in the applicability of the research findings to the farmer's situation.

ACKNOWLEDGEMENTS

This work was funded by the UK Department for International Development and the Government of Tanzania. The views expressed are not necessarily those of DFID (Project R7564 Crop Protection Programme).

REFERENCES

Kwacha J C P H (2001). *Effects of nitrogen and farmyard manure on maize grown in areas under heavy infestation of Striga (Striga asiatica): a case study of Mlingano, Tanga, Tanzania. MSc. Thesis.* Sokoine University of Agriculture, Tanzania. pp. 76.

Lamboll R; Hella J; Riches C R; Mbwaga A M; Ley G (2001a). *Integrated management of Striga species on cereal crops in Tanzania: preliminary study of farmer perceptions of soil resources in Central, Lake and Eastern zones.* Chatham, UK: Natural Resources Institute. pp.43.

Lamboll R; Hella J; Mbwaga A M; Riches C R (2001b). *Striga research activities in Central Zone and Lake Zone of Tanzania: evaluation of on-farm research trials 2000/2001 season.* Chatham, UK: Natural Resources Institute. pp. 65.

Ngalesoni G S (2001) *Relating erosivity factors to soil loss: a case study of Hombolo and Morogoro sites. MSc. Thesis.* Morogoro, Tanzania: Sokoine University of Agriculture. pp. 76.

Pierce S; Mbwaga A M; Ley G; Lamboll R I; Riches C R; Press M C; Scholes J D; Watling J (2003). *Chemical characteristics of soil and sorghum from Striga-infested regions of Tanzania, and the influence of fertiliser application.* Sheffield, UK: University of Sheffield. pp. 29.

Promoting integrated *Striga* management practices in maize in northern Nigeria

I Kureh, M A Hussaini
Institute for Agricultural Research, Ahmadu Bello University, PMB. 1044, Zaria, Nigeria
Email: ikurehng@yahoo.com

D Chikoye, A M Emechebe, P Kormawa, S Schulz, G Tarawali, A C Franke
International Institute of Tropical Agriculture, Ibadan, Nigeria

J Ellis-Jones
Silsoe Research Institute, Wrest Park, Silsoe, Bedfordshire MK45 4HS, UK

ABSTRACT

Striga hermonthica is a serious parasite of cereals that causes substantial yield losses in savannah zones of much of sub-Saharan Africa. Adoption of integrated control methods involving legume-cereal rotations and the use of resistant host cultivars has been less than expected. As a result, a participatory research and extension approach has been used to encourage farmer involvement in improving *Striga* management to promote wider adoption. Integral to the research were two researcher managed "mother" and 155 farmer managed "daughter" trials each learning from the other. In the "mother" trials a *Striga* tolerant maize cv. Across 97 TZLcomp.1-W, produced higher grain yield, supported fewer *Striga* plants, and was less damaged than TZB-SR, a susceptible cultivar widely grown by farmers. Vigour and grain yield of maize was lowest in plots that did not receive N and increased with higher N rates. The incidence of *Striga* and crop damage was higher where no N was applied and decreased with increased N application. The "daughter" trials, provided opportunity for farmer testing, monitoring and evaluation, with most farmers indicating higher productivity with less *Striga* using *Striga* control methods. Net output increased on average by $183/ha over traditional farmer practices with greatest returns being achieved from a maize/soya-bean intercrop.

INTRODUCTION

Striga hermonthica a parasitic weed constitutes one of the greatest biotic constraints to cereal crop production in sub-Saharan African with estimated yield losses up to 46% in the Guinea savannah (GS) of Nigeria, (Oikeh *et al.,* 1996). Continuous cereal mono-cropping has intensified the *Striga* problem with grazing cattle, infected seed, and wind contributing to the spread of the weed (Berner *et al.*, 1996). This is further compounded by *Striga's* reproductive capacity; with a single plant producing over 50,000 seeds, which can remain viable in the soil for 15-20 years (Doggett, 1988). Past research identified several effective control options. These include host plant resistance, use of trap-crops, and the improvement and maintenance of soil fertility through cereal-legume rotation and intercropping (Parker & Riches; 1993, Carsky *et al.*, 2000; Kureh *et al.*, 2000, Schulz *et al.*, 2003). Although the potential of these *Striga* management practices has been demonstrated in researcher-managed trials, adoption by farmers is less than expected. The participatory research and extension approach (PREA) reported in this paper has encouraged farmers to test alternative *Striga* control options under their conditions to facilitate wider adoption (Hagmann *et al.*, 1998). The process consisted of community analysis, problem diagnosis, action planning, experimentation, monitoring and evaluation using a "mother-daughter" approach to the research. Researcher managed "mother" trials with farmer selected and managed on-farm "daughter" trials allowed farmers and extension staff from Government, NGOs, and farmer organizations an opportunity to observe, test and compare different *Striga* management options.

MATERIALS AND METHODS

Community analysis and mobilisation

Community workshops held in 2002, involving 42 villages in northern Nigeria, allowed assessment of livelihood strategies, natural resources problems and their prioritisation, major crops, household resources, local institutions, problems arising from *Striga* infestation, local coping mechanisms and identification of methods farmers saw as priorities for field testing through visits to "mother" trials. As a result, local institutions and farmers were selected by each community to test alternative *Striga* control options, namely, legume trap crops causing *Striga* suicidal germination, *Striga* resistant/tolerant maize varieties and legume-cereal rotations.

Mother trials

Two research managed on-station 'mother' trials were conducted at Samaru ($11°11'$N, $7°36'$E, 686 masl), in the GS of Nigeria. The first investigated the effect of maize cultivar, and legume/maize rotation on incidence and severity of *S. hermonthica* in maize. The treatments consisted of two maize cultivars (Across 97 TZL Comp.1-W, a tolerant cultivar and TZB-SR, a susceptible cultivar, widely grown by farmers, three legume trap-crops (soybean cv. TGX 1448-2E, cowpea cv. IT93K452-1 and groundnut cv. RMP 12), and natural fallow. Treatments were arranged in a randomized complete block design with three replications. Land was ploughed, harrowed, and ridged (0.75 m apart). The experimental field was inoculated with *Striga* seed prior to sowing. Maize, cowpea and groundnut were sown at an intra-row spacing of 25 cm. Two seeds of each crop were seeded per stand and thinned two weeks after sowing (WAS) to one plant per stand. Soya-bean was drilled and thinned to an intra-row spacing of 5 cm.

Maize plots were hoe weeded at 2 WAS, earthed up at 6 WAS followed with hand pulling of weeds, other than *Striga*. Legumes were hoe weeded at 3 and 6 WAS. Fertilizer was applied to maize at a dose of 120 N/ha, 26 kg P/ha and 50 kg K/ha using NPK (15:15:15) and urea. All P and K and half of the N were applied at 2 WAS while the remaining N was top dressed at 6 WAS. Legumes were fertilized with 20 kg N/ha, 18 kg P/ha and 17 kg K/ha using NPK (15:15:15) mixed with single super phosphate (P_2O_5). Cowpeas were sprayed with a mixture of 30 g kg a.i. /ha of cypermethrin and 250 kg a.i. /ha of dimethoate (BASF Corp.) and with 200 g a.i. /ha Benomyl (Dupont Agricultural Products) at flowering and at podding to control diseases and insect pests. Data collected included the *Striga* seedbank at 0-15 cm depth, *Striga* count (11 WAS and at harvest), and grain yield. The *Striga* seedbank was assessed just before planting in 2002 using the elutriation method (Eplee & Norris, 1990). Farmers visited these trials to evaluate and choose treatment for their experimentation. The second on-farm "mother" trial evaluated the interaction between resistant and susceptible maize cultivars and nitrogen rates on the incidence and severity of *Striga* over a two-year period. No trap crops were involved. The treatments consisted of the same cultivars as the first trial and five N levels (0, 40, 80, 120, and 160 kg N/ha). All plots received 27 kg P/ha and 26 kg K/ha using single super phosphate and muriate of potash, respectively, at planting. Half of the N was applied at 2 WAP and the rest at 6 WAP. Data on both trials were analysed using SAS (Littell *et al.*, 1996). Means were separated using the standard error of the mean.

Daughter trials

As a result of the community mobilisation activities and visits to mother trials by farmers, 155 Lead Farmers each representing local groups in 53 villages tested a *Striga* control method of their choosing with support from extension agents (EAs) in 2002. Each trial comprised a split plot of a *Striga* control option and a local practice. Options selected comprised sole leguminous trap crops, mostly soya-bean (over 50% of trials), groundnuts (13%) *Striga* resistant maize (19%) and maize intercropped with a legume trap crop (17%), again mostly soya-bean, the latter being an adaptation of a mother trial treatment. *Striga* control varieties were the same as those on the mother trials. Farmer practices included local varieties of maize, sorghum and legume/cereal intercrops. Mid and end of season evaluations, facilitated by EAs, were undertaken by each group of farmers to identify advantages and disadvantages of the *Striga* control options and to undertake a participatory budgeting exercise comparing *Striga* control with farmer practice. The trials are continuing into a second season so that a two-year rotational effect becomes apparent. Results from the first season are reported in this paper.

RESULTS

Community analysis and mobilisation

Discussions during community workshops indicated that crop production was the main source of livelihood for over 80% of households. Major natural resource problems in priority order were *Striga* infestation, poor soil fertility, lack of fertilizer, other weeds, and lack of improved seeds. The three most important crops in all communities (maize, sorghum and pearl millet) are attacked by *Striga,* causing up to 100% crop loss. Increasing incidence and severity of *Striga* was attributed to lack of capital, decline in soil fertility, and continuous cropping of host crops. Common *Striga* control methods included hoe weeding, hand pulling, application of urea and manure, cereal/legume intercropping and rotations, fallowing. Early planting with legume-cereal intercrops and rotations were the most popular. However no use of leguminous trap crops or resistant varieties had occurred.

Mother trials

Cultivar effect on *Striga* infection and maize performance: *Striga* tolerant maize (Across 97 TZL Comp.1-W) produced 8% more grain yield (P=0.05), supported 98% less *Striga,* exhibited more vigorous growth and had less crop damage than the susceptible cultivar (TZB-SR) (Table 1). The *Striga* seedbank was 63% higher in soils collected from plots where the tolerant maize was grown.

Table 1. Effect of maize cultivar on *Striga* infestation, crop damage severity crop vigour and maize grain yield (Samaru, Nigeria, 2002)

Cultivar	Crop vigour[1]	*Striga* seedbank (no./100g soil)	*Striga* count (no./ha)	*Striga* damage rating[2]	Grain yield (kg /ha)
Across 97 TZL Comp.1-W	8.5	10.6	5985	3.1	4078
TZB-SR	7.9	6.5	11881	3.7	3769
SE	0.2	1.5	1310	0.2	144

[1]Crop vigour score using a scale 1-10; where 1=completely dead plants and 10=healthy plants
[2]*Striga* damage rating using a scale 1-9; where 1=healthy plants and 9=dead plants

Rotation effects on *Striga*. Maize grain yield, averaged over cultivars in the season after the legume trap crop was up to 28% higher than either continuous maize or maize after fallow (Table 2). Maize after fallow or legume trap crop had greater crop vigour and less *Striga* damage than continuous maize. Continuous maize had the highest *Striga* count, followed by maize after fallow with the least being in maize grown after legume trap crops. Maize after groundnut and cowpea supported the lowest incidence of *Striga*. Maize after fallow had the highest incidence of *Striga* in the seedbank.

Table 2. Rotation effect of legume trap-crops on *Striga* incidence, crop damage severity, maize vigour, grain yield averaged over cultivar (Samaru, Nigeria, 2002)

Types of rotation	Crop vigour[1]	*Striga* seed bank (no./100g soil)	*Striga* count (no./ha)	*Striga* damage rating[2]	Grain yield (kg /ha)
Continuous maize	7.5	8.7	11,556	4.1	3402
Maize after Fallow	8.2	13.2	8,519	3.6	3484
Maize after Soybean	8.5	6.2	7,778	3.1	4277
Maize after Cowpea	8.7	6.2	4222	3.0	4363
Maize after Groundnut	8.4	8.7	2593	3.0	4091
SE	0.3	2.4	2071	0.3	228

[1]Crop vigour score using a scale 1-10; where 1=completely dead plants and 10=healthy plants
[2]*Striga* damage rating using a scale 1-9; where 1=healthy plants and 9=dead plants

Nitrogen effects on *Striga* infection and maize performance. Maize vigour and grain yield were lowest where no N was applied and increased with higher N rates (Table 3). *Striga* incidence and crop damage were higher where no N was applied and decreased with higher N rates.

Table 3. Effect of nitrogen on *Striga* and maize grain yield (averaged over cultivar for two seasons, 2001 and 2002)

N level	Crop vigour[1]	*Striga* count (no./ha)	*Striga* damage rating[2]	Grain yield (kg /ha)
0	4.7	5111	7.7	187
40	6.2	3481	4.5	671
80	7.3	1815	2.7	997
120	8.2	3222	3.1	1427
160	7.0	2777	2.8	1402
SE	0.4	1259	0.4	195

[1]Crop vigour score using a scale 1-10; where 1=completely dead plants and 10=healthy plants
[2]*Striga* damage rating using a scale 1-9; where 1=healthy plants and 9=dead plants

Daughter trials

Most farmers achieved higher output with less *Striga*, being the two main advantages identified during farmer evaluations. Other advantages identified by farmers largely related to comparison of soya-bean varieties, where the legume trap crop variety was seen to shatter less, germinate better, grow better, require less fertiliser and be earlier maturing than local varieties. Other perceived advantages included bigger, visually more attractive and better quality grain with greater weed suppression during growth. However in a few cases farmers achieved higher output from their local practice, usually where maize was grown with high rates of inorganic fertiliser, confirming the results shown in the "mother" trials. The most often quoted disadvantage was increased difficulty in planting soya-beans in the narrower rows required to increase plant population sufficiently to encourage greater *Striga* suicidal germination, the benefits of which should be apparent in the following season. Other problems were largely associated with narrower rows, such as greater difficulty in making ridges, fertilising and weeding as well as requiring more seed.

Partial budgets comparing *Striga* control options and farmer practice indicated an overall increased net output of US $183/ha over farmer practice, although this varied considerably between the options tested (Table 4). Maize-soya-bean intercrops gave the highest return ($278/ha), legume trap crops grown on their own gave similar but lower increases ($189/ha in the case of soya-beans and sole maize lower still, $115/ha).

Table 4. Mean increase of *Striga* control[1] over farmer practice[2] (US $ /ha) from 155 farmer trials and demonstrations

	Soya-beans	*Striga* resistant Maize	Maize and soya-beans	Maize and cowpeas	Maize, soya-beans and cowpeas	Groundnuts	Overall
	n=78	n=30	n=20	n=3	n=3	n=20	n=155
Increased benefit							
Grain value	185	157	276	273	153	188	192
Crop residue value	8	6	20	17	29	43	14
Total increased output	193	163	297	289	182	231	206
Increased costs							
Seed cost	4	4	2	8	6	14	5
Fertiliser cost	-32	21	-26	14	18	-18	-17
Labour cost	32	23	44	70	59	56	36
Total increased cost	4	48	19	92	83	53	24
Increased net output	189	115	278	198	99	179	183
Rank	3	5	1	2	6	4	

[1]These were the same cultivars as grown on the "mother" trials.
[2]Farmer practice included local maize, sorghum, legumes and cereal-legume intercropping

CONCLUSIONS

Striga had a greater detrimental effect on growth, development and productivity of TZB-SR, the susceptible cultivar, than on Across. 97 TZL Comp. 1-W, the resistant cultivar. Growing maize in rotation after a leguminous trap crops produced greater crop vigour, less *Striga* and crop damage, higher yield and reduced the *Striga* seedbank compared to two seasons of continuous maize cultivation. Higher doses of nitrogen fertilizer reduced *Striga* damage and increased crop yields, though there seemed little increased *Striga* benefit beyond 40 kg N /ha. Maize yield increase at higher N levels is likely to be related to improved N availability rather than reduced *Striga* infestation. Results from "mother" and "daughter" trials indicate that an integrated *Striga* control strategy with improved nitrogen management (through legumes and better fertilizer and manure management) is most likely to control *Striga* successfully.

The extent to which local farmers tested and demonstrated *Striga* control options show the demand stimulated by using PREA. This indicates a potential for widespread scaling-up, based on local institution and farmer-managed testing and demonstrations of leguminous trap crops, *Striga* resistant maize and inter-planting of these maize and legume varieties. Increases in productivity through both benefit increase and cost reduction, particularly fertiliser reduction mean that these technologies can be used by poorer households.

ACKNOWLEDGEMENTS

This study is partially funded by the United Kingdom Department for International Development (DFID), (Project R7864C). However, DFID cannot be held responsible for any views expressed.

REFERENCES

Berner D K; J K Kling; B B Singh (1996). *Striga* research and control. A Perspective from Africa. *Plant Disease* **79,** 652-660

Eplee R E; Norris A (1990). Soil sampling collection equipment and equipment to separate seeds from the soil. In: *Witchweed research and control in the United States*, eds P F Sand, R E Eplee & RG Westbrooks, pp 126-135. Weed Science Society of America: Champaign, IL 61820, USA.

Carsky R J; Berner D K; Oyewole B D; Dashiell K; Schulz A (2000). Reduction of *Striga hermonthica* parasitism on maize using soybean rotation. *International Journal of Pest Management* **46,** 115-120

Doggett H (1988) Witch weed (*Striga*). In: *Sorghum. 2nd edn*, ed. G Wrigley, pp. 368-404. Longman Scientific and Technical: London, UK.

Hagmann J; Chuma E; Murwira K; Connelly M (1998). *Learning together through participatory extension. A guide to an Approach developed in Zimbabwe*. AGRITEX: Harare, Zimbabwe.

Kureh I; Chiezey U F; Tarfa B D (2000) On-station verification of the use of soybean trap-crop for the control of *Striga* in maize. *African Crop Science Journal* **8,** 295-300

Littell R C; Milliken G A; Stroup W W; Wolfinger R D; (1996) *A setting for Mixed Models Applications: Randomized Blocks Designs*. In *SAS®* System for Mixed Models, pp. 1-29. SAS® Institute Inc.: Cary, NC, USA.

Parker C; Riches C (1993) *Parasitic Weeds of the World: Biology and Control*. CAB International: Wallingford, UK

Oikeh SO; Weber G; Lagoke S T O; A E (1996). Assessment of yield loss from *Striga hermonthica* in farmers' fields in the northern Guinea Savanna. *Nigerian Journal of Weed Science* **9,** 1-6.

Schulz S; Hussaini M A; Kling J G; Berner D K; Ikie F O (2003). Evaluation of integrated *Striga hermonthica* control technologies under farmer management. *Experimental Agriculture* **39,** 99-108

Improving rice-based cropping systems in north-west Bangladesh: diversification and weed management

M Mazid, M A Jabber
Bangladesh Rice Research Institute, Joydepur, Gazipur, 1701, Bangladesh

M Mortimer
International Rice Research Institute, DAPO Box 7777, Metro Manila, Philippines
School of Biological Sciences, University of Liverpool, Liverpool, L69 3BX, UK
Email: A.M.Mortimer@liverpool.ac.uk

L Wade
School of Plant Biology, The University of Western Australia, Crawley WA 6009, Australia

C R Riches, A W Orr
Natural Resources Institute, University of Greenwich, Chatham, Kent ME4 4TB, UK

ABSTRACT

Improving total productivity in the rice-*rabi* cropping system in Bangladesh depends on elevating component yields whilst minimizing the risk of drought to both crops. Direct seeding of rice has the potential of advancing crop establishment with the onset of monsoon rains and allowing greater opportunities for subsequent *rabi* (chick-pea, mustard, linseed) crops on residual moisture as the dry season commences. Agronomic studies over three years indicated that rice yields could be increased over traditional transplanting by use of direct seeding in both a widely used (Swarna) and more recently introduced cultivar (BRRI dhan 39). Oxadiazon applied pre-emergence controlled major weeds but one manual weeding was needed for yield protection from weed competition from *Altenanthera sessilis*, *Cyperus iria* and *Paspalum distichum* in particular. Socio-economic evaluation indicated that adoption of direct seeded rice was more likely to occur on large farms where competition for labour at times of peak demand was intense and where there was a greater proportion of land area favourable for *rabi* cropping.

INTRODUCTION

A single crop of transplanted rainfed rice (TPR), grown in the monsoon *aman* season from June to October provides a major component of rural livelihoods in the High Barind Tract, in NW Bangladesh. *Aman* rice is vulnerable to late-season drought during grain filling in October and in the dry *rabi* (winter) season much of the land lies fallow. Cultivation intensity in much of the Barind is below 175%, and considerably less than in districts where irrigation allows two or three rice crops to be grown each year (Nur-E-Elahi *et al.*, 1999). Farmers' land is typically distributed over a shallow sloping landscape or toposequence. The objective facing agricultural improvement is to simultaneously improve the reliability and yield of *aman* rice while increasing the total system productivity. Mazid *et al.* (2002) have demonstrated that this can be achieved by using direct dry seeded rice (DSR) and planting of short duration *rabi* crops (e.g. mustard, linseed or chickpea) on residual moisture immediately after rice harvest. Late onset of the monsoon or low rainfall can delay rice transplanting as a minimum of 600 mm cumulative rainfall is needed to complete land preparation and transplanting. Direct seeding, on the other hand, can be completed after land preparation by a power tiller with only 150 mm cumulative rainfall (Saleh & Bhuiyan, 1995). The earlier planted DSR crop matures 1-2 weeks before TPR reducing the risk of terminal drought, and allows earlier planting of a following non-rice crop (Saleh *et al.*, 2000).

In comparison to TPR, DSR reduces labour and draught power requirements for rice establishment by 16% and 30% respectively, but weeds are a major constraint to adoption of DSR (Mazid *et al.*, 2002). Monitoring of farmer managed transplanted *aman* rice crops in the Barind revealed that labour availability constrains timeliness of first weeding for many households and with current practices 34% of farmers lose over 0.5 t/ha of the attainable yield due to weed competition (Mazid *et al.*, 2001). This study also reported that the integration of a pre-emergence herbicide with hand weeding has the potential to protect yield in DSR. Farmers in the Barind have a strong preference for the late maturing, but coarse rice cultivar Swarna (a long duration photosensitive cultivar). Use of this cultivar however reduces the opportunity for establishing chickpea or other *rabi* crops on residual moisture, whereas growing earlier maturing modern cultivars may contribute to an earlier harvest. This paper summarises selected findings from a long term field experiment designed to explore the contribution of rice establishment method, rice cultivar duration and weed control practice to *aman* rice performance and the long-term impact on the rice weed flora. Associated investigations of socio-economic factors influencing future adoption of direct seeding and increased *rabi* cropping by Barind farmers are also summarised.

METHODS

From the 2000 planting season, rice establishment, nutrient management and weeding practices have been investigated on farmland at Rajabari, Rajshahi District in the Barind. In this paper we report results for rice crops in 2000, 2001 and 2002, comparing rice crop establishment methods and weed management practices. Treatments were: 1) *Transplanted rice (TPR)* - soil was puddled prior to transplanting rice which was hand weeded twice at 30 and 45 days after transplanting (DAT); 2) *Direct seeded rice (DSR)* - soil was ploughed prior to seeding rice in rows by hand with hand weeding at 21, 33 and 45 days after sowing (DAS); 3) *Direct seeded rice with chemical weed control (DSRH)* -as for DSR but with oxidiazon (375 g a.i./ha) applied 2-4 days after seeding with one hand weeding at 33 DAS. Plots of these treatments were sown to the cultivars Swarna (maturity 140 – 145 days) and BRRI dhan 39 (maturity 120 - 125 days). Biomass of individual weed species was recorded in two quadrats per plot at 28 days DAS/DAT and total weed biomass at 45 DAS/DAT and again at harvest. Information on timeliness of farmer weeding was collected as part of a questionnaire survey of 119 households in Rajshahi district (Orr & Jabbar, 2002). Socio-economic factors likely to influence crop intensification were investigated by a second survey, undertaken after the 2001 rice harvest, of 91 households in 12 villages. This focused on the availability of labour for weeding and the key determinants of *rabi* cropping that will influence the area planted in the post-rice season.

RESULTS

Crop establishment method

With the exception of BRRI dhan 39 in 2000, yields from direct seeding of this and cv. Swarna were as good or better than from transplanting, the usual method of rice culture in the district

(Figure 1). Early season weed control, by pre-emergence application of herbicide resulted in the highest yields except for BRRI dhan 39 in 2000.

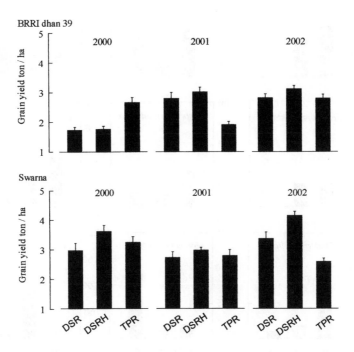

Figure 1. Effect of establishment and weed control practices on the yield (mean ± SEM) of rice cultivars BRRI dhan 39 and Swarna. DSR = direct seeded, hand weeded; DSRH = direct seeded + herbicide; TPR = transplanted rice + hand weeded.

Weed species shifts

The weed flora of rainfed rice in the Barind is diverse and exhibits high inter-seasonal variability depending on water regimes at rice establishment and soil moisture status of toposequence position. Common weed species are *Alternanthera sessilis, Ammania baccifera, Cyanotis axillaris, Cynodon dactylon, Cyperus difformis, Cyperus iria, Cyperus rotundus, Cyperus tenuispica, Echinocloa colona, Eclipta prostrata, Eriocaulon cinereum, Fimbristylis dichotoma, Fimbristylis miliacea, Hedyotis corymbosa, Lindernia ciliata, Ludwigia octovalvis, Monochoria vaginalis, Paspalum distichum, Paspalum distichum, Pseudoraphis spinescens* and *Sphaeranthus indicus*. At harvest there were significantly higher densities of weeds in DSR (228 m^{-2}) in comparison to TPR (75 m^{-2}; $P \leq 0.023$). However as expected at 45 DAS/DAT, least weed density and biomass was recorded in DSRH. The range of responses by individual weed species over three consecutive seasons to crop establishment and weed management practices is shown in Figure 2. Increase in abundance (biomass at 28 DAS/DAT) of the broadleaved species *Alternanthera sessilis, Eclipta prostrata, Lindernia ciliata* and *Ludwigia octovalvis* and the sedges *Cyperus difformis* and *Fimbrystilis miliacea* was noticeable in DSR. Conversely the biomass of *Monochoria vaginalis* was decreased by direct seeding. The most noticeable increase in abundance was seen in the perennial grass *Paspalum distichum*.

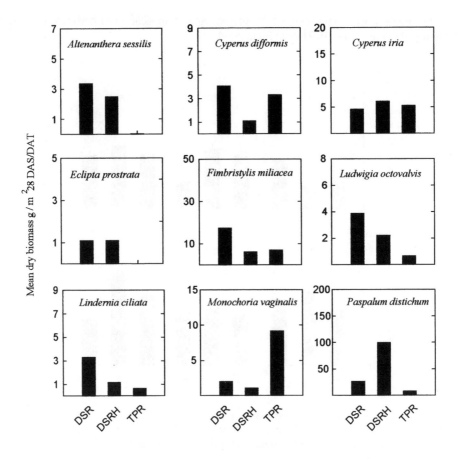

Figure 2. Effect of establishment and weed control practices on the biomass of nine rice weeds at 28 days after planting in unweeded plots. See text for details.

Socio-economics

Survey analysis did not reveal a significant difference in household labour supply by farm size but there was a lower participation rate ($P \leq 0.05$) of male family members on the upper tercile of larger holdings of over 2.7 ha. The area of transplanted *aman* per adult male worker was much higher on the large farms, averaging 2 ha per worker or four times greater than that of the smallest farms (below 0.6 ha in the lower tercile of the sample). Whilst larger farms faced a significant shortage of family labour for weeding, the survey revealed that virtually all rice was weeded with some additional hired labour irrespective of farm size. Results for the *aman* crop in 2000 revealed that farmers weeded rice at 28 and 45 DAT. Late first weeding was more common on large farms and where plots were weeded using hired labour.

Nine in ten farmers planted *rabi* crops in the survey year. Whilst the proportion of farmers planting *rabi* crops did not vary by farm size, the share of land planted to *rabi* crops was significantly higher (45 %) on small farms, although the land area planted to these crops was significantly higher (1.63 acres) on large farms. Overall, *rabi* crops occupied 32 % of the rice area; the remaining 68 % was fallowed. *Rabi* cropping was not significantly associated with land tenure so sharecropped or fixed rent plots were just as likely as owned plots to be planted.

Plotwise analysis (data not presented) revealed that the extent of *rabi* cropping varied significantly by land type, access to irrigation and according to the maturity group of rice cultivar grown in the previous *aman* season. Therefore *rabi* crops were most likely to be found on lower lying fields with moisture retentive soils and to be planted after short duration rice cultivars. This implied that owners of large farms were able to choose plots for *rabi* cultivation in order to reduce risk from moisture stress. By contrast, on small farms *rabi* crops were planted on marginal areas where soils were less favourable, and after cultivation of Swarna. On large farms, Swarna was grown primarily on plots with unfavourable soils that were not planted with rabi crops. On small farms, Swarna was not restricted to unfavourable soils, and plots planted to Swarna were likely to be followed by *rabi* crops. This lack of choice was positively related to subsistence pressure on small farms. For the survey sample as a whole and for small farms, Swarna was more likely to be planted on sharecropped plots. Average yields from Swarna are higher under farmer management than from shorter-duration cultivars, and tenants in consequence expected to retain a higher absolute yield after 50% sharing with the landlord. In the lower tercile of the sample there was 0.11 ha per consumer in each household compared to 0.54 ha in the upper tercile. Smaller farmers share-cropped an average 58% of their farm of which 43% was planted to *rabi* crops, compared to 35% rented with just 25% under *rabi* for the largest holdings.

DISCUSSION AND CONCLUSIONS

The long-term trial has demonstrated that while rice yield can be maintained with the switch from transplanting to direct seeding, farmers will face a greater weed problem early in the crop season. Not only is there an increased burden of weeds in direct seeded rice but the change in establishment practice also leads to a shift in the relative abundance of important species. Use of a herbicide can reverse this trend in some cases, e.g. for *F. miliacea* an important weed in the Barind (Mazid *et al.,*2001) but to prevent the build-up of other species a follow-up hand weeding will be needed, particularly for perennial grasses (*P. distichum*) which are not controlled by oxadiazon. Previous research (Mazid *et al.*, 2002) has indicated that direct seeding was associated with higher labour inputs for first weeding than is the case for transplanting. With the labour constraint, late first weeding, and a significant yield gap due to weeds on many farms in transplanted rice with current weed control practices (Mazid *et al.*, 2001) it is clear that the adoption of direct seeding will need to be associated with use of chemical weed control. At current prices one application of oxidiazon followed by one hand weeding results in a saving of 35% compared to weeding twice by hand with hired labour. Socio-economic analysis suggests that herbicides will find a ready market in Rajshahi district because a) weeding is done almost exclusively by hired labour, and b) the supply of hired labour is local, with very little weeding done by seasonal migrant labour. Together, these factors heighten competition for labour, especially on larger farms that would be intensified by the adoption of direct seeding. This work also suggests that interventions to expand *rabi* cropping in the High Barind may distinguish two broad target groups: (1) larger farms with lower cropping intensity and the potential to grow *rabi* crops under relatively favourable conditions. Interventions for this group should focus on raising the area planted to rabi crops. This may be achieved by adopting direct seeding of lower yielding short duration rice cultivars and herbicides for weed control; (2) smaller farms with higher cropping intensity and limited potential to grow *rabi* crops under favourable conditions.

Interventions for this group should focus on raising yields of rice. Farmers may wish to continue growing higher yielding Swarna rice through transplanting but increase yield by use of herbicides to achieve timely weed control.

Agronomic and socio-economic factors in the Barind Tract (a single rice crop, combined with land pressure and a high level of sharecropping) place a premium on optimising rice yield and household food security. Consequently, the adoption of DSR, and increased post-rice cropping, will depend critically on the availability of a short-duration rice variety that out-yields the long-duration variety currently grown by farmers. This challenge requires a systems approach that combines expertise from rice breeding, agronomy, and weed science.

ACKNOWLEDGEMENTS

This research was conducted in association with the Consortium for Unfavourable Rainfed Environments (IRRI) site at Rajshahi, and was partially funded under the Crop Protection Programme (project R8215) by the United Kingdom Department for International Development. The views expressed are not necessarily those of DFID.

REFERENCES

Mazid, M A; Bhuiyan S I; Mannan M A; Wade L J (2002). Dry–seeded rice for enhanced productivity of rainfed drought-prone lands: lessons from Bangladesh and the Philippines. In: *Direct seeding in Asian rice systems: strategic research issues and opportunities*. eds Pandey S, Mortimer M, Wade L J, Tuong T P & Hardy B. pp 185-201. International Rice Research Institute: Manila, Philippines.

Mazid M A; Jabber M A; Riches C R; Robinson E J Z; Mortimer M; Wade L J (2001). Weed management implications of introducing dry-seeded rice in the Barind Tract of Bangladesh. *Proceedings of the BCPC Conference – Weeds 2001* 1, 211-216.

Nur-E-Elahi A H; Khan M R; Siddique A; Saha M; Nasim M; S M Shahidullah S M (1999) Existing cropping patterns of Bangladesh: Potential techniques and strategies for improving systems productivity. In: *Proceedings of the Workshop on modern rice cultivation in Bangladesh*, ed. M R Mandal, pp 107-169. Bangladesh Rice Research Institute: Gazipur, Bangladesh.

Orr A W; Jabbar M A (2002). *Farmers' Weed Management for T. Aman, Bangladesh*. Natural Resources Institute: Chatham, UK.

Orr, A W; Jabber, M A (2003). *Expanding* rabi *cropping in the High Barind Tract, Bangladesh: a socio-economic perspective*. Natural Resources Institute: Chatham, UK.

Saleh A F M; Bhuiyan S I (1995). Crop and rainwater management strategies for increasing productivity of rainfed lowland rice systems. *Agricultural Systems* 49, 259-276.

Saleh A F M; Mazid M A; Bhuiyan S I (2000). Agrohydrologic and drought risk analyses of rainfed cultivation in northwest Bangladesh. In: *Characterizing and Understanding Rainfed Environments*. eds T P Tuong, S P Kam, L J Wade, S Pandey, B A M Bouman & B Hardy, pp. 233-244 International Rice Research Institute: Manila, Philippines.

Direct seeding as an alternative to transplanting rice for the rice-wheat systems of the Indo-Gangetic Plains: sustainability issues related to weed management

G Singh, Y Singh, V P Singh, R K Singh, Pratibha Singh
G.B. Pant University of Agriculture and Technology, Pantnagar, Uttaranchal, India

D E Johnson, M Mortimer
International Rice Research Institute, DAPO Box 7777, Metro Manila, Philippines

A Orr
Natural Resources Institute, University of Greenwich, Chatham Maritime, ME4 4TB, UK

ABSTRACT

Increasing costs of labour threaten the sustainability of transplanted rice within the rice-wheat systems of the Indo-Gangetic plains. Direct seeding of rice is cheaper, can save water and through earlier rice crop establishment allows earlier sowing of the following wheat crop. In direct seeded rice, the major challenge for farmers is effective weed management. Wet and dry direct-seeded rice establishment methods were tested on farmers' fields and compared to the traditional practice of transplanting. Field experiments, over two years, showed that yields were comparable across all establishment systems, provided competition from weeds was removed. Potential yield losses due to weeds were however much greater in direct seeded rice. On- farm studies recorded similar yields with dry direct seeding compared to transplanting, but that a number of weed species, including *Ischaemum rugosum*, *Leptochloa chinensis* and *Cyperus rotundus* were more abundant in the dry direct seeded crops.

INTRODUCTION

In India, rice grown in the wet summer season (kharif, June – October), followed by wheat in the cooler drier winters (rabi, November – May) contributes 40% of the nation's grain (Sinha *et al.*, 1998). Cropping intensification has raised issues of sustainability due to the need to improve water-use efficiency, soil structure and weed management against a background of increasing labour scarcity for agriculture (Hobbs *et al.*, 2000). As in many parts of South East Asia where there are water and labour shortages for agriculture, in India there is increased interest in direct seeding (Pandey & Velasco, 1999). Direct seeding does not require the large quantities of water required for puddling prior to rice transplanting, nor is labour required for raising nursery beds and transplanting. Farmers growing direct seeded rice are however likely to encounter greater problems related to weed management because of the lack of weed suppression by standing water. The transition to direct seeding of rice can therefore only be successful if accompanied by effective weed management practice. To determine the impact of crop establishment methods on the cropping system, and to improve weed control measures, experiments were designed to explore a range of available options for weed management and direct seeding of rice using either dry or pre-germinated seed.

MATERIALS AND METHODS

Two experimental systems examined weed and crop growth under different methods of establishing rice and wheat. The first, at the research station of G. B. Pant University of Agriculture and Technology, Pantnagar, Uttaranchal, compared five different methods of crop establishment, and was initiated in 2000 and continued in successive seasons. It was complemented by trials conducted in farmers' fields in the vicinity of Pantnagar and compared direct seeded rice with transplanted rice crops, under farm practice. Singh *et al.*, (2001) reported the first year's results.

Comparison of methods of crop establishment

Treatments compared rice establishment methods as main plot treatments with subplots of weed management treatments in rice, as follows. After rice harvest, the experimental area was either sown to wheat after conventional tillage or using zero-tillage (as strips). The overall experimental design was a strip, split-plot design, with four complete randomised replications as follows.

Main plots (60 m^2) - rice establishment :

TP   conventional transplanting of c. 21 day old plants after soil puddling, 20 cm x 20 cm spacing (seedling nursery established at the same time as direct seeding)

WS   wet seeding (pre-germinated (drum seeded, 35 kg/ha) after soil puddling, 20 cm row spacing

DS   dry seeding (50 kg/ha) after conventional tillage, 20 cm row spacing

DSF   dry seeding (50 kg/ha) after conventional tillage but final tillage following a flush irrigation

ZT   dry seeding (50 kg/ha) zero-tillage after flush irrigation (7d before glyphosate application)

Subplots (20m^2) - intensity of weeding, post emergence weed control in rice:

TO   unweeded checks

CW   weed free 'best-bet herbicide treatment' followed by two manual weedings

HW   one manual weeding 30 days after seeding (DAS)

The rice cultivar Sarju-52 was sown throughout. A water depth of c. 10cm was used at transplanting with one plant per hill and maintained for one month, thereafter soil being saturated unless flooding occurred through rainfall. In wet seeded plots, soil was kept saturated by water management for 21 DAS to ensure rice establishment. Dry seeding was into aerobic soil. Main plots were separated by double bunds to preserve differences in water regimes and changes in soil structure and seedbank. Strips (c. 1m) separated subplots. The herbicide treatments in rice for the CW subplots varied according to the establishment method. In TP plots, butachlor (1.5 kg a.i./ha) was applied 2 DAT; on the WS plots anilophos (0.4 kg a.i./ha) was used 5 DAS; and for DS, DSF and ZT, pendimethalin (1.0 kg a.i./ha) was applied, 1 DAS. Herbicide treatments was followed in each case by two hand weedings, 28 and 56 DAS/DAT. From each subplot, weed counts and biomass (fresh weight) by species were taken from two 0.25m x 1m quadrats covering 5 crop rows. In TO and HW subplots sampling occurred at 28, 56, 84 DAS and at 28 DAS/DAT in CW subplots, and in all plots at harvest. Wheat (cv PBW-343 or PBW-154, 100 kg/ha, 20 cm row spacing) was sown in December in either, conventionally prepared plots (harrowed, rotavated and levelled) or, zero-tilled plots (paraquat 0.5 kg a.i./ha), 1 week before seeding. Yield estimates were taken from 5 m^2 areas.

On-farm trials

Paired plots (each c. 0.2 ha) of direct, dry seeded rice after minimum tillage and of transplanted rice after conventional wet tillage (puddling) were established on farmers' fields in villages in the vicinity of Pantnagar. Trials were conducted on six farms in 2001 and on seven farms on 2002. In 2002, at each farm additional plots were established by wet seeding. For weed control, pendimethalin (1.0 kg a.i./ha) was applied to dry seeded rice, butachlor (1.5 kg a.i./ha) to transplanted plots and anilophos under wet seeding. Timing of application was as described above. All plots were subsequently hand weeded once. Two control (T0) plots of 5m x 4m were located at random in each 0.2 ha plot within which no weed control was practised. Weeds were sampled from within 1 m^2 at 28 DAS (days after seeding/transplanting), separated by species and weighed. Rice was harvested from 5 m^2 within each plot and grain weight recorded. Wheat (conventional and zero till) was grown after the rice and grain yield recorded.

RESULTS

In 2001, in on-station, research-managed plots the grain yields from weed free (CW) plots of transplanted rice were equivalent to those of wet-seeded rice, whilst those of dry-seeded rice (DS, DSF & ZT) were less (Table 1). Similar yields were obtained from zero-tilled (ZT) and conventionally tilled plots (DSF, DS). A single hand weeding (HW) was insufficient to prevent major yield loss due to weeds. A similar pattern of results for grain yields was observed in 2002 although yield loss due to weed competition was less severe when a single hand weeding (HW) was employed, and yields in unweeded plots were not reduced to the same extent as in 2001. In 2001 and 2002, wheat yields were not affected by establishment method either of the wheat crop itself (conventional versus zero-till) or of the previous rice crop. Wheat yield under conventional tillage was 4.05 t/ha compared with 4.43 t/ha under zero-tillage in 2001 and 3.84 and 4.08 t/ha, in 2002, respectively.

Table 1. Effects of rice establishment method and weed control on grain yield (t/ha) and standard errors (SE) of rice in 2001 and 2002, on station and on-farm experiments. See text for details

Establishment method	2001 Weed management					2002 Weed management				
	On-station			On-farm		On-station			On-farm	
	CW	HW	T0	CW	T0	CW	HW	T0	CW	T0
TP	7.8	7.2	5.9	4.9	3.4	6.1	5.5	4.6	5.8	3.6
WS	8.1	5.6	1.0	-	-	6.8	5.4	0.9	5.9	2.2
DS	6.1	1.0	0.0	4.9	2.6	6.7	5.1	1.0	6.3	3.6
DSF	6.6	1.6	0.0	-	-	6.1	4.7	0.4	-	-
ZT	6.6	1.5	0.0	-	-	5.9	5.4	0.2	-	-
SE	0.04			0.24		0.24			0.21	

In farm trials, equivalent grain yields were achieved from dry seeded and transplanted rice in 2001 (Table 1), yield depression due to weeds being 30% under transplanting and almost 50% in direct seeding. In 2002, dry direct seeded rice gave the highest yield. Ranked yield suppression by weeds were TP (37%), DS (44%) and WS (62%). There were no significant differences in wheat yields in 2002 arising from the method of establishment of the preceding rice crop (DS = 4.05, TP = 4.23, ± 0.221 t/ha), or due to wheat establishment method (conventional or zero-tillage).

Figure 1 illustrates the weed species shifts in transplanted and dry, drill seeded rice in the absence of weeding evident in the first experiment. Prior to the start of the experiment, all plots had been in commercial rice production and extensively weeded. In the absence of weeding, three seasons of transplanting resulted in the dominance in rank order of *Echinochloa colona*, *Commelina diffusa* and *Ischaemum rugosum*, with *Caesulia axillaris*, *Cyperus rotundus* and *Fimbristylis miliacea* being much less abundant. In contrast in direct seeded plots, *C. diffusa* exhibited equivalent abundance to *E. colona*, *C. rotundus*, with *Cyperus difformis* and *Leptochloa chinensis* being lesser in rank.

Partial budget analysis of rice production by establishment system (Table 2), based on farm yields and detailed costs recorded on-station, indicated that the yields, and gross returns, were broadly similar for each system. However the relative higher costs of nursery beds, land preparation and labour for manual transplanting result in the benefit:cost ratio for rice transplanting being approximately half that of dry seeded rice. Moreover in relative terms, dry seeding used approximately 40% of water by volume as transplanting.

Table 2. Indicative costs and returns for three rice production systems, Uttaranchal, India. Costs exclude those common to all systems (e.g. fixed costs, harvesting and some fertilisers) and reflect appropriate herbicides and levels of hand weeding for each establishment method, as well as differential labour inputs in land preparation

Method of rice establishment	Rice yield (t/ha)	Variable costs (Rs/ha)		Gross benefits (Rs/ha)	Net benefits (Rs/ha)	Benefit : cost ratio
		Labour	Materials			
Transplanting	5.41	6995	2905	23323	13423	1.36
Wet seeding	5.35	5896	2760	25698	17042	1.97
Dry seeding	4.91	4675	2536	25413	18202	2.52

DISCUSSION

These experiments confirm that wet and dry seeded rice yields were comparable to yields from transplanted rice both experimentally and on-farm. These results contrast with those reported earlier (Singh *et al.* 2001) when rice establishment was delayed by early season flooding and low yields were reported. Whilst transplanting into standing water is a risk-averse strategy for farmers when flooding is unpredictable and infrastructure for water management is lacking, direct seeding offers considerable savings in labour and water and

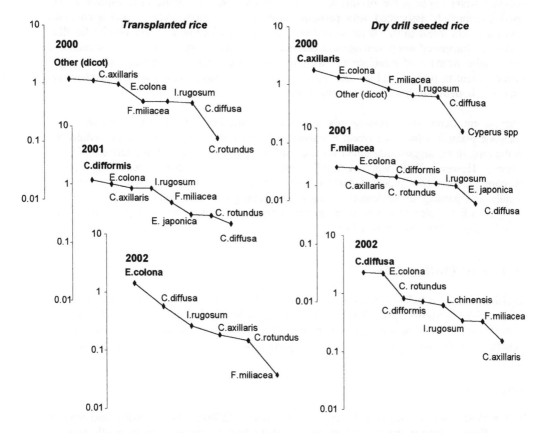

Figure 1. Changes in abundance of weed species in relation to crop establishment method in unweeded plots. Data are the mean (n = 8) abundance of species measured as dry biomass 56 DAS. In each year, species are ranked on a logarithmic scale. Within each year, there were significant differences (P < 0.01) in species composition (MANOVA) and across years significant changes in rank order (P < 0.05) were evident (Page's test, Page, 1963). The most abundant species, in each year, is emboldened.

Caesulia axillaris : C. axillaris   Eragrostis japonica : E. japonica
Commelina diffusa : C. diffusa   Fimbristylis miliacea : F. miliacea
Cyperus difformis : C. difformis   Ischaemum rugosum : I. rugosum
Cyperus rotundus : C. rotundus   Leptochloa chinensis : L. chinensis
Echinochloa colona : E. colona

potentially higher net benefits. These gains however depend upon effective weed management that is critical early in the life of the crop. In these experiments, the yield gap due to weeds was increased under direct seeding but varied between seasons. Mortimer and Hill (1999) have emphasized that temporal variation in water regimes at the start of an irrigated rice cropping season is a critical determinant of the selective recruitment of weed species. In common with local farming practice, flooding was not maintained on fields and irrigation was undertaken only to facilitate crop establishment and prevent moisture stress. The lack of standing water explains the occurrence of *C. rotundus* and *E. colona* in transplanted rice, species commonly associated with partially aerobic, rainfed rice fields. *Cyperus rotundus* poses a severe threat to the direct seeded rice systems examined here, where regular flooding is absent. Integrated weed management practices will be necessary to control this species and will require rotation of establishment methods, herbicides and water management regimes. Other potential threats include the grass weeds *Leptochloa chinensis*, and *Ischaemum rugosum*, both of which are highly competitive.

The current trends of increasing labour costs in many, but not all, regions of the Indo-Gangetic plains in which rice-wheat is grown, and increasing concerns over water availability in the long term, suggest that direct seeding will become an increasingly attractive option for farmers. However DSR will not totally replace the need for hand-weeding and socio-economic studies (not reported here) indicate that rural non-farm employment is growing rapidly and pushing up agricultural wages. The main group that will be affected by these changes will be migrant labour from poorer regions (e.g. Bihar), particularly women, who have largely replaced men in weeding.

ACKNOWLEDGEMENTS

Collaboration with Indian Council for Agricultural Research and the Rice Wheat Consortium is gratefully acknowledged. This research is partially funded by the United Kingdom Department for International Development (DFID) Crop Protection Programme for the benefit of developing countries. The views expressed are not necessarily those of DFID.

REFERENCES

Hobbs P R; Singh Y; Giri G S; Lauren J G; Duxbury J (2000). Direct seeding and reduced tillage options in the rice-wheat systems of the Indo-Gangetic plains of south Asia. In: *Direct seeding in Asian rice systems,* eds S Pandey, T P Tuong, M Mortimer & L J Wade, pp. 201-218, IRRI: Los Baños Laguna, Philippines.

Mortimer M; Hill J E (1999). Weed species shifts in response to broad spectrum herbicides in sub-tropical and tropical crops. *Proceedings of the BCPC Conference Weeds – 1999,* 2, 425 - 437.

Page E B (1963). Ordered hypotheses for multiple treatments: a significance test for linear ranks. *Journal of American Statistical Association,* **58**, 216–230.

Pandey S; Velasco L (1999). Economics of direct seeding in Asia: patterns of adoption and research priorities. *IRRN,* **24**, 2, 6-11.

Singh Y; Singh G; Singh V P; Singh R K; Srivastava R S L; Singh P; Mortimer M; White J L; Johnson D E (2001). Direct seeding of rice in the Rice-Wheat Systems of the Indo-Gangetic Plains and the implications for weed management. *Proceedings of the BCPC Conference - Weeds 2001*, BCPC, Farnham, UK, 187-192.

Sinha S K; Singh G B; Mangla R (1998). *Decline in crop productivity in Haryana and Punjab-Myth or Reality*: Report of the Fact-Finding Committee. ICAR, New Delhi.

Glyphosate and carfentrazone-ethyl mixtures for the control of hard to kill weeds in zero-tillage systems in Brazil.

L L Foloni
Universidade de Campinas, UNICAMP – Feagri, Campinas, SP, 13083-970, Brazil
Email: lfoloni@aol.com

V A Gangora
FMC Química do Brasil Ltda, Campinas, SP, 13010-910, Brazil

E D Vellini
Universidade Estadual Paulista – UNESP, Botucatu, SP, 18.610-000, Brazil.

P J Christoffoleti, J F Barela, M Nicolai
Universidade de São Paulo – USP - Piracicaba, SP,13.418-900, Brazil

ABSTRACT

Successive applications of glyphosate in Brazil have selected weed species hard to kill by usually recommended doses. However tank mixtures with low rates of non-systemic herbicides increase the efficacy of glyphosate. The efficacy on five weed species of glyphosate alone and in mixture with carfentrazone-ethyl (5 ml of carfentrazone/litre of glyphosate), with rainfall simulation after application was studied in the greenhouse. Treatments were also compared under field conditions in a no-till system, with herbicides applied pre-planting, to pasture. The treatments were: glyphosate (formulation 480 g/litre) with carfentrazone at 720 + 2.0; 720 + 3.0; 720 + 4.0; 960 + 2.0; 960 + 3.0 and 960 + 4.0 and glyphosate (formulation 648 g/litre) at 712.8 and 972 g/ha, plus a check plot without herbicide application. The efficacy of glyphosate was enhanced by the addition of 2.0 g/ha of carfentrazone (corresponding to 5 ml of commercial product/litre of glyphosate), being equivalent to the activity of similar rates of the formulation of 648 g/litre. The mixture increased the spectrum and efficiency of control of broad-leaved species, particularly *Commelina benghalensis*, and showed reduced susceptibility to rainfall after application.

INTRODUCTION

Brazilian agricultural is undergoing a transformation with the widespread adoption of zero-tillage systems that allow rational use of water and agrochemicals. Zero-tillage enables farmers to reduce production costs to ensure the competitiveness and sustainability of crops and livestock production on degraded pastures. Among the pre-seeding applied herbicides used in the zero tillage system are the bipyridiliums (paraquat, diquat and paraquat + diuron), glyphosate, sulfosate and mixtures of these herbicides with 2,4-D. Glyphosate is particularly effective on a number of grasses and broad-leaved species but in general it is considered more active on grasses (Ahrens, 1994). Successive applications of glyphosate have led to the build up of some hard to kill, tolerant species including *Sida cordifolia* and *Commelina benghalensis*. A number of studies have demonstrated that the control of these species can be enhanced by using mixtures of glyphosate with other herbicides.

Mixtures of glyphosate with 2,4-D have been particularly useful for pre-plant weed control, with several crops, for example tomato, cotton and grapevine. However, in some Brazilian districts the use of the mixture with 2,4-D is forbidden. Possible replacements for 2,4-D in the mixture with glyphosate or sulfosate, which allow a reduction in the time between spraying and tillage, include sulfentrazone, flumioxazin and carfentrazone-ethyl (Gazziero *et al.*, 2000).

Carfentrazone-ethyl is an aryl triazoline herbicide whose mode of action is inhibition of protoporphyrinogen oxydase (PPO), an important enzyme in chlorophyll biosynthesis (WSSA, 2002). Foloni *et al.*, (2000) reported that rain within 2 hours of treatment did not affect the activity of sulfentrazone + glyphosate or carfentrazone + glyphosate, on *Chenchrus echinatus*, *Commelina benghalensis*, *Bidens pilosa*, *Ipomoea grandifolia* or *Senna obtusifolia*. Werlang and Silva (2002) concluded that the effect of carfentrazone-ethyl in mixture with glyphosate varies depending on the weed species. Rochi *et al.* (2002) evaluated the effectiveness carfentrazone-ethyl alone or in tank-mix with glyphosate or glyphosate-K for the control of *C. benghalensis* and *C. diffusa*, and concluded that the mixtures presented better efficacy on the species than glyphosate alone.

This paper describes the evaluation of mixtures containing a small amount of carfentrazone-ethyl: 5 ml of carfentrazone (formulation 400 g/litre) per litre of glyphosate (formulations containing either 480 g a.e./litre or 648 g a.e./litre) in pre-planting applications, in the zero-till system, for the control of some broad-leaved weed species that are normally hard to kill with glyphosate alone.

MATERIAL AND METHODS

Experiments were conducted in both the glasshouse and in the field. In the glasshouse, weeds were raised to evaluate the rainfastness of a range of herbicide mixtures. Individual seedlings of *Brachiaria plantaginea*, *Digitaria horizontalis*, *Commelina benghalensis* and *Richardia brasiliensis* were transplanted from the field to pots when the plants were about 2-4 leaves stage. These were raised in a greenhouse with temperature ranging from 20-28^{0}C, relative humidity ranging from 60-80%, and watered daily through an automated system. Plants were sprayed 30 days later with the herbicide treatments shown in Table 1. Herbicides were applied through a laboratory sprayer fitted with a fan nozzle (XR110.02E). Rain treatments were applied 2 hours after herbicide application using a rainfall simulator delivering the equivalent of 40 mm rain over a 10 minutes period. The field trial was on an area that had been under pasture for more than 10 years. The experimental design was randomized block, with four replications. Individual plots were 4m x 5 m. Herbicide treatments shown in Table 2 were applied on December 7, 2002 with a CO_2 pressurized backpack sprayer fitted with XR 110.02 nozzles, operating at a pressure of 278 kPa to apply 150 litres/ha. All weeds were at the flowering stage, at 40 and 110 cm height, at spraying.

For both experiments herbicide efficacy was evaluated by visual estimation of percentage control (where 0% no control and 100% total control). Assessments were made at 4, 7, 14 and 28 days after treatments (DAT). Field assessments were made only until 14 DAT.

Table 1. Herbicide treatments applied in the greenhouse experiment to evaluate rainfastness

Treatments	Rates g a.i./ha	
	Brachiaria plantaginea	Other weeds
1. Glyphosate	240	960
2. Glyphosate + Carfentrazone-ethyl	240+1	960+4
3. Glyphosate + Carfentrazone-ethyl	240+2	960+8
4. Glyphosate	324	1296
5. Check	-	-

Table 2. Treatments used in the field experiment.

Treatments	Rates g a.i./ha
1. Glyphosate + Carfentrazone-ethyl	720+2
2. Glyphosate + Carfentrazone-ethyl	720+3
3. Glyphosate + Carfentrazone-ethyl	720+4
4. Glyphosate + Carfentrazone-ethyl	960+2
5. Glyphosate + Carfentrazone-ethyl	960+3
6. Glyphosate + Carfentrazone-ethyl	960+4
7. Glyphosate	712.8
8. Glyphosate	972
9. Check weeded	-

RESULTS

Greenhouse experiment

The data for weed control in the greenhouse are summarised in Tables 3 and 4. The grasses *Brachiaria plantaginea* (low rate) and *Digitaria horizontalis* were controlled by glyphosate without any antagonistic effect with carfentrazone, even though glyphosate alone controlled this weed satisfactorily. *Richardia brasiliensis* and *Commelina benghalensis* were not well controlled by glyphosate alone but up to 55 and 60% control respectively was achieved by the mixture of glyphosate + carfentrazone, as previously shown by Foloni *et al.* (2000), Werlang & Silva (2002). The data obtained in the current study represents control achieved following rainfall simulation immediately after herbicide application indicating that the mixture is likely to be a robust treatment under field conditions. The improved activity of glyphosate with carfentrazone suggests improved absorption by the target weeds.

Table 3. Control of greenhouse grown *Brachiaria plantaginea* and *Digitaria horizontalis* by herbicides at 4, 7 and 14 days after treatment

Treatments	Rate g a.i./ha	Weed control %					
		Brachiaria plantaginea			*Digitaria horizontalis*		
		4	7	14	4	7	14
Glyphosate	960	0	45.0	100	48.75	97.2	100
Glyphosate	1296	0	27.5	100	55.0	97.5	100
Glyphosate + Carfentrazone-ethyl	960+4	0	13.75	100	67.5	93.5	100
Glyphosate + Carfentrazone-ethyl	960+8	10	48.75	100	47.5	98.0	100
Check	-	0	0	0	0	0	0

Table 4. Control of greenhouse grown *Richardia brasiliensis* and *Commelina benghalensis* at 4, 7 and 14 days after treatment

| Treatments | Rate g a.i./ha | Weed control % | | | | | |
| | | *Richardia brasiliensis* | | | *Commelina benghalensis* | | |
		4	7	14	4	7	14
Glyphosate	960	0	0	0	0	0	0
Glyphosate	1296	0	0	0	23.7	30.0	60
Glyphosate + Carfentrazone-ethyl	960+4	0	55.0	75	11.2	31.2	65
Glyphosate + Carfentrazone-ethyl	960+8	13.7	41.2	80	48.7	60.0	85
Check	-	0	0	0	0	0	0

Field experiments

The data for weed control in the field trials are summarized in Tables 5, 6 and 7. The mixture of glyphosate + carfentrazone, applied post-emergence to weeds and pre-planting of the crop did not show synergistic effects for *D. horizontalis* and *E. colonum* control. For *C. benghalensis,* only the higher rates of the mixture glyphosate + carfentrazone (960+2), (960+3) and (960+4 g a.i./ha) provided superior control with over 80% of plants killed. For *I. grandifolia* and *A. viridis* all the treatments showed good control levels, demonstrating that there is no antagonism in the mixture. Control was similar to that achieved with the highest doses of glyphosate used alone. The data show similar results to that reported by Foloni *et al.* (2000).

For *B. decumbens* control in pasture re-habilitation, the results were excellent for all the studied treatments. Therefore for the control of the *B. decumbens* glyphosate alone was sufficient because there was no infestation of broad-leaved weeds at the experimental site. Even though carfentrazone is not necessary to control *B. decumbens* it does not cause any antagonistic effect in the mixture. For pastures infested with broad-leaved weeds that are hard to kill with glyphosate, the mixture of glyphosate with carfentrazone could be a useful alternative. These results also demonstrated that for renewal of pastures, the no-till system can be used. Degraded pasture can be renewed by inter-planting and using the mixture of glyphosate and carfentrazone for weed control

Table 5. Control of *Digitaria horizontalis* and *Echinochloa colonum* in the field with a range of herbicides at 4 to 28 days after treatment

Treatments	Rate g a.i./ha	Weeds control %							
		Digitaria horizontalis				*Echinochloa colonum*			
		4	7	14	28	4	7	14	28
Glyphosate+carfentrazone	720+2	37.5	61.2	71.2	77.5	40.0	62.5	90.0	95.0
Glyphosate+carfentrazone	720+3	41.2	58.7	73.7	77.5	41.2	62.5	88.7	99.2
Glyphosate+carfentrazone	720+4	46.2	72.5	77.5	77.5	41.2	72.5	91.2	97.5
Glyphosate+carfentrazone	960+2	40.0	78.7	88.7	96.2	50.0	78.7	95.5	99.5
Glyphosate+carfentrazone	960+3	41.2	76.2	92.5	97.5	48.7	78.7	93.5	100.0
Glyphosate+carfentrazone	960+4	45.0	75.0	95.0	97.5	47.5	77.5	95.0	100.0
Glyphosate	712,8	41.2	65.0	98.7	100.0	40.0	66.2	92.5	99.5
Glyphosate	972	43.7	76.2	100.0	100.0	45.0	80.0	98.2	100.0
Check weeded	-	0	0	0	0	0	0	0	0
LSD (P=0,05)		17.55	25.00	6.06	7.15	20.39	23.61	15.54	6.44

Table 6. Control of *Commelina benghalensis* and *Ipomoea grandifolia.* in the field by a range of herbicides at 4 to 28 days after treatment

Teatments	Rate g a.i./ha	Weeds control %							
		Commelina benghalensis				*Ipomoea grandifolia*			
		4	7	14	28	4	7	14	28
Glyphosate+carfentrazone	720+2	35.0	55.0	67.8	58.7	51.2	68.0	86.2	85.0
Glyphosate+carfentrazone	720+3	38.7	60.0	68.7	70.0	51.2	75.0	87.5	90.0
Glyphosate+carfentrazone	720+4	42.5	63.7	77.5	70.0	53.7	76.2	92.5	100.0
Glyphosate+carfentrazone	960+2	47.5	68.7	77.5	78.2	58.2	78.7	95.0	98.2
Glyphosate+carfentrazone	960+3	52.5	76.2	80.0	81.2	58.7	80.0	97.5	100.0
Glyphosate+carfentrazone	960+4	55.0	82.5	85.0	83.7	62.5	82.5	98.7	100.0
Glyphosate	712,8	28.0	48.7	75.0	63.7	33.7	72.0	88.7	82.5
Glyphosate	972	37.5	66.2	75.0	78.2	35.0	75.0	90.0	95.0
Check weeded	-	0	0	0	0	0	0	0	0
LSD (P=0,05)		11.85	19.26	12.90	14.44	12.85	15.23	25.43	28.03

Table 7. Control of *Amaranthus hibridus* and *Brachiaria decumbens* in the field by a range of herbicides at 4 to 28 days after treatment

Teatments	Rate g a.i./ha	Weeds control %							
		Amaranthus hibridus				*Brachiaria decumbens*			
		4	7	14	28	4	7	14	28
Glyphosate+carfentrazone	720+2	57.5	78.2	93.7	91.2	32.5	66.2	94.5	97.0
Glyphosate+carfentrazone	720+3	57.5	78.7	95.0	96.2	33.7	68.7	96.0	98.2
Glyphosate+carfentrazone	720+4	61.2	80.0	97.7	99.0	33.7	71.2	96.5	99.5
Glyphosate+carfentrazone	960+2	62.0	82.5	98.0	99.5	36.2	73.7	96.5	98.7
Glyphosate+carfentrazone	960+3	65.0	83.7	95.0	100.0	38.7	78.2	98.0	100.0
Glyphosate+carfentrazone	960+4	70.0	86.2	99.0	100.0	40.0	78.2	99.5	100.0
Glyphosate	712.8	42.5	70.0	90.0	97.5	31.2	73.7	97.2	98.0
Glyphosate	972	50.0	76.2	92.5	98.7	32.5	73.7	99.5	1000
Check weeded	-	0	0	0	0	0	0	0	0
LSD (P=0,05)		7.51	10.43	5.77	10.63	12.49	12.96	4.28	3.95

The overall conclusion of this research is that the addition of a small dose of carfentrazone-ethyl, equivalent to 2 g a.e./litres of glyphosate, improved performance, as well as the absorption speed. The mixture was little affected by rain after application (see greenhouse experiment). The use of this mixture allows the efficient control of the weeds already controlled by glyphosate (without antagonic effects) and provides an additional advantage of controlling species including *C. benghalensis* which are poorly controlled, if at all, by glyphosate alone. The glyphosate + carfentrazone is similar in efficacy to the higher rate of the most concentrated formulation of glyphosate.

REFERENCES

Ahrens W H (1994). *Herbicide Handbook.* 7th edition. pp. 149-152 Weed Science Society of America: Champaign, IL, USA.

Gazziero D L P *et al.* (2000) Herbicide alternatives for 2,4-D in no-till cropping systems. In: *Abstracts, Third International Weed Science Congress.* pp. 134. International Weed Science Society: Corvallis, Oregon, USA.

Hydrick D E; Shaw D R (1994). Effects of tank-mix combinations of non-seletive foliar an selective soil-applied herbicides on three weed species. *Weed Technology* **8**, 129-133.

Malik J; Barry G; Kishore G (1989). The herbicide glyphosate. *Biofactores* **2**, 17-25.

Selleck G W; Baird D D (1981). Antagonism of glyphosate and residual herbicide combinations. *Weed Science* **29**, 185-190.

Vidrine P R *et al.* (1997) Post-emergence weed control in soybeans using glyphosate and chlorimuron. *Proceedings Southern Weed Science Society* **50**, 175.

Foloni L L (2000). *Influence of rainfall on the weed control efficacy of sulfentrazone and carfentrazone tank mixtures with glyphosate,* pp.248. International Weed Science Society, Corvallis, Oregon, USA.

Stark R J; Oliver L R (1998) Interaction of glyphosate with chlorimuron, fomesafen, imazethapyr and sulfentrazone. *Weed Science* **46**, 652-660.

Werlang R C; Silva A A (2002). Integração de glyphosate com carfentrazone-ethyl. *Planta Daninha* **20**, 93-102.

WSSA (2002). *Weed Science Society of America Handbook, 8th Edition.* WSSA: Lawrence, USA.

Modulation of seed dormancy in *Ocimum basilicum* by light, gibberellins (GA3) and abscisic acid (ABA)

D A Dawoud, E A Ahmed, H Khalid, A G T Babiker
Agricultural Research Corporation, P.O. Box 126, Wad Medani, Sudan
Email: agbabiker@hotmail.com

ABSTRACT

Ocimum basilicum L. (Lamiaceae), a common annual weed in central Sudan, is problematic in all crops in the area as it displays no seasonal periodicity in germination and is tolerant to most herbicides. The present study investigated the effects of light, gibberellins (GA3) and abscisic acid (ABA) on germination under a constant temperature of 30°C. The weed did not germinate in the dark. In continuous light, maximum germination (> 95%) was displayed on imbibition in water for 2 days. Germination increased with light duration. Exposure to light for 3, 12 and 21 h induced 8, 48 and 90% germination within 3 days. The light induced germination was inhibited by paclobutrazol (a gibberellin biosynthesis inhibitor). GA3 induced germination in the dark and alleviated, completely, the inhibitory effects of paclobutrazol. ABA reduced and delayed germination. GA3 mitigated the inhibitory effect of ABA. The results, which are consistent with a model in which light induced germination by promoting GAs biosynthesis and ABA catabolism, suggest that deep ploughing and husbandry practices that promote rapid canopy closure may reduce *O. basilicum* infestation in field crops.

INTRODUCTION

Ocimum basilicum L. (Lamiaceae) is a common weed in central Sudan (Braun *et al.*, 1991). The weed, a prodigious seed producer, exhibits negligible germination on burial to a depth of a few mm below the soil surface (Ismail *et al.*, 1990). On wetting, the seeds produce a thick layer of mucilage which helps conserves water and establishes contact with soil (Young & Evans, 1973). The weed displays no seasonal periodicity in germination and is relatively tolerant to several herbicides (Hamdoun & Babiker, 1978; Babiker, 1979; Babiker & Ahmed, 1986).

Previous studies have shown that germination of *O. basilicum* and related species requires light (Ismail *et al.*, 1990; Hamada *et al.*, 1993; Rocha *et al.*, 2002). Light requirement for germination has been associated with the conversion of phytochrome to the active form and stimulation of gibberellins (GAs) biosynthesis (Taylorson, 1982). The present study was therefore designed to investigate the role of light and the phytohormones GA3 and ABA on germination of *O. basilicum*.

MATERIALS AND METHODS

Six experiments were undertaken to study the influence of i) duration of exposure to light ii) the phytohormones gibberellins (GA3) and abscisic acid (ABA), each alone, and in combinations and iii) paclobutrazol (GA – biosynthesis inhibitor) alone and in combinations with GA3 on germination of *O. basilicum* seeds. The seeds were collected from the Gezira Research Station farm at Wad Medani, Sudan in December 2001, cleaned and stored dry at room temperature on an open shelf till used.

GA3 and ABA were dissolved in distilled water whereas, paclobutrazol was dissolved in minimum methanol before completion to volume with distilled water. Methanol at the concentration used did not affect germination.

Seeds of *O. basilicum* (50 each), placed on a filter paper in a Pyrex Petri-dish (9 cm), were moistened with 4 ml of the respective test solution or distilled water. The Petri-dishes were incubated at 30°C in light or dark. Light was provided by 80-W daylight florescent tube. Prior to incubation the Petri-dishes were wrapped in transparent or black polythene for the light and dark treatments, respectively. The treatments were replicated 3-4 times. Each experiment was repeated 3-times. Data presented were means from single complete experiments plus or minus standard deviation ($\pm$ SD). A seed was considered to have germinated on protrusion of the radicle.

RESULTS

Seeds soaked in water and incubated in the dark for 7 days did not germinate. Germination increased, progressively, with time of exposure to light (Figure 1). Seeds exposed to light for 3 h displayed negligible (5%) germination 7 days after treatment, while those exposed for 12 and 21 h, prior to transfer to complete darkness, displayed 55 and 95% germination, respectively.

Seeds soaked in water and incubated in light displayed nearly full germination (>95%) 2 days after treatment (Figure 2a). Paclobutrazol (GA-biosynthesis inhibitor) reduced germination significantly (Figure 2a). The inhibitor at 2 - 10 µM reduced germination by 58 - 87 % 2 days after incubation, respectively and no further germination was displayed on further extension of the incubation period to 10 days. The inhibitory effect of paclobutrazol at 10 µM on germination was partially mitigated by exogenous GA3 at 10 µM and was completely alleviated by the phytohormone at 80 µM (Figure 2b).

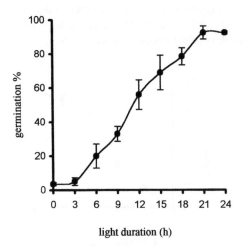

Figure 1.   Effects of duration of exposure to light on germination of *O. basilicum* seeds. Vertical bars represent ± SD.

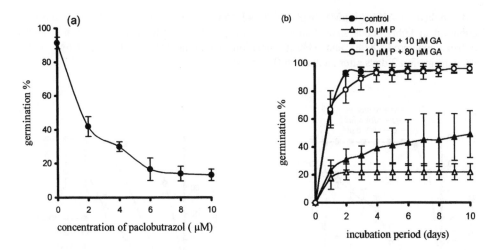

Figure 2.   Effects of different concentrations of paclobutrazol (a) and its mixture with GA3 (b) on germination of light incubated *O. basilicum* seeds. Vertical bars represent ± SD.

Seeds soaked in water and incubated in the dark for 7 days displayed no germination (Figure 3). GA3 promoted germination of dark incubated seeds. The phytohormone at 40, 60 and 80 µM induced 34, 73 and 86% germination, respectively.

ABA delayed and suppressed germination and the effects were concentration dependent. Seeds soaked in water and incubated in light displayed maximum germination (> 95%) 2 days after treatment (Figure 4a). Seeds imbibed in ABA at 4, and 8 µM displayed no germination 3, and 5 days after incubation, respectively. The maximum germination exhibited by seeds imbibed in ABA was 82 and 60%, 12 days after incubation, respectively.

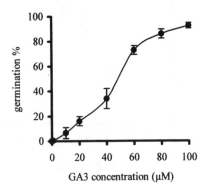

Figure 3.   Effects of GA3 concentration on germination of dark incubated *O. basilicum* seeds. Vertical bars represent ± SD.

Seeds soaked in ABA (4 µM) displayed 1, 43 and 72% germination 2, 4 and 6 days after incubation in light. Seeds soaked in ABA (4 µM) and GA3 (40 µM) mixture and similarly incubated exhibited 28, 83 and 93% germination. Seeds incubated in GA3 (40 µM) showed 93% germination 2 days after incubation (Figure 4b).

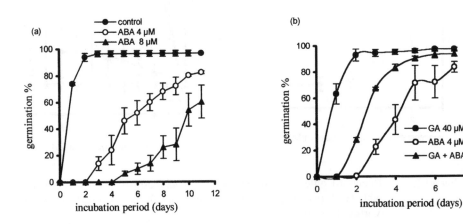

Figure 4.   Effect of different concentrations of ABA (a) and its mixture with GA3 (b) on germination of light incubated *O. basilicum* seeds. Vertical bars represent ± SD.

DISCUSSION

The study, in line with previous reports (Ismail *et al.*, 1990; Hamada *et al.*, 1993), indicated clearly that *O. basilicum* seeds require light for germination (Figure1). The finding that prolonged exposure to light is needed to induce useful germination, is consistent with that noticed for *O. gratissimum* L., a closely related species, and is an indication of a phytochrome dependent germination with a typical High Irradiant Response (Rocha *et al.*, 2002). Light regulation of dormancy in weed seeds is an important ecological adaptation as it restricts germination to conditions conducive to seedling establishment and can be interpreted as a mechanism for gap detection (Taylorson, 1982; Pons, 1992). In the field, *O. basilicum* seeds fail to germinate on shallow burial (Ismail *et al.*, 1990). The seedlings often appear after soil disturbance and/or destruction of established vegetation resulting from manual weeding. It would thus appear that deep ploughing and husbandry practices that promote canopy closure and/or limit soil disturbance, especially when herbicides are used for weed control, may reduce *O. basilicum* infestation in field crops. Experience in Sudan, has shown that delayed supplementary weeding of herbicide treated cotton is more efficient in curtailment of late season weeds, including *O. basilicum*, than early one.

The observations that exogenous GA3 promoted germination in the dark and that light induced germination is inhibited by the gibberellins biosynthesis inhibitor, paclobutrazol, suggest that light-mediated GA synthesis is critical in the signal transduction chain leading to *O. basilicum* germination. GAs were reported (Metzger *et al.*, 1996) to enhance germination of several seeds by promoting enzymatic hydrolysis of endosperms and by increasing growth potential of the embryo. The delay and inhibition of light induced germination of *O. basilicum* by ABA, together with the partial mitigation of the inhibitory effect of ABA by GA3, suggest a possible antagonism between the two phytohormones. This is consistent with the notion that GAs and ABA have antagonistic effects on cell-wall extension with GAs promoting this while ABA had the opposite effects (Karssen, 1995).

For proper management of *O. basilicum,* in field crops, the implication of the light requirement for germination on persistence of the seed bank and the role of ABA as an antagonist of GA need further investigations. Proper understanding of the influence of light and ABA on the germination process may play a pivotal role in designing and implementing an integrated strategy, involving both cultural and chemical methods, for control of *O. basilicum.*

REFERENCES

Babiker A G T (1979). Herbicides in the clay soil of Central Sudan. In: *Proceedings of a symposium Weed Research in Sudan,* eds M E Beshir & W Koch, pp. 1–6. W. Koch and A. Kenmar: Stuttgart, Germany.

Babiker A G T; Ahmed M K (1986). Chemical weed control in transplanted onion (*Allium cepa* L.) in the Sudan Gezira. *Weed Research* **21**, 299 – 306.

Braun M; Burgstaller H; Hamdoun A M; Walter H (1991) *Common Weeds of Central Sudan.* Verlag Josef Margraf: Weikersheim, Germany.

Hamada A A; Koch W; Hamdoun A; Kunisch M; Sauerborn J (1993). Effect of temperature, light and simulated drought on the germination of some weed species from the Sudan. *Angewandte Botanik* **67**, 52 – 55.

Hamdoun A M; Babiker A G T (1978) Effects of some herbicides on cotton weeds in the Sudan Gezira. *Experimental Agriculture* **14,** 137–144.

Ismail A M A; Khalifa F M; Babiker A G T (1990). Age environmental factors, germination and seedling emergence of *Ocimum basilicum* L. *Quatar University Science Bulletin* **10,** 155 – 166.

Karssen C M (1995) Hormonal regulation of seed development, dormancy and germination studied by genetic control. In: *Seed Development and Germination*, eds J Kigel & G Galili, pp. 333–350. Marcel Dekker Inc., New York, USA.

Metzger G L; Fruendt C; Meins F (1996) Effects of gibberellins, darkness and osmotica on endosperm rupture and class I β-1,3-glucanase induction in tobacco seed germination. *Planta* **199**, 282-288.

Pons T L (1992). Seed Responses to light. In: *Seeds the Ecology of Regeneration in Plant Communities,* ed M Fenner pp. 259 – 284. CAB International: Wallingford, UK.

Rocha S F R; Chaves F C M; Ming L C; Scarda F M (2002). Phytochrome and light influence on germination and vigour of *Ocimum gratissimum* L. (lamiaceae) seeds under high irradiance conditions. *Acta Horticulture* **569**, 33-39.

Taylorson R B (1982). Interaction of phytochrome and other factors in seed germination. In: *The physiology and biochemistry of seed development, dormancy and germination,* ed A A Khan, pp. 323–346. Elsevier Biomedical Press: Amsterdam, The Netherlands.

Young J A; Evans R A (1973). Mucilaginous seed coats. *Weed Science* **21**, 52–54.

Response of some important citrus weeds to two formulations of glyphosate applied at three growth stages

M Singh, S Singh

University of Florida, IFAS-Citrus Research and Education Center, 700 Experiment Station Road, Lake Alfred, FL 33850, USA

E-mail: msingh@lal.ufl.edu

ABSTRACT

Experiments were conducted under controlled environmental conditions in the greenhouse to evaluate the efficacy of two formulations of glyphosate (Roundup UltraMax and Touchdown IQ) tank mixed with 2% ammonium sulfate at three application rates (0.32, 0.47 and 0.63 kg a.e./ha) and three stages of weed growth 4, 6 and 8 WAS (weeks after sowing). *Echinochloa crus-galli, Bidens pilosa, Morrenia odorata, Panicum maximum, Ambrosia artemisiifolia* and *Paspalum notatum* were raised in the greenhouse. Herbicide was applied by an air pressure chamber track sprayer fitted with a Teejet 8002 flat fan spray nozzle. Visual observations on percent weed mortality were recorded at weekly intervals for 5 weeks. Delay in application time from 4 to 8 WAS significantly reduced weed mortality from 86 to 58%; reduction was severe on *M. odorata* with 77% lower mortality at 8 than 4 WAS. *A. artemisiifolia* was less affected by delay in application than other weed species, but it was less sensitive to glyphosate compared to *P. notatum* and *B. pilosa*. However, regeneration in *P. notatum* and *B pilosa* was observed 4 weeks after treatment with lower application rates of both formulations of glyphosate, particularly with delayed spraying. Increasing the application rates from 0.32 to 0.63 kg/ha increased weed mortality from 59 to 81%. There was no significant difference between the two formulations of glyphosate with respect to weed mortality when data was averaged over species and rates.

INTRODUCTION

Florida grows citrus on 797,000 acres (Anon. 2002) and is the second largest producer in the world after Brazil. Due to warm growing conditions and sufficient rains, weeds germinate and grow year-around and compete vigorously, particularly with young citrus trees and deprive them of essential resources. The total annual cost of weed control in Florida citrus was estimated at $60 million (Singh, 2000). Weed control accounts for a quarter of citrus production cost. Weeds not only compete for moisture and nutrients, but also interfere with other operations and potentially harbours insects, pathogens, nematodes and rodents which adversely affect citrus trees. During a recent survey in Florida, heavy galling and egg mass development of *Meloidogyne incognita* (root-knot nematodes) was found on the roots of *Amaranthus* spp., *Portulaca oleracea*, *Solanum* spp., *Trifolium* spp., *Sesbania exaltata*, *Geranium carolinianum* and several other weeds (Noling *et al.*, 2003). Weeds also reduce soil and air temperature thus increasing chances of frost damage in the cold season (Tucker & Singh, 1984). Glyphosate is one of the most commonly used herbicides in citrus groves. Glyphosate has no residual soil activity and does not control late emerging weeds; a split or multiple applications at lower rates have been found more effective than a single high rate application (Jordan *et al.*, 1977). Different weed species may respond differently to glyphosate at different growth stages. In general, plants at later growth stages are less sensitive to glyphosate due to reduced uptake and translocation; however some species have shown increased uptake and translocation at later than early growth stages (Rioux *et al.*, 1974; Neal *et al.*, 1985). Variations have also been observed on glyphosate efficacy due to species (Wehtje & Walker, 1997) and formulations (Martini *et al.*, 2002). The objective of this study was to compare the efficacy of two formulations of glyphosate when applied at different growth stages of citrus weeds at three application rates under greenhouse conditions.

MATERIALS AND METHODS

The weed species spanishneedles, *Bidens pilosa*; milkweed or stranglervine, *Morrenia odorata*; common ragweed, *Ambrosia artemisiifolia*; guineagrass, *Panicum maximum*; bahiagrass, *Paspalum notatum*, and barnyardgrass, *Echinochloa crus-galli* which are common weeds present in Florida citrus were assessed for two glyphosate formulations at three growth stages. Five seeds of each species were planted in each well of a 72 well plastic tray using commercial potting medium (Metro-Mix 500, Grace Sierra Company, USA) in a greenhouse under controlled climatic conditions of $25/16\pm2^{O}C$ day/night temperature and $70\pm5\%$ relative humidity. Plants were thinned one week after emergence to one plant per well, maintaining 12 plants of each species per tray. Glyphosate [n-(phosphonomethyl) glycine] formulations, Roundup UltraMax in the form of isopropyl salt (IS) (443 g a.e./L) and Touchdown IQ in the form of diammonium salt (DA) (360 g a.e./L) were compared at 0, 0.315, 0.473 and 0.630 kg a.e./ha. Under greenhouse conditions, these application rates correspond to one quarter, half and recommended field rates of glyphosate. Ammonium sulfate (2% W/V) has been shown to increase glyphosate uptake and translocation (Satchivi et al, 2000), thus was added to all herbicide treatments at spraying. Plants were sprayed at 4, 6 or 8 weeks after sowing (WAS). Spraying was done with an air pressure chamber track sprayer fitted with a Teejet 8002 flat fan spray nozzle delivering 189 L/ha volume at 138 kPa pressure. Four replicate trays for each treatment were arranged in a completely random block design. Experiment was repeated under similar conditions. Visual mortality was recorded at weekly intervals until 35 DAT (days after treatment) when the herbicide effect was stabilized. Mortality data (pooled) was arcsin transformed for ANOVA and further subjected to One Way ANOVA for significance of application rates, time and species effect. Original data is presented in tables and figures.

RESULTS AND DISCUSSION

Maximum mortality of 86% (averaged over species and herbicides) was recorded when plants were sprayed 4 WAS (Table 1). Delay in spraying from 4 to 6 and 8 WAS reduced weed mortality by 20 and 28%, respectively. Increasing herbicide rates from 0.32 to 0.47 and 0.63 kg/ha increased weed mortality from 59 to 70 and 81%, respectively, data averaged over species, herbicides and stages. However, delay in application from 4 to 8 WAS reduced weed mortality by 46, 35 and 20% when glyphosate IS was sprayed at 0.32, 0.47 and 0.63 kg/ha. The corresponding reduction in weed mortality with glyphosate DA was 41, 29 and 28%. Reduction in weed mortality was higher at lower rates when sprayed at 8 than at 4 WAS.

P. notatum (83%) and *B. pilosa* (82%) were more sensitive to glyphosate, whereas *M. odorata* (41%) was least, when data was averaged over growth stage and herbicide rates (Table 2). Delayed application from 4 to 8 WAS resulted in 28-32% lower mortality of *E. crus-galli, P.*

notatum and *P. maximum* compared to 15-18% reduction in *A. artemisiifolia* and *B. pilosa*. The corresponding reduction was 77% in *M. odorata* when glyphosate application was delayed from 4 to 8 WAS. Glyphosate applied 8 WAS to *B. pilosa* and *A. artemisiifolia*, still provided >70% mortality (Table 2). Mortality of *P. maximum* and *A. artemisiifolia* with glyphosate was comparable at 6 and 8 WAS, but was significantly less than 4 WAS.

Table 1. Effect of growth stage on the mortality (%) of six weed species when treated with two glyphosate formulations. Data pooled for all species at 35 DAT

| Weed stage | Herbicide treatments | | | | | |
| | Glyphosate IS (kg a.e./ha) | | | Glyphosate DA (kg a.e./ha) | | |
	0.32	0.47	0.63	0.32	0.47	0.63
4 weeks	80	86	95	75	86	94
6 weeks	54	67	77	57	64	77
8 weeks	43	56	76	44	61	68
LSD (*P*=0.05)			3 (SE = 1.419 at 10 df)			

Table 2. Mortality (%) of six weed species treated by two glyphosate formulations at three growth stages. Data pooled over formulations at 35 DAT

| Weed stage | Weed species | | | | | |
	E. crus -galli	*B. pil -osa*	*M. odo -rata*	*P. maxi -mum*	*A. artemi -siifolia*	*P. nota -tum*
4 weeks	81	90	77	87	83	98
6 weeks	77	81	26	56	73	83
8 weeks	58	74	18	59	71	69
LSD (*P*=0.05)			3 (S E = 1.419 at 10 df)			

Some variations in mortality among weed species were observed with different rates of glyphosate formulations, but both were comparable when data were averaged over rates and species (Table 3). Highest mortality among weed species to glyphosate formulations was recorded in *P. notatum* and *B. pilosa*, however, both species exhibited regeneration 28 DAT. There was significant effect between stage of weeds and application rates on mortality. Regeneration in *P. notatum* was visible 28 DAT when sprayed 4 WAS with glyphosate DA 0.32 kg/ha; delaying application to 8 WAS resulted in regeneration even at higher rates (data not shown). Plants of *P. notatum* and *B. pilosa* treated at 6 WAS with both formulations of glyphosate exhibited regeneration at 0.32 kg/ha application rates.

Glyphosate was very effective on *E. crus-galli* when applied at early growth stage (4 WAS) as it provided >65% mortality at lowest rate of 0.32 kg/ha (Figure 1). Delayed application 8 WAS resulted in significant lower mortality of *E. crus-galli* and *B. pilosa*, particularly at 0.32 and 0.47 kg/ha application rates. There was no difference in the activity of either formulations of glyphosate on *E. crus-galli* or *B. pilosa*, when data averaged over rates at all the stages of application.

Table 3. Susceptibility (% mortality) of weed species to two formulations of glyphosate 35 DAT

| Weed species | Herbicide treatments | | | | | |
| | Glyphosate IS (kg a.e./ha) | | | Glyphosate DA (kg a.e./ha) | | |
	0.32	0.47	0.63	0.32	0.47	0.63
E. crus-galli	56	66	93	58	70	88
B. pilosa	73	83	93	69	83	89
M. odorata	32	42	51	32	37	50
P. maximum	59	65	78	54	71	77
A. artemisiifolia	60	77	89	68	78	84
P. notatum	76	87	93	72	83	90
LSD (P=0.05)	4 (SE 2.006 at 35 df)					

Glyphosate IS and DA applied to 4 weeks old plants of *M. odorata* provided 80 and 75% mortality, respectively when averaged over rates, but mortality was reduced to 26 and 27%, respectively at 6 WAS (Figure 2). Further delay in glyphosate application (8 WAS) resulted in further reduction in activity. The largest reduction in herbicide activity on *P. maximum* was between 4 to 6 WAS. Plants of *P. maximum* had similar mortality when glyphosate was applied at 6 or 8 weeks, but was 30% lower than application at 4 WAS (Figure 2).

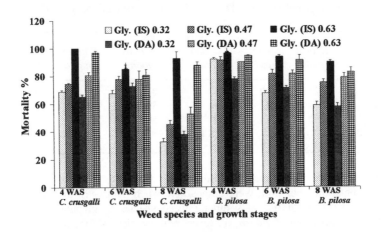

Figure 1. Effect of glyphosate formulations on percent mortality of *E. crus-galli* and *B. pilosa* at 35 DAT, when applied at three growth stages.

Glyphosate IS and DA at 4 WAS provided 81 and 86% control of *A. artemisiifolia*, respectively. Mortality was, however, reduced to <74% at 6 or 8 WAS (Figure 3). *P. notatum* exhibited greater sensitivity at 4 WAS with 90-100% mortality even at 0.32 kg/ha of both formulations; reduction was significant at 6 and 8 WAS.

Previous studies by Ahmadi *et al.* (1980) showed that increase in growth of *E. crus-galli* resulted in decreased glyphosate activity by reduced uptake and translocation. Similarly increase in growth stage of *Solanum nigrum* from 3-4 to 5-6 and 7-9 leaf stage resulted in 7 to 19 fold increase in herbicide dose for the same level of control (Ruiter *et al.*, 1999). Decreas

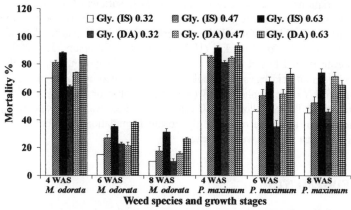

Figure 2.   Effect of glyphosate formulations on percent mortality of *M. odorata* and
P. maximum at 35 DAT, when applied at three growth stages.

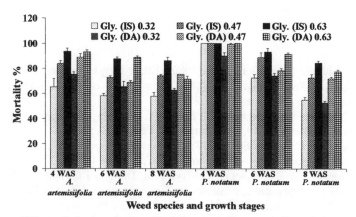

Figure 3.   Effect of glyphosate formulations on percent mortality of *A. artemisiifolia*
and *P. notatum* at 35 DAT, when applied at three growth stages

in glyphosate activity under the present study with delayed spraying from 4 to 6 or 8 weeks
may be due to lower glyphosate uptake possibly due to increased cuticle thickness in older
plants. Other than glyphosate uptake and translocation in the meristems, weed growth stage
might have variations in enzymatic activities (Ruiter *et al.*, 1999). The target site sensitivity
may decrease in older plants. Regeneration of plants 28 DAT in some species at lower
application rates of glyphosate could be due to less inhibition of the enzyme ESPS synthase.
Lowering the application rates may not help due to partial control of weeds; however, field
studies are needed to confirm enhanced efficacy by multiple applications as control varies with
different weed species. Frequent applications of glyphosate at lower rates (Jordan *et al.*, 1977)
may not be helpful in the long run if the growth stage of weeds is advanced with decreased
efficacy and eventually evolution of resistant biotypes as has been observed in many situations
across the globe. Already, the shift in weed flora is visible in citrus groves, where weeds
tolerant to glyphosate are dominating the grove floor. There is increase in the occurrence of
broadleaf weeds with reduced glyphosate susceptibility to *Richardia* spp., *Commelina diffusa*,
B. pilosa, *Scoparia dulcis* and others. Farmers should adopt herbicide rotations to avoid weed
shifts, reduced efficacy of herbicide applications and evolution of resistant biotypes.

No significant variations in the activity of the two formulations of glyphosate were observed when applied to plants at different growth stages. It may not always be accurate to compare the economics of two herbicide formulations as price varies in the market depending on several factors. Enquiry from the local market (Helena Chemical Company, July 2003) revealed the price of glyphosate IS and DA at $50.25 and $42.00 per US gallon, respectively. The cost of both formulations on an acid basis when calculated at the recommended rate of 1.68 kg a.e./ha was $50.70 and $51.79 for glyphosate IS (3.7 lb/US gallon or 443 g/litre of acid equivalent) and glyphosate DA (3 lb/US gallon or 360 g/litre of acid equivalent), respectively. There may be a small variation in the price of these glyphosate formulations, but both were found to be equally effective against the test weed species.

ACKNOWLEDGEMENTS

We thank Gary K Test for technical assistance in conducting these experiments. The research was supported by the Florida Agricultural Experiment Station, and approved for publication as Journal Series No. R-09657.

REFERENCES

Ahmadi M S; Haderlie L C; Wicks G A (1980). Effect of growth stage and water stress on barnyardgrass (*Echinochloa crus-galli*) control and on glyphosate absorption and translocation. *Weed Science* **28**, 277-282.

Anonymous (2002). Florida Agricultural Statistical Service. *Commercial Citrus Inventory Preliminary Report* Sept. 10, 2002, http://www.nass.usda.gov/fl.

Jordan L S; Russell R C; Shaner D L (1977). Citrus weed control with herbicides. *Proceedings of the International Society of Citriculture* 1977, **2**, 140-145.

Martini G; Pedrinho Jr A F F; Felici G V; Pivya F M; Durigan J C (2002). Efficacy of a new formulation of glyphosate for control of Bermuda grass (*Cynodon dactylon*) in citrus orchards. *Revista Brasileira de Fruticulture*, **24**, 683-686.

Neal J C; Skroch W A; Monaco T J (1985). Effects of plant growth stage on glyphosate absorption and transport in Ligustrum (*Ligustrum japonicum*) and Blue Pacific juniper (*Juniperus conferata*). *Weed Science* **34**, 115-121.

Noling, J W; Gilreath, J P; Gilreath, P (2003). Weeds: the nemesis of Florida agriculture. *Citrus and Vegetable Magazine* **67**, 6-8.

Rioux R; Bandeen J D; Anderson G W (1974). Effects of growth stage on translocation of glyphosate in quack grass. *Canadian Journal of Plant Science* **54**, 397-401.

Ruiter H de; Uffing A J M; Dijk N M van (1999) The influence of growth stage of weeds on the glyphosate dose needed. *Proceeding of the BCPC Conference – Weeds* **2**, 615-620.

Satchivi N M; Wax L M; Stoller E W; Briskin D P (2000). Absorption and translocation of glyphosate isopropylamine and trimethylsulfonium salts in *Abutilon theophrasti* and *Setaria faberi*. *Weed Science* **48**, 675-679.

Singh M (2000). Weed management in citrus. *Proceedings of the International Society of Citriculture IX Congress*, Orlando, Florida, US, 2000, **1**, 370-376.

Tucker D P H; Singh M (1984) Florida Citrus Weed Management. In: *Florida Citrus Integrated Pest Management Handbook*, ed. J L Knapp, pp. 12-31 Florida Cooperative Extension Service, University of Florida, Gainesville, USA.

Whetje G; Walker R H (1997) Interaction of glyphosate and 2,4-DB for the control of selected morning-glory (*Ipomoea* spp.) species. *Weed Technology* **11**, 152-156.

Rhizotron study on soil moisture and plant population effect on root competition of cotton and mungbean with *Trianthema portulacastrum* and *Echinochloa crus-galli*

S Singh, A Yadav, R K Malik
Department of Agronomy, CCS Haryana Agricultural University, Hisar-125004, India
Email: Samunder@lal.ufl.edu

M Singh
University of Florida-IFAS, CREC Lake Alfred, FL-33850, USA

ABSTRACT

The effects of soil moisture and plant population on root competition between crop and weed was studied in rhizotron tubes at three levels of irrigation [0.3, 0.6 and 0.9, based on ID/CPE (irrigation depth and cumulative pan evaporation) ratio]. Three plant population ratios of 3:0, 2:1 and 1:2 for crop and weed species for cotton or mungbean (in separate experiments) with *Trianthema portulacastrum* and *Echinochloa crus-galli*, were compared after 50 days for root competition. Root and shoot length, and shoot weight of cotton was unaffected by moisture levels, but root weight increased by 127% with increase in ID/CPE ratio from 0.3 to 0.9. Moisture level or competition with cotton had no effect on root or shoot length of *T. portulacastrum*. One plant of *T. portulacastrum* (1:2 ratio) significantly reduced cotton root/shoot length and dry weight, whereas *T. portulacastrum* root and shoot weight increased by 174 and 252% respectively. Root competition was more severe with *E. crus-galli* compared to *T. portulacastrum* as one plant of *E. crus-galli* (with 2 of cotton) was potent enough to reduce cotton root length and root weight by 33 and 59%, respectively. Shoot and root length of *E. crus-galli* had no effect of moisture level. Competition with cotton (1:2 ratio) reduced shoot and root length of *E. crus-galli*, but its shoot and root weight increased by 177 and 165%, respectively. Increase in moisture level from 0.3 to 0.9 (ID/CPE) had no significant effect on root or shoot length of mungbean or *T. portulacastrum*, but significantly increased their root and shoot weight. Decreasing plant population of mungbean from 3 to 1 significantly reduced its root/shoot length and dry weights, whereas root and shoot weight of *T. portulacastrum* increased by 234 and 218%, respectively. Root length and root weight of mungbean increased with increase in moisture level, but decreased significantly in competition with *E. crus-galli*.

INTRODUCTION

Most weed competition studies are performed on above ground parameters of crop and weeds; not much is known about root competition in the soil. Inter- and intra-specific root competition inhibits root proliferation, upsetting nutrient and moisture absorption thereby affecting above ground growth of plants. The competitive ability of plants depends on several factors including the soil moisture, nutrients and plant population. Carpetweed (*Trianthema portulacastrum*) and barnyardgrass (*Echinochloa colona/crus-galli*) are major weeds infesting mungbean (*Vigna radiata*) and cotton (*Gossypium hirsutum*) in India (Balyan *et al.*, 1995; Panwar *et al.*, 2000) and many other countries. Abundance of moisture in the rainy season and warm temperature stimulates germination and growth of *T. portulacastrum* and *E. crus-galli*. Wide plant spacing and initial slow growth of cotton provides ample space for these weeds to flourish and severely arrest crop growth. Under field conditions of N W India, *T. portulacastrum* is the most competitive and dominant weed in cotton up to 50 days after sowing (DAS), while *E. crus-galli* competes more aggressively between 50 and 100 DAS under higher moisture conditions (Panwar & Malik, 1991). Previous work on root competition between rice and *E. crus-galli* indicates that root effects were more important than shoot effects (Assemat *et al.*, 1981; Perera *et al.*, 1992). Reduction in *Phaseolus vulgaris* yield was 48 and 37% by root and shoot competition with *E. colona*, respectively (Premlal *et al.*, 1998). Gibson *et al.*, (1999) reported that root competition was more important than shoot competition in determining the yield of target species. Rhizotron studies are generally reported for screening genotypes for drought or salt tolerance; not much information is available on root competition with weeds. Studies on root competition could be helpful in better understanding crop-weed interactions as a basis for developing improved control measures.

MATERIALS AND METHODS

In order to understand the effect of soil moisture and plant population on ensuing crop-weed competition, repeat experiments were conducted in rhizotron tubes of 1.25 m length (30 cm diameter) using dunal sand with three replicates. Three trenches of 1.5 m depth were dug in the field and rhizotron tubes filled with dunal sand were placed in trenches after skirting the bottom with 45 cm long polyethylene bags to avoid the interference of groundwater by capillary movement in the tubes. Three irrigation levels (0.3, 0.6 and 0.9) based on ID/CPE (irrigation depth and cumulative pan evaporation) ratio were applied. Three plant population ratios of 3:0, 2:1 and 1:2 for crop and weed species for cotton cv. H-777 and mungbean cv. K-851 with *T. portulacastrum* and *E. crus-galli* in separate experiments, were maintained and compared for root competition. Plants were thinned one week after emergence and 3 plants (pure or mixed with weed/crop species) were maintained. Watering was done as and when required based on ID/CPE ratio and supplemented with Hewitt nutrient solution. Experiments were terminated 50 days after sowing (DAS) and shoot length and dry weight were recorded. The tubes were slit open on a sieve (dimensions 0.2 mm; 1.5 m x 1.0 m) and dipped in a water channel to loosen the sand. Roots were separated by washing with mild water pressure. Root lengths were measured before removing from the tube and later oven dried to record dry weight. Pooled data for both years were subjected to analysis of variance using SPSS.

RESULTS AND DISCUSSION

Effect of *Trianthema* on cotton

Shoot and root length of cotton decreased by 27 and 23%, respectively with one plant of *T. portulacastrum* compared to pure stand (3 plants of cotton) in rhizotron tubes (Figure 1a). Increasing ID/CPE ratio from 0.3 to 0.9 significantly increased cotton shoot length in monoculture, but the same was decreased by 32% in the presence of *T. portulacastrum* even at highest moisture level. There was significant decrease in cotton shoot length in the presence of *T. portulacastrum*. On the other hand *T. portulacastrum* exhibited significant increase in shoot length in 1:2 ratio with cotton at increased moisture level of 0.9 ID/CPE ratio. Root length of cotton and *T. portulacastrum* was non-significant for moisture levels, when data was averaged over populations. Greater reduction in cotton root length was recorded with 2 plants of *T. portulacastrum*; effect of competition was more severe on root than shoot length of cotton. Root length of *T. portulacastrum* was not much affected by plant population or moisture levels, although a significant increase in root length was observed at the highest moisture level in the presence of two plants of cotton (1:2 plant ratio).

There was no significant difference in the shoot weight of cotton at different moisture regimes (SE=0.20 at 2 df), but root weight significantly increased from 1.67 to 2.13 g/plant with increase in ID/CPE ratio from 0.3 to 0.9 (SE=0.08 at 2 df), data averaged over plant ratio (Figure 1b). Shoot weight of cotton decreased by 41 and 49% in the presence of one and two plants of *T. portulacastrum*, respectively compared to cotton alone (3:0). There was some increase in cotton root weight with increase in moisture level, but it was not significant. Shoot and root weight of *T. portulacastrum* increased by 252 and 174%, respectively with reduction in its population from 3 (alone) to 1 plant (with 2 of cotton). The shoot and root weight of *T. portulacastrum* increased exponentially with increase in moisture level in the presence of cotton plants.

Effect of *Echinochloa* on cotton

Shoot length of cotton increased with an increase in moisture level, but the effect of plant ratio was less apparent (Figure 2a). Increase in moisture level significantly increased cotton root length, except in the presence of 2 plants of *E. crus-galli*. *E. crus-galli* was more inhibitory to root length of cotton decreasing it by 25 and 33%, respectively in 2:1 and 1:2 ratio of cotton to *E. crus-galli*. Moisture levels had non-significant effect on shoots and root length of *E. crus-galli*, data averaged over population. In the presence of cotton plants, both shoot and root length of *E. crus-galli* exhibited decreasing trends compared to *E. crus-galli* alone.

Dry matter accumulation by cotton increased with increasing moisture level from 0.3 to 0.9 (ID/CPE ratio), but decreased significantly in the presence of *E. crus-galli* (Figure 2b). Two plants of *E. crus-galli* decreased cotton shoot weight by 49, 46 and 40% respectively, with increasing moisture levels in comparison to pure stand of cotton. Decreasing plant ratio of *E. crus-galli* from 3 to 1 (with 2 plants of cotton) resulted in 177% increase in its dry weight. Moisture levels had no significant effect on *E. crus-galli* shoot weight. However, increase in moisture level was non-significant on cotton root weight, but led to a significant increase in *E. crus-galli* root weight. Compared to monoculture of cotton (3:0), two plants (1:2) of *E. crus-galli* reduced root weight of cotton by 57, 60 and 59%, respectively with increase in moisture level from 0.3 to 0.6 and 0.9. Root dry weight of *E. crus-galli* responded significantly to increase in moisture levels and decrease in its plant population ratio.

Effect of *Trianthema* on mungbean

Effect of moisture on shoot or root length of mungbean was non-significant (data averaged over plant population), but significant decrease in plant height and root length was recorded in the presence of *T. portulacastrum* (Figure 3a). Decreasing population of mungbean or *T. portulacastrum* from 3 to 1 increased the shoot length of *T. portulacastrum* from 79 to 92 cm, but significantly decreased shoot length of mungbean from 43 to 32 cm. Root length of mungbean was not affected by moisture levels, but competition with *T. portulacastrum* resulted in 18-19% reduction in root length. Root length of *T. portulacastrum* was unaffected by moisture level or plant geometry.

Dry matter accumulation by mungbean was affected more than plant height by *T. portulacastrum* (Figure 3b). Increasing the moisture level from 0.3 to 0.9 (ID/CPE ratio) increased both shoot and root weight of mungbean. The decrease in shoot and root weight of mungbean in the presence of *T. portulacastrum* was 14 and 6% only compared to mungbean alone in monoculture. Decreasing the plant ratio from 3 to 1 decreased shoot weight of mungbean, but root weight was less affected. Higher moisture produced significantly higher shoot and root weight of *T. portulacastrum*. One plant of *T. portulacastrum* in the presence of two plants of mungbean resulted in 218 and 234% higher dry matter accumulation of shoot and root, respectively over its pure stand.

Effect of *Echinochloa* on mungbean

Increasing the moisture content from 0.3 to 0.9 (ID/CPE) significantly increased shoot and root length of mungbean, but had no effect on *E. crus-galli* (Figure 4a). Decreasing plant ratio of mungbean to *E. crus-galli* decreased its shoot and root length significantly; the decrease was more on root than shoot length. The shoot length of *E. crus-galli* was unaffected by plant ratio, but root length decreased significantly in competition with mungbean.

Moisture did not contribute significantly to mungbean shoot weight; there was only some increase in shoot weight with increase in moisture level from 0.3 to 0.9 ID/CPE ratio in pure stand (Figure 4b). Shoot and root weight of *E. crus-galli* increased exponentially with increase in moisture level and decreasing *E. crus-galli* from 3 to 1 plants with mungbean. Root weight of mungbean increased with increasing moisture levels, but it was reduced significantly in the presence of *E. crus-galli*.

E. crus-galli has been reported to be competitive even at low moisture with maize (Martinkova & Honek, 1998). Increasing the soil moisture availability resulted in the increase in combined biomass of maize and *E. crus-galli*, but maize shoot weight decreased with increase in root biomass of *E. crus-galli*. In spring planted mungbean, density of *Echinochloa colona* was found to increase with increase in irrigation frequency (Prasad *et al.*, 1989). Balyan and Bhan (1989) reported differential suppression in *T. portulacastrum* dry matter accumulation by some crops, but density was less affected. The suppression of *T. portulacastrum* was more with cowpea than with mungbean. The present study shows that root and shoot growth are closely linked. A single plant of *T. portulacastrum* or *E. crus-galli* could be more competitive than many when moisture and nutrients are not a limiting factor. Root/shoot length of cotton and mungbean and their dry weight increased with increase in moisture level, but only under monoculture. When growing with *T. portulacastrum* and *E. crus-galli*, crop plants failed to utilize additional moisture and nutrients as the same was cornered by the weeds. Suppression in root/shoot lengths of weeds was less by crop plants than vice-versa. *T. portulacastrum* and *E. crus-galli* exhibited better survival even under limited moisture compared to crop plants. Increased root weight directly contributed to higher above ground biomass accumulation by weeds. Even one plant of *T. portulacastrum* or *E. crus-galli* was able to outgrow two plants of cotton or mungbean. Although crop plant height plays a significant role in suppressing weeds, this was not the case with the cultivars tested of cotton or mungbean. The root-shoot dynamics is important for a blue print on competition study with crops for suppression of weed species.

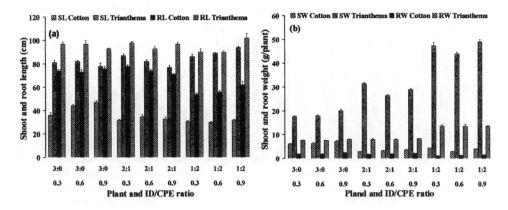

Figure 1. Effect of plant geometry and moisture level on (a) shoot (SL), root length (RL) and (b) shoot (SW) and root (RW) weight of cotton and *T. portulacastrum*.

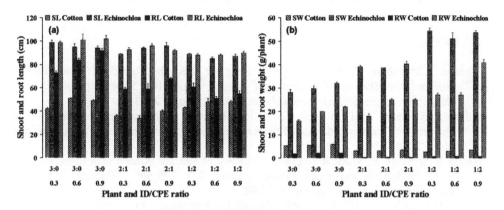

Figure 2. Effect of plant geometry and moisture level on (a) shoot (SL), root length (RL) and (b) shoot (SW) and root (RW) weight of cotton and *E. crus-galli*.

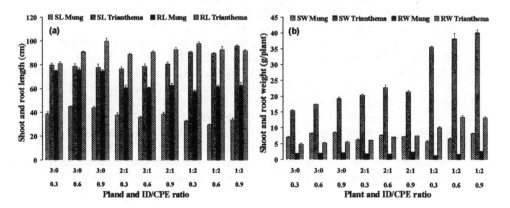

Figure 3. Effect of plant geometry and moisture level on (a) shoot (SL), root length (RL) and (b) shoot (SW) and root (RW) weight of mungbean and *T. portulacastrum*.

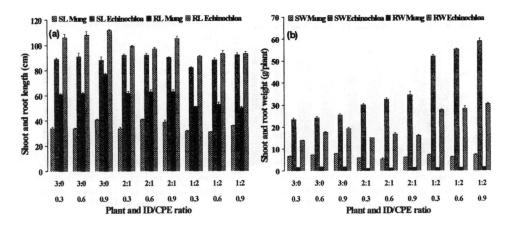

Figure 4. Effect of plant geometry and moisture level on (a) shoot (SL), root length (RL) and (b) shoot (SW) and root (RW) weight of mungbean and *E. crus-galli*.

REFERENCES

Assemat L; Morishima H; Oka H I (1981). Neighbor effects between rice (*Oryza sativa*) and barnyardgrass (*Echinochloa crus-galli* Beauv.) strains II. Some experiments on the mechanism of interaction between plants. *Acta Oceologia* **2**, 63-78.

Balyan R S; Bhan V M (1989). Competing ability of maize, pearlmillet, mungbean and cowpea with carpetweed under different weed management practices. *Crop Research – Hisar* **2**, 147-153.

Balyan R S; Singh S; Malik R K (1995). Efficacy of soil and foliage applied herbicides for weed control in mungbean (*Vigna radiata* (L.) Wilczek. *Haryana Agricultural University Journal of Research* **25**, 35-40.

Gibson K D; Foin T C; Hill J E (1999). The relative importance of root and shoot competition between water-seeded rice and *Echinochloa phyllopogon*. *Weed Research* **39**, 181-190.

Martinkova Z; Honek A (1998). Competition between maize and barnyardgrass (*Echinochloa crus-galli*) at different moisture regimes. *Rostlinna Vyroba* **44**, 65-69.

Panwar R S; Balyan R S; Malik R S (2000) Evaluation of glufosinate for control of weeds in cotton. *Indian Journal of Weed Science* **32**, 94-95.

Panwar R S; Malik R K (1991). Competition and control of weeds in cotton. *Haryana Agricultural University Journal of Research* **21**, 226-234.

Perera K K; Ayres P G; Guanasena H P M (1992) Root growth and the relative importance of root and shoot competition in interaction between rice (*Oryza sativa*) and *Echinochloa crus-galli*. *Weed Research* **32**, 67-76.

Prasad R; Lal B; Singh G (1989). Herbicide use and irrigation effects on weed growth and productivity of spring planted mungbean. *Indian Journal of Weed Science* **21**, 1-8.

Premlal K P S B; Sangakkara U R; Damme P van; Bulcke R (1998). Effect of root and shoot competition of two weeds on *Phaseolus vulgaris* beans. *Proceedings of 50th International Symposium on Crop Protection*, Gent, Belgium, **3**, 727-734.

DISCUSSION SESSION 3

REGULATION OF ADJUVANTS – CURRENT STATUS AND FUTURE PROSPECTS

Chairman and   Dr John Caseley
Session Organiser: *Castan Consultants, Bristol, UK*

Regulation of adjuvants – current status and future prospects

Tank mix adjuvants are widely used to improve the performance of pesticides. Regulations governing the sale and use of adjuvants and inerts vary between countries, but in both Europe and North America requirements for authorisation are being revised and in the future additional information will be required.

This session will start with two short presentations to stimulate discussion.

Rupert Sohm, *Syngenta Crop Protection, Muenchuilen, Switzerland* will give an overview of developments in adjuvant markets worldwide and examples of the current regulations.

Dr Jan Rosenblom, *AkzoNobel Surface Chemistry, Stenungsund, Sweden* will focus on chemical legislation changes and pressures which may affect the cost and availability of tank-mix adjuvants including the re-registration processes in Europe and the USA.

Copies of their presentations are presented in the following pages.

Market and regulatory trends affecting the use of tank mix adjuvants

R H Sohm
Syngenta Crop Protection, Muenchwilen, CH-4333, Switzerland
Email: rupert.sohm@syngenta.com

Many pesticides need to be sprayed in conjunction with inherently non-pesticidal substances in order for the full effect of the pesticide to be delivered.

The potential benefits to the grower include:

- Improved cost-effectiveness of the crop protection products applied – e.g. via the use of wetting/retention aids, bioefficacy enhancement adjuvants, etc.;

- Improved reliability of the crop protection product – e.g. via the use of rainfastness aids, water quality modifiers;

- Avoidance of adverse off-crop effects – e.g. via the use of spray drift reduction additives.

The majority of developments in the use of tank mix adjuvants have been driven by their use with herbicidal products. Of these, the single biggest source of change has resulted from the growth of glyphosate-based products. This active ingredient provides many opportunities for enhancement of product performance through the use of adjuvants.

There is a diversity of grower attitudes towards tank mix adjuvants. Growers managing large acreages tend to have the expertise to gain the maximum benefit from a wide range of tank-mix adjuvants while smallholder farmers tend to prefer products where the adjuvant is co-formulated with the active ingredient. Overall there is a gradual global trend towards 'built-in' products. The primary driver for this is the desire for simplicity in an environment that is becoming increasingly complex.

Manufacturers of crop protection products also prefer 'complete' products. This is driven primarily by the desire to ensure that the benefits of adjuvant technology are not shared with competitors. In many cases such 'built-in' products are not practical due to the wide range of application rates which may be appropriate for an active ingredient.

The regulatory environment is equally diverse. There is a broad spectrum of regulatory data requirements for tank mix adjuvants. One extreme is presented by the USA, where the Environment Protection Agency (EPA) requires little more than proof that the formulants used are exempted from tolerance (i.e. 'approved' by the EPA) and some limited toxicology data. The other extreme may be found in some European markets, where extensive data requirements linking the adjuvant to the a.i. are required. In many such cases extensive biological data needs to be generated (e.g. ecotox, environmental fate and AI residue data in the target crops). The diversity of regulatory requirements in Europe is a consequence of an absence of EU-wide legislation relating to the regulation of tank mix adjuvants. Again, the regulatory environment is not static. Setting aside the pressures upon the suppliers of the formulants there is a trend towards more regulation of adjuvants and therefore more extensive data requirements and therefore higher costs and longer development times for new entrants.

As a consequence both the market and the regulatory environment are driving the crop protection market away from tank-mix adjuvants. This is not a rapid trend, but can be observed in most of the key markets.

A few clear exceptions are expected to emerge:

- Where commercial factors are important – e.g. where distributors/retailers wish to provide a technical service to growers.

- Where vendors of tank mix adjuvants can demonstrate unique benefits – often through novel products generating enhanced benefits.

- Where the adjuvant is required only in specific circumstances and routine use would not be cost effective (e.g. avoidance of spray drift).

- Where the active ingredient has a broad range of application rates making it difficult to build in a single robust and economic level of adjuvant.

The only clear certainty in this market is that it will remain dynamic and evolve with time.

Trends in the chemicals regulatory arena affecting tank mix adjuvant markets

J A Rosenblom
Akzo Nobel Surface Chemistry AB, S-444 85 Stenungsund, Sweden
Email: Jan.Rosenblom@sc.akzonobel.com

Producers of tank mix adjuvants make these products from formulants supplied by chemical manufacturers. While on the one hand there is a trend towards more regulation of adjuvants as such, the development of general chemicals legislation, especially in Europe, may affect both the availability of chemical substances for use as formulants as well as the possibility to protect proprietary formulation know-how.

Some of the drivers for the development of chemical regulations are:

- The current trend of globalization of businesses and information flows, supported by communication technologies like the internet
  - makes issues, perceived or real, travel faster and faster to other regions of the world
  - facilitates copying of legislation from one region to another
  - supports harmonization of regulations between regions

- Increased pressure from non-governmental organisations, consumer groups and other stakeholders
  - Political pressure for more stringent regulations on chemicals
  - Increased pressure for transparency of data and risk assessments

- Political pressure results in
  - Increased regulatory requirements in most regions of the world and in particular in Europe

In Europe the general use and classification and labelling of chemical substances is currently regulated by the Directives on Dangerous Substances, Dangerous Preparations and Safety Data Sheets (SDS). There are no special requirements for testing or registration of a substance before use in a particular application as long as the substance is listed in the inventory of existing chemicals (EINECS) and the application not subject to specific regulations. This may however change in the future according to a proposal for new European chemicals legislation called REACH. The acronym stands for Registration, Evaluation and Authorisation of Chemicals.

REACH will replace the existing European legislation on chemicals which makes a difference between new and existing substances. REACH does not make this difference and covers registration, evaluation and authorization of all substances produced or imported in one single system.

- Registration of substances manufactured in quantities above 1 tonne per year;

- Evaluation by authorities of substances manufactured above 100 tonnes per year or of very high concern;

- Authorisation of substances of very high concern.

The registration will require:

- a dossier with toxicity and ecotoxicity data the scope of which are triggered by volumes produced;

- a human health and environmental risk assessment for <u>all</u> intended uses;

- a chemical safety report including risk management recommendations based on the outcome of the risk assessment

While the current legislation requires authorities to do risk assessments the proposal puts the full responsibility for the safe use of chemical substances on industry including the chain of downstream uses.

While REACH may have an impact on the possibilities to use a specific chemical substance as an ingredient the other competitive strength of a formulator, the formulation know-how, will be affected by another recent regulatory requirement. The new updated European Preparations Directive require all ingredients in a formulation classified as dangerous to human health or environment to be revealed in the obligatory SDS. Since most of the key ingredients in a formulation are revealed in the SDS it will be very difficult to keep propriety technology and knowledge secret which in turn will weaken the contribution of strength in technology to competitiveness.

In the future there will be increasing regulatory burdens which will result in:

- small volume specialty products will have difficulties recovering the costs to comply with regulations;

- the number of available small volume specialty chemicals will probably decrease due to rationalization of product portfolios;

- many small and medium sized companies may have difficulties in recruiting and keeping experts needed as well as finding the financial resources;

- favours the use of global formulations;

- large companies will be favoured being able to capitalize on a larger global market.

DISCUSSION SESSION 4

DOES UK PLANT BIOTECHNOLOGY HAVE A COMMERCIAL FUTURE?

Chairman: Professor John MacLeod
                     RHS Professor of Plant Science,
                     Cambridge, UK

Session Organiser: Dr Rod Morrod
                     Biotech2020 Organising Group Chair,
                     Maidenhead, UK

Does UK plant biotechnology have a commercial future?

In February 2003, BCPC organised a major Forum on plant biotechnology entitled *Biotech2020: Plant Biotechnology in the World of 2020.* This brought together over 50 experts and senior representatives from government, international institutions, research, industry and commerce.

The purpose of the meeting was to identify the emergence by 2020 of new plant science and biotechnology on a global basis and to discuss its interaction with relevant aspects of the world of 2020, including geopolitics, trade, food supply, societal values and the nature of the agri-food market. By focusing on 2020 and creating cross fertilisation between very different disciplines, the Forum provided new insights to those involved in policy making, strategy setting and investment in the UK and Europe. (The Report of the Forum is available from BCPC Publications Sales price £25. Email: publications@bcpc.org).

One of the clearest messages from the Forum was that increased understanding of plants over the next two decades and beyond, will be unprecedented and will provide huge opportunities for mankind throughout the 21st century. The UK, through university groups and research institutes, is at the forefront of this exploration. However, a number of factors were identified that could seriously undermine the conversion of this research into commercial activities with the capability to participate successfully in future European and global biotechnology markets.

The Discussion Session will raise questions on three aspects of the route to market for UK plant science.

1.   What relationship should the UK maintain with the international bioscience companies?

2.   Do we need a new paradigm to achieve impact from UK biotechnology in outlets specific to the UK which is of no commercial interest to the multinationals?

3.   What are the critical issues for the UK's successful involvement in the non-food crops sector, including renewable energy and the replacement of current petro-chemical products?

SESSION 8A

THE ENVIRONMENTAL IMPACT OF GM CROPS: COSTS AND BENEFITS A DECADE AFTER COMMERCIALISATION

Chairman and
Session Organiser:

Dr Alan Raybould
Syngenta, Bracknell, UK

Papers:

8A-1 to 8A-4

An Assessment of the Environmental Impact of Genetically Modified Crops in the US

M J McKee, S Fernandez, T E Nickson, G P Head

Monsanto Company – Ecological Technology Center, 800 North Lindbergh, St. Louis, MO 63141, USA

ABSTRACT

Genetically modified (GM) crops have become important components of modern agriculture in the past ten years. The United States had over 39 million hectares of GM crops grown in 2002 with much of these hectares comprised of Bt corn, Bt cotton, and herbicide tolerant (HT) soybeans. Commercialization of GM crops has been more limited in other areas, such as the EU. This paper describes the information collected to address ecological risks in the US as part of the initial regulatory process and provides a review of new information derived since commercialization, with a focus on field data. Field studies for Bt corn, Bt cotton, and HT crops in the US are reviewed specifically for impacts on arthropod populations and results show no consistent unexpected findings in abundance. Indeed, the adoption of these products can have direct and indirect benefits for the environment by the replacement of broad-spectrum insecticides and the facilitation of reduced tillage. The results of the field studies are discussed within the context of overall biodiversity in agroecosystems.

INTRODUCTION

Genetically modified (GM) crops have become an important tool in agriculture over the past ten years. The initial products have been mainly crops protected from insect damage using insecticidal proteins from the soil bacterium, *Bacillus thuringeinesis* (Bt), and crops made resistant to selected herbicides. GM crops have been commercialized more rapidly in some world areas that others (James, 2002). For example, in Europe, a moratorium has existed for several years on new registrations of GM crops, whereas, GM crops were planted on over 39 million hectares in the US in 2002 (James, 2002). The rapid rate of adoption in the US is likely due to various factors including grower satisfaction with the benefits of using GM crops (Gianessi *et al.*, 2002), consumer confidence relative to food safety regulation, and the suitability of these products with environmentally improved management practices (e.g., conservation tillage and reduced risk to nontarget organisms).

GM soybeans tolerant to Roundup herbicide account for the majority of the GM crop acres in the US. Most of the US GM corn acres were planted in corn expressing the Cry1Ab Bt protein providing European corn borer control. GM cotton expressing the Cry1Ac Bt protein providing tobacco budworm, pink bollworm and cotton bollworm control is also an important part of the U.S. GM crop acres. These products were initially registered in the mid-1990s. During the registration process, the regulating agencies concluded that there were no unreasonable adverse effects on the environment (FR, 1994; US EPA 2003). This paper provides an overview of the type of information collected to address ecological risks in the US for these products and reviews new information derived since commercialization, with a focus on field data and potential implications relative to biodiversity.

US REGULATORY FRAMEWORK

Responsibility for the regulation of GM crops in the US is divided among three federal agencies: the Department of Agriculture (USDA), the Environmental Protection Agency (EPA) and the Food and Drug Administration (FDA). Roles and specific elements of oversight were established in 1986 under the Coordinated Framework for the Regulation of Biotechnology (Federal Register, 1986)

Ecological risk assessment of GM crops falls within the responsibility of one or more US agencies depending on whether the introduced trait contains a plant-incorporated protectant (PIP). GM crops are, at least initially, separated into plant and animal (e.g. insects, birds, fish, wildlife, domestic animals and humans) assessment components. The plant assessment is reviewed primarily by the USDA (Animal Plant Health Inspection Service or APHIS), which focuses on the pest potential of the GM crop and gene flow. The animal assessment is governed by both USDA APHIS regulation and, especially in the case of insecticidal proteins (a specific type of PIP), EPA Federal Insecticide, Fungicide, and Rodenticide Act (FIFRA) regulation under Subdivision M (OPPTS, 1996).

Plant Assessment:

The GM plant is assessed to determine which of its characteristics are "familiar" (OECD, 1993; Hokanson *et al.*, 1999), relative to the parental or control lines. Familiarity enables regulators to focus on those characteristics/properties that require detailed risk assessment. As such familiarity is a characterization endpoint and not a risk conclusion. The basic approach to establish familiarity focuses on phenotypic measurements including germination, growth, time to flowering, pollen morphology, composition and reproduction. In addition to the phenotypic assessment, the potential for altered interactions with known pests (insects and diseases) and biologically meaningful consequences associated with gene flow from the GM crop to other plants is assessed.

Animal Assessment:

Initially the animal assessment focuses on identifying the hazard potential for the introduced trait. Proteins introduced to confer herbicide tolerance may have a history of exposure and/or lack a plausible toxicity mechanism. For these products, the lack of hazard potential may eliminate the need for extensive testing and risk assessment. Other proteins, such as Bt proteins, could potentially be toxic to insect species closely related to the target insect pest species. Therefore, a more comprehensive hazard and exposure assessment may be warranted. For pesticidal traits, the US EPA's Subdivision M (OPPTS, 1996) provides for a series of standard laboratory tests to assess hazard (Table 1).

Using the above-mentioned regulatory framework, the first Bt and herbicide tolerant (HT) crops were found to cause no unreasonable adverse effects to non-target organisms (FR, 1994; US EPA, 2003). No observed effect concentration (NOEC) values for Bt proteins were in excess of expected levels of exposure in the field (Table 1). After a product is registered for commercial use in the US, the ecological risk assessment is updated as new information becomes available. For example, when new information became available in the scientific literature on potential effects of Bt proteins on monarch butterflies (Losey *et al.*, 1999), the ecological risk assessment was re-evaluated and a data call-in was issued by the EPA for additional information. Independent scientists evaluated the information and concluded that Bt pollen had negligible impact on monarch butterfly populations (Sears *et al.*, 2001). Therefore, there was no need to initiate additional regulatory action. This process of updating the ecological risk assessment serves to maintain a robust and transparent technical foundation for GM products.

Table 1. Typical hazard assessment data collected for pesticidal GM products in accordance with US EPA guidelines with NOEC examples for Cry1Ab corn and Cry1Ac cotton.

Specific taxa/species	Test material	Cry1Ab*	Cry1Ac*
Beneficial insects			
Honey bee larva	Pure protein	NOEC>20 ppm	NOEC>20 ppm
Honey bee adult	Pure protein	Not reported	NOEC>20 ppm
Ladybird beetle	Pure protein	NOEC>20 ppm	NOEC>20 ppm
Parasitoid wasp	Pure protein	NOEC>20 ppm	NOEC>20 ppm
Lacewing	Pure protein	NOEC>17 ppm	NOEC>17 ppm
Soil organisms			
Earthworm	Pure protein	NOEC>20 ppm	Not reported
Collembola	Pure protein	NOEC>200 ppm	NOEC>20 ppm
Aquatic animals			
Daphnia	Pollen (only corn)	NOEC >100 mg /L	Not reported
Catfish	Grain/meal	NOEC >35% in diet	Not reported
Birds			
Bobwhite Quail	Grain/seed	NOEC > 100 g/kg diet	Not reported

* Data from from Betz et al. (2000) and Sims (1995). No unreasonable adverse effects are predicted because NOECs are in excess of potential environmental exposures.

Recently, the re-registration process was completed for Bt corn and Bt cotton. The products were again found to cause no unreasonable adverse effects on non-target organisms (US EPA, 2001). The regulators requested that, during the continued growing of these crops, additional data be submitted to confirm these findings, specifically for field arthropod data. Since the initial registrations of these products, a number of field studies have been conducted on the Bt crops and on HT soybeans. The following sections summarize field data currently available for non-target arthropods for Bt corn, Bt cotton and RR soybeans in the US that can confirm the results of the initial assessment. In addition, these data are discussed within a context of biodiversity of agricultural ecosystems.

FIELD EXPERIENCE WITH GMO CROPS IN THE US

Industry and academic scientists have used two basic approaches to field assessment: a plot-based approach where measurements are made on plots, typically smaller than standard fields but replicated for additional statistical power, and a monitoring approach where measurements are made on farm-scale fields under actual use conditions.

Bt cotton

Where the product is used, Bt cotton replaces most insecticide use for tobacco budworm, pink bollworm and bollworm control. If these pests are common, the use of Bt cotton results in a substantial reduction in overall insecticide use. For example, Roof & DuRant (1997) studied 10 pairs of farms with Bt cotton and conventional cotton and found that pesticide applications averaged 1.2 for Bt cotton and 4.8 for conventional cotton. Field studies of the non-target impact of Bt cotton have included comparisons with unsprayed conventional cotton and comparisons with conventional cotton treated as needed with insecticides. The former comparison, while not being agronomically realistic, allows the absolute environmental impact of the plant-expressed Bt protein to be assessed. The latter comparison involves the relative environmental impact of the alternative cropping systems, which is the most relevant comparison. Most studies have focused on measuring generalist predator populations because of their acknowledged importance as biological control agents within cotton agroecosystems.

Researchers working in the field have concluded that there are no significant adverse effects on non-pest arthropods in Bt cotton when compared to non-Bt cotton (Table 2) (Armstrong *et al.*, 2000; Hagerty *et al.*, 2001; Head *et al.*, 2001; Naranjo & Ellsworth, 2003). Importantly, significantly larger arthropod predator populations have been observed in Bt cotton fields than in conventionally managed cotton fields as would have been predicted from what is known of the insecticidal spectrum of the commonly used insecticides compared to Bt proteins (Roof & DuRant, 1997; Head et al., 2001; Naranjo & Ellsworth, 2003). For example, in a replicated farm scale study where Bt cotton was paired with conventional cotton production systems, abundance of *Geocoris, Orius* and spiders, three generalist predators was found to be significantly higher in Bt cotton (Head *et al.*, 2001). This has important consequences for secondary pest control; more outbreaks of secondary pests such as cotton aphids and beet armyworms are observed in sprayed conventional cotton fields than in Bt cotton field. Comparable results have been seen in a multiple year field studies in China where Wu and Guo (2003) found generalist predator populations to be higher in Bt cotton than in appropriately managed conventional cotton which led to fewer outbreaks of cotton aphids in the Bt cotton fields. Presumably consumer taxa other than predatory insects, including insectivorous birds and mammals, also may be affected by these differences in non-target arthropod populations (Firbank *et al.*, 2003; Watkinson *et al.*, 2000). In addition, the reduced insecticide use will have benefits to wildlife outside of the cotton fields because of reduced drift, lower insecticide levels in water, and lower potential for secondary poisoning of birds. Long-term suppression of target lepidopteran pests through the use of Bt crops may lead to even greater reductions in insecticide use in both Bt cotton and conventional cotton fields, with concomitant benefits for non-target populations (Carriere *et al.*, 2003).

Bt Corn

Comparable studies have been performed with Bt corn to those with Bt cotton with generally similar results (Table 2). Generalist predator populations are not significantly different in Bt corn and unsprayed conventional cornfields (Orr & Landis, 1997; Pilcher *et al.*, 1997; Wold *et al.*, 2001; Jasinski *et al.*, 2003). When Bt cornfields are compared with sprayed corn fields, many groups of non-targets are more common in the Bt fields (Orr & Landis, 1997; Dively & Rose, 2003). For example, Orr & Landis (1997) observed that in a

Table 2: Non-target arthropod field studies conducted on Bt cotton expressing CrylAc and Bt corn expressing the CrylAb corn in the US.

Type of Assessment	No. years/ No. sites/ Sample method	Results/Conclusions	Reference
Cotton			
Plot-based (16 rows x 27 m)	1 year/1 site/beat-net	No differences in key insect and spider predators inhabiting Bt vs non-Bt cotton	Armstrong et al., 2000
Plot-based (24-40 rows x 18-46 m)	2 years/1 site/visual observations and beat cloth	No difference in predaceous arthropods between GM and non-GM crops	Hagerty et al., 2001
Plot-based (0.03-0.15 ha)	2 years/1 site/beat sampling, sweep nets, whole plants and pitfalls	No negative impacts of Bt-cotton but strong effects of spraying non Bt-cotton	Naranjo & Ellsworth, 2002
Farm-scale	1 year/10 sites (paired fields)/visual observations	Population of beneficial arthropods slightly greater in Bt-cotton	Roof & DuRant, 1997
Farm-scale	1 year/5 sites/beat net	No differences in key insect and spider predators inhabiting Bt vs non-Bt cotton	Armstrong et al., 2000
Farm-scale	1 year/3 sites (paired fields)/visual observations beat sheets	Bollgard preserves natural enemies populations more effectively than broad spectrum insecticides	Head et al., 2001
Corn			
Plot-based (4 rows x 7.6 m)	2 years/1 site/visual observations	No detrimental effects on abundance of the insects observed	Pilcher et al., 1997
Plot-Based (64 x 63 m)	1 year/1 site/visual observations	No significant differences in pest egg populations or its predators and parasitoids	Orr & Landis, 1997
Plot based (4 rows x 9.14 m and 30 x 24.6 m)	2 years/1 site/visual observations	No significant differences were detected for total predator density, or species diversity, of immature beneficial insects	Wold et al., 2001
Farm-scale	1 year/5 sites (paired fields)/visual observations, sticky traps, soil samples, sweep net samples	No consistent significant effect on NTO populations	Jasinski et al., 2003

couple of sampling periods, abundance of Coccinellid adults and lacewing larvae were significantly higher in Bt corn compared to conventional corn. In the US, the insecticide use associated with lepidopteran pests is much lower in corn than in cotton, so, although the use of Bt corn reduced insecticide use, Bt corn is associated with lower insecticide use reduction than Bt cotton. Thus, comparisons of Bt corn fields with sprayed conventional corn fields only are relevant to corn growing areas with relative high pest infestations.

Impacts of Bt corn on specialist parasitoids also have been quantified. The hymenopteran *Macrocentrus grandii* is a parasitoid of the European corn borer. Not surprisingly, in Bt corn fields where the European corn borer is completely controlled, this parasitoid is rare (Venditti & Steffey, 2003). Presumably any effective control tactic for corn borers would have a similar indirect effect on populations of this parasitoid. At a landscape level, the areas of non-Bt corn that are planted as part of the insect resistance management program for European corn borer also will serve as a refuge for *M. grandii*.

Comparable results have been observed in European studies. For example, Bourguet *et al.* (2002) found no significant effects of Bt corn on a variety of non-target predators and secondary pests. However, as in the US studies and presumably for the same reasons, they did observe some impact on specialist parasitoids.

Herbicide Tolerant Crops

Herbicide tolerant crops are not expected to directly affect animals because of the nature of the protein that is expressed in the plant to confer herbicide tolerance. Nonetheless, several field studies have been conducted on Roundup Ready (RR) and other herbicide tolerant soybean varieties in the US (Table 3). Two plot-based studies indicated no impact of soybeans with the RR trait (Buckelew *et al.*, 2000; McPherson *et al.*, 2003). Variation in insect abundance was noted among varieties, however, the differences were correlated to either plant height (Buckelew *et al.*, 2000) or to maturity (McPherson *et al.*, 2003). Jazinski *et al.* (2003) reported on a farm-scale study comparing paired fields of HT soybeans with non-GM soybeans. Farm-scale monitoring systems compare all aspects of the RR system and separation of effects due to weed control efficiency, varietal differences and weather can be difficult. Results reported by Jazinski *et al.* (2003) indicated that in most of the 6 paired soybean fields observed, no difference in arthropod abundance was noted between conventional and RR soybean fields. Decreased abundance of certain predatory species were associated with the HT fields if data were pooled from all sites, however, as discussed below, these differences could reflect phenotypic differences (height or maturity), or in timing of herbicide application, changes in tillage practices or other differences. Overall these reports indicate no adverse impact of herbicide tolerance trait on arthropods compared to conventional non-transgenic soybeans.

The plot-based studies mentioned above compared soybeans grown under similar tillage systems. An important aspect of the RR system is that producers plant a significantly higher percentage of acres using no-till or reduced tillage systems compared to producers using conventional soybean (American Soybean Association, 2001). A survey conducted by the American Soybean Association (2001) revealed that 54% of farmers interviewed credited RR soybeans as a factor that had the greatest impact in their adoption of reduced tillage or no-tillage in soybean production. Arthropods have been shown to be more abundant and diverse in minimal tillage crop fields compared to crops grown under conventional tillage (Warburton & Klimstra, 1984; Steffey, 1995) likely due to the increased ground cover (Witmer *et al.*, 2003). Although the effect of tillage was not specifically investigated in the soybean studies discussed above, the increase in productivity of soil and arthropods is likely to be associated with increased ground cover from the decreased tillage in RR soybeans.

Table 3: Arthropod field studies conducted on herbicide tolerant soybeans in the US.

Type of Assessment	Number of years/ Number of sites/ Sample method	Results/Conclusions	Reference
Plot-based (6-8 rows x 15.1 m)	2 years/ 5 sites/sweepnet	No differences in seasonal abundance of arthropod pests.	McPherson et al., 2003
Plot-based (6 x 7.3m and 6 x 6 m)	1 year/2 sites/sweep net	No apparent direct effect of RR soybeans on arthropod populations although weed management can affect insect populations.	Buckelew et al., 2000
Farm scale	1 year/6 sites (paired field)/yellow sticky traps and sweep net	No differences in arthropod populations. Reanalysis of data pooled across sites noted lower population of one insect predator in GM soybeans.	Jazinski et al., 2003

Buckelew et al. (2000) and McPherson et al. (2003) demonstrated that the degree of weed control can have significant effects on arthropod abundance. Other studies with RR crops have shown that modification of the timing of herbicide application can lead to different levels of weed biomass and of ground cover (Dewar et al., 2002; Witmer et al., 2003). These studies indicate that herbicide tolerant crops can provide an important tool to manage weed biomass which can lead to in-field increases in invertebrate biodiversity for production systems where that is an objective compatible with crop production.

BIODIVERSITY IN THE AGRICULTURAL LANDSCAPE

The purpose of collecting data on in-field abundance of arthropods for Bt and HT crops is twofold. First, to determine if the genetically modified plant itself or the introduced trait has a direct adverse effect on arthropod abundance. As discussed above, studies to date in the US show no consistent adverse effects. A second purpose is to ascertain if the long-term use of the GM crops will result in changes in biodiversity in the agroecosystem. Recent studies, mainly in the UK, have indicated that the intensification of agriculture, through a variety of mechanisms, can lead to decreases in biodiversity (Robinson & Sutherland, 2002; Weibull et al., 2003). GM crops can potentially mitigate some of the concerns of agricultural intensification providing a highly targeted, highly productive set of pest control solutions that can replace less environmentally compatible pesticide alternatives while, at the same time, increasing agricultural productivity and potentially improving wildlife habitat. In addition, GM crops can provide farmers with greater flexibility in their management operations and can provide opportunities to increase biodiversity within agricultural fields. For example, HT crops facilitate reductions in tillage, as has been observed with RR soybeans in North America which can increase invertebrate productivity (see above). A more innovative example comes from Brooms Barn in the UK where researchers showed that RR sugar beets enabled farmers to delay and reduce herbicide applications, thereby increasing the biomass of weed in sugar beet fields and providing food and shelter for non-target arthropods and other wildlife (Dewar et al., 2002). Of course providing improved tools to farmers is only part of the solution if the aim is to preserve and increase biodiversity in agricultural landscapes. Agricultural policies also must encourage farmers to adopt appropriate agricultural practices. Nevertheless, the demonstrated and potential benefits of GM crops are such that their use can be expected to continue to grow. One of the responsibilities of scientists and policy makers will be to ensure that GM crops are used in ways that maximize their value.

CONCLUSIONS

- No unacceptable adverse effects are predicted for non-target organisms including beneficial insects, soil invertebrates, aquatic organisms, birds and mammals exposed to Bt corn, Bt cotton, and HT soybeans based on regulatory evaluation in the US.
- Many field studies have been conducted and the results to date for specific field tests, as well as some monitoring studies, for both Bt crops and herbicide tolerant crops suggest no consistent unexpected or adverse changes in non-target arthropod abundance relative to direct effects of the introduced trait.
- Both Bt and herbicide tolerant crops have been shown to have direct and indirect benefits for agroecosystems in the US through the replacement of broad-spectrum pesticides and the facilitation of reduce tillage which can lead to increased local biodiversity
- GM crops can potentially mitigate some concerns associated with agricultural intensification by providing a highly targeted, highly productive set of pest control solutions that can replace less environmentally compatible alternatives while, at the same time, increasing agricultural productivity and potentially improving wildlife habitat.

REFERENCES

American Soybean Association (2001). http://www.asa-europe.org/index.shtml.

Armstrong, J S; Leser, J; Kraemer, G (2000). An inventory of the key predators of cotton pests on Bt and non-Bt cotton in west Texas. *Proceedings - Beltwide Cotton Conference,* San Antonio, TX, pp.1030-1033. National Cotton Council, Memphis: TN.

Betz, F S, Hammond, B G, Fuchs, R L (2000). Safety and advantages of *Bacillus thuringiensis*-Protected plants to control insect pests. *Regulatory Toxicology and Pharmacology* **32**:156-173.

Buckelew, L D; Pedigo, L P; Mero, H M; Owen, M D K; Tylka, G L (2000). Effects of weed management systems on canopy insects in herbicide-resistant soybeans. *Journal of Economic Entomology* **93**, 1437-1443.

Bourguet, D; Chaufaux, J; Micoud, A; Delos, M; Naibo, B; Bombarde, F; Marque, G; Eychenne, N; Pagliari, C (2002). *Ostrinia nubilalis* parasitism and the field abundance of non-target insects in transgenic *Bacillus thuringiensis* corn (*Zea mays*). *Environmental Biosafety Research* **1**, 49-60.

Carriere, Y; Ellers-Kirk, C, E-K; Sisterson, M; Antilla, L; Whitlow, M; Dennehy, T J; Tabashnik, B E (2003). Long-term regional suppression of pink bollworm by Bacillus thuringiensis cotton. *Proceedings of the National Academy of Sciences of the United States of America* **100**, 1519-1523

Dewar, M A; May, M J; Woiwod, I P; Haylock, L A, Champion, G T; Garner, B H; Sands, R J N; Qi, A; Pidgeon, J D (2002). A novel approach to the use of genetically modified herbicide tolerant crops for the environmental benefit. *Proceedings of the Royal Society of London* **270**, 335-340.

Dively, G P; Rose, R (2003). Effects of Bt transgenic and conventional insecticide control on the non-target invertebrate community in sweet corn. In *Proceedings of the First International Symposium of Biological Control of Arthropods*, U.S. Forest Service, Amherst, MA. In press.

Federal Register (1986). http://www.epa.gov/opptintr/biotech/biorule.htm

Federal Register (1994). Availability of determination of non-regulated status of Monsanto genetically engineered soybean. *Federal Register* 59(99):26781-26821.

Firbank, L G; Heard, M S; Woiwod, I P; Hawes, C; Haughton, A J; Champion, G T; Scott, R J; Hill, M O; Dewar, A M; Squire, G R; May, M J; Brooks, D R; Bohan, D A; Daniels, R E; Osborne, J L; Roy, D B; Black, H I J; Rothery, P; Perry, J N (2003). An introduction to the Farm-Scale Evaluations of genetically modified herbicide-tolerant crops. *Journal of Applied Ecology* 40, 2-16.

Gianessi, LP., Silvers, CS., Sankula, S. and Carpenter, JE. 2002. Plant Biotechnology: Current and Potential Impact for Improving Pest Management in US Agriculture. An Analysis of 40 Case Studies. National Center for Food & Agricultural Policy. Washington, DC.

Hagerty, A; Turnipseed, S G; Sullivan, M J (2001). Impact of predaceous arthropods in cotton IPM. Proceedings - Beltwide Cotton Conference, Anaheim, CA, pp.812-815. National Cotton Council, Memphis: TN.

Head, G; Freeman, B; Moar, W; Ruberson, J; Turnipseed, S (2001). Natural enemy abundance in commercial Bollgard® and conventional cotton fields. *Proceedings - Beltwide Cotton Conferences*, Anaheim, CA, pp.796-798. National Cotton Council, Memphis, TN.

Hokanson, K; Heron, D; Gupta, S; Koehler, S; Roseland, C; Shantharam, S; Turner, J; White, J; Schechtman, M; McCammon, S; Bech, R (1999). The concept of familiarity and pest resistant plants. In: *Ecological effects of pest resistance genes in managed ecosystems*, eds P L Taylor & J H Westwood, pp.15-19. *Proceedings of a Workshop on: Ecological Effects of Pest Resistance Genes in Managed Ecosystems*: Blacksburg, Virginia.

James, C (2002). Preview: Global Status of Commercialized Transgenic Crops: 2002. *ISAAA Briefs* No. 27. ISAAA: Ithaca: NY.

Jasinski, J R; Eisley, J B; Young, C E; Kovach, J; Willson, H (2003). Select nontarget arthropod abundance in transgenic and nontransgenic field crops in Ohio. *Environmental Entomology* 32, 407-413.

Losey, J E; Rayor, L S; Carter, M E (1999). Transgenic pollen harms monarch larvae. *Nature* 399, 214-214.

McPherson, R M; Johnson, W C; Mullinix Jr, B G; Mills III, W A; Peebles, F S (2003). Influence of herbicide tolerant soybean production systems on insect pest populations and pest-induced crop damage. *Journal of Economic Entomology* 96, 690-698.

Naranjo, S E; Ellsworth, P C (2003). Arthropods communities and transgenic cotton in the Western United States: implications for biological control. In *Proceedings of the First International Symposium of Biological Control of Arthropods*, U.S. Forest Service, Amherst, MA. In press.

OECD (1993). Safety considerations for biotechnology. OECD: Paris.

OPPTS (1996). Microbial Pesticide Guidelines: OPPTS 885.4000 Background for nontarget organism testing of microbial pest control agents. US EPA Office of Prevention, Pesticides, and Toxic Substance. EPA 712-C-96-328.

Orr, D B; Landis, D A (1997). Oviposition of European corn borer (Lepidoptera: Pyralidae) and impact of natural enemy populations in transgenic versus isogenic corn. *Journal of Economic Entomology* 90, 905-909.

Pilcher, C D; Obrycki, J J; Lewis, L C (1997). Preimaginal development, survival, and field abundance of insect predators on transgenic *Bacillus thuringiensis* corn. *Environmental Entomology* **26**, 446-454.

Robinson, R A; Sutherland, W J (2002). Post-war changes in arable farming and biodiversity in Great Britain. *Journal of Applied Ecology* **39**, 157-176.

Roof, M E; DuRant, J A (1997). On-farm experiences with Bt cotton in South Carolina. *Proceedings - Beltwide Cotton Conference*, Anaheim, CA, p.861. National Cotton Council, Memphis: TN.

Sears, M K; Hellmich, R L; Stanley-Horn, D E; Oberhauser, K S; Pleasants, J M; Matilla, H R; Siegfried, B D; Dively, G P (2001). Impact of Bt corn pollen on monarch butterfly populations: A risk assessment. *Proceedings of National Academy of Sciences* **98**, 11937-11942.

Sims, S R (1995) Bacillus thuringiensis Var. Kurtaski (Cry1Ac) protein expressed in transgenic cotton: Effects on beneficial and other non-target insects. *Southwestern Entomologist* **20(4)**: 493-499.

Steffey, K L (1995). Impacts of various tillage practices on insect an insecticides. In: *Farming for a Better Environment*. Soil and Water Conservation Society. Ankeny, Iowa, 26-27.

US EPA (2001). Biopesticides Registration Action Document - *Bacillus thuringiensis* Plant-Incorporated Protectants. http://www.epa.gov/oppbppd1/biopesticides/pips/bt_brad.htm.

US EPA (2003). Plant Incorporated Protectants. http://www.epa.gov/pesticides/biopesticides /pips/index.htm

Venditti, M E; Steffey, K L (2003). Field effects of Bt corn on the impact of parasitoids and pathogens on European corn borer in Illinois. In *Proceedings of the First International Symposium of Biological Control of Arthropods*, U.S. Forest Service, Amherst, MA. In press.

Warburton, D B; Klimstra, W D (1984). Wildlife use of no-till and conventionally tilled corn fields. *Journal of Soil and Water Conservation* **39**, 327-330.

Watkinson, , A R; Freckleton, R P; Robinson, R A; Sutherland, W J. (2000). Predictions of biodiversity responses to genetically modify herbicide-tolerant crops. *Science* **289**, 1554-1557.

Weibull, A-C; Östman, Ö; Granqvist, Å (2003). Species richness in agroecosystems: the effect of landscape, habitat and farm management. *Biodiversity and Conservation* **12**, 1335-1355.

Witmer, J E; Hough-Goldstein, J A; Pesek, J D (2003). Ground-Dwelling and Foliar Arthropods in Four Cropping Systems. *Environmental Entomology* **32**, 366-376.

Wold, S J; Burkness, E C; Hutchison, W D; Venette, R C (2001). In-field monitoring of beneficial insect populations in transgenic corn expressing a Bacillus thuringiensis toxin. *Journal of Entomological Science* **36**, 177-187.

Wu, K M; Guo, Y Y (2003). Influences of *Bacillus thuringiensis* Berliner cotton planting on population dynamics of the cotton aphid, *Aphis gossypii* Glover, in northern China. *Environmental Entomology* **32**, 312-318.

The environmental impact of controlling weeds using broad spectrum herbicides in genetically modified herbicide tolerant crops: the farm scale evaluations explained

A Dewar
IACR-Broom's Barn, Bury St Edmunds, UK

No information could be released for publication at the time of going to press.

Evaluation of transgenic herbicide-resistant oilseed rape and maize with respect to integrated pest management strategies

B Hommel, B Pallutt

Federal Biological Research Centre for Agriculture and Forestry (BBA), Institute for Integrated Plant Protection, Stahnsdorfer Damm 81, D - 14532 Kleinmachnow, Germany
Email: b.hommel@bba.de

ABSTRACT

In the present study, weed control in glufosinate-resistant maize and rape was comparable to that in conventional crops but was associated with fewer biological risks. New weeds emerged after glufosinate treatment. These plants increased the in-field biodiversity during vegetation but deposited their seeds in the soil, which can lead to later weed control problems. In maize, dead floral mulch and new weeds that emerged after treatment provided only a small degree of protection against soil erosion. Out-crossing of transgenic rape into neighbouring non-transgenic rape was far below the proposed thresholds of 0.5 % and 0.9 %. We believe that conservation tillage systems with herbicide-resistant crops have a greater potential in promoting integrated pest management than same systems that do not use transgenic herbicide-resistant varieties.

INTRODUCTION

Of all the options available for indirect and direct plant protection in integrated pest management (IPM), the application of pesticides should be used as the last choice and should be minimised to reduce the risk of harm to non-target organisms (Burth & Freier, 1996). Farmers growing transgenic herbicide-resistant (HR) crops commit themselves at a very early stage to use a specific herbicide. Alternative weed control measures then play a subordinate role. Without herbicides, many crops cannot be grown economically in accordance with the principles of IPM. This is especially relevant to countries like Germany, where an increasing proportion of farming land is managed by conservation tillage. Hence, the negative and positive economic and ecological effects of HR crops must be carefully considered when attempting to implement IPM strategies in agricultural practice.

Since 1996, the Biologische Bundesanstalt (BBA) in Kleinmachnow has been conducting a long-term field trial in conventional and HR maize and rape to elucidate the following key issues:

1. Effects of frequent glufosinate use on field flora after several crop rotations;
2. Consequences of volunteer HR rape in maize resistant to the same herbicide;
3. Ecological effects of new weeds that emerge in maize fields after glufosinate treatment;
4. Ecotoxicological differences in herbicide treatment strategies in conventional and herbicide-resistant maize and oilseed rape;
5. Potential impact of out-crossing of different rape varieties on the coexistence of farms cultivating transgenic and non-transgenic oilseed rape.

MATERIALS AND METHODS

The BBA trial of transgenic HR rape and maize was performed in fields in Dahnsdorf, Brandenburg, a site characterised by silty sandy soil with 1.42 % organic matter, an annual mean temperature of 8.4 °C, an average annual precipitation of 536 mm, and a pronounced pre-summer dryness period. The study, which was initiated in 1996, was designed as a randomised block field trial with four replicates and four courses of crop rotation, from winter rape to winter rye to maize to winter wheat (figure 1). Each crop rotation field (18 m x 20 m = 360 m²) was divided into three plots of equal size, where the following variants of oilseed rape and maize were grown:

Variant 1: Conventional rape treated as needed with metazachlor, quinmerac, carbetamide, dimefuron or fluazifop-P, and conventional maize treated as needed with metolachlor, pyridate or terbuthylazin.

Variant 2: Glufosinate-resistant rape (event GS 40/90) and maize (event T 25) with intensive glufosinate treatment, i.e. high-dose or two applications.

Variant 3: Glufosinate-resistant rape (event GS 40/90) and maize (event T 25) with extensive glufosinate treatment, i.e. low-dose or one application.

All three variants were subjected to uniform tillage, fertilisation and other plant protection measures. The kind of weed species and their abundance (weed-coverage) were determined before and after herbicide treatment. The yield of oilseed rape, maize, rye and wheat, and the feed values of maize were also determined. An ecotoxicological analysis based on the SYNOPS model (Gutsche & Roßberg, 1997), which considers the biological risk potentials of herbicides for fish, daphnia, earthworm and alga, was also performed in all three variants of maize and rape.

In order to reduce the transmission of transgenic rape pollen to fields with conventional rape, ruderal rape or wild relatives, the 16 test fields were surrounded by an unbroken strip of isogenic rape (7.5 m in width) positioned 15 to 35 m away (figure 1). To calculate the proportion of out-crossing, the rape seedlings yielded in the catch crop strip were treated with glufosinate under greenhouse conditions, and the survivors were genetically tested by PCR.

Figure 1.   Aerial view showing the 4 fields of transgenic herbicide-resistant winter rape and maize surrounded by a strip of isogenic rape positioned a variable distance away; here, one crop rotation with rye and wheat has been completed. (Photo: Baier, 05/2001)

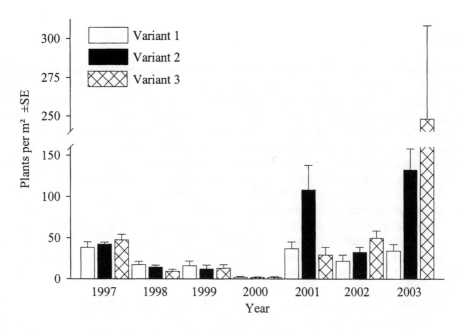

Figure 2.   Annual abundance of *Chenopodium album* in maize before herbicide treatment (first crop rotation 1997 – 2000).

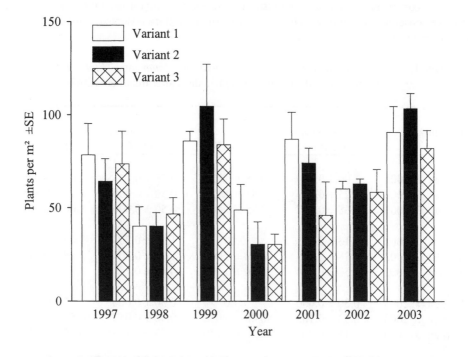

Figure 3.   Annual abundance of *Viola arvensis* in maize before herbicide treatment (first crop rotation 1997 – 2000).

RESULTS

Chenopodium album and *Viola arvensis* were the most commonly observed weed species in the maize fields. *C. album* had similar abundance in all variants during the first crop rotation (1997 – 2000), but a marked annual increase has been observed in variants 2 and 3 since the second crop rotation in 2001 (figure 2). In the case of *V. arvensis*, the abundance levels registered during the first rotation persisted during the second crop rotation in all variants (figure 3). *Polygonum spp.*, another frequent weed genus, showed a trend similar to that of *C. album*.

In maize variant 1, *C. album* and *V. arvensis* coverage has remained very low 4 weeks after herbicide treatment since 1997 (table 1), and a small degree of diversity and abundance of associated floral species has persisted until the September harvest each year. New *C. album* emerged after glufosinate application in maize variants 2 and 3. In 2 of 3 years, *C. album* was almost as abundant 4 weeks after treatment as before treatment (table 1). In most cases, *V. arvensis* was not satisfactory controlled by glufosinate (table 1). The high degree of coverage by *V. arvensis* 4 weeks after treatment was usually attributable to growing plants which had already emerged before glufosinate treatment. The degree of coverage of *Polygonum* spp. in all maize variants did not exceed 0.2 % until 4 weeks after treatment.

Beginning with the second rotation in 2001, glufosinate-resistant volunteer oilseed rape emerged in maize variants 2 and 3; these plants predictably survived glufosinate treatment. Glufosinate was successfully supplemented with nicosulfuron or rimsulfuron in 2001 and 2002, respectively. Both of these herbicides and variable doses of glufosinate have adequately controlled weed growth in the HR crops during last 7 years. Yields of rape and maize variants 2 and 3 were comparable to those of the respective standard crop (variant 1), i.e. no significant differences observed. The pretty higher percentage of crude fibre observed in maize variants 2 and 3 in certain years was not significant.

Table 1. Effect of herbicide on *Chenopodium album* and *Viola arvensis* coverage (% ± SE) in maize 0 and 28 days after treatment (DAT).

Variant	Chenopodium album		Viola arvensis	
	0 DAT	28 DAT	0 DAT	28 DAT
Variant_1_2001	1.00 ± 0.204	0.08 ± 0.025	0.75 ± 0.144	0.08 ± 0.025
Variant_2_2001	1.25 ± 0.323	0.88 ± 0.125	0.50 ± 0.000	1.13 ± 0.125
Variant_3_2001	0.68 ± 0.197	0.75 ± 0.166	0.50 ± 0.000	1.00 ± 0.000
Variant_1_2002	1.13 ± 0.375	0.00	1.00 ± 0.204	0.03 ± 0.025
Variant_2_2002	0.88 ± 0.125	0.10 ± 0.000	1.00 ± 0.204	1.88 ± 0.315
Variant_3_2002	1.50 ± 0.204	0.20 ± 0.100	0.88 ± 0.125	1.50 ± 0.204
Variant_1_2003	0.30 ± 0.000	0.00	0.30 ± 0.000	0.00
Variant_2_2003	0.53 ± 0.165	0.40 ± 0.058	0.40 ± 0.058	0.53 ± 0.165
Variant_3_2003	1.15 ± 0.202	0.58 ± 0.149	0.53 ± 0.103	0.45 ± 0.050

The proportion of out-crossing of HR transgenic rape into the conventional rape cultivated as a catch crop strip around the experimental fields ranged from a mean 0.026 % to 0.13 % (table 2).

The distance between the transgenic pollen donor and the nearest recipient was roughly 25 m, 35 m and 15 m in 1998, 1999 and 2001, respectively. In the isogenic rape (variant 1), the percentage of out-crossing ranged between 1 % and 3 %.

Table 2.   Occurrence of transgenic HR rape seeds in isogenic rape harvested in a pollen catch crop strip (approx. 0.5 ha) in 1998, 1999 and 2001.

Season	Number of sampling points	Seeds per sample	Plants treated (total)	Surviving plants (total)	Out-crossing rate [%]
1997/98	187	200	35,599	31	0.090
1997/98	14	1,000	13,396	18	0.130
1998/99	222	ca. 200	ca. 42,000	11	0.026
1998/99	14	1,000	13,641	10	0.070
2000/01	116	1,000	107,957	37	0.034

DISCUSSION

Allowing a pretty wide period for herbicide application in all HR crops increases the flexibility of weed control and enables better compliance with herbicide thresholds (Hommel & Pallutt, 2000). The addition of glufosinate to the list of post-emergence herbicides for oilseed rape and maize is therefore in the interest of IPM. Nevertheless, a second application of glufosinate is often required about 2 to 3 weeks after initial treatment for adequate weed control in maize. This increase in treatment intensity prevents the excessive accumulation of *C. album* seeds in the soil. The unsatisfactory effect of glufosinate on *V. arvensis* was reflected by a moderate to high abundance of this weed species in oilseed rape and maize. However, this gap in glufosinate activity in these crops is ecologically desirable because of the low competitive ability of *V. arvensis* (Schulte, 1999).

Except for the occurrence of HR volunteer rape in maize as a new competitive weed, the different glufosinate treatment intensities (from 0 litre/ha to 14.5 litres/ha) in the three rape and maize variants did not lead to differences in weed species diversity in any of the 7 years studied (Hommel & Pallutt, 2002).

The volunteer rape made it necessary to supplement glufosinate with another herbicide (Stelling, et al., 2000), which naturally offsets the economic and ecological advantages of HR crops. Therefore, when cultivating HR rape according to the principles of IPM, another crop resistant to the same herbicide should not be used within a given crop rotation.

Neither the dead mulch in maize nor the newly emerged weeds that survived 1 or 2 glufosinate treatments reached coverage levels capable of protecting the soil from wind or water erosion. None the less, the diversity and abundance of epigeous fauna in HR maize fields was probably still greater than that in conventional maize. The use of HR crops in special erosion-prevention systems with conservation tillage has some advantages over the use of conventional crops. For example, the intensity of herbicide use (e.g. dose, number of active compounds) is often lower, and the wider spraying window gives the farmer increased flexibility in selecting an optimum spraying date.

The out-crossing of transgenic HR rape to conventional rape can not be entirely prevented (Dietz-Pfeilstetter, et al., 2003). Therefore, practicable thresholds like 0.5 % for non-commercialised and 0.9 % for commercialised transgenic varieties, as recommended by the EC, are absolutely necessary. Abstention from transgenic rape growing in certain regions also seems to be an acceptable solution. Because of the long dormancy of oilseed rape (Pekrun, et al., 1997), the occurrence of volunteer transgenic rape in conventional rape fields poses an important obstacle to their coexistence. However, this problem is still less often investigated because the pollen donor plants can probably cause higher proportions of out-crossing than transgenic pollen originating from outside the field.

Compared to conventional oilseed rape and maize managed with herbicides such as metazachlor, quinmerac, carbetamide, dimefuron, fluazifop-P, metolachlor, pyridate, and terbuthylazin, the use of glufosinate in herbicide-resistant transgenic rape and maize has distinct ecotoxicological advantages because of glufosinate's lack of effect in the soil, the often later need for herbicide application, and the subsequently higher degree of crop and weed coverage, which reduces the biological risks of chemical weed control (Hommel & Pallutt, 2000).

ACKNOWLEDGEMENTS

We thank the breeders who supplied us with transgenic oilseed rape and maize seed and Anne-Georgia Metke for her excellent technical assistance.

REFERENCES

Burth U; Freier B (1996). The development of the concept of integrated plant protection and what it includes. Plant Research and Development **43**, 7-15.

Dietz-Pfeilstetter A; Bübl W; Stelling D (2003). Occurrence of transgenic progenies in the harvest of winter oilseed rape variety trials. Nachrichtenbl. Deut. Pflanzenschutzd. **55**, 134-137.

Gutsche V; Rossberg D (1997). Die Anwendung des Modells SYNOPS 1.2 zur synoptischen Bewertung des Risikopotentials von Pflanzenschutzmittelwirkstoffgruppen für den Naturhaushalt. Nachrichtenbl. Deut. Pflanzenschutzd. **49**, 273-285.

Hommel B; Pallutt B (2000). Bewertung der Herbizidresistenz für den integrierten Pflanzenschutz im System einer 4-feldrigen Fruchtfolge mit Glufosinat-resistentem Raps und Mais. Z. PflKrankh. PflSchutz, Sonderh. XVII, 411-420.

Hommel B; Pallutt B (2002). Bewertung der Glufosinatresistenz bei Raps und Mais aus der Sicht des integrierten Pflanzenschutzes – Ergebnisse eines 1996 begonnenen Langzeitversuchs unter besonderer Berücksichtigung von Veränderungen in der Ackerbegleitflora. Z. PflKrankh. PflSchutz, Sonderh. XVIII, 985-994.

Pekrun C; Potter T C; Lutman P J W (1997). Genotypic variation in the development of secondary dormancy in oilseed rape and its impact on the persistence of volunteer rape. Brighton Crop Protection Conf. – Weeds, 243-248.

Schulte E (1999). LibertyLink im Winterraps. Ein Beitrag zur Entwicklung unweltfreundlicher Anbauverfahren. Report. Aventis CropScience, 79 pp.

Stelling D; Schulte M; Amann A (2000). Strategien der Unkrautbekämpfung mit Liberty® in LibertyLink® Mais. Mitt. Biol. Bundesanst. Land- Forstwirtsch. **376**, 154-155.

Life cycle and gene dispersal of oilseed rape volunteers (*Brassica napus* L.)

S Gruber, C Pekrun, W Claupein
*University of Hohenheim, Institute for Crop Production and Grassland Research, Fruwirthstr.
23, 70599 Stuttgart, Germany*
Email: grubersf@uni-hohenheim.de

ABSTRACT

To assess gene dispersal from oilseed rape volunteers, the whole life cycle of
deliberately broadcast seeds and seed losses during harvest was observed in four
different tillage operations. Treatments 1 and 3 were immediate stubble tillage,
later followed by primary tillage with a plough or cultivator. In treatment 2, the
stubble tillage was delayed for four weeks and later followed by primary tillage
ploughing. Treatment 4 was zero tillage. The following crop in all treatments was
winter wheat. In autumn, between about 7 and mostly less than 50% of the initial
rape seeds emerged, whereas volunteer emergence was less than 0.01% in spring.
Depending on the treatment, a seed bank was built up reaching up to 30% of the
initial number of seeds. The seed bank was largest when seeds were immediately
incorporated into the soil by stubble tillage. Up to 85% of seeds could not be
found; the heaviest losses occurring when the seeds remained on the soil surface
for a while in treatments 2 and 4. When volunteers flowered at the same time as an
oilseed rape crop, gene dispersal in space by pollen transfer was possible.
Flowering volunteer plants could be observed mainly in treatments 3 and 4, at a
population density of up to 0.78 plants m^{-2} in treatment 3. A new generation of
seeds could be produced by the volunteers that may found a further cohort of
volunteers and enable gene dispersal in time or, in case of volunteers emerging in a
rape crop, be harvested with the crop.

INTRODUCTION

With regard to a future labelling threshold of genetically modified (GM) food or feed in the
EU, possible mixing of transgenic and conventionally bred crops is gaining in importance.
Mixing of GM and conventional crops could occur by pollen-mediated gene flow between
fields or by GM volunteers appearing within a conventional crop and then outcrossing within
the field or being harvested. Since oilseed rape pods are not completely resistant to shattering,
considerable seed losses can occur before or during harvest. Additionally, these seeds can
become secondarily dormant under particular environmental conditions (Pekrun et al., 1998),
persist for years in the soil (Roller, 2002) and emerge from this soil seed bank years later.
Although volunteers are quite easily controlled by mechanical or chemical operations, control
of volunteer rape in a rape crop is not possible. Soil tillage after oilseed rape harvest can affect
whether spilled seeds become secondarily dormant or persistent (Gruber et al., 2003) by
shifting the seeds into particular soil layers with different light, water or gaseous conditions.
Therefore, the number of volunteer plants can be expected to vary depending on the method of
tillage. Since it is known from laboratory experiments (Pekrun et al., 1997; Gruber et al., 2002)
that genotypic differences exist in the level of dormancy, this capacity could additionally affect
the number of emerging volunteers. The aim of this study was to observe the life cycle of
volunteers from rape seed artificially broadcast on the soil in a defined number and from seed

losses obtained under normal conditions during harvest. Different rape seed genotypes and tillage operations after harvest were factors to be examined for their effects on the number and time of emergence of volunteers, their flowering and seed production and subsequently their potential for gene flow.

MATERIALS AND METHODS

The experiments were set up 2001 and 2002 on the experimental station of the University of Hohenheim 'Ihinger Hof' near Stuttgart in south-west Germany (N 48° 44'/ E 8° 55'; altitude 450 m a. s. l., 689 mm mean annual precipitation, 8.0 °C mean annual temperature) on a loamy soil. In the first experiment (E1, artificial seed losses, established 2001 and 2002), 10,000 rape seeds were broadcast in July on a clean cereal stubble simulating harvest losses of a rape crop. The rape seed cultivars tested were Liberator and Artus, both near-isogenic to the transgenic, herbicide-tolerant cultivars Lilly^{LL} and Avalon^{LL}. In the second experiment (E2, practical seed losses, established 2002) the oilseed rape cultivar Liberator was grown and harvested normally. The experimental design was a split plot design with four replications in E1 and a block design with four replications in E2. The extent of seed loss was determined by catching the seeds on cloths sized 50 x 70 cm that were placed under the standing rape crop shortly before harvesting. After seeds had arrived at the soil surface either by broadcasting or by practical shedding, four different treatments of soil cultivation were performed (Table 1).

Table 1. Tillage treatments, implements and cultivation depth used in the experiments

Treatment	Stubble tillage (rotary tiller, 10 cm)	Primary tillage in autumn
T 1	Immediately	Plough (25 cm)
T 2	4 weeks delayed	Plough (25 cm)
T 3	Immediately	Cultivator (15 cm)
T 4	None	None

Stubble tillage followed immediately (within 24 hrs) after seeds had dropped to the soil in T1 and T3, or with four weeks delay in T2. No tillage was performed in the zero tillage treatment T4. The primary tillage in T1 and T2 was ploughing, and cultivating with a rigid tine cultivator in T3, all shortly before sowing the following crop winter wheat. Sowing in T4 was performed by direct drilling. A germination test determined the viability of the seeds used in the field.

Because of wet weather in autumn 2002, primary tillage and subsequent sowing of winter wheat was done with about two months delay (E1: January 9th 2002; E2: December 9th 2003) compared to the previous year (E1: October 31st 2001) and to the common sowing date for this region. Before drilling, a non-selective herbicide was applied in all treatments. No further herbicides were used after drilling to enable rape volunteers to grow.

In autumn and spring following the harvest of oilseed rape or the broadcast of seeds the mean emergence of rape volunteer seedlings was recorded on 0.25 cm^{-2} (total of 10 single positions) per plot shortly before stubble tillage (only T2) and/or primary tillage or direct drilling (all treatments). For determination of the soil seed bank, 40 soil samples were taken in a depth of 0-30 cm in spring in each plot. In 2002, soil sampling took place when the seed germination had already started, and shortly before this date in the year 2003. During the following vegetation period, the number and date of flowering and fruiting rape seed volunteers in the winter wheat was determined until harvest. In experiment 1 set up in 2001, seedlings emerging from the soil seed bank in the second spring (2003) after broadcast of seeds were also counted.

The statistical analysis was performed in SAS with the MIXED procedure and Satterthwaite's test. To meet the standards of the ANOVA, data were transformed ln $(x + 0.1)$ if necessary.

RESULTS AND DISCUSSION

Seed outcome experiment 1 (artificial seed losses)

In experiment 1, about 50 to 85% of the seeds could not be registered in one of the surveys in both experimental years (Tables 2 and 3). The highest unknown losses occurred in T2 and T4 in both years, when seeds laid on the soil surface for a while.

Table 2.   Outcome (mean) of broadcast rape seeds from two cultivars in E1 affected by tillage treatments from 2001 until 2002 (according to Gruber et al., 2003)

Survey	% of 10,000 seeds m^{-2} initially broadcast			
	T 1	T 2	T 3	T 4
		Liberator		
Autumn emergence 2001	12.3	12.0	12.4	7.1
Spring emergence 2002	0.0	0.0	5^{-3}	0.0
Seed bank spring 2002	0.8	0.0	1.9	0.0
Non viable	18.7	18.7	18.7	18.7
Unregistered loss	68.2	69.3	67.0	74.2
Spring emergence 2003	9^{-3}	8.8^{-4}	3.13^{-3}	1.81^{-3}
		Artus		
Autumn emergence 2001	25.9	12.6	19.1	11.3
Spring emergence 2002	1.0^{-2}	0.0	9.0^{-2}	8.8^{-4}
Seed bank spring 2002	4.1	1.5	9.8	0.0
Non viable	3.5	3.5	3.5	3.5
Unregistered loss	66.5	82.4	67.5	85.2
Spring emergence 2003	5.0^{-2}	1.1^{-3}	8.9^{-3}	3.1^{-4}

Table 3.   Outcome (mean) of broadcast rape seeds from two cultivars in E1 affected by tillage treatments from 2002 until 2003

Survey	% of 10,000 seeds m^{-2} initially broadcast			
	T 1	T 2	T 3	T 4
		Liberator		
Autumn emergence 2002	26.0	34.4	26.4	22.4
Spring emergence 2002	1.1^{-3}	0.0	1.3^{-2}	4.0^{-4}
Seed bank spring 2003	9.8	0.0	14.0	0.8
Non viable	13.0	13.0	13.0	13.0
Unregistered loss	51.1	52.6	46.6	63.8
		Artus		
Autumn emergence 2002	31.1	35.3	32.7	22.1
Spring emergence 2002	7.0^{-4}	0.0	6.4^{-3}	2.0^{-4}
Seed bank spring 2003	7.9	0.4	3.8	1.5
Non viable	1.7	1.7	1.7	1.7
Unregistered loss	59.3	62.6	61.8	74.7

The second highest sink of the seeds was the autumn emergence ranging from about 7 to 35% of all initial seeds depending on cultivar and treatment. The smallest emergence was observed in the direct drilling treatment T4.

A maximum of 0.09% of the broadcast seeds was recorded as seedlings by the spring counting. The soil seed bank consisted of up to 14% of all broadcast seeds, depending on treatment and year. The highest levels resulted T1 and T3 with an immediate incorporation of the seeds in the soil after broadcasting. Differences observed in 2001 were only significant between the treatments within the cultivar Artus. In 2002 significant differences in the soil seed bank occurred between T1 and T3 on the one hand and T2 and T4 on the other hand within both cultivars (Table 4).

Table 4.　Soil seed bank of oilseed rape seeds affected by tillage operations derived from harvest seed losses or deliberately broadcast seeds. In italics: *transformed data*, E1 2002 *ln (x + 0.1)*; SEM E1 2001: 141.0, E1 2002 (*transformed*): *1.30*, E2: 63.0; no significant differences (Satterthwaite's formula, $\alpha=0.05$) between values with same letters; comparison within one experiment (E2) or within the same cultivar and year (E1) only.

Expe-riment	Cultivar	Soil seed bank (mean number of seeds m^{-2}, *transformed data*)				Soil seed bank (mean number of seeds m^{-2}, absolute data)			
		T1	T2	T3	T4	T1	T2	T3	T4
2001									
E1	Liberator	-	-	-	-	76^A	0^A	189^A	0^A
	Artus	-	-	-	-	416^B	151^{B,C}	982^A	0^C
2002									
E1	Liberator	*6,81^A*	*-2,30^B*	*7,05^A*	*-0.30^B*	983	0	1399	75
	Artus	*6,59^A*	*-0.47^B*	*5.70^A*	*-0.13^B*	794	38	378	151
E2	Liberator	-	-	-	-	378^A	38^B	189^{A,B}	227^{A,B}

These results can be attributed to the tillage operations that shifted the seeds in deeper, dry and dark soil layers in T1 and T3 where secondary dormancy can be induced. When lying on the soil surface for a longer period, seeds cannot become secondarily dormant and can be destroyed or damaged by seed predators and other environmental factors. If the seeds germinated, soil cultivation, herbicides and herbivores would also lead to a reduction of the plants. In spring 2003, a maximum of 0.05% of the seed bank recorded in E1 in the previous year emerged in the second following crop (maize). Overall, most plants were found in T1 with both cultivars tested. In the second experimental year, the autumn emergence was higher than 2001, probably due to the wet weather conditions. Nevertheless, a similar or higher level of persistent seeds was found in the soil seed bank in 2002 compared to 2001. Due to the increase of autumn emergence and the size of the soil seed bank, fewer seeds vanished without leaving recorded traces in the second experimental year.

Seed outcome experiment 2 (practical seed losses)

The harvest losses in experiment 2 were 1324 seeds m^{-2} on average, about 1.5% of the yield. Except T4, the main outcome of the seeds was the autumn emergence 2002 (Table 5).

Table 5. Outcome (mean) of seed losses during harvest from the cultivar Liberator in E2 affected by tillage treatments from 2002 until 2003

	(% of 1324 initial seeds lost m^{-2})			
Survey	T 1	T 2	T 3	T 4
	Liberator			
Autumn emergence 2002	49.0	90.4	61.1	32.2
Spring emergence 2002	0.0	0.0	0.04	0.07
Seed bank spring 2003	28.5	2.9	14.3	17.1
Non viable	0.3	0.3	0.3	0.3
Unregistered loss	22.1	6.4	24.3	50.3

Nearly 90% of all seeds emerged after delayed stubble tillage and primary tillage plough (T2), and about 60% and 50% in T3 and T1 respectively. A third of all lost seeds germinated without any tillage (T4). The high autumn emergence in T2 may be a result of the delayed stubble tillage that enabled ungerminated seeds to emerge after being triggered by soil cultivation. Because of high autumn germination, numbers entering the seed bank and unregistered losses were low. Maybe this mechanism particularly worked in the wet autumn 2002 and under the straw mulch in experiment 2, since it is not so apparent in experiment 1.

Between about 3 and 30% of the seeds were incorporated into the soil seed bank, with the smallest contribution to the seed bank occurred in T2 and the highest in T1. Only the differences between T1 and T2 were significant (Table 4, last line). Also in T4, without any soil movement by tillage, a considerable soil seed bank was built up by 17% of the seed losses. The level of germinated or otherwise registered outcome of seeds was higher in experiment 2 than in experiment 1. Seeds may have had better protection from predators or better germination conditions under the straw mulch in experiment 2. Also the comparatively high soil seed bank – even in T4 without any soil movement – may be a result of the covering straw mulch that kept the seeds in darkness and led to a better induction of secondary dormancy.

Flowering volunteers

Most flowering volunteers were observed in T3 and T4 (Table 6) with up to almost 0.8 plants

Table 6. Flowering oilseed rape volunteers of two cultivars affected by different tillage treatments T1-T4 in two experiments and years; results E1 2001 according to Gruber et al. 2003, May 2002, E1 and E2 2002: June 2003. No significant differences (Satterthwaite's formula, $\alpha=0.05$) between treatments with same letters; comparison within the same cultivar and year only

	T1	T2	T3	T4	SEM
	Mean of plants m^{-2}				
E1 2001					0.02
Liberator	0.00^A	0.00^A	0.03^A	0.05^A	
Artus	0.00^C	0.00^C	0.09^B	0.33^A	
E1 2002					0.05
Liberator	0.11^B	0.01^B	0.78^A	0.07^B	
Artus	0.03^{A,B}	0.01^B	0.15^A	0.02^{A,B}	
E2 2002					0.04
Liberator	0.13^B	0.11^B	0.59^A	0.55^A	

m^{-2} in experiment 1 from 2002. The highest number of flowering volunteers in experiment 1 established 2001 was observed in T4 with a volunteer density of about 0.3 plants m^{-2}, and in experiment 2 in T3 and T4, both with nearly 0.6 plants m^{-2}. In contrast to the first experimental year when volunteers and sown rape crop flowered simultaneously, the volunteers from harvest 2002 started flowering at the end of the common flowering period of oilseed rape in the region. Gene transfer by pollen consequently was possible in the 2001 experiments, though not likely in the 2002 experiments. It has to be proved whether the volunteers of the current year will produce ripe and viable seeds as they did the year before.

CONCLUSIONS

In terms of the whole life cycle, autumn emergence could contribute to the rapid removal of all spilled seeds, maybe especially in wet years. Hence stubble cultivation for inducing maximal emergence seems to be useful, although the time of the tillage operation is critical to prevent the build up of a soil seed bank. Since the persistence was higher when seeds were immediately incorporated into the soil compared to (temporarily) uncovered seeds, the cultivation system 'immediately incorporated' would entail the highest risk of gene flow in time. To minimise the soil seed bank and subsequent gene dispersal, the first soil cultivation after seed shedding should be delayed. A zero tillage system can result in many flowering volunteers. Therefore gene transfer by pollen and newly produced seeds can be minimised according to this study with delayed stubble tillage and subsequent use of plough for primary tillage. Although no reproducible differences could be observed between the cultivars in both experimental years, an influence of genotype on seed persistence generally seems to exist.

ACKNOWLEDGEMENTS

This project is financed by the German Federal Ministry for Education and Research. Support by BayerCropScience, NPZ and DSV is gratefully acknowledged.

REFERENCES

Gruber S, Pekrun C, Claupein W (2002). Variation of secondary dormancy in genetically modified and conventionally bred oilseed rape. VII. Congress of the European Society of Agronomy, Cordoba, Spain, 15th-18th July 2002, 187-188.

Gruber S, Pekrun C, Claupein W (2003). Population dynamics of volunteer oilseed rape (Brassica napus L.) affected by tillage. European Journal of Agronomy, in press.

Pekrun C, Potter TC, Lutman PJW (1997). Genotypic variation in the development of secondary dormancy in oilseed rape and its impact on the persistence of volunteer rape. Proceedings of the 1997 Brighton Crop Protection Conference – Weeds, pp. 243-248.

Pekrun C, Hewitt JDJ, Lutman PJW (1998). Cultural control of volunteer oilseed rape. Journal of Agricultural Science **130**, 155-163.

Roller A, Beismann H, Albrecht H (2002). Persistence of genetically modified, herbicide-tolerant oilseed rape – first observations under practically relevant conditions in South Germany. Journal of Plant Diseases and Protection, XVIII (Special issue), 255-260.

SESSION 8B

CROP PRODUCTION
WITH REDUCED INPUTS

Chairman and Session Organiser:	Professor Bob Naylor *Trelareg Consultants, Aberdeen, UK*
Papers:	8B-1 to 8B-3

A rational basis for the design of wheat canopy ideotypes

S R Parker
Central Science Laboratory, Sand Hutton, York YO41 1LZ, UK

P M Berry, N D Paveley
ADAS High Mowthorpe, Duggleby, Malton North Yorkshire, YO17 8BP, UK

F van den Bosch, D J Lovell
Rothamsted Research, Harpenden, Hertfordshire AL5 2JQ

ABSTRACT

Canopy architecture influences the capture and use of radiation and the susceptibility of crops to disease and lodging. Architecture traits are heritable, and might therefore be exploited to develop more sustainable wheat varieties. However, a 'phenotype gap' exists between knowledge of the wheat genome and understanding of sustainable phenotypes that can provide commercially acceptable varieties. Previous research, done separately on radiation use, disease and lodging suggests that trade-offs will be necessary to optimise the benefits conferred by canopy traits (e.g. tall plants escape disease but are more prone to lodging). This paper describes work in progress to investigate whether a mathematical framework can be developed, which relates canopy traits with crop productivity, via their effect on radiation use, disease and lodging. The outputs of such a framework could be compared against benchmarks defined to measure sustainability.

INTRODUCTION

Canopy architecture is crucial to the capacity of crops to exploit their environment because it is a key determinant of the interception of incoming radiation and the efficiency with which dry matter is produced. In wheat, canopy architecture is also a key determinant of 'field resistance' to disease (Lovell *et al.*, 1997; Parker *et al.*, 2002) and lodging (Baker *et al.*, 1998). Growers are currently dependent on agrochemical inputs to ameliorate losses in productivity caused by disease and lodging. Progress in developing efficient and environmentally responsible production systems is most likely to be achieved through better understanding and exploitation of crop genetic potential. Part of this will involve combining canopy traits that trap and use radiation efficiently whilst also minimising the risk of disease and lodging. Research done separately on radiation use, disease and lodging suggests that trade-offs will be necessary to optimise the benefits conferred by canopy traits (e.g. tall plants escape disease but are more prone to lodging).

This paper describes work in progress to investigate whether a mathematical framework can be developed, which relates canopy traits with crop productivity, via their effect on radiation use, disease and lodging. This approach will help the development of canopy ideotypes, which Donald (1968) proposed as a method for improving the effectiveness of breeding programmes.

APPROACH

Models exist that describe how aspects of canopy architecture interrelate with (1) radiation interception and use efficiency (Campbell and Norman, 1998; Choudhury, 2000), (2) escape of splash borne foliar diseases (Parker *et al.*, 2002) and (3) lodging risk (Baker *et al.*, 1998). Only the radiation model output is a measure of crop productivity (dry matter accumulation), with the others calculating the area of disease infected leaves and lodging risk respectively. Therefore, the first objective of this paper is to identify 'coupling points' that enable the disease and lodging models to be integrated with the radiation model. The coupling points could be at the initial input stage of the radiation model or at one of the intermediate processes; radiation interception or radiation use efficiency (RUE). The concept of coupling points is well established for linking pests to crop growth models to predict yield reductions (Boote *et al.*, 1983), but is not well developed for ideotype design. As will be shown, the identification of coupling points requires the development of the disease and lodging models. The primary canopy traits that are considered by the models include leaf area index and leaf angle by the radiation model, crop height and leaf angle by the disease model and ear area, shoot height at centre of gravity and natural frequency by the lodging model. The models must consider the same traits to enable them to be optimised for productivity. Therefore the second objective of this paper will be to develop the models so that their inputs include similar canopy traits. This exercise has initially been carried out for crop height and leaf angle to demonstrate a method of working that could be applied for other characters.

RESULTS

Canopy and radiation

Theoretical models exist that describe how crop canopies intercept radiation (Campbell and Norman, 1998), photosynthesize and respire (Choudhury, 2000). These models can be combined to calculate dry matter accumulation from canopy architecture traits (leaf area, angle and nitrogen content) and from incoming radiation levels. We developed the models to make them more applicable to UK wheat and used them to investigate whether crop height has a significant effect on radiation capture and use.

Crop height determines the ratio of leaf area to stem area. There are two routes by which this ratio can affect the amount of radiation captured and the efficiency of dry matter production;
   (1) Rate of photosynthesis - due to different light response curves of lamina and sheath.
   (2) Rate of respiration – because stems have a greater N content per unit area of their photosynthesizing tissue, which will increase maintenance respiration.

To investigate how crop height might affect productivity we modelled the response of a crop without stems, using a leaf area index (LAI) of 4.5 and a canopy nitrogen content of 500 mmol m^{-2}. Then the amount of light intercepted, gross photosynthesis and respiration was calculated. The procedure was then repeated with the same LAI with a typical stem area index. This required several assumptions:
- that for a typical crop of 1m height, 25% of green area is contributed by the stem and that 50% of the canopy nitrogen is contained by the stems (Critchley, 2001). These assumptions require the addition of 1.5 units of stem area to the LAI and 500 mmol N m^{-2} to the canopy nitrogen content.

- To account for changes in the mean orientation of the photosynthetic tissue due to the inclusion of stems, the leaves were assumed to have a mean angle of 57° (from horizontal) and the stems a mean angle of 90°. This gives a mean angle of 65° for the leaves and stems combined.

The mean concentration of radiation intercepted by the stems was estimated from their projected area, which is appropriate for sunny periods, and cylindrical sheath area was used for cloudy periods. Methods described by Choudhury (2000) were used to estimate the light response curve for a leaf sheath from its nitrogen content (Critchley, 2001), and this was used to estimate its gross rate of photosynthesis. Additional respiratory losses arising from the stems were also estimated. The calculations were repeated for other stem lengths by assuming that each 1 cm of stem adds 0.015 stem area index and 5 mmol N m^{-2} of ground.

The model outputs indicated that increased stem height produced only small increases in gross photosynthesis and this was cancelled by an increase in respiratory losses. The leaf sheath makes a small contribution of photo-assimilate because it intercepts small amounts of light (due to its relatively small area and orientation) and because it has a low photosynthetic rate (about 25% of leaves). The latter is caused by the low nitrogen content of sheaths and is supported by measurements by Angus et al. (1972). Therefore it appears that the main effect of reducing height is to allow more assimilate to be partitioned to the developing ear, which results in more grains per ear and a larger sink (Calderini et al., 1995; Fischer, 1984). This part of the work showed that radiation interception and use can be estimated from area, angle and nitrogen content of leaves

Canopy and disease

Foliar diseases decrease radiation interception, primarily by reducing the LAI. Parker et al. (2002) have identified canopy architecture traits (internode length, leaf insertion angle, leaf length and stem extension rate) that allow the upper leaves to distance themselves from sporulating lesions on leaves lower down the canopy. The main effect of crop architecture is a shift in the epidemic curve, along the time axis. This shift is the result of less spores arriving on upper leaves when the crop is taller and internodes longer (Fraaije et al., 2003). This is explained by the dependence of spore dispersal on rain splash height, a variable that can be predicted from the kinetic energy of raindrops (Lovell et al., 2002; Pietravalle et al., 2001). Crop height thus influences the amount of inoculum initiating the epidemic on the top three leaf layers. We have modelled the relationship between plant canopy (plant height and leaf angle) and symptom area index by a two-step process. First, the step from canopy architecture to spore arrival and then the step from spore arrival to symptom area index.

The effects of disease on yield are due primarily to the associated reduction in LAI and hence impairment of light capture during the crucial grain filling period (Parker et al., 2002). The disease models we have developed could therefore be coupled to the radiation model, described above, through LAI. By this route the effect of disease could be expressed in terms of dry matter accumulation.

Canopy and lodging

Baker et al. (1998) outlined a model that predicts lodging when the leverage force of the shoots exceed the strength of the stem base or anchorage system. Recently this model was validated by Berry *et al.* (2003).

Alterations to canopy architecture will have a direct effect on the leverage component of the lodging model by altering the traits that determine it: height at centre of gravity, natural frequency, ear area and shoot number per plant. Changes to ear area and shoot number are easy to quantify and are measured commonly in field experiments. However, height at centre of gravity and natural frequency are more difficult to quantify and might more appropriately be estimated through their relationships to more commonly measured variables.

Height at centre of gravity can be estimated by a function of its principal components; stem height, stem and leaf fresh weight, ear fresh weight and ear length. Berry (1998) showed that the non-uniform weight distribution of the shoot (heavier base) must be taken into account for the above function to calculate height at centre of gravity accurately. A sensitivity analysis showed that the most influential component of height at centre of gravity is stem height, that stem/leaf fresh weight and ear fresh weight are moderately important and variation in ear length has a negligible effect. This analysis indicates that leaf angle will not affect lodging. Berry *et al.* (2000) showed how natural frequency can be estimated from height at centre of gravity using an empirical relationship. Hence, the effect of changes in canopy traits, such as stem height, on plant leverage can be modelled by first calculating height at centre of gravity and using this to estimate natural frequency, which can then be used to derive shoot leverage. The results of this exercise show that plant leverage increases exponentially with height.

As a gross simplification we may assume that any change in the probability of lodging, due to altering shoot leverage, will equate to the mean percentage area lodged over a large run of years. The percentage area lodged could then be related to a reduced rate of dry matter accumulation since RUE appears to be reduced by 0.5% for each percentage area of crop lodged, when averaged over each day of grain filling (Stapper and Fischer, 1990). The relationship between lodging and reduction in RUE requires testing, but this illustrates how the lodging and radiation models could be coupled via RUE.

DISCUSSION

The ongoing work, described in this paper, identifies coupling points for linking disease and lodging models with a model for calculating radiation capture and use. These coupling points are described in Figure 1, in which the models are represented by a series of steps in which the dependent variable in one step forms the independent variable in the next step. This coupling enables the models to estimate crop productivity, in terms of dry matter accumulation ($g^{-1}m^{-2}day^{-1}$), as a common output. This paper also describes how the models can be developed to make use of common inputs describing the crop canopy. This has been done for crop height and leaf angle. The importance of using common inputs and a common output is that the canopy traits may now be optimised for crop productivity. Sylvester-Bradley *et al.* (1997) and Paveley *et al.* (2001) demonstrated the value of this approach by using it to predict the prime influences on optimum nitrogen and fungicide dose respectively.

Future work must now couple these models explicitly and carry out the model development necessary to include more canopy traits (e.g. LAI and leaf N) as inputs that are common to all of the models. Specific experimentation will be required to test some of the less well understood parts of these models. The resulting model could then be used to design crop ideotypes that are best suited to different environments and management systems. The predicted performance of different ideotypes could be tested using doubled haploid mapping populations that segregate for the important canopy traits. The plant breeding and research communities have invested substantial monies into developing mapping populations of elite genetic material, many of which already segregate for some of the traits described here.

In time, the above framework could be usefully linked with the new canopy simulation implemented in SIRIUS (described in Parker *et al.*, 2003). This simulates the development of LAI according to environmental factors such as thermal time, water and N availability. The process of simulating inter-leaf distances has also been started. Linking these models would be mutually beneficial because it would enable SIRIUS to account for more of the processes that determine dry matter accumulation. The ideotype framework would benefit from a consideration of how environmental factors during crop development determine canopy traits. The models may also be adapted to help explain competition between weed and crop growth.

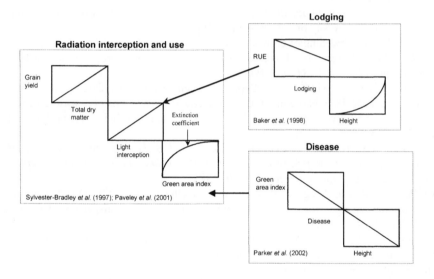

Figure 1.   Hypothetical framework for integrating light, disease and lodging models for optimising wheat canopy ideotypes. In these sequences of steps the dependent variable of one step forms the independent variable of the next step.

REFERENCES

Angus J F; Jones R; Wilson J H (1972). A comparison of barley cultivars with different leaf inclinations. *Australian Journal of Agricultural Research* **23**, 945-957.

Baker C J; Berry P M; Spink J H; Sylvester-Bradley R; Griffin J M; Scott R K; Clare R W (1998). A method for the assessment of the risk of wheat lodging. *Journal of Theoretical Biology* **194**, 587-603.

Berry P M (1998). *Predicting lodging in winter wheat*. PhD thesis. The University of Nottingham, UK, 210pp.

Berry P M; Griffin J M; Sylvester-Bradley R; Scott R K; Spink J H; Baker C J; Clare, R.W (2000). Controlling plant form through husbandry to minimise lodging in wheat. *Field Crops Research* **67**, 59-81.

Berry P M; Sterling M; Baker C J; Spink J H; Sparkes D L (2003). A calibrated model of wheat lodging compared with field measurements. *Agricultural and Forest Meteorology* In press.

Boote K J; Jones J W; Mishoe J W; Berger R D (1983). Coupling pests to crop growth simulators to predict yield reductions. *Phytopathology* **73**, 1581-1587.

Calderini D F; Derccer M F; Slafer G A (1995). Genetic improvements in wheat yield and associated traits. A re-examination of previous results and latest trends. *Plant Breeding* **114**, 108–112.

Campbell G S; Norman J M (1998). An Introduction to Environmental Biophysics, 2nd Edition. Springer, London.

Choudhury B J (2000). A Sensitivity analysis of the radiation use efficiency for gross photosynthesis and net carbon accumulation by wheat. *Agricultural and Forest Meteorology* **101**, 217-234.

Critchley C S (2001). *A physiological explanation for the nitrogen requirement of winter wheat*. PhD thesis, University of Nottingham, 231pp.

Donald C M (1968). The breeding of crop ideotypes. *Euphytica* **17**, 385-403.

Fischer R A (1984). Wheat. In: Potential productivity of field crops under different environments, pp. 129-154. IRRI : Los Banos.

Fraaije B A; Lovell D J; Baldwin S (2002). Septoria epidemics on wheat: Combined use of visual assessment and PCR-based diagnostics to identify mechanisms of disease escape. Proceedings of the 6th Conference EFPP 2002, Prague. Plant Prot. Sci., 38 (Special issue 2), 421-424.

Lovell D J; Parker S R; Hunter T; Royle D J; Coker R R (1997). The influence of growth habit and architecture on the risk of epidemics of *Mycosphaerella graminicola (Septoria tritici)* in winter wheat. *Plant Pathology* **47**,126-138.

Lovell D J; Parker S R; van Petegham P; Webb D A; Welham S J (2002). Quantification of raindrop kinetic energy for improved prediction of splash-dispersed pathogens. *Phytopathology* **92**, 497-503.

Parker S R; Lovell D J; Foulkes M J; Worland A J; Paveley N D (2002). Improving and exploiting self defence against wheat diseases. Proceedings of the Brighton Crop Protection Conference, Pests and Diseases, 919-924.

Parker S R: Berry P M; Paveley N D; van den Bosch F; Lovell D J (2003). A rational basis for the design of wheat canopy ideotypes in UK environments. Defra Project No AR0906.

Paveley N D; Sylvester-Bradley R; Scott R K; Craigon J; Day W (2001). Steps in predicting the relationship of yield on fungicide dose. *Phytopathology* **91**, 708-716.

Pietravalle S; van den Bosch F; Welham S J; Parker S R; Lovell D J (2001). Prediction of rainsplash height and risks of spread of splash-dispersed diseases. *Agricultural and Forest Meteorology* **109**,171-185.

Stapper M; Fischer R A (1990). Genotype, sowing date and plant spacing influence on high-yielding irrigated wheat in Southern New South Wales. I. Potential yields and optimum flowering dates. *Australian Journal of Agricultural Research* **41**, 1043-1056.

Sylvester-Bradley R; Scott R K; Stokes D T; Clare R W (1997). The significance of crop canopies for N nutrition. *Aspects of Applied Biology* **50**, 103-116.

Novel sensors for measuring soil nitrogen, water availability and strength

A J Miller, D M Wells
Rothamsted Research, Harpenden, Hertfordshire AL5 2JQ, UK
Email: tony.miller@bbsrc.ac.uk

J Braven, L Ebdon, T Le Goff
University of Plymouth, Drake Circus, Plymouth, Devon PL4 8AA, UK

L J Clark, W R Whalley
Silsoe Research Institute, Wrest Park, Silsoe, Bedford, MK45 4HS, UK

D J G Gowing
Open University, Walton Hall, Milton Keynes MK7 6BT, UK

P B Leeds-Harrison
National Soil Resources Institute, Cranfield University, Silsoe, MK45 4DT, UK

ABSTRACT

The availability of water and nitrogen to plant roots are very important factors determining the yield of crops. In soil these two factors are closely linked as nitrogen is chiefly available to crops as nitrate that is very soluble in water. Therefore environmental monitoring of both soil water and nitrate availability is important for crop production with reduced inputs. Progress in this area is limited by the lack of methods for *in situ* estimates of nitrogen status, soil strength and water availability in the field. In this paper we describe approaches to measure these soil variables in the field environment. We describe the development of sensors to measure soil matric potential between 0 to −300 kPa. An explanation of how these data can be used with soil water content data to estimate soil strength is presented. In other research, flexible N-sensors suitable for monitoring soil mineral nitrogen have been developed. These probes have been produced using a new type of nitrate-selective electrode that has been successfully used in rivers and drainage waters for environmental monitoring. The information obtained from the electrodes can be used to provide diagnostic decision support for fertiliser recommendations and for more general field monitoring by farmers.

INTRODUCTION

The root environment has a major effect on crop growth, both directly through the supply of water and nutrients to the shoot, and indirectly through root to shoot signalling (Mulholland *et al.*, 1996). Developing more sustainable agriculture systems requires accurate and easy to use methods for measuring the main soil parameters that are likely to limit yield. Water and nitrogen supply are the two most important parameters for most UK crops. Measuring soil water and nitrogen availability and then matching supply to the changing crop demands is important for improving the efficient use of these resources. An imbalance between supply and demand leads to waste that has both economic and environmental costs.

Better management of crop root systems through agronomic practice and breeding has the potential to improve the efficiency of water and nutrient uptake, and limit root restrictions to crop growth. However, progress in this area is currently limited by the lack of sensors for *in situ* estimates of soil water, strength and nutritional status in the field. The challenge is to develop sensors that will report these parameters during the growing season of a crop which will then permit greater precision in the targeting and management of inputs.

In this paper we describe new types of sensors to directly measure soil strength, matric potential and nitrate availability. For the soil matric potential measurements, an explanation of how to use the effective stress theory to estimate soil strength from water content and matric potential data is presented, together with a laboratory validation of the effective stress theory. The nutrient measurements have adapted ion-selective electrode technology to give a robust sensor that can be directly inserted into the soil to report the concentration of nitrate that is available to the plant.

MATERIALS AND METHODS

Sensor for soil water matric potential

Hydraulic tensiometers can measure the matric potential of soil water between 0 (saturation) and approximately −85 kPa. In drier soils there are currently no reliable sensors available to measure matric potential. Whalley *et al.* (2001) describe the development of a sensor to measure matric potential, in the range 0 to −60 kPa, which is based on the measurement of the water content of a porous ceramic in hydraulic equilibrium with the soil. In this work, Whalley *et al.* (2001) described how to take hysteresis into account to achieve a better accuracy when calculating matric potential from the measured water content of the ceramic and the sensor worked over a narrow range of water potentials. Here, we have developed a sensor that can give estimates of matric potential between 0 and −300 kPa. We measured the water retention characteristics of a number of ceramics and selected one of these to form the basis of our porous material sensor of soil water matric potential. We used the method of Gaskin & Miller (1996) to measure the water content of the selected ceramic. This gives us the possibility of a sensor that can be powered by a 12V battery and therefore an easily-logged analogue output.

Use of effective stress to predict soil strength

Soil tensile strength can be predicted using the effective stress theory which states that the tensile strength, Y, of a soil is given by,

$$Y = c - \left\{ \frac{\chi \psi}{f(s)} \right\}$$

where c is the soil's cohesion, χ is a factor that takes into account the proportion of failure surface occupied by water films at a matric potential of ψ and $f(s)$ is a pore shape factor Mullins (2000). In wet soils, $f(s)$ is a constant and χ is approximately equal to the degree of saturation, S. As the matric potential, ψ, can be estimated over a wide range of soil moisture with the new sensor and S can be estimated from dielectric sensors of soil water content, we can in principle calculate soil tensile strength from soil moisture measurement. In this paper we will examine if the theory of effective stress can be used to give a calibration between soil moisture status (i.e. the product ψS) and soil penetrometer strength in a range relevant to root growth.

We measured the pressure needed to push a rotating penetrometer into two soils packed to dry bulk densities of 1.2 and 1.7 g cm^{-3} at matric potentials between 0 and −300 kPa. The silty soil contained 19% clay, 70% silt and 11% sand and the sandy soil contained 9% clay, 24% silt and 67% sand. A rotating penetrometer is thought to give good estimates of the pressure that roots need to exert to deform soil (Bengough *et al.,* 1997). For these soils, in work not reported here, we confirmed that a common relationship existed between soil tensile strength and effective stress.

Sensor for soil nitrate measurements

Nitrate-sensors for long term monitoring of nitrate in drainage water have recently been developed (Le Goff *et al.,* 2002a). These nitrate-selective electrodes are made by covalently bonding the sensor molecule N,N,N-triallyl leucine betaine chloride to a polystyrene-*block* - polybutadiene-*block*-polystyrene polymer (SBS rubber). In river waters these electrodes have been used for two months continuous measurement of nitrate (NO_3^-) without any major decline in the response of the electrode. The characteristics of this electrode were a linear Nernstian range of 1 M to 5 x 10^{-6} M NO_3^-, a limit of detection of 3.4 x 10^{-7} M NO_3^-, with response times of 1 min or less and a three-fold selectivity for nitrate against chloride. These figures represented a significant improvement on current commercial NO_3^- sensors and their stability of response and electrode lifetime in continuous use was also very satisfactory. The SBS rubber NO_3^- sensor membranes have been further improved by the addition of clay to the membrane to give a threefold improvement in both tensile strength and resistance to penetration relative to the clay-free membranes (Le Goff *et al.,* 2003b). Field performance was also improved by at least a 20% increase in lifetime. These nitrate-electrodes are being tested for their feasibility to monitor soil NO_3^- availability.

RESULTS

A porous material for the matric potential of soil water

The full design of this new sensor will be described in a later paper. In Figure 1 the output of our new sensor is given as a function of matric potential. The buriable part of the sensor is shown in the insert in Figure 1.

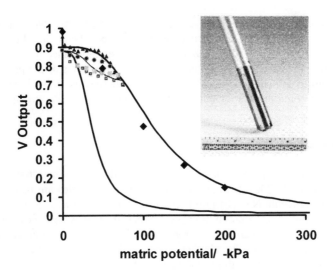

Figure 1. The voltage output of the porous material sensor of matric potential as a function of matric potential. Between matric potentials of 0 and −70 kPa wetting and drying scanning curves are shown. These are used in the calibration of the sensor with a model of hysteresis described by Whalley *et al.* (2001).

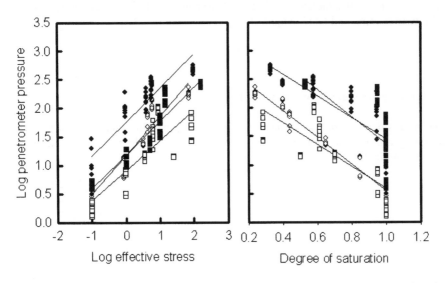

Figure 2. Log penetrometer pressure plotted against log effective stress (left panel) and the degree of saturation (right panel). The data shown is for a sandy soil (circles) and for a silty soil (squares). The soil was packed to bulk densities of 1.7 g cm^{-3} (closed symbols) and 1.2 g cm^{-3} (open symbols). The linear fits shown were all significant to $P<0.001$ and the percentage of variance accounted for is given in Table 1.

Table 1.   Percentage of variance accounted for on the fits shown in Figure 2.

Soil type	Bulk Density g cm^{-3}	Percentage of variance accounted for between Log (Q) and	
		S	Log (ψ S)
Sandy	1.2	87	96
soil	1.7	76	62
Silty	1.2	59	63
soil	1.7	43	88

Predicting soil strength from soil moisture status

Figure 2 shows penetrometer pressure for two soils at two densities plotted against effective stress and the degree of saturation. Interestingly the relationship between penetrometer pressure and effective stress is linear on a log-log plot. It is already accepted that the relationship between penetrometer pressure and the degree of water saturation is linear when plotted as a log-linear plot. When the log of penetrometer pressure is plotted against degree of saturation, the data group according to bulk density. The use of effective stress reduced the grouping effect that resulted from bulk density, but did not eliminate it.

Electrode measurements of soil nitrate availability

The nitrate-selective membranes are hot-pressed at 150 °C and 220 kN as described previously (LeGoff *et al.*, 2002a) and then small circular discs of 7 mm diameter are cut and pre-conditioned in 100 mM potassium nitrate solution for at least 7 days. Each disc was then clamped into a nylon housing that could be directly inserted into the soil. The final dimensions of the probe are very similar to those of the matric potential probe shown in Figure 1. The NO_3^- probe was calibrated before and after three days of continuous recording in soil. The sample was a silty clay loam topsoil taken from the Broadbalk wheat experiment at Rothamsted (Goulding *et al.*, 2000) to which 1 ml of distilled water per 2g of dried soil had been added 6 h before the NO_3^- recordings were started. This soil was taken from the plot receiving no additional fertiliser and the soil water has a pH of 8.3.

The NO_3^- electrode calibration measurements show that the detection limit of the electrodes (0.013-0.018 mM) is much lower than the values recorded from a soil that had received no additional fertilizer. These measurements were made on soil that had been previously air-dried and sieved, so after re-hydration of the soil there was a gradual decrease in NO_3^- concentration from 15 mM after 6 h to a value of 2.5 mM after 3 days.

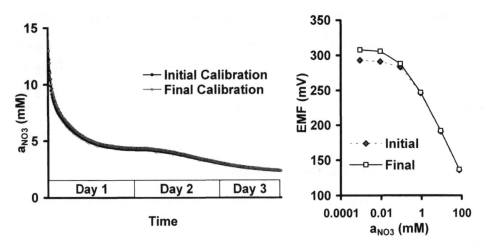

Figure 3. Continuous NO₃⁻ electrode recording for 3 days in soil (left) showing the calibration before and after the measurement (right). Calibration shows electrode output (EMF) plotted against the $\log_{10}$ nitrate activity.

DISCUSSION

The porous material sensors for soil water matric potential described in this paper are currently being tested in field experiments. The sensors will help us understand how crop growth is affected by soil strength and water stress in the field. The data in Figure 2 shows that it is possible to achieve high soil strengths (up to an equivalent root growth pressure of 400 kPa) at matric potentials as high as –300 kPa. This suggests that in UK conditions it is more likely that soil strength will limit plant growth than water stress. The integration of the assessment of water stress and soil strength will be an important tool in determining the plant response to the root growth environment.

Nitrate availability in the soil after the addition of water to an air dried sample has been measured using the electrode measuring system. The soil NO_3^- concentrations are within the range of values obtained from porous suction cup samples collected under a similar type of soil (Barraclough, 1986). One major advantage of this type of soil measuring system is that the electrodes only report the local NO_3^- concentrations that are available to the plant. An electrode placed alongside a root will directly report the NO_3^- that is available to the plant in the soil.

In Figure 3 the gradual decrease in soil nitrate availability may result from an initial flush of bacterial denitrification, after an initial release of NO_3^- on the addition of water. Nitrate is the main form of soil available nitrogen for crops, but in more acidic soils and at low temperatures more nitrogen is available as ammonium. Soil ammonium can also be measured using an ammonium-selective electrode (Wells & Miller, 2000).

Preliminary results for these two new types of soil sensing probes suggest an opportunity for the direct measurement of soil parameters that are major determinants of crop yield. By measuring water matric potential and nitrate availability in the soil these measurements can identify environmental conditions that may limit yield long before symptoms appear in the crop itself. These measurements can be used to feedback advice to management decisions thus enabling more efficient targeting of fertiliser and water to the crops requirements. However, these are early days for these new sensor systems and more work is required to establish how these measurements compare with current soil evaluation methods and to relate the data obtained to crop yields. For example, the relationship between soil depth and nitrate concentration that is optimal for crop yield but giving minimal leaching can be measured.

ACKNOWLEDGEMENTS

The authors wish to thank DEFRA for funding the development of these soil sensors (grants AR0910 and AR0913). Rothamsted Research and Silsoe Institute are grant-aided by the Biotechnology and Biological Sciences Research Council of the UK.

REFERENCES

Barraclough P (1986). The growth and activity of winter wheat roots in the field: nutrient inflows of high-yielding crops. *Journal of Agricultural Science Camb.* **106**, 53-59.

Bengough A G; Mullins C E; Wilson G (1997). Estimating soil frictional resistance to metal probes and its relevance to the penetration of soil by roots. *European Journal of Soil Science* **48**, 603-612.

Gaskin G J; Miller J D (1996). Measurement of soil water content using a simplified impedance measuring technique. *Journal of Agricultural Engineering Research* **63**, 153-159.

Goulding K W T; Poulton P R; Webster C P; Howe M T (2000). Nitrate leaching from the Broadbalk wheat experiment, Rothamsted, UK as influenced by fertilizer and manure inputs and the weather. *Soil Use and Management* **16**, 244-250.

Le Goff T; Braven J; Ebdon L; Chilcott N P; Scholefield D; Wood J W (2002a). An accurate and stable nitrate-selective electrode for the *in situ* determination of nitrate in agricultural drainage waters. *The Analyst* **127**, 507-511.

Le Goff T; Marsh J; Braven J; Ebdon L; Scholefield D (2002b). A solvent-free method for preparing improved quality ion-selective electrode membranes. *Green Chemistry* **4**, 486-491.

Mulholland B J; Black C R; Taylor I B; Roberts J A; Lenton J R (1996). Effect of soil compaction on barley (*Hordeum vulgare* L.) growth I. Possible role for ABA as a root-sourced chemical signal. *Journals of Experimental Botany* **46**, 539-549.

Mullins C E (2000) Hardsetting soils. In: *Handbook of soil,* ed M Sumner, pp G65-G87. CRC Press: Boca Raton, Florida.

Wells D M; Miller A J (2000). Intracellular measurement of ammonium in *Chara corallina* using ion-selective microelectrodes. *Plant and Soil* **221**, 105-108.

Whalley W R; Watts C W; Hilhorst M A; Bird N R A; Balendonck J; Longstaff D J (2001). The design of porous material sensors to measure matric potential of water in soil. *European Journal of Soil Science* **53**, 511-519.

Adjusting the fungicide input in winter wheat depending on variety resistance

L N Jørgensen, L Hagelskjær
Danish Institute of Agricultural Sciences, Research Centre Flakkebjerg, 4200 Slagelse, Denmark
Email: LiseN.Jorgensen@agrsci.dk

G C Nielsen
Danish Agricultural Advisory Service, Udkærvej 14, 8200 Århus N, Denmark

ABSTRACT

For 3 seasons, different fungicide input was tested in varieties with different degrees of resistance to septoria (*Septoria tritici*) and yellow rust (*Puccinia striiformis*). The yearly variation in benefits from fungicide application was considerable due to differences in climate and disease pressure. In individual years the differences in margin over fungicide cost from different fungicide inputs were small compared with the yearly variations. The economic optimum in resistant varieties was a TFI (Treatment Frequency Index) between 0.25 and 0.5. Most typically, only an ear application was profitable. In more susceptible varieties, the optimum TFI was 0.5-0.9, and a 2-spray programme gave a larger flexibility with regard to the dose needed at the 2nd application. The decision support system Crop Protection Online gave competitive disease control and margin over fungicides cost in line with or better than the standard treatments. A general TFI in winter wheat lower than the present target figure at 0.75 is possible if varieties with good resistance to septoria diseases and yellow rust increase significantly in area.

INTRODUCTION

More than a 50% reduction in fungicide input in winter wheat has taken place during the last 20 years mainly due to use of appropriate and reduced dosages. Input of pesticides in Denmark is today generally measured as Treatment Frequency Index (TFI), which quantifies the number of full dosages applied in the field. The target figure in Pesticide Action Plan II for fungicide input in winter wheat has been recommended to 0.75. This target has generally been reached in 2002 (Anon., 2003). On average the number of treatments is two, and the average dose/TFI of fungicides is 0.35 per treatment (Farmstat & Kleffmann, 2002).

If further reduction plans are to be suggested, cropping of resistant varieties and adjusting of fungicide input according to the need in specific varieties are believed to become of increasing importance. In order to establish the economic optimal input of fungicides in varieties with different degrees of resistance, trials were carried out investigating the response from different input of TFI. The trials were carried out by both the Danish Institute of Agricultural Sciences (DIAS) and the Danish Agricultural Advisory Service (DAAS).

MATERIALS AND METHODS

For 3 seasons (2000-2002), trials have been carried out investigating the response from different inputs of fungicides in varieties with significant differences in resistance levels. Following the national resistance ratings, varieties are grouped according to the degree of resistance (0-3; 3 = most susceptible). In this investigation, a variety is categorised as resistant if the variety has shown good resistance to both *Septoria tritici* and yellow rust (*Puccinia striiformis*). Severe attack of mildew (*Erysiphe graminis*) is regarded as having less impact on yields and is therefore not included in the categorisation in this paper. The following fungicides were used in the trials:

Products	normal rate	active ingredients per litre	Code
Amistar	1.0 l/ha	Azoxystrobin (250 g)	Az;
Folicur EW	1.0 l/ha	Tebuconazole (250g)	Teb;
Opus	1.0 l/ha	Epoxiconazole (125 g)	Epo;
Opus Team	1.5 l/ha	Epoxiconazole (84 g) + fenpropimorph (250g)	EpoFen.

Control of diseases in 4 varieties with different dosages at heading (DIAS).

Four varieties (Table 1) were investigated using 3 different dosages of the tankmix Azoxytrobin + Tebuconazole as well as testing the recommendation given by the decision support system (DSS) Crop Protection Online (Hagelskjær & Jørgensen 2002) based on weekly assessments. In 2 of the 3 trial years, only applications at heading were investigated. In the 3rd year, ear treatments were tested with and without application at GS 31 (0,25 of normal dose of EpoFen). Ear treatments were in all 3 years:
1) Untreated; 2) 0.75 TFI (GS 51-55); 3) 0.5 TFI (GS 51-55); 4) 0.25 TFI (GS 51-55); 5) Recommendation given by Crop Protection Online.

Table 1. Number of trials and varieties investigated in the trials with different degrees of resistance. R= resistant; S = Susceptible.

	2000	2001	2002
No. of trials (DIAS)	2	2	2
Varieties	Variety mixture	Variety mixture	Variety mixture
	Ritmo (S)	Ritmo (S)	Ritmo (S)
	Stakado (R)	Stakado (R)	Stakado (R)
	Hussar (S)	Hussar (S)	Kris (S)
No. of trials (DAAS)	8	13	9
Varieties	Kris (S)	Kris (S)	Kris (S)
	Ritmo (S)	Ritmo (S)	Baltimor (S)
	Stakado (R)	Stakado (R)	Boston (R)

Control of diseases in 3 varieties with different TFI's during the season (DAAS).

For 3 seasons, DAAS has carried out trials with different numbers of treatments and TFI applied in 3 major variety types (Table 1). The total input varied between 0.25 and 1.25 TFI divided into 1, 2 or 3 treatments (Table 2). A total of 30 trials were carried out according to these plans.

Net yield is calculated in dt/ha as the yield response in treated plots compared with untreated plots with costs of fungicides and application subtracted. The cost of application is set at 8 EUR per hectare, and the grain price at 8.7 EUR per decitonne.

Table 2. Trial plan carried out in DAAS trials 2000-2002 with variable numbers of treatments and dosages.

Trial plan 2000-2001 Treatments (g a.i/ha)	GS	TFI	Trial plan 2002 Treatments (g a.i/ha)	GS	TFI
a. Untreated			a. Untreated		
b. EpoFen (32+94)	30-31	0.88	b. EpoFen (32+94)	30-31	0.88
Teb (31) + Az (31)	35-37		Epo (16) + Az (31)	35-37	
Teb (31) + Az (31)	59-61		Epo (16) + Az (31)	59-61	
c. EpoFen (63+188)	35-37	1.25	c. Epo (16) + Az (31)	35-37	0.50
Teb (63) + Az (63)	59-61		Epo (16) + Az (31)	59-61	
d. EpoFen (32+94)	31-32	0.63	d. EpoFen (32+94)	31-32	0.63
Teb (31) + Az (31)	45-51		Epo (16) + Az (31)	45-51	
e. EpoFen (32+94)	31-32	0.88	e. EpoFen (32+94)	31-32	0.88
Teb (63) + Az (63)	45-51		Epo (31) + Az (63)	45-51	
f. Teb (31) + Az (31)	45-51	0.25	f. Epo (16) + Az (31)	45-51	0.25
g. Teb (63) + Az (63)	45-51	0.50	g. Epo (31) + Az (63)	45-51	0.50

RESULTS

Control of diseases in 4 varieties using different dosages for ear-application (DIAS).

In the 3 seasons, large differences in disease levels and obtained yield responses from ear application were found (Table 3). 2002 was a year with a very severe attack of septoria and high yield responses. The difference in yield response between varieties was only significant in 2002, where Stakado gave the lowest yield increase (Table 3; Figure 1). In 2000 and 2001, the net yields were only marginal. The dose response curves in all 3 years were very flat for the 3 tested dosages.

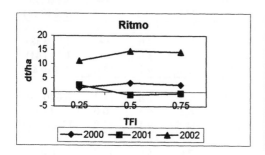
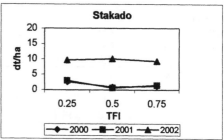

Figure 1. Margin over fungicide cost in Ritmo and Stakado using 3 different TFIs for ear treatments. Data from 3 years. 2 trials per year.

There is a tendency to an input of 0.5 TFI being optimal on Ritmo and Kris and 0.25 on Stakado (Figure 1). This was particularly the case in 2002 where the septoria attack was severe. Crop Protection Online has given a margin over fungicide cost at the same level as the best standard treatments (Table 3). The input from Crop Protection Online in the resistant variety Stakado was lower in 2 of the 3 years compared with the other varieties.

Trials in 2002 showed that treatment at GS 31 had a positive effect on net yield on susceptible varieties like Kris and Ritmo but not on the resistant variety Stakado (Figure 2). The results on Ritmo indicated that ear treatments with TFI =0.5 (63 g a.i. Az + 63 g a.i. Teb) were optimum. If no treatment had been applied earlier, an ear application of TFI = 0.25 was sub-optimal. If treatments had been applied before ear application, very little difference was seen between the 3 tested dosages investigated at heading, indicating that in susceptible varieties an early treatment (T1) gave a higher degree of flexibility regarding the choice of dose at heading. For the resistant variety Stakado, the optimum in 2002 was half dose both with and without treatment at GS 31; however, only with a minor and not significant difference to ¼ dose. Growing the variety mixtures generally reduced the level of septoria marginally compared with individual varieties and the optimum input was in line with susceptible varieties.

Table 3. Gross and net yield (dt/ha) in 4 varieties treated with different ear treatments in 3 years, 2 trials per year. In brackets under Crop Protection Online is given the TFI in the specific year and variety.

Variety and year	0.75 N 94 g a.i. Az + 94 g a.i. Teb		0.5 N 63 g a.i. Az + 63 g a.i. Teb		0.25 N 31 g a.i. Az + 31 g a.i. Teb		Crop Protection Online	
	gross	net	gross	net	Gross	net	gross	net
Variety mixture*	-	-	-	-	-		-	
2000	5.7	-0.6	5.4	0.9	2.1	-0.6	5.6	0.9 (0.5)
2001	7.7	1.4	8.0	3.5	5.0	2.3	10.5	6.2 (0.56)
2002	18.5	12.2	16.6	12.1	13.6	10.9	19.0	11.7 (0.75)
Ritmo	-	-	-	-	-		-	
2000	8.8	2.5	7.7	3.2	3.8	1.1	7.2	2.5 (0.5)
2001	5.8	-0.5	3.5	-1.0	5.2	2.5	5.4	1.1 (0.56)
2002	20.5	14.2	19.1	14.6	13.8	11.1	22.4	15.0 (0.76)
Stakado	-	-	-	-	-		-	
2000	7.5	1.2	5.4	0.9	5.3	2.6	4.6	1.0 (0.38)
2001	7.8	1.5	3.9	-0.6	5.7	3.0	4.8	1.3 (0.41)
2002	15.6	9.3	14.5	10.1	12.4	9.7	17.0	9.4 (0.8)
Hussar/Kris	-	-	-	-	-		-	
2000	8.5	2.2	7.2	2.7	5.3	2.6	11.3	6.0 (0.57)
2001	8.8	2.5	8.3	3.8	6.8	4.1	10.0	5.8 (0.56)
2002	20.0	13.7	17.2	12.7	11.8	9.1	20.0	12.8 (0.74)
Average	11.3	5.0	9.7	5.2	7.6	5.0	11.2	6.0

*Variety mixture =Ritmo. Stakado. Hussar/Kris

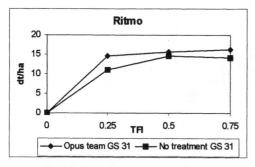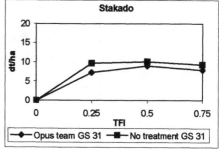

Figure 2. Margin over fungicide cost for ear application with 3 different dosages of the tank mix Amistar + Folicur in Ritmo and Stakado. The ear application is done with and without a treatment at GS 31 using EpoFen (32+94 g a.i./ha).

Control of diseases in 3 varieties with different TFI's during the season (DAAS).

Results from the DAAS trials carried out showed generally small differences in margin over fungicide cost from the different input of fungicides measured as TFI (Figure 3-4). Stakado and Boston, which both have shown good resistance to septoria and yellow rust, generally gave the greatest margin over fungicide cost using TFI between 0.25 and 0.5. A single ear application was sufficient in those resistant varieties. In more susceptible varieties, the best margin was obtained using 0.5-0.9 TFI. Fungicide input above TFI = 1 generally did not give the optimal net return. In 2 trials with Stakado, the variety developed a severe attack of brown rust (*Puccinia recondita*). In those trials, higher net yields were obtained but one single ear application using 0.5 TFI gave the best margin. In 3 trials with Baltimor and Kris, a severe attack of yellow rust developed. In those trials, a TFI of 0.5-0.88 has been the optimal divided into 2 or 3 applications.

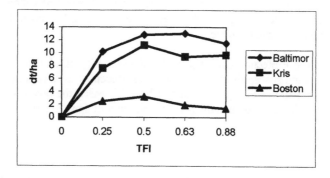

Figure 3. Margin over fungicide cost from different fungicide input (TFI) in 3 varieties with different resistance. 9 trials 2002.

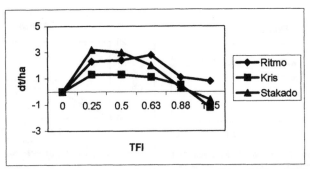

Figure 4. Margin over fungicide cost from different input of fungicides (TFI) in 3 varieties with different resistance. 21 trials 2000-2001.

DISCUSSION

The optimal input with fungicides in wheat depends on the disease pressure and the climate in the individual season, but the susceptibility of the variety also plays a major role for the optimal input. The difference in margin between resistant and susceptible varieties was greatest in seasons with severe attacks of septoria and yellow rust. One single ear treatment was often sufficient in varieties with good resistance to rust and *Septoria tritici,* where more susceptible varieties needed 2 and more rarely 3 applications.

The dose-response curves for ear treatment were generally very flat. This was particularly the case if treatments at GS 31-32 had been applied prior to ear treatment leaving a great deal of flexibility regarding the choice of dose. In the most resistant varieties, a fungicide input of 0.25-0.5 TFI applied as an ear application gave the best economic result in all 3 seasons. A quarter dose was optimal at low levels of attack and a half dose in severe attacks. In more susceptible varieties, a fungicide input of 0.25-0.5 TFI was optimal under moderate attack, while 0.5-0.75 TFI was optimal under more severe attacks. Control of yellow rust generally required 2-3 treatments depending on when the epidemic starts. For control of this disease timing is more important than the dose.

Use of DSS like Crop Protection Online provide the possibility of adjusting input depending on disease pressure and susceptibility of the varieties. Recently, new varieties on the Danish market with good resistance to septoria and rust have increased the possibilities of reducing the TFI in wheat to a lower level than the present TFI input of approximately 0.75.

REFERENCES

Anon. (2003). Bekæmpelsesmiddelstatistik 2003. Orientering nr. 5 2003. Miljøstyrelsen. Miljøministeriet.
Kleefman; Farmstat (2002) . Statistical data on pesticide use in DK (Company data)
Hagelskær L; Jørgensen LN (2003). A web-based DSS for integrated management of diseases and pest in cereals. EPPO bulletin (in press)

SESSION 8C

NEW APPROACHES TO CROP PROTECTION BY EXPLOITING STRESS-RELATED SIGNALLING IN PLANTS

Chairman and Session Organiser:	Professor John Pickett *Rothamsted Research, Harpenden, UK*
Papers:	8C-1 to 8C-4

Exploring multi-trophic plant-herbivore interactions for new crop protection methods

H J Bouwmeester, F W A Verstappen, A Aharoni, J Lücker, M A Jongsma
Plant Research International, P.O. Box 16, 6700 AA Wageningen, The Netherlands
E-mail: harro.bouwmeester@wur.nl

I F Kappers, L L P Luckerhoff, M Dicke
Laboratory of Entomology, Wageningen University, P.O. Box 8031, 6700 EH Wageningen,
The Netherlands

ABSTRACT

Biological control of arthropod herbivores in agricultural crops depends on antagonists or enemies of the pest organisms. To minimise damage to a crop, it is crucial that the biological control agents are able to find their prey efficiently. Here we discuss the finding that when herbivores feed, plants produce volatiles that are attractive to the predators. The effects of biotic, abiotic and genetic factors on volatile formation and the biochemical and molecular regulation of this indirect defence mechanism are reviewed. The opportunities to use genetically modified plants to further understanding this complex interaction and the possibilities of using our knowledge to improve biological control in agricultural crops are discussed.

INTRODUCTION

Environmentally benign protection of crops against arthropod herbivores can use either direct host plant resistance or biological control. These two approaches are fundamentally different in that host plant resistance depends on direct – constitutive or feeding-induced - defence traits of the crop plants (such as trichomes, toxic secondary metabolites or proteins, and repellents), whereas biological control depends on the use of antagonists or enemies of the pest organisms. For the latter to be effective, it is crucial that the biological control agents are able to find their prey efficiently enough to minimise damage to the crop.

More than a decade ago it was discovered that when herbivores feed, the plants produce volatiles that are attractive to the natural enemies of the herbivore (Dicke *et al.*, 1990a; Turlings *et al.*, 1990) (Figure 1). Thus, plants indirectly defend themselves by enhancing the effectiveness of the natural enemies of the herbivores. The use of predators and parasitoids for biological control is receiving more and more attention and for many years it has been common practice in a number of crops in glasshouse as well as open fields (Van Lenteren, 2000; Kfir *et al.*, 2002). Nevertheless, breeders and agronomists have so far paid little attention to the optimisation of biological control. This is probably due to the relatively recent discovery of the phenomenon of indirect defence, the more complex relationships involved and the difficulties associated with quantification of the effects.

Here we will discuss the principles of plant-mediated multitrophic interactions involved in biological control and our research into the possibilities of using this principle to design new control methods. We use a combination of scientific disciplines varying from ethological studies of predators to plant molecular biology. We focus our work on the induction of volatiles by spider mites in a number of plant species, such as cucumber and potato, and the effects of abiotic and biotic factors on this induction, and we study the effects of the volatiles on the behaviour of predators such as predatory mites. The biochemical and molecular regulation of volatile formation is investigated using enzymology and cDNA microarray technology and genes involved in volatile formation are cloned from a variety of plant species. These genes are then used to transform plants, including model plants such as tobacco and arabidopsis, to change their volatile profile and study the effects on the behaviour of parasitoids and predators.

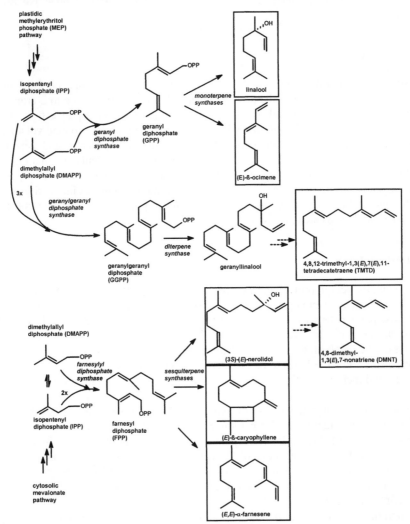

Figure 1.   Examples of isoprenoid volatiles that have been shown to be induced in a range of plant species by a range of arthropod herbivores (boxed compounds) and schematic representation of biosynthetic pathways involved in their formation. (Broken) arrows indicate (putative) enzymatic steps.

VOLATILE INDUCTION AND EFFECTS ON PREDATOR BEHAVIOUR

The importance of the third trophic level for plant defence was first suggested by Price et al (Price *et al.*, 1980), and was followed by the discovery of the herbivory-induced volatiles that attract parasitoids and predators (Dicke *et al.*, 1990a; Turlings *et al.*, 1990). Upon infestation with two-spotted spider mites (*Tetranychus urticae*), lima bean plants responded by emitting a mixture of volatiles attracting the predatory mite *Phytoseiulus persimilis* (Dicke *et al.*, 1990b) that effectively eliminated local populations of the spider mites (Dicke *et al.*, 1990a). Similarly, corn plants respond to feeding damage of *Spodoptera exigua* caterpillars with the production of volatiles that attracted the parasitoid *Cotesia marginiventris* (Turlings *et al.*, 1990). Since then, it has been shown that this is a common mechanism employed by many plant species in the interaction with many different herbivores, and that these volatiles are not usually emitted in response to mechanical wounding (Dicke *et al.*, 2003).

Figure 2 shows a typical example of the induction of volatiles in cucumber and Figure 3 the results obtained in Y-tube olfactometer experiments on predator attraction by induced plants for a number of plant species. Although treatment with jasmonic acid mimics fairly well the effect of spider mite infestation, some differences (e.g. peak 5, (*E,E*)-α-farnesene) can be found in the volatile blend (Figure 2). Typical volatiles released from a multitude of species after herbivory are the so-called green leaf volatiles such as C6-alcohols, -aldehydes, and - esters, derivatives of the shikimate pathway such as methyl salicylate, and isoprenoids such as (*E*)-ß-ocimene, linalool, (*E*)-ß-caryophyllene, (*E,E*)-α-farnesene and the homoterpenes 4,8-dimethyl-1,3(*E*),7-nonatriene and 4,8,12-trimethyl-1,3(*E*),7(*E*),11-tetradecatetraene (Figure 1). The isoprenoids are by far the most important components of the induced volatile blend and hence this is the class we focus on.

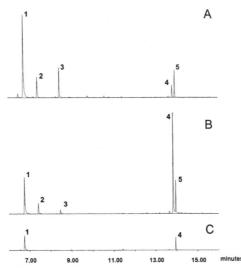

Figure 2.   Induction of volatiles in cucumber by spider mite feeding (A) and jasmonic acid spraying (B). Panel C shows the response of control leaves. Peaks are: (*Z*)-3-hexen-1-yl acetate (1), (*E*)-ß-ocimene (2), 4,8-dimethyl-1,3(*E*),7-nonatriene (DMNT) (3), (*E,E*)- α-farnesene (4), 4,8,12-trimethyl-1,3(*E*),7(*E*),11-tridecatraene (5).

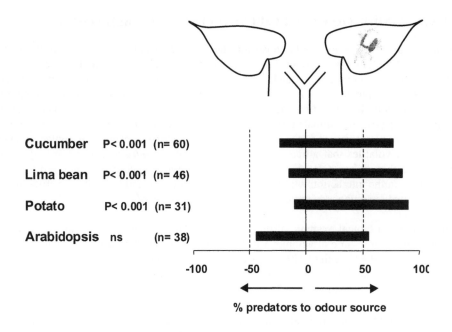

Figure 3. Predator attraction (*Phytoseiulus persimilis*) by spider mite infested cucumber, lima bean, potato and arabidopsis plants in a Y-tube olfactometer.

FACTORS AFFECTING INDUCED VOLATILE FORMATION

Biotic and abiotic factors

Plants have been shown to respond to different herbivore species with quantitatively and qualitatively different volatile blends allowing predators to respond to their specific prey (Sabelis & van der Baan, 1983; Takabayashi *et al.*, 1991; De Moraes *et al.*, 1998; Du *et al.*, 1998). Within a plant species, the quality of the volatile blend may be affected by the developmental stage of the herbivore (Takabayashi *et al.*, 1995), and the volatiles induced by insect egg deposition differ from those induced by feeding (Wegener *et al.*, 2001; Hilker & Meiners, 2002).

There are many reports that the production of non-herbivore induced secondary metabolites by plants is influenced by environmental conditions. It is therefore likely that this also holds for herbivory-induced volatiles and knowledge of these effects may be important for improvement of biological control, e.g. by using optimal conditions for efficient signalling. Some of the factors that have been shown to affect secondary metabolite production such as light, temperature and water availability have also been investigated for their effect on herbivore-induced volatile biosynthesis. High light intensity and water stress are generally reported to increase induced volatile production and/or predator attraction for example in Lima bean, kidney bean, maize and cotton (Loughrin *et al.*, 1994; Takabayashi *et al.*, 1994; Turlings *et al.*, 1995; Gouinguene & Turlings, 2002).

Genetic variation

If conventional plant breeding is to be used to improve biological control through enhanced volatile production there has to be genetic variation in the ability to produce herbivore-induced, predator-attracting volatiles. In gerbera, a number of cultivars differed in composition and amount of volatiles produced after spider mite feeding (Krips *et al.*, 2001) and there were differences between the cultivars in the odour-preference of predatory mites. The composition of the volatile blend seemed to be more important for this difference than the total amount of volatiles produced, and the terpenoids (*E*)-ß-ocimene and linalool were possible candidates in determining the difference in attractiveness between cultivars. Also maize cultivars and *Zea* spp. showed large differences in the composition of the volatile blend induced by the application of the oral secretion of *Spodoptera littoralis* to mechanically damaged leaves (Gouinguene *et al.*, 2001).

There are several problems associated with comparing genotypes for their production of induced volatiles, when other differences between the genotypes can not be controlled (Krips *et al.*, 2001). For example, there may be differences in direct defence causing differences in developmental rate of herbivores leading to differences in volatile formation. To circumvent this problem, in addition to spider mite infestation we also used jasmonic acid (JA) treatment in a comparison between seven cucumber genotypes. Earlier research had shown that JA treatment mimics the effect of spider mite infestation in lima bean, gerbera and cucumber plants (Dicke *et al.*, 1999; Gols *et al.*, 1999) (H J Bouwmeester *et al.*, unpublished data). Figure 4 shows that there are large differences in the response of cucumber genotypes to spider mite infestation. In addition, there are similar differences in volatile production among cucumber genotypes after JA treatment. There is a fair correlation between the response to spider mites and JA (e.g. high production in genotypes 1, 6 and 7 for both treatments and low for genotypes 2 and 3). In a preliminary Y-tube olfactometer experiment, the attractiveness of genotypes 1, 4, and 7 to predatory mites upon spider mite infestation was compared, showing a small, but significant preference towards genotype 1 (data not shown).

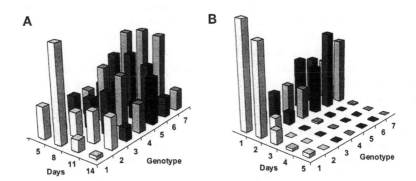

Figure 4.   A, Time course of total volatile induction by spider mite feeding and B, jasmonic acid spraying in seven cucumber genotypes. A. 2-Wks old plants were infested with 50 spider mites on day 0. Leaves were sampled after 5, 8, 11 and 14 days for headspace analysis. B. 2-Wks old plants were sprayed with jasmonic acid on day 0. Leaves were sampled after 1, 2, 3, 4 and 5 days for headspace analysis.

HOW IS VOLATILE INDUCTION REGULATED?

Using $^{13}CO_2$ pulse-labeling experiments it was demonstrated that most of the induced volatiles are biosynthesised *de novo* in response to herbivory (Pare & Tumlinson, 1997). This has led to the search for the induced enzymes involved in the formation of these volatiles. The first herbivory-induced enzyme to be identified was (3S)-(E)-nerolidol synthase in cucumber and lima bean (Bouwmeester et al., 1999). This enzyme catalyses the conversion of farnesyl diphosphate to (3S)-(E)-nerolidol, a sesquiterpene alcohol, likely an intermediate in the formation of 4,8-dimethyl-1,3(E),7-nonatriene (DMNT) (Donath et al., 1994; Donath and Boland, 1995) (Figure 1). Indeed DMNT is one of the major induced volatiles of cucumber (Figure 2) and all the evidence suggests that (3S)-(E)-nerolidol synthase is the regulatory step en route to this compound. DMNT is also an important constituent of the induced volatiles of other plant species such as lima bean, maize and cotton (Dicke et al., 1990a; Turlings et al., 1990; Takabayashi et al., 1991; Loughrin et al., 1994; Takabayashi et al., 1994) and seems responsible for the attraction of the predatory mite *P. persimilis* to Lima bean and cucumber plants infested with the spider mite *T. urticae* (Dicke et al., 1990b). A synthetic mixture of volatiles, including DMNT, that mimics the blend of volatiles that is emitted by corn plants infested with *S. exigua* caterpillars, attracted the parasitoid *C. marginiventris* which parasitizes the caterpillars (Turlings et al., 1991).

MOLECULAR TOOLS

Elucidation of mechanisms

As mentioned, the elucidation of genotype differences and the role of individual volatiles in herbivory-induced indirect defence, is hindered by the lack of genotypes that differ in one factor only (*e.g.* only differ in the level of volatile production, not in composition and/or direct defence level) (Dicke & Hilker, 2003), but see (Van Poecke & Dicke, 2002) for a first example). With the advent of molecular tools, the use of transgenic plants is now becoming a feasible and exciting way to unravel not only the importance of individual compounds but also the regulation of their induction. Research in our laboratories has focussed on the major components of the blends of induced volatiles, the terpenoids. We have isolated and characterised a multitude of genes involved in terpene biosynthesis such as the monoterpene synthases (+)-limonene synthase, ß-pinene synthase and γ-terpinene synthase from lemon (Lücker et al., 2002), α-pinene synthase from strawberry (Aharoni et al., 2003b), the sesquiterpene synthases amorpha-4,11-diene synthase from *Artemisia annua* (Mercke et al., 2000; Wallaart et al., 2001), two isoforms of germacrene A synthase from chicory (Bouwmeester et al., 2002), (+)- and (-)-germacrene D synthase, α-gurjunene synthase and cascarilladiene synthase from *Solidago canadensis* (I G Altug, W A König & H J Bouwmeester, unpublished) and a combined mono-/sesquiterpene synthase linalool/nerolidol synthase from strawberry (Aharoni et al., 2003b). Most of these enzymes are involved in the constitutive (or developmentally regulated) biosynthesis of essential oils or flavour compounds in these plant species. They were cloned using PCR with degenerate primers or cDNA microarray analyses from plant tissues that were shown to produce the corresponding products, and hence needed no induction by herbivores.

Some of these enzymes catalyse the formation of compounds that have been shown, in other plant species, to be produced upon induction by herbivores. Examples are limonene and linalool (Dicke *et al.*, 1990a; De Moraes *et al.*, 1998), germacrene A (Van den Boom *et al.*, 2002) and nerolidol. Nerolidol is found in the induced volatile blend of for example maize but is, more importantly, the first dedicated intermediate *en route* to DMNT (Bouwmeester *et al.*, 1999; Degenhardt & Gershenzon, 2000) (Figure 1). In addition, we have cloned two spider mite induced sesquiterpene synthases from cucumber, (*E,E*)-α-farnesene synthase and (*E*)-ß-caryophyllene synthase (P M Mercke, I F Kappers, F W A Verstappen, M Dicke & H J Bouwmeester, unpublished), two other major contributors to the induced volatile blend of many plant species (Dicke *et al.*, 1990a; De Moraes *et al.*, 1998) (Figure 1). In addition to the directed cloning of genes encoding enzymes involved in terpenoid biosynthesis, we and others use more generic approaches such as cDNA microarray analysis (Reymond *et al.*, 2000; Schenk *et al.*, 2000; P M Mercke, I F Kappers, F W A Verstappen, M Dicke & H J Bouwmeester, unpublished) or DDRT-PCR (Hermsmeier *et al.*, 2001) to explore genes which are regulated by herbivory.

Use of transgenic plants

With the cloning of the genes involved in volatile biosynthesis it is becoming feasible to produce transgenic plants with overexpression or antisense/silencing to produce a new volatile blend. Alternatively, eventually transcription factors may be cloned that could be used to upregulate entire indirect defence pathways. Such plants would be the perfect tools to study the importance of individual compounds, blends, timing and magnitude of the plant's response for predator behaviour. In our laboratories, we have used a number of terpene synthases to transform model plant species. One of the first studies reported the transformation of petunia with the *Clarkia breweri* linalool synthase (Lücker *et al.*, 2001). Instead of the expected emission of linalool, transgenic plants were demonstrated to contain appreciable amounts of linalyl-ß-D-glucoside, a non-volatile storage form of linalool, likely formed through the action of an endogenous petunia glycosyltransferase (Lücker *et al.*, 2001). In potato, transformation with a strawberry linalool synthase also led to the formation of glycosides of linalool, and also high amounts of free linalool were emitted, particularly from young plants (A Aharoni, H J Bouwmeester, M A Jongsma *et al.*, unpublished) (Figure 5). The difference between the transgenic and wild type plants could easily be detected with the (untrained) human nose.

More straightforward results, i.e. with less side effects caused by endogenous enzymes, were obtained with other monoterpene synthases in tobacco. Tobacco was transformed with three lemon monoterpene synthases that were combined into one plant by crossing (Lücker *et al.*, 2002; Lücker *et al.*, 2003). Transgenic tobacco plants were obtained that produced up to seven new monoterpenes in leaves and flowers (three major products (-)-ß-pinene, (+)-limonene and γ-terpinene plus some side products that had also been detected upon heterologous expression in *E. coli*) (Lücker *et al.*, 2003). Finally, the recent successful transformation of arabidopsis with a strawberry linalool/nerolidol synthase (Aharoni *et al.*, 2003a) brings the molecular advantages of arabidopsis into research on the effects of altered volatile blends on multi-trophic interactions. Arabidopsis has shown to be a good model plant for the investigation of induced indirect defence: feeding by the crucifer specialist *Pieris rapae* as well as other herbivorous arthropods results in the emission of volatiles that attract the parasitoid *Cotesia rubecula* (Van Poecke *et al.*, 2001; Van Poecke *et al.*, 2003). Preliminary Y-tube olfactometer experiments with the transgenic potato plants showed that the attractiveness to predators is enhanced by the introduction (or increase) of a single component in the volatile blend (Figure 5).

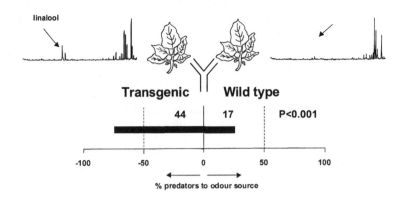

Figure 5.   Attractiveness of non-damaged wild type and transgenic, linalool producing potato leaves to predatory mites. Bars represent choices of predatory mites reared on lima bean. Chromatograms show GC-MS analysis of the headspace of the odour sources.

CONCLUSIONS AND OPTIONS FOR NEW CONTROL METHODS

This review shows that our understanding of tritrophic interactions and the chemical signalling molecules and mechanisms involved is increasing rapidly. The use of this knowledge for the design of new control methods will depend on the agricultural system for which the method is intended. Biological control of herbivores in a glasshouse, for example, usually depends on the introduction of the predators, whereas in open systems natural enemies may be present or attracted from elsewhere (although also there it is feasible that introduction of natural enemies will become increasingly important). The introduction of enemies is of course costly and it is important that they survive for some time (which may mean a threshold level of their prey has to be accepted) and are able to find and control their prey quickly once it reaches a threshold level. The advantage of introduction is that the predators are reared under controlled conditions (constant quality) and can even be trained (Dicke *et al.*, 1990c). In open agricultural systems, the farmer in principle depends on the natural presence or invasion of predators, which also have to be kept alive, present and active when necessary. Now that many of the induced volatile blends have been identified, artificial mixtures could be used or alternatively, crops could be sprayed with jasmonic acid to induce volatile production that should lead to the increased presence of natural enemies (Thaler, 1999). However, there are examples where this approach has been unsuccessful (Chiri & Legner, 1983) and several authors have expressed the feeling that this approach will fail because the presence of the volatile cue and the prey are uncoupled (Dicke *et al.*, 1990a; Degenhardt *et al.*, 2003).

If the volatile cues and the presence of the prey are not uncoupled (*i.e.* attractive volatiles are only or mainly produced upon herbivory) then an adequate response of the crop to herbivory is most important. We have reviewed several studies in which the effect of environmental conditions on volatile production and herbivore attraction has been demonstrated and these results should be taken into account when designing future experiments. However, for a practical application, such as the optimisation of biological control, these factors may be important and it would be of interest to see whether environmental conditions that stimulate induced volatile formation actually improve biological control in a field situation. Another as yet completely ignored factor in the optimisation of biological control is the selection for genotypes with improved (faster, stronger) response. Our results on cucumber (Figure 4), and results with other plant species, demonstrate that genetic variation for this response is available. Further research should demonstrate the effectiveness and the best and easiest way to exploit this variation in breeding.

Finally, it is tempting to speculate about the opportunities that lie within molecular approaches. The knowledge about the molecular regulation of indirect defence volatile formation is rapidly increasing, a multitude of structural genes are already available, and we have shown ample evidence that expression of these structural genes in plants can lead to the production of the expected volatiles. Making this volatile production dependent on herbivore-feeding is only a small step away that will be facilitated by our hunt for herbivore-feeding induced gene expression and hence inducible promoters. There are several indications in the literature that even though the induced volatile blends are sometimes extremely complex mixtures, there are major contributors to the attractive effect of these blends, which increases the chances for success of a molecular approach. Such a molecular approach could include genetic modification or the use of genetic (gene) markers in the selection process. Finally, it is conceivable that changes in the (induced) volatile production in commercial crops could lead to the development of biological control packages in which biological control agents trained specifically for the modified crop are included. It will be exciting to see whether these approaches can lead to plants with altered (improved) predator behaviour and to crops with improved biological control.

ACKNOWLEDGEMENTS

We thank the Dutch Technology Foundation for their support (to IFK and LLPL) (STW project WPB.5479).

REFERENCES

Aharoni A; Giri A P; Deuerlein S; Appel M; Griepink F; Verstappen F W A; Verhoeven H A; Jongsma M A; Schwab W; Bouwmeester H J (2003a). Terpenoid metabolism in wild-type and transgenic *Arabidopsis thaliana* plants. *The Plant Cell* submitted.

Aharoni A; Giri A P; Verstappen F W A; Bertea C; Sevenier R; Zhongkui S; Jongsma M A; Schwab W; Bouwmeester H J (2003b). Molecular evolution of fruit flavor: Biosynthesis of terpenoids in wild and cultivated strawberry. *The Plant Cell* submitted.

Bouwmeester H J; Kodde J; Verstappen F W A; Altug I G; De Kraker J W; Wallaart T E (2002). Isolation and characterization of two germacrene A synthase cDNA clones from chicory. *Plant Physiology* **129,** 134-144.

Bouwmeester H J; Verstappen F W A; Posthumus M A; Dicke M (1999). Spider mite-induced $(3S)$-(E)-nerolidol synthase activity in cucumber and lima bean. The first dedicated step in acyclic C11-homoterpene biosynthesis. *Plant Physiology* **121,** 173-180.

Chiri A A; Legner E F (1983). Field applications of host-searching kairomones to enhance parasitization of the pink bollworm (Lepidoptera: Gelechiidae). *Journal of Economic Entomology* **76,** 254-255.

De Moraes C M; Lewis W J; Pare P W; Alborn H T; Tumlinson J H (1998). Herbivore-infested plants selectively attract parasitoids. *Nature London* **393,** 570-573.

Degenhardt J; Gershenzon J (2000). Demonstration and characterization of (*E*)-nerolidol synthase from maize: a herbivore-inducible terpene synthase participating in (*3E*)-4,8-dimethyl-1,3,7-nonatriene biosynthesis. *Planta* **210,** 815-822.

Degenhardt J; Gershenzon J; Baldwin I T; Kessler A (2003). Attracting friends to feast on foes: engineering terpene emission to make crop plants more attractive to herbivore enemies. *Current opinion in biotechnology* **14,** 169-176.

Dicke M; Gols R; Ludeking D; Posthumus M A (1999). Jasmonic acid and herbivory differentially induce carnivore-attracting plant volatiles in Lima bean plants. *Journal of Chemical Ecology* **25,** 1907-1922.

Dicke M; Hilker M (2003). Induced plant defences: from molecular biology to evolutionary ecology. *Basic and Applied Ecology* **4,** 3-14.

Dicke M; Sabelis M W; Takabayashi J; Bruin J; Posthumus M A (1990a). Plant strategies of manipulating predator-prey interactions through allelochemicals: prospects for application in pest control. *Proceedings of Semiochemicals and Pest Control - Prospects for New Applications*. Wageningen, the Netherlands, pp. 3091-3118.

Dicke M; Van Beek T A; Posthumus M A; Ben Dom N; Van Bokhoven H; De Groot A (1990b). Isolation and identification of volatile kairomone that affects acarine predator-prey interactions. Involvement of host plant in its production. *Journal of Chemical Ecology* **16,** 381-396.

Dicke M; Van der Maas K J; Takabayashi J; Vet L E M (1990c). Learning affects response to volatile allelochemicals by predatory mites. *Proceedings of 1st annual meeting of the section of Experimental and Applied Entomology of the Netherlands Entomological Society*. Utrecht, the Netherlands, pp. 31-36.

Dicke M; Van Poecke R M P; De Boer J G (2003). Inducible indirect defence of plants: from mechanisms to ecological functions. *Basic and Applied Ecology* **4,** 27-42.

Donath J; Boland W (1995). Biosynthesis of acyclic homoterpenes: enzyme selectivity and absolute configuration of the nerolidol precursor. *Phytochemistry* **39,** 785-790.

Donath J; Boland W; Golz A (1994). Biosynthesis of acyclic homoterpenes in higher plants parallels steroid hormone metabolism. *Journal of Plant Physiology* **143,** 473-478.

Du Y; Poppy G M; Powell W; Pickett J A; Wadhams L J; Woodcock C M; Du Y J (1998). Identification of semiochemicals released during aphid feeding that attract parasitoid *Aphidius ervi*. *Journal of Chemical Ecology* **24,** 1355-1368.

Gols R; Posthumus M A; Dicke M (1999). Jasmonic acid induces the production of gerbera volatiles that attract the biological control agent *Phytoseiulus persimilis*. *Entomologia Experimentalis et Applicata* **93,** 77-86.

Gouinguene S; Degen T; Turlings T C J (2001). Variability in herbivore-induced odour emissions among maize cultivars and their wild ancestors (teosinte). *Chemoecology* **11,** 9-16.

Gouinguene S P; Turlings T C J (2002). The effects of abiotic factors on induced volatile emissions in maize plants. *Plant Physiology* **129,** 1296-1307.

Hermsmeier D; Schittko U; Baldwin I T (2001). Molecular interactions between the specialist herbivore *Manduca sexta* (Lepidoptera, Sphingidae) and its natural host *Nicotiana attenuata*. I. Large-scale changes in the accumulation of growth- and defense-related plant mRNAs. *Plant Physiology* **125,** 683-700.

Hilker M; Meiners T (2002). Induction of plant responses to oviposition and feeding by herbivorous arthropods: a comparison. *Entomologia Experimentalis et Applicata* **104**, 181-192.

Kfir R; Overholt W A; Khan Z R; Polaszek A (2002). Biology and management of economically important lepidopteran cereal stem borers in Africa. *Annual Review of Entomology* **47**, 701-731.

Krips O E; Willems P E L; Gols R; Posthumus M A; Gort G; Dicke M (2001). Comparison of cultivars of ornamental crop *Gerbera jamesonii* on production of spider mite-induced volatiles, and their attractiveness to the predator *Phytoseiulus persimilis*. *Journal of Chemical Ecology* **27**, 1355-1372.

Loughrin J H; Manukian A; Heath R R; Turlings T C J; Tumlinson J H (1994). Diurnal cycle of emission of induced volatile terpenoids by herbivore-injured cotton plants. *Proceedings of the National Academy of Sciences of the United States of America* **91**, 11836-11840.

Lücker J; Bouwmeester H J; Schwab W; Blaas J; van der Plas L H W; Verhoeven H A (2001). Expression of *Clarkia S*-linalool synthase in transgenic petunia plants results in the accumulation of *S*-linalyl-beta-D-glucopyranoside. *Plant Journal* **27**, 315-324.

Lücker J; El Tamer M K; Schwab W; Verstappen F W A; van der Plas L H W; Bouwmeester H J; Verhoeven H A (2002). Monoterpene biosynthesis in lemon (*Citrus limon*) cDNA isolation and functional analysis of four monoterpene synthases. *European Journal of Biochemistry* **269**, 3160-3171.

Lücker J; Schwab W; van Hautum B; Blaas J; van der Plas L H W; Bouwmeester H J; Verhoeven H A (2003). Increased and altered fragrance of tobacco plants after metabolic engineering using three monoterpene synthases from lemon. *Plant Physiology* accepted.

Mercke P; Bengtsson M; Bouwmeester H J; Posthumus M A; Brodelius P E (2000). Molecular cloning, expression, and characterization of amorpha-4,11-diene synthase, a key enzyme of artemisinin biosynthesis in *Artemisia annua* L. *Archives of Biochemistry and Biophysics* **381**, 173-180.

Pare P W; Tumlinson J H (1997). De novo biosynthesis of volatiles induced by insect herbivory in cotton plants. *Plant Physiology* **114**, 1161-1167.

Price P W; Bouton C E; Gross P; McPheron B A; Thompson J N; Weis A E (1980). Interactions among three trophic levels: influence of plants on interactions between insect herbivores and natural enemies. *Annual Review of Ecology and Systematics* **11**, 41-65.

Reymond P; Weber H; Damond M; Farmer E E (2000). Differential gene expression in response to mechanical wounding and insect feeding in *Arabidopsis*. *Plant Cell* **12**, 707-719.

Sabelis M W; van der Baan H E (1983). Location of distant spider mite colonies by phytoseiid predators: demonstration of specific kairomones emitted by *Tetranychus urticae* and *Panonychus ulmi*. *Entomologia Experimentalis et Applicata* **33**, 303-314.

Schenk P M; Kazan K; Wilson I; Anderson J P; Richmond T; Somerville S C; Manners J M (2000). Coordinated plant defense responses in *Arabidopsis* revealed by microarray analysis. *Proceedings of the National Academy of Sciences of the United States of America* **97**, 11655-11660.

Takabayashi J; Dicke M; Posthumus M A (1991). Variation in composition of predator-attracting allelochemical emitted by herbivore-infested plants: relative influence of plant and herbivore. *Chemoecology* **2**, 1-6.

Takabayashi J; Dicke M; Posthumus M A (1994). Volatile herbivore-induced terpenoids in plant-mite interactions: variation caused by biotic and abiotic factors. *Journal of Chemical Ecology* **20,** 1329-1354.

Takabayashi J; Takahashi S; Dicke M; Posthumus M A (1995). Developmental stage of herbivore *Pseudaletia separata* affects production of herbivore-induced synomone by corn plants. *Journal of Chemical Ecology* **21,** 273-287.

Thaler J S (1999). Jasmonate-inducible plant defences cause increased parasitism of herbivores. *Nature London* **399,** 686-688.

Turlings T C J; Loughrin J H; McCall P J; Rose U S R; Lewis W J; Tumlinson J H (1995). How caterpillar-damaged plants protect themselves by attracting parasitic wasps. *Proceedings of the National Academy of Sciences of the United States of America* **92,** 4169-4174.

Turlings T C J; Tumlinson J H; Heath R R; Proveaux A T; Doolittle R E (1991). Isolation and identification of allelochemicals that attract the larval parasitoid, *Cotesia marginiventris* (Cresson), to the microhabitat of one of its hosts. *Journal of Chemical Ecology* **17,** 2235-2251.

Turlings T C J; Tumlinson J H; Lewis W J (1990). Exploitation of herbivore-induced plant odors by host-seeking parasitic wasps. *Science Washington* **250,** 1251-1253.

Van den Boom C E M; Van Beek T A; Dicke M (2002). Attraction of *Phytoseiulus persimilis* (Acari: Phytoseiidae) towards volatiles from various *Tetranychus urticae*-infested plant species. *Bulletin of Entomological Research* **92,** 539-546.

Van Lenteren J C (2000) Success in biological control of arthropods by augmentation of natural enemies. In: *Biological Control: Measures of Success*, eds G Gurr & S Wratten, pp. 77-103. Kluwer Academic Publishers: Dordrecht.

Van Poecke R M P; Dicke M (2002). Induced parasitoid attraction by *Arabidopsis thaliana*: involvement of the octadecanoid and the salicylic acid pathway. *Journal of Experimental Botany* **53,** 1793-1799.

Van Poecke R M P; Posthumus M A; Dicke M (2001). Herbivore-induced volatile production by *Arabidopsis thaliana* leads to attraction of the parasitoid *Cotesia rubecula*: chemical, behavioral, and gene-expression analysis. *Journal of Chemical Ecology* **27,** 1911-1928.

Van Poecke R M P; Roosjen M; Pumarino L; Dicke M (2003). Attraction of the specialist *Cotesia rubecula* to *Arabidopsis thaliana* infested by host or non-host herbivores. *Entomologia Experimentalis et Applicata* **107,** 229-236.

Wallaart T E; Bouwmeester H J; Hille J; Poppinga L; Maijers N C A (2001). Amorpha-4,11-diene synthase: cloning and functional expression of a key enzyme in the biosynthetic pathway of the novel antimalarial drug artemisinin. *Planta* **212,** 460-465.

Wegener R; Schulz S; Meiners T; Hadwich K; Hilker M (2001). Analysis of volatiles induced by oviposition of elm leaf beetle *Xanthogaleruca luteola* on *Ulmus minor*. *Journal of Chemical Ecology* **27,** 499-515.

Plant activation of barley by intercropped conspecifics and weeds: allelobiosis

J Pettersson, V Ninkovic, R Glinwood
Department of Entomology, Box 7044, SE-750 07 Uppsala, Sweden
Email: jan.pettersson@entom.slu.se

ABSTRACT

Experiments with components of a barley cropping system are summarised in a tritrophic context with reference to allelochemical communication between undamaged plants. The results are discussed with regards to different mechanistic explanations. With reference to the different roles of allelochemicals in plant/plant communication in a "winner-loser" perspective, it is suggested that the term "allelobiosis" is used to denote this type of interaction.

INTRODUCTION

The impression of peaceful coexistence in a eutrophic flowering meadow might be an anthropomorphic misinterpretation of the real situation. Even if attacks by herbivores are common, it is fair to assume that the most serious biotic challenge for an individual plant is sharing and competing for space and resources with other plants. Thus the meadow is a battlefield upon which all kinds of weaponry are used to gain ecological advantages, and similarities in resource patterns between plant individuals intensifies the struggle. Many aspects of this fight for survival and ecological success have been studied thoroughly and are described and discussed in most standard ecological textbooks.

Even though the existence of plant/plant competition is mentioned in ancient Greek literature (Plinius first century A.D.), an important step towards a mechanistic understanding was taken when it was shown that allelochemicals could assist in mediating plant dominance (allelopathy sensu Molisch 1937). Since then the literature on this topic has grown rapidly and there are several known examples of the potential competitive value for a plant individual of emitting allelopathically active semiochemicals. Effects of the emitted substances can be manifested as profound changes in the physiology and development of neighbouring plants (Rice 1984). Classic examples of chemo-dominance are the sage bush and the eucalyptus (Harborne 1993), and the literature on this and related topics is vast. Since investigations on chemical plant/plant communication are usually focussed on the rhizosphere and on non volatile soil borne substances (for a review see Rice 1984), it is not always obvious whether the substances are produced by the plants themselves – true exudates - or by associated micro-organisms in the rhizosphere.

The term "allelopathy" was originally formulated to denote plant/plant communication as a means by which one plant individual can suppress other plants. However, we hypothesize that it may, in the long run, be favourable for a "listening plant" individual to be able to detect the presence of its neighbours. For example, elegant studies have shown that when herbivores attack a plant, the wound responses in this individual can promote reduced herbivore acceptance of neighbouring plants (Bruin *et al.*, 1995; Bruin & Dicke, 2001; Farmer 2001) and promote searching behaviour of natural enemies of the herbivores (Dicke *et al.* 1999). To what extent similar effects can occur also between undamaged plants is still an open question. However, it is obvious that chemical plant/plant communication can favour both the emitting plant and the receiving plant.

There is some justification in speculating that allelobiotic plant interactions can affect susceptibility to herbivores. In many respects plant responses to different types of biotic stress are reasonably uniform (Lambers *et al.* 1998). For example, volatile messenger substances emitted by *Artemisia* have been shown to promote, via aerial allelopathy, induced resistance to herbivores (Farmer & Ryan 1990), supporting the thoughts on similarities between plant/plant and herbivore-induced stress.

The classical view of allelopathy as a term to denote plant-plant interactions via semiochemicals may be misleading. It implies that a plant individual emitting allelobiotically active substances benefits by doing so if it reduces competition with other individuals for available resources. In principle, this is a form of chemical warfare and the winner is the emitter of the active substances. Under certain conditions however, the winning concept may derive from perceiving stimuli from a neighbouring plant, if those stimuli induce favourable modifications in growth patterns, such as a reinforced water uptake capacity through a promoted root growth capacity as reported by Ninkovic (2003). Therefore we suggest using the term "allelobiosis" which is neutral with regards to the winner-loser perspective. This term would also be more appropriate to cover the situation in which volatiles from a herbivore-attacked plant promote defence in a neighbouring plant.

Superficially, the structure of agricultural monocultures invites competition for the same set of resources by plants with very similar resource need profiles in dense stands. However, human screening and breeding efforts have modified what may have been the original characteristics of the plants, and to what extent allelobiotically based mechanisms are still important in these cropping systems is unknown. Although mixed cropping is a traditional, and often successful, strategy to increase plant protection, data on the effects of allelobiosis on higher trophic levels are lacking (Vandermeer 1992).

Allelobiotic mechanisms operate on a time scale set by plant phenology, and herbivores closely adapted to this are likely to be more affected than others. Aphids are phloem feeders with a sophisticated capacity for host plant discrimination and feeding site evaluation (Dixon 1998; Pickett *et al.,* 1992). The importance of plant volatiles in the settling process, and of food quality in terms of free amino acids and secondary metabolites have been demonstrated (Pickett *et al.* 1992; Hardie *et al.* 1994; Pettersson *et al.* 1994; Pettersson *et al.* 1996). Thus aphids may be a group of herbivores likely to respond to allelobiotically-induced changes in host plant traits such as phloem transport and the pattern of emitted volatiles.

In this presentation we summarise the results of experiments in which a barley crop (*Hordeum vulgare*) is used as a model system for studies of tritrophic effects promoted by allelobiosis. We summarise the results from a series of experiments based on the common conditions in a barley crop in central Sweden. The overall objective is to contribute to a general understanding of how allelobiotic mechanisms can have effects spanning different tritrophic levels of the model system. Hypothetically these mechanisms may form a link between botanical and faunistic biodiversity, and contribute to the development of new approaches to plant protection.

MATERIAL AND METHODS

Four commercial barley cultivars (Frida, Alva, Hulda and Kara) were chosen from field experiments on intercropping to control powdery mildew (Wiik 1987). These genotypes are comparable, with regards to agronomic characters, but differ with respect to genes for resistance to powdery mildew. No differences with regards to aphid responses in olfactometer, preference or settling tests are apparent (Pettersson *et al.*, 1999; Ninkovic 2002).

Barley plants were exposed individually to air that had passed over another plant in a twin cage system with a one-way-airflow-system (Pettersson *et al.*, 1999) (Figure 1). Each cage unit consisted of two chambers and air passed first through one of these and then through the second and out via a vacuum tank. The chamber units could also be rearranged to make exposures to root exudates. The treatments were randomly distributed and each twin unit was regarded as a replicate.

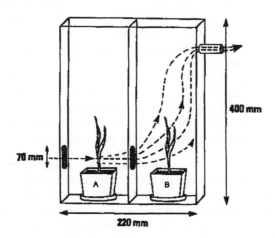

Figure 1. Twin cage system.

The herbivore chosen for the experiments was the bird cherry-oat aphid, *Rhopalosiphum padi* (L.), a key pest in spring-sown cereals. It is a host-alternating aphid that is monophagous on its winter host plant, *Prunus padus* L. but has a broad range of grasses as summer hosts (Wiktelius *et al.*, 1990). A common predator of *R.. padi*, the seven spotted ladybird *Coccinella septempunctata* L. was chosen to represent the third trophic level.

Plant responses to treatments were evaluated through estimates of changes in biomass allocation (Ninkovic 2003) and changes in leaf temperature, measured with an infrared camera (Pettersson *et al.*, 1999).

The following methods were used to evaluate aphid responses to plant treatment

1. preference in host plant choice experiments – initial laboratory experiments (Pettersson *et al.* 1999)

2. settling measured in a no choice test – in field and laboratory experiments (Ninkovic *et al.* 2002)
3. olfactometer responses (Ninkovic 2002; Glinwood *et al.* 2003;).

Ladybird responses were recorded from field observations and olfactometer experiments (Ninkovic *et al.*, 2001; Ninkovic & Pettersson 2003).

RESULTS AND DISCUSSION

Barley/barley allelobiosis

Changes in biomass allocation and leaf temperature. In specific cultivar combinations, plants exposed to volatiles from another cultivar allocated more biomass to roots compared with plants exposed to air from the same cultivar, or to clean air (Ninkovic 2003). There were no significant changes in relative growth rate (RGR, increase in biomass per unit biomass per unit time) and unit leaf ratio (ULR, increase in biomass per unit time and leaf area) but there was a significant increase in specific leaf area (SLA, leaf area per leaf dry weight). Thus allelobiotic interaction between two barley cultivars may not affect total biomass production, but rather alters biomass allocation in individual plants. This is in line with previous studies (Aerst *et al.*, 1991; Boot & Den Duddelden, 1990) showing that reduced biomass allocation to leaves can be compensated for by high SLA. The observed influence of one cultivar on another probably has implications for competition. More roots may be of advantage in dry situations, increasing stress tolerance. Obviously, such variation would increase the phenotypic stability of mixtures and thus be of competitive advantage.

Effects of allelobiosis on plant leaf temperature were measured by infrared imaging (Pettersson *et al.*, 1999). Comparisons were made between plants exposed to air passed over (i) a plant of a different genotype (ii) a plant of the same genotype (self-induced control) and (iii) no plant at all (clean air control). Significant decreases in temperature were recorded in response to air passed over a different genotype in eight of 12 cultivar combinations when compared to clean air controls. When compared to self induced controls, leaf temperature effects were found in four combinations. Significant self-inducing effects were found in two of four tested cultivars.

Effects of allelobiosis between barley genotypes on aphid olfactory responses, preferences and settling in laboratory bioassays

Preference test. Effects on aphid host plant preference were examined in a choice test with treated plants (exposure period 6 days) compared to one of two types of control treatment: (i) self inducing control, (ii) non self inducing control. Significant reduction of aphid preference was found in seven of the 16 possible combinations (Pettersson *et al.*, 1999), including the combination Alva-Kara (Figure 2). It is also interesting to note that plant individuals of two genotypes also showed a change with regards to aphid response when exposed to volatiles from the same cultivar. The results of the study indicate that this phenomenon is genotype specific, not only for responding cultivars but for the inducing cultivar.

Olfactometry Aphids did not show any intrinsic preference or aversion for any of the four tested cultivars, based on the inherent odour composition of unexposed plants. Two series of olfactometer tests were made with exposed plants, one in which the inducing plants were retained as part of the overall odour stimulus, and one in which they were removed. This was to test whether aphids responded to allelobiosis-induced changes in the exposed plant or merely to an increased complexity of volatiles in the mixture. The aphid visiting frequencies were significantly lower in arm zones with volatiles from cv Kara exposed to cvs. Alva or Frida when the inducing plants were retained (Figure 3). With the inducing plants removed, the response to the Frida-Kara combination disappeared (Figure 3). This indicates that exposure to volatiles from another cultivar may induce a systemic change in the volatile profile of a responding cultivar.

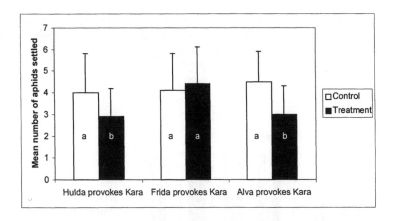

Figure 2.   Changes of aphid settling in the preference test after exposure of one cultivar to another.

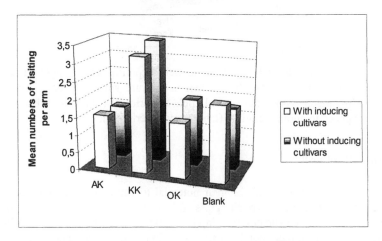

Figure 3. Olfactometer data for aphid responses. Change in aphid plant attraction of cv. Kara after exposure to cv. Alva. AK is a cultivar combination where cv. Kara was exposed to cv. Alva. KK is a cultivar combination where cv. Kara was exposed to the same cultivar (self-induced control). OK is a combination where Kara was exposed to no plant volatiles (clean air control).

Field experiments. All cultivars were sown in pair wise combinations in field plots under conditions i dentical t o c ommon a gricultural m ethods. C areful w eeding was d one b y h and. Aphid response to treated plants was estimated with a no-choice settling test when the plants were at the two leaf stage. Ten aphids were released in a clear plastic tube placed over the youngest leaf of the barley plants in the field plots. The number of aphids settling on the leaf was recorded after two hours and used as an estimate of settling. This estimate of the aphid response was used to make statistical comparisons. The same test of aphid settling responses was a pplied t o a s et o f p lant g enotype c ombinations u sing t he t win c age sy stem f or p lant exposure.

When aphid responses in plots with only one c ultivar were c ompared with plots with two cultivars, significant differences were found in three of the eight possible combinations. No difference was found between plots with one cultivar (Figure 4).

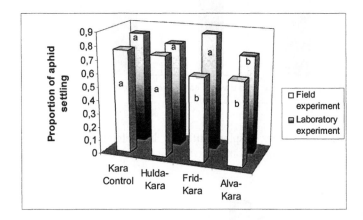

Figure 4. Settling data from laboratory and field experiments. Changes in aphid settling on cv. Kara when grown in mixture with another cultivar, in comparison with a pure stand (field experiment), and when Kara was exposed to another cultivar (laboratory experiment).

Weed-barley allelobiosis

Some common weeds were tested for their potential to cause, via allelobiosis, changes in aphid acceptance of barley. Couch grass (*Elytrigia repens*) is known to produce allelobiotically-active root exudates (Hagin, 1989; Hagin & Bobnick, 1991). When barley plants were exposed to either root leachates from living *E. repens* plants, or to solutions containing known *E. repens* root exudates, settling by *R. padi* was significantly reduced (Glinwood *et al.*, 2003) (Figure 5). Barley plants exposed to root exudates also became less attractive then unexposed plants in an olfactometer, suggesting that allelobiosis changed the volatile profile. Thistles in the genus *Cirsium* are also known to exert allelobiotic effects on other plants (Kazinczi *et al.*, 2001). Exposure of barley to root leachates from *Cirsium vulgare* or *C. arvense* did not affect aphid settling, however when plants were e xposed to volatiles from either thistle species, settling by *R. padi* and *S. avenae* was significantly reduced (Glinwood *et al*, unpublished). *Cirsium*-exposed plants were also less attractive than unexposed plants to aphids in an olfactometer.

A further weed species, *Stellaria media*, exerted similar allelobiotic effects on aphid acceptance of barley via its root leachates but not via volatiles (Fig 5). However, the common aggressive stinging nettle, *Urtica dioica*, did not affect aphid responses to barley after exposure to either root leachates or volatiles (Figure 5). These results indicate that the expected effects of plant-plant allelobiosis on herbivores is likely to be dependent upon the specific combinations of plant species, and thus difficult to predict without experimental study.

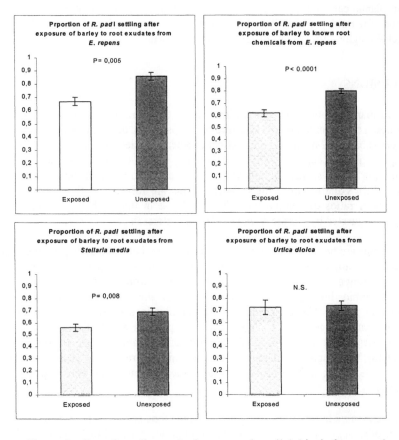

Figure 5.   *R. padi* settling on barley exposed to allelobiosis from weeds.

Allelobiosis and natural enemies

Field observations.   Observations in a barley field showed that *C. septempunctata* was significantly aggregated to patches with *Elytrigia repens* and *Cirsium vulgare* although no obvious food resource such as pollen or aphids or other small prey insects were abundant (Ninkovic & Pettersson 2003).

Olfactometry. In olfactometer experiments adult ladybirds showed no preference for either of the three plant species. However, a significant preference was shown for a mixture of barley odour together with each of the two weeds. The effect on barley exposed to volatiles from *E. repens* and *C. arvense* differed in that barley plants exposed to *C. arvense* remained attractive when the weed was taken away whereas those exposed to *E. repens* lost their attractiveness. This indicates that the positive effect of the barley/*E. repens* combination may merely be an effect of mixed volatiles, whereas the barley/*C. arvense* mixture is likely to represent a more complex mechanism involving allelobiosis.

Several experimental studies have shown how natural enemies respond to volatiles from plants attacked by herbivores. There is also convincing evidence showing that volatiles from attacked plants can induce responses in neighbouring plants that encourage searching behaviour of natural enemies. To what extent the volatile profile of the attacked plants and the affected neighbouring plants differ is still not known.

CONCLUSIONS

When two plant genotypes or species are mixed, there are at least three possible ways to explain how semiochemicals can interfere with host plant discrimination by herbivores. (i) Messenger substances from one plant affect another via allelobiosis, and cause changes that affect aphid plant acceptance. (ii) Behaviourally active components from one plant are enriched in, or on the surface of, an exposed plant and then released thus affecting herbivore responses. (iii) Volatiles from the different plants are mixed and this mixture offers new components or ratios of components. This would be in line with the concept of olfactory masking as suggested by Hardie *et al.* (1994) and Pettersson *et al.* (1994)

Further studies are necessary to clarify the mechanisms, but the results presented support the hypothesis that allelobiosis influences aphid host plant acceptance. The experiments with barley and known allelobiotic messenger substances from *E .repens* show a significant change in aphid host plant responses, although the substances are not themselves behaviourally active. The experiments with combinations of barley genotypes show that allelobiosis causes significant changes in growth patterns and leaf temperatures (Ninkovic 2003a; Pettersson *et al* 1999), and that the effects are limited to specific genotype combinations. Although no inherent differences in the preference of aphids to unexposed cultivars were found, differences were found after the cultivars were exposed to volatile allelobiosis.

Ladybird responses to volatiles from plant combinations appear to be complex. Olfactometer responses of *C. septempunctata* to volatiles from barley exposed to *E. repens* and *C. arvense* indicated attraction. However, when the weed plants were removed from the odour stimulus, barley plants exposed to *C. arvense* remained attractive while those exposed to *E. repens* plants lost their attractiveness. This indicates that the positive effect of the barley/*E. repens* combination is merely an effect of mixed volatiles (cf. iii above) while with the barley/*C. arvense* mixture may constitute a more complex mechanism in line with type *i)* or *ii)* as described above.

From an applied point of view, the findings contribute to two plant protection approaches. The first is an increased understanding of the mechanisms potentially active in different systems for intercropping and mixed cropping. Obviously, the positive effects of these cropping strategies are a combination of several mechanisms, of which allelobiosis has been less recognised until now. Increased knowledge should contribute to the search for more effective combinations of plants. The second contribution will be to increase our understanding of the extent to which active substances can be used to manipulate induced resistance in plants. Further knowledge might also favour breeding for cultivars that combine high yield with a capacity to allocate resources depending on prevailing conditions.

The results presented deal with experiments in which two plant species or genotypes have been combined. The extent to which the effects shown operate in natural plant communities is still an open question. If they do, it would be a contribution to our understanding of how plant community composition contributes to entomological diversity via allelobiosis.

REFERENCES

Aerts R; Boot R G A; Van der Aart P J M (1991). The relation between above- and below-ground biomass allocation patterns and competitive ability. *Oecologia* **87**, 551-559.

Boot R G A; Den-Dubbelden K C (1990). Effects of nitrogen supply on growth allocation and gas exchange characteristics of two perennial grasses from inland dunes. *Oecologia* **85**, 115-121.

Bruin J; Dicke M (2001). Chemical information transfer between wounded and unwouded plants: backing up future. *Biochemical Systematics and Ecology* **29**, 1103-1113.

Bruin J; Sabelis M W; Dicke M (1995). Do plants tap SOS signals from their infested neighbours? *Trends in Ecology and Evolution* **10**, 167-170.

Dicke M (1999). Are herbivore-induced plant volatiles reliable indicators of herbivore identity to foraging carnivorous arthropods? *Entomologia Experimentalis et Applicata* **91**, 131-142.

Dixon A F G (1998). Aphid ecology. 2nd edition. Chapman & Hall: London.

Farmer E E (2001). Surface-to -air signals. *Nature* **411**, 854-856.

Farmer E E; Ryan C A (1990). Interplant communication: Airborne methyl jasmonate induces synthesis of proteinase inhibitors in plant leaves. *Proceedings of the National Academy of Sciences of the United States of America USA* **87**, 7713-7716.

Glinwood RT; Pettersson J; Ninkovic V; Ahmed E; Birkett M; Pickett J A (2003). Change in acceptability of barley plants to aphids after exposure to allelochemicals from couch-grass (Elytrigia repens). *Journal of Chemical Ecology* **29**, 259-272

Hagin R D (1989). Isolation and identification of 5-hydroxyindoleacetic acid and 5-hydroxytryptophan, major allelopathic aglycons in quackgrass (Agropyron repens, L. Beauv.). *Journal of Agricultural Food Chemistry* **37**, 1143-1149.

Hagin R D; Bobnick S J (1991). Isolation and indentification of a slug-specific molluscicide from quackgrass (Agropyron repens, L. Beauv.). *Journal of Agricultural Food Chemistry* **39**, 192-196.

Harborne J B (1993). *Introduction to Ecological Biochemistry*. 4th edition. Academic press: London.

Hardie J; Isaacs R; Pickett J A; Wadhams L J; Woodcock C M (1994). Methyl salicylate and (-)-(1R,5S)-myrtenal are plant-derived repellents for black bean aphid, *Aphis fabae* Scop. (Homoptera:Aphididae). *Journal of Chemical Ecology* **20**, 2847-2855.

Kazinczi G; Beres I; Narwal S S (2001). Allelopathic plants. 1. Canada thistle (*Cirsium arvense* (L.) Scop.). *Allelopathy Journal* **8**, 29-40.

Lambers H; Chapin F S; Pons T L (1998). Plant Physiological Ecology. Springer-Verlag: New York.

Molisch H (1937). Der Einfluss einer Planze auf die andere Allelopathie. Verlag von Gustav Fischer, Jena, Germany.

Ninkovic V (2003). Volatile communication between barley plants affects biomass allocation. *Journal of Experimental Botany* **54**, 1931-1939.

Ninkovic V (2002). Plant volatiles mediate tritrophic interactions - barley aphids and ladybirds. *PhD Thesis, Swedish University of Agricultural Sciences*, Uppsala, Sweden.

Ninkovic V; Pettersson J (2003). Searching behaviour of sevenspotted ladybird, *Coccinella septempunctata* – effects of plant-plant odour interaction. *OIKOS* **100**, 65-70.

Ninkovic V; Al Albasi A; Pettersson J (2001). The influence of aphid-induced plants volatiles on ladybird beetle searching. *Biological Control* **21**, 191-195.

Ninkovic V; Olsson U; Pettersson J (2002). Mixing barley cultivars affects aphid host plant acceptance in field experiments. *Entomologia Experimentalis at Applicata* **102**, 177-182.

Pettersson J; Ninkovic V; Ahmed E (1999). Volatiles from different barley cultivars affect aphid acceptance of neighbouring plants. *Acta Agriculture Scandinavica Section B, Plant and Soil* **49**, 152-157.

Pettersson J; Quiroz A; Fahad A E (1996). Aphid antixenosis mediated by volatiles in cereals. *Acta Agriculturae Scandinavica. Section B, Soil and Plant Science* **49**, 152-157.

Pettersson J; Pickett J A; Pye B J; Quiroz A; Smart L E; Wadhams L J; Woodcock C M (1994). Winter host component reduces colonization of summer hosts by the bird cherry-oat aphid, *Rhopalosipum padi* (L.). and other aphids in cereal fields. *Journal of Chemical Ecology* **20**, 2565-2574.

Pickett J A; Wadhams L J; Woodcock C M; Hardie J (1992). The chemical ecology of aphids. *Annual Review of Entomology* **37**, 67-90.

Plinus Secundus, C. A.D. 1. *Natural History*, 10 vols (Engl. Transl. By H. Rackam, W.H.S. Jones & D.E. Eichholz), pp. 1938-1963. Harvard University Press: Cambridge, Massachusetts, UK.

Rice E L (1984). *Allelopathy*. Academic press INC: Orlando, Florida, USA.

Vandermeer J (1992). *The ecology of intercropping*. 2nedition. Cambridge University Press: Cambridge, UK.

Wiik L (1987). Cultivars of spring barley and powdery mildew (*Erysiphe graminis* f. sp. hordei) in Sweden. In: *Integrated Control of Cereal Mildews*, eds. E Limpert & M S Wolfe, Volume 22, pp. 103-112. Martinus Nijhoff: Dordrecht, The Netherlands.

Wiktelius S; Weibull J; Pettersson J (1990). Aphid host plant ecology: the bird cherry-oat aphid as a model. In: *Aphid-plant Genotype Interactions*, eds. R K Campbell & R D Eikenbary, pp. 21-36. Elsevier: Amsterdam, The Netherlands.

Plant-fungal interactions mediated by volatile signals

J A Lucas

Plant-Pathogen Interactions Division,Rothamsted Research, Harpenden, Herts, AL5 2JQ,UK
Email: john.lucas@bbsrc.ac.uk

ABSTRACT

Previous exposure of plants to attack by pests or pathogens can alter the response of such plants to subsequent challenge. The molecular basis of this induced resistance is now well documented and the signal networks are being dissected through the analysis of mutants in plant genetic models such as *Arabidopsis*. Circumstantial evidence is accumulating that plants neighbouring those subject to attack or infection may also be altered in response, implicating the involvement of volatile signals. Experimental work to test the hypothesis that volatile emissions from plants infected by pathogens can induce resistance in adjacent plants, using barley seedlings and the necrotrophic fungi *Rhynchosporium* and *Pyrenophora,* is described. Practical exploitation of this phenomenon in crop protection, for instance through chemical elicitors or the use of responsive crop genotypes in variety mixtures, will depend upon identification of the key signals involved and a better understanding of the molecular and physiological basis of the induced resistance.

INTRODUCTION

Higher plants have evolved a range of surveillance and defence systems that enable them to recognise and respond to pests and potentially pathogenic organisms. Recent molecular analyses have shown that defence genes may be expressed locally in the proximity of pathogen challenge as well as in tissues remote from the initial challenge. The involvement of a complex of signalling networks is implicated by genetic and molecular analyses (Dangl & Jones, 2001; Asai *et al.*, 2002). Identification of the key signals involved in the induction and regulation of defence networks is a major objective of current research to elucidate the mechanisms by which plants resist potential pathogens.

Plants exposed to stress, including attack by herbivorous insect or mites, emit a range of volatile chemicals (Koch *et al.*,1999). Some of these volatiles are known to act as signals that either repel the herbivore or attract natural predators of the pest. Such stress signals can also switch on so-called defence genes, the products of which have been implicated in plant resistance to both pests and pathogens (Pickett & Poppy, 2001). There is also the possibility that volatile stress signals might induce similar responses in neighbouring plants not yet exposed to attack (Farmer, 2001). To date, most of the experimental evidence concerns the effects of plant volatiles on insect pests. Much less is known about potential effects on plant pathogenic microorganisms.

Two main induced defence pathways have been identified in plants, in which either salicylic acid (systemic acquired resistance: SAR) or jasmonic acid and ethylene (induced systemic resistance: ISR) play key roles. These compounds are anticipated to serve as endogenous signals, although ethylene has long been recognised as a volatile hormone with potential effects on plant disease. Recent work has confirmed this, for instance in tomato exposed to an ethylene pre-treatment the expression of several pathogenesis-related (PR) protein genes was induced, and resistance to the necrotrophic pathogen *Botrytis cinerea* was increased (Diaz *et al.*, 2002). Volatile analogues of other signal molecules have also been implicated in the induction of plant defence. In tobacco plants forming local lesions in response to infection by tobacco mosaic virus, the emission of gaseous methyl salicylate was suggested to be at levels sufficient to induce PR proteins and to increase resistance in nearby healthy plants (Shulaev *et al.*, 1997). Methyl salicylate has also been detected in volatile samples from peanut plants infected with the white mould fungus *Sclerotium rolfisii* (Cardoza *et al.*, 2002). In this case direct effects of volatile compounds on the growth of the pathogen were reported.

Circumstantial e vidence t hat i nteractions b etween i nfected and h ealthy p lants m ediated b y external signals might influence resistance to pathogens comes from studies on crop variety mixtures in which the levels of disease observed in the mixture are often lower than would be expected from the resistance or susceptibility of the individual component genotypes. One mechanism might be the induction of resistance in genetically susceptible genotypes by volatile signals emitted from nearby infected plants. Testing this hypothesis under field conditions is problematical in the absence of information on the identity of the likely signal molecules and their effects on host-pathogen interactions at defined physiologically-active concentrations.

A MODEL SYSTEM

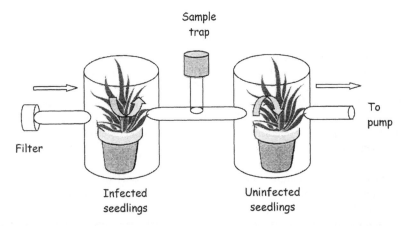

Figure 1. Two compartment system for testing emission and effect of volatile compounds.

We established a model system using commercial cultivars of barley (*Hordeum vulgare*) and two foliar fungal pathogens, leaf scald (*Rhynchosporium secalis*) and net blotch (*Pyrenophora teres*). Air from chambers containing susceptible barley seedlings inoculated with the pathogen was transferred to uninfected seedlings in a second chamber (Figure 1). The barley seedlings exposed in this way were then inoculated with spores of the same pathogen and disease severity on individual leaves scored after 7 and 14 days. Control plants were exposed to air from uninfected seedlings. Figure 2 shows disease severity data for leaf scald 14 days after inoculation. Disease severity on leaf 3 (the youngest leaf at the time of exposure) was reduced by around 50% compared with plants exposed to the air from healthy control seedlings. Furthermore, in exposed plants the onset of leaf scald symptom expression was also delayed by 48 hours. A similar reduction in disease severity was observed in barley plants inoculated with *P. teres* and scored at 7 days. These results suggest that volatile compounds emitted by infected barley plants c an trigger c hanges in uninfected plants that induce or enhance resistance to subsequent pathogen attack.

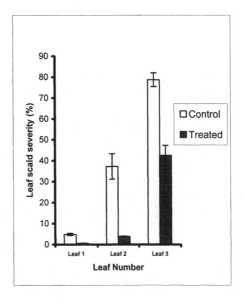

Figure 2. *Rhynchosporium* disease severity in control and treated barley seedlings 14 days after inoculation.

The volatile profiles of headspace samples from infected plants were analysed by high-resolution gas chromatogaphy-coupled mass spectroscopy (GC/MS) (Birkett *et al.*, 2000). Known signal molecules such as methyl jasmonate and methyl salicylate were at the limits of detection.

DISCUSSION

Communication b etween p lants mediated b y v olatile s ignals i s k nown t o affect r esistance t o herbivorous insects, but effects on pathogens including fungi are less well documented. Volatiles released following wounding have been shown to induce changes in tobacco plants that reduce damage by insects under field conditions (Karban *et al.*, 2000). Petterson *et al.* (1999) demonstrated that volatiles from barley seedlings may affect aphid acceptance of neighbouring exposed plants. In the present experiments changes in leaf reaction type to two necrotrophic barley pathogens were observed after exposure to atmospheres from compartments containing diseased plants. The identity and activity of the potential signal(s) involved is not yet known. Further work is also required to establish whether plant to plant communication might be one mechanism underlying the enhanced resistance of mixtures of crop genotypes to pathogens, including barley leaf scald (Newton *et al.* 1997).

ACKNOWLEDGEMENTS

I thank Olu Latunde-Dada for constructive input to this paper. Rothamsted Research receives grant-aided support from the Biotechnology and Biological Science Research Council of the UK.

REFERENCES

Asai, T; Tena, G; Potnikova, J; Willman, M R; Chiu, W L; Gomez-Gomez, L; Boller, T; Ausubel, F M; Sheen J (2002) MAP kinase signalling in *Arabidopsis* innate immunity. *Nature* **415**, 977-983.

Birkett, M A; Campbell, C A M; Chamberlain, K; Guerrieri, E; Hick, A J; Martin, J L; Matthes, M; Napier, J A; Pettersson, J; Pickett, J A; Poppy, G M; Pow, E M; Pye, B. J., Smart, L E; Wadhams, G H; Wadhams, L J; Woodcock, C M (2000). New roles for cis-jasmone as an insect semiochemical and in plant defense. *Proceedings National Academy of Sciences USA* **97**, 9329-9334.

Cardoza, Y J; Alborn, H T; Tumlinson, J H (2002). In vivo volatile emissions from peanut plants induced by simultaneous fungal infection and insect damage. *Journal of Chemical Ecology* **28**, 161-174.

Dangl, J L; Jones,J D G (2001).Plant pathogens and integrated defence responses to infection. *Nature* **411**, 826-833.

Diaz, J; ten Have, A; van Kan, J A L (2002) The role of ethylene and wound signalling in reistance of tomato to *Botrytis cinerea*. *Plant Physiology* **129**, 1341-1351.

Farmer, E E (2001). Surface to air signals. *Nature* **411**, 854-856.

Karban, R; Baldwin, I T; Baxter, K J; Laue, G; Felton, G W (2000). Communication between plants; induced resistance in wild tobacco plants following clipping of neighboring sagebrush. *Oecologia* **125**, 66-71.

Koch, T; Krumm, T; Jung, V; Engelberth, J; Boland, W (1999). Differential induction of plant volatile biosynthesis in the lima bean by early and late intermediates of the octadecanoid-signaling pathway. *Plant Physiology* **121**, 153-162.

Newton, A C; Ellis, R P; Hackett, C A; Guy, DC (1997) The effect of component number on *Rhynchosporium secalis* infection and yield in mixtures of winter barley cultivars. *Plant Pathology* **45**, 930-938.

Pettersson, J; Ninkovic, V; Ahmed, E (1999). Volatiles from different barley cultivars affect aphid acceptance of neighbouring plants. *Acta Agriculturae Scandinavica* **49**, 152-157.

Pickett, J A; Poppy, G (2001) Switching on plant genes by external chemical signals. *Trends in Plant Science* **6**, 137-139.

Shulaev, V; Silverman, P; Raskin, I (1997). Airborne signalling by meythyl jasmonate in plant pathogen resistance. *Nature* **385**, 718-721.

Registration opportunities for natural products versus synthetic plant stress signals (or plant activators) for crop protection

T E Tooby
JSC International Ltd, Osborne House, 20 Victoria Avenue, Harrogate, HG1 5QY, UK
Email: Terry.Tooby@jsci.co.uk

ABSTRACT

Policies to reduce the use of plant protection products are being developed in many Member States of the EU and elsewhere in the world. To meet such objectives, viable low risk alternative products need to be developed and authorised. Until now the regulatory procedures based on synthetic chemical active substances have been regarded as a barrier to the commercialisation of alternative products. The EU is now taking steps to encourage the development of natural plant extracts by proposing reduced data requirements.

INTRODUCTION

To gain any insight into the often difficult and constantly changing European regulatory requirements, an understanding of both the procedures and the wider political issues are necessary. Over the last 10 years, since the implementation of Council Directive 91/414/EEC (Council Directive, 1991), policies have been developed at both EU and Member State level in response to perceived and real risks both to the environment and to humans through the food chain. Initiatives such as the 6th Environment Action Programme (Commission Decision, 2002), the Precautionary Principle (Commission Communication, 2000) and the setting up of the European Food Safety Authority (Commission Regulation, 2002a) have wide reaching implications for the use and regulation of all plant protection products. Unfortunately they may not always keep pace with the rapidly developing sectors of science and technology and the development of plant protection by plant extracts seems a far cry from the situation found over a decade ago which prompted the need for EU-wide legislation.

Data requirements necessarily reflect the political climate of the day and much has evolved since the establishment of the regulatory framework for plant protection products. The European Commission has indicated that the Directive will have to be amended to reflect the current policies. The main issues were included in a report submitted to the European Parliament in 2001 (SANCO, 2001a). These were expanded and discussed with stakeholders at a meeting held in Corfu in 2002 (SANCO, 2002). Not all stakeholders attending this meeting supported the continued use of plant protection products on the current scale. For example, PAN Europe presented a position paper on behalf of a number of NGOs on Pesticide Use Reduction in Europe (PURE) (PAN, 2002). This paper outlined the position over the need, as they saw it, for mandatory Community-wide targets and a clear timetable for achieving the reduction in use of plant protection products throughout Europe.

Regulatory science and risk assessment practices also are evolving continuously. Data requirements together with risk assessment guidelines have been developed globally and have added hugely to the burden of the notifier. When drafting legislation there has always been a tendency to attempt to cover all regulatory eventualities. So the lists of data requirements have increased alarmingly and are based almost exclusively on synthetic chemical active substances and extreme worst-case scenarios. Of course the key to developing a data package to support any application is to navigate the most appropriate path through this list and provide the most relevant data. However, this assumes that Regulatory Authorities have the necessary experience and expertise to evaluate dossiers based on scientific argument rather than compliance with a list of requirements. No matter what size of enterprise involved, regulatory requirements now present a major financial hurdle to every applicant. Clearly SMEs will find this burden disproportionately large compared to the turnover expected from any product marketed.

Can there really be hope for SMEs involved with the development of plant extracts and niche products? This paper intends to present the current regulatory position and also to explore the wider issues in order to put the requirements into some context and offer some hope. It assumes some knowledge of Directive 91/414/EEC and the control of plant protection products.

PLANT EXTRACTS AND THE SCOPE OF 91/414/EEC

Plant extracts intended for use as plant protection products are covered by the legislation. In the Commission report to Parliament (SANCO, 2001a), plant extracts were identified as needing to be in the list of substances to be included in the 4th stage of the EU Review Programme. This recognised that plant extracts were already on the market and needed to be included in the scope of the legislation. The Commission stated that a host of new niche companies developing environmentally friendly alternative methods of plant protection were emerging. These were almost always SMEs adopting innovatory approaches to existing problems. Nurturing their continued development by not imposing impossible regulatory hurdles in their path, whilst guaranteeing health and environmental safety and effective crop protection, would be a big challenge for the future.

Subsequently, the Commission Regulation (Commission Regulation, 2002b), laying down the rules for the 4th stage of the EU Review Programme, included plant extracts in the list of substances under review. It stated that detailed provisions concerning the submission of dossiers and deadlines will be established by a further Regulation in due course. In the meantime a list of all of the existing active substances that were notified by companies willing to support their continued use has been published (SANCO, 2003). Although the list now includes many plant extracts such as essential oils, plant oils, seaweed and seaweed extract, it is far from exhaustive. Any active substance not on this list and which is being actively developed will need to be registered as a new active substance. One of the biggest challenges will be the recognition that the use of such technology differs fundamentally from the use of chemical plant protection products (A Hamer, personal communication). The main objective of most plant protection products is to eradicate a pest, disease or weed. The novel approach being developed is completely different with the aim, for example, to improve defence systems. This will require a completely different approach to both risk assessment and efficacy evaluation.

The attraction of plant extracts appears to be associated with the likely low adverse impact on crops or stored products themselves or on human health. They also appear to be biodegradable so the likely environmental impact is low (Velcheva, *et al.*, 2001). For some uses the results seem very promising and range from direct effects on pests and diseases (Boeke, *et al.*, 2001; Parimelazhagan, 2001; Thacker, *et al.*, 2002) to plant activators (J Pickett, personal communication).

The realisation that regulatory requirements need to be scaled down for certain groups of plant protection products with reduced risks has been picked up by two Member States. The Dutch have produced guidelines for plant strengtheners with low risk profiles (SANCO, 2001b) and the French Authorities have developed a draft working document on plant extracts (A Hamer, personal communication). Before the French proposals are discussed it might be helpful to explore the wider initiatives that have prompted the need to develop such guidance.

SIXTH ENVIRONMENT ACTION PROGRAMME

The 6th Environment Action programme (Commission Decision, 2002), whilst recognising Directive 91/414/EEC, goes further by proposing a two-track approach to minimise the risks due to the use and misuse of plant protection products. This initiative is interesting as it identifies the thinking in the Commission outside the group directly involved with Directive 91/414/EEC. It is clear that plant protection products are still regarded with suspicion and despite the huge data package developed to support safe use, the risks are still perceived to be high. The first track of the proposal is to ban or severely limit the placing on the market and use of the most *hazardous* and *risky* plant protection products. The words in italics are the actual words used in the proposal. It does not indicate how this would be done or whether it would be based on a risk assessment or on cut-off values related to the hazard classification of the active substance. The second track is to ensure that best practice is adopted regarding the use of those plant protection products that are authorised.

To assist with the general aims of the Action Programme, a Thematic Strategy on Sustainable Use of Pesticides has been developed (Commission Communication, 2002) which aims to provide a general overview of the risk reduction efforts and policies. The main objectives include the need

- to minimise the hazards and risks to health and the environment from the use and distribution of plant protection products;

- to reduce the levels of harmful active substances, in particular by replacing the most dangerous by safer (including non-chemical) alternatives;

- to encourage the use of low-input or pesticide-free crop farming particularly by raising the user's awareness, promoting the use of codes of good practices and consideration of the possible application of financial instruments.

The first of these aims has been taken up already by a number of Member States where national plant protection product reduction programmes have been introduced. In future a policy will be developed to cover a reduction plan and efforts to increase IPM, pest forecasting and biological control methods.

US EPA REQUIREMENTS

In the US the Environmental Protection Agency (EPA) has also recognised that "biopesticides", covering microbial products and biochemicals which include plant extracts, differ markedly from traditional synthetic chemical plant protection products. The EPA take the line that such products occur in nature and affect pests by means other than toxicity. Therefore, the extent of the data required to support a typical biopesticide is very much reduced compared to the requirements for synthetic chemicals. The key data requirements (Table 1) are very similar to those proposed by the European Union with a few notable exceptions. This list represents the requirements for active substances produced synthetically but based on natural products. Plant extracts would not be expected to trigger the need for higher tier testing regimes.

Table 1. Data requirements for "biochemicals"* – US EPA

1	Product Identity and Composition		
2	Analysis and Certified Limits		
3	Physical and Chemical Characteristics		
4	Toxicology data requirements	Tier I	Acute toxicity, skin sensitisation, hypersensitivity incidents, genotoxicity, immunotoxicity, 90-day studies, teratogenicity (1 sp)
		Tier II	Mammalian mutagenicity studies, immune response
		Tier III	Chronic exposure, carcinogenicity
6	Chemical Identity		
7	Directions for use		
8	Nature and Magnitude of Residues		
9	Impact on non-target organisms	Tier I	Acute toxicity on bird, fish, aquatic invertebrate, non-target plant, non-target insect testing
		Tier II	Environmental Fate
		Tier III	Terrestrial Wildlife (determined on a case-by-case basis)

* Details on US EPA website: www.epa.gov/pesticides/biopesticides/regtools/guidelines/biochem_gdlns.htm

OECD ACTIVITY

The Organisation for Economic Co-operation and Development (OECD), under the Pesticide Programme, has been working on the harmonisation of their plant protection product review procedures, sharing the evaluation of plant protection products and proposing policies for the reduction of risks associated with plant protection product use. The OECD together with the FAO held workshops on Integrated Pest Management and Pesticide Risk Reduction in Neuchâtel, Switzerland in 1998 (OECD, 1999). Rather than be restricted to a single definition of Integrated Pest Management (IPM), the workshop developed an approach which was to combine a variety of methods to control pests rather than relying on chemical plant protection products alone. Alternative methods included cultural strategies and biological methods. They discussed the role of IPM in plant protection product risk reduction. This theme was developed through reducing plant protection product usage and promoting reduced risk products. The group recognised that the take-up of IPM and plant protection product risk reduction would be slow because of the lack of viable alternative control methods and, in general, regulatory procedures not being flexible enough to deal with biological or reduced risk products. The rigid regulatory procedures developed for synthetic chemical products were seen as a barrier to the development of alternative strategies and achieving the aim of reduced plant protection product usage.

The OECD has maintained its active role in this area, developing a guidance document for the preparation of a dossier to support pheromones and other semiochemicals (OECD, 2002). They recognise that semiochemicals act by modifying the behaviour of pest species rather than killing them and can be target specific. They are used at very low rates, are non-toxic and dissipate rapidly. Therefore, they can be regarded as low risk and the data requirements are not as onerous as for synthetic chemical substances.

EU REQUIREMENTS

For the EU, the French Authorities have prepared a draft working document on the preparation of dossiers for plant protection products made from plants or plant extracts and have distributed it to Member States and Trade Associations such as the International Biocontrol Manufacturers Association (IBMA) for comment. The working document is intended to cover plant protection products made from plants or plant extracts, pheromones and [other] semiochemicals and commodity chemical substances. Although commodity chemicals have been included in the title, the French intend to cover this group in another document, which is in preparation. Also the French intend to use the guidance already in existence and developed by the OECD for pheromones and other semiochemicals (OECD, 2002).

The document now under discussion develops ideas on the data needed to support products made from plants or plant extracts. It is understood that all plant protection products must be authorised and must be supported by sufficient data to satisfy Articles 4 and 5 of Directive 91/414/EEC. These state that authorisation cannot be granted unless it can be demonstrated that there is no risk to human and animal health or the environment. The proposal is for the minimum data requirements to be applied to extracts obtained from plants included in a reference list (Table 2). This list contains plants authorised as herbal drugs in the European pharmacopoeia which are known to possess plant protection properties and would be expected to present a reduced risk. It is also the intention to up-date this list regularly.

Table 2. Proposed list of authorised plants

Common name of plant	Species	Part of plant used
Sweet chamomile	*Anthemis nobiilis*	Whole plant
Bladder wrack	*Fucus vesiculosus*	Thallus
Feverfew	*Chrysanthemum parthenium*	Whole plant
Lavender	*Lavandula officinalis*	Whole plant
Nettle	*Urtica spp,*	Whole plant
Rhubarb	*Rheum officinale*	Rhizome

The French have proposed that plant protection products made from plants or plant extracts should be defined as "mixtures or solutions comprising two or more substances intended for use as a plant protection product". They define plants as being "live or dried plants and live or dried parts of plants including seeds and fruit" and a plant extract is "obtained by concentrating, through evaporation, distillation or some other process, a solution achieved by treating plants or parts of them with a liquid such as water and ethanol".

It is proposed that there should be a tiered approach to the generation and evaluation of data. The data requirements proposed have been tabulated in a very brief format in Table 3. Two examples are given

- Case 1 - Plant protection products made from plants included in the reference list and mixed with water, possibly with formulants added, and used directly on the crop
- Case 2 - Water/ethanol extracts of plants included in the reference list and possibly with formulants added. In this example it is assumed that an extract would be prepared but not used directly as a plant protection product. Data would be expected to be generated for the initial plant extract in addition to the plant protection product

Table 3. Proposed data requirements for plant extracts

	Data	Case 1	Case 2 Extract	Case 2 Product
	Plant nomenclature			
	description	✓	✓	
	origin	✓	✓	
1	Identity of water ethanol extract			
	Particulars of extraction		✓	
	Specification		✓	
	Identity of plant protection product			
	Particulars of preparation	✓		✓
	Specification	✓		✓
	Full list of ingredients	✓		✓
2	Physical and chemical properties	✓	✓	✓
3	Data on application	✓		✓
4	Further information on plant protection product	✓		✓
5	Analytical methods	✓	✓	✓
6	Efficacy data	✓		✓
7	Toxicological studies			
	Acute oral, dermal and inhalation		✓	✓
	Skin and eye irritation	✓	✓	✓
	Skin sensitivity	✓	✓	✓
	Other toxicity data from literature		✓	✓
	SDS on formulants if added	✓		✓
	Risk assessment for operator and workers	✓		✓
8	Ecotoxicological studies			
	From literature	✓	✓	✓
	SDS on formulants if added	✓		✓
9	Classification and labelling	✓	✓	✓

It is expected that the package could rely heavily on data in the published literature. The proposals have enough detail to determine that a flexible approach will be taken. For example, analytical methods should be developed as far as possible. If the active components of the extract are unknown, a representative marker chemical should be used. Also since natural products often do not act directly on harmful organisms, the initial efficacy package need not reach the same level as for chemical products. So the scale of all of the requirements is vastly reduced from those expected for active substances based on synthetic chemicals provided that the extract is from a plant that is included in the reference list.

The document also states that for plants or plant extracts not included in the reference list, the requirements of Annexes II and III of the Directive 91/414/EEC must be fulfilled. Similarly synthetic active substances based on plant extracts will need to satisfy the relevant Annexes. For both of these examples a flexible approach to the selection of studies will be acceptable to most authorities but the extent of the data package will depend on the perceived degree of risk.

CONCLUSION

Policies developed from within the EU and from groups elsewhere in the world have stated the need to reduce traditional plant protection product usage. One of the options available to achieve this aim is to use low risk alternatives. Most authorities now accept that such low risk active substances must be treated in a different manner compared with synthetic substances. The political climate is changing and alternative strategies are being sought. Hope and encouragement lies in the French proposals to reduce the list of requirements needed to support natural products. However, there has been very little experience gained with assessing the risk of these products. A few examples are needed to act as pilot compounds to develop the system and give confidence to the proposed procedures.

REFERENCES

Boeke S J; van Loon J J A; van Huis A; Kossou D K; Dicke M (2001). The use of plant material to protect stored leguminous seeds against seed beetles: a review. *Wageningen University Papers 2001 – 2003.* Backhuys Publishers. 2001.

Commission Communication (2000). Communication from the Commission on the precautionary principle COM(2000) 1 Brussels, 02.02.2000.

Commission Communication (2002). Towards a Thematic Strategy on the Sustainable Use of pesticides. *Communication from the Commission to the Council, the European Parliament and the Economic and Social Committee.* Brussels, XX.XX.2002. COM (2002).

Commission Decision (2002). Decision No. 1600/2002/EC of the European Parliament and of the Council of 22 July 2002 laying down the Sixth Community Environment Action Programme.

Commission Regulation (2002a). Regulation (EC) No. 178/2002 of the European Parliament and of the Council of 28 January 2002 Laying down the general principles and requirements of food law, establishing the European Food Safety Authority and laying down procedures in matters of food safety.

Commission Regulation (2002b) Commission Regulation (EC) No. 1112/2002 of 20 June 2002 laying down the detailed rules for the implementation of the fourth stage of the programme of work referred to in Article 8(2) of Council Directive 91/414/EEC.

Council Directive (1991). Council Directive 91/414/EEC of 15 July 1991 concerning the placing of plant protection products on the market.

OECD (1999). Report of the OECD/FAO workshop on Integrated Pest Management and Pesticide Risk Reduction. *OECD Series on Pesticides*. Number 8. ENV/JM/MONO (99) 7. 14 April 1999.

OECD (2002). OECD Guidance for Industry Data Submissions for Pheromones and Other Semiochemicals and their active substances (Dossier Guidance for Pheromones and Other Semiochemicals) PART 1. *OECD Series on Pesticides*. Number 16. September 2002.

Parimelazhagan T (2001). Botanical fungicide for the control of rice blast disease. *Bioved* **12**, 11 – 15.

PAN (2002). Suggested text for a Directive of the European Parliament and of the Council on measures for a reduction of use and of impacts to health and environment from pesticides. *PAN Europe*, May 2002. ISBN 0 9521656 4 3.

SANCO (2001a). Report from the Commission to the European Parliament and the Council. Evaluation of the active substances of plant protection products (submitted in accordance with Article 8(2) of Council Directive 91/414/EEC on the placing of plant protection products on the market. SANCO/822/2001 rev. 3. Brussels, 12.7.2001.

SANCO (2001b). Dossier requirements for plant strengtheners with low risk profile. Draft working document. SANCO/1003/2000 rev. 3. 21,06,2001.

SANCO (2002). Workshop on the amendment of Council Directive 91/414/EEC held on 10 – 12 July 2002 in Corfu. Conclusions of the Workshop. SANCO/10351/2002. Corfu, 12 July 2002.

SANCO (2003). List of active substances and notifiers for which a notification in accordance with Article 4 of Commission Regulation (EC) No. 1112/2002 has been assessed and appears to be admissible. SANCO/10179/2002 rev. 3. 24.06.2003.

Thacker J R M; Bryan W; McGinley C; Heritage S; Strang R H C (2002). Field and laboratory studies on the effects of a neem-based plant extract on the activity of the large pine weevil, *Hylobius abietis. Proceedings of the BCPC Conference – Pests & Diseases 2002*, **1**, 45 – 50.

Velcheva N; Atanassov N; Velchev V; Vulcheva R; Karadjova O; Velichkova M (2001). Toxic action of plant extracts on some pests of economic importance. *Bulgarian Journal of Agricultural Science* **7**, 133 – 139.

SESSION 9A

THE ENVIRONMENTAL IMPACT OF GM CROPS: SAFETY TESTING, RISK ASSESSMENT AND REGULATION

Chairman and Session Organiser:	Dr Alan Raybould *Syngenta, Bracknell, UK*
Papers:	9A-1 to 9A-4

The use of ecological endpoints and other tools from ecological risk assessment to create a more conceptual framework for assessing the environmental risk of GM plants

G M Poppy

Biodiversity and Ecology Division, School of Biological Sciences, University of Southampton, SO16 7PX, UK

Email gmp@soton.ac.uk

ABSTRACT

Genetically Modified (GM) plants are heralded as a "second green revolution", but in order to gain the benefits they can offer we must also understand the risks they pose in order to allow cost/benefit analyses to be undertaken. Assessing the risks of a biotic introduction to the environment is very complex, and has not been helped by the lack of information flow from traditional risk assessment to GM biosafety research. At present we lurch from one small study to the next and really don't have a robust framework or any form of conceptual model into which the studies can fit together to complete the jigsaw. The introduction of tiered risk assessment methodologies have helped address a number of key ecological and environmental questions but such schemes need to be considered within a broader perspective so that other areas of risk can be considered and we can adopt comparative risk assessment of GM technology compared with alternative agricultural practices. Ecological risk assessments have been widely developed for assessing the impact of "contaminants" (usually an abiotic chemical input). Such assessments involve problem formulation and the development of a conceptual model into which studies gathering data can be placed. The use of assessment and measurement endpoints allow clear integration between the collection of data and the management goal and thus allow risks to be characterised, assessed and managed. A similar approach for assessing GM plants would be a powerful advance on the current risk assessment framework, and may allow scientists involved in detailed laboratory studies to fit their research into the bigger picture. Using Bt maize as an example endpoints and a conceptual model are developed.

INTRODUCTION

The debate concerning the ecological impact of genetically modified (GM) plants still rages, frequently fuelled by the media. A recent comprehensive scientific review highlighted the need for more studies to ascertain the environmental impact of GM crops (DTI, 2003). One of the biggest challenges will be developing the best framework for assessing the past and future studies that are generating extensive data on the risks and impact of GM crops. Too many studies have been conducted without reference to a conceptual framework/model. This has led to numerous scare stories which in turn have obscured considerable research addressing the same questions but part of a more complete risk assessment framework. The best example relates to the risk posed to the Monarch butterfly by pollen from Bt maize. John Losey and colleagues at Cornell University showed that Monarch butterfly larvae could be killed by pollen from Bt maize in a classical first-tier "worst-case scenario" experiment (Losey *et al.*,

1999). The identification of this hazard generated tremendous media and public attention and even speculation that Monarch migrations may be a thing of the past. A comprehensive risk assessment was then undertaken by many scientists in North America resulting in a series of papers published in Proceedings of National Academy of Sciences (PNAS, 2001). These concluded that the risk to Monarch butterflies from Bt maize is very low and that there are ways to manage the risk One could ask the simplistic question as to why it took a preliminary scientific study and tremendous media attention to initiate a comprehensive risk assessment of Bt maize and Monarch butterflies. However, it should be noted that the Bt maize had been through a risk assessment prior to commercial release but this did not appear to cover many of the questions which were now being asked.

There have been other similar cases to the "Monarch story" and there will be more unless we are more careful in how we interpret and most importantly frame scientific Biosafety studies on the environmental and ecological impacts of GM plants (Poppy, 2000). One way in which progress has been made is the use of tiered risk assessment schemes similar to that used for assessing pesticides. There is not room in this paper to comprehensively outline such a scheme (see previous BCPC proceedings paper by Schuler *et al.*, 2000), but such a framework does allow hazards to be identified and subsequently risks quantified. Such a tiered approach can also be extended to address other risks such as that posed by geneflow (Wilkinson *et al.*, 2003) This has offered a major advance to the risk assessment of GM plants and is allowing studies to be placed in context and risks to be compared. However, there are still many discrepancies in how this process is completed and at what thresholds (trigger values) different tiers are adopted. There is too little interaction between many scientists working on GM biosafety and the wider risk-assessment community. This may be because of the terminology being used and the differences between principally abiotic changes by man as opposed to the biotic change (a living GM plant) but I still think we have a lot to learn and would benefit from "borrowing" methods and approaches from the broader risk assessment community. This paper will take some of these concepts and try to incorporate them into the assessment of GM plants.

ECOLOGICAL RISK ASSESSMENTS (ERA)

The US Environmental Protection Agency (EPA) defines ecological risk assessment as "an evaluation of the likelihood that adverse ecological effects could result from exposure to one or more stressors" (USEPA, 1998)). An ecological risk assessment does not consider the impacts to humans or domesticated species. The goal of the risk assessment is to evaluate actual and predicted potential effects on plant and animal populations by principally addressing the following three questions:

1) Do current stressor levels pose a current or future ecological risk?
2) What portions of the site should be monitored or be subjected to remediation?
3) Have past activities adversely affected biodiversity?

The number of steps in the process vary according to degree of splitting and/or clumping of components. EPA recommend an eight-step process, but for clarity for non-specialists in risk assessment, this paper will only highlight three basic parts to the ecological risk assessment: Problem Formulation, Analysis Phase and Risk Characterisation.

Problem formulation

As the name suggests this is a systematic planning step that identifies the major factors to be considered in the risk assessment. For example, if considering the impact on a site, it reviews all the existing data relating to that site. The process will deliver a conceptual model that identifies the characteristics of the stressors (an abiotic or biotic entity that can cause an adverse effect), the ecosystems potentially at risk, and the ecological effects to be evaluated. During this process, the assessment and measurement endpoints (see next section) for the ecological risk assessment are identified.

Analysis phase

This phase can usually be considered in two parts.

The first is called an exposure assessment which quantifies the exposures of ecological receptors (animals, plants, microorganisms) to the stressor. Key aspects in this assessment involve quantification of the "substance" acting as the stressor, its migration and fate in the environment, and determining which organism are exposed and at what levels. There are numerous factors which influence exposure which relate both to the nature of the contaminant or ecology and behaviour of the receptor (ecological entity being exposed).

A second phase called the ecological effects assessment attempts to create a dose response relationship by linking concentration of contaminant to adverse effects in receptors. A range of lab and field tests are conducted to establish links between cause and effect (contaminants causing ecological effects).

Risk characterization

The final phase of the assessment compares the results from the exposure and ecological effects assessments. This allows hazards to be identified and the risks they pose to be quantified. If the process is successful it will allow a risk description to be developed in both numerical and descriptive terms. It is important to be able to link this back to the endpoints developed in the problem formulation part of the process. This will identify thresholds for adverse effects and provide an indication of the confidence the risk assessor has in the results.

ECOLOGICAL ENDPOINTS

Ecological endpoints are critical both in the problem formulation at the start of the assessment and in the risk characterisation stage at the end of the ecological risk assessment when risks are related back to the assessment endpoints. Ecological endpoints are thus critical in ecological risk assessment and warrant detailed consideration in a risk assessment of GM plants. The concept of Assessment and Measurement endpoints was initially described by Suter (1989, 1990) and appeared shortly after in the USEPA Guidance in the Framework for ERA (USEPA 1992).

Assessment endpoints

"Explicit expression of the actual environmental values that are to be protected, operationally defined by an ecological entity and its attributes" (USEPA 1992, 1998).

These are critical in establishing the rigour of an ecological risk assessment and should be selected in light of goals and methodology to be used in the assessment. They are also subject to public perception since there is little point establishing endpoints for unfavoured groups of organism (e.g. soil microorganisms), unless they are considered as part of an ecosystem attribute which is to be measured. A critical factor relates to the site management goals and objectives which can guide and influence the assessment endpoints and thus need to be identified and developed prior to selection of assessment endpoints in the problem formulation stage of the assessment. A significant problem relating to GM crops is the lack of agreement about site management goals which is discussed in more detail later in this paper.

Assessment endpoints are typically identified at the population, community or ecosystem level of biological organisation (USEPA 1996) in contrast to measurement endpoints which tend to focus on the individual level of organisation. A range of criteria are used in selecting the endpoints which can have either ecological or societal relevance. However, they all must be unambiguous, accessible to prediction and susceptible to the stressor. Commonly used assessment endpoints include variables relating to biodiversity, sensitive species and important ecosystem functions.

It is worth remembering that specific clearly defined assessment endpoints allow answers to be determined for specific questions, something critical for a good risk assessment framework. By developing specific assessment endpoints, it is easier to produce robust measurement endpoints and thus allow the two classes of endpoint to fully integrate, thus providing confidence in the risk assessment.

Measurement endpoints

"Measurable responses to a stressor that are related to the valued characteristic chosen as the assessment Endpoints" (Suter, 1989, USEPA 1992)

If the appropriate measurement endpoints are selected, these can be used to infer a measure of protection or evaluate risk to the assessment endpoints. A number of subclasses have been defined which include "Measures of effect", "Measures of Exposure" and "Measures of ecosystem and receptor characteristics) but these are beyond the scope of this paper (see USEPA 1998), but are used in Figure 1 which outlines management goals, assessment and measurement endpoints for Bt maize.

In some cases the measurement endpoint can be the same as the assessment endpoint, but usually they are measurable responses which relate to the assessment endpoint. They are usually at a lower level of biological organisation, principally focussing at the individual physiological, morphological or anatomical levels of organisation. Again a range of criteria are used in selecting the measurement endpoints including: relevance to assessment endpoint, high signal to noise ratio, sensitivity and response time, practicality and of high diagnostic ability.

USING ENDPOINTS FOR ASSESSING GM PLANTS

Although members of national risk assessment committees for GM crops may be familiar with the ideas associated with generic risk assessment such as ecological risk assessment as outlined above, not all practicing research scientists are familiar with the framework, let alone the terms. One could criticise those scientists who have failed to read the extensive literature, although this may be explained by the ecologists struggling to understand details relating to the science and terminology of GM biotechnology. However, it should be noted that the literature on ecological risk assessment abounds with acronyms, flow charts and diagrams which can make the topic unapproachable. Hopefully, such barriers will breakdown and the useful aspects of conventional ecological risk assessments can be adopted and translated for GM plants, allowing more time to focus on fine tuning the system for the stressor (GM plant) and the receptors (ecological entities being exposed to GM plant) at risk.

During the problem formulation process of an ecological risk assessment, the ecological endpoints are determined and a conceptual model developed. It is this stage which appears to be lacking in GM risk assessment and is why there has been little consensus into acceptability of the risks associated with GM. There has been considerable effort in the analysis phase, but how can one characterise the risks using the data from the analysis phase if the problem has not been formulated.

A conceptual model is a written description and visual representation of predicted relationships between ecological entitities and the stressors to which they are exposed. It is thus possible to develop such a model for a GM risk assessment, but the harder aspect is determining the endpoints around which the whole assessment will be based. (See Figures 1 and 2 for examples of ecological endpoints and a conceptual model relating to the risks posed to parasitoids and predators by Bt maize).

In order to generate a series of management goals for GM crops, it is important to be clear about what type of environment you require during the problem formulation part of the ecological risk assessment. In agroecosystems, there are conflicting interests and much uncertainty about what we want from our agricultural environment. As consumers, we require high quality cheap food, whereas as land users, we demand a beautiful countryside which is full of wildlife. A recent discussion meeting at the Royal Society tried to explore the impact of farming on the environment and the implications of adding GM crops into the equation (Royal Society, 2003). A principal area of discussion related to how we want farming to be like in the future and the roadmap for getting to that point. This was in contrast to the approach of describing the current baseline and looking for perturbation from that point. Unfortunately what we require from Agriculture is not clear due to conflicting issues and agendas, but it does seem that we wish to have food security with a minimum ecological footprint. There are various ways of achieving this involving a number of factors relating to productivity, scale of production area and biodiversity. For example one question we may need to consider relates to whether it is better for biodiversity to produce more food from less land or farm less intensively on greater land areas?

GOAL: Sustain populations of natural enemies (predators and parasitoids)

Assessment endpoint:
- Survival and reproduction of generalist and specialist predators/parasitoid

Measurement endpoints:

a) **Measure of effects:**
- Analysis of adverse effects to adult parasitoid/predators (specialist/generalist on European cornborer and other non-target herbivores e.g. *Trichrogramma* spp., *Chrysoperla, Cotresia margineventris, Aphidius rhopalosiphi*)
- Reproductive success of above species of parasitoid/predator
- Population structure of above species of parasitoid/predator
- Parasitoid/Predator Community analysis in Bt fields and margins

b) **Measures of ecosystem and receptor charcteristics**
- Abundance and distribution of prey/hosts and other food sources (nectar, pollen)
- Quality and size of habitat (floral/faunal diversity, refugia size, spatial arrangement)
- Environmental conditions (e.g. temp, management regime – sprays etc.)

c) **Measures of exposure**
- Bt expression levels in the plant tissue (e.g. leaves, pollen, nectar) and in the tissue of hosts/prey

Figure 1.   Management goal, assessment endpoint and measurement endpoints for Bt maize and insect natural enemies.

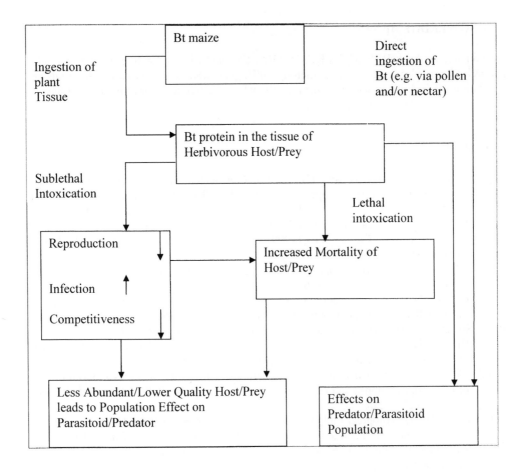

Figure 2. A conceptual model for assessing the impacts of Bt maize on insect natural enemies

CONCLUSIONS

The risk assessment of GM crops is a young science which has made progress, but it is important that it does not reinvent the wheel. Much can be learnt from more generic risk assessment, especially that used for assessing pesticides and other stressors which affect ecological systems. Although the terminology can seem difficult, the use of conceptual frameworks and endpoints allow quantitative assessments and decisions to be made about safety. If we ignore this approach, we are in danger of going round in circles and not really differentiating between degrees of risk and thus wasting our resources focussing on issues which don't require the degree of testing of another trait. We all speak of the need for case by case analysis, but we don't seem to have the necessary conceptual frameworks, endpoints or trigger values (values which mean further testing is required) to allow for joined up decision making. If the regulators and company regulatory specialists have produced such a system, then let's ensure that the practising scientists utilise it rather than continue to mechanistically take systems apart without really knowing the question for which they seek the answer.

ACKNOWLEDGEMENTS

I would like to thank BBSRC, NERC, DEFRA, ESF and EU for funding my GM Biosafety research. I am also grateful to numerous colleagues who have discussed the trials and tribulations of GM plants and the general public who have frequently informed me of the non-scientific issues which need considering.

REFERENCES

Department for Trade and Industry (2003). The GM Science Review Panel. GM Science Review (First Report): An Open Review Of The Science Relevant To GM Crops And Food Based On Interests And Concerns Of The Public.(http://www.gmsciencedebate.org.uk/report/default.htm)

Losey JE; Rayor LS; Carter ME (1999).Transgenic pollen harms monarch larvae *Nature* **399**, 214-214

Poppy G (2000) GM crops: environmental risks and non-target effects *Trends in Plant Sciences* **5**, 4-6

Proceedings of the National Academy of Sciences (2001) a series of 6 papers relating to Bt maize pollen and Monarch butterflies. *PNAS* **98**, 11908-11942

Royal Society (2003). GM crops, modern agriculture and the environment - Transcript of a Royal Society Discussion meeting held on 11 February 2003 (see http://www.royalsoc.ac.uk/policy/transcript11FebGMCrops.pdf)

Schuler TH; Poppy GM; Denholm I (2000). Recommendations for the assessment of effects of GM crops on non-target organisms. *Proceedings of the BCPC- Pests and Diseases 2000*, **3**, 1221-1228

Suter GW II (1989) Ecological Endpoints. In: Ecological Assessments of Hazaradous Waste Sites: a Field and Laboraotory Reference Document, eds. W. Warren-Hicks; BR Parkhurst; SS Baker Jr, EPA/600/3-89/013, U.S.Environmental Protection Agency, Wahington DC.

Suter GW II (1990) Endpoints for Regional Ecological Risk Assessments. *Environmental Management* **14**, 19-23.

United States Environmental Protection Agency (USEPA) (1992). Framework for Ecological Risk Assessment. EPA/630/R-92/001. Risk Assessment Forum, Washington DC.

USEPA (1996). Eco Update: Ecological Significance and Selection of candidate Assessment Endpoints. EPA/540/F-95?037. Office of Solid Waste and Emergency Response, Washington DC.

USEPA (1998). Guidelines for Ecological Risk Assessment. EPA/630/R-95?002F. Risk Assessment Forum, Washington DC.

Wilkinson MJ; Sweet J; Poppy GM (2003). Risk assessment of GM plants: avoiding gridlock? *Trends in Plant Sciences* **8**, 208-212

Rethinking the herbicide development and regulation process post GM crop environment impact studies

J Pidgeon
IACR-Broom's Barn, Bury St Edmunds, UK

No information could be released for publication at the time of going to press.

An assessment of the level of crop to crop gene flow in forage maize crops in the UK

R Weekes, C Henry, D Morgan
Central Science Laboratory, Sand Hutton, York YO41 1LZ, UK
Email: r.weekes@csl.gov.uk

R Daniels, C Boffey
Centre for Ecology and Hydrology, Winfrith Technology Centre, Dorchester, Dorset DT2 8ZD, UK

ABSTRACT

Farm-scale evaluation (FSE) trials were established to assess the effects on farmland biodiversity of weed management methods associated with the use of genetically modified herbicide tolerant (GM HT) crops compared with conventional crops. Gene flow was monitored at the FSE sites of fodder maize over the duration of the 3-year trial. The trial sites had a split field layout; one half of the field was planted with the GM HT crop, the other half with a conventional equivalent of the same crop. Maize samples were collected from the conventional crop halves of FSE sites at a range of distances from the GM crop. GM/non-GM hybridization was detected and quantified using molecular methods. Additional data on wind direction and landscape were also collected for each trial site. The results show that the rates of cross-pollination decreased over distance and followed the expected pollen dispersal curve. Evidence of cross-pollination was found up to 200m away from the GM/non-GM junction in the crop. There was significant variation in levels of cross-pollination between sites in each year ($p < 0.01$), although the variation between years across all sites was not significant ($p > 0.05$). The importance of isolation distances in contributing to reducing adventitious pollen intrusion will be discussed with respect to sustainable co-existence of GM, conventional and organic crops.

INTRODUCTION

There is currently (August, 2003) a moratorium on the commercial planting of genetically modified (GM) crops in the UK. The government will make a decision on whether or not GM crops should be cultivated following publication of the results of the Farm-Scale Evaluations, reviews of the costs and benefits of GM crops (Strategy Unit of the Cabinet Office, 2003) and a review of the science relevant to GM crops and food based on interests and concerns of the public (King *et al.*, 2003).

In 1999, the Department for Environment, Food and Rural Affairs (Defra) established farm-scale evaluation (FSE) trials to assess the effects on farmland biodiversity of the weed management methods associated with the cultivation of GM herbicide tolerant crops compared with conventional (non-GM) crops. In conjunction with these trials, a study of gene flow from the GM to conventional crops was also established, using the FSE sites of winter and spring oilseed rape and fodder maize, genetically modified to be herbicide tolerant (HT). This paper reports the results of the forage maize trials.

A review, which addressed the issue of separation distances between GM and other crops, was published in 2000 by the Ministry of Agriculture, Fisheries and Food (Ingram, 2000). Currently the minimum separation distance required in the European Union is 200m for all categories of seed production, which is believed to be sufficient to maintain inbred lines at 99.9% purity (Ingram, 2000). The recommended separation distances for non-GM crops from the Supply Chain Initiative on Modified Agricultural Crops (SCIMAC) guidelines for growing GM HT crops are 200m for sweetcorn and 80m for forage maize. However, whilst no maize seed is currently produced in the UK fodder maize is grown and harvested for silage, and sweetcorn is also grown in some areas.

A number of factors affect pollination rates in maize. Most of the pollen is shed from the plants before the silks are receptive, but there is some overlap, resulting in up to 5% self pollination (at least 95% of ovules are fertilised by pollen from other plants). Pollen viability can vary between 2h and 8 days, depending on environmental conditions. The impaction rate (settling velocity) of maize pollen is 30-40 cm s^{-1} so the pollen normally only travels short distances. Pollination rates can also be affected by competition from pollen from other sources. Finally, wind speed, wind direction and surface turbulence can also affect pollination rates. These factors make it difficult to predict the effect of one maize field on another. A higher wind speed will cause the pollen to travel further downwind but the impaction rate of the pollen will also increase. Other factors that will affect the rate of cross-pollination between fields are synchronisation of flowering, the relative concentration of the pollen in the donor and receptor plot (the protective strength of the field pollen cloud), the levels of selfing and the density of the stands.

Although hybrid corn production practices have remained basically unchanged for the last thirty years (Burris, 2002), there is limited literature available on gene flow from pollen. Reports of outcrossing rates range from 40% at 2.5m (Bateman, 1947), 4.5% at 3m (Jugenheimer, 1976), 1.11% at 200m (Burris, 2002) and 2.47% at 200m (Jones & Brookes, 1950). Under very arid, calm conditions, outcrossing was not detected beyond 200m (Baltazar and Schoper, 2002). Previous studies on gene flow from maize have not been carried out on a commercial scale (with the exception of Burris in the USA). The FSE offered the opportunity to sample a large number of fields in a wide range of locations and environments in England. This paper presents quantitative results from years 2000 to 2002 for the extent of transfer of the GM herbicide tolerance gene to conventional fodder maize at different distances from the GM crop unit.

MATERIALS AND METHODS

The gene flow study commenced after the FSE biodiversity study had been established. Sites consisted of a split field design, half planted with Liberty Link™, line T25 (containing the *pat* gene), which is tolerant to Liberty™, a broad spectrum, non-residual, glufosinate ammonium herbicide and the other half with a conventional equivalent maize variety. A total of 55 trial sites were used in the maize study (Figure 1). Samples were taken from the conventional crop halves of the fields, along transects, at 2, 5, 10, 20, 50 and 150m from the division between the crop units. Transect positions were determined to be approximately one quarter, one half and three quarters of the distance across the width of each field.

Covariate data were collected for each of the fields sampled. The FSE dataset was used to provide data on the size, aspect, orientation and slope of the fields. Field boundary attributes describing the type, height and completeness of boundaries round the sampled fields were also extracted from the dataset. These covariate data were used in conjunction with the PCR data to explain patterns of hybridisation and gene flow from the GM crop to the conventional.

The maize samples were tested for the presence of the *pat* gene using real time (TaqMan) PCR. Briefly, a reporter dye and a quencher dye are attached to the 5' and 3' ends of a TaqMan probe. When both dyes are attached to the probe, reporter dye emission is quenched. During each PCR extension cycle, the *Taq* DNA polymerase cleaves the probe when bound to the template ahead of the *Taq*, which separates the dyes. Once separated from the quencher, the reporter dye emits its characteristic fluorescence. The fluorescence is detected using an ABI Prism 7700 sequence detection system. Results are in the form of Ct values, which represent the PCR cycle at which an increase in reporter fluorescence can first be detected. Primers (and probe) were designed using published sequence data for the *pat* gene for maize (T25) (referred to as the target genes). In addition to the GM detection primers (and probe), primers and a probe were also required to detect an endogenous reference for relative quantification of the target. The rationale behind the design of these primers was to pick a single copy gene that was specific to that species of plant. For maize the endogenous control *Zea mays cdc2* was used.

Genomic DNA was extracted from maize using the Promega Wizard Magnetic DNA purification system and the Labsystems KingFisher ml Magnetic Particle Processor. DNA standards (used for quantification of unknown samples) were produced using known quantities of genomic T25 DNA and making a dilution series in DNA extracted from *Nicotiana tabacum*. Standard curves were created by plotting the Ct values of the known standards against the log of the concentration of DNA. Data for the unknown samples was then calculated from the standard curves. A normalized amount of target DNA was obtained by dividing the target value by the endogenous control reference amount. The normalized TaqMan data was expressed as a GM: non-GM ratio. The T25 maize was heterozygous for the transgene and this was taken as being 100% (i.e. 1:1 ratio) reference material.

To stabilise variances all results of the proportion of GM DNA (*pat* gene) detected in the field, samples were subjected to a probit transformation (Armitage, 1983). To determine the effect of year and site on proportion of GM cross-pollination, field sites that had been sampled in more than one year were chosen. The transformed results were analysed using General Linear Model (GLM) Analysis of Variance (ANOVA) (McCullagh & Nelder, 1989). To determine the spatial spread of the *pat* gene, results collected at different distances along transects established in the fields were used. The results were subjected to non-linear regression analysis to estimate the extent of gene flow with distance from source.

RESULTS

A total of 55 FSE sites were sampled during the three years of the study. The sites were at a range of locations across England (Figure 1) and were representative of some of the main maize growing regions. Evidence of gene flow by cross-pollination was detected at all the sites that were sampled. Overall the results showed a decrease in the rate of cross-pollination with increasing distance from the GM crop unit (Figure 2). There was a rapid decrease in the rate of cross-pollination within the first 20m from the donor crop and beyond this distance the rate of decrease was much slower. The average GM: non-GM ratio was 0.06 (6%) in the first 2m of the crop, this decreased to approximately 0.0003 (0.03%) at 200m. At two of the sites a number of samples were taken (with the kind permission from the grower) from the facing edge of forage maize fields nearest to the trial sites. One positive result was obtained at a distance of 650m from the GM source.

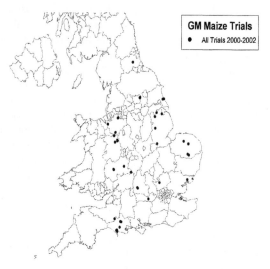

Figure 1.   Location of maize FSE sites from 2000-02. A total of 54 sites were used, some of the sites were used for more than one year and other sites were relatively close to each other.

Taking the 99.9% purity threshold for seed production and a 50m-isolation distance for forage maize, the fields were scored according to how many had GM: non-GM levels greater that 0.1% at a distance of 50m or more. Evidence of cross-pollination was found beyond the 50m-isolation distance in 42 out of 54 fields. Of these 34, were at a level of ≥0.1% and 23 of these fields were found to have levels ≥0.3%. At 150m from the GM source there was evidence of cross-pollination in 19 of 44 fields and of these 12 were ≥0.1% and 7 were ≥0.3%. In all cases where there was evidence of cross-pollination at 150m there was also cross-pollination at 50m.

Results of the GLM ANOVA indicated that GM: non-GM cross-pollination was significantly different between sampling locations on the field transects with distance (t = -5.67, d.f. = 65, p < 0.001) and between field sites (t = -3.32; d.f. = 65; p = 0.001) but not between years (t = -1.18; d.f. = 65; p = 0.241). A comparison of different non-linear equations indicated that a negative power regression explained most of the variation in the experimental results and thus, was chosen for subsequent analysis. Results of the non-linear regression analysis further indicated that gene flow was highly dependent upon distance from the source of GM DNA (F = 30.4; d.f. = 2,8; p < 0.001; Figure 2).

The regression equation was validated against field results not used in its derivation. The model predicted that at 650m from a source of GM maize, cross-pollination would be 0.04 %, whereas a mean value of 0.02 % was recorded. Further examination of the predicted equation indicated that at a distance of 80m cross-pollination levels would be less than 0.3%. To ensure contamination levels of less than 0.9% and 0.1% crops would need to be located at distances greater than 24.4m and 257.7m, respectively.

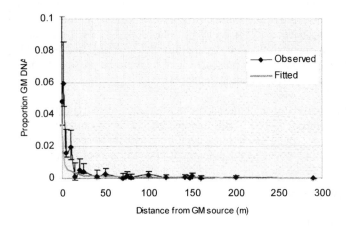

Figure 2.   Comparison of fitted and observed GM DNA cross-pollination against distance from GM source in metres.

DISCUSSION

To our knowledge this is the first study on crop-to-crop gene flow in maize at a farm-scale level in the UK. This study is unique both in the size and range of the trial sites and in the molecular approach to quantification of gene flow. The FSE trials were set up to compare effects on biodiversity of GM and conventional weed control practices and not explicitly to determine the extent of gene flow. However, these trials represent the potential for gene flow under realistic agricultural conditions rather than either small-scale trial plots or a number of GM plants in the middle of a conventional field.

The original aim of this project was to validate assumptions made in risk assessments concerning gene flow by pollen from the farm-scale evaluations and to ensure that the guidelines issued by SCIMAC stipulate an effective separation distance for the crop. It is evident from the results that cross pollination events occurred not only beyond the 80m isolation distance recommended for forage/fodder crops by SCIMAC, but also beyond the 200m distance recommended for sweetcorn and organic crops. Although these trials did not use sweetcorn, it is reasonable to assume that pollen distribution from the two crops would be similar. It is important to emphasise that the whole of the plant is harvested in forage crops and thus any cross-pollination events will be 'diluted' out in the final product. Sweetcorn presents more of a problem in that individual cobs will be consumed. So, even if a field was well below the threshold (currently at 0.9% for the labelling of GM food and feed), individual cobs may not be.

If the aim is to maintain a 99.9% purity level then an 80m-separation distance will not be enough. The current proposed threshold for the adventitious presence of GM seeds in certified seed lots is now 0.3% for authorized events and 0.1%-nil for unauthorized events (under part C of Directive 2001/18/EC). A recent report published by the European Commission (Block *et al.*, 2002) suggested that for maize, a threshold of 0.1% would be extremely difficult to achieve for any farming scenarios (conventional and organic farms). The report also pointed out that in less intensive maize growing regions it would be possible to meet a 1% threshold providing some changes were made to farming practices (assuming a GM adventitious presence of 0.3% or less). Maize seed is not produced in this country, therefore it is more important to consider the threshold for food and feed, which is currently set at 0.9 %. Based on the results presented here it would be possible to meet this threshold with an increase to the current isolation distances.

A more in depth analysis of the landscape characteristics of individual fields will be carried out using the data collected. It is hoped that this huge data set can be used to give us a better understanding of how typical UK farming conditions and landscape can be utilised to limit the extent of gene flow and maximise the potential for co-existence of the two farming practices.

ACKNOWLEDGEMENTS

We would like to thank Defra for funding this work (project EPG 1/5/138), also Bayer CropScience for kindly providing the positive control T25 maize seed and finally we would like to thank all those involved with sample collection and lab work at CEH, IACR, SCRI and CSL.

REFERENCES

Armitage, P. 1974. Statistical Methods in Medical Research. Blackwell, Oxford.

Baltazar B M; Schoper J B (2002). Crop-to-crop gene flow: dispersal of transgenes in maize, during field tests and commercialization. *Proceedings of the 7th International Symposium on The Biosafety of Genetically Modified Organisms.*

Bateman A J (1947). Contamination of seed crops – II. Wind pollination. *Heredity, 1*, 257-275.

Block A K, Lheureux K, Libeau-Dulos M, Nilsagard H and Rodriguez-Cerezo E (2002). Scenarios for co-existence of genetically modified and conventional and organic crops in European agriculture. A synthesis report prepared for the European Commission.

Burris J S (2002). Adventitious pollen intrusion into hybrid maize seed production fields. Statement representing the Association of Official Seed Certifying Agencies, http://www.amseed.com/.

Ingram J (2000). Report on the separation distances required to ensure cross-pollination is below specified limits in non-seed crops of sugar beet, maize and oilseed rape. *MAFF project number RG0123.*

Jugenheimer R W (1976). In: *Corn improvement, seed production and uses.* Published by Wiley Interscience.

King D K *et al.* (2003). GM science review (first report). An open review of the science relevant to GM crops and food based on interests and concerns of the public. Available at http://www.gmsciencedebate.org.uk .

McCullagh P. & Nelder, J.A. 1989. Generalized Linear Models. Chapman and Hall, London.

Strategy Unit of the Cabinet Office (2003). Field work: weighing up the costs and benefits of GM crops. Available at http://www.strategy.gov.uk

Containment and mitigation of transgene flow from crops

J Gressel, H I Al-Ahmad
Department of Plant Sciences, Weizmann Institute of Science, Rehovot, 76100, Israel
Email: Jonathan.Gressel@weizmann.ac.il

ABSTRACT

There are many ways to prevent transgene introgression from crops to other varieties, or to related weeds or wild species (containment strategies), as well as to preclude the impact should containment fail (mitigation strategies). The needs are most acute with rice and sunflowers, which have con-specific weeds, and with oilseed rape, sorghum, barley, which have closely related weeds. Containment and mitigation are critical for pharmaceutical crops, where gene flow from the crop to edible varieties must be precluded. Some gene flow (leakage) is inevitable with all containment mechanisms and once leaked, could then move throughout populations of undesired species, unless their spread is mitigated. Leakage even occurs with chloroplast-encoded genes, a >0.03% pollen transmission was found in the field. We focused on mitigation, which should be coupled with containment as a last resort. A mechanism for mitigation was proposed where the primary transgene (herbicide resistance, etc.) is tandemly coupled with flanking genes that could be desirable or neutral to the crop, but unfit for the rare weed into which the gene introgresses. Mitigator traits include dwarfing, non-bolting, no secondary dormancy, no seed shattering, and poor seed viability, depending on the instance. We demonstrated the potential utility of the concept using tobacco as a model, and dwarfing as the mitigator with herbicide resistance as the primary gene. Hybrids with the tandem construct were unable to reach maturity when grown interspersed with the wild type. Such mitigation should greatly decrease risk of transgene movement especially when coupled with containment technologies, allowing cultivation of transgenic crops having related weeds. As the number of transgenic plants being released is increasing, and the problems of monitoring such genes increases geometrically, we suggest that a uniform biobarcode[TM] system be used, where a small piece of non-coding DNA carrying an assigned variable region is used to mark transgenic crops, allowing monitoring.

INTRODUCTION

Farmers in most of the world have begun to realize the benefits that accrue from cultivating transgenic crops, whether to prevent soil erosion by using post-emergence herbicides or use less expensive/toxic insecticides while contributing to farmer and environmental health and safety. Herbicide resistant crops are especially useful for controlling crop-related weeds where there had been no herbicide selectivity. Several crops (e.g., wheat, barley, sorghum, rice, squash, sunflower, sugarbeets, oats, and oilseed rape) can naturally interbreed with closely related weedy relatives under field conditions, in both directions (Ellstrand *et al.*, 1999; Gressel, 2002). There is a concern that transgenes may escape from engineered crops into related weedy species by hybridization and backcrossing. This could potentially result in hybrids and their progeny with enhanced invasiveness or weediness (Ellstrand *et al.*, 1999).

Many of the engineered genes such as those conferring resistance to herbicides, diseases, and to stresses may grant a fitness advantage to a weedy species growing in the same agricultural ecosystem. There is also the rather emotive issue of transgene flow from crops such as maize bearing transgenes encoding pharmaceuticals to other varieties. Farm produced pharmaceuticals especially enzymes and antibodies, can be produced inexpensively in plants, without the need for animal tissue culture cells grown in a medium of expensive serum albumin that is all too easily contaminated with pathogenic mycoplasms, prions and viruses. Still, there is reason not to want the pharmaceutical transgenes in other varieties of the crop.

Two general approaches are discussed below to deal with the problems of transgene flow: containment of the transgenes within the transgenic crop; transgenic mitigation of the effects of the primary transgenic trait should it escape and move to an undesired target. While most containment mechanisms will severely restrict gene flow, some gene flow (leakage) is inevitable and could then spread through the population of undesired species, unless mitigated.

CONTAINING TRANSGENE FLOW

Several molecular mechanisms have been suggested to contain the transgene within the crop (i.e. to prevent outflow to related species), or to mitigate the effects of transgene flow once it has occurred (Gressel, 1999, 2002; Daniell, 2002). The containment mechanisms include utilization of partial genome incompatibility with crops such as wheat and oilseed rape having multiple genomes derived from different progenitors. When only one of these genomes is compatible for interspecific hybridization with weeds, the risk of introgression could be reduced if the transgene was inserted into the unshared genome where there is presumed to be no homeologous introgression between the non-homologous chromosomes. It has not been reported if this mechanism works in wheat, and it was modeled to be ineffectual for oilseed rape (Tomiuk et al., 2000) due to considerable recombination between the A and C genomes.

Another containment possibility is to integrate the transgene in the plastid or mitochondrial genomes (Maliga, 2002). The opportunity of gene outflow is limited due to maternal inheritance of these genomes. This technology does not preclude the weed from pollinating the crop, and then acting as the recurrent pollen parent. The claim of no paternal inheritance of plastome encoded traits (Bock, 2001; Daniell, 2002), was not substantiated. Tobacco (Avni & Edelman, 1991) and other species (Darmency, 1994) often have between a 10^{-3}–10^{-4} frequency of pollen transfer of plastid inherited traits in the laboratory. Pollen transmission of plastome traits can only be easily detected using both large samples and selectable genetic markers. A large-scale field experiment utilized a *Setaria italica* (foxtail or birdseed millet) with chloroplast-inherited atrazine resistance (bearing a nuclear dominant red leaf base marker) crossed with five different male sterile yellow- or green-leafed herbicide susceptible lines. Chloroplast-inherited resistance was pollen transmitted at a 3×10^{-4} frequency in >780,000 hybrid offspring (Wang et al., 2003). At this transmission frequency, the probability of herbicide resistance form plastomic gene flow is orders of magnitude greater than by spontaneous nuclear genome mutations. Chloroplast transformation is probably unacceptable for preventing transgene outflow, unless stacked with additional mechanisms.

A novel additional combination that considerably lowers the risk of plastome gene outflow within a field (but not gene influx from related strains or species) can come from utilizing male sterility with transplastomic traits (Wang et al., 2003). Introducing plastome inherited traits into varieties with complete male sterility would vastly reduce the risk of transgene flow, except in the small isolated areas required for line maintenance. Such a double failsafe containment method might be considered sufficient where there are highly stringent requirements for preventing gene outflow to other varieties (e.g. to organically cultivated ones), or where pharmaceutical or industrial traits are engineered into a species. Plastome-encoded transgenes for non-selectable traits (e.g. for pharmaceutical production) could be transformed into the chloroplasts together with a trait such as tentoxin or atrazine resistance as a selectable plastome marker. With such mechanisms to further reduce out-crossing risk, plastome transformation can possibly meet the initial expectations.

Other molecular approaches suggested for crop transgene containment include: seed sterility, utilizing the genetic use restriction technologies (GURT) (Oliver *et al.*, 1998), and recoverable block of function (Kuvshinov *et al.*, 2001). Such proposed technologies control out-crossing and volunteer seed dispersal, but theoretically if the controlling element of the transgene is silenced, expression will occur. Another approach includes the insertion of the transgene behind a chemically-induced promoter so that it will be expressed upon chemical induction (Jepson, 2002). However, there is a possibility of an inducible promoter mutating to become constitutive. Schernthaner *et al.* (2003) proposed an impractical technology using a "repressible seed-lethal system". The seed-lethal trait and its repressor must be simultaneously inserted at the same locus on homologous chromosomes in the hybrid the farmer sows to prevent recombination (crossing over), technology that is not yet workable in plants. The hemizygote transgenic seed lethal parent cannot reproduce by itself, as its seeds are not viable. If the hybrid could be made, half the progeny would not carry the seed lethal trait (or the trait of interest linked to it) and they will have to be culled, which would not be easy without a marker gene. The results of selfing or cross pollination within the crop and leading to volunteer weeds where 100% containment is needed, would leave only 25% dead and 50% like the hybrid parents and 25% with just the repressor. Thus, the repressor can cross from the volunteers to related weeds as can the trait of choice linked with the lethal, and viable hybrid weeds could form. The death of some seed in all future weed generations is inconsequential to weeds that copiously produce seed, as long as the transgenic trait provides some selective advantage.

None of the above containment mechanisms is absolute, but risk can be reduced by stacking containment mechanisms together, compounding the infrequency of gene introgression. Still, even at very low frequencies of gene transfer, once it occurs, the new bearer of the transgene can disperse throughout the population if it has just a small fitness advantage.

MITIGATING FURTHER FLOW OF 'LEAKED' TRANSGENES

If the transgene has a small fitness disadvantage, it will remain localized as a very small proportion of the population. Therefore, gene flow should be mitigated by lowering the fitness of recipients below the fitness of the wild type so that they will not spread. A concept of "transgenic mitigation" (TM) was proposed (Gressel, 1999), in which mitigator genes are added to the desired primary transgene, which would reduce the fitness advantage to hybrids and their rare progeny, and thus considerably reduce risk. This TM approach is based on the premises that: 1) tandem constructs act as tightly linked genes, and their segregation from each other is exceedingly rare; 2) The TM traits chosen are neutral or favorable to crops, but deleterious to non-crop progeny due to a negative selection pressure; and 3) Individuals bearing even mildly harmful TM traits will be kept at very low frequencies in weed populations because weeds typically have a very high seed output and strongly compete among themselves eliminating even marginally unfit individuals (Gressel, 1999). Thus, it was predicted that if the primary gene of agricultural advantage being engineered into a crop is flanked by TM gene(s), such as dwarfing, uniform seed ripening, non-shattering, anti-secondary dormancy, or non-bolting genes in a tandem construct, the overall effect would be deleterious after introgression into weeds, because the TM genes will reduce the competitive ability of the rare transgenic hybrids so that they cannot compete and persist in easily noticeable frequencies in agroecosystems (Gressel, 1999). Weeds are usually copious pollen producers and set large numbers of seeds, many of which germinate during the following season.

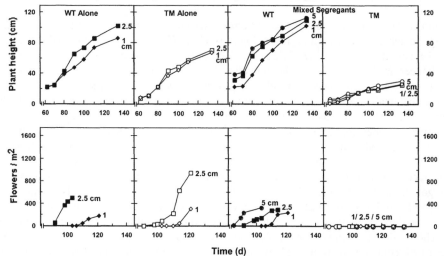

Figure 1. Suppression of growth and flowering of TM (transgenic mitigator) bearing tobacco plants carrying a dwarfing gene in tandem with a herbicide resistance gene (open symbols) when in competition with the wild type (closed symbols) (right panels), and their normal growth when cultivated separately without herbicide (left panels). The wild type and transgenic hemizygous semi-dwarf/herbicide resistant plants were planted at 1, 2.5, and 5 cm from themselves or each other, in soil. See Al-Ahmad et al. (2003) for further details.

We used tobacco (*Nicotiana tabacum*) as a model plant to test the TM concept: a tandem construct was made containing an *ahas*[R] (acetohydroxy acid synthase) gene for herbicide resistance as the primary desirable gene, and the dwarfing Δ*gai* (gibberellic acid-insensitive) mutant gene as a mitigator (Al-Ahmad et al., 2003). Dwarfing would be disadvantageous to the rare weeds introgressing the TM construct, as they could no longer compete with other crops or with fellow weeds, but is desirable in many crops, preventing lodging and producing less straw with more yield. The dwarf and imazapyr resistant TM transgenic hybrid tobacco plants (simulating a TM introgressed hybrid) were more productive than the wild type when cultivated alone. They formed many more flowers than the wild type, which is an indication of a higher harvest index (Figure 1). Conversely, the TM transgenics were weak competitors and highly unfit when co-cultivated with the wild type in ecological simulation competition experiments (Figures 1, 2). The lack of flowers on the TM plants in the competitive situation (Figure 1) led to a zero reproductive fitness of the TM plants grown in a 1:1 mixture with the wild type at the spacings used, which are representative of those of weeds in the field (Figure 2). The highest vegetative fitness was less than 30% of the wild type (Figure 2). Thus, it is clear that transgenic mitigation should be advantageous to a crop growing alone, while disadvantageous to a crop-weed hybrid living in a competitive environment. If a rare pollen grain bearing tandem transgenic traits bypasses containment, it must compete with multitudes of wild type pollen to produce a hybrid. Its rare progeny must then compete with more fit wild type cohorts during self-thinning and establishment. Even a small degree of unfitness encoded in the TM construct would bring about the elimination of the vast majority of progeny in all future generations as long as the primary gene provides no selective advantage while the linked gene confers unfitness. Further large-scale field studies will be needed with crop/weed pairs to continue to evaluate the positive implications of risk mitigation. We have inserted the same construct into oilseed rape and are testing the selfed progeny, as well as hybrids with the weed *Brassica campestris=B.rapa.* The rare hybrid offspring from escaped pollen bearing transgenic mitigator genes would not pose a dire threat, especially to wild species outside fields, as the amount of pollen reaching the pristine wild would be minimal. Pollen flow decreases exponentially with distance, belying the unbased 'demographic swamping' by 'Trojan genes' giving rise to 'migrational meltdown', as predicted by Haygood et al. (2003).

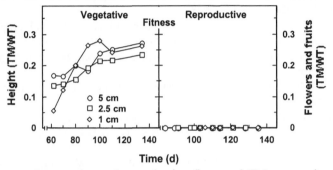

Figure 2. Suppressed vegetative and reproductive fitness of TM transgenics in competition with wild type tobacco. The points represent the calculated ratio of data for TM to wild type plants in Figure 1.

The containment of pharmaceutical transgenes has been physical, and as evidenced by recent human error that allowed temporary volunteer escape of "Prodigene" maize with such genes. The biological containment strategies described above may be preferable to depending on humans, and the mitigation strategies should work as well. Maize pharmaceutical transgenes are expressed in embryo tissues, and a potential tandem mitigating gene could be any dominant gene that affects the endosperm, e.g. the various "shrunken seed" loci, especially those where sugar transformation to starch is inhibited. Such shrunken seeds, with their high sugar content, are somewhat harder to store than normal maize but are extremely unfit in the field, and are unlikely to over winter. Because the endosperm of corn is 67% pollen genes, it is important that expression of pharmaceutical encoding genes be only in the embryo.

MONITORING TRANSGENE MOVEMENT

Using the various containment and mitigation strategies it should be possible to keep 'leaks' below risk thresholds, which should be mandated by science-based regulators on a case-to-case basis. As the numbers of transgenic species being released is increasing, and the problems of monitoring for such genes increases geometrically, we suggest that a uniform biobarcode[TM] system be used, where a small piece of non-coding DNA with uniform recognition sites are at the ends (for single PCR primer pair amplification) with an assigned variable region in between. Thus, PCR-automated sequencing could be used to determine the origin of 'leaks', contamination, liability, as well as intellectual property violations (Gressel & Ehrlich, 2002).

ACKNOWLEDGEMENTS

The research on transgenic mitigation was supported by the Levin Foundation, by INCO–DC, contract no. ERB IC18 CT 98 0391, H.I. A.-A. by a bequest from Israel and Diana Safer, and J.G. by the Gilbert de-Botton chair in plant sciences.

REFERENCES

Al-Ahmad, H I; Galili S; Gressel J (2003). Tandem constructs to mitigate risks of transgene flow: tobacco as a model. *(submitted)*.

Avni, A; Edelman M (1991). Direct selection for paternal inheritance of chloroplasts in sexual progeny of *Nicotiana*. *Molecular & General Genetics* **225**, 273-277.

Bock, R (2001). Transgenic plastids in basic research and plant biotechnology. *Journal of Molecular Biology* **312**, 425-438.

Daniell, H (2002). Molecular strategies for gene containment in transgenic crops. *Nature Biotechnology* **20**, 581-586.

Darmency, H (1994). Genetics of herbicide resistance in weeds and crops, In: *Herbicide Resistance in Plants: Biology and Biochemistry*, eds S B Powles & J A M Holtum, pp. 263-298. Lewis: Boca-Raton.

Ellstrand, N C; Prentice H C; Hancock J F (1999). Gene flow and introgression from domestic plants into their wild relatives. *Annual Review of Ecology and Systematics* **30**, 539-563.

Gressel, J (1999). Tandem constructs: preventing the rise of superweeds. *Trends in Biotechnology* **17**, 361-366.

Gressel, J (2002). *Molecular biology of weed control* Taylor and Francis, London.

Gressel, J; Ehrlich G (2002). Universal inheritable barcodes for identifying organisms. *Trends in Plant Science* **7**, 542-544.

Haygood, R; Ives, AR; Andow, DA (2003) Consequences of recurrent gene flow from crops to wild relatives. *Proceedings of the Royal Society: Biological Sciences* (in press).

Jepson, I (2002). Inducible herbicide resistance. *US Patent 6380463*.

Kuvshinov, V; Koivu K; Kanerva A; Pehu E (2001). Molecular control of transgene escape from genetically modified plants. *Plant Science* **160**, 517-522.

Maliga, P (2002). Engineering the plastid genome of higher plants. *Current Opinion in Plant Biology* **5**, 164-172.

Oliver, M J; Quisenberry J E; Trolinder N L G; Keim D L (1998). Control of plant gene expression. *United States Patent 5,723,765*.

Schernthaner, J P; Fabijanski S F; Arnison P G; Racicot M; Robert L S (2003). Control of seed germination in transgenic plants based on the segregation of a two-component genetic system. *Proceedings of the National Academy of Sciences USA* **100**, 6855-6859.

Tomiuk, J; Hauser T P; Bagger-Jørgensen R (2000). A- or C-chromosomes, does it matter for the transfer of transgenes from *Brassica napus*. *Theoretical and Applied Genetics* **100**, 750-754.

Wang, T; Li Y; Shi Y; Reboud X; Darmency H; Gressel J (2003). Low frequency transmission of a plastid encoded trait in *Setaria italica*. *Theoretical and Applied Genetics* (in press).

SESSION 9B

IMPACT OF CHANGING WEATHER PATTERNS ON CROP PROTECTION AND CROP PRODUCTION

Chairman: Dr Anthony Biddle
                     Processors and Growers Research
                     Organisation, Peterborough, UK

Session Organiser: Dr Keith Walters
                     Central Science Laboratory, York, UK

Papers: 9B-1 to 9B-4

Linking climate change predictions with crop simulation models

M A Semenov

Rothamsted Research, Harpenden, Herts, AL5 2JQ, UK

E-mail:mikhail.semenov@bbsrc.ac.uk

ABSTRACT

Assessment of the effects of climate change on crop yields is based on two integral parts: (1) crop simulation models, and (2) climate change scenarios. Crop simulation models are used for analysing the causes of yield variations in response to climate and environmental variability and operate on a spatial scale of one kilometre and with daily time steps. Climate change scenarios are based on global or regional climate models (GCMs or RegCMs) with spatial and temporal resolutions inappropriate for crop simulations. Output on the scale of hundreds of kilometeres and monthly time-scale needs to be spatially and temporally downscaled. One down-scaling method, which is capable of producing daily site-specific weather, is a stochastic weather generator. By combining the output from GCMs with a stochastic weather generator we are able to produce climate scenarios with high spatial and temporal resolution, which are suitable as input for crop simulation models. An alternative approach to linking GCMs with crop simulation models is the development of a simplified crop simulation model, a metamodel, that is able to use the output from GCMs at coarse spatial and temporal resolutions. An example of the development of a metamodel based on analysis of the structure of the Sirius wheat simulation model is given.

INTRODUCTION

Crop simulation models have proved themselves to be powerful tools for analysing the causes of production variations in many crops. A common need of most crop simulation models is daily weather data as the principle driving variables. Such models are useful for impact assessment when linked with climate change predictions, assessing crop responses to potential climate changes. They are also useful for seasonal yield predictions when linked with seasonal weather forecasts, guiding management early in the season well before most growth has occurred.

Global climate models (GCMs), the tools most widely used for climate predictions, are very complex and their demand for computational power limits their output to spatial and temporal scales inappropriate for crop simulation. Output is on the scale of hundreds of kilometres and the associated time-scale is monthly, which means that sub-grid scale processes on a short time-scale, such as precipitation, are not adequately represented. Stochastic weather generators lack the predictive power of GCMs, but are able to reproduce site-specific climates on a daily time-scale quite well (Semenov *et al.*, 1998). The combination of these two methodologies should allow the development of climate scenarios for agricultural applications that (1) are site-specific with daily temporal resolution; (2) include the full set of climate variables required by the crop model; (3) contain an adequate number of years to permit risk analysis; and (4) include changes in means and climate variability. By combining the output from GCMs with a stochastic weather generator we are able to produce climate change scenarios with high spatial and temporal resolution. The importance of downscaling and the incorporation of climate variability into climate change scenarios are demonstrated in the next section of this paper.

An alternative to downscaling from GCMs is upscaling crop simulation models by simplifying them to metamodels with fewer parameters and equations, and that may run on inputs of coarser temporal resolution, e.g. monthly weather. An example of development of a metamodel from the Sirius wheat simulation model is presented in the third section of the paper, together with some performance data in comparison with its parent.

NON-LINEARITY IN CLIMATE CHANGE IMPACT ASSESSMENT

Climate change scenarios with high spatial and temporal resolution were constructed and used in agricultural impact assessments at two selected sites, Rothamsted (UK) and Seville (Spain). The climate change scenarios were produced in two steps. First, a stochastic weather generator (LARS-WG) was run for observed weather at each site, and parameter files characterising typical weather at these sites were generated. Second, changes in climate characteristics, derived from GCMs (including changes in mean and variability), were applied to these parameters. New parameter files were used to generate site-specific climate change scenarios with a daily time-step. To construct scenarios, we used data from the UK Met. Office GCM transient experiments (UKTR; Murphy & Mitchell, 1995). Instead of using climate change integration fields themselves, the change fields were constructed by calculating the difference between a period in the climate change integration and the corresponding years of the control integration.

In order to produce scenarios of climate change at a site scale required by crop simulation models, it was necessary to downscale the coarse spatial resolution GCM data to a site level. This procedure involved the development of relationships between the coarse- and local-scale data for the climate variables concerned. There are currently a number of downscaling methodologies in use, including circulation patterns (e.g. Bardossy & Plate, 1991; Matyasovszky *et al.*, 1993) and regression techniques (e.g. Kim *et al.*, 1984; Wigley *et al.*, 1990). Both methods use existing instrumental databases to determine the relationships between large-scale and local climate. Regression techniques develop statistical relationships between local station data and grid-box scale, area-average values of say, temperature and precipitation and other meteorological variables. The circulation pattern approach classifies atmospheric circulation according to type and then determines links between the circulation type and precipitation. At the selected sites, regression relationships were calculated between local station data (temperature and precipitation; i.e., the predictants) and grid-box scale, monthly anomalies of mean sea level pressure, the north-south and east-west pressure gradients, temperature and precipitation (i.e., the predictors). The regression relationships were based on anomalies from the long-term mean in order to facilitate the use of the GCM-derived changes in the equations. To calculate changes in climatic variability, daily data for the appropriate grid boxes from the control and perturbed integrations of the UKTR experiment were used to calculate changes in precipitation intensity, duration of wet and dry spells and temperature variances. These changes were then applied to the LARS-WG parameters previously calculated from the observed daily data at each site.

Incorporation of changes in variability into climate change scenarios could have a significant effect on agricultural impact assessments (Porter & Semenov, 1999), although it does not effect monthly statistics such as, for example, monthly total precipitation or monthly mean temperature. These means were compared for the UKTR scenarios with and without variability for Seville. There is no significant difference between monthly mean temperatures for the scenarios with and without variability for all months. Results from a t-test indicate that precipitation totals were significantly different for four months out of seven during the vegetation period for winter wheat (January - July) (Semenov & Barrow, 1997). For three of these months (May, June & July) precipitation for both scenarios was so low that it did not make a big difference to total precipitation over the vegetation period, 184 mm and 210 mm with and without variability, respectively, compared to 496 mm for the base climate. The effect of climate change scenarios with and without changes in variability for simulated crop yield is significant. This is partly because crop simulation models have non-linear responses to environmental variables (Semenov & Porter, 1995). For the base climate the grain yield simulated by the Sirius wheat simulation model (Jamieson et al., 1998) was 5.6 t/ha and its coefficient of variation (CV) was 0.24 (Table 1). According to the UKTR scenario without variability, the grain yield does not change much (5.2 t/ha) and the CV remains about the same (0.23). If changes in climate variability are considered the results are very different. The grain yield drops to 3.9 t/ha and the CV almost doubles to 0.48. The reason for this is not the total amount of precipitation, but the change in precipitation distribution over the vegetation period and the prolonged dry spells. The probability of producing yields less than 3.5 t/ha is almost 50% for the UKTR scenario with variability and only about 10% for the UKTR scenario without variability or for the baseline climate. The high probability of obtaining low grain yields may make wheat an economically unsuitable crop in Spain under this climate change scenario.

The disadvantage of regression downscaling is that it is data intensive; observed data from several sites are required in order to calculate observed means and anomalies. Construction of site-specific scenarios of climate change may be aided by the current development of Regional Climate model (RegCMs). This methodology has been recently developed for climate change studies (Giorgi & Mearns, 1991; Mearns et al., 1999). The RegCM is run with a high grid resolution (approximately 50km) over a limited area of interest. The RegCM is a physically based model nested into the GCM and is able to reproduce regional climate in more detail than the GCM itself. The UK Climate Impact Programme has made available climate change scenarios, based on HadRM3 regional model with the spatial resolution of 50 km and monthly temporal resolution (Hulme *et al.*, 2002). Work on the validation of a RegCM has shown that there may be still large differences between model output and observed weather statistics, especially in the case of climate variability (Mearns *et al.*, 1995). This means that the construction of local climate change scenarios from these models may be as problematic as from GCMs and will require the use of a stochastic weather generator for temporal downscaling. Mearns *et al.*, 1999 recently compared scenarios, which have been produced using a regional climate model and a statistical downscaling method based on atmospheric circulation patterns. They demonstrated that

Table 1. The effect of climate variability on crop yield and its coefficient of variation (CV), as simulated by SIRIUS Wheat, for UKTR scenario at Seville, Spain. Total precipitation and cumulative mean temperature were calculated for the winter wheat vegetation period from January to July.

	Base	UKTR	UKTR with variability
Grain yield, t/ha	5.6	5.2	3.9
CV of yield	0.24	0.23	0.48
Total precipitation January-July, mm	296	210	184
Cum. Temperature January-July, °C	3630	4293	4323

substantial differences in the regional climate details of climate change are produced by two different means of downscaling from the same large-scale GCM experiments.

SIMPLIFYING CROP SIMULATION MODEL

An alternative approach to linking global climate models with crop simulation models is the development of a simplified crop simulation model that is able to use the output from GCMs at course spatial and temporal resolutions. Recently a sensitivity analysis and analysis of the structure of the Sirius wheat simulation model led to the development of a simpler meta-model that used relationships between simulated crop variables and aggregations of weather input variables (Brooks et al., 2000). The metamodel produced very similar yield predictions to its parent, Sirius, for both potential and water-limited yields where nitrogen was not a limiting factor. The meta-model aggregates the three main Sirius components, the calculation of leaf area index, the soil water balance and the evapotranspiration calculations, into simpler equations. This reduces the requirements for calibration to fewer model parameters and allows weather variables to be provided on a monthly rather than daily time-step, because the meta-model is able to use cumulative values of weather variables. This makes the meta-model a valuable tool for regional impact assessments with seasonal weather predictions, when detailed input data are not available. A brief description of the metamodel follows.

The metamodel calculates potential yield and then reduces it using a drought stress index. The essential elements of the metamodel are calculation of phenology to determine the duration of the main growth phases, calculation of the biomass accumulated during those phases, and calculation of a drought stress index.

The phenological submodel of Sirius is based primarily on the prediction of the rate of leaf production and the numbers of leaves produced on the mainstem of wheat, in response to temperature and daylength. This part of the model has been retained intact in the metamodel, but there are prospects for simplifying it. It is important because it determines both the duration of growth and weather experienced by the crop during the critical grain growth period. The timing of anthesis is important within the metamodel because biomass accumulated by this time makes a contribution to grain yield.

Biomass accumulated from sowing to anthesis A is calculated from the ratio of mean daily solar radiation to mean temperature during this phase, and the phase duration. The simplified relationship encapsulates canopy response to temperature, affecting the amount of solar radiation captured by the crop, and the solar radiation itself. Similarly, the biomass accumulated after anthesis G, most of which is grain, is calculated from a single equation involving the ratio of mean solar radiation and temperature during the grain filling period. Potential grain yield is calculated as $0.25A + G$. This is reduced by a drought stress factor based on a simplified calculation of the crop water balance, and the ratio between potential evapotranspiration and water supply, analogous to the Penman drought response model (Penman, 1971).

A major difference of the metamodel from Sirius is that the growth of the plant is not simulated on a daily basis but, rather, biomass is related to the accumulated weather variables. Indeed, the only daily calculations are the adding up of the weather variables. An important characteristic is that the meta-model contains very little interaction between components. Once the anthesis date and leaf number are known, the anthesis biomass, the post-anthesis potential biomass and the water stress yield loss are all calculated separately.

The meta-model was run for Rothamsted 1961 – 1990 with 50% precipitation and for Edinburgh with a soil of low water holding capacity and the results compared with those from Sirius. Daily weather data was used in both cases. The scenarios were chosen to give a wide range of yields mainly due to variations in water stress. In both cases the meta-model performed well giving a root mean square error (RMSE) of 0.68 and 0.83 t ha^{-1} respectively on yields of 4-11 t ha^{-1} (cf. standard deviations in Sirius yields of 1.3 and 2.2 t ha^{-1}) and correlation coefficients of 0.92 and 0.95.

The good match of the meta-model yield values with those of Sirius indicates that the meta-model contains the most important aspects of Sirius and, in particular, that there are no other mechanisms within Sirius that substantially affect yield. The meta-model is based on analysis of the Sirius model, rather than just on its output, so it should be able to match the Sirius output well for most scenarios in Britain (e.g., different sowing dates or cultivars) and probably for many other climates, without serious modifications.

The parameters and data used by the meta-model are the ones that need to be determined accurately for Sirius to perform well. As noted above, phenological development is crucial, so the parameters governing plant performance (responses to daylength and temperature) need to be well known, and temperature well specified. Solar radiation is important because it affects both potential yield and the water deficit. However, solar radiation is often not directly measured but is estimated, for example from sunshine hours. To some extent the accuracy of the model will depend on the accuracy of those estimates.

Because the meta-model uses accumulated values of the weather variables, it is able to perform well with just monthly weather data. To demonstrate this, it was run at Rothamsted with 50% precipitation and at Edinburgh for the soil with low AWC (80 mm), using daily weather data and 30-days moving average weather data. The results of metamodel runs for daily and monthly weather were compared. RMSE for the anthesis day and water-limited yield are 1 day and 147 kg/ha, and 1.7 days and 470 kg/ha for Rothamsted and Edinburgh, respectively. Hence replacing daily data with disaggregated monthly data in the metamodel is unlikely to change the output significantly. This makes the concept of this type of model really useful in the forecasting arena where trends rather than daily weather data are the likely outputs of weather forecasting.

CONCLUSIONS

In this paper it has been shown that methodology exists for linking climate change predictions with crop models to allow agricultural risk assessment, either by downscaling GCM data, or by upscaling crop simulation models.

ACKNOWLEDGEMENTS.

Rothamsted Research receives grant-aided support from the Biotechnology and Biological Sciences Research Council of the United Kingdom.

REFERENCES

Bardossy A; Plate E J (1991). Modelling daily rainfall using a semi-Markov representation of circulation pattern occurrence. *Journal of Hydrology* **122**, 33-47.

Brooks R J; Semenov M A; Jamieson P D (2000). Simplifying Sirius: sensitivity analysis and development of a meta-model for wheat yield prediction. *European Journal of Agronomy* **14**, 43-60.

Hulme M *et al.* (2002). Climate Change Scenarios for the United Kingdom: The UKCIP02 Scientific Report. *Tyndall Centre for Climate Change Research and School of Environmental Sciences*, University of East Anglia.

Giorgi F; Mearns L O (1991). Approaches to the simulation of regional climate change: a review. *Review of Geophysics* **29**, 191-216.

Jamieson P D; Semenov M A; Brooking I R; Francis G S (1998). Sirius: a mechanistic model of wheat response to environmental variation. *Field Crop Research* **8**, 161-179.

Kim, J W; Chang, J T; Baker N L; Wilks D S; Gates W L; (1984). The statistical problem of climate inversion: Determination of the relationship between local and large-scale climate. *Monthly Weather Review* **112**, 2069-2077.

Matyasovszky I; Bogardi I; Bardossy A; Duckstein L (1993). Space-time precipitation reflecting climate change. *Hydrological Sciences* **38**, 539-558.

Mearns L O; Giorgi F; Mcdaniel L; Shields C (1995). Analysis of variability and diurnal range of daily temperature in a nested regional climate model - comparison with observations and doubled CO_2 results. *Climate Dynamics* **11**, 193-209.

Mearns L O; Bogardi I; Giorgi F; Matyasovskey I; Paleski M (1999). Comparison of climate change scenarios generated from regional climate model experiments and statistical downscaling. *Journal of Geophysical Research* **104**, 6603-6621.

Murphy J M; Mitchell J F B (1995). Transient response of the Hadley Centre coupled ocean-atmosphere model to increasing carbon dioxide. Part II: Spatial and temporal structure of the response. *Journal of Climate* **8**, 57-80.

Penman H L (1971). Irrigation at Woburn VII. *Report Rothamsted Experimental Station for 1970*, Part 2, 147-170.

Porter J R; Semenov M A (1999). Climate variability and crop yields in Europe. *Nature* **400**, N 6746, 724.

Semenov M A; Barrow E M (1997). Use of a stochastic weather generator in the development of climate change scenarios. *Climatic Change* **35**, 397-414.

Semenov M A; Brooks R J; Barrow E M; Richardson C W (1998). Comparison of the WGEN and LARS-WG stochastic weather generators in diverse climates. *Climate Research* **10**:95-107.

Semenov M A; Porter J R (1995). Climatic variability and the modelling of crop yields. *Agricultural and. Forest Meteorology* **73**, 265-283.

Wigley T M L; Jones P D; Briffa K R; Smith G (1990). Obtaining sub-grid-scale information from coarse-resolution general circulation model output. *Journal of Geophysical Research* **95**, 1943-1953.

Climate change and decreasing herbicide persistence

S W Bailey
ADAS, Woodthorne, Wergs Road, Wolverhampton, WV6 8TQ, UK
Email: steven.bailey@adas.co.uk

ABSTRACT

A herbicide degradation model, run with historical weather data, was used to study the change in duration of weed control by autumn-applied isoproturon over the period 1980-2001. The results suggest that soil residues fell to the minimum for weed control by a mean of approximately 30 days earlier during the last five years of this period than in the first five years, equivalent to a reduction of approximately 25% in duration of weed control. This decline in persistence is attributed to increasing soil temperature. The results are discussed in relation to recent observations and predictions of climate change and their relevance to other autumn-applied pesticides and future weed control is considered.

INTRODUCTION

The herbicide degradation model developed by Walker and Eagle (Walker & Eagle, 1983) uses standard records of air temperature and rainfall to estimate soil moisture content and temperature at short time intervals. These in turn are used to calculate rates of degradation in the field of pesticides with different half-lives, using observed effects of soil moisture and temperature on degradation rate, (previously measured in laboratory incubation experiments). Each day, for a given meteorological area and pesticide laboratory half-life, the amount of pesticide remaining undegraded in the soil at the end of the day can be estimated as a percentage of that present at the start. Residues remaining at the end of longer periods, eg. months, can be determined by successive daily estimates.

A similar model (Walker & Barnes, 1981) has formed the basis of the degradation routine in other more complete pesticide dissipation models, in particular PELMO (Klein, 1991) and MACRO (Jarvis, 1993). The Walker & Eagle (1983) model is not used to estimate actual residues at a site, but to compare estimated residues in one year to those in others. By assessing relative changes in residues, the model has been used to give farm advice on either herbicide carryover risk to following crops, or the persistence of weed control in one year compared to others.

As an example of the former, atrazine residues at the end of September can be estimated, after its use on maize in May. If the estimated residues are found to be higher than the estimated long-term average, advice can be given that the risk of atrazine carryover into following crops is higher than normal. This might have major implications for cultivations and crop sowing dates. The persistence of weed control can be estimated in a similar manner. For example, the herbicide isoproturon, which has both foliar and soil activity, is applied to winter cereals in the UK, most commonly in November. By the end of the following February farmers need to establish whether any soil activity remains. The model is run for the period 1 November – 28

February and if the resulting estimated residues are less than the estimated long-term average, advice may be given that the duration of weed control is likely to be shorter than normal.

During the 1990s, it was noticed that estimates of isoproturon persistence at the end of February were less than the long-term average in almost every year. This paper investigates the trend using a 22-year dataset, from 1980 and relates the findings to observed changes in climate during this period.

METHODS

The original version of the Walker & Eagle (1983) model used weather data from a limited number of sites in England and Wales and provided little opportunity to the manipulate data. In January 1999, the model was upgraded. Daily meteorological data are now supplied for 650 areas covering the whole of Great Britain. Daily data are available for all 650 sites from January 1999. Retrospective data were also supplied from January 1980 onwards for six of these areas, selected from across England to represent arable farming in a range of climates, (Brize Norton in Oxfordshire; Heathrow near London; Leeming in North Yorkshire; Marham in Norfolk; Shawbury in Shropshire; Yeovilton in Devon). The updated model was used to estimate degradation for each month from January 1980, for four laboratory half-life categories (20, 40, 60 and 80 days, to reflect a range of pesticides), for these six areas. This required approximately 6300 runs of the model. The results were entered into spreadsheets, so that trends could be investigated.

These data were used first to estimate the residues of isoproturon remaining at the end of February, following an application on 1 November, for each year from 1980. Two of the six sites were chosen, Brize Norton representing a southern site and Leeming in the North. A 20-day laboratory half-life was selected, as suggested by Walker & Eagle (1983) for this herbicide.

The resulting change in persistence was then related to changes in the duration of weed control. To do this a threshold concentration of isoproturon in the soil was required, below which there would be little or no herbicidal activity. Little information was available to determine this threshold. However, previous research on damaging isoproturon levels for various crops (ADAS, 1983) had found that a soil concentration of 0.19 mg kg^{-1} in the top 15 cm was the minimum to cause damage to grass and a range of cereals. Assuming a soil bulk density of 1.3g cm^{-3} and an isoproturon application rate of 1500 g ha^{-1}, this residue is equivalent to approximately 25% of the applied rate. The model could now be run to estimate the date on which residues from a 1 November application declined to 25% of the initial amount, for each year from November 1980.

RESULTS

Figure 1 shows the estimated residue at the end of February, following an application on 1 November, for Brize Norton over the period 1980-2001. There is a downward trend in the five-year running average, suggesting there has been a general decrease in persistence over the 22 year period investigated.

The estimated dates on which residues declined to the minimum for weed control, at Brize Norton and Leeming, are shown in Figure 2. A trend to an earlier date on which the threshold was reached can be clearly seen. The threshold was usually reached slightly later at Leeming than Brize Norton.

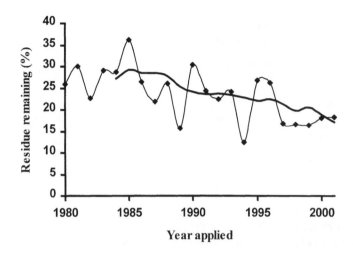

Figure 1: Estimated isoproturon residue on 28 February at Brize Norton (-•-), following application on 1 november (% of applied amount), and five-year running average (-), 1980-2001.

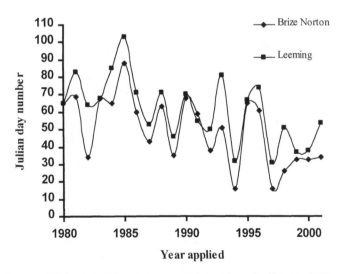

Figure 2: Estimated Julian date on which residues declined to 25% of the amount applied on 1 November, 1980-2001.

Table 1 presents the average date on which the 25% threshold was reached, for the first and last five year periods (1980-84 and 1997-01). These results suggest that isoproturon residues fell to below the 25% threshold on average 32 and 31 days earlier in the last five years than in the first five years of this period, for Brize Norton and Leeming respectively.

Table 1.   Estimated average date for isoproturon residues to fall to 25% of the initial amount applied, following application on 1 November.

Area	1980[a] –1984[a]	1997[a] – 2001[a]
Brize Norton	1 March	28 January
Leeming	14 March	11 February

[a] Application year

DISCUSSION

The results suggest that the period over which isoproturon gives effective weed control has reduced by approximately 30 days since the early 1980s. This is a reduction of approximately 25% in the duration of efficacy and represents a major decline in persistence.

A reduction in persistence of this magnitude would be expected to have a noticeable effect on weed control. Such an effect has frequently been reported by farmers and agronomists and attributed to a number of factors. Firstly, the maximum rate of isoproturon normally applied has declined over the 22-year period of this study, from 2500 g ha^{-1} in the 1980's, to 1500 g ha^{-1} in the winter of 2001-2. This, however, makes little difference to the predictions made by the model. The time taken to fall to the threshold concentration of 0.19 mg kg^{-1} is extended by four to five weeks by the higher application rate, but the date on which this concentration is reached still advances by approximately four weeks over the 22-year period of study. Weed resistance to herbicides is a widely reported phenomenon and has also been implicated to explain the declining levels of control, (Moss et al., 1999). Thirdly, enhanced degradation of isoproturon by soil microorganisms, due to microbial adaptation, has been reported, (Cox et al., 1996).

In addition to these factors, the above results suggest the weather has had a major effect over the last 22 years. Soil temperature and moisture content are the two environmental factors having the greatest effect on pesticide degradation in soil. Soil moisture content is unlikely to have been a major limiting factor on degradation over winter during the period studied, with soils close to field capacity. Hence, the trends found are likely to be primarily a result of changing temperatures. Records of the mean November – February air temperature (which directly affects soil temperature variation) for Brize Norton over this period reveals a clear upward trend. The slightly longer persistence of isoproturon in most years at Leeming than Brize Norton, shown in Figure 2, reflects the slightly lower temperatures at the more northerly site. The wide variation in dates shown in Figure 2 would also account for a large part of the year-to-year variation in weed control from isoproturon often remarked upon by agronomists.

Whether the effects found are the result of anthropogenic climate change is more equivocal. However, the trends are broadly consistent with some weather effects now being attributed to climate change. The recently published "Climate Change Scenarios for the United Kingdom" (UK Climate Impacts Programme or UKCIP02; Hulme *et al.*, 2002) reports that the annual average temperature for central England has increased by almost 1°C during the twentieth century and that the 1990's was the warmest decade in central England since records began in the 1660's. This is broadly consistent with the trend in estimated herbicide persistence described above.

The same report also presents four alternative scenarios of how climate change may affect UK climate over the next hundred years, based on a range of future global emissions of greenhouse gases. Of particular relevance are the following key projections:

by the 2080's, the annual average temperature across the UK may rise by between 1°C (low emissions scenario) and 5°C (high emissions scenario), with greater warming in the south and east;
winters are likely to become up to 30% wetter over the same period.

The time-scale of these projections is very long, but the magnitude of the changes could be considerably greater than those seen so far. The projections suggest that the persistence of herbicides such as isoproturon may be reduced further and that even over a timescale similar to that studied in this paper, the reduction could be much greater than has taken place so far.

It is important to stress that such an effect would not be limited to isoproturon. All autumn and winter-applied, soil active herbicides are likely to be affected in a broadly similar manner, as indeed would other pesticides present in UK soils at this time of year, because of the temperature dependence of degradation. Isoproturon is an old herbicide, but there are many other residual, autumn-applied herbicides in use (Table 2) and new ones continue to be developed.

Table 2.   Autumn-applied herbicides with residual activity

Crop	Herbicides
Cereals	chlorotoluron, DFF, flufenacet, flupyrsulfuron-methyl, pendimethalin, propoxycarbazone-sodium, trifluralin
Winter beans	clomazone, simazine
Winter oilseed rape	cyanazine, metazachlor, propyzamide, quinmerac

The results suggest that the persistence of pesticide residues in soils over winter in the UK will have declined since 1980 and the magnitude of the effect will depend on the laboratory half-life of the pesticide. The Walker & Eagle (1983) model used in this study can be applied to all pesticides in soil for which there is a well-defined laboratory half-life and for which a first order degradation curve is a reasonable approximation. If the model were to be used to make the same estimates for other pesticides as for isoproturon, similar percentage declines in persistence are likely to be predicted. For pesticides that may contaminate water by movement through the soil, this loss of persistence may be of benefit to the environment. However, for pesticides with soil activity, such as residual herbicides, a significant loss of pest control is likely.

The overall effects of climate change on pesticides in general and weed control in particular are difficult to predict, because there will be many interacting factors involved. However, recent work by Harris & Hossell (2001) has suggested that predicted higher soil moisture deficits in autumn might bring fields to a condition which is too wet to conduct fieldwork at an earlier date than at present. This might encourage the earlier application of autumn herbicides. If this is combined with a reduction in herbicide persistence, autumn and winter weed control may become much more difficult than at present (Bailey, in Press).

REFERENCES

ADAS (1983). Research and Development Report *Pesticide Science 1983*, p.37. MAFF Reference Book252 (83), HMSO, London.

Bailey S W. Climate change and decreasing herbicide persistence. *Pest Management Science, (in Press)*.

Cox L; Walker A; Welch S J (1996). Evidence for the accelerated degradation of isoproturon in soils. *Pesticide Science* **48,** 253-260.

Harris D; Hossell J E (2001). Weed management constraints under climate change. *Proceedings of the BCPC Conference – Weeds 2001*, **1,** 91-96.

Hulme M; Jenkins G J; Lu X; Turnpenny J R; Mitchell T D; Jones R G; Lowe J; Murphy J M; Hassell D; Boorman P; McDonald R; Hill S (2002). In: *Climate Change Scenarios for the United Kingdom: The UKCIP02 Scientific Report,* Tyndall Centre for Climate Change Research, School of Environmental Sciences, University of East Anglia, Norwich.

Klein M (1991). PELMO Release 1.0. Fraunhoffer Gesselschaft, Schmallenberg, Germany

Jarvis N J (1993). MACRO Release 3.0. Swedish Environmental Protection Agency, Swedish University of Agricultural Sciences, Uppsala, Sweden.

Moss S R; Clarke J H; Blair A M; Culley T N; Read M A; Ryan P J; Turner M (1999). The occurrence of herbicide-resistant grass weeds in the United Kingdom and a new system for designating resistance in screening assays. *Proceedings of the BCPC Conference – Weeds 1999*, **1,** 179-184.

Walker A; Barnes A (1981). Simulation of herbicide persistence in soil; a revised computer model. *Pesticide Science* **12,** 123-132.

Walker A; Eagle D J (1983). Prediction of herbicide residues in soil for advisory purposes. *Aspects of Applied Biology 4, 1983, Influence of environmental factors on herbicide performance and crop and weed biology*, 503-509.

Turning up the heat on pests and diseases: a case study for Barley yellow dwarf virus

R Harrington
Rothamsted Research, Harpenden, Hertfordshire, AL5 2JQ, UK
Email: richard.harrington@bbsrc.ac.uk

ABSTRACT

Interactions between the various factors influencing the incidence of pests and diseases are always very complex, making modelling and prediction difficult. Environmental changes add another layer of problems and may influence the longevity of decision support systems. In many areas Barley yellow dwarf virus is likely to become more troublesome. In the UK, indications are that the risk of increase in BYDV incidence in autumn-sown cereals is greatest in the west where milder winters are expected to be accompanied by wetter summers than will occur in the east, both these factors aiding aphid survival.

INTRODUCTION

The World is getting warmer (I.P.C.C., 2001) and it is certain that this will affect arable agriculture. Whether the effect is positive or negative will depend on location and crops grown. It will also depend on the affect of changes in temperature and other factors, perhaps especially rainfall, not only on the crops themselves but also on their competitors, the pests and diseases of the crops and their own competitors, and the natural enemies of the pests. Indeed, even this is a gross oversimplification as the interactions between these factors are highly complex.

There are good reasons for trying to predict the impacts of climate change within the context of the protection of crops from pests and diseases. We need to determine whether we will be able to manage pests and diseases in the future as we do currently or, if not, the options that will be open to us. So far, generalisations have proved elusive and methodological frameworks controversial. However, the more diverse the range of problems studied and the methodologies used, the more likely it is that generic insights will emerge. In the mean time, the daunting task of integration should not deter studies of specific systems.

Potential means by which changes in climate may lead to changes in pest status of species, for example through changes in the physiology, phenology, distribution and abundance and through impacts on our ability to control pest species, have been reviewed elsewhere (Harrington *et al.*, 2001). This paper concentrates on how climatic changes may affect the incidence of Barley yellow dwarf viruses (collectively here termed BYDV) and some of their aphid vectors.

BYDV EPIDEMIOLOGY

Several authors have drawn attention specifically to the complexities of BYDV epidemiology (*e.g.* Irwin & Thresh, 1990; Burgess *et al.*, 1999). The so-called disease triangle, made into a pyramid by adding interactions with the environment to those between the viruses, vectors and host plants, is a bit hackneyed. However, it still serves a useful purpose in drawing attention to some of the issues that need to be addressed when considering potential impacts of climate change, and a brief summary is warranted.

The viruses

There are at least two species and a whole raft of strains and isolates involved in barley yellow dwarf disease, each of which may interact differently with vectors, host plants and the environment.

The vectors

Being a persistent, phloem-limited virus, aphids have to feed to acquire BYDV, rather than just probe for host plant identification cues. At least 28 species can do this, although it is probable that only a sub-set of these is important. Nonetheless this presents multiple complications, as the aphid species have different life cycles, fly at different times and in different places and have different behaviour patterns. Different clones within species may also vary in some or all of these characteristics. Environmental change will certainly have a different impact between, or even within, species.

The host plants

There is a whole range of crops and other *Poaceae* that are hosts to BYDV. All are potential reservoirs of infection and, again, they will respond differently to environmental changes. Changes to cropping patterns, such as the introduction of *Miscanthus* as a renewable energy source, will increase the potential BYDV reservoir and might also provide a green bridge for the disease. Expansion of the area of maize also has the potential to alter dramatically patterns of BYDV spread through its influence on aphid incidence and species composition and on virus strains present.

Virus - vector interactions

Some species of aphid can transmit more than one virus strain efficiently and some virus strains can be transmitted efficiently by more than one aphid species. Different clones of aphids also differ in their vectoring efficiency (Guo *et al.*, 1996) and behaviour. Furthermore a given virus isolate can be transmitted with different efficiency by different clones of a given aphid species and a given aphid clone can transmit different isolates with different efficiencies. Yet another complication is that the species of aphid which inoculated the virus may have a significant effect on the efficiency with which different aphid species can subsequently transmit virus (Gray *pers. comm.*). It is possible that such effects are even seen at aphid clonal level.

Virus - host plant interactions

Symptoms in host plants differ with virus strain or isolate, making it difficult to assign resistance ratings to cultivars. Also, under this heading, the latent period in the plant must be considered, *i.e.* the time between the plant becoming infected and itself acting as a virus source. This is affected by growth stage, virus strain and environmental conditions.

Vector - host plant interactions

Different aphids have different host plant preferences and this will clearly affect disease epidemiology. Also, crop growth stage will affect both aphid feeding behaviour and host plant preference.

Virus - vector - host plant interactions

Considering just the virus, the host range of each BYDV strain is similar. However, in the field there are differences in which virus strains are prevalent in different hosts. For example *Rhopalosiphum maidis* does not tend to feed on oats and so RMV, a virus strain which relies on this vector, is not usually a problem in oats. Changes in cultivars may have profound effects on epidemiology through effects on the vectors and viruses.

ENVIRONMENTAL CONSIDERATIONS AND CLIMATE CHANGE

Environmental factors interact strongly at every stage discussed above and make predictions of climate change impacts somewhat circumspect. However, there are some pointers.

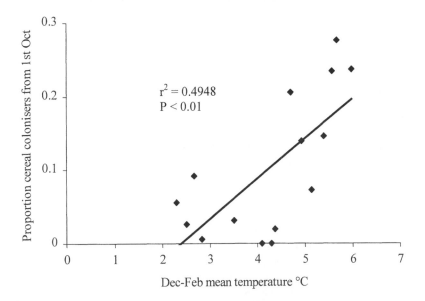

Figure 1. Relationship between previous winter temperature and proportion of cereal-colonising forms of the aphid *Rhopalosiphum padi* trapped at Rothamsted in autumn 1986-2000.

In the UK, general experience and some empirical evidence suggest that BYDV problems are greatest following two consecutive mild winters with a wet summer in between. The first mild winter leads to a high proportion of anholocyclic clones of *Rhopalosiphum padi*, a major vector, in the following year (Fig. 1). The anholocyclic clones are those which over-winter in the active stage on grasses, including cereals, rather than as an egg on their primary host, *Prunus padus*. Therefore, only the anholocyclic clones are important in transmission of BYDV in autumn-sown crops. The active forms are far less tolerant of low temperature than are the eggs and a tendency can be seen for the proportion of anholocyclic forms in autumn to be related to temperature in the previous winter, with a higher proportion following a mild winter. If, in the mean time, the summer is wet, there is a plentiful supply of good quality grasses to tide the aphids over between the ripening of one crop and emergence of the next. In the UK, there is a weak but significant relationship between numbers of *R. padi* in autumn, and summer rainfall. A second mild winter allows all these aphids of the right morph to move around the newly emerged crop, spreading virus. Thus, two mild winters with a wet summer in between provides the basis for increased risk of economically damaging virus spread. Figure 2 shows how the probability of encountering two consecutive mild winters (defined here as December to February mean temperature exceeding 4.5°C), with a wet summer in between (defined here as precipitation from June to August exceeding 190mm), is likely to change in different regions of the UK according to climate predictions to the end of this century. The BYDV risk is predicted to rise particularly in Northwest England and Southwest England. In other parts, although the criterion of warm winters is met more often in the future, the summers are expected to be particularly dry, hence reducing risk.

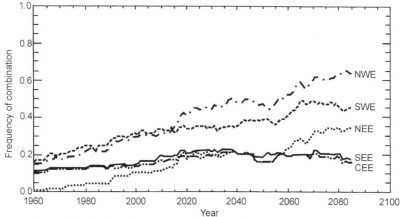

Figure 2   Probability of two mild winters with an intervening wet summer in Northeast England (NEE), Southeast England (SEE), Central and Eastern England (CEE), Northwest England (NWE) and Southwest England (SWE).

Drought stress during the growing season can increase risk of spread. In laboratory experiments in which trays of plants were subjected to different levels of drought stress, aphids visited more plants at higher temperatures and at higher drought stress levels, and this was reflected in the number of plants infected with BYDV (Smyrnioudis *et al.*, 2000). There was a temperature - drought stress interaction: high levels of drought stress had a particularly strong effect at higher temperatures. Furthermore, there is likely to be an interaction between drought stress and BYDV with respect to plant vigour. Drought stress is likely to weaken the plant and increase its susceptibility to the disease. On the other hand BYDV is likely to weaken the plant and make it more susceptible to drought.

Climatic change may influence the prevalence of particular virus isolates in a region and the efficiency of their transmission by particular aphid species. For example, the RMV strain of BYDV is currently unimportant in small grain cereals in the UK. It is transmitted by *R. maidis*, which is uncommon compared to other vectors. With climate warming, maize may become more widespread, as may the maize-preferring strain of the aphid, which does not produce an egg and hence is not tolerant of cold winters. At higher temperatures, the more common vectors in the UK may become capable of transmitting the RMV strain to cereals such as wheat and barley (Lucio-Zavaleta *et al.*, 2001). Therefore, warmer conditions, through their effect on interactions between host plants, aphids and viruses, may render the maize strain of BYDV important in wheat and barley for the first time in the UK.

These examples serve to remind us that changes in climatic variables may have unexpected effects on BYDV epidemiology. Thus, the extrapolation based on mild winters and wet summers (above) could turn out to be grossly over simplistic, whilst process-based modelling could turn out to be grossly over complex.

Extrapolation from current distribution

What can the distribution of BYDV incidence around the World today tell us about expected impacts of climate change in a given region? Can we find areas where the climate today is similar to that expected in our particular area of interest fifty years hence and infer that BYDV problems will be similar? Again, this is too simplistic. For example, even though climate may be matched, photoperiod may not, and that influences plant growth, insect life cycles and hence epidemiology in a range of ways. However, the review by Lister & Ranieri (1995) shows clearly that where there are cereals there is BYDV and, although prevalent strains and isolates may change in a given area, the disease is likely to be sufficiently adaptable to continue to be ubiquitous no matter how the climate changes. Nonetheless, there currently exists no summary of which strains of BYDV are prevalent in which areas of the World, and how abundant and damaging they tend to be in those areas. Such information would provide a useful base on which to build testable hypotheses concerning climate change impacts on BYDV.

Impacts on decision support

Various decision support systems (DSS) aimed at rationalising the use of insecticides to control BYDV are in operation or are under development (Knight & Thackray, in press). A major concern with any DSS is its upkeep following development and launch. This is particularly important in the case of computer-based systems which, if not updated, can become scientifically outdated surprisingly quickly whilst continuing to present a beguiling façade to users. We have seen that a BYDV DSS has to account for a large number of biotic and abiotic components of the disease system and for primary and lower level interactions between them. If any of these changes, the model parameters may become inappropriate. For example, new cereal varieties may interact in different ways to current varieties with the aphids and the viruses. In the longer term, environmental changes may have important effects. If a new DSS is found to be successful, growers should be prepared to reinvest some of the money saved through its use in its continued scientific development. The challenge for DSS developers is to provide systems that take account of the huge amount of variation, and potential for change that goes with any pest and disease problem and hence produce a system with wide and enduring applicability.

Wider considerations and mitigation options

There are at least three major problems when trying to assess mitigation options to offset the impacts of climate change on pests and diseases. The first is that generalisations are proving elusive. Even quite closely related pests or diseases respond to changes in different ways. The second is that pests and diseases are only a small component of agronomic considerations. For both of these reasons it is quite possible that changes designed to reduce one problem will exacerbate another. The third problem relates to the sheer complexity of interactions within and between the abiotic and biotic components of change (not only in climate) and the immense difficulty in accounting for this complexity in models. It is right the agricultural community is aware of what may lie ahead and that mitigation options are explored but there is much still to do to raise understanding to a level that can be translated into a holistic approach for growers.

ACKNOWLEDGEMENTS

I am grateful to Monique Henry (CIMMYT), Stewart Gray (Cornell University), Martin Parry (Jackson Environment Institute, University of East Anglia) and Ilias Smyrnioudis (University of Thessaloniki). Rothamsted Research receives grant aided support from the Biotechnology and Biological Sciences Research Council of the United Kingdom.

REFERENCES

Burgess A J; Harrington R; Plumb R T (1999). Barley and cereal yellow dwarf virus epidemiology and control strategies. In: *The Luteoviridae*, eds H G Smith & H Barker, pp. 248-261. CABI Publishing: Wallingford.

Guo J Q; Moreau J P; Lapierre H (1996). Variability among aphid clones of *Rhopalosiphum padi* L. and *Sitobion avenae* Fabr. (Homoptera: Aphididae) in transmission of three PAV isolates of barley yellow dwarf viruses. *Canadian Entomologist* **128**, 209-217.

Harrington R; Fleming R A; Woiwod I P (2001). Climate change impacts on insect management and conservation in temperature regions: can they be predicted? *Agricultural and Forest Entomology* **3**, 233-240.

IPCC (2001). *Climate change 2001: the scientific basis. Summary for policymakers and technical summary of the working group 1 report.* Cambridge University Press, Cambridge.

Irwin M E; Thresh J M (1990). Epidemiology of barley yellow dwarf: a study in ecological complexity. *Annual Review of Phytopathology* **28**, 393-424.

Knight J D; Thackray D J (in press). Decision support systems. In: *Aphids as Crop Pests*, eds H F van Emden and R Harrington, CABI Publishing: Wallingford.

Lister R M; Ranieri R (1995). Distribution and economic importance of barley yellow dwarf. In: *Barley yellow dwarf 40 years of progress*, eds C J D'Arcy & P A Burnett, pp. 29-35. APS Press: St Paul.

Lucio-Zavaleta E; Smith D M; Gray S M (2001). Variation in transmission efficiency among barley yellow dwarf virus - RMV isolates and clones of the normally inefficient aphid vector, *Rhopalosiphum padi*. *Phytopathology* **91**, 792-796.

Smyrnioudis I N; Harrington R; Katis N; Clark S J (2000). The effect of drought stress and temperature on spread of barley yellow dwarf virus (BYDV). *Agricultural and Forest Entomology* **3**, 161-166.

Predicting the potential distribution of alien pests in the UK under global climate change:
Diabrotica virgifera virgifera

R H A Baker, R J C Cannon, A MacLeod
Central Science Laboratory, Sand Hutton, York, YO41 1LZ, UK
Email: r.baker@csl.gov.uk

ABSTRACT

Diabrotica virgifera virgifera, the western corn rootworm, a North American species, was first found in Yugoslavia in 1992, and has since spread widely in central Europe. In 2002, it was found near Paris, raising concerns regarding its potential threat to UK maize crops. The computer program CLIMEX was used to identify the critical parameter – accumulated temperature – which defines the northward limit of distribution of *D. virgifera virgifera* in North America, and this threshold was then applied to the UK, at improved spatial and temporal resolutions, under current and predicted future climates. Under current climate conditions, *D. virgifera virgifera*, appears to be at the edge of its range in the UK but by 2050, under global warming, a large area of SE England will be suitable for this species.

INTRODUCTION

The growth in the volume, frequency, diversity and speed of global plant, animal and commodity movements through man's activities has provided increasing opportunities for species to spread beyond their natural range (Levine & D'Antonio, 2003). In England and Wales, approximately 500 taxa are identified from organisms detected in imported consignments each year (C Malumphy, *pers.comm*). Pest risk analyses are undertaken to determine the likelihood of these species establishing and causing serious economic or environmental damage, and the strength of any measures that should be imposed (FAO, 2001). Assuming entry, successful establishment in a new area depends on the suitability of both abiotic factors, e.g. climate, and biotic factors, e.g. the presence of hosts. The extent to which intrinsic attributes, e.g. the reproductive rate, favour colonisation must also be taken into account (Baker, 2002). While all such factors and attributes may influence establishment, the suitability of the climatic conditions is fundamental (Baker, *et al.,* 2000). Reliable assessments of the climatic suitability of a new area depend on the extent to which the species' climatic responses are known or can be inferred, climatic data are available or can be predicted for the time period of interest, interpolation techniques accurately predict climatic conditions over the landscape and differences between the micro-climate in the species' niche and locations where the climate recording instruments are situated can be taken into account.

Taking climate change into account is also critical to the assessments, since, for example, increasing temperatures may make habitats which are currently marginal more suitable to warmth-loving organisms over time. Temperature directly affects herbivorous insects, and in general terms, insect pests are expected to become more abundant as temperatures increase, through a number of inter-related processes, including range extensions and phenological changes, as well as increased rates of population development, growth, migration and over-wintering (Bale, *et al.*, 2002; Cannon, 1998; Masters, *et al.*, 1998). Species range expansions, in response to the increased favourability of habitats could have a marked influence in countries, such as the UK, which include a large number of species at, or near, the limit of their current northern distributions. The ranges of many, non-migratory European butterflies shifted northwards, between 35 to 240 km, in response to increasing temperatures during the 20th Century (Parnesian, *et al.*, 1999).

For insects and other invertebrates, which are regularly moving in or on traded plants or plant products, an increase in the suitability – or establishment potential – of their favoured habitat, can have a marked influence on their occurrence and abundance. For example, the UK Plant Health Service has become aware of a number of newly established species in recent years, particularly those with a Mediterranean or southern European distribution (see Cannon, *et al.*, 2003). For example, the Cottony cushion scale (*Icerya puchasi*) has recently bred and over-wintered outdoors in Britain (London) for the first time (Watson & Malumphy, *pers. comm*). Whilst not all of these invasions have been directly linked to climate change, increasing temperatures combined with a human intervention, have probably been major factors in enabling them to increase their natural range.

Previous studies have focused on predictions of potential distributions under current and future climates for species such as the Colorado beetle, *Leptinotarsa decemlineata*, which have well known climatic responses, threaten areas and spend critical periods of their life cycle above ground where the micro-climate is not too dissimilar to that recorded by weather stations (Baker *et al.*, 1998). Predicting the distribution of species which spend most or part of their life cycle in environments which are markedly different from those where climatic conditions are recorded, e.g. soil, wood or artificial environments, is much more difficult. In this paper, we describe how we have attempted to predict the potential UK distribution of a species which, apart from the adult stage, spends all of its life cycle in the soil. Originally from North America where it is one of the most serious pests of maize (Oerke *et al.*, 1994), the western corn rootworm, *Diabrotica virgifera virgifera*, was first found in Yugoslavia in 1992 and has since spread widely in central Europe and to three locations in northern Italy. In 2002, it was found near Paris (EPPO, 2003). Larval root feeding is the primary source of damage, reducing nutrient uptake and growth (Gavloski *et al.*, 1992) weakening plants and making them more susceptible to lodging which can cause serious losses in yield, particularly where the crop is grown continuously. Evidence from European countries suggests that there is a time lag of approximately five years between the first finding of *D. virgifera virgifera* and reports of economic damage. During 1999, in counties of Yugoslavia where damage occurred, the mean yield of maize was reduced by an estimated 30% (EPPO, 2000).

MATERIALS AND METHODS

Although there is a considerable and growing literature covering all aspects of the distribution and biology of *D. virgifera virgifera*, the data on its distribution and climatic responses is difficult to interpret for three main reasons. Firstly, although the current distribution of *D. virgifera virgifera* in North America and Europe is well documented, since it is rapidly spreading in Europe, it is difficult to judge the extent to which the current limits to its distribution are caused by unfavourable climate or simply by the fact that *D. virgifera virgifera* has not yet had sufficient opportunity to spread further. Secondly, all stages, except the adults, live in the soil, whereas the temperature data which are primarily used for predicting climatic suitability are all based on measurements above ground and there is no simple relationship between air and soil temperatures. Environmental conditions in the soil depend on ground cover, soil type, water retention capabilities, conductivity and other factors. Thirdly the estimated environmental responses in the literature, particularly those which have been used to attempt to predict *D. virgifera virgifera* phenology in the soil based on air temperatures, show considerable variability (Elliott *et al.*, 1990). Soil type, maize variety and genetic variation in *D. virgifera virgifera* populations clearly all play a role in addition to the fact that individuals can be found at a range of depths down to 23 cm with larvae occurring between 0-15 cm (Bergman & Turpin, 1986).

To take account of these difficulties, CLIMEX (Sutherst *et al.*, 1999), a program which matches and configures climatic responses to the current distribution of the species and extrapolates these to the PRA area, has been applied to predict the distribution of *D. virgifera virgifera* in France (Reynaud, 1998) and Germany (Baufeld *et al.*, 1996). Climatic responses calculated originally for the soil have been applied even though CLIMEX only uses air temperatures. The key parameter chosen is an 11°C minimum threshold for development and the minimum number of degree days for the completion of *D. virgifera virgifera*'s life cycle is given as 670 based on studies by Jackson & Elliot (1988). Although these parameters overestimate the southern limits to its distribution in North America, the northern limits in North America predicted by CLIMEX are similar to those in the literature (Krysan & Miller, 1986), justifying the use of these parameters to predict the northern limit of climatic suitability in Europe. The annual total of degree-days was found to be critical for establishment at the northern boundary.

CLIMEX includes 1931-1960 monthly averages for 285 European weather stations. These data have two main disadvantages: firstly the climate has warmed up considerably since 1931-1960 and, secondly, the stations may be unrepresentative of the areas where crops are grown. Accordingly, we loaded CLIMEX with 1961-1990 mean monthly climate interpolated to a 0.5° latitude/longitude grid by New *et al.* (1999). However, whereas the 1931-1960 data indicate that four UK weather stations are climatically suitable for *D. virgifera virgifera*, none of the 0.5° latitude/longitude 1961-90 UK grid cells were found to be suitable. Examination of the outputs revealed that failure to reach the 670 degree days at a base of 11°C defines the northern limit to the distribution. We therefore concluded that climatic suitability maps for *D. virgifera virgifera* in the UK could be estimated from calculating accumulated temperatures without using CLIMEX and displaying these in a proprietary geographical information system (GIS). In the UK, maize is usually harvested by the end of October, so this was chosen as the cut-off date for degree day calculations.

In order to determine whether the apparent unsuitability of the UK climate based on 0.5° latitude/longitude 1961-90 grid cells was due to the use of data which are either at too coarse a spatial and temporal scale or reflect a cooler historical past, additional climatic datasets were employed. We increased the spatial resolution from 0.5° latitude/longitude to 5 km, and the temporal resolution from 30-year mean monthly data to annual means (using datasets from the

UK Met. Office). The maize distribution for England, also at a 5 km resolution, was provided by the Defra Economics and Statistics Division and so, using a GIS mask facility, accumulated temperature data for only the 5 km grids where maize is currently grown could be calculated and displayed. Accumulated temperature data were calculated at 5 km resolution for a cool (1996) and a hot (1995) year to provide an improved representation of the extremes of current climate and compared to the four UKCIP02 climate change scenarios predicting climates in 2050 under low, medium low, medium high and high emission scenarios (Hulme *et al.*, 2002). To explore the inter-annual fluctuation in degree days over a 30 year period, daily maximum and minimum air temperatures were obtained for 1970-1999 from Gatwick Airport.

RESULTS

The numbers of 5 km grid cells where accumulated temperatures reached 670 for the UK under current and climate change conditions are given in Table 1. By masking out those cells not used for maize production in 2001, it was found that only 3 cells in 1996 and 2333 cells in 1995 were both climatically suitable and likely to contain maize.

Table 1.   Comparison of the number of 5 km grid cells in the UK climatically suitable for *Diabrotica virgifera virgifera* under current and future climatic conditions based on a threshold of 670 degree days above a base of 11°C.

Year	Number of climatically suitable 5 km cells
Hot year (1995)	4852
Cool Year (1996)	34
2050 UKCIP02 high emissions scenario	5137
2050 UKCIP02 medium high emissions scenario	4667
2050 UKCIP02 medium low emissions scenario	4407
2050 UKCIP02 low emissions scenario	3879

Figure 1 shows that the area suitable for *D. virgifera virgifera* establishment in the hot year of 1995 is very similar to predictions for the UKCIP02 high emission scenario for 2050. Figure 2 gives the annual variation in accumulated temperatures base 11°C for Gatwick airport from 1970-1999 and clearly shows how the years have become warmer over the 30 year period (maximum 1032 in 1995). For nine years out of the thirty analysed, annual accumulated temperatures were less than 670. The date when 670 degree days are achieved is also becoming earlier (earliest 14th August in 1995). An insignificant amount of degree days above 11°C is accumulated in November and December, so there is little difference between the annual accumulated temperature total and that reached at the end of October, by which time the maize is harvested.

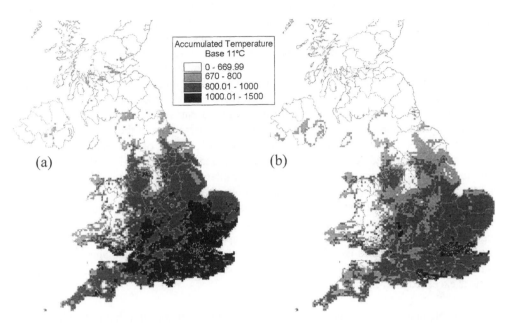

Figure 1.   Comparison of the area of the UK climatically suitable for establishment by *Diabrotica virgifera virgifera* in (a) 1995 (a hot year) and (b) 2050 (under the UKCIP02 high emissions climate change scenario).

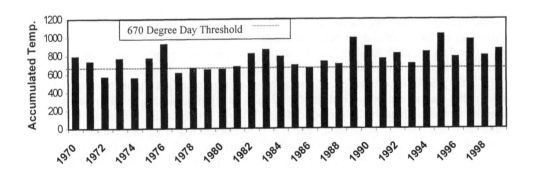

Figure 2.   Annual accumulated temperature base 11°C calculated from daily 1970-1999 data at Gatwick Airport, UK

DISCUSSION

The procedure adopted here, applying CLIMEX to identify the parameter which is critical to defining the northward limit of distribution in North America, i.e. an accumulated temperature threshold, and then applying this to the UK at improved spatial and temporal resolutions under current and future climates, depends for its success on a number of assumptions. The host plant is grown widely in England but other biotic factors must also be non-limiting. For example, although crop rotation is an effective control method, a small proportion of eggs may exhibit prolonged diapause (Levine et al., 1992). Since CLIMEX predictions of potential distribution are partly based on existing distributions, differences between the microclimate at climate stations and the pest niche are accounted for to some extent. An alternative approach would require comprehensive soil temperature profiles for the maize crop in the UK or could follow Elliot et al., (1990), who adapted models by Gupta et al., (1983) of soil temperature profiles related to above ground temperatures, the soil type and the crop. Soil temperature data at various depths under a grass sward are available for a few locations in the UK, though they are usually recorded at 9 am and are thus not a mean which can be used to calculate degree days. We conducted an exploratory study of locations south of London with hourly temperature measurements and a soil temperature profile, and found that, at 10 cm depth, annual temperature accumulations at a base of 11°C are approximately 200 day degrees higher than those above ground. If this is added to the 1970-1999 annual accumulated air temperatures at Gatwick airport, then the 670 day degree threshold for D. virgifera virgifera to complete its life cycle is exceeded in every year.

Considerable uncertainty remains as to the choice of the minimum threshold of 11°C and the limit to the annual accumulated temperature being set at 670. Jackson & Elliott (1988) and Davis et al. (1996) highlight the difficulties of estimating the minimum threshold for development and the appropriate number of degree days for the development of each life stage. D. virgifera virgifera is extremely adaptable and environmental response data taken from populations in Ontario, at the current northerly limit to its distribution in North America, and from European populations would be more appropriate.

Increasing the spatial and temporal resolution of climatic data significantly influences predictions of the establishment potential of warmth loving organisms in the UK. The 5 km resolution data for 1995 and 1996 show that there is considerable annual variation in the area available for establishment. However, by 2050 under global warming the very hot summer of 1995, with its large area suitable for D. virgifera virgifera, is likely to be representative of the mean rather than an exception (Hulme et al., 2002). At 5 km resolution, monthly accumulated temperature calculations for 1996 produced only 34 cells above the 670 threshold, one on the south coast and the rest in London, whereas daily calculations from one location, Gatwick airport, for the same year produced a total of 783 degree days. This strengthens the conclusions of Jarvis & Baker (2001) who showed how increasing the spatial and temporal resolution of climatic data influences predictions of climatic suitability.

Under current climate conditions, D. virgifera virgifera, appears to be at the edge of its range in the UK. Predictions of climatic suitability for D. virgifera virgifera are not easy to make because all stages, except the adult, live in the soil. Similarly, D. virgifera virgifera's environmental responses which have been reported in the literature are difficult to extrapolate to UK conditions primarily because there are no comprehensive soil temperature profiles for the maize crop in the UK. Nevertheless, comparisons of air and soil temperatures at different depths from locations south of London indicate that D. virgifera virgifera could complete its life cycle in most if not all of the last thirty years and the warmer summer temperatures in the most recent years have greatly increased the likelihood of this occurring. Outside southern England, the likelihood of *D. virgifera virgifera* completing its life cycle rapidly diminishes. The increasing area of forage maize, sweet corn and game cover are also enhancing the potential for *D. virgifera virgifera* establishment in the UK.

ACKNOWLEDGEMENTS

We thank Plant Health Division, Defra for funding and CSL colleagues, in particular Chris Malumphy for discussion of the manuscript.

REFERENCES

Baker R H A (2002). Predicting the limits to the potential distribution of alien crop pests. In: *Invasive arthropods in agriculture. Problems and solutions*, eds. Hallman, G J and Schwalbe, C P pp. 207-241. Science Publishers Inc: Enfield, USA.

Baker R H A; MacLeod A; Cannon R J C; Jarvis C H ; Walters K F A; Barrow E M; Hulme M (1998). Predicting the impacts of a non-indigenous pest on the UK potato crop under global climate change: reviewing the evidence for the Colorado beetle, *Leptinotarsa decemlineata*. *Proceedings of the BCPC Conference - Pests and Diseases 1998*, **3**, 979-984.

Baker R H A; Sansford C E; Jarvis C H; Cannon R J C; MacLeod A; Walters K F A (2000). The role of climatic mapping in predicting the potential distribution of non-indigenous pests under current and future climates. *Agriculture, Ecosystems & Environment* **82**, 57-71.

Bale J S; Masters G J; Hodkinson I D; Awmack C; Bezemer T M; Brown V K; Butterfield J; Buse A; Coulson J C; Farrar J; Good J E G; Harrington R; Hartley S; Jones T H; Lindroth R L; Press M C; Symrnioudis I; Watt A D; Whittaker J B (2002). Herbivory in global climate change research: direct effects of rising temperature on insect herbivores. *Global Climate Change* **8**, 1-6.

Baufeld P; Enzian S; Motte G (1996). Establishment potential of *Diabrotica virgifera* in Germany. *EPPO Bulletin* **26**, 511-518.

Bergman M K; Turpin F T (1986). Phenology of field populations of corn rootworms (Coleoptera: Chrysomelidae) relative to calendar data and heat units. *Environmental Entomology* **15**, 109-112.

Cannon R J C (1998). The implications of predicted climate change for insect pests in the UK, with emphasis on non-indigenous species. *Global Change Biology* **4**, 785-796.

Cannon R J C; Bartlett P W; Tuppen R J (2003). Introduction to the statutory responsibilities of the Plant Health Service in Great Britain. *Antenna* **27**, 87-94.

Davis P M; Brenes N; Allee L L (1996). Temperature dependent models to predict regional differences in corn rootworm (Coleoptera: Chrysomelidae) phenology. *Environmental Entomology* **25**, 767-775.

Elliott N C; Jackson J J; Gustin R D (1990). Predicting western corn rootworm beetle (Coleoptera: Chrysomelidae) emergence from the soil using soil or air temperature. *Canadian Entomology* **122**, 1079-1091.

EPPO (2000). Situation of *Diabrotica virgifera* in the EPPO region. *EPPO Reporting Service* (2000/031).

EPPO (2003). The situation of *Diabrotica virgifera virgifera* (Coleoptera: Chrysomelidae) in Europe. *EPPO Reporting Service* (2003/001).

FAO (2001). Pest risk analysis for quarantine pests. *International Standards for Phytosanitary Measures* 11. FAO: Rome.

Gavloski J E; Whitfield G H; Ellis C R (1992). Effect of larvae of western corn rootworm and of mechanical root pruning on sap flow and growth of corn. *Journal of Economic Entomology* **85**, 1434-1441.

Gupta S C; Larson W E; Linden D R (1983). Effect of tillage and surface residues on soil temperatures. I. Upper boundary temperature. *Soil Science Society of America Journal* **47**,1212-1218.

Hulme M; Jenkins G J; Lu X; Turnperry J R; Mitchell T D; Jones R G; Lowe J; Murphy J M; Hassell D; Boorman P; McDonald R; Hill S (2002). *Climate change scenarios for the United Kingdom: the UKCIP02 scientific report.* Tyndall Centre for Climate Change Research, School of Environmental Sciences, University of East Anglia, Norwich UK.

Jackson, J J; Elliott N C (1988). Temperature-dependent development of immature stages of the western corn rootworm, *Diabrotica virgifera virgifera* (Coleoptera: Chrysomelidae). *Environmental Entomology* **17**, 166-171.

Jarvis C H; Baker R H A (2001). Risk assessment for nonindigenous pests: 1. Mapping the outputs of phenology models to assess the likelihood of establishment. *Diversity and Distributions* **7**, 223-235.

Krysan J L; Miller T A (1986). *Methods for the Study of Pest Diabrotica.* Springer Verlag: New York.

Levine E; Oloumi-Sadeghi H; Ellis C R (1992). Thermal requirements, hatching patterns, and prolonged diapause in western corn rootworm (Coleoptera: Chrysomelidae) eggs. *Journal of Economic Entomology* **85**, 2425-2432.

Levine J M; D'Antonio C M (2003). Forecasting biological invasions with increasing international trade. *Conservation Biology* **17**, 322-326.

Masters G J; Brown V K; Clarke I P; Whittaker J B; Hollier J A (1998). Direct and indirect effects of climate change on insect herbivores: Auchenorrhyncha (Homoptera). *Ecological Entomology* **23**, 45-52.

New M; Hulme M; Jones P D (1999). Representing twentieth century space-time climate variability. Part 1: development of a 1961-90 mean monthly terrestrial climatology. *Journal of Climate* **12**, 829-856.

Oerke E C; Dehne H W; Schonbeck F; Weber A (1994). *Crop production and crop protection - estimated losses in major food and cash crops*, Elsevier, 808pp.

Parnesan C; Ryrholm N; Stefanescu C; Hill J K; Thomas C D; Descimon H; Huntley B; Kaila L; Kullberg J; Tammaru T; Tennent W J; Thomas J A; Warren M. (1999). Poleward shifts in geographical ranges of butterfly species associated with regional warming. *Nature* **399**, 579-583.

Reynaud P (1998). Risk assessment of *Diabrotica virgifera virgifera* Le Conte in France. *Pflanzenschutzberichte* **57**, 46-51.

Sutherst R W; Maywald G F; Yonow T; Stevens P M (1999). *CLIMEX. Predicting the effects of climate on plants and animals. User's guide.* CSIRO Publishing: Collingwood, Australia.

SESSION 9C

NEW APPROACHES TO CROP PROTECTION BY EXPLOITING STRESS-RELATED SIGNALLING IN PLANTS

Chairman: Dr Harro Bouwmeester
Plant Research International,
Wageningen, The Netherlands

Session Organiser: Professor John Pickett
Rothamsted Research, Harpenden, UK

Papers: 9C-1 to 9C-4

Plant defense-inducing *N*-acylglutamines from insect guts: structural diversity and microbe-assisted biosynthesis

L Ping, D Spiteller, W Boland
Max Planck Institute for Chemical Ecology, Hans-Knöll-Straße 8, D-07745 Jena, Germany
Email: Boland@ice.mpg.de

ABSTRACT

N-Acylglutamines are ubiquitously present in the regurgitants of herbivorous insects. The compounds comprise a larger family containing fatty acids of different degrees of unsaturation and chain length. Further modifications occur in the fatty acid moiety by oxidative transformations to secondary alcohols and epoxides. By hydrolysis (epoxide), acylation or phosphorylation of the alcohols the diversity of the compounds is further increased. Screening of cultivable gut bacteria from several Lepidopterans revealed that many of the commensal microorganims are principally able to synthesize the *N*-acylglutamines. From *Microbacterium arborescens* the first pure *N*-acyl synthase was isolated and characterized as an homooligomeric enyzme with a protomer size of 17.2 kDa. The enzyme displays a pH optimum at pH 8 and second plateau of even higher activity between pH 9-12 corresponding to the strongly alkaline conditions in the insect gut. The enzyme catalyses amide formation between a wide range of free fatty acid and most proteinogenic amino acids. Preceding activation of the acyl moiety is not required.

INTRODUCTION

Plants under attack by a herbivorous insect often release a blend of *de novo* synthesised volatiles that may attract the natural enemies of the attacking insect (Dicke *et al*. 1990; Turlings *et al*. 1993). While the mechanical damage of the feeding process only effects the release of pre-formed volatiles and that from rapid degradation processes, low- and high-molecular weight components (elicitors) from the simultaneously introduced salivary secretions modify the plant's gene expression activating a *de novo* biosynthesis of defensive compounds (Mattiaci *et al*., 1995; Paré *et al*., 1997). These secretions may be composed of glandular components from the mouth area and enteric fluids from the foregut from regurgitation. In 1997 Alborn *et al*. isolated in a bioassay guided fractionation of an elicitor-active regurgitate from Spodoptera exigua larvae *N*-(17-hydroxylinolenoyl)-glutamine (volicitin) as the first member of a family of *N*-acyl glutamines which was able to trigger volatile emission from corn plants (*Zea mais*). In some insects, for example in the oral secretions of the tobacco hornworm (*Manduca sexta*) the amino acid glutamine is replaced by glutamate (Halitschke *et al*., 2001).

Structural diversity of *N*-acylglutamines

Besides the simple conjugates of glutamine with saturated or unsaturated fatty acids (Figure 1, Type I), there exist more complex structures with functionalized fatty acid moieties that were isolated recently from regurgitates of lepidopteran larvae (*S. frugiperda*, *S. exigua* and *Heliothis virescens*) (Paré *et al*., 1998; Pohnert *et al*., 1999).

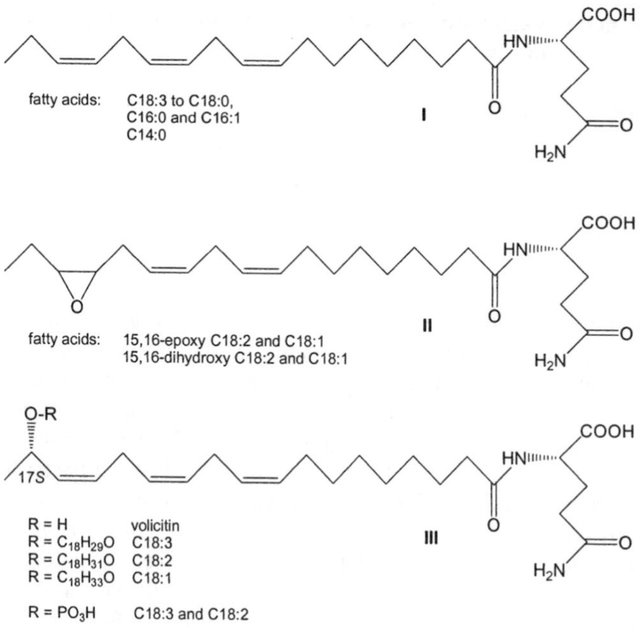

Figure 1.   Structural diversity of *N*-acyl glutamines isolated from regurgitants of various lepidopteran larvae.

Additional oxidative transformations of either the intact *N*-acyl-glutamines or their precursor fatty acids lead to *N*-(15,16-epoxy-linoleoyl)-glutamine and *N*-(15,16-dihydroxy-linoleoyl)-glutamine (Figure 1, Type II) (Spiteller & Boland, 2003a). Another family of conjugates is generated by acylation of volicitin-type precursors which result in very unpolar and rather unstable compounds such as *N*-(17-linolenoxy-linolenoyl)-glutamine (Figure 1, Type III) (Spiteller & Boland, 2003b). The latter exhibit striking structural similarities to the mayolenes previously isolated from defensive secretions of the Lepidopteran *Pieris rapae* (Smedley et al., 2002). Most surprising was the recent discovery of a C(17)-phosphorylated conjugate (Figure 1, Type III), which represents the first alkyl-chain phosphorylated fatty acid derivative in nature (Spiteller & Boland, unpublished results). The chiral centre of the functionalized linolenic acid moiety of volicitin was determined as (17*S*, >94% ee) (Spiteller et al,. 2001). In case, that volicitin serves as a common precursor *en route* to the more complex structures (Figure 1, compounds of type III), the same configuration is to be expected for the other conjugates.

Biosynthesis of *N*-acyl conjugates by commensal gut bacteria of insects

N-acylamino acid conjugates such as *N*-acylornithines or *N*-acylserines are long known as metabolites of microorganisms (Asselineau, 1991) and, in fact, in a recent study we presented first evidence that microorganisms may be also involved in the biosynthesis of *N*-acylglutamines in insect guts (Spiteller et al., 2001). From gut segments of *Spodoptera exigua*, *Mamestra brassicae* and *Agrotis segetum* c. 30 bacterial strains could be isolated, cultured and identified by sequencing of their 16S rDNA. Many of them (c. 50%) were able to synthesise the typical lepidopteran *N*-acylamino acids from externally added precursors (Spiteller, 2002). Moreover, the extent of conjugate biosynthesis in the insect could be suppressed to a certain extent by pre-treatment of the food with antibiotics. The effect was, however, in general not very pronounced, but in the case of larvae of *Spodoptera frugiperda* with the antibiotic fosmidom-ycin and lima bean as the host plant a significant reduction of conjugate biosynthesis was observed (c. 90% reduction).

Isolation of a novel *N*-acyl synthase from *Microbacterium arborescens*

Three non-related microorganisms representing diverse bacterial groups were selected to study the biosynthesis of *N*-acyl glutamines in detail. *Providencia rettgeri* is a Gram negative patho-gen causing nosocomial infections. It has been also isolated from oil fly (Kadavy *et al.*, 2000). *Microbacterium arborescens* is a free living Gram positive species with a high GC content (Rainey *et al.*, 1994), and the third species, *Bacillus pumilus* is a low GC content Gram positive soil bacterium (Hallmann *et al.*, 1999). Owing to the wide distribution of the two Gram positive bacteria (for example on leaf surfaces), they will, upon feeding, opportu-nistically colonize the insect gut. Although the three microorganisms displayed different growth kinetics, amide formation consistently increased at the early stationary phase. At that time, nutrient depletion occurs. Such stringent conditions appear to be general for bacteria colonizing higher organisms, and a number of bacterial genes, especially those responsible for colonization and pathogenicity, are known to be regulated by lag phase signaling systems (Parsek & Greenberg, 2000). Hence, the precise controlled time window of this bio-transformation (Figure 2) may suggest a defined interaction between bacteria and their insect hosts.

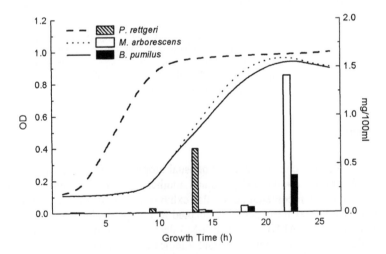

Figure 2.   Time course of *N*-acylglutamine biosynthesis in growing microbial cultures. Bacteria were grown in BHI medium at 37°C. Cell density was measured at 600 nm (left axis). Linolenic acid and glutamine were added into the growing culture and samples were taken in four hour intervals and analysed by HPLC. Bars indicate the amount of *N*-acyl glutamine formed (right axis).

M. arborescens, isolated from the regurgitate of *Spodoptera exigua*, was recognized as an fficient producer of *N*-linolenoyl-glutamine and was therefore chosen as a source for the isolation of the catalytically active protein(s). Bacterial cells were harvested at the early stationary phase and yielded an active homogenate after cell rupture. Obviously, the enzyme is not secreted into the medium, since control experiments with the medium indicated much lower catalytic activity. Owing to the high stability and the large molecular weight (> 100 KDa) of the protein ultrafiltration through Vivaspin 20 columns (100 kDa cut off) allowed a very simple removal of lower-molecular weight compounds; c. 90% of active protein was retrieved in the supernatant (Figure 3a). Subsequent treatment with ammonium sulphate resulted in precipitation of the protein between 25-65% (Figure 3b) suggesting that protein surface is not highly charged. Accordingly, an attempt to purify the biocatalyst by chromatography on hydrophobic columns failed due to very tight binding. Further purification was achieved by anion exchange (ResourceQ) and chromatography on Superdex 200 HR. Based on the purification procedure, we conclude that there is only a single active protein present in M. arborescens (Ping *et al.*, unpublished results).

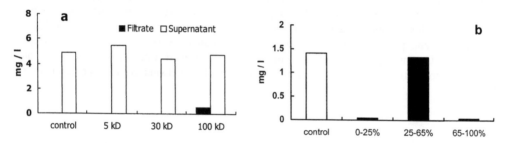

Figure 3.   Effect of major purification steps; Figure 3a: Vivaspin 20 passage, Figure 3b: ammonium sulphate precipitation. After each step, the fraction was desalted. The catalytic activity was determined by addition of aliquots to a standardized solution of linolenic acid and glutamine followed by HPLC-analysis of the products.

Enzyme characteristics

First studies with the pure enzyme revealed unusual properties of the biocatalyst. The enzyme displays two pH-optima; one around pH 8 and another as an activity plateau between pH 9-12. Since the foregut of lepidopteran larvae also exhibits a strongly basic milieu in the range of pH 9-11, the bacterial enzyme is perfectly adapted to this particular environment. Characterization of the protein by MALDI-TOF or ESI-MS demonstrated the presence of a protomer of 17.2 kDa, while size exclusion chromatography indicated an apparent molecular weight of c. 310 kDa suggesting a high degree of association of the protomers.

The protein catalyses amide formation between free fatty acids and glutamine without the need for previous activation. Activated derivatives such as acyl-CoA esters, acylglycerides, or phospholipids were not converted into glutamine conjugates. On the other hand, all fatty acids and almost all proteinogenic amino acids (except of Glc, Asp, and Pro) were accepted as substrates. Thus, a single enzyme is able to produce a very large number of different N-acyl amino acids. Interestingly, similar observations were made with growing cultures of *M. arborescens*. Since there is no evidence from the purification protocol for additional enzymes of this kind in *M. arborescens*, apparently a single enzyme is sufficient to generate the broad product spectrum that can be generated by the microorganisms from a mixture of precursors.

The physiological function of the N-acyl conjugates in the insect and in the herbivore-damaged plants remains to be clarified. It has been previously postulated that the compounds might serve the insect as biosurfactants to aid digestions of plant-derived lipids (Collatz & Mommsen, 1974). This assumption appears to be justified by the very broad distribution of N-acyl amino acid conjugates in many different arthropods and even beyond (e.g. spiders and crabs) (Pohnert *et al.*, 1999). Although their mode of action as elicitors is not yet known, the surface active N-acylamides act on plant tissue by causing a massive influx of extracellular Ca^{2+} into the cells (unpublished results). Whether or not this is the major signalling pathway leading to the up-regulation of plant defence responses remains to be clarified.

REFERENCES

Asselineau, J (1991). In: *Progress in the Chemistry of Organic Natural Products*, eds W Herz, H Grisebach, G W Kirby & C Thamm, pp. 1-85. Springer: Wien, New York, 1991.

Alborn H T; Turlings T C J; Jones T H; Stenhagen G; Loughrin J H; Tumlinson J H (1997). An elicitor of plant volatiles from beet armyworm oral secretion. *Science* **276**, 945-949.

Collatz K G; Mommsen T J (1974). Structure of emulsifying substances in several invertebrates *Comparative Physiology* **94**, 339-352.

Dicke M; Sabelis M W; Takabayashi J; Bruin J; Posthumus M A (1990). Plant strategies of manipulating predator-prey interactions through allelochemicals – prospects for application in pest control. *Journal of Chemical Ecology* **16**, 3091-3118.

Halitschke R; Schittko U; Pohnert G; Boland W; Baldwin I T (2001). Molecular interactions between the specialist herbivore *Manduca sexta* (Lepidoptera, Sphingidae) and its natural host *Nicotiana attenuata*. III. Fatty acid-amino acid conjugates in herbivore oral secretions are necessary and sufficient for herbivore-specific plant responses. *Plant Physiology*, **125**, 711-717.

Hallmann J; Rodríguez-Kábana R; Kloepper J W (1999). Chitin-mediated changes in bacterial communities of the soil, rhizosphere and within roots of cotton in relation to nematode control. *Soil Biology and Biochemistry* **31**, 551-560.

Kadavy D R; Hornby J M; Haverkost T; Nickerson K W (2000). Natural antibiotic resistance of bacteria isolated from larvae of the oil fly, *Helaeomyia petrolei*. *Applied Environmental Microbiology* **66**, 4615-4619.

Mattiacci M L; Dicke M; Posthumus M A (1995). Beta-glucosidase – An elicitor of herbivore-induced plant odor that attracts host-searching parasitic wasps. *Proceedings of the National Academy of Sciences USA* **92**, 2036.

Paré P W; Alborn H T; Tumlinson J H (1998). Concerted biosynthesis of an insect elicitor of plant volatiles. *Proceedings of the National Academy of Sciences USA* **95**, 13971-13975.

Paré P W; Tumlinson J H (1997). Induced synthesis of plant volatiles. *Nature* **385**, 30-31.

Parsek M R; Greenberg E P (2000). Acyl-homoserine lactone quorum sensing in Gram-negative bacteria: a signaling mechanism involved in associations with higher organisms. *Proceedings of the National Academy of Sciences USA* **97**, 8789-8793.

Pohnert G; Jung V; Haukioja E; Lempa K; Boland W (1999). New fatty acid amides from regurgitant of lepidopteran (Noctuidae, Geometridae) caterpillars. *Tetrahedron* **55**, 11275-11280.

Rainey F; Weiss N; Prauser H; Stackelbrandt E (1994). Further evidence for the phylogenetic coherence of actinomycetes with group B-peptidoglycan and evidence for the phylogenetic intermixing of the genera *Microbacterium* and *Aureobacterium* as determined by 16S rDNA analysis. *FEMS Microbiology Letters* **118**, 135-140.

Smedley S R; Schroeder F C; Weibel D B; Meinwald J; Lafleur K A; Renwick J A; Rutowski R; Eisner T (2002). Mayolenes: Labile defensive lipids from the glandular hairs of a caterpillar (*Pieris rapae*). *Proceedings of the National Academy of Sciences USA* **99**, 6822-6827.

Spiteller D; Dettner K; Boland W (2000). Gut bacteria may be involved in interactions between plants, herbivores and their predators: Microbial biosynthesis of *N*-acylglutamine surfactants as elicitors of plant volatiles. *Biological Chemistry* **381**, 755-762.

Spiteller D; Pohnert G; Boland W (2001). Absolute configuration of volicitin, an elicitor of plant volatile biosynthesis from lepidopteran larvae. *Tetrahedron Letters* **42**, 1483-1485

Spiteller D (2002). Ph.D. Thesis, University of Jena.

Spiteller D; Boland W (2003a). *N*-(15,16-Dihydroxylinoleoyl)-glutamine and *N*-(15,16-epoxylinoleoyl)-glutamine isolated from oral secretions of lepidopteran larvae. *Tetrahedron* **59**, 135-139.

Spiteller D; Boland W (2003b). *N*-(17-Acyloxy-acyl)-glutamines; Novel Surfactants From Oral Secretions of Lepidopteran Larvae. *Journal of Organic Chemistry,* in press.

Turlings T C J; McCall H; Alborn H T; Tumlinson J H (1993). An elicitor in caterpillar oral secretions that induces corn seedlings to emit chemical signals attractive to parasitic wasps. *Journal of Chemical Ecology* **19**, 411.

Synthetic herbivore-induced plant volatiles as field attractants for beneficial insects

D G James
Department of Entomology, Washington State University, Prosser, Washington, USA
Email: djames@tricity.wsu.edu

ABSTRACT

Evidence for field attraction by beneficial insects to synthetic herbivore-induced plant volatiles (HIPV's) is presented. Three synthetic HIPV's (methyl salicylate, (Z)-3-hexenyl acetate and (E)-4,8-dimethyl-1,3,7-nonatriene) were evaluated in a Washington State hop yard during April-October 2002, for attractiveness to beneficial insects. The predatory mirid, *Deraeocoris brevis* and the anthocorid, *Orius tristicolor* were attracted to sticky cards baited with (E)-3-hexenyl acetate, while the geocorid, *Geocoris pallens* and hover flies (Syrphidae) were attracted to methyl salicylate-baited cards. The coccinellid, *Stethorus punctum picipes* was attracted to both HIPV's in July and September. (E)-4,8-dimethyl-1,3,7- nonatriene did not attract any beneficial insects. *Lygus hesperus*, *Leptothrips mali*, *Anagrus* spp., other Miridae, Coccinellidae and parasitic Hymenoptera were not attracted to the three HIPV's tested. The possible exploitation of HIPV's in enhancing spring populations of beneficial insects, and conservation biological control in cropping systems is discussed.

INTRODUCTION

Some plants respond to herbivore damage by producing volatiles that attract natural enemies of the herbivores responsible for the damage (Dicke *et al.*, 1990a). The qualitative and quantitative characteristics of herbivore-induced plant volatiles (HIPV's) can vary according to the herbivore involved, the plant species and even the genotype. The phenolic compound, methyl salicylate, has been identified in the HIPV blends from at least 10 plant species including lima bean damaged by spider mites, *Tetranychus urticae* (Dicke *et al.*, 1990a), cucumber [*T. urticae*] (Agrawal *et al.*, 2002), cabbage [caterpillars, *Pieris* sp.] (Geervliet *et al.*, 1997), pear [psyllids] (Scutareanu *et al.*, 1997), hops [aphids, *Phorodon humuli*] (Campbell *et al.*, 1993), bird cherry [aphids, *Rhopalosiphum padi*] (Glinwood & Petterson, 2000), potato [beetles, *Leptinotarsa decemlineata*] (Bolter *et al.*, 1997), *Nicotiana attenuata* [caterpillars, *Manduca quinquemaculata*, leaf bugs, *Dicyphus minmus*, flea beetles, *Epitrix hirtipennis*] (Kessler & Baldwin, 2001), and *Lotus japonicus* [*T. urticae*] (Ozawa *et al.*, 2000). Tobacco plants innoculated with tobacco mosaic virus also produced methyl salicylate (Shulaev *et al.*, 1997). Two other common HIPV's identified from a range of arthropod-damaged plants (e.g. corn, cabbage, beans, pear, cotton) are the terpene, (E)-4,8-dimethyl-1,3,7-nonatriene and the ester (Z)-3-hexenyl acetate (Dicke *et al.*, 1990a).

Laboratory studies have demonstrated that methyl salicylate is attractive to the predatory mite, *Phytoseiulus persimilis* (Dicke *et al.*, 1990a, b) and the predatory bug, *Anthocoris nemoralis* (Drukker *et al.*, 2000). In contrast, olfactometer studies showed methyl salicylate to be repellent to the aphid pests, *Aphis fabae* and *Sitobion avenae* (Hardie *et al.*, 1994).

Similarly, field experiments showed methyl salicylate reduced trap catches of the aphid, *P. humuli*, during spring colonization of hop yards (Losel *et al.*, 1996). Ninkovic *et al.* (2003) demonstrated that methyl salicylate significantly delayed establishment and reduced infestation of the bird cherry oat aphid (*R. padi*) in oats treated with a pellet formulation of the semiochemical. James (2003) in hop yard experiments in Washington State, showed synthetic methyl salicylate to be an attractant for the green lacewing, *Chrysopa nigricornis*.

(Z)-3-hexenyl acetate, a 'green leaf volatile' emitted by many plants following herbivore or artificial mechanical damage, is attractive to a number of natural enemies including the aphid parasitoid, *Aphidius ervi* (Du *et al.*, 1996). (E)-4,8-dimethyl-1,3,7-nonatriene is a common HIPV resulting from spider mite feeding and is attractive to *P. persimilis* (Dicke *et al.*, 1990a, b).

Most of the research to date on HIPV's and the response by natural enemies has been conducted under laboratory conditions. If these semiochemicals are to realize their potential in applied entomology, then more studies on HIPV's and natural enemy responses in the field environment need to be conducted. In Washington hop yards, effective conservation biological control of mites and aphids appears to depend on spring recruitment of winged predators (James *et al.*, 2003). The use of synthetic HIPVs to enhance the recruitment of beneficial insects in early season hops might provide a useful pest management tool.

MATERIALS AND METHODS

A trapping experiment was conducted in an unsprayed 1 ha hop yard at WSU-Prosser from 11 April-24 October 2002 to determine whether three synthetic HIPV's were attractive to beneficial arthropods. Yellow sticky cards (23 X 18 cm) baited with 2 ml glass vials (containing 1 ml of HIPV solutions or left unbaited) were tied to wooden poles ~ 2 m above the ground. The glass vials were 3.5 cm in length and 1 cm wide with a 5 mm internal diameter of the opening. HIPV's tested were methyl salicylate (99%), (Z)-3-hexenyl acetate (98%), and (E)-4,8-dimethyl-1,3,7-nonatriene (10 mg in 2 ml hexane). (E)- 4,8-dimethyl-1,3,7-nonatriene was replaced weekly; the other two chemicals were replaced fortnightly. The release rates for methyl salicylate and (Z)-3-hexenyl acetate were similar (~ 0.5 ml/fortnight) while 1 ml of (E)-4,8-dimethyl-1,3,7-nonatriene evaporated within 4-6 days. Bait vials were taped vertically to the lower edge of the cards which were placed in a 3 X 4 grid with at least 10 m between the randomized treatments. All treatments were replicated three times and the treatment area occupied about half of the 1 ha hop yard. Sticky cards were replaced weekly and examined under a stereomicroscope for beneficial arthropods. Eleven groups or species of predators or parasitoids were sufficiently numerous to allow assessment of attraction: *Deraeocoris brevis* (Hemiptera: Miridae), *Geocoris pallens* (Hemiptera: Geocoridae), *Orius tristicolor* (Hemiptera: Anthocoridae), *Lygus hesperus* (Hemiptera: Miridae), *Stethorus punctum picipes* (Coleoptera: Coccinellidae), *Leptothrips mali* (Thysanoptera: Phlaeothripidae), *Anagrus* spp. (Hymenoptera: Mymaridae), Miridae (excluding *D. brevis* and *L. hesperus*), Syrphidae, Coccinellidae (excluding *S. punctum picipes*) and Hymenoptera (parasitic families including Ichneumonidae, Scelionidae, Encyrtidae and Mymaridae (excluding *Anagrus* spp.)). Miridae were considered to be beneficial arthropods in this study because most species have at least some carnivorous behavior. Coccinellidae were comprised mostly of the three aphidophagous species, *Coccinella transversoguttata*, *Hippodamia convergens* and *Harmonia axyridis*. *Anagrus* spp were evaluated separately because of our experience with this genus. Data were log $(x + 1)$ transformed to equalize variance and analyzed using analysis of variance and Fisher's least significant difference procedure.

RESULTS

The predatory mirid, *D. brevis*, and the anthocorid, *O. tristicolor*, were trapped in significantly higher numbers on (Z)-3-hexenyl acetate-baited cards than on unbaited, methyl salicylate, or (E)-4,8-dimethyl-1,3,7-nonatriene-baited cards (*D. brevis*: $F = 3.36$, df = 3, 68, $P = 0.03$; *O. tristicolor*: $F = 4.20$, df = 3, 68, $P = 0.0088$) (Table 1). The difference for *D. brevis* was most pronounced in August when populations were largest (Figure 1). For both species, attraction to (Z)-3-hexenyl acetate did not occur when populations were small. The geocorid predator, *G. pallens*, and hover flies (Syrphidae) were significantly attracted to methyl salicylate-baited cards compared to unbaited, (Z)-3-hexenyl acetate or (E)-4,8-dimethyl-1,3,7-nonatriene-baited cards (*G. pallens*: $F = 3.71$, df = 3, 68, $P = 0.0156$; Syrphidae: $F = 16.1$, df = 3, 68, $P = 0.0000$) (Table 1). Once again, attraction was most pronounced when populations were large, during June-August for *G. pallens* and in July, September and October for syrphids (Fig.1). No attempt was made to identify syrphid species. Although *S. punctum picipes* was not significantly attracted to any of the HIPV's when analyzed over the entire trapping period (Table 1), significantly greater numbers of this coccinellid were caught on methyl salicylate and (Z)-3-hexenyl acetate-baited cards in July and September (July: $F = 13.2$, df = 3, 12, $P = 0.0004$; September: $F = 3.37$, df = 3, 12, $P = 0.05$) (Fig.1). No attraction to the HIPV's was detected for *L. hesperus*, *L. mali*, *Anagrus* spp., other Miridae, other Coccinellidae or parasitic Hymenoptera ($P > 0.05$) (Table 1). No attraction by any insect species or group was noted for (E)-4,8-dimethyl–1,3,7–nonatriene.

Table 1.   Season means (± SE) for beneficial insects trapped on sticky cards baited with methyl salicylate, (Z)-3-hexenyl acetate, (E)-4,8-dimethyl-1,3,7-nonatriene or left unbaited. Experiment conducted in a Washington State hop yard during April-October 2002. For each species or group, means followed by a different letter are significantly different ($P < 0.05$)

beneficial insect (species, genus, family or order)	methyl salicylate	(Z)-3-hexenyl acetate	(E)-4,8-dimethyl-1,3,7-nonatriene	unbaited
Deraeocoris brevis	2.2 (0.6)a	5.2 (1.6)b	1.7 (0.6)a	1.0 (0.5)a
Orius tristicolor	2.3 (0.6)a	6.9 (0.4)b	2.0 (0.4)a	1.4 (0.5)a
Geocoris pallens	5.7 (0.7)b	1.4 (0.7)a	0.8 (0.4)a	0.8 (0.4)a
Syrphidae	2.2 (0.3)b	0.7 (0.3)a	0.4 (0.2)a	0.5 (0.2)a
Stethorus p. picipes	2.8 (0.7)a	2.6 (0.7)a	2.8 (0.6)a	1.7 (0.4)a
Lygus hesperus	1.4 (0.5)a	1.3 (0.3)a	2.5 (0.8)a	1.7 (0.5)a
Leptothrips mali	5.0 (1.5)a	7.5 (2.6)a	4.7 (1.0)a	8.1 (2.1)a
Anagrus spp.	2.0 (1.3)a	5.2 (2.9)a	2.8 (1.3)a	3.1 (1.5)a
Miridae	6.0 (1.7)a	5.2 (1.4)a	6.0 (1.9)a	4.2 (1.4)a
Coccinellidae	1.1 (0.2)a	0.7 (0.2)a	0.5 (0.1)a	1.0 (0.2)a
Hymenoptera	8.6 (1.6)a	9.0 (0.8)a	9.7 (0.8)a	8.2 (0.9)a

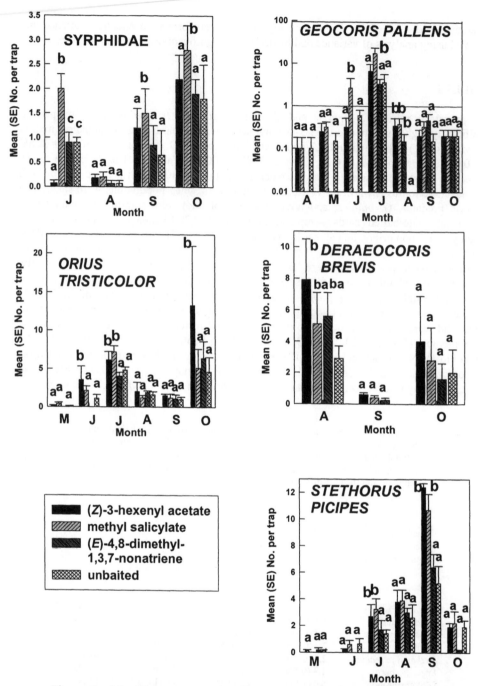

Figure 1. Monthly mean trapping frequency of Syrphidae, *Geocoris pallens*, *Orius tristicolor*, *Deraeocoris brevis*, and *Stethorus punctum picipes* on yellow sticky cards baited with HIPVs or left unbaited in a Washington hop yard in 2002. Error bars represent standard errors with different letters on columns within months indicating significant differences ($P < 0.05$).

DISCUSSION

Although laboratory evidence for plant volatiles manipulating the foraging of natural enemies is now overwhelming, very few studies have been published showing natural enemy responses to plant volatiles under field conditions. In addition, the few outdoor studies that have been published were often correlative (higher densities of predators around pest-infested plants than uninfested plants, or involved inducing HIPV's from plants (without other predator-associated cues) and measuring responses by natural enemies. Field attraction of beneficial insect species to synthetic HIPV's was shown in studies by Flint *et al.* (1979), Zhu *et al.* (1999), and more recently by James (2003).

The present study showed that methyl salicylate is an attractant for the bigeyed bug, *G. pallens* and hover flies and (Z)-3-hexenyl acetate is an attractant for the mirid, *D. brevis* and the minute pirate bug, *O. tristicolor.* In addition, both chemicals appeared to have some attractiveness to the mite-eating ladybeetle, *S. punctum picipes.* Previously, methyl salicylate was demonstrated to be attractive to the predatory mite, *P. persimilis,* the pirate bug, *A. nemoralis* and the green lacewing, *C. nigricornis* (Dicke *et al.,* 1990a, b, Ozawa *et al.,* 2000, James, 2 003). D emonstration o f f ield a ttraction of s pecies o f p redatory true b ugs, b eetles, flies and lacewings to these two HIPV's suggests that synthetic HIPV formulations might be used in integrated pest management programs to aid conservation biological control.

The results reported here indicate the potential of HIPV's as field attractants for beneficial arthropods. This research is being undertaken in an effort to increase early season recruitment of winged beneficial arthropods to hop yards. Conservation biological control has been shown to aid in the management of the principal pests of hop, twospotted spider mite, *T. urticae,* and hop aphid, *P. humuli* in Washington (James *et al.,* 2003). A key component in the success of this strategy is spring colonization of hop yards by winged, generalist predators of mites and aphids. The current study suggests that deployment of methyl salicylate and (Z)-3- hexenyl acetate dispensers in spring hops may enhance recruitment of key natural enemies like *O. tristicolor, G. pallens* and *D. brevis.* Methyl salicylate was shown by Losel *et al.* (1996) to reduce trap catches of *P. humuli* in a hop yard. These authors concluded that methyl salicylate was repellent to *P. humuli,* thus the use of this semiochemical in hop yards may serve two benefits to pest management; enhanced recruitment of beneficial insects and repellency of the pest, *P. humuli.*

REFERENCES

Agrawal, A A; Janssen A; Bruin J; Posthumus M A; Sabelis M W (2002). An ecological cost of plant defence: attractiveness of bitter cucumber plants to natural enemies of herbivores. *Ecological Letters* **5**, 377-385.

Campbell, C A M; Petterson J; Pickett J; Wadhams L J; Woodcock C M (1993). Spring migration of Damson-Hop aphid, *Phorodon humuli* (Homoptera: Aphididae), and summer host plant-derived semiochemicals released on feeding. *Journal of Chemical Ecology* **19**,1569-1576.

Dicke M; Sabelis M W; Takabayashi J; Bruin J; Posthumus M A (1990a). Plant strategies of manipulating predator-prey interactions through allelochemicals: Prospects for application in pest control. *Journal of Chemical Ecology* **16**, 3091-3118.

Dicke M; van Beck T A; Posthumus M A; Ben Dom M; van Bokhoven H; de Groot A (1990b). Isolation and identification of volatile kairomone that affects acarine predator-prey interactions: involvement of host plant in its production. *Journal of Chemical Ecology* **16**, 81-396.

Drukker B; Bruin J; Sabelis M W (2000). Anthocorid predators learn to associate herbivore-induced plant volatiles with presence or absence of prey. *Physiological Entomology* **25**, 260-265.

Du Y; Poppy G M; Powell J; Pickett J A; Wadhams L J; Woodcock C M (1998). Identification of semiochemicals released during aphid feeding that attract the parasitoid *Aphidius ervi. Journal of Chemical Ecology* **24**, 1355-1368.

Flint H M; Slater S S; Walters S (1979). Caryophyllene: an attractant for the green lacewing. *Environmental Entomology* **8**, 1123-1125.

Geervliet J B F; Posthumus M A; Vet L E M; Dicke M (1997). Comparative analysis of headspace volatiles from different caterpillar-infested and uninfested food plants of *Pieris* species. *Journal of Chemical Ecology* **23**, 2935-2954.

Glinwood R; Petterson J (2000). Host plant choice in *Rhopalosiphum padi* spring migrants and the role of olfaction in winter host leaving. *Bulletin of Entomological Research* **90**, 57-61.

Hardie J; Isaacs R; Pickett J A; Wadhams L J; Woodcock C M (1994). Methyl salicylate and (-)-(1R,5S)-myrtenal are plant-derived repellents for black bean aphid, *Aphis fabae* Scop. (Homoptera: Aphididae). *Journal of Chemical Ecology* **20**, 2847-2855.

James D G (2003). Field evaluation of herbivore-induced plant volatiles as attractants for beneficial insects: methyl salicylate and the green lacewing, *Chrysopa nigricornis. Journal of Chemical Ecology* **29**, 1601-1609.

James D G; Price T S; Wright L C (2003). Mites and aphids in Washington hops: candidates for augmentative or conservation biological control? *Proceedings 1st International Symposium on Biological Control of Arthropods* (in press).

Kessler A; Baldwin L T (2001). Defensive function of herbivore-induced plant volatile emissions in nature. *Science* **291**, 2141-2144.

Losel P M; Lindemann M; Scherkenbeck J; Maier J; Engelhard B; Campbell C A; Hardie J; Pickett J A; Wadhams L J; Elbert A; Thielking G (1996). The potential of semiochemicals for control of *Phorodon humuli* (Homoptera: Aphididae). *Pesticide Science* **48**, 293-303.

Ninkovic V; Ahmed E; Glinwood R; Petterson J (2003). Effects of two types of semiochemical on population development of the bird cherry oat aphid *Rhopalosiphum padi* in a barley crop. *Agricultural and Forest Entomology* **5**, 27-33.

Ozawa R; Shimoda T; Kawaguchi M; Arimura G; Horiuchi J; Nishioka T; Takabayashi J (2000). *Lotus japonicus* infested with herbivorous mites emits volatile compounds that attract predatory mites. *Journal of Plant Research* **113**, 427-433.

Scutareanu P; Drukker B; Bruin J; Posthumus M A; Sabelis M W (1997). Volatiles from *psylla*-infested pear trees and their possible involvement in attraction of anthocorid predators. *Journal of Chemical Ecology* **23**, 2241-2260.

Shulaev V; Silverman P; Raskin I (1997). Airborne signalling by methyl salicylate in plant pathogen resistance. *Nature* **385**, 718-721.

Zhu J; Cosse A A; Obrycki J J; Boo K S; Baker T C (1999). Olfactory reactions of the twelve-spotted lady beetle, *Coleomegilla maculata* and the green lacewing, *Chrysoperla carnea* to semiochemicals released from their prey and host plants: electroantennogram and behavioral responses. *Journal of Chemical Ecology* **25**, 1163-1177.

Evaluation of the plant defence booster, acibenzolar-S-methyl, for use in Australian agriculture

I L Macleod, R Walker, I M Inglis
Serve-Ag Research, PO Box 690 Devonport Tasmania 7310 Australia
Email: imacleod@serve-ag.com.au

ABSTRACT

Acibenzolar-S-methyl was screened for its efficacy against a range of diseases in Australian crops. Crop phytotoxicity was also assessed. Trial results in tomatoes, lettuce, cucurbits, ornamentals and various other crops indicated that acibenzolar-S-methyl has potential as an alternative crop protection tool. In tomatoes, acibenzolar-S-methyl applied at 50 g a.i /ha was significantly more effective than copper hydroxide for management of *Xanthomonas campestris pv. vesicatoria* (bacterial spot). In watermelon, acibenzolar-S-methyl was as effective as the conventional copper treatment for control of the bacterium *Acidovorax avenae* subsp. *citrulli* (bacterial blotch).

There was a tendency for increased disease control when lower rates of acibenzolar-S-methyl were used in combination with conventional chemicals. Higher rates alone often resulted in disease control equivalent to the lower rates used in conjunction with conventional chemistry. However, in a number of trials, the higher rates of acibenzolar-S-methyl resulted in crop phytotoxicity.

INTRODUCTION

Plant defence boosters act by triggering plants' natural defence mechanisms. Acibenzolar-S-methyl (Bion) has been shown to induce disease resistance in a number of monocotyledon and dicotyledon plants (e.g Friedrich *et al.*, 1996; Graves & Alexander, 2002; Romero *et al.*, 2001). The mode of action is through initiation of the systemic acquired resistance (SAR) pathway in plants (Kessmann *et al.*, 1996) which leads to specific plant defence genes being activated. Pathogensis-related proteins (PR proteins) are synthesised, and accumulate in intercellular spaces, where pathogenic microbes grow before they attack cells. PR proteins include beta-1,3-glucanases and chitinases, enzymes which can degrade fungal and bacterial cell walls.

MATERIALS AND METHODS

Sixteen trials were conducted across Australia as part of a three-year project to evaluate acibenzolar-S-methyl for disease control efficacy and crop phytotoxicity.

In all trials, a range of product rates was used, typically including 12.5, 25, and 50 grams active ingredient/hectare (g a.i./ha). These rates of acibenzolar-S-methyl were also evaluated in combination with conventional crop protection products applied at recommended crop rates.

Treatments were applied to replicated plots (minimum four replicates) in commercial crops using appropriate nozzles. With the exception of three glasshouse trials, all trials were conducted in the field, generally using commercial crops, although three trials were established on governmental research stations. Applications were made using appropriate cone jet spray nozzles, with recommended water rates. Three trials required disease inoculation, while the remainder had sufficient natural disease pressure. Eight trials were conducted in tomatoes, five trials in lettuce and two in cucumbers. Additional trials were conducted in roses, spring onions, grapes (Semillon Blanc) and strawberries.

RESULTS

Results were highly variable between crops, with acibenzolar-S-methyl causing different disease efficacy and phytotoxic responses, depending on the target crop. Results were particularly promising in tomatoes, with the finding that acibenzolar-S-methyl applied at 50 g a.i./ha was significantly more effective than copper hydroxide for management of *Xanthomonas campestris pv. vesicatoria* (bacterial spot) (Figure 1). This trial was conducted in the field and the trial was inoculated with disease.

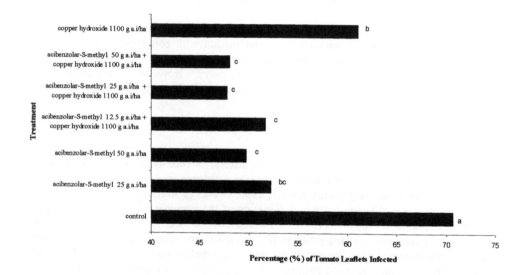

Figure 1. Incidence of *Xanthomonas campestris pv. vesicatoria* (bacterial spot) infection in tomato plants .

Good results were also obtained for control of *Acidovorax avenae subsp. citrulli* (bacterial blotch) in watermelon, with acibenzolar-S-methyl being as effective as the conventional copper treatment (Table 1). This trial was conducted in a glasshouse, and the trial plants were inoculated with disease. The implications of these results in tomatoes and watermelons are significant because sole reliance on copper as a tool for managing bacteria can lead to pathogen resistance, and copper toxicity problems.

Table 1. Mean disease severity of *Acidovorax avenae subsp. citrulli* (bacterial blotch) in watermelon plants receiving weekly sprays of acibenzolar-S-methyl and copper hydroxide. Disease assessments made at 7 and 10 days after inoculation. *0-6 disease severity rating scale was as follows: 0:no disease symptoms, 1:<1% leaf area affected (laa), 2:1-<5% laa, 3:5-<10% laa, 4:10-<25% laa, 5:25-<50% laa, 6:>50% leaf area affected.* Means followed by the same letter were not significantly different (P<0.05).

Treatment	Bacterial blotch severity (0-6)			
	7 days		10 days	
acibenzolar-S-methyl 10 g a.i./100L	0.03	e	0.00	e
acibenzolar-S-methyl 5 g a.i./100L	0.09	e	0.19	de
acibenzolar-S-methyl 2.5 g a.i./100L	0.15	e	0.31	de
acibenzolar-S-methyl 1.0 g a.i./100L	0.40	de	0.78	cd
acibenzolar-S-methyl 0.5 g a.i./100L	0.81	cd	1.19	bc
acibenzolar-S-methyl 0.1 g a.i./100L	1.06	bc	1.75	b
acibenzolar-S-methyl 0.01 g a.i./100L	1.57	a	2.49	a
copper hydroxide 120 g a.i./100L	0.56	c	0.56	d
control	1.87	a	2.75	a
lsd (P<0.05)	*0.55*		*0.62*	

Acibenzolar-S-methyl was also effective against a range of fungal diseases including *Pseudoperonospora cubensis* (downy mildew) and *Sphaerotheca fuliginea* (powdery mildew) in cucumbers, *Stemphylium solani* (grey leaf mould) in tomatoes and *Marssonia rosae* (black spot) in roses.

There was a general trend for increased disease control when lower rates of acibenzolar-S-methyl were used in combination with conventional chemicals. Higher rates of acibenzolar-S-methyl alone often resulted in disease control equivalent to the lower rates used in conjunction with conventional chemistry.

Phytotoxicity appeared to be a concern in some crops, particularly at the higher dose rates, although no phytotoxicity was reported in any of the tomato trials. Acibenzolar-S-methyl-induced phytotoxicity was more obvious in the glasshouse trials, where plants were stressed and phytotoxic responses such as stunting and leaf curling were more common. Cumulative phytotoxicity in some crops may be an issue, and additional research is required to refine product rates and timings to avoid plant damage.

DISCUSSION

Acibenzolar-S-methyl represents a new approach to plant disease management, and such a product will require excellent product stewardship. There are practical issues such as timing of product application, which dramatically influence efficacy. For example, acibenzolar-S-methyl must be applied before any disease symptoms appear, in order to allow time for stimulation of plant defence mechanisms before pathogen development.

Currently, the most fundamental limitation to the development of acibenzolar-S-methyl in Australia is a lack of management and responsibility for product development. Product ownership is uncertain, and this issue must be resolved in order to progress preparation of data submissions to relevant government agencies such as the Australian Pesticides and Veterinary Medicines Authority and the Therapeutic Goods Administration.

Specific recommendations for prioritising development of acibenzolar-S-methyl to commercial availability in Australia are listed below.

- Complete the development of acibenzolar-S-methyl for control of bacterial spot and *Stemphyllium* in tomatoes to enable an application for registration to be made as soon as practical.
- Generate data on the other major diseases of tomatoes with a view of including them in the first, or failing that, a subsequent submission.
- Once a maximum residue limit - temporary or otherwise - is established, measure the contribution a schedule of acibenzolar-S-methyl sprays makes to a tomato crop when applied in conjunction with a standard programme.
- Test the efficacy of acibenzolar-S-methyl on as wide a range of bacterial and viral diseases of vegetables as possible to determine where else it brings benefits to vegetable growers.
- Conduct field phytotoxicity work on all cucurbit crops to determine if acibenzolar-S-methyl can be safely developed for use in all or some cucurbits.

In order to progress these recommendations, significant corporate investment in the product will be required.

ACKNOWLEDGEMENTS

Syngenta Crop Protection Pty Ltd, IHD PTY LTD and Horticulture Australia Ltd provided funding for this project. We thank all growers who kindly provided trial sites. We also thank all researchers who undertook trials as part of this project. Researchers included R O'Brien, K Lewis, E Minchinton, N Kita and P Sadler.

REFERENCES

Friedrich L; Lawton K; Ruess W; Masner P; Specker N; Gut Rella M; Meier B; Dincher S; Staub T; Uknes S; Metraux, J.-P; Kessmann H; Ryals J. (1996). A benzothiadiazole derivative induces systemic acquired resistance in tobacco. *The Plant Journal*, **10**, 61-70.

Graves A S; Alexander S A. (2002). Managing bacterial speck and spot of tomato with acibenzolar-S-methyl in Virginia. Online. *Plant Health Progress* doi:10.1094/PHP-2002-0220-01 RS.

Kessmann H; Oostendorp M; Staub T; Gorlach J; Friedrich L; Lawton K; Ryals J. (1996). CGA 2455704: Mode of action of a new plant activator. *Brighton Crop Protection Conference*, 961-966.

Romero A M; Kousik C S; Ritchie D F. (2001). Resistance to bacterial spot in bell pepper induced by acibenzolar-S-methyl. *Plant Disease*, **85**, 189-194.

New chemical signals in plant protection against herbivores and weeds

M Matthes, J A Napier, J A Pickett, C M Woodcock
Rothamsted Research, Harpenden, Hertfordshire, AL5 2JQ, UK
Email: john.pickett@bbsrc.ac.uk

ABSTRACT

Studies leading to the identification of *cis*-jasmone as a plant derived signal of potential value in protection of cereals against aphids are described. Unpublished work on understanding the molecular mechanisms by which *cis*-jasmone exerts a persistent effect is reviewed, in particular the potential role of *cis*-jasmone in upregulating expression, in *Arabidopsis thaliana*, of genes potentially associated with its own biosynthesis and response by plants. The possibility for similar approaches to weed control is evidenced, using the example of allelopathic control of the witchweed *Striga hermonthica* in subsistence cereals by intercropping with the forage legume *Desmodium uncinatum*.

INTRODUCTION

There are still many new opportunities for the design of novel molecular structures for development as pesticides and herbicides. However, the selection of pests and weeds for resistance to these agents remains an attendant problem to commercialisation, even of the most novel molecular structures. Some examples now exist of cross-resistance to compounds, even before commercialisation (G D Moores, personal communication). These problems are exacerbated by continually growing demands for food to be produced without detectable pesticide residues, even though health or environmental risks are minimal. This continues to inflate the cost of registration, where cost recovery for anything but major pest targets is impossible. Thus, we see a loss of recognised and established pesticides from smaller niche markets and a reluctance to develop new pesticides unless these have a wide range of applications, or at least one major economic pest target. The early promise of using genetically modified plants that express resistance genes and their products has yielded relatively few commercial successes. These are almost entirely based on expression of genes associated with the *Bacillus thuringiensis* endotoxins for insect control, or to a relatively limited range of genes giving herbicide tolerance in crop plants. In addition to the reluctance of sections of the world community to accept food produced by genetically modified crops, there is an over-concern regarding human health and possible environmental impacts which delay commercial introduction, restrict use of genetically modified crop plants, and require increased resources directed at safety and away from technological improvement or innovation in this area.

Fuelled by these problems, but also because of recent scientific advances, induced response to pest attack is seen as offering opportunities for novel approaches to the protection of crop plants against pests and weeds. Thus, we now see attempts worldwide to exploit the responses of plants to attack by herbivores and other antagonistic organisms, including pathogens and competing plants or weeds. In reviewing induced responses to herbivory,

Karban & Baldwin (1997) listed over 20 field and orchard crops upon which one organism could induce resistance against a pest species. Another advantage of induced responses to pest attack is that organisms antagonistic to the pest, either as predators or parasites, can be exploited to a greater extent than normally occurs in monocrop agriculture. In considering the evolution of induced indirect defence of plants, Dicke (1999) referenced over 50 plant/herbivore interactions in which a species antagonistic to the herbivore was attracted on damage by the herbivore. There can also be useful crossovers between organisms from completely different taxa. Thus, the silverleaf whitefly, *Bemisia argentifolii*, alters host plant physiology during feeding to reduce development of phytopathogens (Mayer, *et al.*, 2002).

Natural products have long been viewed as having potential for weed management and include inducible phytotoxins, often exuded from one plant to affect another (Duke, *et al.*, 2002). However, there is now real potential for using induced or constitutive chemical signals to switch on effects in weeds that are deleterious to their competitive development (Birkett, *et al.*, 2001). Such plant/plant interactions occur aerially and in the rhizosphere. They provide chemicals for switching on plant defence, and also an opportunity to use the plants themselves as a means of releasing signals which benefit plants with which they are intercropped. The first notable example (Farmer & Ryan, 1990) involved methyl jasmonate released from one plant and which induces synthesis of proteinase inhibitors active against herbivores in a neighbouring plant. Methyl jasmonate is formed from linolenic acid via jasmonic acid (Figure 1). Jasmonic acid itself is created by epimerisation of the original natural product, *epi*-jasmonic acid, during storage and release. However, if the emitting plant, in the case of this first study the sagebrush, *Artemisia tridentata*, is freshly clipped, then methyl *epi*-jasmonate is released, which has a stronger effect on, for example, wild tobacco, *Nicotiana attenuata*, in terms of inducing defence (Karban, *et al.*, 2000; Preston, *et al.*, 2002) Such induction can take place in other plant taxa, for example in the brassicaceous plant oilseed rape, *Brassica napus*. Here, methyl jasmonate aerially applied above intact plants causes induction of certain defensive secondary metabolites, the glucosinolates (Doughty, *et al.*, 1995).

Defence chemistry is not limited to the lipoxygenase pathway, and methyl salicylate, produced either by the inducible phenylalanine ammonialyase pathway or, as more recently suggested, via isochorismate synthase (Wildermuth, *et al.*, 2001), also aerially applied, can cause induction of PR proteins and associated pathogen resistance (Shulaev *et al.*, 1997). Other compounds have been implicated, but methyl jasmonate and methyl salicylate have attracted most attention. Both are methyl esters, thereby deriving volatility for aerial transport compared with the free acids, jasmonic acid and salicylic acid, already established as internally acting plant hormones in their own right. As such, these two esters may also exert deleterious effects on plants treated for protection against pests and diseases. None the less, it is clear that damaged plants, and even intact plants, can transfer other signals, beyond methyl jasmonate and methyl salicylate, that can be beneficial to the recipient plants. Aggressive weeds such as couch grass, *Elytrigia repens*, and thistles, *Cirsium* spp., can also induce repellency against aphids in neighbouring barley plants, although the weeds themselves are not intrinsically repellent (Glinwood, *et al.*, unpublished data). Furthermore, even certain intact barley cultivars can, by aerial transmission of signals, induce defence in neighbouring barley plants of different cultivars (Ninkovic, *et al.*, 2002).

Thus, the scene is set for the identification of new externally acting chemical signals. Although it might initially be considered that, where such signals are volatile, they may be too ephemeral to use practically, the role in switching on defence, rather than needing to be present continuously, obviates this problem. By use of synthetic compound screening from the original lead of salicylate, the compound acibenzolar-S-methyl has been developed for the induction of plant defence and demonstrates the possibility for commercialisation. Furthermore, by understanding the effects of the natural plant-activating signals themselves on gene expression, it may be possible to exploit these processes more extensively. It is already known that methyl jasmonate influences a range of pathways, for example polyamine metabolism and the induction of systemic protection against powdery mildew in barley plants (Walters, *et al.*, 2002). Also, attempts at profiling the response of plants to herbivorous insects by microarray techniques is set to provide new opportunities in inducible defence gene expression (Schenk, *et al.*, 2000; Korth, 2003).

THE IDENTIFICATION OF NEW CHEMICAL SIGNALS

Chemical signals (semiochemicals) active at the sensory nervous system of animals are identified, in the case of non-sentient taxa such as insects and other arthropods, by means of electrophysiological preparations, involving recording from whole sensory organs or even from individual olfactory neurons (Pickett *et al.*, 1998). Semiochemicals released by plants under pest attack, and which influence defence metabolism in neighbouring plants, are difficult to identify since they are produced, as are most semiochemicals, in very small amounts, but in this case do not interact with as yet identifiable receptor systems. Bioassay linked fractionation could lead to the identification of active compounds, but it is clear that a large number of different molecular structures are involved in the profile of damaged plants. It was noticed that the plant semiochemical methyl salicylate is also used by herbivores, often as a repellent since it denotes plant damage, and at the higher trophic level by organisms that are parasitic on the herbivores as an attractant or foraging cue (Hardie, *et al.*, 1994; Pettersson, *et al.*, 1994). Many insects studied, from five insect orders, had olfactory neurons responding specifically to methyl salicylate or at least evidence of a highly specific response to this compound (Pickett, *et al.*, 1999; Chamberlain, *et al.*, 2000). Thus, it was suggested that insect electrophysiology might also provide a means of identifying semiochemicals that were plant activators of defence.

In the ensuing investigations a number of candidate compounds were found, with the most interesting to date proving to be *cis*-jasmone. *cis*-Jasmone is considered to be biosynthesised by the same pathway that gives rise to jasmonic acid (Figure 1), but in a route that leads off from *epi*-jasmonic acid prior to methylation (Koch, *et al.*, 1997). Indeed, by decarboxylation, *cis*-jasmone represents a more volatile metabolite than methyl jasmonate and so could be a more useful external measure of plant defence, based on the activation of this biosynthetic pathway, compared with methyl jasmonate. Initially, the lettuce aphid, *Nasonovia ribis-nigri*, was found to be repelled by *cis*-jasmone. This was based on the aphid's response via olfactory neurons selectively responsive to *cis*-jasmone, with only a very weak response to the structurally and biosynthetically related methyl jasmonate (Birkett, *et al.*, 2000). It was subsequently shown that other herbivores were repelled, including the hop aphid, *Phorodon humuli*. At the same time, *cis*-jasmone itself was found to attract ladybirds, which are predators of aphids, and parasitoids that also attack these pests (Birkett, *et al.*, 2000). Thus, in addition to the relationship between *cis*-jasmone and methyl jasmonate, and its putative biosynthesis by a stress-related pathway, *cis*-jasmone appeared to be a potent insect semiochemical, antagonistic to herbivores but giving a positive response with their antagonists (Birkett, *et al.*, 2000).

When bean plants, *Vicia faba*, were treated with *cis*-jasmone from air held above intact plants, these plants remained repellent to herbivores, but attractive to parasitoids, long after the *cis*-jasmone had disappeared. It was therefore decided to investigate the potential field use of *cis*-jasmone in inducing resistance against herbivorous pests, and also to investigate the molecular biological mechanisms by which *cis*-jasmone caused this plant activation.

It is anticipated that other plant signals having better properties than *cis*-jasmone will be identified, particularly by use of insect electrophysiology and new postgenomic approaches to exploiting insect olfaction. However, it was felt that the field demonstration of *cis*-jasmone in controlling pests by inducing plant defence would demonstrate the principle of using essentially ephemeral plant volatiles, as opposed to purely synthetic, relatively persistent compounds such as acibenzolar-S-methyl. Furthermore, by understanding the processes by which *cis*-jasmone is detected by plants at the molecular level and by which it derives its persistent activity, this would pave the way to exploiting these mechanisms more widely.

FIELD APPLICATION OF *cis*-JASMONE AGAINST CEREAL APHIDS

Initial laboratory studies (Birkett, *et al.*, 2000) were made by placing bean plants, *V. faba*, in a bell jar into which a small dose of *cis*-jasmone had been evaporated. This was selectively absorbed by the plant, leaving behind contaminants comprising compounds with closely related structures to that of *cis*-jasmone (Chamberlain, *et al.*, 2001). For field work, it was decided to investigate the protection of winter wheat against cereal aphids, comprising the grain aphid, *Sitobion avenae*, the rose-grain aphid, *Metopolophium dirhodum*, and the bird-cherry-oat aphid, *Rhopalosiphum padi*. In this crop, application via the air could not be made in the field, so treatment was achieved by using an emulsifiable concentrate formulated using the surfactant Ethylan BV, with *cis*-jasmone being applied at the rate of 50 g/ha. Clearly, a large percentage of this application would be lost to the atmosphere, with only a small proportion entering the plant compared to the situation of the bell jar application to bean plants. However, it was intended that any success in the field with this simple emulsifiable concentrate approach would be followed by further studies on more economic and effective application systems (Bruce, *et al.*, 2003a).

Field trials have been made in each year between 1999-2002 and, with the exception of 2001, there was a statistically significant reduction in aphid populations, with, for example in 2000, a 50% reduction in aphid populations one month after application of the *cis*-jasmone. Unfortunately, throughout, there were insufficient aphid parasitoids to determine if there was an associated effect on parasitoid populations. However, in the laboratory, the aphid parasitoid *Aphidius ervi* spent significantly longer foraging on wheat seedlings previously treated with *cis*-jasmone (Bruce, *et al.*, 2003b).

INVESTIGATIONS INTO THE MOLECULAR MECHANISM OF *cis*-JASMONE AS A PLANT ACTIVATOR

Initially, the technique of differential display of genes caused to be expressed by *cis*-jasmone in *V. faba* was investigated. Although demonstrating clearly that *cis*-jasmone was indeed causing specific gene expression (Birkett, *et al.*, 2000), this work did not identify genes apparently associated with either the persistent effect of *cis*-jasmone, or receptor systems by which the plant could respond to this signal. None the less, it was subsequently shown that *cis*-jasmone affected the acceptability to aphids of a plant more useful for molecular genetic studies. This was the thale cress, *Arabidopsis thaliana* (T J Bruce, personal communication). Information was first acquired from *A. thaliana* gene expression by means of a limited microarray, involving genes already known to be associated with plant stress (E E Farmer, personal communication). This demonstrated that the gene responsible for reduction of the oxophytodienoic acid (Figure 1) in the biosynthetic pathway to jasmonic acid, and the putative pathway to *cis*-jasmone, was upregulated by *cis*-jasmone.

It was therefore decided to investigate the effects of *cis*-jasmone on gene expression in *A. thaliana* by using the Stanford *Arabidopsis* microarray facility, and that the effects of *cis*-jasmone would be tested against a control comprising plants treated in the same way with methyl jasmonate. Thus, intact eight-week old *A. thaliana*, ecotype Columbia, were exposed for 24 h in sealed Plexiglass boxes, 3.7 litres, to methyl jasmonate or *cis*-jasmone as a vapour from 1 µl released from a cotton wick. Following combinations and the respective technical replicates, the extracted messenger RNA was hybridised to the Stanford array giving the following comparisons: control against *cis*-jasmone, control against methyl jasmonate, *cis*-jasmone against methyl jasmonate.

There were about 30 genes upregulated by exposure to *cis*-jasmone. Confirmation of this upregulation was obtained for a subset of the initially recognised genes by differential expression to *cis*-jasmone using Northern blots, and included genes annotated as a cytochrome P450, a 4-methyl-5(2-hydroxyethyl)thiazole monophosphate biosynthase and an oxophytodienoic acid reductase gene, OPR1/2. It would be expected that products from genes upregulated by plant activators would be enzymes involved in the generation of herbivore repellents and foraging stimulants for predators and parasitoids. The cytochrome P450 may fulfil such a role, but this has not yet been determined. Alternatively, the cytochrome P450 could be involved in the selective discrimination of *cis*-jasmone as the activating signal. It is now known that OPR3, rather than OPR1/2, is responsible for the reduction step in the specific biosynthesis of jasmonic acid from oxophytodienoic acid (Schaller, *et al.*, 2000; Schaller, 2001). OPR1 and OPR2 are considered likely to be involved in the removal of isomers different from the 9*S*,13*S*- isomer of the oxophytodienoic acid, which has the appropriate stereochemistry to be the precursor of *epi*-jasmonic acid. It may be that, since methyl jasmonate was also observed to upregulate OPR3 and only *cis*-jasmone upregulated OPR1/2, this latter gene might be involved in the specific biosynthesis of *cis*-jasmone as part of a feedback loop which might account for the persistent effect of *cis*-jasmone. However, this mode of action is still under investigation.

In addition to progress towards uncovering the mechanism by which *cis*-jasmone is detected and gives a persistent response, the molecular biological studies have also demonstrated another principle of potential practical value. The promoter sequence for one of the genes upregulated by *cis*-jasmone has been cloned and linked to a marker gene encoding a

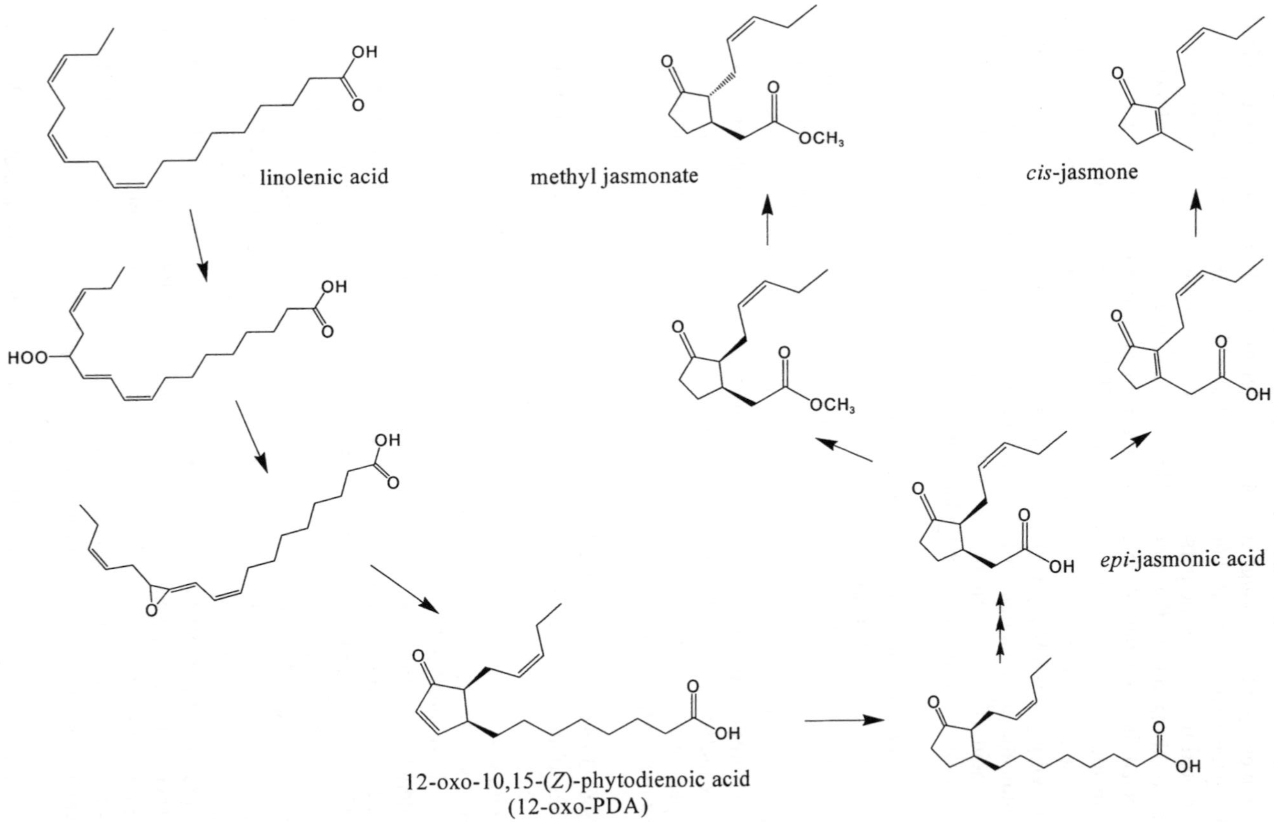
OH
O
linolenic acid
HOO
methyl jasmonate
OCH3
cis-jasmone
epi-jasmonic acid
12-oxo-10,15-(Z)-phytodienoic acid
(12-oxo-PDA)

Figure 1. Putative biosynthetic pathway to methyl jasmonate and *cis*-jasmone.

luciferase and then expressed transgenically in *A. thaliana*. Thus, when this transgenic plant is exposed to *cis*-jasmone from the air, the luciferase gene is expressed and the plant emits light when treated with the substrate luciferin, whereas without *cis*-jasmone, the gene remains inactivated. This demonstrates the principle of using *cis*-jasmone with *cis*-jasmone responsive promoters to switch on other genes, not merely acting as markers but of potential value. Such genes could relate to other aspects of plant protection; for example, the activator promoter sequence could be linked to *Bacillus thuringiensis* insect defence genes, or even genes associated with agronomic traits such as water stress, whereby plant respiration could be shut down during drought (Matthes, *et al.*, 2002).

POTENTIAL FOR WEED CONTROL

Although work in this direction is not as advanced as the development of aerial plant activators, discoveries have been made in the control of the parasitic African witchweed, *Striga hermonthica*, that demonstrate the principle of using plant signals. As part of a programme in East Africa against witchweeds and stem borer pests damaging subsistence maize and sorghum crops, it has been found that forage legumes, e.g. *Desmodium uncinatum*, when intercropped with maize or sorghum, gives very effective control of *S. hermonthica*. The mechanism involves an allelopathic signalling system in which there is initially a stimulated germination of *S. hermonthica* seeds. However, the seeds do not develop to colonise the cereal crop effectively, and there are overall reductions in the seed bank and in the amount of infestation of *S. hermonthica* within the crop (Khan, *et al.*, 2002). Although the chemical identification of active components is still continuing, the compound named, uncinone C, having the novel isoflavanone structure given (Figure 2), moderately inhibited the development of the radicle after germination of *S. hermonthica* (Tsanuo, *et al.*, in press).

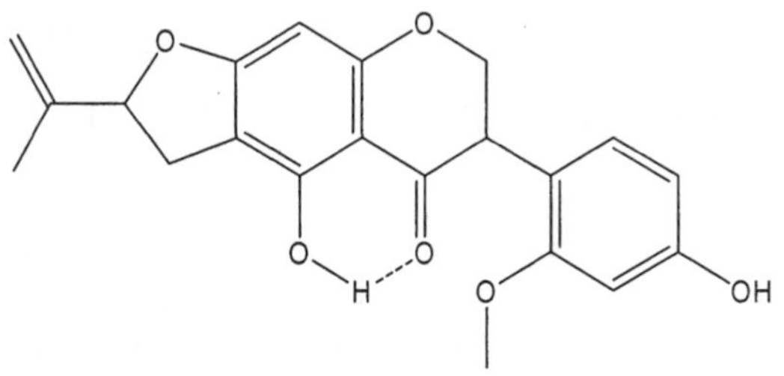

Figure 2.   Structure of uncinone C, a novel isoflavanone from *Desmodium uncinatum* which controls witchweed in cereals.

Since the activity of the natural system has not yet been accounted for in the identification work, it would be premature to consider how this signal chemistry can be developed in detail. None the less, knowledge of the chemical structures involved will allow wider screening of legumes to find more economically useful cultivars and more effective plants with respect to control of *S. hermonthica*, and particularly that can deal with the varied agricultural ecosystems present in sub-Saharan Africa, where the main problem with witchweeds occurs.

CONCLUSIONS

New chemical signals, exemplified by *cis*-jasmone, can be identified which cause natural gene expression conferring pest resistance in agricultural crops. The novel role observed for *cis*-jasmone in causing defence gene expression allows the intellectual property embodied therein to be protected by patenting, and shows commercial potential for natural products as new plant activators for plant protection. Initial investigations into new signal compounds, and t he m olecular m echanisms b y w hich c is-jasmone a cts, s how considerable p romise f or further developments in this area. Initial studies in the control of the parasitic weed *S. hermonthica* suggest that plant signals may also find use, beyond protection of plants against pests, to weed control.

ACKNOWLEDGEMENTS

Rothamsted Research receives grant-aided support from the Biotechnology and Biological Sciences Research Council of the United Kingdom. This work was in part supported by the United Kingdom Department for Environment, Food and Rural Affairs.

REFERENCES

Birkett M A; Campbell C A M; Chamberlain K; Guerrieri E; Hick A J; Martin J L; Matthes M; Napier J A; Pettersson J; Pickett J A; Poppy G M; Pow E M; Pye B J; Smart L E; Wadhams G H; Wadhams L J; Woodcock C M (2000). New roles for *cis*-jasmone as an insect semiochemical and in plant defense. *Proceedings of the National Academy of Sciences USA* **97**, 9329-9334.

Birkett M A; Chamberlain K; Hooper A M; Pickett J A (2001). Does allelopathy offer real promise for practical weed management and for explaining rhizosphere interactions involving higher plants? *Plant and Soil* **232**, 31-39.

Bruce T J A; Martin J L ; Pickett J A; Pye B J; Smart L E; Wadhams L J (2003a). *cis*-Jasmone treatment induces resistance in wheat plants against the grain aphid, *Sitobion avenae* (Fabricius) (Homoptera: Aphididae). *Pest Management Science* **59**, 1031-1036.

Bruce T J; Pickett J A; Smart L E (2003b). *Cis*-jasmone switches on plant defence against insects. *Pesticide Outlook* **14**, 96-98.

Chamberlain K; Pickett J A; Woodcock C M (2000). Plant signalling and induced defence in insect attack. *Molecular Plant Pathology* **1**, 67-72.

Chamberlain K; Guerrieri E; Pennachio F; Pettersson J; Pickett J A; Poppy G M; Powell W; Wadhams L J; Woodcock C M (2001). Can aphid-induced plant signals be transmitted aerially and through the rhizosphere? *Biochemical Systematics and Ecology* **29**, 1063-1074.

Dicke M (1999). Evolution of induced indirect defense of plants. In: *The ecology and evolution of inducible defenses*, eds. R Tollrian & C D Harvell, pp. 62-88. Princeton University Press: Princeton, New Jersey.

Doughty K J; Kiddle G A; Pye B J; Wallsgrove R M; Pickett J A (1995). Selective induction of glucosinolates in oilseed rape leaves by methyl jasmonate. *Phytochemistry* **38**, 347-350.

Duke S O; Dayan F E; Rimando A M; Schrader K K; Aliotta G; Oliva A; Romagni J G (2002). Chemicals from nature for weed management. *Weed Science* **50**, 138-151.

Farmer E E; Ryan C A (1990). Interplant communication: airborne methyl jasmonate induces synthesis of proteinase inhibitors in plant leaves. *Proceedings of the National Academy of Sciences USA* **87**, 7713-7716.

Hardie J; Isaacs R; Pickett J A; Wadhams L J; Woodcock C M (1994). Methyl salicylate and (-)-(1*R*,5*S*)-myrtenal are plant-derived repellents for black bean aphid, *Aphis fabae* Scop. (Homoptera: Aphididae). *Journal of Chemical Ecology* **20**, 2847-2855.

Karban R; Baldwin I T (1997). Induced Responses to Herbivory. The University of Chicago: Chicago.

Karban R; Baldwin I T; Baxter K J; Laue G; Felton G W (2000). Communication between plants: induced resistance in wild tobacco plants following clipping of neighboring sagebrush. *Oecologia* **125**, 66-71.

Khan Z R; Hassanali A; Overholt W; Khamis T M; Hooper A M; Pickett J A; Wadhams L J; Woodcock C M (2002). Control of witchweed *Striga hermonthica* by intercropping with *Desmodium* spp., and the mechanism defined as allelopathic. *Journal of Chemical Ecology* **28**, 1871-1885.

Korth K L (2003). Profiling the response of plants to herbivorous insects. *Genome Biology* **4**, 221.1-4.

Matthes M C; Pickett J A; Napier J A (2002). *Cis*-Jasmone as a novel signalling molecule in plant gene expression. Poster at XIII International Conference on Arabidopsis Research, Seville, Spain, June 28 – July 2, 2002. (Full paper in preparation).

Mayer R T; Inbar M; McKenzie C L; Shatters R; Borowicz V; Albrecht U; Powell C A; Doostdar H (2002). Multitrophic interactions of the silverleaf whitefly, host plants, competing herbivores, and phytopathogens. *Archives of Insect Biochemistry and Physiology* **51**, 151-169.

Ninkovic V; Olsson U; Pettersson J (2002). Mixing barley cultivars affects aphid host plant acceptance in field experiments. *Entomologia Experimentalis et Applicata* **102**, 177-182.

Pettersson J; Pickett J A; Pye B J; Quiroz A; Smart L E; Wadhams L J; Woodcock C M (1994). Winter host component reduces colonization by bird-cherry-oat aphid, *Rhopalosiphum padi* (L.) (Homoptera, Aphididae), and other aphids in cereal fields. *Journal of Chemical Ecology* **20**, 2565-2574.

Pickett J A; Wadhams L J; Woodcock C M (1998). Insect supersense: mate and host location by insects as model systems for exploiting olfactory interactions. *The Biochemist*, August 1998, 8-13.

Pickett J A; Chamberlain K; Poppy G M; Woodcock C M (1999). Exploiting insect responses in identifying plant signals. In: *Insect-Plant Interactions and Induced Plant Defence. Novartis Foundation Symposium 223*, ed. J Goode, pp. 253-265. John Wiley & Sons Ltd.: Chichester.

Preston C A; Betts H; Baldwin I T (2002). Methyl jasmonate as an allelopathic agent: sagebrush inhibits germination of a neighboring tobacco, *Nicotiana attenuata*. *Journal of Chemical Ecology* **28**, 2343-2369.

Schaller F; Biesgen C; Müssig C; Altmann T; Weiler E W (2000). 12-Oxophytodienoate reductase 3 (OPR3) is the isoenzyme involved in jasmonate biosynthesis. *Planta* **210**, 979-984.

Schaller F (2001). Enzymes of the biosynthesis of octadecanoid-derived signalling molecules. *Journal of Experimental Botany* **52**, 11-23.

Schenk P M; Kazan K; Wilson I; Anderson J P; Richmond T; Somerville S C; Manners J M (2000). Coordinated plant defense responses in *Arabidopsis* revealed by microarray analysis. *Proceedings of the National Academy of Sciences USA* **97**, 11655-11660.

Shulaev V; Silverman P; Raskin I (1997). Airborne signalling by methyl salicylate in plant pathogen resistance. *Nature* **385**, 718-721.

Tsanuo M K; Hassanali A; Hooper A M; Khan Z R; Kaberia F; Pickett J A; Wadhams L J. Isoflavanones from the allelopathic root exudate of *Desmodium uncinatum*. *Phytochemistry* (in press).

Walters D; Cowley T; Mitchell A (2002). Methyl jasmonate alters polyamine metabolism and induces systemic protection against powdery mildew infection in barley seedlings. *Journal of Experimental Botany* **53**, 747-756.